Modern Young's Literal Translation™
New Testament with Psalms & Proverbs

Translated by
Robert Young

Edited by
Allen K. LeClaire

Greater Truth Publishers

Copyright © 2005 by Allen K. LeClaire
All Rights Reserved

ISBN 0965307875

The Modern Young's Literal Translation™ (MYLT™) text may be quoted and/or reprinted up to and inclusive of one thousand verses (1,000) without express written consent of the copyright holder, providing the verses quoted do not constitute a complete book of the Bible, nor account for as much as 50% of the total work in which they are quoted. Notice of copyright must appear on the title or copyright page of the work as follows:

"Scripture taken from the Modern Young's Literal Translation™
Copyright © 2005
By Allen K. LeClaire
Used by permission of the copyright holder."

When quotations from the MYLT are used in media not for sale, such as church bulletins, orders of service, posters, transparencies, or similar media, the initials MYLT may be used at the end of each quotation. Quotations and/or reprints in excess of one thousand (1,000) verses, or other permission requests must be directed to and approved in writing by Allen K. LeClaire through a request directed to the publisher.

The name Modern Young's Literal Translation™ and the initials MYLT™ are trademarked by Greater Truth Publishers and the trademark symbol must accompany the name and/or initials whenever possible.

Published by:
Greater Truth Publishers
PO Box 4332
Lafayette, IN 47903

Editor's Preface

For over 100 years, the Young's Literal Translation of the Bible has been considered to be one of the most accurate and literal Bibles ever produced. A great many years of study and work by Robert Young went into this Bible. However, even though he was doing this in the middle to late 1800's, he used the same Elizabethan language that the King James Version used, since that was the type of language that most people were used to reading in their Bible. This, coupled with Mr. Young's writing down the English words mostly in the order that the Hebrew and Greek words were translated, has made this translation harder to read than the King James Version. Young's Literal Translation was not meant to replace the King James Version, but to supplement it as a study resource. While it is more accurate and more literal than the King James Version, the King James Version has remained the most popular by far. In fact, most people have not even heard of Young's Literal Translation of the Bible.

Mr. Young translated the Young's Literal Translation from the same texts that the King James Version was translated from. He used the Masoretic Text for the Old Testament and the Textus Receptus (Received Text) for the New Testament. So, the Young's Literal Translation and now the Modern Young's Literal Translation™ are among the few translations today that are translated from these texts, the others include the Literal Translation of the Bible by Jay P. Green Sr.; the King James 3, also by Jay P. Green Sr.; the Interlinear Hebrew Greek English Bible, by Jay P. Green Sr., and possibly the New King James Version (we have read different things put out by Thomas Nelson, each stating a different text).

To help modern readers better understand the Young's Literal Translation, we have decided to modernize the text. If modern readers can better read and understand it, more people will benefit from the accurateness and the literalness of it. After all, all of us want an fairly easy to read Bible that is as close to the original meanings as humanly possible.

We have not changed any of the meaning of the text and we have not subtracted from the literalness of Young's Literal Translation. We have changed some of the words from the Elizabethan language to language used today. We have re-arranged the sentence structures to more reflect the sentence structures used today, to help the language flow better without seeming so silted at times. We have not attempted to "revise" the translation, just to modernize it.

To some people, re-arranging the sentence structure will mean that the literalness is now missing. This is far from the case. It is not writing down the English words in the exact order that the Hebrew and Greek is translated that makes a literal translation. It is using every word that is translated and using it in the way that it was meant to be used. If you were translating from Spanish or French (or any other language) into English and the exact format of the words was "the day second", you would automatically translate it as "the second day". This has not altered the meaning of the text nor made it less literal. It still means the same exact thing, but in a way that is easier to read and to understand.

We hope that people will like this new translation, but understand that there will be people who have suggestions or comments. We invite those people to write to us concerning those suggestions or comments. We thank you for having a look at this translation (and hopefully adopting it as your new version of choice), we thank you on behalf of myself and my proofreaders.

We have also added notations to the forms of "you" to denote singluar or plural usage. A small "S" above the word denotes singular usage and a small "P" above the word denotes plural usage. This was done in response to reader comments that in places it could be difficult to figure out whether the word usage was singular or plural. We think that this will improve the readability of our edition and we wish to thank our readers who contributed to this change.

Thank you,
Allen K. LeClaire

Table of Contents

The Gospel according to
MATTHEW

CHAPTER 1

1 A roll of the birth of Jesus Christ, son of David, son
of Abraham.
2 Abraham fathered Isaac, and Isaac fathered Jacob,
and Jacob fathered Judah and his brethren,
3 and Judah fathered Pharez and Zarah of Tamar, and
Pharez fathered Hezron, and Hezron fathered Ram,
4 and Ram fathered Amminadab, and Amminadab
fathered Nahshon, and Nahshon fathered Salmon,
5 and Salmon fathered Boaz of Rahab, and Boaz fathered
Obed of Ruth, and Obed fathered Jesse,
6 and Jesse fathered David the king. And David the
king fathered Solomon, of her [who had been] Uriah's,
7 and Solomon fathered Rehoboam, and Rehoboam
fathered Abijah, and Abijah fathered Asa,
8 and Asa fathered Jehoshaphat, and Jehoshaphat
fathered Joram, and Joram fathered Uzziah,
9 and Uzziah fathered Jotham, and Jotham fathered Ahaz,
and Ahaz fathered Hezekiah,
10 and Hezekiah fathered Manasseh, and Manasseh
fathered Amon, and Amon fathered Josiah,
11 and Josiah fathered Jeconiah and his brethren, at
the Babylonian removal.
12 And after the Babylonian removal, Jeconiah fathered
Shealtiel, and Shealtiel fathered Zerubbabel,
13 and Zerubbabel fathered Abiud, and Abiud fathered
Eliakim, and Eliakim fathered Azor,
14 and Azor fathered Sadok, and Sadok fathered Achim,
and Achim fathered Eliud,
15 and Eliud fathered Eleazar, and Eleazar fathered
Matthan, and Matthan fathered Jacob,
16 and Jacob fathered Joseph, the husband of Mary, of
whom was begotten Jesus, who is named Christ.
17 All the generations, therefore, from Abraham unto
David [are] fourteen generations, and from David unto
the Babylonian removal fourteen generations, and from
the Babylonian removal unto the Christ, fourteen
generations.
18 And of Jesus Christ, the birth was thus: For His
mother Mary having been engaged to Joseph, before
their coming together she was found to have conceived
from the Holy Spirit,
19 and her husband Joseph being righteous, and not
willing to make an example of her, did wish to send her
away privately.
20 And on his thinking of these things, behold, a
messenger of the Lord appeared to him in a dream,
saying, 'Joseph, son of David, you[S] need not fear to
receive Mary your[S] wife, for that which was begotten in
her [is] of the Holy Spirit,
21 and she shall bring forth a son, and you[S] shall call
His name Jesus, for He shall save His people from their
sins.'
22 And all this had come to pass, that it may be fulfilled
that was spoken by the Lord through the prophet,
saying,
23 'Behold, the virgin shall conceive, and she shall bring
forth a son, and they shall call His name Emmanuel,'
which is, being interpreted 'With us [He is] God.'
24 And Joseph, having risen from the sleep, did as the
messenger of the Lord directed him, and received his wife,
25 and did not know her till she brought forth her son
— the first-born, and he called his name Jesus.

CHAPTER 2

1 And Jesus having been born in Beth-Lehem of Judea,
in the days of Herod the king, behold, mages from the
east came to Jerusalem,
2 saying, 'Where is He who was born king of the Jews?
for we saw His star in the east, and we came to bow to
Him.'
3 And Herod the king having heard, was stirred, and all
Jerusalem with him,
4 and having gathered all the chief priests and scribes
of the people, he was inquiring from them where the
Christ is born.
5 And they said to him, 'In Beth-Lehem of Judea, for
thus it has been written through the prophet,

6 And you[S], Beth-Lehem, the land of Judah, you[S] are by
no means the least among the leaders of Judah, for out
of you[S] shall come one leading, who shall feed My
people Israel.'
7 Then Herod, having privately called the mages, did
inquire exactly from them the time of the appearing star,
8 and having sent them to Beth-Lehem, he said, 'Having
gone — inquire you[P] exactly for the child, and whenever
you[P] may have found, bring me back word, that I may
also come bow to Him.'
9 And they, having heard the king, departed, and behold,
the star, that they did see in the east, did go before them,
till, having come, it stood over where the child was.
10 And having seen the star, they rejoiced with
exceeding great joy,
11 and having come to the house, they found the child
with Mary His mother, and having fallen down they
bowed to Him, and having opened their treasures, they
presented to Him gifts, gold, and frankincense, and
myrrh,
12 and having been divinely warned in a dream not to
turn back unto Herod, they withdrew through another
way to their own region.
13 And on their having withdrawn, behold, a messenger
of the Lord did appear in a dream to Joseph, saying,
'Having risen, take the child and His mother, and flee to
Egypt, and be you[S] there till I may speak to you[S], for
Herod is about to seek the child to destroy Him.'
14 And he, having risen, took the child and his mother
by night, and withdrew to Egypt,
15 and he was there till the death of Herod, that it might
be fulfilled that was spoken by the Lord through the
prophet, saying, 'Out of Egypt I did call My Son.'
16 Then Herod, having seen that he was deceived by
the mages, was very angry, and having sent forth, he
slew all the male children in Beth-Lehem, and in all its
borders, from two years and under, according to the time
that he inquired exactly from the mages.
17 Then was fulfilled that which was spoken by Jeremiah
the prophet, saying,
18 'A voice in Ramah was heard — lamentation and
weeping and much mourning — Rachel weeping [for]
her children, and she would not be comforted because
they are not.'
19 And Herod having died, behold, a messenger of the
Lord did appear in a dream to Joseph in Egypt,
20 saying, 'Having risen, take the child and His mother,
and be going to the land of Israel, for they have died —
those seeking the life of the child.'
21 And he, having risen, took the child and His mother,
and came to the land of Israel,
22 and having heard that Archelaus did reign over Judea
instead of Herod his father, he was afraid to go there,
and having been divinely warned in a dream, he withdrew
to the parts of Galilee,
23 and coming, he dwelt in a city named Nazareth, that
it might be fulfilled that was spoken through the
prophets, that 'He shall be called a Nazarene.'

CHAPTER 3

1 And in those days came John the Baptist, proclaiming
in the wilderness of Judea,
2 and saying, 'Reform, for the reign of the heavens
comes near,'
3 for this is he who was spoken of by Isaiah the prophet,
saying, 'A voice of one crying in the wilderness, Prepare
you[P] the way of the Lord, you[P] make straight His paths.'
4 And this John had his clothing of camel's hair, and a
girdle of skin round his loins, and his nourishment was
locusts and honey of the field.
5 Then were going forth unto him Jerusalem, and all
Judea, and all the region round about the Jordan,
6 and they were baptized in the Jordan by him,
confessing their sins.
7 And having seen many of the Pharisees and
Sadducees coming about his baptism, he said to them,
'Brood of vipers! who did show you[P] to flee from the
coming wrath?
8 bear, for that reason, fruits worthy of the reformation,
9 and do not think to say in yourselves[P], A father we
have — Abraham, for I say to you[P], that God is able to
raise children to Abraham out of these stones,
10 and now also, the axe is laid unto the root of the
trees, for that reason every tree not bearing good fruit
is hewn down, and is cast to fire.
11 'I indeed do baptize you[P] with water to reformation,
but He who is coming after me is mightier than I, of whom
I am not worthy to bear the sandals, He shall baptize
you[P] with the Holy Spirit and with fire,
12 whose fan [is] in His hand, and He will thoroughly
cleanse His floor, and will gather His wheat to the
storehouse, but the chaff He will burn with fire
unquenchable.'
13 Then came Jesus from Galilee upon the Jordan, unto
John to be baptized by him,
14 but John was forbidding Him, saying, 'I have need

to be baptized by You[S]— and You[S] do come unto me!'
15 But Jesus answering said to him, 'Allow [it] now, for
thus it is becoming to us to fulfill all righteousness,' then
he did allow Him.
16 And having been baptized, Jesus went up
immediately from the water, and behold, the heavens
were opened to Him, and He saw the Spirit of God
descending as a dove, and coming upon Him,
17 and behold, a voice out of the heavens, saying, 'This
is My Son — the Beloved, in whom I did delight.'

CHAPTER 4

1 Then Jesus was led up to the wilderness by the Spirit,
to be tempted by the Devil,
2 and having fasted forty days and forty nights,
afterwards He did hunger.
3 And the Tempter having come to Him said, 'If You[S] are
Son of God — speak that these stones may become
loaves.'
4 But He answering said, 'It has been written, Not upon
bread alone does man live, but upon every word coming
forth from the mouth of God.'
5 Then did the Devil take Him to the [holy] city, and did
set Him on the pinnacle of the temple,
6 and said to Him, 'If You[S] are Son of God — throw
Yourself[S] down, for it has been written, that, He shall
charge His messengers concerning You[S], and they shall
bear You[S] up on [their] hands, that You[S] may not strike
Your[S] foot on a stone.'
7 Jesus said to him again, 'It has been written, You[S]
shall not tempt the Lord your[S] God.'
8 Again did the Devil take Him to a very high mount,
and did show all the kingdoms of the world and the glory
of them to Him,
9 and said to Him, 'All these I will give to You[S], if falling
down You[S] may bow to me.'
10 Then Jesus said to him, 'Go — Adversary, for it has
been written, You[S] shall bow to the Lord your God, and
you[S] shall only serve Him.'
11 Then did the Devil leave Him, and behold, messengers
came and were ministering to Him.
12 And Jesus having heard that John was delivered up,
did withdraw to Galilee,
13 and having left Nazareth, having come, He dwelt at
Capernaum that is by the sea, in the borders of Zebulun
and Naphtalim,
14 that it might be fulfilled that was spoken through
Isaiah the prophet, saying,
15 'Land of Zebulun and land of Naphtali, way of the
sea, beyond the Jordan, Galilee of the nations! —
16 the people that is sitting in darkness saw a great
light, and to those sitting in a region and shadow of
death — light arose to them.'
17 From that time Jesus began to proclaim and to say,
'Reform you[P], for the reign of the heavens has come
near.'
18 And Jesus, walking by the sea of Galilee, saw two
brothers, Simon named Peter and Andrew his brother,
casting a drag into the sea — for they were fishers —
19 and He said to them, 'Come you[P] after me, and I will
make you[P] fishers of men,'
20 and they, immediately, having left the nets, did follow
Him.
21 And having advanced there, He saw other two
brothers, James of Zebedee, and John his brother, in the
boat with Zebedee their father, refitting their nets, and
He called them,
22 and they, immediately, having left the boat and their
father, did follow Him.
23 And Jesus was going about all Galilee teaching in
their synagogues, and proclaiming the good news of the
reign, and healing every disease, and every sickness
among the people,
24 and His fame went forth to all Syria, and they brought
to Him all having ailments, pressed with various
sicknesses and pains, and demoniacs, and lunatics, and
paralytics, and He healed them.
25 And there followed Him many multitudes from Galilee,
and Decapolis, and Jerusalem, and Judea, and beyond
the Jordan.

CHAPTER 5

1 And having seen the multitudes, He went up to the
mount, and He having sat down, His disciples came to
Him,
2 and having opened His mouth, He was teaching them,
saying:
3 'Happy [are] the poor in spirit — because theirs is the
reign of the heavens.
4 'Happy [are] the mourning — because they shall be
comforted.
5 'Happy [are] the meek — because they shall inherit
the land.
6 'Happy [are] those hungering and thirsting for

righteousness — because they shall be filled.
7 ‘Happy [are] the kind — because they shall find
kindness.
8 ‘Happy [are] the clean in heart — because they shall
see God.
9 ‘Happy [are] the peacemakers — because they shall
be called Sons of God.
10 ‘Happy [are] those persecuted for righteousness’
sake — because theirs is the reign of the heavens.
11 ‘Happy are you[P] whenever they may reproach you[P],
and may persecute, and may say any evil thing against
you[P] falsely for My sake —
12 rejoice you[P] and be glad, because your[P] reward [is]
great in the heavens, for so did they persecute the
prophets who were before you[P].
13 ‘You[P] are the salt of the land, but if the salt may lose
flavor, in what shall it be salted? it is good for nothing
afterwards , except to be cast out, and to be walked upon
by men.
14 ‘You[P] are the light of the world, a city set upon a
mount is not able to be hid;
15 nor do they light a lamp, and put it under the measure,
but on the lamp-stand, and it shines to all those in the
house;
16 so let your[P] light shine before men, that they may
see your[P] good works, and may glorify your[P] Father who
[is] in the heavens.
17 ‘Do not suppose that I came to throw down the law
or the prophets — I did not come to throw down, but to
fulfill;
18 for, truly I say to you[P], till that the heaven and the
earth may pass away, one iota or one tittle may not pass
away from the law, till that all may come to pass.
19 ‘Whoever consequently may loose one of these
commands — the least — and may teach men so, he
shall be called least in the reign of the heavens, but
whoever may do and may teach [them], he shall be called
great in the reign of the heavens.
20 ‘For I say to you[P], that if your[P] righteousness may
not abound above that of the scribes and Pharisees, you[P]
may not enter to the reign of the heavens.
21 ‘You[P] heard that it was said to the ancients: You[S]
shall not kill, and whoever may kill shall be in danger of
the judgment;
22 but I — I say to you[P], that every one who is angry at his
brother without cause, shall be in danger of the judgment,
and whoever may say to his brother, Empty fellow! shall
be in danger of the sanhedrim, and whoever may say, Rebel!
shall be in danger of the gehenna of the fire.
23 ‘If, therefore, you[S] may bring your[S] gift to the altar,
and there may remember that your[S] brother has anything
against you[S],
24 leave your[S] gift there before the altar, and go — first
be reconciled to your[S] brother, and then having come
bring your[S] gift.
25 ‘Be agreeing with your[S] opponent quickly, while you[S]
are in the way with him, that the opponent may not
deliver you[S] to the judge, and the judge may deliver you[S]
to the officer, and you[S] may be cast to prison,
26 truly I say to you[S], you[S] may not come forth from
there till that you[S] may pay the last farthing.
27 ‘You[P] heard that it was said to the ancients: You[S]
shall not commit adultery;
28 but I — I say to you[P], that every one who is looking
on a woman to desire her, did already commit adultery
with her in his heart.
29 ‘But, if your[S] right eye does cause you[S] to stumble,
pluck it out and cast from you[S], for it is good to you[S]
that one of your[S] members may perish, and not your[S]
whole body be cast to gehenna.
30 ‘And, if your[S] right hand does cause you[S] to stumble,
cut it off, and cast from you[S], for it is good to you[S] that
one of your[S] members may perish, and not your[S] whole
body be cast to gehenna.
31 ‘And it was said, That whoever may put away his
wife, let him give to her a writing of divorce;
32 but I — I say to you[P], that whoever may put away
his wife, save for the matter of whoredom, does make
her to commit adultery; and whoever may marry her who
has been put away does commit adultery.
33 ‘Again, you[P] heard that it was said to the ancients:
You[S] shall not swear falsely, but you[S] shall pay your[S]
oaths to the Lord;
34 but I — I say to you[P], not to swear at all; neither by
the heaven, because it is the throne of God,
35 nor by the earth, because it is His footstool, nor by
Jerusalem, because it is a city of a great king,
36 nor may you[S] swear by your[S] head, because you[S] are
not able to make one hair white or black;
37 but let your[P] word be, Yes, Yes, No, No, and that
which is more than these is of the evil.
38 ‘You[P] heard that it was said: Eye for eye, and tooth
for tooth;
39 but I — I say to you[P], not to resist the evil, but
whoever shall slap you[S] on your[S] right cheek, turn the
other to him also;
40 and whoever is willing to take you[S] to law, and to
take your[S] coat — allow the cloak to him also.

41 ‘And whoever shall impress you[S] one mile, go with
him two,
42 to him who is asking of you[S] be giving, and him who
is willing to borrow from you[S] may not turn away.
43 ‘You[P] heard that it was said: You[S] shall love your[S]
neighbor, and shall hate your[S] enemy;
44 but I — I say to you[P], Love your[P] enemies, bless
those cursing you[P], do good to those hating you[P], and
pray for those falsely accusing you[P], and persecuting
you[P],
45 that you[P] may be sons of your[P] Father in the heavens,
because He does cause His sun to rise on evil and good,
and He does send rain on righteous and unrighteous.
46 ‘For, if you[P] may love those loving you[P], what reward
have you[P]? do not the tax-gatherers the same also?
47 and if you[P] may salute your[P] brethren only, what do
you[P] abundant? do not the tax-gatherers so also?
48 you[P] shall therefore be perfect, as your[P] Father who
[is] in the heavens is perfect.

CHAPTER 6

1 ‘Take heed not to do your[P] kindness before men, to
be seen by them, and if not — you[P] have not reward
from your[P] Father who [is] in the heavens;
2 whenever, for that reason, you[S] may do kindness, you[S]
may not sound a trumpet before you[S] as the hypocrites
do, in the synagogues, and in the streets, that they may
have glory from men; truly I say to you[P] — they have
their reward!
3 ‘But you[S], doing kindness, let your[S] left hand not know
what your[S] right hand does,
4 that your[S] kindness may be in secret, and your[S] Father
who is seeing in secret shall reward you[S] Himself
obviously.
5 ‘And when you[S] may pray, you[S] shall not be as the
hypocrites, because they love in the synagogues, and
in the corners of the broad places — standing — to pray,
that they may be seen of men; truly I say to you[P], that
they have their reward.
6 ‘But you[S], when you[S] may pray, go into your[S] chamber,
and having shut your[S] door, pray to your[S] Father who
[is] in secret, and your[S] Father who is seeing in secret,
shall reward you[S] obviously.
7 ‘And — praying — you[P] may not use vain repetitions
like the nations, for they think that in their much speaking
they shall be heard,
8 for that reason you[P] be not like to them, for your[P]
Father does know those things that you[P] have need of
before your[P] asking Him;
9 thus for that reason pray you[P]: ‘Our Father who [is] in
the heavens! hallowed be Your[S] name.
10 ‘Your[S] reign come: Your[S] will come to pass, on the
earth as in heaven also.
11 ‘Give us our appointed bread today.
12 ‘And forgive us our debts, as also we forgive our
debtors.
13 ‘And may You[S] lead us not to temptation, but deliver
us from the evil, because Yours[S] is the reign, and the
power, and the glory — to the ages. Amen.
14 ‘For, if you[P] may forgive men their trespasses He
also will forgive you[P] — your[P] Father who [is] in the
heavens;
15 but if you[P] may not forgive men their trespasses,
neither will your[P] Father forgive your[P] trespasses.
16 ‘And when you[P] may fast, be you[P] not as the
hypocrites, of sour countenances, for they disfigure their
faces, that they may appear to men fasting; truly I say
to you[P], that they have their reward.
17 ‘But you[S], fasting, anoint your[S] head, and wash your[S]
face,
18 that you[S] may not appear to men fasting, but to your[S]
Father who [is] in secret, and your[S] Father, who is seeing
in secret, shall reward you[S] obviously.
19 ‘Treasure not up to yourselves[P] treasures on the
earth, where moth and rust disfigure, and where thieves
break through and steal,
20 but treasure up to yourselves[P] treasures in heaven,
where neither moth nor rust does disfigure, and where
thieves do not break through nor steal,
21 for where your[P] treasure is, there will be also your[P]
heart.
22 ‘The lamp of the body is the eye, if, for that reason,
your[S] eye may be perfect, all your[S] body shall be
enlightened,
23 but if your[S] eye may be evil, all your[S] body shall be
dark; if, for that reason, the light that [is] in you[S] is
darkness — the darkness, how great!
24 ‘None is able to serve two lords, for either he will
hate the one and love the other, or he will hold to the
one, and despise the other; you[P] are not able to serve
God and Mammon.
25 ‘Because of this I say to you[P], be not anxious for
your[P] life, what you[P] may eat, and what you[P] may drink,
nor for your[P] body, what you[P] may put on. Is not the life
more than the nourishment, and the body than the
clothing?

26 look to the fowls of the heaven, for they do not sow,
nor reap, nor gather into storehouses, and your[P]
heavenly Father does nourish them; are not you[P] much
better than they?
27 'And who of you[P], being anxious, is able to add to
his age one cubit?
28 and why are you[P] anxious about clothing? consider
well the lilies of the field; how do they grow? they do
not labor, nor do they spin;
29 and I say to you[P], that not even Solomon in all his
glory was arrayed as one of these.
30 'And if the herb of the field, that today is, and
tomorrow is cast to the furnace, God does so clothe —
not much more you[P], O you[P] of little faith?
31 therefore you[P] may not be anxious, saying, What
may we eat? or, What may we drink? or, What may we
put round?
32 for all these do the nations seek for, for your[P]
heavenly Father does know that you[P] have need of all
these;
33 but seek you[P] first the reign of God and His
righteousness, and all these shall be added to you[P].
34 For that reason be not anxious for the morrow, for
the morrow shall be anxious for its own things; sufficient
for the day [is] the evil of it.

CHAPTER 7

1 'Judge not, that you[P] may not be judged,
2 for in what judgment you[P] judge, you[P] shall be judged,
and in what measure you[P] measure, it shall be measured
to you[P].
3 'And why do you[S] behold the mote that [is] in your[S]
brother's eye, and do not consider the beam that [is] in
your[S] own eye?
4 or, how will you[S] say to your[S] brother, Allow me to
cast the mote out from your[S] eye, and behold, the beam
[is] in your[S] own eye?
5 Hypocrite, first cast out the beam out of your[S] own
eye, and then you[S] shall see clearly to cast out the mote
out of your[S] brother's eye.
6 'You[P] may not give that which is [holy] to the dogs,
nor cast your[P] pearls before the swine, that they may
not trample them among their feet, and having turned
— may rend you[P].
7 'Ask, and it shall be given to you[P]; seek, and you[P]
shall find; knock, and it shall be opened to you[P];
8 for every one who is asking does receive, and he who
is seeking does find, and to him who is knocking it shall
be opened.
9 'Or what man is of you[P], of whom, if his son may ask a
loaf — will he present a stone to him?
10 and if he may ask a fish — will he present a serpent
to him?
11 if, for that reason, you[P] being evil, have known to
give good gifts to your[P] children, how much more shall
your[P] Father who [is] in the heavens give good things
to those asking him?
12 'All things, for that reason, whatever you[P] may will
that men may be doing to you[P], so also do to them, for
this is the law and the prophets.
13 'Go you[P] in through the strait gate, because wide [is]
the gate, and broad the way that is leading to the
destruction, and many are those going in through it;
14 how strait [is] the gate, and compressed the way that
is leading to the life, and those finding it are few!
15 'But, take heed of the false prophets, who come unto
you[P] in sheep's clothing, and inwardly are ravening
wolves.
16 From their fruits you[P] shall know them; do [men]
gather from thorns grapes? or from thistles figs?
17 so every good tree does yield good fruits, but the
bad tree does yield evil fruits.
18 A good tree is not able to yield evil fruits, nor a bad
tree to yield good fruits.
19 Every tree not yielding good fruit is cut down and is
cast to fire:
20 for that reason you[P] shall know them from their fruits.
21 'Not every one who is saying to Me Lord, Lord, shall
come into the reign of the heavens; but he who is doing
the will of My Father who is in the heavens.
22 Many will say to Me in that day, Lord, Lord, have we
not prophesied in Your[S] name? and cast out demons in
Your[S] name? and done many mighty things in Your[S]
name?
23 and then I will acknowledge to them, that — I never
knew you[P], depart from Me you[P] who are working
lawlessness.
24 'For that reason, every one who does hear of Me
these words, and does do them, I will liken him to a wise
man who built his house upon the rock;
25 and the rain did descend, and the streams came, and
the winds blew, and they beat on that house, and it fell
not, for it had been founded on the rock.
26 'And every one who is hearing of Me these words,
and is not doing them, shall be likened to a foolish man
who built his house upon the sand;

27 and the rain did descend, and the streams came, and
the winds blew, and they beat on that house, and it fell,
and its fall was great.'
28 And it came to pass, when Jesus ended these words,
the multitudes were astonished at His teaching,
29 for He was teaching them as having authority, and
not as the scribes.

CHAPTER 8

1 And when He came down from the mount, great
multitudes did follow Him,
2 and behold, a leper having come, was bowing to Him,
saying, 'Sir, if You[S] are willing, You[S] are able to cleanse me;'
3 and having stretched forth the hand, Jesus touched
him, saying, 'I will, be you[S] cleansed,' and immediately
his leprosy was cleansed.
4 And Jesus said to him, 'See, you[S] may tell no one, but
go, show yourself[S] to the priest, and bring the gift that
Moses commanded for a testimony to them.'
5 And Jesus having entered into Capernaum, there came
to Him a centurion calling upon Him,
6 and saying, 'Sir, my young man has been laid in the
house a paralytic, fearfully afflicted,'
7 and Jesus said to him, 'I, having come, will heal him.'
8 And the centurion answering said, 'Sir, I am not worthy
that You[S] may enter under my roof, but only say a word,
and my servant shall be healed;
9 for I also am a man under authority, having under
myself soldiers, and I say to this one, Go, and he goes,
and to another, Be coming, and he comes, and to my
servant, Do this, and he does [it].'
10 And Jesus having heard, did wonder, and said to
those following, 'Truly I say to you[P], not even in Israel
have I found so great faith;
11 and I say to you[P], that many from east and west shall
come and recline (at meat) with Abraham, and Isaac, and
Jacob, in the reign of the heavens,
12 but the sons of the reign shall be cast forth to the
outer darkness — there shall be the weeping and the
gnashing of the teeth.'
13 And Jesus said to the centurion, 'Go, and as you[S]
did believe let it be to you[S];' and his young man was
healed in that hour.
14 And Jesus having come into the house of Peter, saw
his mother-in-law laid, and fevered,
15 and He touched her hand, and the fever left her, and
she arose, and was ministering to them.
16 And evening having come, they brought to Him many
demoniacs, and He did cast out the spirits with a word,
and did heal all who were ill,
17 that it might be fulfilled that was spoken through
Isaiah the prophet, saying, 'Himself took our infirmities,
and He did bear the sicknesses.'
18 And Jesus having seen great multitudes about Him,
did command to depart to the other side;
19 and a certain scribe having come, said to Him,
'Teacher, I will follow You[S] wherever You[S] may go;'
20 and Jesus said to him, 'The foxes have holes, and
the birds of the heaven places of rest, but the Son of
Man has not where He may lay the head.'
21 And another of His disciples said to Him, 'Sir, permit
me first to depart and to bury my father;'
22 and Jesus said to him, 'Follow Me, and allow the
dead to bury their own dead.'
23 And when He entered into the boat His disciples did
follow Him,
24 and behold, a great tempest arose in the sea, so that
the boat was being covered by the waves, but He was
sleeping,
25 and His disciples having come to Him, awoke Him,
saying, 'Sir, save us; we are perishing.'
26 And He said to them, 'Why are you[P] fearful, O you[P]
of little faith?' Then having risen, He rebuked the winds
and the sea, and there was a great calm;
27 and the men wondered, saying, 'What kind — is this,
that even the wind and the sea do obey Him?'
28 And He having come to the other side, to the region
of the Gergesenes, there two demoniacs met Him , coming
forth out of the tombs, very fierce, so that no one was
able to pass over by that way,
29 and behold, they cried out, saying, 'What — to us
and to You[S], Jesus, Son of God? did You[S] come here,
before the time, to afflict us?'
30 And there was far off from them a herd of many swine
feeding,
31 and the demons were calling on Him, saying, 'If You[S] do
cast us forth, permit us to go away to the herd of the swine;'
32 and He said to them, 'Go.' And having come forth,
they went to the herd of the swine, and behold, the whole
herd of the swine rushed down the steep, to the sea,
and died in the waters,
33 and those feeding did flee, and, having gone to the
city, they declared all, and the matter of the demoniacs.
34 And behold, all the city came forth to meet Jesus,
and having seen Him, they called on [Him] that He might
depart from their borders.

CHAPTER 9

1 And having gone to the boat, He passed over, and came to His own city,
2 and behold, they were bringing to Him a paralytic, laid upon a couch, and Jesus having seen their faith, said to the paralytic, 'Be of good courage, child, your[S] sins have been forgiven you[S].'
3 And behold, certain of the scribes said within themselves, 'This one does speak evil.'
4 And Jesus, having known their thoughts, said, 'Why think you[P] evil in your[P] hearts?
5 for which is easier? to say, The sins have been forgiven to you[S]; or to say, Rise, and walk?
6 'But, that you[P] may know that the Son of Man has power upon the earth to forgive sins — (then He said to the paralytic) — having risen, take up your[S] couch, and go to your[S] house.'
7 And he, having risen, went to his house,
8 and the multitudes having seen, wondered, and glorified God, who did give such power to men.
9 And Jesus passing by there, saw a man sitting at the tax-office, named Matthew, and said to him, 'Be following Me,' and he, having risen, did follow Him.
10 And it came to pass, He reclining (at meat) in the house, that behold, many tax-gatherers and sinners having come, were lying (at meat) with Jesus and His disciples,
11 and the Pharisees having seen, said to His disciples, 'Why does your[P] teacher eat with the tax-gatherers and sinners?'
12 And Jesus having heard, said to them, 'They who are whole have no need of a physician, but they who are ill;
13 but having gone, learn you[P] what is, Kindness I will, and not sacrifice, for I did not come to call righteous men, but sinners, to reformation.'
14 Then do the disciples of John come to Him, saying, 'Why do we and the Pharisees fast much, and Your[S] disciples fast not?'
15 And Jesus said to them, 'Can the sons of the bride-chamber mourn, so long as the bridegroom is with them? but days shall come when the bridegroom may be taken from them, and then they shall fast.
16 'And no one does put a patch of undressed cloth on an old garment, for its filling up does take from the garment, and a worse rent is made.
17 'Nor do they put new wine into old skins, and if not — the skins burst, and the wine does run out, and the skins are destroyed, but they put new wine into new skins, and both are preserved together.'
18 While He is speaking these things to them, behold, a ruler having come, was bowing to Him, saying that 'My daughter just now died, but, having come, lay Your[S] hand upon her, and she shall live.'
19 And Jesus having risen, did follow him, also His disciples,
20 and behold, a woman having an issue of blood twelve years, having come to Him behind, did touch the fringe of His garments,
21 for she said within herself, 'If only I may touch His garment, I shall be saved.'
22 And Jesus having turned about, and having seen her, said, 'Be of good courage, daughter, your[S] faith has saved you[S],' and the woman was saved from that hour.
23 And Jesus having come to the house of the ruler, and having seen the minstrels and the multitude making tumult,
24 He said to them, 'Withdraw, for the damsel did not die, but does sleep,' and they were deriding Him;
25 but, when the multitude was put forth, having gone in, He took hold of her hand, and the damsel arose,
26 and the fame of this went forth to all the land.
27 And Jesus passing on from there, two blind men followed Him, calling and saying, 'Deal kindly with us, Son of David.'
28 And He having come to the house, the blind men came to Him, and Jesus said to them, 'Believe you[P] that I am able to do this?' They say to Him, 'Yes, sir.'
29 Then He touched their eyes, saying, 'According to your faith let it be to you[P],'
30 and their eyes were opened, and Jesus strictly charged them, saying, 'See, let no one know;'
31 but they, having gone forth, did spread His fame in all that land.
32 And as they are coming forth, behold, they brought to Him a man dumb, a demoniac,
33 and the demon having been cast out, the dumb spoke, and the multitude did wonder, saying that 'It was never so seen in Israel:'
34 but the Pharisees said, 'By the ruler of the demons he does cast out the demons.'
35 And Jesus was going up and down all the cities and the villages, teaching in their synagogues, and proclaiming the good news of the reign, and healing every sickness and every malady among the people.
36 And having seen the multitudes, He was moved with

compassion for them, that they were faint and cast aside,
as sheep not having a shepherd,
37 then He said to His disciples, 'The harvest indeed
[is] abundant, but the workmen few;
38 therefore implore you[P] the Lord of the harvest, that
He may put forth workmen to His harvest.'

CHAPTER 10

1 And having called to Him His twelve disciples, He
gave to them power over unclean spirits, so as to be
casting them out, and to be healing every sickness, and
every malady.
2 And of the twelve apostles the names are these: first,
Simon, who is called Peter, and Andrew his brother;
James of Zebedee, and John his brother;
3 Philip, and Bartholomew; Thomas, and Matthew the
tax-gatherer; James of Alpheus, and Lebbeus who was
surnamed Thaddeus;
4 Simon the Cananite, and Judas Iscariot, who did also
deliver Him up.
5 These twelve did Jesus send forth, having given
command to them, saying, 'To the way of the nations
go not away, and into a city of the Samaritans go not in,
6 and be going rather unto the lost sheep of the house
of Israel.
7 'And, going on, proclaim saying that, the reign of the
heavens has come near;
8 be healing infirm ones, be cleansing lepers, be raising
dead, be casting out demons — freely you[P] did receive,
freely give.
9 'Provide not gold, nor silver, nor brass in your[P] girdles,
10 nor scrip for the way, nor two coats, nor sandals, nor
staff — for the workman is worthy of his nourishment.
11 'And into whatever city or village you[P] may enter,
inquire you[P] who in it is worthy, and there abide, till you[P]
may go forth.
12 And coming to the house salute it,
13 and if indeed the house be worthy, let your[P] peace
come upon it; and if it be not worthy, let your[P] peace
turn back to you[P].
14 'And whoever may not receive you[P] nor hear your[P]
words, coming forth from that house or city, shake the
dust off of your[P] feet,
15 truly I say to you[P], It shall be more tolerable for the
land of Sodom and Gomorrah in the day of judgment
than for that city.
16 'Behold, I do send you[P] forth as sheep in the midst
of wolves, be you[P] for that reason wise as the serpents,
and simple as the doves.
17 And, take you[P] heed of men, for they will give you[P]
up to sanhedrims, and they will scourge you[P] in their
synagogues,
18 and you[P] shall be brought before governors and kings
for My sake, for a testimony to them and to the nations.
19 'And whenever they may deliver you[P] up, be not
anxious how or what you[P] may speak, for it shall be given
you[P] in that hour what you[P] shall speak;
20 for you[P] are not the speakers, but the Spirit of your[P]
Father that is speaking in you[P].
21 'And brother shall deliver up brother to death, and
father child, and children shall rise up against parents,
and shall put them to death,
22 and you[P] shall be hated by all because of My name,
but he who has endured to the end, he shall be saved.
23 'And whenever they may persecute you[P] in this city,
flee to the other, for truly I say to you[P], you[P] may not
have completed the cities of Israel till the Son of Man
may come.
24 'A disciple is not above the teacher, nor a servant
above his lord;
25 sufficient to the disciple that he may be as his teacher,
and the servant as his lord; if the master of the house
they did call Beelzeboul, how much more those of his
household?
26 'You[P] may not, for that reason, fear them, for there is
nothing covered, that shall not be revealed, and hid, that
shall not be known;
27 that which I tell you[P] in the darkness, speak in the
light, and that which you[P] hear at the ear, proclaim on
the house-tops.
28 'And be not afraid of those killing the body, and are
not able to kill the soul, but rather fear Him who is able
to destroy both soul and body in gehenna.
29 'Are not two sparrows sold for an assar? and one of
them shall not fall on the ground without your[P] Father;
30 and of you[P] — even the hairs of the head are all
numbered;
31 for that reason be not afraid, you[P] are better than
many sparrows.
32 'Every one, consequently, who shall confess in Me
before men, I will also confess in him before My Father
who is in the heavens;
33 and whoever shall deny Me before men, I will also
deny him before My Father who is in the heavens.
34 'You[P] may not suppose that I came to put peace on
the earth; I did not come to put peace, but a sword;

35 for I came to set a man at variance against his father,
and a daughter against her mother, and a daughter-in-
law against her mother-in-law,
36 and the enemies of a man are those of his household.
37 'He who is loving father or mother above Me, is not
worthy of Me, and he who is loving son or daughter
above Me, is not worthy of Me,
38 and whoever does not receive his cross and follow
after Me, is not worthy of Me.
39 'He who found his life shall lose it, and he who lost
his life for My sake shall find it.
40 'He who is receiving you[P] does receive Me, and he
who is receiving Me does receive Him who sent Me,
41 he who is receiving a prophet in the name of a
prophet, shall receive a prophet's reward, and he who is
receiving a righteous man in the name of a righteous
man, shall receive a righteous man's reward,
42 and whoever may give a cup of cold water only to
drink to one of these little ones in the name of a disciple,
truly I say to you[P], he may not lose his reward.'

CHAPTER 11

1 And it came to pass, when Jesus ended directing His
twelve disciples, He departed from there to teach and to
preach in their cities.
2 And John having heard in the prison the works of the
Christ, having sent two of his disciples,
3 said to Him, 'Are You[S] He who is coming, or do we
look for another?'
4 And Jesus answering said to them, 'Having gone,
declare to John the things that you[P] hear and see,
5 blind receive sight, and lame walk, lepers are cleansed,
and deaf hear, dead are raised, and poor have good news
proclaimed,
6 and happy is he who may not be stumbled in Me.'
7 And as they are going, Jesus began to say to the
multitudes concerning John, 'What went you[P] out to
the wilderness to view? — a reed shaken by the wind?
8 'But what went you[P] out to see? — a man clothed in
soft garments? behold, those wearing the soft things
are in the kings' houses.
9 'But what went you[P] out to see? — a prophet? yes, I
say to you[P], and more than a prophet,
10 for this is he of whom it has been written, Behold, I
do send My messenger before Your[S] face, who shall
prepare Your[S] way before You[S].
11 Truly I say to you[P], there has not risen, among those
born of women, a greater than John the Baptist, but he
who is least in the reign of the heavens is greater than
he.
12 'And, from the days of John the Baptist till now, the
reign of the heavens does suffer violence, and violent
men do take it by force,
13 for all the prophets and the law till John did prophesy,
14 and if you[P] are willing to receive [it], he is Elijah who
was about to come;
15 he who is having ears to hear — let him hear.
16 'And to what shall I liken this generation? it is like
little children in market-places, sitting and calling to their
comrades,
17 and saying, We piped unto you[P], and you[P] did not
dance, we lamented to you[P], and you[P] did not strike the
breast.
18 'For John came neither eating nor drinking, and they
say, He has a demon;
19 the Son of Man came eating and drinking, and they
say, Behold, a man, a glutton, and a wine-drinker, a friend
of tax-gatherers and sinners, and wisdom was justified
of her children.'
20 Then He began to reproach the cities in which were
done most of His mighty works, because they did not
reform.
21 'Woe to you[S], Chorazin! woe to you[S], Bethsaida!
because, if the mighty works that were done in you[P] had
been done in Tyre and Sidon, they would have reformed
long ago in sackcloth and ashes;
22 but I say to you[P], it shall be more tolerable to Tyre
and Sidon in a day of judgment than for you[P].
23 'And you[S], Capernaum, which was exalted unto the
heaven, shall be brought down unto hades, because if
the mighty works that were done in you[S] had been done
in Sodom, it would have remained unto this day;
24 but I say to you[P], it shall be more tolerable to the
land of Sodom in a day of judgment than to you[S].'
25 At that time Jesus answering said, 'I do confess to
You[S], Father, Lord of the heavens and of the earth, that
You[S] did hide these things from wise and understanding
ones, and did reveal them to babes.
26 Yes, Father, because it was good pleasure before You[S].
27 'All things were delivered to Me by My Father, and
none does know the Son, except the Father, nor does
any know the Father, except the Son, and he to whom
the Son may wish to reveal [Him].
28 'Come unto Me, all you[P] laboring and burdened ones,
and I will give you[P] rest,
29 take up My yoke upon you[P], and learn from Me,

because I am meek and humble in heart, and you[P] shall
find rest to your[P] souls,
30 for My yoke [is] easy, and My burden is light.'

CHAPTER 12

1 At that time did Jesus go on the sabbaths through the
corn, and His disciples were hungry, and they began to
pluck ears, and to eat,
2 and the Pharisees having seen, said to Him, 'Behold,
Your[S] disciples do that which it is not lawful to do on a
sabbath.'
3 And He said to them, 'Did you[P] not read what David
did, when he was hungry, himself and those with him —
4 how he went into the house of God, and did eat the loaves
of the presentation, which it is not lawful to him to eat, nor
to those with him, except to the priests alone?
5 'Or did you[P] not read in the Law, that on the sabbaths
the priests in the temple do profane the sabbath, and
are blameless?
6 and I say to you[P], that a greater than the temple is here;
7 and if you[P] had known what is: Kindness I will, and
not sacrifice — you[P] would not have condemned the
blameless,
8 for the son of man is lord even of the sabbath.'
9 And having departed from there, He went to their
synagogue,
10 and behold, there was a man having the hand
withered, and they questioned Him, saying, 'Is it lawful
to heal on the sabbaths?' that they might accuse Him.
11 And He said to them, 'What man shall be of you[P],
who shall have one sheep, and if this may fall into a ditch
on the sabbaths, will not lay hold on it and raise [it]?
12 How much better, therefore, is a man than a sheep?
— so that it is lawful on the sabbaths to do good.'
13 Then He said to the man, 'Stretch forth your[S] hand,'
and he stretched [it] forth, and it was restored whole as
the other.
14 And the Pharisees having gone forth, held a
consultation against Him, how they might destroy Him,
15 and Jesus having known, withdrew from there, and there
followed Him great multitudes, and He healed them all,
16 and did charge them that they might not make Him
obvious,
17 that it might be fulfilled that was spoken through
Isaiah the prophet, saying,
18 'Behold, My servant, whom I did choose, My
beloved, in whom My soul did delight, I will put My
Spirit upon Him, and He shall declare judgment to the
nations,
19 He shall not strive nor cry, nor shall any hear His
voice in the broad places,
20 a bruised reed He shall not break, and smoking flax
He shall not quench, till He may put forth judgment to
victory,
21 and shall nations hope in His name.'
22 Then was brought to Him a demoniac, blind and
dumb, and He healed him, so that the blind and dumb
both spoke and saw.
23 And all the multitudes were amazed, and said, 'Is
this the Son of David?'
24 but the Pharisees having heard, said, 'This one does
not cast out demons, except by Beelzeboul, ruler of the
demons.'
25 And Jesus, knowing their thoughts, said to them,
'Every kingdom having been divided against itself is
desolated, and no city or house having been divided
against itself, does stand,
26 and if the Adversary does cast out the Adversary,
he was divided against himself, how then does his
kingdom stand?
27 'And if I, by Beelzeboul, do cast out the demons,
your[P] sons — by whom do they cast out? because of
this they — they shall be your[P] judges.
28 'But if I, by the Spirit of God, do cast out the demons,
then the reign of God did come already unto you[P].
29 'Or how is one able to go into the house of the strong
man, and to plunder his goods, if he may not first bind
the strong man? and then he will plunder his house.
30 'He who is not with Me is against Me, and he who is
not gathering with Me, does scatter.
31 Because of this I say to you[P], all sin and evil speaking
shall be forgiven to men, but the evil speaking of the
Spirit shall not be forgiven to men.
32 And whoever may speak a word against the Son of
Man it shall be forgiven to him, but whoever may speak
against the Holy Spirit, it shall not be forgiven him,
neither in this age, nor in that which is coming.
33 'Either make the tree good, and its fruit good, or make
the tree bad, and its fruit bad, for from the fruit is the
tree known.
34 'Brood of vipers! how are you[P] able to speak good
things — being evil? for the mouth does speak out of
the abundance of the heart.
35 The good man does put forth the good things out of
the good treasure of the heart, and the evil man does
put forth evil things out of the evil treasure.

36 'And I say to you[P], that every idle word that men
may speak, they shall give a reckoning for it in a day of
judgment;
37 for from your[S] words you[S] shall be declared righteous,
and from your[S] words you[S] shall be declared
unrighteous.'
38 Then answered certain of the scribes and Pharisees,
saying, 'Teacher, we will to see a sign from You[S].'
39 And He answering said to them, 'A generation, evil
and adulterous, does seek a sign, and a sign shall not
be given to it, except the sign of Jonah the prophet;
40 for, as Jonah was in the belly of the fish three days
and three nights, so shall the Son of Man be in the heart
of the earth three days and three nights.
41 'Men of Nineveh shall stand up in the judgment with
this generation, and shall condemn it, for they reformed
at the proclamation of Jonah, and behold, a greater than
Jonah here!
42 'A queen of the south shall rise up in the judgment
with this generation, and shall condemn it, for she came
from the ends of the earth to hear the wisdom of
Solomon, and behold, a greater than Solomon here!
43 'And, when the unclean spirit may go forth from the
man, it does walk through dry places seeking rest, and
does not find;
44 then it says, I will turn back to my house from where
I came forth; and having come, it finds [it] unoccupied,
swept, and adorned:
45 then does it go, and take with itself seven other spirits
more evil than itself, and having gone in they dwell there,
and the last of that man does become worse than the
first; so shall it be also to this evil generation.'
46 And while He was yet speaking to the multitudes,
behold, His mother and brethren had stood without,
seeking to speak to Him,
47 and one said to Him, 'Behold, Your[S] mother and Your[S]
brethren do stand without, seeking to speak to You[S].'
48 And He answering said to him who spoke to Him,
'Who is My mother? and who are My brethren?'
49 And having stretched forth His hand toward His
disciples, He said, 'Behold, My mother and My brethren!
50 for whoever may do the will of My Father who is in
the heavens, he is My brother, and sister, and mother.'

CHAPTER 13

1 And in that day Jesus, having gone forth from the
house, was sitting by the sea,
2 and gathered together unto Him were many multitudes,
so that He having gone into the boat did sit down, and
all the multitude on the beach did stand,
3 and He spoke to them many things in similes, saying:
'Behold, the sower went forth to sow,
4 and in his sowing, some indeed fell by the way, and
the fowls did come and devour them,
5 and others fell upon the rocky places, where they had
not much earth, and immediately they sprang forth,
through not having depth of earth,
6 and the sun having risen they were scorched, and
through not having root, they withered,
7 and others fell upon the thorns, and the thorns did
come up and choke them,
8 and others fell upon the good ground, and were giving
fruit, some indeed a hundredfold, and some sixty, and
some thirty.
9 He who is having ears to hear — let him hear.'
10 And the disciples having come near, said to Him,
'Why do You[S] speak to them in similes?'
11 And He answering said to them that — 'To you[P] it
has been given to know the secrets of the reign of the
heavens, and to these it has not been given,
12 for whoever has, it shall be given to him, and he shall
have overabundance, and whoever has not, even that
which he has shall be taken from him.
13 'Because of this, do I speak to them in similes,
because seeing they do not see, and hearing they do
not hear, nor understand,
14 and fulfilled on them is the prophecy of Isaiah, that
said, With hearing you shall hear, and you shall not
understand, and seeing you shall see, and you shall not
perceive,
15 for made gross was the heart of this people, and with
the ears they heard heavily, and they did close their eyes,
for fear that they might see with the eyes, and might
hear with the ears, and understand with the heart, and
turn back, and I might heal them.
16 'And happy are your[P] eyes because they see, and
your[P] ears because they hear,
17 for truly I say to you[P], that many prophets and
righteous men did desire to see that which you[P] look
on, and they did not see, and to hear that which you[P]
hear, and they did not hear.
18 'You[P], for that reason, hear you[P] the simile of the
sower:
19 Every one hearing the word of the reign, and not
understanding — the evil one does come, and does
catch that which has been sown in his heart; this is that

sown by the way.
20 'And that sown on the rocky places, this is he who
is hearing the word, and immediately is receiving it with
joy,
21 and he has not root in himself, but is temporary, and
persecution or tribulation having happened because of
the word, immediately he is stumbled.
22 'And that sown toward the thorns, this is he who is
hearing the word, and the anxiety of this age, and the
deceitfulness of the riches, do choke the word, and it
becomes unfruitful.
23 'And that sown on the good ground: this is he who
is hearing the word, and is understanding, who indeed
does bear fruit, and does make, some indeed a
hundredfold, and some sixty, and some thirty.'
24 Another simile He set before them, saying: 'The reign
of the heavens was likened to a man sowing good seed
in his field,
25 and, while men are sleeping, his enemy came and
sowed darnel in the midst of the wheat, and went away,
26 and when the herb sprang up, and yielded fruit, then
the darnel appeared also.
27 'And the servants of the householder, having come
near, said to him, Sir, did you[S] not sow good seed in
your[S] field? from where then has it the darnel?
28 And he said to them, A man, an enemy, did this; and
the servants said to him, Will you[S], then, [that] having
gone away we may gather it up?
29 'And he said, No, for fear — gathering up the darnel
— you[P] root up the wheat with it,
30 allow both to grow together till the harvest, and in
the time of the harvest I will say to the reapers, Gather
up first the darnel, and bind it in bundles, to burn it, and
gather up the wheat into my storehouse.'
31 Another simile He set before them, saying: 'The reign
of the heavens is like to a grain of mustard, which a man
having taken, did sow in his field,
32 which is, indeed, less than all the seeds, but when it
may be grown, is greatest of the herbs, and becomes a
tree, so that the birds of the heaven do come and rest in
its branches.'
33 Another simile He spoke to them: 'The reign of the
heavens is like to leaven, which a woman having taken,
hid in three measures of meal, till the whole was
leavened.'
34 Jesus spoke all these things in similes to the
multitudes, and He was not speaking to them without a
simile,
35 that it might be fulfilled that was spoken through the
prophet, saying, 'I will open my mouth in similes, I will
utter things having been hidden from the foundation of
the world.'
36 Then having let away the multitudes, Jesus came to
the house, and His disciples came near to Him, saying,
'Explain to us the simile of the darnel of the field.'
37 And He answering said to them, 'He who is sowing
the good seed is the Son of Man,
38 and the field is the world, and the good seed, these
are the sons of the reign, and the darnel are the sons of
the evil one,
39 and the enemy who sowed them is the devil, and the
harvest is a full end of the age, and the reapers are
messengers.
40 'As, then, the darnel is gathered up, and is burned
with fire, so shall it be in the full end of this age,
41 the Son of Man shall send forth his messengers, and
they shall gather up out of his kingdom all the stumbling-
blocks, and those doing the unlawlessness,
42 and shall cast them to the furnace of the fire; there
shall be the weeping and the gnashing of the teeth.
43 'Then shall the righteous shine forth as the sun in
the reign of their Father. He who is having ears to hear
— let him hear.
44 'Again, the reign of the heavens is like to treasure
hid in the field, which a man having found did hide, and
from his joy went, and all, as much as he had, he sold,
and bought that field.
45 'Again, the reign of the heavens is like to a man, a
merchant, seeking goodly pearls,
46 who having found one pearl of great price, having gone
away, had sold all, as much as he had, and bought it.
47 'Again, the reign of the heavens is like to a net that
was cast into the sea, and did gather together of every
kind,
48 which, when it was filled, having drawn up again
upon the beach, and having sat down, they gathered
the good into vessels, and they did cast out the bad,
49 so shall it be in the full end of the age, the messengers
shall come forth and separate the evil out of the midst
of the righteous,
50 and shall cast them to the furnace of the fire, there
shall be the weeping and the gnashing of the teeth.'
51 Jesus said to them, 'Did you[P] understand all these?'
They say to Him, 'Yes, sir.'
52 And He said to them, 'Because of this every scribe
having been discipled in regard to the reign of the
heavens, is like to a man, a householder, who does bring
forth out of his treasure things new and old.'

53 And it came to pass, when Jesus finished these
similes, He removed from there,
54 and having come to His own country, He was
teaching them in their synagogue, so that they were
astonished, and were saying, 'From where to this one
this wisdom and the mighty works?
55 is this not the carpenter's son? is His mother not
called Mary, and His brethren James, and Joses, and
Simon, and Judas?
56 and His sisters — are they not all with us? from where,
then, to this one all these?'
57 and they were stumbled at Him. And Jesus said to
them, 'A prophet is not without honor except in his own
country, and in his own house:'
58 and He did not many mighty works there, because of
their unbelief.

CHAPTER 14

1 At that time did Herod the tetrarch hear the fame of
Jesus,
2 and said to his servants, 'This is John the Baptist, he
did rise from the dead, and because of this the mighty
energies are working in him.'
3 For Herod having laid hold on John, did bind him, and
did put him in prison, because of Herodias his brother
Philip's wife,
4 for John was saying to him, 'It is not lawful to you[S] to
have her,'
5 and, willing to kill him, he feared the multitude, because
they were holding him as a prophet.
6 But the birthday of Herod being kept, the daughter of
Herodias danced in the midst, and did please Herod,
7 upon which with an oath he professed to give her
whatever she might ask.
8 And she having been instigated by her mother — 'Give
me (says she) here the head of John the Baptist upon a
plate;
9 and the king was grieved, but because of the oaths
and of those reclining with him, he commanded [it] to be
given;
10 and having sent, he beheaded John in the prison,
11 and his head was brought upon a plate, and was
given to the damsel, and she brought [it] near to her
mother.
12 And his disciples having come, took up the body,
and buried it, and having come, they told Jesus,
13 and Jesus having heard, withdrew from there in a
boat to a desolate place by Himself, and the multitudes
having heard did follow Him on land from the cities.
14 And Jesus having come forth, saw a great multitude,
and was moved with compassion upon them, and did
heal their infirm;
15 and evening having come, His disciples came to Him,
saying, 'The place is desolate, and the hour has now
past, send away the multitudes that, having gone to the
villages, they may buy to themselves food.'
16 And Jesus said to them, 'They have no need to go
away – you[P] give them to eat.'
17 And they say to Him, 'We have not here except five
loaves, and two fishes.'
18 And He said, 'You[P] bring them to Me here.'
19 And having commanded the multitudes to recline
upon the grass, and having taken the five loaves and
the two fishes, having looked up to the heaven, He did
bless, and having broken, He gave the loaves to the
disciples, and the disciples to the multitudes,
20 and they did all eat, and were filled, and they took up what
was over of the broken pieces twelve hand-baskets full;
21 and those eating were about five thousand men, apart
from women and children.
22 And immediately Jesus constrained His disciples to
go into the boat, and to go before Him to the other side,
till He might send away the multitudes;
23 and having sent away the multitudes, He went up to
the mountain by Himself to pray, and evening having
come, He was there alone,
24 and the boat was now in the midst of the sea,
distressed by the waves, for the wind was contrary.
25 And in the fourth watch of the night Jesus went away
to them, walking upon the sea,
26 and the disciples having seen Him walking upon the
sea, were troubled saying — 'It is an apparition,' and
they cried out from the fear;
27 and immediately Jesus spoke to them, saying, 'Be of
good courage, I am [He], be not afraid.'
28 And Peter answering Him said, 'Sir, if it is You[S], bid
me come to You[S] upon the waters;'
29 and He said, 'Come;' and having gone down from
the boat, Peter walked upon the waters to come unto
Jesus,
30 but seeing the wind vehement, he was afraid, and
having begun to sink, he cried out, saying, 'Sir, save
me.'
31 And immediately Jesus, having stretched forth the
hand, laid hold of him, and said to him, 'Little faith! for
what did you[S] waver?'

32 and they having gone to the boat the wind lulled,
33 and those in the boat having come, did bow to him,
saying, 'Truly – You[S] are God's Son.'
34 And having passed over, they came to the land of
Gennesaret,
35 and having recognized Him, the men of that place
sent forth to all that region round about, and they
brought to Him all who were ill,
36 and were calling on Him that they might only touch
the fringe of His garment, and as many as did touch were
saved.

CHAPTER 15

1 Then do they come unto Jesus from Jerusalem —
scribes and Pharisees — saying,
2 'Why do Your[S] disciples transgress the tradition of
the elders? for they do not wash their hands when they
may eat bread.'
3 And He answering said to them, 'Why do you[P] also
transgress the command of God because of your[P]
tradition?
4 for God did command, saying, Honor your[S] father and
mother; and, he who is speaking evil of father or mother
— let him die the death;
5 but you[P] say, Whoever may say to father or mother, An
offering [is] whatever you[S] may be profited by me; —
6 and he may not honor his father or his mother, and
you[P] did set aside the command of God because of your[P]
tradition.
7 'Hypocrites, well did Isaiah prophesy of you[P], saying,
8 This people do draw near to Me with their mouth, and
with the lips it does honor Me, but their heart is far off
from Me;
9 and in vain do they worship Me, teaching teachings
— commands of men.'
10 And having called near the multitude, He said to them,
'Hear and understand:
11 that which is coming into the mouth does not defile
the man, but that which is coming forth from the mouth,
this defiles the man.'
12 Then His disciples having come near, said to Him,
'Have You[S] known that the Pharisees, having heard the
word, were stumbled?'
13 And He answering said, 'Every plant that my
heavenly Father did not plant shall be rooted up;
14 leave them alone, guides they are — blind of blind;
and if blind may guide blind, both shall fall into a ditch.'
15 And Peter answering said to Him, 'Explain to us this
simile.'
16 And Jesus said, 'Are you[P] also yet without
understanding?
17 do you[P] not understand that all that is going into the
mouth does pass into the belly, and is cast forth into
the drain?
18 but the things coming forth from the mouth do come
forth from the heart, and these defile the man;
19 for out of the heart come forth evil thoughts, murders,
adulteries, whoredoms, thefts, false witnessings, evil
speakings:
20 these are the things defiling the man; but to eat with
unwashed hands does not defile the man.'
21 And Jesus having come forth from there, withdrew
to the parts of Tyre and Sidon,
22 and behold, a woman, a Canaanitess, from those
borders having come forth, did call to Him, saying, 'Deal
kindly with me, Sir — Son of David; my daughter is
miserably demonized.'
23 And He did not answer her a word; and His disciples
having come to Him, were asking him, saying — 'Send
her away, because she cries after us;'
24 and He answering said, 'I was not sent except to the
lost sheep of the house of Israel.'
25 And having come, she was bowing to Him, saying,
'Sir, help me;'
26 and He answering said, 'It is not good to take the
children's bread, and to cast to the little dogs.'
27 And she said, 'Yes, sir, for even the little dogs do eat
of the crumbs that are falling from their lords' table;'
28 then answering, Jesus said to her, 'O woman, great
[is] your[S] faith, let it be to you[S] as you[S] want;' and her
daughter was healed from that hour.
29 And Jesus having passed from there, came near unto
the sea of Galilee, and having gone up to the mountain,
He was sitting there,
30 and there came to Him great multitudes, having with
them lame, blind, dumb, maimed, and many others, and
they did cast them at the feet of Jesus, and He healed
them,
31 so that the multitudes did wonder, seeing dumb ones
speaking, maimed whole, lame walking, and blind seeing;
and they glorified the God of Israel.
32 And Jesus having called His disciples near, said, 'I
have compassion upon the multitude, because now three
days they continue with me, and they have not what
they may eat; and I will not send them away fasting, for
fear that they faint in the way.'

33 And His disciples say to Him, 'From where to us, in a
wilderness, so many loaves, as to fill so great a
multitude?'
34 And Jesus said to them, 'How many loaves have
you[P]?' and they said, 'Seven, and a few little fishes.'
35 And He commanded the multitudes to sit down upon
the ground,
36 and having taken the seven loaves and the fishes,
having given thanks, He did break, and gave to His
disciples, and the disciples to the multitude.
37 And they did all eat, and were filled, and they took
up what was left over of the broken pieces seven baskets
full,
38 and those eating were four thousand men, apart from
women and children.
39 And having sent away the multitudes, He went into
the boat, and did come to the borders of Magdala.

CHAPTER 16

1 And the Pharisees and Sadducees having come,
tempting, did question Him, to show to them a sign from
the heaven,
2 and He answering said to them, 'Evening having come,
you[P] say, Fair weather, for the heaven is red,
3 and at morning, Foul weather today, for the heaven is
red — gloomy; hypocrites, the face of the heavens
indeed you[P] do know to discern, but the signs of the
times you[P] are not able!
4 'A generation evil and adulterous does seek a sign,
and a sign shall not be given to it, except the sign of
Jonah the prophet;' and having left them He went away.
5 And His disciples having come to the other side, forgot
to take loaves,
6 and Jesus said to them, 'Beware, and take heed of the
leaven of the Pharisees and Sadducees;'
7 and they were reasoning in themselves, saying,
'Because we took no loaves.'
8 And Jesus having known, said to them, 'Why reason
you[P] in yourselves[P], you[P] of little faith, because you[P]
took no loaves?
9 you[P] do not yet understand, nor remember the five
loaves of the five thousand, and how many hand-
baskets you[P] took up?
10 nor the seven loaves of the four thousand, and how
many baskets you[P] took up?
11 how do you[P] not understand that I did not speak to
you[P] of bread — to take heed of the leaven of the
Pharisees and Sadducees?'
12 Then they understood that He did not say to take
heed of the leaven of the bread, but of the teaching, of
the Pharisees and Sadducees.
13 And Jesus, having come to the parts of Caesarea
Philippi, was asking His disciples, saying, 'Who do men
say Me to be — the Son of Man?'
14 and they said, 'Some, John the Baptist, and others,
Elijah, and others, Jeremiah, or one of the prophets.'
15 He said to them, 'And you[P] — who do you[P] say Me
to be?'
16 and Simon Peter answering said, 'You[S] are the Christ,
the Son of the living God.'
17 And Jesus answering said to him, 'Happy are you[S],
Simon Bar-Jona, because flesh and blood did not reveal
[it] to you[S], but My Father who is in the heavens.
18 'And I also say to you[S], that you[S] are a rock, and
upon this rock I will build my assembly, and gates of
Hades shall not prevail against it;
19 and I will give to you[S] the keys of the reign of the
heavens, and whatever you[S] may bind upon the earth
shall be having been bound in the heavens, and
whatever you[S] may loose upon the earth shall be having
been loosed in the heavens.'
20 Then did He charge His disciples that they may say
to no one that He is Jesus the Christ.
21 From that time began Jesus to show to His disciples
that it is necessary for Him to go away to Jerusalem,
and to suffer many things from the elders, and chief
priests, and scribes, and to be put to death, and the third
day to rise.
22 And having taken Him aside, Peter began to rebuke
Him, saying, 'Be kind to Yourself[S], sir; this shall not be
to You[S];'
23 and He having turned, said to Peter, 'Get you[S] behind
Me, adversary! you[S] are a stumbling-block to Me, for
you[S] do not mind the things of God, but the things of
men.'
24 Then said Jesus to His disciples, 'If any one does
will to come after Me, let him disown himself, and take
up his cross, and follow Me,
25 for whoever may will to save his life, shall lose it,
and whoever may lose his life for My sake shall find it,
26 for what is a man profited if he may gain the whole
world, but suffer loss of his life? or what shall a man
give as an exchange for his life?
27 'For, the Son of Man is about to come in the glory of
His Father, with His messengers, and then He will reward
each, according to His work.

28 Truly I say to you[P], there are certain of those standing
here who shall not taste of death till they may see the
Son of Man coming in His reign.'

CHAPTER 17

1 And after six days Jesus took Peter, and James, and
John his brother, and did bring them up to a high mount
by themselves,
2 and He was transfigured before them, and His face
shone as the sun, and His garments did become white
as the light,
3 and behold, Moses and Elijah did appear to them,
talking together with Him.
4 And Peter answering said to Jesus, 'Sir, it is good to
us to be here; if You[S] want, we may make three booths
here – one for You[S], and one for Moses, and one for
Elijah.'
5 While he is yet speaking, behold, a bright cloud
overshadowed them, and behold, a voice out of the
cloud, saying, 'This is My Son, — the Beloved, in whom
I did delight; hear Him.'
6 And the disciples having heard, did fall upon their
face, and were exceedingly afraid,
7 and Jesus having come near, touched them, and said,
'Rise, be not afraid,'
8 and having lifted up their eyes, they saw no one, except
Jesus only.
9 And as they are coming down from the mount, Jesus
charged them, saying, 'Say to no one the vision, till the
Son of Man may rise out of the dead.'
10 And His disciples questioned Him, saying, 'Why then
do the scribes say it was necessary that Elijah to come
first?'
11 And Jesus answering said to them, 'Elijah does
indeed come first, and shall restore all things,
12 and I say to you[P] — Elijah did already come, and
they did not know him, but did whatever they would
with him, so also the Son of Man is about to suffer by
them.'
13 Then the disciples understood that He spoke
concerning John the Baptist to them.
14 And when they came unto the multitude, there came
to Him a man, kneeling down to Him,
15 and saying, 'Sir, deal kindly with my son, for he is
lunatic, and does suffer miserably, for he does often fall
into the fire, and often into the water,
16 and I brought him near to Your[S] disciples, and they
were not able to heal him.'
17 And Jesus answering said, 'O generation,
unsteadfast and perverse, till when shall I be with you[P]?
till when shall I bear you[P]? bring him here to Me;'
18 and Jesus rebuked him, and the demon went out of
him, and the lad was healed from that hour.
19 Then the disciples having come to Jesus by Himself,
said, 'Why were we not able to cast him out?'
20 And Jesus said to them, 'Through your[P] want of faith;
for truly I say to you[P], if you[P] may have faith as a grain
of mustard, you[P] shall say to this mount, Remove from
here to yonder place, and it shall remove, and nothing
shall be impossible to you[P],
21 and this kind does not go forth except in prayer and
fasting.'
22 And while they are living in Galilee, Jesus said to
them, 'The Son of Man is about to be delivered up to
the hands of men,
23 and they shall kill Him, and the third day He shall
rise,' and they were exceeding sorry.
24 And they having come to Capernaum, those receiving
the didrachms came near to Peter, and said, 'Your[S] teacher
— does he not pay the didrachms?' He said, 'Yes.'
25 And when he came into the house, Jesus anticipated
him, saying, 'What do you[S] think, Simon? the kings of
the earth — from whom do they receive custom or poll-
tax? from their sons or from the strangers?'
26 Peter said to Him, 'From the strangers.' Jesus said to
him, 'Then are the sons free;
27 but, that we may not cause them to stumble, go to
the sea, cast a hook, and take you[S] up the fish that has
come up first, and having opened its mouth, you[S] shall
find a stater, that having taken, give to them for Me and
you[S].'

CHAPTER 18

1 At that hour came the disciples near to Jesus, saying,
'Who, now, is greater in the reign of the heavens?'
2 And Jesus having called near a child, did set him in
the midst of them,
3 and said, 'Truly I say to you[P], if you[P] may not be turned
and become as the children, you[P] may not enter into the
reign of the heavens;
4 whoever then may humble himself as this child, he is
the greater in the reign of the heavens.
5 'And he who may receive one such child in My name,
does receive Me,

6 and whoever may cause one of those little ones who
are believing in Me to stumble, it is better for him that a
weighty millstone may be hanged upon his neck, and
he may be sunk in the depth of the sea.
7 'Woe to the world from the stumbling-blocks! for there
is a necessity for the stumbling-blocks to come, but woe
to that man through whom the stumbling-block does
come!
8 'And if your[S] hand or your[S] foot does cause you[S] to
stumble, cut them off and cast from you[S]; it is good for
you[S] to enter into the life lame or maimed, rather than
having two hands or two feet, to be cast to the fire the
age-during.
9 'And if your[S] eye does cause you[S] to stumble, pluck it
out and cast from you[S]; it is good for you[S] to enter into
the life one eyed, rather than having two eyes to be cast
to the gehenna of the fire.
10 'Beware! — you[P] may not despise one of these little
ones, for I say to you[P], that their messengers in the
heavens do always behold the face of My Father who is
in the heavens,
11 for the Son of Man did come to save the lost.
12 'What think you[P]? if a man may have an hundred
sheep, and there may one of them go astray, does he
not — having left the ninety-nine, having gone on the
mountains — seek that which is gone astray?
13 and if it may come to pass that he does find it, truly I
say to you[P], that he does rejoice over it more than over
the ninety-nine that have not gone astray;
14 so it is not will in presence of your[P] Father who is in
the heavens, that one of these little ones may perish.
15 'And if your[S] brother may sin against you[S], go and
show him his fault between you[S] and him alone, if he
may hear you[S], you[S] did gain your[S] brother;
16 and if he may not hear, take one or two with you[S] yet,
that by the mouth of two witnesses or three every word
may stand.
17 'And if he may not hear them, say [it] to the assembly,
and if he also may not hear the assembly, let him be to
you[S] as the heathen man and the tax-gatherer.
18 'Truly I say to you[P], Whatever things you[P] may bind
upon the earth shall be having been bound in the
heavens, and whatever things you[P] may loose on the
earth shall be having been loosed in the heavens.
19 'Again, I say to you[P], that, if two of you[P] may agree
on the earth concerning anything, whatever they may
ask — it shall be done to them from My Father who is in
the heavens,
20 for where there are two or three gathered together —
to My name, there am I in the midst of them.'
21 Then Peter having come near to Him, said, 'Sir, how
often shall my brother sin against me, and I forgive him
— till seven times?'
22 Jesus said to him, 'I do not say to you[S] till seven
times, but till seventy times seven.
23 'Because of this was the reign of the heavens likened
to a man, a king, who did will to take reckoning with his
servants,
24 and he having begun to take account, there was
brought near to him one debtor of a myriad of talents,
25 and he having nothing to pay, his lord did command
him to be sold, and his wife, and the children, and all,
whatever he had, and payment to be made.
26 The servant then, having fallen down, was bowing
to him, saying, Sir, have patience with me, and I will pay
you[S] all;
27 and the lord of that servant having been moved with
compassion did release him, and he forgave him the debt.
28 'And, that servant having come forth, found one of
his fellow-servants who was owing him an hundred
denaries, and having laid hold, he took him by the throat,
saying, Pay me that which you[S] owe.
29 His fellow-servant then, having fallen down at his
feet, was calling on him, saying, Have patience with me,
and I will pay you[S] all;
30 and he would not, but having gone away, he cast
him into prison, till he might pay that which was owing.
31 'And his fellow-servants having seen the things that
were done, were grieved exceedingly, and having come,
showed fully to their lord all the things that were done;
32 then having called him, his lord said to him, Evil
servant! I did forgive you[S] all that debt, seeing you[S] did
call upon me,
33 was it not necessary also you[S] to have dealt kindly
with your[S] fellow-servant, as I also dealt kindly with
you[S]?
34 'And having been angry, his lord delivered him to
the inquisitors, till he might pay all that was owing to
him;
35 so also My heavenly Father will do to you[P], if you[P]
may not forgive each one his brother from your[P] hearts
their trespasses.'

CHAPTER 19

1 And it came to pass, when Jesus finished these words,
He removed from Galilee, and did come to the borders of

Judea, beyond the Jordan,
2 and great multitudes followed Him, and He healed them
there.
3 And the Pharisees came near to Him, tempting Him,
and saying to Him, 'Is it lawful for a man to put away his
wife for every cause?'
4 And He answering said to them, 'Did you[P] not read,
that He who made [them], from the beginning a male and
a female made them,
5 and said, For this cause shall a man leave father and
mother, and cleave to his wife, and they shall be — the
two — for one flesh?
6 so that they are no more two, but one flesh; for that
reason what God did join together, let no man put
asunder.'
7 They say to Him, 'Why then did Moses command to
give a roll of divorce, and to put her away?'
8 He said to them — 'Moses did allow you[P] to put away
your[P] wives for your[P] stiffness of heart, but from the
beginning it has not been so.
9 'And I say to you[P], that, whoever may put away his
wife, if not for whoredom, and may marry another, does
commit adultery; and he who did marry her that has been
put away, does commit adultery.'
10 His disciples say to Him, 'If the case of the man with
the woman is so, it is not good to marry.'
11 And He said to them, 'All do not receive this word,
but those to whom it has been given;
12 for there are eunuchs who from the mother's womb
were so born; and there are eunuchs who were made
eunuchs by men; and there are eunuchs who kept
themselves eunuchs because of the reign of the heavens:
he who is able to receive [it] — let him receive.'
13 Then were brought near to Him children that He might
put hands on them and pray, and the disciples rebuked
them.
14 But Jesus said, 'Allow the children, and forbid them
not, to come unto Me, for of such is the reign of the
heavens;'
15 and having laid [His] hands on them, He departed
from there.
16 And behold, one having come near, said to Him,
'Good teacher, what good thing shall I do, that I may
have life age-during?'
17 And He said to him, 'Why do you[S] call Me good? no
one [is] good except One — God; but if you[S] do want to
enter into the life, keep the commands.'
18 He said to him, 'What kind?' And Jesus said, 'You[S]
shall not kill, you[S] shall not commit adultery, you[S] shall
not steal, you[S] shall not bear false witness,
19 honor your[S] father and mother, and, you[S] shall love
your[S] neighbor as yourself[S].'
20 The young man said to Him, 'All these did I keep
from my youth; what do I yet lack?'
21 Jesus said to him, 'If you[S] do want to be perfect, go
away, sell what you[S] have, and give to the poor, and
you[S] shall have treasure in heaven, and come, follow
Me.'
22 And the young man, having heard the word, went
away sorrowful, for he had many possessions;
23 and Jesus said to His disciples, 'Truly I say to you[P],
that hardly shall a rich man enter into the reign of the
heavens;
24 and again I say to you[P], it is easier for a camel to go
through the eye of a needle, than for a rich man to enter
into the reign of God.'
25 And His disciples having heard, were amazed
exceedingly, saying, 'Who, then, is able to be saved?'
26 And Jesus having earnestly beheld, said to them,
'With men this is impossible, but with God all things are
possible.'
27 Then Peter answering said to Him, 'Behold, we did
leave all, and follow You[S], what then shall we have?'
28 And Jesus said to them, 'Truly I say to you[P], that
you[P] who did follow Me, in the regeneration, when the
Son of Man may sit upon a throne of His glory, shall sit
— you[P] also — upon twelve thrones, judging the twelve
tribes of Israel;
29 and every one who left houses, or brothers, or sisters,
or father, or mother, or wife, or children, or fields, for My
name's sake, an hundredfold shall receive, and life age-
during shall inherit;
30 and many first shall be last, and last first.

CHAPTER 20

1 'For the reign of the heavens is like to a man, a
householder, who went forth with the morning to hire
workmen for his vineyard,
2 and having agreed with the workmen for a denary a
day, he sent them into his vineyard.
3 'And having gone forth about the third hour, he saw
others standing in the market-place idle,
4 and to these he said, Go you[P] — also you[P] — to the
vineyard, and I will give you[P] whatever may be
righteous;
5 and they went away. 'Again, having gone forth about

the sixth and the ninth hour, he did in like manner.
6 And about the eleventh hour, having gone forth, he
found others standing idle, and said to them, Why have
you[P] stood here idle all the day?
7 they say to him, Because no one did hire us; he said
to them, Go you[P] — you[P] also — to the vineyard, and
you[P] shall receive whatever may be righteous.
8 'And evening having come, the lord of the vineyard
said to his steward, Call the workmen, and pay them the
reward, having begun from the last — unto the first.
9 And they of about the eleventh hour having come,
did receive each a denary.
10 'And the first having come, did suppose that they
shall receive more, and they received, they also, each a
denary,
11 and having received [it], they were murmuring against
the householder, saying,
12 that these, the last, worked one hour, and you[S] did
make them equal to us, who were bearing the burden of
the day — and the heat.
13 'And he answering said to one of them, Comrade, I
do no unrighteousness to you[S]; did not you[S] agree with
me for a denary?
14 take that which is yours[S], and go; and I will to give
to this, the last, also as to you[S];
15 is it not lawful to me to do what I will in mine own? is
your[S] eye evil because I am good?
16 So the last shall be first, and the first last, for many
are called, and few chosen.'
17 And Jesus going up to Jerusalem, took the twelve
disciples by themselves in the way, and said to them,
18 'Behold, we go up to Jerusalem, and the Son of Man
shall be delivered to the chief priests and scribes,
19 and they shall condemn Him to death, and shall
deliver Him to the nations to mock, and to scourge, and
to crucify, and the third day He will rise again.'
20 Then the mother of the sons of Zebedee came near
to Him, with her sons, bowing and asking something
from Him,
21 and He said to her, 'What do you[S] want?' She said to
Him, 'Say, that they may sit — these my two sons —
one on Your[S] right hand, and one on the left, in Your[S]
reign.'
22 And Jesus answering said, 'You[P] have not known
what you[P] ask for yourselves[P]; are you[P] able to drink of
the cup that I am about to drink? And to be baptized
with the baptism that I am baptized with?' They say to
Him, 'We are able.'
23 And He said to them, 'Of My cup indeed you[P] shall
drink, and with the baptism that I am baptized with you[P]
shall be baptized; but to sit on My right hand and on
My left is not Mine to give, but — to those for whom it
has been prepared by My father.'
24 And the ten having heard, were much displeased with
the two brothers,
25 and Jesus having called them near, said, 'You[P] have
known that the rulers of the nations do exercise lordship
over them, and those great do exercise authority over
them,
26 but not so shall it be among you[P], but whoever among
you[P] may want to become great, let him be your[P]
ministrant;
27 and whoever may want to be first among you[P], let
him be your[P] servant;
28 even as the Son of Man did not come to be ministered
to, but to minister, and to give His life a ransom for many.'
29 And they going forth from Jericho, there followed
Him a great multitude,
30 and behold, two blind men sitting by the way, having
heard that Jesus did pass by, cried, saying, 'Deal kindly
with us, sir — Son of David.'
31 And the multitude charged them that they might be
silent, and they cried out the more, saying, 'Deal kindly
with us sir — Son of David.'
32 And having stood, Jesus called them, and said, 'What
will you[P] [that] I may do to you[P]?'
33 they say to Him, 'Sir, that our eyes may be opened;'
34 and having been moved with compassion, Jesus
touched their eyes, and immediately their eyes received
sight, and they followed Him.

CHAPTER 21

1 And when they came near to Jerusalem, and came to
Bethphage, unto the mount of the Olives, then Jesus
sent two disciples,
2 saying to them, 'Go on to the village over-against you[P],
and immediately you[P] shall find an ass bound, and a colt
with her — having loosed, bring you[P] to Me;
3 and if any one may say anything to you[P], you[P] shall
say, that the lord has need of them, and immediately he
will send them.'
4 And all this came to pass, that it might be fulfilled that
was spoken through the prophet, saying,
5 'Tell you[P] the daughter of Zion, Behold, your[S] king
does come to you[S], meek, and mounted on an ass, and a
colt, a foal of a beast of burden.'

6 And the disciples having gone and having done as
Jesus commanded them,
7 brought the ass and the colt, and did put their garments
on them, and set [Him] upon them;
8 and the very great multitude spread their own garments
in the way, and others were cutting branches from the
trees, and were strewing in the way,
9 and the multitudes who were going before, and who
were following, were crying, saying, 'Hosanna to the Son
of David, blessed is He who is coming in the name of
the Lord; Hosanna in the highest.'
10 And He having entered into Jerusalem, all the city
was moved, saying, 'Who is this?'
11 And the multitudes said, 'This is Jesus the prophet,
who [is] from Nazareth of Galilee.'
12 And Jesus entered into the temple of God, and did
cast forth all those selling and buying in the temple, and
He overturned the tables of the money-changers, and
the seats of those selling the doves,
13 and He said to them, 'It has been written, My house
shall be called a house of prayer, but you[P] did make it a
den of robbers.'
14 And there came to Him blind and lame men in the
temple, and He healed them,
15 and the chief priests and the scribes having seen the
wonderful things that He did, and the children crying in
the temple, and saying, 'Hosanna to the Son of David,'
were much displeased;
16 and they said to Him, 'You[S] hear what these say?'
And Jesus said to them, 'Yes, did you[P] never read, that,
Out of the mouth of babes and sucklings You[S] did
prepare praise?'
17 And having left them, He went forth out of the city
to Bethany, and did lodge there,
18 and in the morning turning back to the city, He
hungered,
19 and having seen a certain fig-tree on the way, He
came to it, and found nothing in it except leaves only,
and He said to it, 'No more may fruit be from you[S] — to
the age;' and immediately the fig-tree withered.
20 And the disciples having seen, did wonder, saying,
'How did the fig-tree immediately wither?'
21 And Jesus answering said to them, 'Truly I say to
you[P], if you[P] may have faith, and may not doubt, not
only shall you[P] do this of the fig-tree, but even if you[P]
may say to this mount, Be lifted up and be cast into the
sea, it shall come to pass;
22 and all — as much as you[P] may ask in the prayer,
believing, you[P] shall receive.'
23 And He having come to the temple, there the chief
priests and the elders of the people came to Him when
teaching, saying, 'By what authority do You[S] do these
things? and who gave You[S] this authority?'
24 And Jesus answering said to them, 'I will ask you[P]
— I also — one word, which if you[P] may tell Me, I will
also tell you[P] by what authority I do these things;
25 the baptism of John, from where was it? — from
heaven, or from men?' And they were reasoning with
themselves, saying, 'If we should say, From heaven; He
will say to us, Why, then, did you[P] not believe him?
26 and if we should say, From men, we fear the multitude,
for all hold John as a prophet.'
27 And answering Jesus they said, 'We have not
known.' He said to them — he also — 'Neither do I tell
you[P] by what authority I do these things.
28 'And what think you[P]? A man had two children, and
having come to the first, he said, Child, go, be working
in my vineyard today.'
29 And he answering said, 'I will not,' but at last, having
repented, he went.
30 'And having come to the second, he said in the same
manner, and he answering said, I [go], sir, and went not;
31 which of the two did the will of the father?' They say
to Him, 'The first.' Jesus said to them, 'Truly I say to
you[P], that the tax-gatherers and the harlots do go into
the reign of God before you[P],
32 for John came unto you[P] in the way of righteousness,
and you[P] did not believe him, and the tax-gatherers and
the harlots did believe him, and you[P], having seen,
repented not at last — to believe him.
33 'Hear you[P] another simile: There was a certain man, a
householder, who planted a vineyard, and did put a
hedge round it, and dug in it a wine-press, and built a
tower, and gave it out to husbandmen, and went abroad.
34 'And when the season of the fruits came near, he
sent his servants unto the husbandmen, to receive the
fruits of it,
35 and the husbandmen having taken his servants, one
they scourged, and one they killed, and one they stoned.
36 'Again he sent other servants more than the first,
and they did to them in the same manner.
37 'And at last he sent unto them his son, saying, They
will reverence my son;
38 and the husbandmen having seen the son, said
among themselves, This is the heir, come, we may kill
him, and may possess his inheritance;
39 and having taken him, they cast [him] out of the
vineyard, and killed him;

40 whenever therefore the lord of the vineyard may come, what will he do to these husbandmen?'

41 They say to Him, 'Evil men — he will evilly destroy them, and will give out the vineyard to other husbandmen, who will give back to him the fruits in their seasons.'

42 Jesus said to them, 'Did you[P] never read in the Writings, A stone that the builders disallowed, it became head of a corner; this has come to pass from the Lord, and it is wonderful in our eyes.

43 'Because of this I say to you[P], that the reign of God shall be taken from you[P], and given to a nation bringing forth its fruit;

44 and he who is falling on this stone shall be broken, and on whomsoever it may fall it will crush him to pieces.'

45 And the chief priests and the Pharisees having heard His similes, knew that He spoke of them,

46 and seeking to lay hold on Him, they feared the multitudes, seeing they were holding Him as a prophet.

CHAPTER 22

1 And Jesus answering, again spoke to them in similes, saying,

2 'The reign of the heavens was likened to a man, a king, who made marriage-feasts for his son,

3 and he sent forth his servants to call those having been called to the marriage-feasts, and they were not willing to come.

4 'Again he sent forth other servants, saying, Say to those who have been called: Behold, I prepared my dinner, my oxen and the fatlings have been killed, and all things [are] ready, come you[P] to the marriage-feasts;

5 and they, having disregarded [it], went away, the one to his own field, and the other to his merchandise;

6 and the rest, having laid hold on his servants, did insult and slay [them].

7 'And the king having heard, was angry, and having sent forth his soldiers, he destroyed those murderers, and he set their city on fire;

8 then said he to his servants, The marriage-feast indeed is ready, and those called were not worthy,

9 be going, then, on to the cross-ways, and as many as you[P] may find, call you[P] to the marriage-feasts.

10 'And those servants, having gone forth to the ways, did gather all, as many as they found, both bad and good, and the marriage-feast apartment was filled with those reclining.

11 'And the king having come in to view those reclining, saw there a man not clothed with clothing of the marriage-feast,

12 and he said to him, Comrade, how did you[S] come in here, not having clothing of the marriage-feast? and he was speechless.

13 'Then said the king to the ministrants, Bind his feet and hands, take him up and cast forth to the outer darkness, there shall be the weeping and the gnashing of the teeth;

14 for many are called, and few chosen.'

15 Then the Pharisees having gone, took counsel how they might ensnare Him in words,

16 and they send to Him their disciples with the Herodians, saying, 'Teacher, we have known that You[S] are true, and You[S] do teach the way of God in truth, and You[S] are not caring for any one, for You[S] do not look to the face of men;

17 tell us, therefore, what do You[S] think? is it lawful to give tribute to Caesar or not?'

18 And Jesus having known their wickedness, said, 'Why do you[P] tempt Me, hypocrites?

19 show Me the tribute-coin?' and they brought to Him a denary;

20 and He said to them, 'Whose [is] this image and the inscription?'

21 they say to Him, 'Caesar's;' then He said to them, 'For that reason render the things of Caesar to Caesar, and the things of God to God;'

22 and having heard they wondered, and having left Him they went away.

23 In that day there came near to Him Sadducees, who are saying there is not a rising again, and they questioned Him, saying,

24 'Teacher, Moses said, If any one may die not having children, his brother shall marry his wife, and shall raise up seed to his brother.

25 'And there were seven brothers with us, and the first having married did die, and not having seed, he left his wife to his brother;

26 in like manner also the second, and the third, unto the seventh,

27 and last of all died also the woman;

28 therefore in the rising again, of which of the seven shall she be wife — for all had her?'

29 And Jesus answering said to them, 'You[P] go astray, not knowing the Writings, nor the power of God;

30 for in the rising again they do not marry, nor are they given in marriage, but are as messengers of God in heaven.

31 'And concerning the rising again of the dead, did
you[P] not read that which was spoken to you[P] by God,
saying,
32 I am the God of Abraham, and the God of Isaac, and
the God of Jacob? God is not a God of dead men, but of
living.'
33 And having heard, the multitudes were astonished
at His teaching;
34 and the Pharisees, having heard that He did silence
the Sadducees, were gathered together unto Him;
35 and one of them, a lawyer, did question, tempting
Him, and saying,
36 'Teacher, which [is] the great command in the Law?'
37 And Jesus said to him, 'You[S] shall love the Lord your[S]
God with all your[S] heart, and with all your[S] soul, and
with all your[S] understanding —
38 this is a first and great command;
39 and the second [is] like to it, You[S] shall love your[S]
neighbor as yourself[S];
40 on these — the two commands — all the law and the
prophets do hang.'
41 And the Pharisees having been gathered together,
Jesus did question them,
42 saying, 'What do you[P] think concerning the Christ?
of whom is he son?' They say to him, 'Of David.'
43 He said to them, 'How then did David in the Spirit
call him lord, saying,
44 The Lord said to my lord, Sit at my right hand, till I
may make your[S] enemies your[S] footstool?
45 If then David did call him lord, how is he his son?'
46 And no one was able to answer Him a word, nor did
any from that day question Him any more.

CHAPTER 23

1 Then Jesus spoke to the multitudes, and to His
disciples,
2 saying, 'The scribes and the Pharisees sat down on
the seat of Moses;
3 all, then, as much as they may say to you[P] to observe,
observe and do, but do not according to their works, for
they say, and do not;
4 for they bind together burdens heavy and grievous
to be borne, and lay upon the shoulders of men, but
with their finger they will not move them.
5 'And they do all their works to be seen by men, and
they make their phylacteries broad, and enlarge the
fringes of their garments,
6 they also love the chief couches in the supper, and
the chief seats in the synagogues,
7 and the salutations in the market-places, and to be
called by men, Rabbi, Rabbi.
8 'And you[P] — you[P] may not be called Rabbi, for one is
your[P] director — the Christ, and you[P] are all brethren;
9 and you[P] may not call [any] your[P] father on the earth,
for one is your[P] Father, who is in the heavens,
10 nor may you[P] be called directors, for one is your[P]
director — the Christ.
11 And the greater of you[P] shall be your[P] ministrant,
12 and whoever shall exalt himself shall be humbled,
and whoever shall humble himself shall be exalted.
13 'Woe to you[P], Scribes and Pharisees, hypocrites!
because you[P] shut up the reign of the heavens before
men, for you[P] do not go in, nor do you[P] allow those going
in to enter.
14 'Woe to you[P], Scribes and Pharisees, hypocrites!
because you[P] eat up the houses of the widows, and make
long prayers for a pretense, because of this you[P] shall
receive more abundant judgment.
15 'Woe to you[P], Scribes and Pharisees, hypocrites!
because you[P] go round the sea and the dry land to make
one proselyte, and whenever it may happen — you[P]
make him a son of gehenna twofold more than
yourselves[P].
16 'Woe to you[P], blind guides, who are saying, Whoever
may swear by the sanctuary, it is nothing, but whoever
may swear by the gold of the sanctuary — is debtor!
17 Fools and blind! for which [is] greater, the gold, or
the sanctuary that is sanctifying the gold?
18 'And, whoever may swear by the altar, it is nothing;
but whoever may swear by the gift that is upon it — is
debtor!
19 Fools and blind! for which [is] greater, the gift, or the
altar that is sanctifying the gift?
20 ' For that reason he who did swear by the altar, did
swear by it, and by all things on it;
21 and he who did swear by the sanctuary, did swear
by it, and by Him who is dwelling in it;
22 and he who did swear by the heaven, did swear by
the throne of God, and by Him who is sitting upon it.
23 'Woe to you[P], Scribes and Pharisees, hypocrites!
because you[P] give tithe of the mint, and the dill, and the
cumin, and did neglect the weightier things of the Law —
the judgment, and the kindness, and the faith; it is
necessary for [you[P]] to do these, and not to neglect those.
24 'Blind guides! who are straining out the gnat, and
are swallowing the camel.

25 'Woe to you[P], Scribes and Pharisees, hypocrites!
because you[P] make clean the outside of the cup and the
plate, and within they are full of rapine and incontinence.
26 'Blind Pharisee! first cleanse the inside of the cup
and the plate, that the outside of them may also become
clean.
27 'Woe to you[P], Scribes and Pharisees, hypocrites!
because you[P] are like to whitewashed sepulchres, which
outwardly indeed do appear beautiful, and within are full
of bones of dead men, and of all uncleanness;
28 so also you[P] outwardly indeed do appear to men
righteous, and within you[P] are full of hypocrisy and
lawlessness.
29 'Woe to you[P], Scribes and Pharisees, hypocrites!
because you[P] build the sepulchres of the prophets, and
adorn the tombs of the righteous,
30 and say, If we had been in the days of our fathers,
we would not have been partakers with them in the blood
of the prophets.
31 So that you[P] testify to yourselves[P], that you[P] are
sons of them who did murder the prophets;
32 and you[P] — you[P] fill up the measure of your[P] fathers.
33 'Serpents! brood of vipers! how may you[P] escape
from the judgment of the gehenna?
34 'Because of this, behold, I send to you[P] prophets,
and wise men, and scribes, and of them you[P] will kill and
crucify, and of them you[P] will scourge in your[P]
synagogues, and will pursue from city to city;
35 that on you[P] may come all the righteous blood being
poured out on the earth from the blood of Abel the
righteous, unto the blood of Zacharias son of Barachias,
whom you[P] slew between the sanctuary and the altar:
36 truly I say to you[P], all these things shall come upon
this generation.
37 'Jerusalem, Jerusalem, that are killing the prophets,
and stoning those sent unto you[S], how often did I will
to gather your[S] children together, as a hen does gather
her own chickens under the wings, and you[P] did not
will.
38 Behold, your[P] house is left desolate to you[P];
39 for I say to you[P], you[P] may not see Me from this time
forth, till you[P] may say, Blessed [is] He who is coming in
the name of the Lord.'

CHAPTER 24

1 And having gone forth, Jesus departed from the
temple, and His disciples came near to show Him the
buildings of the temple,
2 and Jesus said to them, 'Do you[P] not see all these?
truly I say to you[P], There may not be left a stone upon a
stone here, that shall not be thrown down.'
3 And when He is sitting on the mount of the Olives,
the disciples came near to Him by Himself, saying, 'Tell
us, when shall these be? and what [is] the sign of Your[S]
presence, and of the full end of the age?'
4 And Jesus answering said to them, 'Take heed that
no one may lead you[P] astray,
5 for many shall come in My name, saying, I am the
Christ, and they shall lead many astray,
6 and you[P] shall begin to hear of wars, and reports of
wars; see, be not troubled, for it is necessary for all
[these] to come to pass, but the end is not yet.
7 'For nation shall rise against nation, and kingdom
against kingdom, and there shall be famines, and
pestilences, and earthquakes, in divers places;
8 and all these [are] the beginning of sorrows;
9 then they shall deliver you[P] up to tribulation, and shall
kill you[P], and you[P] shall be hated by all the nations
because of My name;
10 and then shall many be stumbled, and they shall
deliver up one another, and shall hate one another.
11 'And many false prophets shall arise, and shall lead
many astray;
12 and because of the abounding of the lawlessness,
the love of the many shall become cold;
13 but he who did endure to the end, he shall be saved;
14 and this good news of the reign shall be proclaimed
in all the world, for a testimony to all the nations; and
then shall the end arrive.
15 'Whenever, for that reason, you[P] may see the
abomination of the desolation, that was spoken of
through Daniel the prophet, standing in the holy place
(whoever is reading let him observe)
16 then those in Judea — let them flee to the mounts;
17 he on the house-top — let him not come down to
take up any thing out of his house;
18 and he in the field — let him not turn back to take his
garments.
19 'And woe to those with child, and to those giving
suck in those days;
20 and pray you[P] that your[P] flight may not be in winter,
nor on a sabbath;
21 for there shall be then great tribulation, such as was not
from the beginning of the world till now, no, nor may be.
22 And if those days were not shortened, no flesh would
have been saved; but because of the chosen, shall those

days be shortened.
23 'Then if any one may say to you[P], Behold, here [is]
the Christ! or here! you[P] may not believe;
24 for there shall arise false Christs, and false prophets,
and they shall give great signs and wonders, so as to
lead astray, if possible, also the chosen.
25 Behold, I did tell you[P] beforehand.
26 'If consequently they may say to you[P], Behold, he is
in the wilderness, you[P] may not go forth; behold, in the
inner chambers, you[P] may not believe;
27 for as the lightning does come forth from the east,
and does appear unto the west, so shall be also the
presence of the Son of Man;
28 for wherever the carcass may be, there shall the eagles
be gathered together.
29 'And immediately after the tribulation of those days,
the sun shall be darkened, and the moon shall not give
her light, and the stars shall fall from the heaven, and
the powers of the heavens shall be shaken;
30 and then shall appear the sign of the Son of Man in
the heaven; and then shall all the tribes of the earth smite
the breast, and they shall see the Son of Man coming
upon the clouds of the heaven, with power and much
glory;
31 and He shall send His messengers with a great sound
of a trumpet, and they shall gather together His chosen
from the four winds, from the ends of the heavens unto
the ends thereof.
32 'And from the fig-tree learn you[P] the simile: When
already its branch may have become tender, and the
leaves it may put forth, you[P] know that summer [is] near,
33 so also you[P], when you[P] may see all these, you[P] know
that it is near — at the doors.
34 Truly I say to you[P], this generation may not pass
away till all these may come to pass.
35 The heaven and the earth shall pass away, but my
words shall not pass away.
36 'And concerning that day and the hour no one has
known — not even the messengers of the heavens —
except my Father only;
37 and as the days of Noah — so shall be also the
presence of the Son of Man;
38 for as they were, in the days before the flood, eating,
and drinking, marrying, and giving in marriage, till the
day Noah entered into the ark,
39 and they did not know till the flood came and took all
away; so shall be also the presence of the Son of Man.
40 Then two men shall be in the field, the one is received,
and the one is left;
41 two women shall be grinding in the mill, one is
received, and one is left.
42 'Watch you[P] for that reason, because you[P] have not
known in what hour your[P] Lord does come;
43 and this know, that if the master of the house had
known in what watch the thief did come, he had watched,
and not allowed his house to be broken through;
44 because of this also you[P], become you[P] ready,
because in what hour you[P] do not think, the Son of Man
does come.
45 'Who, then, is the servant, faithful and wise, whom
his lord did set over his household, to give them the
nourishment in season?
46 Happy that servant, whom his lord, having come,
shall find doing so;
47 truly I say to you[P], that he will set him over all his
substance.
48 'And, if that evil servant may say in his heart, My
Lord does delay to come,
49 and may begin to beat the fellow-servants, and to
eat and to drink with the drunken,
50 the lord of that servant will arrive in a day when he
does not expect, and in an hour of which he does not
know,
51 and will cut him off, and his portion with the
hypocrites will appoint; there shall be the weeping and
the gnashing of the teeth.

CHAPTER 25

1 'Then shall the reign of the heavens be likened to ten
virgins, who, having taken their lamps, went forth to meet
the bridegroom;
2 and five of them were prudent, and five foolish;
3 they who were foolish having taken their lamps, did
not take oil with themselves;
4 and the prudent took oil in their vessels, with their
lamps.
5 'And the bridegroom tarrying, they all nodded and
were sleeping,
6 and in the middle of the night a cry was made, Behold,
the bridegroom does come; go you[P] forth to meet him.
7 'Then rose all those virgins, and trimmed their lamps,
8 and the foolish said to the prudent, Give us of your[P]
oil, because our lamps are going out;
9 and the prudent answered, saying — Lest there may
not be sufficient for us and you[P], go you[P] rather unto
those selling, and buy for yourselves[P].

10 'And while they are going away to buy, the bridegroom came, and those ready went in with him to the marriage-feasts, and the door was shut;
11 and afterwards come also do the rest of the virgins, saying, Sir, sir, open to us;
12 and he answering said, Truly I say to you[P], I have not known you[P].
13 ' For that reason watch, for you[P] have not known the day nor the hour in which the Son of Man does come.
14 'For — as a man going abroad did call his own servants, and did deliver to them his substance,
15 and to one he gave five talents, and to another two, and to another one, to each according to his several ability, went abroad immediately.
16 'And he who did receive the five talents, having gone, worked with them, and made other five talents;
17 in like manner also he who [received] the two, he gained, also he, other two;
18 and he who did receive the one, having gone away, dug in the earth, and hid his lord's money.
19 'And after a long time comes the lord of those servants, and takes reckoning with them;
20 and he who did receive the five talents having come, brought other five talents, saying, 'Sir, you[S] did deliver five talents to me; behold, I did gain five other talents besides them.
21 'And his lord said to him, Well done, servant, good and faithful, you[S] were faithful over a few things, I will set you[S] over many things; enter into the joy of your[S] lord.
22 'And he who also did receive the two talents having come, said, Sir, you[S] did deliver two talents to me; behold, I did gain two other talents besides them.
23 'His lord said to him, Well done, servant, good and faithful, you[S] were faithful over a few things, I will set you[S] over many things; enter into the joy of your[S] lord.
24 'And he also who had received the one talent having come, said, Sir, I knew you[S], that you[S] are a hard man, reaping where you[S] did not sow, and gathering from where you[S] did not scatter;
25 and having been afraid, having gone away, I hid your[S] talent in the earth; behold, you[S] have your[S] own!
26 'And his lord answering said to him, Evil servant, and slothful, you[S] had known that I reap where I did not sow, and I gather where I did not scatter!
27 it was necessary for you[S] then to put my money to the money-lenders, and having come I had received mine own with increase.
28 'For that reason take consequently the talent from him, and give to him having the ten talents,
29 for to every one having shall be given, and he shall have overabundance, and from him who is not having, even that which he has shall be taken from him;
30 and you[P] cast the unprofitable servant forth to the outer darkness; there shall be the weeping and the gnashing of the teeth.
31 'And whenever the Son of Man may come in His glory, and all the holy messengers with Him, then He shall sit upon a throne of His glory;
32 and all the nations shall be gathered together before Him, and He shall separate them from one another, as the shepherd does separate the sheep from the goats,
33 and He shall set the sheep indeed on His right hand, and the goats on the left.
34 'Then the King shall say to those on His right hand, Come you[P], the blessed of My Father, inherit the reign that has been prepared for you[P] from the foundation of the world;
35 for I did hunger, and you[P] gave Me to eat; I did thirst, and you[P] gave Me to drink; I was a stranger, and you[P] received Me;
36 naked, and you[P] put around Me; I was infirm, and you[P] looked after Me; I was in prison, and you[P] came unto Me.
37 'Then shall the righteous answer Him, saying, Lord, when did we see You[S] hungering, and we nourished? or thirsting, and we gave to drink?
38 and when did we see You[S] a stranger, and we received? or naked, and we put around?
39 and when did we see You[S] infirm, or in prison, and we came unto You[S]?
40 'And the king answering, shall say to them, Truly I say to you[P], inasmuch as you[P] did [it] to one of these My brethren — the least — you[P] did [it] to Me.
41 Then shall He also say to those on the left hand, Go you[P] from Me, the cursed, to the fire, the age-during, that has been prepared for the Devil and his messengers;
42 for I did hunger, and you[P] gave Me not to eat; I did thirst, and you[P] gave Me not to drink;
43 I was a stranger, and you[P] did not receive Me; naked, and you[P] put not around Me; infirm, and in prison, and you[P] did not look after Me.
44 'Then shall they answer, they also, saying, Lord, when did we see You[S] hungering, or thirsting, or a stranger, or naked, or infirm, or in prison, and we did not minister to You[S]?
45 'Then shall He answer them, saying, Truly I say to you[P], Inasmuch as you[P] did [it] not to one of these, the

least, you[P] did [it] not to Me.
46 And these shall go away to punishment age-during, but the righteous to life age-during.'

CHAPTER 26

1 And it came to pass, when Jesus finished all these words, He said to His disciples,
2 'You[P] have known that after two days the Passover comes, and the Son of Man is delivered up to be crucified.'
3 Then were gathered together the chief priests, and the scribes, and the elders of the people, to the court of the chief priest who was called Caiaphas;
4 and they consulted together that they might take Jesus by guile, and kill [Him],
5 and they said, 'Not in the feast, that there may not be a tumult among the people.'
6 And Jesus having been in Bethany, in the house of Simon the leper,
7 there came to Him a woman having an alabaster box of ointment, very precious, and she poured on His head as He is reclining (at meat).
8 And having seen [it], His disciples were much displeased, saying, 'To what purpose [is] this waste?
9 for this ointment could have been sold for much, and given to the poor.'
10 And Jesus having known, said to them, 'Why do you[P] give trouble to the woman? for she worked a good work for Me;
11 for the poor you[P] always have with you[P], and you[P] have not Me always;
12 for she having put this ointment on My body — she did [it] for My burial.
13 Truly I say to you[P], Wherever this good news may be proclaimed in the whole world, what this [one] did shall also be spoken of — for a memorial of her.'
14 Then one of the twelve, who is called Judas Iscariot, having gone unto the chief priests, said,
15 'What are you[P] willing to give me, and I will deliver Him up to you[P]?' and they weighed out thirty silverlings to him,
16 and from that time he was seeking a convenient season to deliver Him up.
17 And on the first [day] of the unleavened food came the disciples near to Jesus, saying to Him, 'Where will You[S] [that] we may prepare for You[S] to eat the Passover?'
18 and He said, 'Go away to the city, unto such a one, and say to him, The Teacher says, My time is near; I keep the Passover near you[S], with My disciples;'
19 and the disciples did as Jesus appointed them, and prepared the Passover.
20 And evening having come, He was reclining (at meat) with the twelve,
21 and while they are eating, He said, 'Truly I say to you[P], that one of you[P] shall deliver Me up.'
22 And being grieved exceedingly, they began to say to Him, each of them, 'Is it I, Sir?'
23 And He answering said, 'He who did dip the hand in the dish with Me, he will deliver Me up;
24 the Son of Man does indeed go, as it has been written concerning Him, but woe to that man through whom the Son of Man is delivered up! it were good for him if that man had not been born.'
25 And Judas — he who delivered Him up — answering said, 'Is it I, Rabbi?' He said to him, 'You[S] have said.'
26 And while they were eating, Jesus having taken the bread, and having blessed, did break, and was giving to the disciples, and said, 'Take, eat, this is My body;'
27 and having taken the cup, and having given thanks, He gave to them, saying, 'Drink you[P] of it — all;
28 for this is My blood of the new covenant, that is being poured out for many — to remission of sins;
29 and I say to you[P], that I may not drink from this time forth on this produce of the vine, till that day when I may drink it with you[P] new in the reign of My Father.'
30 And having sung a hymn, they went forth to the mount of the Olives;
31 then said Jesus to them, 'All you[P] shall be stumbled at Me this night; for it has been written, I will smite the shepherd, and the sheep of the flock shall be scattered abroad;
32 but, after My having risen, I will go before you[P] to Galilee.'
33 And Peter answering said to him, 'Even if all shall be stumbled at You[S], I will never be stumbled.'
34 Jesus said to him, 'Truly I say to you[S], that, this night, before cock-crowing, you[S] will deny Me three times.'
35 Peter said to Him, 'Even if it may be necessary for me to die with You[S], I will not deny You[S];' all the disciples also said in like manner.
36 Then Jesus did come with them to a place called Gethsemane, and He said to the disciples, 'Sit you[P] here, till having gone away, I shall pray yonder.'
37 And having taken Peter, and the two sons of Zebedee, He began to be sorrowful, and to be very heavy;
38 then He said to them, 'My soul is exceedingly

sorrowful — unto death; you[P] abide here, and watch
with Me.'
39 And having gone forward a little, He fell on His face,
praying, and saying, 'My Father, if it be possible, let
this cup pass from Me; nevertheless, not as I will, but
as You[S].'
40 And He came unto the disciples, and found them
sleeping, and He said to Peter, 'So! you[P] were not able
to watch with Me one hour!
41 watch, and pray, that you[P] may not enter into
temptation: the spirit indeed is forward, but the flesh
weak.'
42 Again, a second time, having gone away, He prayed,
saying, 'My Father, if this cup cannot pass away from
Me except I drink it, Your[S] will be done;'
43 and having come, He found them sleeping again, for
their eyes were heavy.
44 And having left them, having gone away again, He
prayed a third time, saying the same word;
45 then He came unto his disciples, and said to them,
'Sleep on from this time forth, and rest! behold, the hour
has come near, and the Son of Man is delivered up to
the hands of sinners.
46 Rise, let us go; behold, he who is delivering Me up
has come near.'
47 And while He is yet speaking, behold, Judas, one of
the twelve did come, and with him a great multitude, with
swords and sticks, from the chief priests and elders of
the people.
48 And he who did deliver Him up did give them a sign,
saying, 'Whomsoever I will kiss, it is He: lay hold on
Him;'
49 and immediately, having come to Jesus, he said, 'Hail,
Rabbi,' and kissed Him;
50 and Jesus said to him, 'Comrade, for what are you[S]
present?' Then having come near, they laid hands on
Jesus, and took hold on Him.
51 And behold, one of those with Jesus, having
stretched forth the hand, drew his sword, and having
struck the servant of the chief priest, he took off his ear.
52 Then said Jesus to him, 'Turn back your sword to its
place; for all who did take the sword, shall perish by the
sword;
53 do you[S] think that I am not able now to call upon My
Father, and He will place beside Me more than twelve
legions of messengers?
54 how then may the Writings be fulfilled, that thus it
was necessary to happen?'
55 In that hour said Jesus to the multitudes, 'You[P] did
come forth as against a robber, with swords and sticks,
to take Me! I was sitting with you[P] daily teaching in the
temple, and you[P] did not lay hold on Me;
56 but all this has come to pass, that the Writings of the
prophets may be fulfilled;' then all the disciples, having
left Him, fled.
57 And those laying hold on Jesus led [Him] away unto
Caiaphas the chief priest, where the scribes and the
elders were gathered together,
58 and Peter was following Him afar off, unto the court
of the chief priest, and having gone in within, he was
sitting with the officers, to see the end.
59 And the chief priests, and the elders, and all the
council, were seeking false witness against Jesus, that
they might put Him to death,
60 and they did not find; and many false witnesses
having come near, they did not find; and at last two false
witnesses having come near,
61 said, 'This one said, I am able to throw down the
sanctuary of God, and to build it after three days.'
62 And the chief priest having stood up, said to Him,
'You[S] do answer nothing! what do these witness against
You[S]?
63 and Jesus was silent. And the chief priest answering
said to Him, 'I appeal You[S], by the living God, that You[S]
may say to us, if You[S] are the Christ — the Son of God.'
64 Jesus said to him, 'You[S] have said; nevertheless I
say to you[P], hereafter you[P] shall see the Son of Man
sitting on the right hand of the power, and coming upon
the clouds, of the heaven.'
65 Then the chief priest rent his garments, saying, —
'He has spoken evil; what need have we yet of
witnesses? behold, now you[P] heard His evil speaking;
66 what think you[P]?' and they answering said, 'He is
worthy of death.'
67 Then did they spit in His face and buffet Him, and
others did slap,
68 saying, 'Declare to us, O Christ, who he is that struck
You[S]?'
69 And Peter was without sitting in the court, and there
came near to him a certain maid, saying, 'And you[S] were
with Jesus of Galilee!'
70 And he denied before all, saying, 'I have not known
what you[S] say.'
71 And he having gone forth to the porch, another
female saw him, and said to those there, 'And this one
was with Jesus of Nazareth;'
72 and again did he deny with an oath — 'I have not
known the man.'

73 And after a little those standing near having come,
said to Peter, 'Truly you[S] are also of them, for even your[S]
speech does make you[S] known.'
74 Then began he to anathematise, and to swear — 'I
have not known the man;' and immediately did a cock
crow,
75 and Peter remembered the saying of Jesus, He having
said to him — 'Before cock-crowing, you[S] will deny Me
three times;' and having gone without, he did weep
bitterly.

CHAPTER 27

1 And morning having come, all the chief priests and
the elders of the people took counsel against Jesus, so
as to put Him to death;
2 and having bound Him, they did lead away, and
delivered Him up to Pontius Pilate, the governor.
3 Then Judas — he who delivered Him up — having
seen that He was condemned, having repented, brought
back the thirty silverlings to the chief priests, and to the
elders, saying,
4 'I did sin, having delivered up innocent blood;' and
they said, 'What — to us? you[S] shall see!'
5 and having cast down the silverlings in the sanctuary,
he departed, and having gone away, he did strangle
himself.
6 And the chief priests having taken the silverlings, said,
'It is not lawful to put them to the treasury, seeing it is
the price of blood;'
7 and having taken counsel, they bought with them the
field of the potter, for the burial of strangers;
8 therefore was that field called, 'Field of blood,' unto
this day.
9 Then was fulfilled that spoken through Jeremiah the
prophet, saying, 'And I took the thirty silverlings, the
price of Him who had been priced, whom they of the
sons of Israel did price,
10 and gave them for the field of the potter, as the Lord
did appoint to me.'
11 And Jesus stood before the governor, and the
governor did question Him, saying, 'Are You[S] the king
of the Jews!' And Jesus said to him, 'You[S] say .'
12 And in His being accused by the chief priests and
the elders, He did not answer any thing,
13 then Pilate said to Him, 'Do You[S] not hear how many
things they witness against You[S]?'
14 And He did not answer him, not even to one word,
so that the governor did wonder greatly.
15 And at the feast the governor had been accustomed
to release one to the multitude, a prisoner, whom they
willed,
16 and they had then a noted prisoner, called Barabbas,
17 they therefore having been gathered together, Pilate
said to them, 'Whom will you[P] I shall release to you[P]?
Barabbas or Jesus who is called Christ?'
18 for he had known that because of envy they had
delivered Him up.
19 And as he is sitting on the tribunal, his wife sent
unto him, saying, 'Nothing — to you[S] and to that
righteous one, for many things did I suffer today in a
dream because of Him.'
20 And the chief priests and the elders did persuade
the multitudes that they might ask for themselves
Barabbas, and might destroy Jesus;
21 and the governor answering said to them, 'Which of
the two will you[P] [that] I shall release to you[P]?' And they
said, 'Barabbas.'
22 Pilate said to them, 'What then shall I do with Jesus
who is called Christ?' They all say to him, 'Let be
crucified!'
23 And the governor said, 'Why, what evil did He?' and
they were crying out the more, saying, 'Let be crucified.'
24 And Pilate having seen that it profited nothing, but
rather a tumult is made, having taken water, he did wash
the hands before the multitude, saying, 'I am innocent
from the blood of this righteous one; you[P] — you[P] shall
see;'
25 and all the people answering said, 'His blood [is]
upon us, and upon our children!'
26 Then did he release to them Barabbas, and having
scourged Jesus, he delivered [Him] up that He may be
crucified;
27 then the soldiers of the governor having taken Jesus
to the Praetorium, did gather all the band to Him;
28 and having unclothed Him, they put a crimson cloak
around Him,
29 and having braided Him a crown out of thorns they
put [it] on His head, and a reed in His right hand, and
having kneeled before Him, they were mocking Him,
saying, 'Hail, the king of the Jews.'
30 And having spit on Him, they took the reed, and
were smiting on His head;
31 and when they had mocked Him, they took the cloak
off from Him, and put His own garments on Him, and led
him away to crucify [Him].
32 And coming forth, they found a man, a Cyrenian, by

name Simon: they impressed him that he might bear His
cross;
33 and having come to a place called Golgotha, that is
called Place of a Skull,
34 they gave Him vinegar mixed with gall to drink, and
having tasted, He would not drink.
35 And having crucified Him, they divided His garments,
casting a lot, that it might be fulfilled that was spoken
by the prophet, 'They divided My garments to
themselves, and over My vesture they cast a lot;'
36 and sitting down, they were watching Him there,
37 and they put up over His head, His accusation
written, 'This is Jesus, the king of the Jews.'
38 Then crucified with Him are two robbers, one on the
right hand, and one on the left,
39 and those passing by were speaking evil of Him,
wagging their heads,
40 and saying, 'You[S] that are throwing down the
sanctuary, and in three days building [it], save Yourself[S];
if You[S] are Son of God, come down from the cross.'
41 And in like manner also the chief priests mocking,
with the scribes and elders, said,
42 'Others He saved; He is not able to save Himself! If
He be King of Israel, let Him come down now from the
cross, and we will believe Him;
43 He has trusted on God, let Him now deliver Him, if
He wish Him, because He said – I am Son of God;'
44 with the same also the robbers, who were crucified
with Him, were reproaching Him.
45 And from the sixth hour darkness came over all the
land unto the ninth hour,
46 and about the ninth hour Jesus cried out with a great
voice, saying, 'Eli, Eli, lama sabachthani?' that is, 'My
God, my God, why did You[S] forsake Me?'
47 And certain of those standing there having heard,
said — 'He does call Elijah;'
48 and immediately, one of them having run, and having
taken a sponge, having filled [it] with vinegar, and having
put [it] on a reed, was giving Him to drink,
49 but the rest said, 'Let alone, let us see if Elijah does
come — about to save Him.'
50 And Jesus having again cried with a great voice,
yielded the spirit;
51 and behold, the veil of the sanctuary was rent in two
from top unto bottom, and the earth did quake, and the
rocks were rent,
52 and the tombs were opened, and many bodies of the
saints who have fallen asleep, arose,
53 and having come forth out of the tombs after His rising,
they went into the holy city, and appeared to many.
54 And the centurion, and those with him watching
Jesus, having seen the earthquake, and the things that
were done, were exceedingly afraid, saying, 'Truly this
was God's Son.'
55 And there were there many women beholding from
afar, who did follow Jesus from Galilee, ministering to
Him,
56 among whom was Mary the Magdalene, and Mary
the mother of James and of Joses, and the mother of the
sons of Zebedee.
57 And evening having come, there came a rich man,
from Arimathea, named Joseph, who also himself was
discipled to Jesus,
58 he having gone near to Pilate, asked for himself the
body of Jesus; then Pilate commanded the body to be
given back.
59 And having taken the body, Joseph wrapped it in
clean linen,
60 and laid it in his new tomb, that he hewed in the rock,
and having rolled a great stone to the door of the tomb,
he went away;
61 and there were there Mary the Magdalene, and the
other Mary, sitting over-against the sepulchre.
62 And on the morrow that is after the preparation, were
gathered together the chief priests, and the Pharisees,
unto Pilate,
63 saying, 'Sir, we have remembered that that deceiver
said while yet living, After three days I do rise;
64 command, then, the sepulchre to be made secure till
the third day, for fear that His disciples, having come by
night, may steal Him away, and may say to the people,
He rose from the dead, and the last deceit shall be worse
than the first.'
65 And Pilate said to them, 'You[P] have a watch, go away,
make secure — as you[P] have known;'
66 and they, having gone, did make the sepulchre secure,
having sealed the stone, together with the watch.

CHAPTER 28

1 And on the eve of the sabbaths, at the dawn, toward
the first of the sabbaths, came Mary the Magdalene, and
the other Mary, to see the sepulchre,
2 and behold, there came a great earthquake, for a
messenger of the Lord, having come down out of
heaven, having come, did roll away the stone from the
door, and was sitting upon it,

3 and his countenance was as lightning, and his clothing
white as snow,
4 and the keepers did shake from the fear of him, and
they became as dead men.
5 And the messenger answering said to the women, 'Fear
not you[P], for I have known that Jesus, who has been
crucified, you[P] seek;
6 He is not here, for He rose, as He said; come, see the
place where the Lord was lying;
7 and having gone quickly, say you[P] to His disciples,
that He rose from the dead; and behold, He does go
before you[P] to Galilee, there you[P] shall see Him; behold,
I have told you[P].'
8 And having gone forth quickly from the tomb, with
fear and great joy, they ran to tell to His disciples;
9 and as they were going to tell to His disciples, then
behold, Jesus met them, saying, 'Hail!' and they having
come near, laid hold of His feet, and did bow to Him.
10 Then said Jesus to them, 'Fear you[P] not, go away,
tell to My brethren that they may go away to Galilee,
and there they shall see Me.'
11 And while they are going on, behold, certain of the
watch having come to the city, told to the chief priests
all the things that happened,
12 and having been gathered together with the elders,
counsel also having taken, they gave much money to
the soldiers,
13 saying, 'Say you[P], that His disciples having come by
night, stole Him — we being asleep;
14 and if this be heard by the governor, we will persuade
him, and keep you free from anxiety.'
15 And they, having received the money, did as they
were taught, and this account was spread abroad among
Jews till this day.
16 And the eleven disciples went to Galilee, to the mount
where Jesus appointed them,
17 and having seen Him, they bowed to Him, but some
did waver.
18 And having come near, Jesus spoke to them, saying,
'All authority in heaven and on earth was given to Me;
19 having gone, then, disciple all the nations, (baptizing
them — to the name of the Father, and of the Son, and
of the Holy Spirit,
20 teaching them to observe all, whatever I did command
you[P],) and behold, I am with you[P] all the days — till the
full end of the age.'

The Gospel according to
MARK

CHAPTER 1

1 A beginning of the good news of Jesus Christ, Son of God.
2 As it has been written in the prophets, 'Behold, I send My messenger before Your[S] face, who shall prepare Your[S] way before You[S],' —
3 'A voice of one calling in the wilderness, Prepare you[P] the way of the Lord, you[P] make straight His paths,' —
4 John came baptizing in the wilderness, and proclaiming a baptism of reformation — to remission of sins,
5 and there were going forth to him all the region of Judea, and they of Jerusalem, and they were all baptized by him in the river Jordan, confessing their sins.
6 And John was clothed with camel's hair, and a girdle of skin around his loins, and eating locusts and honey of the field,
7 and he proclaimed, saying, 'He does come — who is mightier than I — after me, of whom I am not worthy — having stooped down — to loose the latchet of His sandals;
8 I indeed did baptize you[P] with water, but He shall baptize you[P] with the Holy Spirit.'
9 And it came to pass in those days, Jesus came from Nazareth of Galilee, and was baptized by John at the Jordan;
10 and immediately coming up from the water, He saw the heavens dividing, and the Spirit as a dove coming down upon Him;
11 and a voice came out of the heavens, 'You[S] are My Son — the Beloved, in whom I did delight.'
12 And immediately did the Spirit put Him forth to the wilderness,
13 and He was there in the wilderness forty days, being tempted by the Adversary, and He was with the beasts, and the messengers were ministering to Him.
14 And after the delivering up of John, Jesus came to Galilee, proclaiming the good news of the reign of God,
15 and saying — ' The time has been fulfilled, and the reign of God has come near, reform you[P], and believe in the good news.'
16 And, walking by the sea of Galilee, He saw Simon, and Andrew his brother, casting a drag into the sea, for they were fishers,
17 and Jesus said to them, 'Come you[P] after Me, and I shall make you[P] to become fishers of men;'
18 and immediately, having left their nets, they followed Him.
19 And having gone on from there a little, He saw James of Zebedee, and John his brother, and they were in the boat refitting the nets,
20 and immediately He called them, and, having left their father Zebedee in the boat with the hired servants, they went away after Him.
21 And they go on to Capernaum, and immediately, on the sabbaths, having gone into the synagogue, He was teaching,
22 and they were astonished at His teaching, for He was teaching them as having authority, and not as the scribes.
23 And there was in their synagogue a man with an unclean spirit, and he cried out,
24 saying, 'Away! what — to us and to You[S], Jesus the Nazarene? You[S] did come to destroy us; I have known You[S] who You[S] are — the Holy One of God.'
25 And Jesus rebuked him, saying, 'Be silenced, and come forth out of him,'
26 and the unclean spirit having torn him, and having cried with a great voice, came forth out of him,
27 and they were all amazed, so as to reason among themselves, saying, 'What is this? what new teaching [is] this? that with authority He commands the unclean spirits also, and they obey Him!'
28 And the fame of Him went forth immediately to all the region, round about, of Galilee.
29 And immediately, having come forth out of the synagogue, they went to the house of Simon and Andrew, with James and John,
30 and the mother-in-law of Simon was lying fevered, and immediately they tell Him about her,
31 and having come near, He raised her up, having laid

hold of her hand, and the fever left her immediately, and she was ministering to them.

32 And evening having come, when the sun did set, they brought unto Him all who were ill, and who were demoniacs,

33 and the whole city was gathered together near the door,

34 and He healed many who were ill of various diseases, and He cast forth many demons, and was not allowing the demons to speak, because they knew Him.

35 And very early, it being yet night, having risen, He went forth, and went away to a desert place, and was there praying;

36 and Simon and those with him went in quest of Him,

37 and having found Him, they say to Him, — 'All do seek You[S];'

38 and He said to them, 'We may go to the next towns, that I may preach there also, I came forth for this.'

39 And He was preaching in their synagogues, in all Galilee, and is casting out the demons,

40 and there does come to Him a leper, calling on Him, and kneeling to Him, and saying to Him — 'If You[S] may will, You[S] are able to cleanse me.'

41 And Jesus having been moved with compassion, having stretched forth the hand, touched him, and said to him, 'I will; be you[S] cleansed;'

42 and He having spoken, immediately the leprosy went away from him, and he was cleansed.

43 And having sternly charged him, immediately He put him forth,

44 and said to him, 'See you[S] may say nothing to any one, but go away, show yourself[S] to the priest, and bring near the things Moses directed for your[S] cleansing, for a testimony to them.'

45 And he, having gone forth, began to proclaim much, and to spread abroad the thing, so that no more was He able openly to enter into the city, but He was without in desert places, and they were coming unto Him from every quarter.

CHAPTER 2

1 And again He entered into Capernaum, after [some] days, and it was heard that He is in the house,

2 and immediately many were gathered together, so that there was no more room, not even at the door, and He was speaking to them the word.

3 And they come unto Him, bringing a paralytic, borne by four,

4 and not being able to come near to Him because of the multitude, they uncovered the roof where He was, and, having broken [it] up, they let down the couch on which the paralytic was lying,

5 and Jesus having seen their faith, said to the paralytic, 'Child, your[S] sins have been forgiven you[S].'

6 And there were certain of the scribes there sitting, and reasoning in their hearts,

7 'Why does this one thus speak evil words? who is able to forgive sins except one — God?'

8 And immediately Jesus, having known in His spirit that they thus reason in themselves, said to them, 'Why these things reason you[P] in your[P] hearts?

9 which is easier, to say to the paralytic, The sins have been forgiven to you[S]? or to say, Rise, and take up your[S] couch, and walk?

10 'And, that you[P] may know that the Son of Man has authority on the earth to forgive sins — (He said to the paralytic) —

11 I say to you[S], Rise, and take up your[S] couch, and go away to your[S] house;'

12 and he rose immediately, and having taken up the couch, he went forth before all, so that all were astonished, and do glorify God, saying — 'Never did we see thus.'

13 And He went forth again by the sea, and all the multitude was coming unto Him, and He was teaching them,

14 and passing by, he saw Levi of Alpheus sitting at the tax-office, and said to him, 'Be following Me,' and he, having risen, did follow Him.

15 And it came to pass, in His reclining (at meat) in his house, that many tax-gatherers and sinners were reclining (at meat) with Jesus and His disciples, for there were many, and they followed Him.

16 And the scribes and the Pharisees, having seen Him eating with the tax-gatherers and sinners, said to His disciples, 'Why — that he does eat and drink with the tax-gatherers and sinners?'

17 And Jesus, having heard, said to them, 'They who are strong have no need of a physician, but they who are ill; I came not to call righteous men, but sinners to reformation.'

18 And the disciples of John and those of the Pharisees were fasting, and they come and say to Him, 'Why do the disciples of John and those of the Pharisees fast, and Your[S] disciples do not fast?'

19 And Jesus said to them, 'Are the sons of the bride-

chamber able, while the bridegroom is with them, to fast?
so long time as they have the bridegroom with them they
are not able to fast;
20 but days shall come when the bridegroom may be
taken from them, and then they shall fast — in those
days.
21 'And no one does sew a patch of undressed cloth
on an old garment, and if not — the new filling it up
does take from the old and the rent does become worse;
22 and no one does put new wine into old skins, and if
not — the new wine does burst the skins, and the wine
is poured out, and the skins will be destroyed; but new
wine is to be put into new skins.'
23 And it came to pass — He is going along through
the corn-fields on the sabbaths — and His disciples
began to make a way, plucking the ears,
24 and the Pharisees said to Him, 'Behold, why do they
that which is not lawful on the sabbaths?'
25 And He said to them, 'Did you[P] never read what David
did, when he had need and was hungry, he and those
with him?
26 how he went into the house of God, (at 'Abiathar the
chief priest,') and did eat the loaves of the presentation,
which it is not lawful to eat, except to the priests, and he
gave also to those who were with him?'
27 And He said to them, 'The sabbath for man was made,
not man for the sabbath,
28 so that the son of man is lord also of the sabbath.'

CHAPTER 3

1 And He entered again into the synagogue, and there
was there a man having the hand withered,
2 and they were watching Him, whether He will heal him
on the sabbaths, that they might accuse Him.
3 And He said to the man having the hand withered,
'Rise up in the midst.'
4 And He said to them, 'Is it lawful to do good on the
sabbaths, or to do evil? to save life, or to kill?' but they
were silent.
5 And having looked round upon them with anger, being
grieved for the hardness of their heart, He said to the
man, 'Stretch forth your[S] hand;' and he stretched forth,
and his hand was restored whole as the other;
6 and the Pharisees having gone forth, immediately, with
the Herodians, were taking counsel against Him how
they might destroy Him.
7 And Jesus withdrew with His disciples unto the sea,
and a great multitude from Galilee followed Him, and from
Judea,
8 and from Jerusalem, and from Idumea and beyond the
Jordan; and they about Tyre and Sidon — a great
multitude — having heard how He was doing great
things, came unto Him.
9 And He said to His disciples that a little boat may wait
on Him, because of the multitude, that they may not
press upon Him,
10 for He did heal many, so that they threw themselves
on Him, in order to touch Him — as many as had plagues;
11 and the unclean spirits, when they were seeing Him,
were falling down before Him, and were crying, saying
— 'You[S] are the Son of God;'
12 and many times He was charging them that they might
not make Him known.
13 And He went up to the mountain, and did call whom
He willed near, and they went away to Him;
14 and He appointed twelve, that they may be with Him,
and that He may send them forth to preach,
15 and to have power to heal the sicknesses, and to
cast out the demons.
16 And He put on Simon the name Peter;
17 and James of Zebedee, and John the brother of James,
and He put on them names — Boanerges, that is, 'Sons
of thunder;'
18 and Andrew, and Philip, and Bartholomew, and
Matthew, and Thomas, and James of Alpheus, and
Thaddeus, and Simon the Cananite,
19 and Judas Iscariot, who did also deliver Him up; and
they come into a house.
20 And come together again did a multitude, so that
they are not able even to eat bread;
21 and His friends having heard, went forth to lay hold
on Him, for they said that He was beside Himself,
22 and the scribes who [are] from Jerusalem having come
down, said — 'He has Beelzeboul,' and — 'By the ruler
of the demons He does cast out the demons.'
23 And, having called them near, in similes He said to
them, 'How is the Adversary able to cast out the
Adversary?
24 and if a kingdom be divided against itself, that
kingdom cannot be made to stand;
25 and if a house be divided against itself, that house
cannot be made to stand;
26 and if the Adversary did rise against himself, and
has been divided, he cannot be made to stand, but has
an end.
27 'No one is able to spoil the vessels of the strong

man — having entered into his house, if he may not bind the strong man first, and then he will spoil his house.

28 'Truly I say to you[P], that all the sins shall be forgiven to the sons of men, and evil speakings with which they might speak evil,

29 but whoever may speak evil in regard to the Holy Spirit has not forgiveness — to the age, but is in danger of age-during judgment;'

30 because they said, 'He has an unclean spirit.'

31 Then His brethren and mother do come, and standing without, they sent unto Him, calling Him,

32 and a multitude was sitting about Him, and they said to Him, 'Behold, Your[S] mother and Your[S] brethren without do seek You[S].'

33 And He answered them, saying, 'Who is My mother, or My brethren?'

34 And having looked round in a circle to those sitting about Him, He said, 'Behold, My mother and My brethren!

35 for whoever may do the will of God, he is My brother, and My sister, and mother.'

CHAPTER 4

1 And again He began to teach by the sea, and there a great multitude was gathered unto Him, so that He, having gone into the boat, sat in the sea, and all the multitude was near the sea, on the land,

2 and He taught them many things in similes, and He said to them in His teaching:

3 'Listen, behold, the sower went forth to sow;

4 and it came to pass, in the sowing, some fell by the way, and the fowls of the heaven did come and devour it;

5 and other fell upon the rocky ground, where it had not much earth, and immediately it sprang forth, because of not having depth of earth,

6 and the sun having risen, it was scorched, and it did wither because of not having root;

7 and other fell toward the thorns, and the thorns did come up, and choke it, and it gave not fruit;

8 and other fell to the good ground, and was giving fruit, coming up and increasing, and it bare, one thirty-fold, and one sixty, and one an hundred.'

9 And He said to them, 'He who is having ears to hear — let him hear.'

10 And when He was alone, those about Him, with the twelve, did ask Him of the simile,

11 and He said to them, 'To you[P] it has been given to know the secret of the reign of God, but to those who are without, are all the things done in similes;

12 that seeing they may see and not perceive, and hearing they may hear and not understand, for fear that they may turn, and the sins may be forgiven them.'

13 And He said to them, 'Have you[P] not known this simile? and how shall you[P] know all the similes?

14 He who is sowing does sow the word;

15 and these are they by the way where the word is sown: and whenever they may hear, immediately comes the Adversary, and he takes away the word that has been sown in their hearts.

16 'And these are they, in like manner, who on the rocky ground are sown: who, whenever they may hear the word, immediately with joy do receive it,

17 and have not root in themselves, but are temporary; afterward tribulation or persecution having come because of the word, immediately they are stumbled.

18 'And these are they who toward the thorns are sown: these are they who are hearing the word,

19 and the anxieties of this age, and the deceitfulness of the riches, and the desires concerning the other things, entering in, choke the word, and it becomes unfruitful.

20 'And these are they who on the good ground have been sown: who do hear the word, and receive, and do bear fruit, one thirty-fold, and one sixty, and one an hundred.'

21 And He said to them, 'Does the lamp come that it may be put under the measure, or under the couch — not that it may be put on the lamp-stand?

22 for there is not anything hid that may not be made known, nor was anything kept hid but that it may come to light.

23 If any has ears to hear — let him hear.'

24 And He said to them, 'Take heed what you[P] hear; in what measure you[P] measure, it shall be measured to you[P]; and to you[P] who hear it shall be added;

25 for whoever may have, there shall be given to him, and whoever has not, also that which he has shall be taken from him.'

26 And He said, 'Thus is the reign of God: as if a man may cast the seed on the earth,

27 and may sleep, and may rise night and day, and the seed spring up and grow, he has not known how;

28 for the earth of itself does bear fruit, first a blade, afterwards an ear, afterwards full corn in the ear;

29 and whenever the fruit may yield itself, immediately he does send forth the sickle, because the harvest has come.'

30 And He said, 'To what may we liken the reign of God,
or may we compare it in what simile?
31 As a grain of mustard, which, whenever it may be
sown on the earth, is less than any of the seeds that are
on the earth;
32 and whenever it may be sown, it comes up, and does
become greater than any of the herbs, and does make
great branches, so that under its shade the fowls of the
heaven are able to rest.'
33 And with many such similes He was speaking to them
the word, as they were able to hear,
34 and He was not speaking to them without a simile,
and by themselves, to His disciples He was expounding
all.
35 And He said to them on that day, evening having
come, 'We may pass over to the other side;'
36 and having sent away the multitude, they take Him
up as He was in the boat, and other little boats also were
with Him.
37 And there came a great storm of wind, and the waves
were beating on the boat, so that it is now being filled,
38 and He Himself was upon the stern, upon the pillow
sleeping, and they wake Him up, and say to Him,
'Teacher, are You^{S} not caring that we perish?'
39 And having waked up, He rebuked the wind, and
said to the sea, 'Peace, be stilled;' and the wind did lull,
and there was a great calm:
40 and He said to them, 'Why are you^{P} so fearful? how
have you^{P} not faith?'
41 and they feared a great fear, and said one to another,
'Who, then, is this, that even the wind and the sea do
obey Him?'

CHAPTER 5

1 And they came to the other side of the sea, to the
region of the Gadarenes,
2 and He having come forth out of the boat, immediately
there met Him out of the tombs a man with an unclean spirit,
3 who had his dwelling in the tombs, and not even with
chains was any one able to bind him,
4 because that he had been bound many times with
fetters and chains, and the chains had been pulled in
pieces by him , and the fetters broken in pieces, and none
was able to tame him,
5 and always, night and day, in the mountains, and in
the tombs he was, crying and cutting himself with
stones.
6 And, having seen Jesus from afar, he ran and bowed
before Him,
7 and having called with a loud voice, he said, 'What
— to me and to You^{S}, Jesus, Son of God the Most High?
I appeal to You^{S} by God, may You^{S} not afflict me!'
8 (for He said to him, 'Come forth, unclean spirit, out of
the man,')
9 and He was questioning him, 'What [is] your^{S} name?'
and he answered, saying, 'Legion [is] my name, because
we are many;'
10 and he was calling on Him much, that He may not
send them out of the region.
11 And there was there, near the mountains, a great herd
of swine feeding,
12 and all the demons did call upon Him, saying, 'Send
us to the swine, that we may enter into them;'
13 and immediately Jesus gave them leave, and having
come forth, the unclean spirits did enter into the swine,
and the herd did rush down the steep place to the sea
— and they were about two thousand — and they were
choked in the sea.
14 And those feeding the swine did flee, and told in the
city, and in the fields, and they came forth to see what it
is that has been done;
15 and they come unto Jesus, and see the demoniac,
sitting, and clothed, and right-minded — him having had
the legion — and they were afraid;
16 and those having seen [it], declared to them how it
had come to pass to the demoniac, and about the swine;
17 and they began to call upon Him to go away from
their borders.
18 And He having gone into the boat, the demoniac
was calling on Him that he may be with Him,
19 and Jesus did not allow him, but said to him, 'Go
away to your^{S} house, unto your^{S} own [friends], and tell
them how the Lord did great things to you^{S}, and dealt
kindly with you^{S};
20 and he went away, and began to proclaim in the
Decapolis how Jesus did great things to him, and all were
wondering.
21 And Jesus having passed over to the other side in
the boat again, there was gathered a great multitude to
Him, and He was near the sea,
22 and behold, there does come one of the chiefs of the
synagogue, by name Jairus, and having seen Him, he
does fall at His feet,
23 and he was calling upon Him much, saying — 'My
little daughter is at the last extremity — that having come,
You^{S} may lay [Your^{S}] hands on her, so that she may be

saved, and she shall live;'
24 and He went away with him. And there was following
him a great multitude, and they were thronging Him,
25 and a certain woman, having an issue of blood twelve
years,
26 and having suffered many things under many
physicians, and having spent all that she had, and having
profited nothing, but rather having come to the worse,
27 having heard about Jesus, having come in the
multitude behind, she touched His garment,
28 for she said — 'If I may touch even His garments, I
shall be saved;'
29 and immediately the fountain of her blood was dried
up, and she knew in the body that she had been healed
of the plague.
30 And immediately Jesus having known in Himself that
power had gone forth out of Him, having turned about
in the multitude, said, 'Who did touch My garments?'
31 and His disciples said to Him, 'You[S] see the multitude
thronging You[S], and You[S] say, 'Who did touch Me!'
32 And He was looking round to see her who did this,
33 and the woman, having been afraid, and trembling,
knowing what was done on her, came, and fell down
before Him, and told Him all the truth,
34 and He said to her, 'Daughter, your[S] faith has saved
you[S]; go away in peace, and be whole from your[S] plague.'
35 As He is yet speaking, there come from the chief of
the synagogue's [house, certain], saying — 'Your[S]
daughter did die, why do you[S] still harass the Teacher?'
36 And Jesus immediately, having heard the word that
is spoken, said to the chief of the synagogue, 'Be not
afraid, only believe.'
37 And He did not allow any one to follow with Him,
except Peter, and James, and John the brother of James;
38 and He came to the house of the chief of the
synagogue, and saw a tumult, much weeping and
wailing;
39 and having gone in He said to them, 'Why do you[P]
make a tumult, and weep? the child did not die, but does
sleep;
40 and they were laughing at Him. And He, having put
all forth, did take the father of the child, and the mother,
and those with Him, and went in where the child is lying,
41 and, having taken the hand of the child, He said to
her, 'Talitha cumi;' which is, being interpreted, 'Damsel
(I say to you[S]), arise.'
42 And immediately the damsel arose, and was walking,
for she was twelve years [old]; and they were amazed
with a great amazement,
43 and He charged them much, that no one may know
this thing, and He said that there be given to her to eat.

CHAPTER 6

1 And He went forth from there, and came to His own
country, and His disciples do follow Him,
2 and Sabbath having come, He began to teach in the
synagogue, and many hearing were astonished, saying,
'From where has this one these things? and what the
wisdom that was given to Him, that also such mighty
works are done through His hands?
3 Is this not the carpenter, the son of Mary, and brother
of James, and Joses, and Judas, and Simon? and are not
His sisters here with us?' — and they were being
stumbled at Him.
4 And Jesus said to them — 'A prophet is not without
honor, except in his own country, and among his kindred,
and in his own house;'
5 and He was not able to do any mighty work there,
except on a few infirm people having put hands He did
heal [them];
6 and He wondered because of their unbelief. And He
was going round the villages, in a circle, teaching,
7 and He does call the twelve near, and He began to
send them forth two by two, and He was giving them
power over the unclean spirits,
8 and He commanded them that they may take nothing
for the way, except a staff only — no scrip, no bread, no
brass in the girdle,
9 but having been shod with sandals, and you[P] may
not put on two coats.
10 And He said to them, 'Whenever you[P] may enter
into a house, remain there till you[P] may depart from there,
11 and as many as may not receive you[P], nor hear you[P],
going out from there, shake off the dust that is under
your[P] feet for a testimony to them; truly I say to you[P], It
shall be more tolerable for Sodom or Gomorrah in a day
of judgment than for that city.'
12 And having gone forth they were preaching that
[men] might reform,
13 and they were casting out many demons, and they
were anointing many infirm with oil, and they were
healing [them].
14 And the king Herod heard, (for His name became
public,) and he said — 'John the Baptist was raised out
of the dead, and because of this the mighty powers are
working in him.'

15 Others said — 'It is Elijah,' and others said — 'It is a
prophet, or as one of the prophets.'
16 And Herod having heard, said — 'He whom I did
behead — John — this is he; he was raised out of the
dead.'
17 For Herod himself, having sent forth, did lay hold on
John, and bound him in the prison, because of Herodias
the wife of Philip his brother, because he married her,
18 for John said to Herod — 'It is not lawful to you[S] to
have the wife of your[S] brother;'
19 and Herodias was having a quarrel with him, and
was willing to kill him, and was not able,
20 for Herod was fearing John, knowing him a righteous
and holy man, and was keeping watch over him, and
having heard him, was doing many things, and hearing
him gladly.
21 And a seasonable day having come, when Herod on
his birthday was making a supper to his great men, and
to the chiefs of thousands, and to the first men of Galilee,
22 and the daughter of that Herodias having come in,
and having danced, and having pleased Herod and those
reclining (at meat) with him, the king said to the damsel,
'Ask of me whatever you[S] will, and I will give to you[S],'
23 and he swore to her — 'Whatever you[S] may ask me,
I will give to you[S] — unto the half of my kingdom.'
24 And she, having gone forth, said to her mother, 'What
shall I ask for myself?' and she said, 'The head of John
the Baptist;'
25 and having come in immediately with swiftness unto
the king, she asked, saying, 'I will that you[S] may give
me presently, upon a plate, the head of John the Baptist.'
26 And the king — made very sorrowful — because of
the oaths and of those reclining (at meat) with him, would
not put her away,
27 and immediately the king having sent a guardsman,
did command his head to be brought,
28 and he having gone, beheaded him in the prison,
and brought his head upon a plate, and did give it to the
damsel, and the damsel did give it to her mother;
29 and having heard, his disciples came and took up
his corpse, and laid it in the tomb.
30 And the apostles are gathered together unto Jesus,
and they told Him all, and how many things they did,
and how many things they taught,
31 and He said to them, 'Come you[P] yourselves[P] apart
to a desert place, and rest a little,' for those coming and
those going were many, and not even had they
opportunity to eat,
32 and they went away to a desert place, in the boat, by
themselves.
33 And the multitudes saw them going away, and many
recognized Him, and by land from all the cities they ran
there, and went before them, and came together to Him,
34 and having come forth, Jesus saw a great multitude,
and was moved with compassion on them, that they were
as sheep not having a shepherd, and He began to teach
many things.
35 And now the hour being advanced, His disciples
having come near to Him, say, — 'The place is desolate,
and the hour is now advanced,
36 send them away, that, having gone away to the
surrounding fields and villages, they may buy to
themselves loaves, for they have not what they may eat.'
37 And He answering said to them, 'You[P] give them to
eat,' and they say to Him, 'Having gone away, may we
buy two hundred denaries' worth of loaves, and give to
them to eat?'
38 And He said to them, 'How many loaves have you[P]?
go and see;' and having known, they say, 'Five, and two
fishes.'
39 And He commanded them to make all recline in
companies upon the green grass,
40 and they sat down in squares, by hundreds, and by
fifties.
41 And having taken the five loaves and the two fishes,
having looked up to the heaven, He blessed, and broke
the loaves, and was giving to His disciples, that they
may set before them, and He divided the two fishes to
all,
42 and they did all eat, and were filled,
43 and they took up of broken pieces twelve hand-
baskets full, and of the fishes,
44 and those eating of the loaves were about five
thousand men.
45 And immediately He constrained His disciples to go
into the boat, and to go before to the other side, unto
Bethsaida, till He may send the multitude away,
46 and having taken leave of them, He went away to the
mountain to pray.
47 And evening having come, the boat was in the midst
of the sea, and He alone upon the land;
48 and He saw them harassed in the rowing, for the wind
was against them, and about the fourth watch of the
night He did come to them walking on the sea, and
wished to pass by them.
49 And they having seen Him walking on the sea,
thought [it] to be an apparition, and cried out,
50 for they all saw Him, and were troubled, and

immediately He spoke with them, and said to them, 'Take
courage, I am [He], be not afraid.'
51 And He went up to the boat unto them, and the wind
lulled, and greatly out of measure were they amazed in
themselves, and were wondering,
52 for they understood not concerning the loaves, for
their heart has been hard.
53 And having passed over, they came upon the land
of Gennesaret, and drew to the shore,
54 and they having come forth out of the boat,
immediately having recognized Him,
55 having run about through all that region round about,
they began to carry about those ill upon the couches,
where they were hearing that He is,
56 and wherever He was going, to villages, or cities, or
fields, in the market-places they were laying the infirm,
and were calling upon Him, that they may touch if it were
but the fringe of His garment, and as many as were
touching Him were saved.

CHAPTER 7

1 And gathered together unto Him are the Pharisees,
and certain of the scribes, having come from Jerusalem,
2 and having seen certain of His disciples with defiled
hands — that is, unwashed — eating bread, they found
fault;
3 for the Pharisees, and all the Jews, if they do not wash
the hands to the wrist, do not eat, holding the tradition
of the elders,
4 and, [coming] from the market-place, if they do not
baptize themselves, they do not eat; and there are many
other things that they received to hold, baptisms of cups,
and pots, and brazen vessels, and couches.
5 Then do the Pharisees and the scribes question Him,
'Why do Your[S] disciples not walk according to the
tradition of the elders, but do eat the bread with
unwashed hands?'
6 and He answering said to them — 'Well did Isaiah
prophesy concerning you[P], hypocrites, as it has been
written, This people do honor Me with the lips, and their
heart is far from Me;
7 and in vain do they worship Me, teaching teachings,
commands of men;
8 for, having put away the command of God, you[P] hold
the tradition of men, baptisms of pots and cups; and
many other such like things you[P] do.'
9 And He said to them, 'Well do you[P] put away the
command of God that your[P] tradition you may keep;
10 for Moses said, Honor your[S] father and your[S] mother;
and, He who is speaking evil of father or mother — let
him die the death;
11 and you[P] say, If a man may say to father or to mother,
Korban (that is, a gift), [is] whatever you[S] may be profited
out of mine,
12 and no more do you[P] allow him to do anything for
his father or for his mother,
13 setting aside the word of God for your[P] tradition that
you[P] delivered; and many such like things you[P] do.'
14 And having called near all the multitude, He said to
them, 'Listen to Me, you all, and understand;
15 there is nothing from without the man entering into
him that is able to defile him, but the things coming out
from him, those are the things defiling the man.
16 If any has ears to hear — let him hear.'
17 And when He entered into a house from the multitude,
His disciples were questioning Him about the simile,
18 and He said to them, 'So you[P] are without
understanding also! Do you[P] not perceive that nothing
from without entering into the man is able to defile him?
19 because it does not enter into his heart, but into the belly,
and into the drain it does go out, purifying all the meats.'
20 And He said — 'That which is coming out from the
man, that does defile the man;
21 for from within, out of the heart of men, the evil
reasonings do come forth, adulteries, whoredoms,
murders,
22 thefts, covetous desires, wickedness, deceit,
arrogance, an evil eye, evil speaking, pride, foolishness;
23 all these evils do come forth from within, and they
defile the man.'
24 And from there having risen, He went away to the
borders of Tyre and Sidon, and having entered into the
house, He wished none to know, and He was not able to
be hid,
25 for a woman having heard about Him, whose little
daughter had an unclean spirit, having come, fell at His
feet, —
26 and the woman was a Greek, a Syro-Phenician by
nation — and was asking Him, that He may cast the
demon forth out of her daughter.
27 And Jesus said to her, 'First allow the children to be
filled, for it is not good to take the children's bread, and
to cast [it] to the little dogs.'
28 And she answered and said to Him, 'Yes, sir; for the
little dogs do eat of the children's crumbs under the table
also.'

29 And He said to her, 'Because of this word go; the
demon has gone forth out of your^{S} daughter;'
30 and having come away to her house, she found the
demon gone forth, and the daughter laid upon the couch.
31 And again, having gone forth from the coasts of Tyre
and Sidon, He came unto the sea of Galilee, through the
midst of the coasts of Decapolis,
32 and they bring to Him a deaf, stuttering man, and
they call on Him that He may put the hand on him.
33 And having taken him away from the multitude by
Himself, He put His fingers to his ears, and having spit,
He touched his tongue,
34 and having looked to the heaven, He sighed, and
said to him, 'Ephphatha,' that is, 'Be you^{S} opened;'
35 and immediately were his ears opened, and the string
of his tongue was loosed, and he was speaking plain.
36 And He charged them that they may tell no one, but
the more He was charging them, the more abundantly
they were proclaiming [it],
37 and they were being astonished beyond measure,
saying, 'Well has He done all things; He does both make
the deaf to hear, and the dumb to speak.'

CHAPTER 8

1 In those days the multitude being very great, and not
having what they may eat, Jesus having called near His
disciples, said to them,
2 'I have compassion upon the multitude, because now
they do continue with me three days, and they have not
what they may eat;
3 and if I shall send them away fasting to their home,
they will faint in the way, for certain of them are come
from far.'
4 And His disciples answered Him, 'From where shall
any one be able to feed these here with bread in a
wilderness?'
5 And He was questioning them, 'How many loaves
have you^{P}?' and they said, 'Seven.'
6 And He commanded the multitude to sit down upon
the ground, and having taken the seven loaves, having
given thanks, He broke, and was giving to His disciples
that they may set before [them]; and they did set before
the multitude.
7 And they had a few small fishes, and having blessed,
He said to set them before [them] also;
8 and they did eat and were filled, and they took up that
which was over of broken pieces — seven baskets;
9 and those eating were about four thousand. And He
sent them away,
10 and immediately having entered into the boat with
His disciples, He came to the parts of Dalmanutha,
11 and the Pharisees came forth, and began to dispute
with Him, seeking from Him a sign from the heaven,
tempting Him;
12 and having sighed deeply in His spirit, He said, 'Why
does this generation seek after a sign? Truly I say to
you^{P}, no sign shall be given to this generation.'
13 And having left them, having entered again into the
boat, He went away to the other side;
14 and they forgot to take loaves, and except one loaf
they had nothing with them in the boat,
15 and He was charging them, saying, 'Take heed,
beware of the leaven of the Pharisees, and of the leaven
of Herod,'
16 and they were reasoning with one another, saying
— 'Because we have no loaves.'
17 And Jesus having known, said to them, 'Why do
you^{P} reason, because you^{P} have no loaves? do you^{P} not
yet perceive, nor understand, yet have you^{P} your^{P} heart
hardened?
18 Having eyes, do you^{P} not see? and having ears, do
you^{P} not hear? and do you^{P} not remember?
19 When the five loaves I did break to the five thousand,
how many hand-baskets full of broken pieces took you^{P}
up?' they say to Him, 'Twelve.'
20 'And when the seven to the four thousand, how many
hand-baskets full of broken pieces took you^{P} up?' and
they said, 'Seven.'
21 And He said to them, 'How do you^{P} not understand?'
22 And He came to Bethsaida, and they bring to Him
one blind, and call upon Him that He may touch him,
23 and having taken the hand of the blind man, He led
him forth without the village, and having spit on his eyes,
having put [His] hands on him, He was questioning him
if he did behold anything:
24 and he, having looked up, said, 'I behold men, as I
see trees, walking.'
25 Afterwards again He put [His] hands on his eyes,
and made him look up, and he was restored, and
discerned all things clearly,
26 and He sent him away to his house, saying, 'Neither
to the village may you^{S} go, nor tell [it] to any in the
village.'
27 And Jesus went forth, and His disciples, to the
villages of Caesarea Philippi, and in the way He was
questioning His disciples, saying to them, 'Who do men

say Me to be?'

28 And they answered, 'John the Baptist, and others Elijah, but others one of the prophets.'

29 And He said to them, 'And you[P] — who do you[P] say Me to be?' and Peter answering said to Him, 'You[S] are the Christ.'

30 And He strictly charged them that they may tell no one about it,

31 and began to teach them, that it is necessary for the Son of Man to suffer many things, and to be rejected by the elders, and chief priests, and scribes, and to be killed, and after three days to rise again;

32 and openly He was speaking the word. And Peter having taken Him aside, began to rebuke Him,

33 and He, having turned, and having looked on His disciples, rebuked Peter, saying, 'Get behind Me, Adversary, because you[S] do not mind the things of God, but the things of men.'

34 And having called near the multitude, with His disciples, He said to them, 'Whoever does will to come after Me — let him disown himself, and take up his cross, and follow Me;

35 for whoever may will to save his life shall lose it; and whoever may lose his life for My sake and for the good news' sake, he shall save it;

36 for what shall it profit a man, if he may gain the whole world, and forfeit his life?

37 Or what shall a man give as an exchange for his life?

38 for whoever may be ashamed of Me, and of My words, in this adulterous and sinful generation, the Son of Man also shall be ashamed of him, when He may come in the glory of His Father, with the holy messengers.'

CHAPTER 9

1 And He said to them, 'Truly I say to you[P], That there are certain of those standing here, who may not taste of death till they see the reign of God having come in power.'

2 And after six days did Jesus take Peter, and James, and John, and brought them up to a high mount by themselves, alone, and He was transfigured before them,

3 and His garments became glittering, white exceedingly, as snow, so as a fuller upon the earth is not able to whiten [them].

4 And there appeared to them Elijah with Moses, and they were talking with Jesus.

5 And Peter answering said to Jesus, 'Rabbi, it is good to us to be here; and we may make three booths, one for You[S], and one for Moses, and one for Elijah:'

6 for he was not knowing what he might say, for they were greatly afraid.

7 And there came a cloud overshadowing them, and there came a voice out of the cloud, saying, 'This is My Son — the Beloved, you[P] hear Him;'

8 and suddenly, having looked around, they saw no one any more, but Jesus only with themselves.

9 And as they are coming down from the mount, He charged them that they may declare to no one the things that they saw, except when the Son of Man may rise out of the dead;

10 and the thing they kept to themselves, questioning together what the rising out of the dead is.

11 And they were questioning Him, saying, that the scribes say that it is necessary for Elijah to come first.

12 And He answering said to them, 'Elijah indeed, having come first, does restore all things; and how has it been written concerning the Son of Man, that many things He may suffer, and be set at nothing?

13 But I say to you, That also Elijah has come, and they did to him what they willed, as it has been written of him.'

14 And having come unto the disciples, He saw a great multitude about them, and scribes questioning with them,

15 and immediately, all the multitude having seen Him, were amazed, and running near, were saluting Him.

16 And He questioned the scribes, 'What dispute you[P] with them?'

17 and one out of the multitude answering said, 'Teacher, I brought my son unto You[S], having a dumb spirit;

18 and wherever it does seize him, it does tear him, and he foams, and gnashes his teeth, and pines away; and I spoke to Your[S] disciples that they may cast it out, and they were not able.'

19 And He answering him, said, 'O unbelieving generation, till when shall I be with you[P]? till when shall I suffer you[P]? bring him unto Me;'

20 and they brought him unto Him, and he having seen Him, immediately the spirit tore him, and he, having fallen upon the earth, was wallowing — foaming.

21 And He questioned his father, 'How long time is it since this came to him?' and he said, 'From childhood,

22 and many times also it cast him into fire, and into water, that it might destroy him; but if You[S] are able to do anything, help us, having compassion on us.'

23 And Jesus said to him, 'If you[S] are able to believe! all things are possible to the one that is believing;'

24 and immediately the father of the child, having cried
out, with tears said, 'I believe, sir; be helping mine
unbelief.'
25 Jesus having seen that a multitude does run together,
rebuked the unclean spirit, saying to it, 'Spirit — dumb
and deaf — I charge you[S], come forth out of him, and no
more may you[S] enter into him;'
26 and having cried, and rent him much, it came forth,
and he became as dead, so that many said that he was
dead,
27 but Jesus, having taken him by the hand, lifted him
up, and he arose.
28 And He having come into the house, His disciples
were questioning Him by Himself — 'Why were we not
able to cast it forth?'
29 And He said to them, 'This kind is able to come forth
with nothing except with prayer and fasting.'
30 And having gone forth from there, they were passing
through Galilee, and He did not wish that any may know,
31 for He was teaching His disciples, and He said to
them, 'The Son of Man is being delivered to the hands
of men, and they shall kill Him, and having been killed
the third day He shall rise,'
32 but they were not understanding the saying, and
they were afraid to question Him.
33 And He came to Capernaum, and being in the house,
He was questioning them, 'What were you[P] reasoning
in the way among yourselves[P]?'
34 and they were silent, for they did reason with one
another in the way who is greater;
35 and having sat down He called the twelve, and He
said to them, 'If any does will to be first, he shall be last
of all, and minister of all.'
36 And having taken a child, He set him in the midst of
them, and having taken him in His arms, said to them,
37 'Whoever may receive one of such children in My
name, does receive me, and whoever may receive Me,
does not receive Me, but Him who sent Me.'
38 And John did answer Him, saying, 'Teacher, we saw
a certain one casting out demons in Your[S] name, who
does not follow us, and we forbade him, because he does
not follow us.'
39 And Jesus said, 'Forbid him not, for there is no one
who shall do a mighty work in My name, and shall be
readily able to speak evil of Me:
40 for he who is not against us is for us;
41 for whoever may give you[P] a cup of water to drink in
My name, because you[P] are Christ's, truly I say to you[P],
he may not lose his reward;
42 and whoever may cause one of the little ones
believing in Me to stumble, is it better for him if a
millstone is hanged about his neck, and he had been
cast into the sea.
43 'And if your[S] hand may cause you[S] to stumble, cut it
off; it is better for you[S] to enter into the life maimed, than
having the two hands, to go away to the gehenna, to
the fire — the unquenchable —
44 where there worm is not dying, and the fire is not
being quenched.
45 'And if your[S] foot may cause you[S] to stumble, cut it
off; it is better for you[S] to enter into the life lame, than
having the two feet to be cast to the gehenna, to the fire
— the unquenchable —
46 where there worm is not dying, and the fire is not
being quenched.
47 And if your[S] eye may cause you[S] to stumble, cast it
out; it is better for you[S] to enter into the reign of God
one-eyed, than having two eyes, to be cast to the
gehenna of the fire —
48 where their worm is not dying, and the fire is not
being quenched;
49 for every one with fire shall be salted, and every
sacrifice with salt shall be salted.
50 The salt [is] good, but if the salt may become saltless,
in what will you[P] season [it]? Have in yourselves[P] salt,
and have peace in one another.'

CHAPTER 10

1 And having risen from there, He did come to the coasts
of Judea, through the other side of the Jordan, and again
do multitudes come together unto Him, and, as He had
been accustomed, again He was teaching them.
2 And the Pharisees, having come near, questioned Him,
if it is lawful for a husband to put away a wife, tempting
Him,
3 and He answering said to them, 'What did Moses
command you[P]?'
4 and they said, 'Moses allowed to write a bill of divorce,
and to put away.'
5 And Jesus answering said to them, 'For the stiffness
of your[P] heart he wrote you[P] this command,
6 but from the beginning of the creation, a male and a
female God did make them;
7 on this account shall a man leave his father and mother,
and shall adhere unto his wife,
8 and they shall be — the two — for one flesh; so that

they are no more two, but one flesh;
9 what therefore God did join together, let not man put
asunder.'
10 And in the house again His disciples questioned Him
of the same thing,
11 and He said to them, 'Whoever may put away his
wife, and may marry another, does commit adultery
against her;
12 and if a woman may put away her husband, and is
married to another, she commits adultery.'
13 And they were bringing to Him children, that He might
touch them, and the disciples were rebuking those
bringing them,
14 and Jesus having seen, was much displeased, and
He said to them, 'Allow the children to come unto Me,
and forbid them not, for of such is the reign of God;
15 truly I say to you[P], whoever may not receive the reign
of God, as a child — he may not enter into it;'
16 and having taken them in His arms, having put [His]
hands upon them, He was blessing them.
17 And as He is going forth into the way, one having
run and having kneeled to Him, was questioning Him,
'Good teacher, what may I do, that I may inherit life age-
during?'
18 And Jesus said to him, 'Why do you[S] call Me good?
no one [is] good except One — God;
19 the commands you[S] have known: You[S] may not
commit adultery, You[S] may do no murder, You[S] may not
steal, You[S] may not bear false witness, You[S] may not
defraud, Honor your[S] father and mother.'
20 And he answering said to Him, 'Teacher, all these
did I keep from my youth.'
21 And Jesus having looked upon him, did love him,
and said to him, 'One thing you[S] do lack; go away,
whatever you[S] have — sell, and give to the poor, and
you[S] shall have treasure in heaven, and come, be
following Me, having taken up the cross.'
22 And he — gloomy at the word — went away
sorrowing, for he was having many possessions.
23 And Jesus having looked round, said to His disciples,
'How hardly shall they who have riches enter into the
reign of God!'
24 And the disciples were astonished at His words, and
Jesus again answering said to them, 'Children, how hard
is it to those trusting on the riches to enter into the reign
of God!
25 It is easier for a camel to enter through the eye of the
needle, than for a rich man to enter into the reign of God.'
26 And they were astonished beyond measure, saying
unto themselves, 'And who is able to be saved?'
27 And Jesus, having looked upon them, said, 'With
men it is impossible, but not with God; for all things are
possible with God.'
28 And Peter began to say to Him, 'Behold, we left all,
and we followed You[S].'
29 And Jesus answering said, 'Truly I say to you[P], there
is no one who left house, or brothers, or sisters, or father,
or mother, or wife, or children, or fields, for My sake,
and for the good news',
30 who may not receive an hundredfold now in this time,
houses, and brothers, and sisters, and mothers, and
children, and fields, with persecutions, and in the age
that is coming, life age-during;
31 and many first shall be last, and the last first.'
32 And they were in the way going up to Jerusalem,
and Jesus was going before them, and they were amazed,
and following they were afraid. And having again taken
the twelve, He began to tell them the things about to
happen to Him,
33 — 'Behold, we go up to Jerusalem, and the Son of
Man shall be delivered to the chief priests, and to the
scribes, and they shall condemn Him to death, and shall
deliver Him to the nations,
34 and they shall mock Him, and scourge Him, and spit
on Him, and kill Him, and the third day He shall rise
again.'
35 And there James and John, the sons of Zebedee,
come near to Him saying, 'Teacher, we wish that
whatever we may ask for ourselves, You[S] may do for us;'
36 and He said to them, 'What do you[P] wish Me to do
for you[P]?'
37 and they said to Him, 'Grant to us that, one on Your[S]
right hand and one on Your[S] left, we may sit in Your[S]
glory;'
38 and Jesus said to them, 'You[P] have not known what
you[P] ask; are you[P] able to drink of the cup that I drink
of, and with the baptism that I am baptized with — to be
baptized?'
39 And they said to Him, 'We are able;' and Jesus said
to them, 'Of the cup indeed that I drink of, you[P] shall
drink, and with the baptism that I am baptized with, you[P]
shall be baptized;
40 but to sit on My right and on My left, is not Mine to
give, but — to those for whom it has been prepared.'
41 And the ten having heard, began to be much
displeased at James and John,
42 but Jesus having called them near, said to them, 'You[P]
have known that they who are considered to rule the

nations do exercise lordship over them, and their great
ones do exercise authority upon them;
43 but it shall not be so among you[P]; but whoever may
will to become great among you[P], he shall be your[P]
minister,
44 and whoever of you[P] may will to become first, he
shall be servant of all;
45 for even the Son of Man came not to be ministered
to, but to minister, and to give His life a ransom for many.'
46 And they come to Jericho, and as He is going forth
from Jericho, with His disciples and a great multitude, a
son of Timaeus — Bartimaeus the blind — was sitting
beside the way begging,
47 and having heard that it is Jesus the Nazarene, he
began to cry out, and to say, 'The Son of David — Jesus!
deal kindly with me;'
48 and many were rebuking him, that he might keep
silent, but the more abundantly he cried out, 'Son of
David, deal kindly with me.'
49 And Jesus having stood, He commanded him to be
called, and they call the blind man, saying to him, 'Take
courage, rise, He does call you[S];'
50 and he, having cast away his garment, having risen,
did come unto Jesus.
51 And answering, Jesus said to him, 'What will you[S] I
may do to you[S]?' and the blind man said to Him,
'Rabboni, that I may see again;'
52 and Jesus said to him, 'Go, your[S] faith has saved
you[S]:' and immediately he saw again, and was following
Jesus in the way.

CHAPTER 11

1 And when they come near to Jerusalem, to Bethphage,
and Bethany, unto the mount of the Olives, He sent forth
two of His disciples,
2 and said to them, 'Go away to the village that is over-
against you[P], and immediately, entering into it, you[P] shall
find a colt tied, on which no one of men has sat, having
loosed it, bring [it]:
3 and if any one may say to you[P], Why do you[P] this?
you[P] say that the lord has need of it, and immediately he
will send it here.'
4 And they went away, and found the colt tied at the
door without, by the two ways, and they loose it,
5 and certain of those standing there said to them, 'What
do you[P] — loosing the colt?'
6 and they said to them as Jesus commanded, and they
allowed them.
7 And they brought the colt unto Jesus, and did cast
their garments upon it, and He sat upon it,
8 and many did spread their garments in the way, and
others were cutting down branches from the trees, and
were spreading in the way.
9 And those going before and those following were
crying out, saying, 'Hosanna! blessed [is] He who is
coming in the name of the Lord;
10 blessed is the coming reign, in the name of the Lord,
of our father David; Hosanna in the highest.'
11 And Jesus entered into Jerusalem, and into the
temple, and having looked round on all things, it being
now evening, He went forth to Bethany with the twelve.
12 And on the morrow, they having come forth from
Bethany, He hungered,
13 and having seen afar off a fig-tree having leaves, He
came, if perhaps He shall find anything in it, and having
come to it, He found nothing except leaves, for it was
not a time of figs,
14 and Jesus answering said to it, 'No more from you[S]
— to the age — may any eat fruit;' and His disciples
were hearing.
15 And they come to Jerusalem, and Jesus having gone
into the temple, began to cast forth those selling and
buying in the temple, and He overthrew the tables of
the money-changers and the seats of those selling the
doves,
16 and He did not allow that any might bear a vessel
through the temple,
17 and He was teaching, saying to them, 'Has it not
been written — My house shall be called a house of
prayer for all the nations, and you[P] did make it a den of
robbers?'
18 And the scribes and the chief priests heard, and they
were seeking how they shall destroy Him, for they were
afraid of Him, because all the multitude was astonished
at His teaching;
19 and when evening came, He was going forth without
the city.
20 And in the morning, passing by, they saw the fig-
tree having been dried up from the roots,
21 and Peter having remembered said to Him, 'Rabbi,
behold, the fig-tree that You[S] did curse is dried up.'
22 And Jesus answering said to them, 'Have faith of
God;
23 for truly I say to you[P], that whoever may say to this
mount, Be taken up, and be cast into the sea, and may
not doubt in his heart, but may believe that the things

that he said do come to pass, it shall be to him whatever
he may say.
24 Because of this I say to you[P], all whatever — praying
— you[P] do ask, believe that you[P] receive, and it shall be
to you[P].
25 'And whenever you[P] may stand praying, forgive, if
you[P] have anything against any one, that your[P] Father
also who is in the heavens may forgive you[P] your[P]
trespasses;
26 and, if you[P] do not forgive, neither will your[P] Father
who is in the heavens forgive your[P] trespasses.'
27 And they come again to Jerusalem, and in the temple,
as He is walking, there come unto Him the chief priests,
and the scribes, and the elders,
28 and they say to Him, 'By what authority do You[S]
these things? and who gave You[S] this authority that You[S]
may do these things?'
29 And Jesus answering said to them, 'I will question
you[P] — I also — one word; and answer Me, and I will
tell you[P] by what authority I do these things;
30 the baptism of John – was it from heaven? or from
men? answer Me.'
31 And they were reasoning with themselves, saying,
'If we may say, From heaven, He will say, Why, then,
did you[P] not believe him?
32 But if we may say, From men,' — they were fearing
the people, for all were holding John that he was indeed
a prophet;
33 and answering they say to Jesus, 'We have not
known;' and Jesus answering said to them, 'Neither do
I tell you[P] by what authority I do these things.'

CHAPTER 12

1 And He began to speak to them in similes: 'A man
planted a vineyard, and put a hedge around, and dug an
under-wine-vat, and built a tower, and gave it out to
husbandmen, and went abroad;
2 and he sent a servant unto the husbandmen at the
due time, that he may receive from the fruit of the
vineyard from the husbandmen,
3 and they, having taken him, did severely beat [him],
and did send him away empty.
4 'And again he sent another servant unto them, and
having cast stones at that one, they wounded [him] in
the head, and sent away — dishonored.
5 'And again he sent another, and that one they killed;
and many others, some beating, and some killing.
6 'Having yet therefore one son — his beloved — he
sent him also unto them last, saying — They will
reverence my son;
7 and those husbandmen said among themselves —
This is the heir, come, we may kill him, and ours shall be
the inheritance;
8 and having taken him, they did kill, and cast [him]
forth without the vineyard.
9 'What therefore shall the lord of the vineyard do? he
will come and destroy the husbandmen, and will give
the vineyard to others.
10 And this Writing did you[P] not read: A stone that the
builders rejected, it did become the head of a corner:
11 this was from the Lord, and it is wonderful in our
eyes.'
12 And they were seeking to lay hold on Him, and they
feared the multitude, for they knew that He spoke the
simile against them, and having left Him, they went away;
13 and they send unto Him certain of the Pharisees and
of the Herodians, that they may ensnare Him in
discourse,
14 and they having come, say to Him, 'Teacher, we have
known that You[S] are true, and You[S] are not caring for
any one, for You[S] do not look to the face of men, but do
teach the way of God in truth; is it lawful to give tribute
to Caesar or not? may we give, or may we not give?'
15 And He, knowing their hypocrisy, said to them, 'Why
do you[P] tempt Me? bring Me a denary, that I may see;'
16 and they brought, and He said to them, 'Whose image
[is] this, and the inscription?' and they said to Him,
'Caesar's;'
17 and Jesus answering said to them, 'Give the things
of Caesar back to Caesar, and the things of God to God;'
and they did wonder at Him.
18 And the Sadducees come unto Him, who say there is
not a rising again, and they questioned Him, saying,
19 'Teacher, Moses wrote to us, that if any one's brother
may die, and may leave a wife, and may leave no children,
that his brother may take his wife, and raise up seed to
his brother.
20 'There were then seven brothers, and the first took a
wife, and dying, he left no seed;
21 and the second took her, and died, neither left he
seed, and the third in like manner,
22 and the seven took her, and left no seed, last of all
died also the woman;
23 in the rising again, then, whenever they may rise, of
which of them shall she be wife — for the seven had her
as wife?'

24 And Jesus answering said to them, 'Do you[P] not go astray because of this, not knowing the Writings, nor the power of God?

25 for when they may rise out of the dead, they neither marry nor are they given in marriage, but are as messengers who are in the heavens.

26 'And concerning the dead, that they rise: have you[P] not read in the Book of Moses (at The Bush), how God spoke to him, saying, I [am] the God of Abraham, and the God of Isaac, and the God of Jacob;

27 he is not the God of dead men, but a God of living men; you[P] then go astray greatly.'

28 And one of the scribes having come near, having heard them disputing, knowing that He answered them well, questioned Him, 'Which is the first command of all?'

29 and Jesus answered him — 'The first of all the commands [is], Hear, O Israel, the Lord is our God, the Lord is one;

30 and you[S] shall love the Lord your[S] God out of all your[S] heart, and out of your[S] soul, and out of all your[S] understanding, and out of all your[S] strength — this [is] the first command;

31 and the second [is] like [it], this, You[S] shall love your[S] neighbor as yourself[S]; — there is no other command greater than these.'

32 And the scribe said to Him, 'Well, Teacher, in truth You[S] have spoken that there is one God, and there is none other but He;

33 and to love Him out of all the heart, and out of all the understanding, and out of all the soul, and out of all the strength, and to love one's neighbor as one's self, is more than all the whole burnt-offerings and the sacrifices.'

34 And Jesus, having seen him that he answered with understanding, said to him, 'You[S] are not far from the reign of God;' and no one any more dare question Him.

35 And Jesus answering said, teaching in the temple, 'How say the scribes that the Christ is son of David?

36 for David himself said in the Holy Spirit, The Lord said to my lord, Sit you[S] on My right hand, till I place your[S] enemies — your[S] footstool;

37 therefore David himself said of him Lord, and how is he his son?' And the great multitude were hearing Him gladly,

38 and He was saying to them in his teaching, 'Beware of the scribes, who will to walk in long robes, and love salutations in the market-places,

39 and first seats in the synagogues, and first couches in suppers,

40 who are devouring the widows' houses, and for a pretense are making long prayers; these shall receive more abundant judgment.'

41 And Jesus having sat down over-against the treasury, was beholding how the multitude do put brass into the treasury, and many rich were putting in much,

42 and having come, a poor widow did put in two mites, which are a farthing.

43 And having called near His disciples, He said to them, 'Truly I say to you[P], that this poor widow has put in more than all those putting into the treasury;

44 for all, out of their abundance, put in, but she, out of her want, put in all that she had — all her living.'

CHAPTER 13

1 And as He is going forth out of the temple, one of His disciples said to Him, 'Teacher, see! what stones! and what buildings!'

2 and Jesus answering said to him, 'You[S] see these great buildings? there may not be left a stone upon a stone, that may not be thrown down.'

3 And as He is sitting at the mount of the Olives, over-against the temple, Peter, and James, and John, and Andrew, were questioning Him by Himself,

4 'Tell us when these things shall be? and what [is] the sign when all these may be about to be fulfilled?'

5 And Jesus answering them, began to say, 'Take heed for fear that any one may lead you[P] astray,

6 for many shall come in My name, saying — I am [he], and they shall lead many astray;

7 and when you may hear of wars and reports of wars, be not troubled, for these are necessary to be, but the end [is] not yet;

8 for nation shall rise against nation, and kingdom against kingdom, and there shall be earthquakes in various places, and there shall be famines and troubles; these [are] beginnings of sorrows.

9 'And you[P] take heed to yourselves[P], for they shall deliver you[P] up to sanhedrims, and to synagogues, you[P] shall be beaten, and you[P] shall be set before governors and kings for My sake, for a testimony to them;

10 and it is necessary first that the good news be proclaimed to all the nations.

11 'And when they may lead you[P], delivering up, be not anxious beforehand what you[P] may speak, nor premeditate, but whatever may be given to you[P] in that

hour, that speak you[P], for it is not you[P] who are speaking, but the Holy Spirit.

12 'And brother shall deliver up brother to death, and father child, and children shall rise up against parents, and shall put them to death,

13 and you[P] shall be hated by all because of My name, but he who has endured to the end — he shall be saved.

14 'And when you[P] may see the abomination of the desolation, that was spoken of by Daniel the prophet, standing where it ought not, (whoever is reading let him understand), then those in Judea, let them flee to the mountains;

15 and he upon the house-top, let him not come down to the house, nor come in to take anything out of his house;

16 and he who is in the field, let him not turn to the things behind, to take up his garment.

17 'And woe to those with child, and to those giving suck, in those days;

18 and you[P] pray that your[P] flight may not be in winter,

19 for those days shall be tribulation, such as has not been from the beginning of the creation that God created, till now, and may not be;

20 and if the Lord did not shorten the days, no flesh had been saved; but because of the chosen, whom He did choose to Himself, He did shorten the days.

21 'And then, if any may say to you[P], Behold, here [is] the Christ, or, Behold, there, you[P] may not believe;

22 for there shall rise false Christs and false prophets, and they shall give signs and wonders, to seduce, if possible, also the chosen;

23 and you[P], take heed; behold, I have foretold you[P] all things.

24 'But in those days, after that tribulation, the sun shall be darkened, and the moon shall not give her light,

25 and the stars of the heaven shall be falling, and the powers that are in the heavens shall be shaken.

26 'And then they shall see the Son of Man coming in clouds with much power and glory,

27 and then He shall send His messengers, and gather together His chosen from the four winds, from the end of the earth unto the end of heaven.

28 'And from the fig-tree you[P] learn the simile: when the branch may already become tender, and may put forth the leaves, you[P] know that the summer is near;

29 so you[P], also, when you[P] may see these coming to pass, you[P] know that it is near, at the doors.

30 Truly I say to you[P], that this generation may not pass away till all these things may come to pass;

31 the heaven and the earth shall pass away, but My words shall not pass away.

32 'And concerning that day and the hour no one has known — not even the messengers who are in the heaven, not even the Son — except the Father.

33 Take heed, watch and pray, for you[P] have not known when the time is;

34 as a man who is gone abroad, having left his house, and given to his servants the authority, and to each one his work, did command also the porter that he may watch;

35 watch you[P], for that reason, for you[P] have not known when the lord of the house does come, at even, or at midnight, or at cock-crowing, or at the morning;

36 that, having come suddenly, he may find you[P] sleeping;

37 and what I say to you[P], I say to all, Watch.'

CHAPTER 14

1 And the Passover and the unleavened food were after two days, and the chief priests and the scribes were seeking how, by guile, having taken hold of Him, they might kill Him;

2 and they said, 'Not in the feast, lest there shall be a tumult of the people.'

3 And He, being in Bethany, in the house of Simon the leper, at His reclining (at meat), there came a woman having an alabaster box of ointment, of spikenard, very precious, and having broken the alabaster box, did pour on His head;

4 and there were certain much displeased within themselves, and saying, 'For what has this waste of the ointment been made?

5 for this could have been sold for more than three hundred denaries, and given to the poor;' and they were murmuring at her.

6 And Jesus said, 'Let her alone; why are you[P] giving her trouble? she worked a good work on Me;

7 for you[P] always have the poor with you[P], and whenever you[P] may will you[P] are able to do them good, but you[P] have not Me always;

8 what she could she did, she anticipated to anoint My body for the embalming.

9 Truly I say to you[P], wherever this good news may be proclaimed in the whole world, what this woman did shall also be spoken of — for a memorial of her.'

10 And Judas the Iscariot, one of the twelve, went away unto the chief priests that he might deliver Him up to them,

11 and having heard, they were glad, and promised to give him money, and he was seeking how, conveniently, he might deliver Him up.
12 And the first day of the unleavened food, when they were killing the Passover, His disciples say to Him, 'Where will You[S], [that,] having gone, we may prepare, that You[S] may eat the Passover?'
13 And He sent forth two of His disciples, and said to them, 'Go you[P] away to the city, and there you[P] shall meet a man bearing a pitcher of water, follow him;
14 and wherever he may go in, say you[P] to the master of the house — The Teacher said, Where is the guest-chamber, where I may eat the Passover, with My disciples?
15 and he will show you[P] a large upper room, furnished, prepared — there make ready for us.'
16 And His disciples went forth, and came to the city, and found as He said to them, and they made ready the Passover.
17 And evening having come, He came with the twelve,
18 and as they are reclining, and eating, Jesus said, 'Truly I say to you[P] — one of you[P], who is eating with Me — shall deliver Me up.'
19 And they began to be sorrowful, and to say to Him, one by one, 'Is it I?' and another, 'Is it I?'
20 And He answering said to them, 'One of the twelve who is dipping with Me in the dish;
21 the Son of Man does indeed go, as it has been written concerning Him, but woe to that man through whom the Son of Man is delivered up; good were it to him if that man had not been born.'
22 And as they are eating, Jesus having taken bread, having blessed, broke, and gave to them, and said, 'Take, eat; this is My body.'
23 And having taken the cup, having given thanks, He gave to them, and they drank of it — all;
24 and He said to them, 'This is My blood of the new covenant, which is being poured out for many;
25 truly I say to you[P], that no more may I drink of the produce of the vine till that day when I may drink it new in the reign of God.'
26 And having sung an hymn, they went forth to the mount of the Olives,
27 and Jesus said to them — 'All you[P] shall be stumbled at Me this night, because it has been written, I will strike the shepherd, and the sheep shall be scattered abroad,
28 but after My having risen I will go before you[P] to Galilee.'
29 And Peter said to Him, 'And if all shall be stumbled, yet not I;'
30 And Jesus said to him, 'Truly I say to you[S], that today, this night, before a cock shall crow twice, you[S] shall deny Me three times.'
31 And he spoke the more vehemently, 'If it may be necessary for me to die with You[S] — I will in no wise deny You[S];' and they all said in like manner also.
32 And they come to a spot, the name of which [is] Gethsemane, and He said to His disciples, 'You[P] sit here till I may pray;'
33 and He took Peter, and James, and John with Him, and began to be amazed, and to be very heavy,
34 and He said to them, 'My soul is exceeding sorrowful — to death; remain here, and watch.'
35 And having gone forward a little, He fell upon the earth, and was praying, that, if it be possible the hour may pass from Him,
36 and He said, 'Abba, Father; all things are possible to You[S]; make this cup pass from Me; but, not what I will, but what You[S].'
37 And He came, and found them sleeping, and said to Peter, 'Simon, you[S] do sleep! you[S] were not able to watch one hour!
38 You[P] watch and pray, that you[P] may not enter into temptation; the spirit indeed is forward, but the flesh weak.'
39 And again having gone away, He prayed, the same word saying;
40 and having returned, He found them again sleeping, for their eyes were heavy, and they had not known what they might answer Him.
41 And He came the third time, and said to them, 'Sleep on for now, and rest — it is over; the hour did come; behold, the Son of Man is delivered up to the hands of the sinful;
42 rise, we may go, behold, he who is delivering Me up has come near.'
43 And immediately — while He is yet speaking — Judas came near, one of the twelve, and with him a great multitude, with swords and sticks, from the chief priests, and the scribes, and the elders;
44 and he who is delivering Him up had given a token to them, saying, 'Whomsoever I shall kiss, He it is, lay hold on Him, and lead Him away safely,'
45 and having come, immediately, having gone near Him, he said, 'Rabbi, Rabbi,' and kissed Him.
46 And they laid their hands on Him, and kept hold on Him;
47 and a certain one of those standing by, having drawn

the sword, struck the servant of the chief priest, and took off his ear.
48 And Jesus answering said to them, ‘ You^{P} came out as against a robber, with swords and sticks, to take Me!
49 I was with you^{P} daily in the temple teaching, and you^{P} did not lay hold on Me — but that the Writings may be fulfilled.’
50 And having left Him they all fled;
51 and a certain young man was following Him, having put a linen cloth about [his] naked body, and the young men lay hold on him,
52 and he, having left the linen cloth, did flee from them naked.
53 And they led away Jesus unto the chief priest, and come together to him do all the chief priests, and the elders, and the scribes;
54 and Peter did follow Him afar off, to the inside of the hall of the chief priest, and he was sitting with the officers, and warming himself near the fire.
55 And the chief priests and all the sanhedrim were seeking testimony against Jesus — to put Him to death, and they were not finding,
56 for many were bearing false testimony against Him, and their testimonies were not alike.
57 And certain having risen up, were bearing false testimony against Him, saying —
58 ‘We heard Him saying — I will throw down this sanctuary made with hands, and by three days, I will build another made without hands;’
59 and neither so was their testimony alike.
60 And the chief priest, having risen up in the midst, questioned Jesus, saying, ‘You^{S} do not answer anything! what do these testify against You^{S}?’
61 and He was keeping silent, and did not answer anything. Again the chief priest was questioning Him, and said to Him, ‘Are You^{S} the Christ — the Son of the Blessed?’
62 and Jesus said, ‘I am; and you^{P} shall see the Son of Man sitting on the right hand of the power, and coming with the clouds, of the heaven.’
63 And the chief priest, having rent his garments, said, ‘What need have we yet of witnesses?
64 You^{P} heard the evil speaking, what appears to you^{P}?’ and they all condemned Him to be worthy of death,
65 and certain began to spit on Him, and to cover His face, and to buffet Him, and to say to Him, ‘Prophesy;’ and the officers were striking Him with their palms.
66 And Peter being in the hall beneath, there did come one of the maids of the chief priest,
67 and having seen Peter warming himself, having looked on him, she said, ‘And you^{S} were with Jesus of Nazareth!’
68 and he denied, saying, ‘I have not known [Him], neither do I understand what you^{S} say;’ and he went forth without to the porch, and a cock crew.
69 And the maid having seen him again, began to say to those standing near — ‘This is of them;’
70 and he was again denying. And after a little again, those standing near said to Peter, ‘Truly you^{S} are of them, for you^{S} are a Galilean also, and your^{S} speech is alike;’
71 and he began to curse, and to swear — ‘I have not known this man of whom you^{P} speak;’
72 and a second time a cock crew, and Peter remembered the saying that Jesus said to him — ‘Before a cock crow twice, you^{S} may deny Me three times;’ and having thought thereon — he was weeping.

CHAPTER 15

1 And immediately, in the morning, the chief priests having made a consultation, with the elders, and scribes, and the whole sanhedrim, having bound Jesus, did lead away, and delivered [Him] to Pilate;
2 and Pilate questioned Him, ‘Are You^{S} the king of the Jews?’ and He answering said to him, ‘You^{S} do say [it].’
3 And the chief priests were accusing Him of many things, [but He answered nothing.]
4 And Pilate again questioned Him, saying, ‘You^{S} do not answer anything! behold, how many things they do testify against You^{S}!’
5 and Jesus did no more answer anything, so that Pilate wondered.
6 And at every feast he was releasing to them one prisoner, whomsoever they were asking;
7 and there was [one] named Barabbas, bound with those making insurrection with him, who had in the insurrection committed murder.
8 And the multitude having cried out, began to ask for themselves as he was always doing to them,
9 and Pilate answered them, saying, ‘Will you^{P} [that] I shall release to you^{P} the king of the Jews?’
10 for he knew that the chief priests had delivered Him up because of envy;
11 and the chief priests did move the multitude, that he might rather release Barabbas to them.
12 And Pilate answering, again said to them, ‘What, then, will you^{P} [that] I shall do to him whom you^{P} call king of the Jews?’

13 and they again cried out, 'Crucify Him.'
14 And Pilate said to them, 'Why — what evil did He?' and they cried out the more vehemently, 'Crucify Him;'
15 and Pilate, wishing to content the multitude, released to them Barabbas, and delivered up Jesus — having scourged [Him] — that He might be crucified.
16 And the soldiers led Him away into the hall, which is Praetorium, and call together the whole band,
17 and clothe Him with purple, and having woven a crown of thorns, they put [it] on Him,
18 and began to salute Him, 'Hail, King of the Jews.'
19 And they were smiting Him on the head with a reed, and were spitting on Him, and having bent the knee, were bowing to Him,
20 and when they [had] mocked Him, they took the purple from off Him, and clothed Him in His own garments, and they led Him forth, that they may crucify Him.
21 And they impress a certain one passing by — Simon, a Cyrenian, coming from the field, the father of Alexander and Rufus — that he may bear His cross,
22 and they bring Him to the place Golgotha, which is, being interpreted, 'Place of a skull;'
23 and they were giving Him to drink wine mingled with myrrh, and He did not receive.
24 And having crucified Him, they were dividing His garments, casting a lot upon them, what each may take;
25 and it was the third hour, and they crucified Him;
26 and the inscription of His accusation was written above — 'The King of the Jews.'
27 And they crucify two robbers with Him, one on the right hand, and one on His left,
28 and the Writing was fulfilled that is saying, 'And He was numbered with lawless ones.'
29 And those passing by were speaking evil of Him, shaking their heads, and saying, 'Ah, the thrower down of the sanctuary, and in three days the builder!
30 save Yourself[S], and come down from the cross!'
31 And in like manner also the chief priests, mocking with one another, with the scribes, said, 'Others He saved; He is not able to save Himself.
32 The Christ! the king of Israel — let Him come down now from the cross, that we may see and believe;' and those crucified with Him were reproaching Him.
33 And the sixth hour having come, darkness came over the whole land till the ninth hour,
34 and at the ninth hour Jesus cried with a great voice, saying, 'Eloi, Eloi, lamma sabachthani?' which is, being interpreted, 'My God, My God, why did You[S] forsake Me?'
35 And certain of those standing by, having heard, said, 'Behold, He does call Elijah;'
36 and one having run, and having filled a sponge with vinegar, having put [it] also on a reed, was giving Him to drink, saying, 'Let alone, let us see if Elijah does come to take him down.'
37 And Jesus having uttered a loud cry, yielded the spirit,
38 and the veil of the sanctuary was torn in two, from top to bottom,
39 and the centurion who was standing over-against Him, having seen that, having so cried out, He yielded the spirit, said, 'Truly this man was Son of God.'
40 And there were also women afar off beholding, among whom was also Mary the Magdalene, and Mary of James the less, and of Joses, and Salome,
41 (who also, when He was in Galilee, were following Him, and were ministering to Him,) and many other women who came up with Him to Jerusalem.
42 And now evening having come, seeing it was the preparation, that is, the fore-sabbath,
43 Joseph of Arimathea, an honorable counselor, who also himself was waiting for the reign of God, came, boldly entered in unto Pilate, and asked the body of Jesus.
44 And Pilate wondered if he were already dead, and having called near the centurion, did question him if he were long dead,
45 and having known [it] from the centurion, he granted the body to Joseph.
46 And he, having brought fine linen, and having taken Him down, wrapped him in the linen, and laid Him in a sepulchre that had been hewn out of a rock, and he rolled a stone unto the door of the sepulchre,
47 and Mary the Magdalene, and Mary of Joses, were beholding where He is laid.

CHAPTER 16

1 And the sabbath having past, Mary the Magdalene, and Mary of James, and Salome, bought spices, that having come, they may anoint Him,
2 and early in the morning of the first of the sabbaths, they come unto the sepulchre, at the rising of the sun,
3 and they said among themselves, 'Who shall roll away for us the stone out of the door of the sepulchre?'
4 And having looked, they see that the stone had been rolled away — for it was very great,
5 and having entered into the sepulchre, they saw a

young man sitting on the right hand, arrayed in a long white robe, and they were amazed.

6 And he said to them, 'Be not amazed, you[P] seek Jesus the Nazarene, the crucified: He did rise — He is not here; behold, the place where they laid Him!

7 and go, say to His disciples, and Peter, that He does go before you[P] to Galilee; there you[P] shall see Him, as He said to you[P].'

8 And, having come forth quickly, they fled from the sepulchre, and trembling and amazement had seized them, and to no one said they anything, for they were afraid.

9 And He, having risen in the morning of the first of the sabbaths, did appear first to Mary the Magdalene, out of whom He had cast seven demons;

10 she having gone, told those who had been with Him, mourning and weeping;

11 and they, having heard that He is alive, and was seen by her, did not believe.

12 And after these things, to two of them, as they are going into a field, walking, He was obviously in another form,

13 and they having gone, told to the rest; not even them did they believe.

14 Afterwards, as they are reclining (at meat), He was made known to the eleven, and did reproach their unbelief and stiffness of heart, because they believed not those having seen Him being raised;

15 and He said to them, 'Having gone to all the world, proclaim the good news to all the creation;

16 he who has believed, and has been baptized, shall be saved; and he who has not believed, shall be condemned.

17 'And signs shall accompany those believing these things; in My name they shall cast out demons; they shall speak with new tongues;

18 they shall take up serpents; and if they may drink any deadly thing, it shall not hurt them; they shall lay hands on the ailing, and they shall be well.'

19 The Lord, then, indeed, after speaking to them, was received up to the heaven, and sat on the right hand of God;

20 and they, having gone forth, did preach everywhere, the Lord working with [them], and confirming the word, through the signs following. Amen.

The Gospel according to
LUKE

CHAPTER 1

1 Seeing that many did take in hand to set in order a
narration of the matters that have been fully assured
among us,
2 as they did deliver to us, who from the beginning
became eye-witnesses, and officers of the Word, —
3 it seemed good also to me, having followed from the
first after all things exactly, to write to you[S] in order, most
noble Theophilus,
4 that you[S] may know the certainty of the things wherein
you[S] were instructed.
5 There was in the days of Herod, the king of Judea, a
certain priest, by name Zacharias, of the course of
Abijah, and his wife of the daughters of Aaron, and her
name Elisabeth;
6 and they were both righteous before God, going on
blameless in all the commands and righteousnesses of
the Lord,
7 and they had no child, because that Elisabeth was
barren, and both were advanced in their days.
8 And it came to pass, in his acting as priest, in the
order of his course before God,
9 according to the custom of the priesthood, his lot was
to make perfume, having gone into the sanctuary of the
Lord,
10 and all the multitude of the people were praying
without, at the hour of the perfume.
11 And there appeared to him a messenger of the Lord
standing on the right side of the altar of the perfume,
12 and Zacharias, having seen, was troubled, and fear
fell on him;
13 and the messenger said unto him, 'Fear not,
Zacharias, for your[S] supplication was heard, and your[S]
wife Elisabeth shall bear a son to you[S], and you[S] shall
call his name John,
14 and there shall be joy to you[S], and gladness, and
many shall joy at his birth,
15 for he shall be great before the Lord, and he may not
drink wine and strong drink, and he shall be full of the
Holy Spirit, even from his mother's womb;
16 and he shall turn many of the sons of Israel to the
Lord their God,
17 and he shall go before Him, in the spirit and power of
Elijah, to turn hearts of fathers unto children, and
disobedient ones to the wisdom of righteous ones, to
make ready for the Lord, a people prepared.'
18 And Zacharias said unto the messenger, 'How shall
I know this? for I am aged, and my wife is advanced in
her days?'
19 And the messenger answering said to him, 'I am
Gabriel, who have been standing near before God, and I
was sent to speak unto you[S], and to proclaim these good
news to you[S],
20 and behold, you[S] shall be silent, and not able to speak,
till the day that these things shall come to pass, because
you[S] did not believe my words, that shall be fulfilled in
their season.'
21 And the people were waiting for Zacharias, and
wondering at his tarrying in the sanctuary,
22 and having come out, he was not able to speak to
them, and they perceived that he had seen a vision in
the sanctuary, and he was beckoning to them, and did
remain dumb.
23 And it came to pass, when the days of his service
were fulfilled, he went away to his house,
24 and after those days, his wife Elisabeth conceived,
and hid herself five months, saying —
25 'Thus has the Lord done to me, in days in which He
looked upon [me], to take away my reproach among
men.'
26 And in the sixth month was the messenger Gabriel
sent by God, to a city of Galilee, the name of which [is]
Nazareth,
27 to a virgin, betrothed to a man, whose name [is]
Joseph, of the house of David, and the name of the virgin
[is] Mary.
28 And the messenger having come in unto her, said,
'Hail, favored one, the Lord [is] with you[S]; you[S] [are]
blessed among women;'
29 and she, having seen, was troubled at his word, and

was reasoning of what kind this salutation may be.
30 And the messenger said to her, 'Fear not, Mary, for
you[S] have found favor with God;
31 and behold, you[S] shall conceive in the womb, and
shall bring forth a son, and call His name Jesus;
32 He shall be great, and He shall be called Son of the
Highest, and the Lord God shall give Him the throne of
David His father,
33 and He shall reign over the house of Jacob to the
ages; and there shall be no end of His reign.'
34 And Mary said unto the messenger, 'How shall this
be, seeing I do not know a husband?'
35 And the messenger answering said to her, 'The Holy
Spirit shall come upon you[S], and the power of the
Highest shall overshadow you[S], therefore also the holy-
begotten thing shall be called Son of God;
36 and behold, Elisabeth, your kinswoman, she has also
conceived a son in her old age, and this is the sixth month
to her who was called barren;
37 because nothing shall be impossible with God.'
38 And Mary said, 'Behold, the maid-servant of the
Lord; let it be to me according to your[S] saying,' and the
messenger went away from her.
39 And Mary having arisen in those days, went to the
hill-country, with haste, to a city of Judea,
40 and entered into the house of Zacharias, and saluted
Elisabeth.
41 And it came to pass, when Elisabeth heard the
salutation of Mary, the babe did leap in her womb; and
Elisabeth was filled with the Holy Spirit,
42 and spoke out with a loud voice, and said, 'Blessed
[are] you[S] among women, and blessed [is] the fruit of
your[S] womb;
43 and what [is] this to me, that the mother of my Lord
might come unto me?
44 for, behold, when the voice of your[S] salutation came
to my ears, the babe in my womb did leap in gladness;
45 and happy [is] she who did believe, for there shall be
a completion to the things spoken to her from the Lord.'
46 And Mary said, 'My soul does magnify the Lord,
47 And my spirit was glad on God my Savior,
48 Because He looked on the lowliness of His maid-
servant, For, behold, from here on all the generations
shall call me happy,
49 For He who is mighty did great things to me, And
holy [is] His name,
50 And His kindness [is] to generations of generations,
To those fearing Him,
51 He did powerfully with His arm, He scattered abroad
the proud in the thought of their heart,
52 He brought down the mighty from thrones, And He
exalted the lowly,
53 He did fill the hungry with good, And He sent the
rich away empty,
54 He received Israel His servant again, To remember
kindness,
55 As He spoke unto our fathers, To Abraham and to
his seed — to the age.'
56 And Mary remained with her about three months,
and turned back to her house.
57 And to Elisabeth was the time fulfilled for her bringing
forth, and she bare a son,
58 and the neighbors and her kindred heard that the
Lord was making His kindness great with her, and they
were rejoicing with her.
59 And it came to pass, on the eighth day, they came to
circumcise the child, and they were calling him by the
name of his father, Zacharias,
60 and his mother answering said, 'No, but he shall be
called John.'
61 And they said unto her — 'There is none among
your[S] kindred who is called by this name,'
62 and they were making signs to his father, what he
would wish him to be called,
63 and having asked for a tablet, he wrote, saying, 'John
is his name;' and they did all wonder;
64 and his mouth was opened presently, and his tongue,
and he was speaking, praising God.
65 And fear came upon all those dwelling around them,
and all these sayings were spoken of in all the hill-
country of Judea ,
66 and all who heard did lay them up in their hearts,
saying, 'What then shall this child be?' and the hand of
the Lord was with him.
67 And Zacharias his father was filled with the Holy
Spirit, and did prophesy, saying,
68 'Blessed [is] the Lord, the God of Israel, Because He
did look upon, And worked redemption for His people,
69 And did raise an horn of salvation to us, In the house
of David His servant,
70 As He spoke by the mouth of His holy prophets,
Which have been from the age;
71 Salvation from our enemies, And out of the hand of
all hating us,
72 To do kindness with our fathers, And to be mindful
of His holy covenant,
73 An oath that He swore to Abraham our father,
74 To give to us, without fear, having been delivered

out of the hand of our enemies,

75 To serve Him, before Him in holiness and righteousness, all the days of our life.

76 And you[S], child, you[S] shall be called Prophet of the Highest; For you[S] shall go before the face of the Lord, To prepare His ways.

77 To give knowledge of salvation to His people in remission of their sins,

78 Through the tender mercies of our God, In which the rising from on high did look upon us,

79 To give light to those sitting in darkness and death-shade, To guide our feet to a way of peace.'

80 And the child grew, and was strengthened in spirit, and he was in the deserts till the day of his showing unto Israel.

CHAPTER 2

1 And it came to pass in those days, there went forth a decree from Caesar Augustus, that all the world be enrolled —

2 this enrolment first came to pass when Cyrenius was governor of Syria —

3 and all were going to be enrolled, each to his proper city,

4 and Joseph also went up from Galilee, out of the city of Nazareth, to Judea, to the city of David, that is called Bethlehem, because of his being of the house and family of David,

5 to enroll himself with Mary his betrothed wife, being with child.

6 And it came to pass, in their being there, the days were fulfilled for her bringing forth,

7 and she brought forth her son — the first-born, and wrapped Him up, and laid Him down in the manger, because there was not a place for them in the guest-chamber.

8 And there were shepherds in the same region, lodging in the field, and keeping the night-watches over their flock,

9 and behold, a messenger of the Lord stood over them, and the glory of the Lord shone around them, and they feared a great fear.

10 And the messenger said to them, 'Fear not, for behold, I bring you[P] good news of great joy, that shall be to all the people —

11 because there was born to you[P] today a Savior — who is Christ the Lord — in the city of David,

12 and this [is] to you the sign: You[P] shall find a babe wrapped up, lying in the manger.'

13 And suddenly there came with the messenger a multitude of the heavenly host, praising God, and saying,

14 'Glory in the highest to God, and upon earth peace, among men — good will.'

15 And it came to pass, when the messengers were gone away from them to the heavens, that the men, the shepherds, said unto one another, 'We may go over indeed unto Bethlehem, and see this thing that has come to pass, that the Lord did make known to us.'

16 And they came, having hurried, and found both Mary, and Joseph, and the babe lying in the manger,

17 and having seen, they made known abroad concerning the saying spoken to them concerning the child.

18 And all who heard, did wonder concerning the things spoken by the shepherds unto them;

19 and Mary was preserving all these things, pondering in her heart;

20 and the shepherds turned back, glorifying and praising God, for all those things they heard and saw, as it was spoken unto them.

21 And when eight days were fulfilled to circumcise the child, then was His name called Jesus, having been so called by the messenger before his being conceived in the womb.

22 And when the days of their purification were fulfilled, according to the law of Moses, they brought Him up to Jerusalem, to present to the Lord,

23 as it has been written in the Law of the Lord, — 'Every male opening a womb shall be called holy to the Lord,'

24 and to give a sacrifice, according to that said in the Law of the Lord, 'A pair of turtle-doves, or two young pigeons.'

25 And behold, there was a man in Jerusalem, whose name [is] Simeon, and this man is righteous and devout, looking for the comforting of Israel, and the Holy Spirit was upon him,

26 and it had been divinely told him by the Holy Spirit — not to see death before he may see the Christ of the Lord.

27 And he came in the Spirit to the temple, and in the parents bringing in the child Jesus, for their doing according to the custom of the law regarding Him,

28 then he took Him in his arms, and blessed God, and he said,

29 'Now You[S] do send Your[S] servant away, Lord,

according to Your[S] word, in peace,
30 because mine eyes did see Your[S] salvation,
31 which You[S] did prepare before the face of all the
peoples,
32 a light to the uncovering of nations, and the glory of
Your[S] people Israel.'
33 And Joseph and His mother were wondering at the
things spoken concerning Him,
34 and Simeon blessed them, and said unto Mary his
mother, 'Behold, this [one] is set for the falling and rising
again of many in Israel, and for a sign spoken against —
35 (and also your[S] own soul shall a sword pass through)
— that the reasonings of many hearts may be revealed.'
36 And there was Anna, a prophetess, daughter of
Phanuel, of the tribe of Asher, she was much advanced
in days, having lived with an husband seven years from
her virginity,
37 and she [is] a widow of about eighty-four years, who
did not depart from the temple, with fasts and
supplications serving, night and day,
38 and she, at that hour, having come in, was confessing,
likewise, to the Lord, and was speaking concerning Him,
to all those looking for redemption in Jerusalem.
39 And when they finished all things, according to the
Law of the Lord, they turned back to Galilee, to their
city Nazareth;
40 and the child grew and was strengthened in spirit,
being filled with wisdom, and the grace of God was upon
Him.
41 And His parents were going to Jerusalem yearly, at
the feast of the Passover,
42 and when He became twelve years old, they having
gone up to Jerusalem, according to the custom of the
feast,
43 and having finished the days, in their returning the
child Jesus remained behind in Jerusalem, and Joseph
and His mother did not know,
44 and, having supposed Him to be in the company,
they went a day's journey, and were seeking Him among
the kindred and among the acquaintances,
45 and having not found Him, they turned back to
Jerusalem seeking Him.
46 And it came to pass, after three days, they found
Him in the temple, sitting in the midst of the teachers,
both hearing them and questioning them,
47 and all those hearing Him were astonished at His
understanding and answers.
48 And, having seen Him, they were amazed, and His
mother said unto him, 'Child, why did You[S] thus to us?
behold, Your[S] father and I, sorrowing, were seeking You[S].'
49 And He said unto them, 'Why [is it] that you[P] were
seeking Me? did you[P] not know that it is necessary for
Me to be in the things of My Father?'
50 and they did not understand the saying that He spoke
to them,
51 and He went down with them, and came to Nazareth,
and He was subject to them, and His mother was keeping
all these sayings in her heart,
52 and Jesus was advancing in wisdom, and in stature,
and in favor with God and men.

CHAPTER 3

1 And in the fifteenth year of the government of Tiberius
Caesar — Pontius Pilate being governor of Judea, and
Herod tetrarch of Galilee, and Philip his brother, tetrarch
of Ituraea and of the region of Trachonitis, and Lysanias
tetrarch of Abilene —
2 Annas and Caiaphas being chief priests — there came
a word of God unto John the son of Zacharias, in the
wilderness,
3 and he came to all the region round the Jordan,
proclaiming a baptism of reformation — to remission of
sins,
4 as it has been written in the scroll of the words of
Isaiah the prophet, saying, 'A voice of one crying in the
wilderness, Prepare you[P] the way of the Lord, you[P] make
straight His paths;
5 every valley shall be filled, and every mountain and
hill shall be made low, and the crooked shall become
straightness, and the rough become smooth ways;
6 and all flesh shall see the salvation of God.'
7 Then he said to the multitudes coming forth to be
baptized by him, 'Brood of vipers! who did prompt you[P]
to flee from the coming wrath?
8 make, for that reason, fruits worthy of the reformation,
and begin not to say within yourselves[P], We have a
father — Abraham; for I say to you[P], that God is able to
raise children to Abraham out of these stones;
9 and already also the axe is laid unto the root of the
trees, every tree, consequently, not making good fruit
is cut down, and it is cast to fire.'
10 And the multitudes were questioning him, saying,
'What, then, shall we do?'
11 and he answering said to them, 'He having two coats
— let him impart to him having none, and he having
victuals — in like manner let him do.'

12 And there came also tax-gatherers to be baptized,
and they said unto him, 'Teacher, what shall we do?'
13 and he said unto them, 'Exact no more than that
directed you[P].'
14 And questioning him also were those warring, saying,
'And we, what shall we do?' and he said unto them, 'Do
violence to no one, nor accuse falsely, and be content
with your[P] wages.'
15 And the people are looking forward, and all are
reasoning in their hearts concerning John, whether or
not he may be the Christ;
16 John answered, saying to all, 'I indeed with water do
baptize you[P], but he who comes is mightier than I, of
whom I am not worthy to loose the latchet of his sandals
— he shall baptize you[P] with the Holy Spirit and with
fire;
17 whose winnowing shovel [is] in his hand, and he
will thoroughly cleanse his floor, and will gather the
wheat to his storehouse, and the chaff he will burn with
fire unquenchable.'
18 And, for that reason, indeed with many other things,
exhorting, he was proclaiming good news to the people,
19 and Herod the tetrarch, being reproved by him
concerning Herodias the wife of Philip his brother, and
concerning all the evils that Herod did,
20 added also this to all, that he shut up John in the
prison.
21 And it came to pass, in all the people being baptized,
Jesus also being baptized, and praying, the heaven was
opened,
22 and the Holy Spirit came down in a bodily appearance,
as if a dove, upon Him, and a voice came out of heaven,
saying, 'You[S] are My Son — the Beloved, in You[S] I did
delight.'
23 And Jesus himself was beginning to be about thirty
years of age, being, as was supposed, son of Joseph,
24 the [son] of Eli, the [son] of Matthat, the [son] of
Levi, the [son] of Melchi, the [son] of Janna, the [son]
of Joseph,
25 the [son] of Mattathias, the [son] of Amos, the [son]
of Naum, the [son] of Esli,
26 the [son] of Naggai, the [son] of Maath, the [son] of
Mattathias, the [son] of Semei, the [son] of Joseph, the
[son] of Juda,
27 the [son] of Joanna, the [son] of Rhesa, the [son] of
Zerubbabel, the [son] of Shealtiel,
28 the [son] of Neri, the [son] of Melchi, the [son] of
Addi, the [son] of Cosam, the [son] of Elmodam, the
[son] of Er,
29 the [son] of Jose, the [son] of Eliezer, the [son] of
Jorim, the [son] of Matthat,
30 the [son] of Levi, the [son] of Simeon, the [son] of
Juda, the [son] of Joseph, the [son] of Jonan, the [son]
of Eliakim,
31 the [son] of Melea, the [son] of Mainan, the [son] of
Mattatha, the [son] of Nathan,
32 the [son] of David, the [son] of Jesse, the [son] of
Obed, the [son] of Booz, the [son] of Salmon, the [son]
of Nahshon,
33 the [son] of Amminadab, the [son] of Aram, the [son]
of Esrom, the [son] of Pharez,
34 the [son] of Judah, the [son] of Jacob, the [son] of
Isaac, the [son] of Abraham, the [son] of Terah, the [son]
of Nahor,
35 the [son] of Serug, the [son] of Reu, the [son] of
Peleg, the [son] of Eber,
36 the [son] of Salah, the [son] of Cainan, the [son] of
Arphaxad, the [son] of Shem, the [son] of Noah, the [son]
of Lamech,
37 the [son] of Methuselah, the [son] of Enoch, the [son]
of Jared, the [son] of Mahalaleel,
38 the [son] of Cainan, the [son] of Enos, the [son] of
Seth, the [son] of Adam, the [son] of God.

CHAPTER 4

1 And Jesus, full of the Holy Spirit, turned back from
the Jordan, and was brought in the Spirit to the
wilderness,
2 being tempted by the Devil forty days, and He did not
eat anything in those days, and they having been ended,
He afterward hungered,
3 and the Devil said to Him, 'If You[S] are Son of God,
speak to this stone that it may become bread.'
4 And Jesus answered him, saying, 'It has been written,
that, man shall not live on bread only, but on every
saying of God.'
5 And the Devil having brought Him up to an high
mountain, showed to Him all the kingdoms of the world
in a moment of time,
6 and the Devil said to Him, 'To You[S] I will give all this
authority, and their glory, because it has been delivered
to me, and to whomsoever I will, I do give it;
7 You[S], then, if You[S] may bow before me — all shall be
Yours[S].'
8 And Jesus answering him said, 'Get you[S] behind me,
Adversary, for it has been written, You[S] shall bow before

the Lord your[S] God, and Him only shall you[S] serve.'
9 And he brought Him to Jerusalem, and set Him on the
pinnacle of the temple, and said to Him, 'If You[S] are the
Son of God, cast Yourself[S] down from here,
10 for it has been written — To His messengers He will
give charge concerning You[S], to guard over You[S],
11 and — On hands they shall bear You[S] up, for fear
that at any time You[S] may dash Your[S] foot against a
stone.'
12 And Jesus answering said to him — 'It has been
said, You[S] shall not tempt the Lord your God.'
13 And having ended all temptation, the Devil departed
from Him till a convenient season.
14 And Jesus turned back in the power of the Spirit to
Galilee, and a fame went forth through all the region
round about concerning Him,
15 and He was teaching in their synagogues, being
glorified by all.
16 And He came to Nazareth, where He had been brought
up, and He went in, according to His custom, on the
sabbath-day, to the synagogue, and stood up to read;
17 and there was given over to Him a roll of Isaiah the
prophet, and having unfolded the roll, He found the
place where it had been written:
18 'The Spirit of the Lord [is] upon Me, Because He did
anoint Me; To proclaim good news to the poor, Sent Me
to heal the broken of heart, To proclaim to captives
deliverance, And to blind receiving of sight, To send
away the bruised with deliverance,
19 To proclaim the acceptable year of the Lord.'
20 And having folded the roll, having given [it] back to
the officer, He sat down, and the eyes of all in the
synagogue were gazing on Him.
21 And He began to say unto them — 'Today has this
writing been fulfilled in your[P] ears;'
22 and all were bearing testimony to Him, and were
wondering at the gracious words that are coming forth
out of His mouth, and they said, 'Is this not the son of
Joseph?'
23 And He said unto them, 'Certainly you[P] will say to
Me this simile, Physician, heal Yourself[S]; as great things
as we heard done in Capernaum, do here in Your[S] country
also;'
24 and He said, 'Truly I say to you[P] — No prophet is
accepted in his own country;
25 and of a truth I say to you[P], Many widows were in
the days of Elijah, in Israel, when the heaven was shut
for three years and six months, when great famine came
on all the land,
26 and unto none of them was Elijah sent, but — to
Sarepta of Sidon, unto a woman, a widow;
27 and many lepers were in the time of Elisha the prophet,
in Israel, and none of them was cleansed, but — Naaman
the Syrian.'
28 And all in the synagogue were filled with wrath,
hearing these things,
29 and having risen, they put Him forth without the city,
and brought Him unto the brow of the hill on which their
city had been built — to cast Him down headlong,
30 and He, having gone through the midst of them, went
away.
31 And He came down to Capernaum, a city of Galilee,
and was teaching them on the sabbaths,
32 and they were astonished at His teaching, because
His word was with authority.
33 And in the synagogue was a man, having a spirit of
an unclean demon, and he cried out with a great voice,
34 saying, 'Away, what — to us and to You[S], Jesus, O
Nazarene? You[S] did come to destroy us; I have known
You[S] who You[S] are — the Holy One of God.'
35 And Jesus did rebuke him, saying, 'Be silenced, and
come forth out of him;' and the demon having cast him
into the midst, came forth from him, having not hurt him;
36 and amazement came upon all, and they were
speaking together, with one another, saying, 'What [is]
this word, that with authority and power He does
command the unclean spirits, and they come forth?'
37 and there was going forth a fame concerning Him to
every place of the region round about.
38 And having risen out of the synagogue, He entered
into the house of Simon, and the mother-in-law of Simon
was pressed with a great fever, and they did ask Him
about her,
39 and having stood over her, He rebuked the fever,
and it left her, and presently, having risen, she was
ministering to them.
40 And at the setting of the sun, all, as many as had any
ailing with various sicknesses, brought them unto Him,
and He having put [His] hands on each one of them, did
heal them.
41 And demons also were coming forth from many,
crying out and saying — 'You[S] are the Christ, the Son
of God;' and rebuking, He did not allow them to speak,
because they knew Him to be the Christ.
42 And day having come, having gone forth, He went
on to a desert place, and the multitudes were seeking
Him, and they came unto Him, and were staying Him —
not to go on from them,

43 and He said unto them — ' It is necessary for Me to
proclaim good news of the reign of God to the other cities
also, because I have been sent for this;'
44 and He was preaching in the synagogues of Galilee.

CHAPTER 5

1 And it came to pass, in the multitude pressing on Him
to hear the word of God, that He was standing beside
the lake of Gennesaret,
2 and He saw two boats standing beside the lake, and
the fishers, having gone away from them, were washing
the nets,
3 and having entered into one of the boats, that was
Simon's, He asked him to put back a little from the land,
and having sat down, was teaching the multitudes out
of the boat.
4 And when He left off speaking, He said unto Simon,
'Put back to the deep, and let down your[P] nets for a haul;'
5 and Simon answering said to Him, 'Master, through
the whole night, having labored, we have taken nothing,
but at Your[S] saying I will let down the net.'
6 And having done this, they enclosed a great multitude
of fishes, and their net was breaking,
7 and they beckoned to the partners, who [are] in the
other boat, having come, to help them; and they came,
and filled both the boats, so that they were sinking.
8 And Simon Peter having seen, fell down at the knees
of Jesus, saying, 'Depart from me, because I am a sinful
man, O Lord;'
9 for astonishment seized him, and all those with him, at
the haul of the fishes that they took,
10 and in like manner also James and John, sons of
Zebedee, who were partners with Simon; and Jesus said
unto Simon, 'Fear not, from now on you[S] shall catching
men;'
11 and they, having brought the boats upon the land,
having left all, did follow Him.
12 And it came to pass, in His being in one of the cities,
that behold, a man full of leprosy, and having seen Jesus,
having fallen on [his] face, he begged Him, saying, 'Sir,
if You[S] may will, You[S] are able to cleanse me;'
13 and having stretched forth [His] hand, He touched
him, having said, 'I will; be you[S] cleansed;' and
immediately the leprosy went away from him.
14 And He charged him to tell no one, 'But, having gone
away, show yourself[S] to the priest, and bring near for
your[S] cleansing according as Moses directed, for a
testimony to them;'
15 but the more was the report going abroad concerning
Him, and great multitudes were coming together to hear,
and to be healed by Him of their infirmities,
16 and He was withdrawing Himself in the desert places
and was praying.
17 And it came to pass, on one of the days, that He was
teaching, and there were sitting by Pharisees and
teachers of the Law, who were come out of every village
of Galilee, and Judea, and Jerusalem, and the power of
the Lord was — to heal them.
18 And behold, men bearing upon a couch a man, who
had been struck with palsy, and they were seeking to
bring him in, and to place before Him,
19 and not having found by what way they may bring
him in because of the multitude, having gone up on the
house-top, they let him down through the tiles, with the
little couch, into the midst before Jesus,
20 and He having seen their faith, said to him, 'Man,
your[S] sins have been forgiven you[S].'
21 And the scribes and the Pharisees began to reason,
saying, 'Who is this that does speak evil words? who is
able to forgive sins, except God only?'
22 And Jesus having known their reasonings,
answering, said unto them, 'Why reason you[P] in your[P]
hearts?
23 which is easier — to say, Your[S] sins have been
forgiven you[S]? or to say, Arise, and walk?
24 'And that you[P] may know that the Son of Man has
authority upon the earth to forgive sins — (He said to
the one struck with palsy) — I say to you[S], Arise, and
having taken up your[S] little couch, be going on to your[S]
house.'
25 And presently having risen before them, having taken
up [that] on which he was lying, he went away to his
house, glorifying God,
26 and astonishment took all, and they were glorifying
God, and were filled with fear, saying — 'We saw strange
things today.'
27 And after these things He went forth, and beheld a
tax-gatherer, by name Levi, sitting at the tax-office, and
said to him, 'Be following Me;'
28 and he, having left all, having arisen, did follow Him.
29 And Levi made a great entertainment to Him in his
house, and there was a great multitude of tax-gatherers
and others who were with them reclining (at meat),
30 and the scribes and the Pharisees among them were
murmuring at His disciples, saying, 'Why do you[P] eat
and drink with tax-gatherers and sinners?'

31 And Jesus answering said unto them, 'They who are
well have no need of a physician, but they that are ill:
32 I came not to call righteous men, but sinners, to
reformation.'
33 And they said unto Him, 'Why do the disciples of
John fast often, and make supplications — in like manner
also those of the Pharisees — but Yours[S] do eat and
drink?'
34 And He said unto them, 'Are you[P] able to make the
sons of the bride-chamber — in the bridegroom being
with them — to fast?
35 but days will come, and, when the bridegroom may
be taken away from them, then they shall fast in those
days.'
36 And He spoke a simile unto them also — 'No one
does put a patch of new clothing on old clothing, and if
otherwise, the new also does make a tear, and with the
old the patch does not agree, that [is] from the new.
37 'And no one does put new wine into old skins, and if
otherwise, the new wine will burst the skins, and itself
will be poured out, and the skins will be destroyed;
38 but new wine is to be put into new skins, and both
are preserved together;
39 and no one having drunk old [wine], does immediately
wish new, for he says, The old is better.'

CHAPTER 6

1 And it came to pass, on the second-first Sabbath, as
He is going through the corn fields, that His disciples
were plucking the ears, and were eating, rubbing with
the hands,
2 and certain of the Pharisees said to them, 'Why do
you[P] that which is not lawful to do on the Sabbaths?'
3 And Jesus answering said unto them, 'Did you[P] not
even read this that David did, when he hungered, himself
and those who are with him,
4 how he went into the house of God, and did take the
loaves of the presentation, and did eat, and gave also to
those with him, which it is not lawful to eat, except only
to the priests?'
5 and He said to them, — 'The Son of Man is lord also
of the Sabbath.'
6 And it came to pass also, on another Sabbath, that He
went into the synagogue, and taught, and there was
there a man, and his right hand was withered,
7 and the scribes and the Pharisees were watching Him,
if He will heal on the Sabbath, that they might find an
accusation against Him.
8 And He Himself had known their reasonings, and said
to the man having the withered hand, 'Rise, and stand
in the midst;' and he having risen, stood.
9 Then said Jesus unto them, 'I will question you[P]
something: Is it lawful to do good on the Sabbaths, or
to do evil? to save life or to kill?'
10 And having looked round on them all, He said to the
man, 'Stretch forth your[S] hand;' and he did so, and his
hand was restored whole as the other;
11 and they were filled with madness, and were speaking
with one another what they might do to Jesus.
12 And it came to pass in those days, He went forth to
the mountain to pray, and was passing the night in the
prayer of God,
13 and when it became day, He called near His disciples,
and having chosen from them twelve, whom also He
named apostles,
14 (Simon, whom also He named Peter, and Andrew his
brother, James and John, Philip and Bartholomew,
15 Matthew and Thomas, James of Alphaeus, and Simon
called Zelotes,
16 Judas of James, and Judas Iscariot, who also became
betrayer;)
17 and having come down with them, He stood upon a
level spot, and a crowd of his disciples, and a great
multitude of the people from all Judea, and Jerusalem,
and the maritime Tyre and Sidon, who came to hear Him,
and to be healed of their sicknesses,
18 and those harassed by unclean spirits, and they were
healed,
19 and all the multitude were seeking to touch Him,
because power was going forth from Him, and He was
healing all.
20 And He, having lifted up his eyes to His disciples,
said: 'Happy the poor — because yours[P] is the reign of
God.
21 'Happy those hungering now — because you[P] shall
be filled. 'Happy those weeping now — because you[P]
shall laugh.
22 'Happy are you[P] when men shall hate you[P], and when
they shall separate you[P], and shall reproach, and shall cast
forth your[P] name as evil, for the Son of Man's sake —
23 rejoice in that day, and leap, for behold, your[P] reward
[is] great in the heaven, for according to these things
were their fathers doing to the prophets.
24 'But woe to you[P] — the rich, because you[P] have got
your[P] comfort.
25 'Woe to you[P] who have been filled — because you[P]

shall hunger. 'Woe to you[P] who are laughing now —
because you[P] shall mourn and weep.
26 'Woe to you[P] when all men shall speak well of you[P]
— for according to these things were their fathers doing
to false prophets.
27 'But I say to you[P] who are hearing, Love your[P]
enemies, do good to those hating you[P],
28 bless those cursing you[P], and pray for those accusing
you[P] falsely;
29 and to him striking you[S] upon the cheek, give also
the other, and from him taking away the mantle from you[S],
you[S] may not keep back the coat also.
30 'And to every one who is asking of you[S], be giving;
and from him who is taking away your[S] goods, be not
asking again;
31 and as you[P] wish that men may do to you[P], do you[P]
also to them in like manner;
32 and — if you[P] love those loving you[P], what grace
have you[P]? for also the sinful love those loving them;
33 and if you[P] do good to those doing good to you[P],
what grace have you[P]? for also the sinful do the same;
34 and if you[P] lend [to those] of whom you[P] hope to
receive back, what grace have you[P]? for also the sinful
lend to sinners — that they may receive again as much.
35 'But love your[P] enemies, and do good, and lend,
hoping for nothing again, and your[P] reward will be great,
and you[P] shall be sons of the Highest, because He is
kind unto the ungracious and evil;
36 be you[P] therefore merciful, as also your[P] Father is
merciful.
37 'And judge not, and you[P] may not be judged;
condemn not, and you[P] may not be condemned; release,
and you[P] shall be released.
38 'Give, and it shall be given to you[P]; good measure,
pressed, and shaken, and running over, they shall give
into your[P] bosom; for with that measure with which you[P]
measure, it shall be measured to you[P] again.'
39 And He spoke a simile to them, 'Is blind able to lead
blind? shall they not both fall into a pit?
40 A disciple is not above his teacher, but every one
perfected shall be as his teacher.
41 'And why do you[S] behold the mote that is in your[S]
brother's eye, and do not consider the beam that [is] in
your[S] own eye ?
42 or how are you[S] able to say to your[S] brother, Brother,
allow, I may take out the mote that [is] in your[S] eye —
yourself[S] not beholding the beam in your[S] own eye?
Hypocrite, take first the beam out of your[S] own eye, and
then you[S] shall see clearly to take out the mote that [is]
in your[S] brother's eye.
43 'For there is not a good tree making bad fruit, nor a
bad tree making good fruit;
44 for each tree is known from its own fruit, for they do
not gather figs from thorns , nor do they crop a grape
from a bramble.
45 'The good man does bring forth that which [is] good
out of the good treasure of his heart; and the evil man
does bring forth that which [is] evil out of the evil
treasure of his heart; for his mouth does speak out of
the abounding of the heart.
46 'And why do you[P] call me, Lord, Lord, and do not
what I say?
47 Every one who is coming unto me, and is hearing my
words, and is doing them, I will show you[P] to whom he
is like;
48 he is like to a man building a house, who did dig, and
deepen, and laid a foundation upon the rock, and a flood
having come, the stream broke forth on that house, and
was not able to shake it, for it had been founded upon
the rock.
49 'And he who heard and did not, is like to a man having
built a house upon the earth, without a foundation,
against which the stream broke forth, and immediately it
fell, and the ruin of that house became great.'

CHAPTER 7

1 And when He completed all His sayings in the ears of
the people, He went into Capernaum;
2 and a certain centurion's servant being ill, was about
to die, who was much valued by him,
3 and having heard about Jesus, he sent unto Him elders
of the Jews, begging Him, that having come He might
thoroughly save his servant.
4 And they, having come near unto Jesus, were calling
upon Him earnestly, saying — 'He is worthy to whom
You[S] shall do this,
5 for he does love our nation, and he did build the
synagogue to us.'
6 And Jesus was going on with them, and now when
He is not far distant from the house the centurion sent
unto Him friends, saying to Him, 'Sir, be not troubled,
for I am not worthy that You[S] may enter under my roof;
7 for I thought myself not even worthy to come unto
You[S], but say in a word, and my lad shall be healed;
8 for I also am a man placed under authority, having
under myself soldiers, and I say to this [one], Go, and

he goes; and to another, Be coming, and he comes; and
to my servant, Do this, and he does [it].'
9 And having heard these things Jesus wondered at
him, and having turned to the multitude following Him,
He said, 'I say to you[P], not even in Israel did I find so
much faith;'
10 and those sent, having turned back to the house,
found the ailing servant in health.
11 And it came to pass, on the next day, He was going
on to a city called Nain, and there were going with Him
many of his disciples, and a great multitude,
12 and as He came near to the gate of the city, then,
behold, one dead was being carried forth, an only son
of his mother, and she a widow, and a great multitude of
the city was with her.
13 And the Lord having seen her, was moved with
compassion towards her, and said to her, 'Be not
weeping;'
14 and having come near, He touched the bier, and those
bearing [it] stood still, and He said, 'Young man, to you[S]
I say, Arise;'
15 and the dead sat up, and began to speak, and He
gave him to his mother;
16 and fear took hold of all, and they were glorifying
God, saying — 'A great prophet has risen among us,'
and — 'God did look upon His people.'
17 And the account of this went forth in all Judea about
Him, and in all the region around.
18 And the disciples of John told him about all these
things,
19 and John having called near a certain two of his
disciples, sent unto Jesus, saying, 'Are You[S] He who is
coming, or do we look for another?'
20 And having come near to Him, the men said, 'John
the Baptist sent us unto You[S], saying, Are You[S] He who
is coming, or do we look for another?'
21 And in that hour He cured many from sicknesses,
and plagues, and evil spirits, and He granted sight to
many blind.
22 And Jesus answering said to them, 'Having gone
on, report to John what you[P] saw and heard, that blind
men do see again, lame do walk, lepers are cleansed, deaf
do hear, dead are raised, poor have good news
proclaimed;
23 and happy is he whoever may not be stumbled in
Me.'
24 And the messengers of John having gone away, He
began to say unto the multitudes concerning John:
'What have you[P] gone forth to the wilderness to look
on? a reed shaken by the wind?
25 but what have you[P] gone forth to see? a man clothed
in soft garments? behold, they in splendid clothing, and
living in luxury, are in the houses of kings!
26 'But what have you[P] gone forth to see? a prophet?
Yes, I say to you[P], and much more than a prophet:
27 this is he concerning whom it has been written,
Behold, I send my messenger before Your[S] face, who
shall prepare Your[S] way before You[S];
28 for I say to you[P], there is not a greater prophet, among
those born of women, than John the Baptist; but the
least in the reign of God is greater than he.'
29 And all the people having heard, and the tax-
gatherers, declared God righteous, having been baptized
with the baptism of John,
30 but the Pharisees, and the lawyers, did put away the
counsel of God for themselves, not having been baptized
by him.
31 And the Lord said, 'To what, then, shall I liken the
men of this generation? and to what are they like?
32 they are like to children, to those sitting in a market-
place, and calling one to another, and saying, We piped
to you[P], and you[P] did not dance, we mourned to you[P],
and you[P] did not weep!
33 'For John the Baptist came neither eating bread nor
drinking wine, and you[P] say, He has a demon;
34 the Son of Man came eating and drinking, and you[P]
say, Behold, a man, a glutton, and a wine drinker, a friend
of tax-gatherers and sinners;
35 and the wisdom was justified from all her children.'
36 And a certain one of the Pharisees was asking Him
that He might eat with him, and having gone into the
house of the Pharisee He reclined (at meat),
37 and behold, a woman in the city, who was a sinner,
having known that He reclined (at meat) in the house of
the Pharisee, having provided an alabaster box of
ointment,
38 and having stood behind, beside His feet, weeping,
she began to wet His feet with the tears, and with the
hairs of her head she was wiping, and was kissing His
feet, and was anointing with the ointment.
39 And the Pharisee who did call Him, having seen,
spoke within himself, saying, 'This one, if He were a
prophet, would have known who and of what kind [is]
the woman who does touch Him, that she is a sinner.'
40 And Jesus answering said unto him, 'Simon, I have
something to say to you[S];' and he said, 'Teacher, say on.'
41 'Two debtors were to a certain creditor; the one was
owing five hundred denaries, and the other fifty;

42 and they not having [wherewith] to give back, he
forgave both; which then of them, say you[S], will love
him more?'
43 And Simon answering said, 'I suppose that to whom
he forgave the more;' and He said to him, 'You[S] did judge
rightly.'
44 And having turned unto the woman, He said to
Simon, 'You[S] see this woman? I entered into your[S] house;
you[S] did not give water for My feet, but this woman with
tears did wet My feet, and with the hairs of her head did
wipe;
45 you[S] did not give a kiss to Me, but this woman, from
what [time] I came in, did not cease kissing My feet;
46 you[S] did not anoint My head with oil, but this woman
did anoint My feet with ointment;
47 therefore I say to you[S], her many sins have been
forgiven, because she did love much; but to whom little
is forgiven, little does he love.'
48 And He said to her, 'Your[S] sins have been forgiven;'
49 and those reclining with Him (at meat) began to say
within themselves, 'Who is this, who does forgive sins
also?'
50 and He said unto the woman, 'Your[S] faith have saved
you[S], be going on to peace.'

CHAPTER 8

1 And it came to pass thereafter, that He was going
through every city and village, preaching and
proclaiming good news of the reign of God, and the
twelve [are] with Him,
2 and certain women, who were healed of evil spirits
and infirmities, Mary who is called Magdalene, from
whom seven demons had gone forth,
3 and Joanna wife of Chuza, steward of Herod, and
Susanna, and many others, who were ministering to Him
from their substance.
4 And a great multitude having gathered, and those who
were coming from city and city unto Him, He spoke by a
simile:
5 'The sower went forth to sow his seed, and in his sowing
some indeed fell beside the way, and it was trodden down,
and the fowls of the heaven did devour it.
6 'And other fell upon the rock, and having sprung up,
it did wither, through not having moisture.
7 'And other fell amidst the thorns, and the thorns
having sprung up with it, did choke it.
8 'And other fell upon the good ground, and having
sprung up, it made fruit an hundred fold.' These things
saying, He was calling, 'He having ears to hear — let
him hear.'
9 And His disciples were questioning Him, saying,
'What may this simile be?'
10 And He said, 'To you[P] it has been given to know the
secrets of the reign of God, and to the rest in similes;
that seeing they may not see, and hearing they may not
understand.
11 'And this is the simile: The seed is the word of God,
12 and those beside the way are those hearing, then
comes the Devil, and takes up the word from their heart,
lest having believed, they may be saved.
13 'And those upon the rock: They who, when they
may hear, do receive the word with joy, and these have
no root, who for a time believe, and in time of temptation
fall away.
14 'And that which fell to the thorns: These are they
who have heard, and going forth, through anxieties, and
riches, and pleasures of life, are choked, and bear not to
completion.
15 'And that in the good ground: These are they, who
in an upright and good heart, having heard the word, do
retain [it], and bear fruit in continuance.
16 'And no one having lighted a lamp does cover it
with a vessel, or does put [it] under a couch; but he does
put [it] upon a lamp-stand, that those coming in may
see the light,
17 for nothing is secret, that shall not become known,
nor hid, that shall not be known, and become known.
18 'See, for that reason, how you[P] hear, for whoever
may have, there shall be given to him, and whoever may
not have, also what he seems to have, shall be taken
from him.'
19 And there came unto Him His mother and brethren,
and they were not able to get to Him because of the
multitude,
20 and it was told Him, saying, 'Your[S] mother and Your[S]
brethren do stand without, wishing to see You[S];'
21 and He answering said unto them, 'My mother and
My brethren! they are those who are hearing the word
of God, and doing.'
22 And it came to pass, on one of the days, that He
Himself went into a boat with His disciples, and He said
unto them, 'We may go over to the other side of the
lake;' and they set forth,
23 and as they are sailing He fell deeply asleep, and
there came down a storm of wind to the lake, and they
were filling, and were in peril.

24 And having come near, they awoke Him, saying, 'Master, Master, we perish;' and He, having arisen, rebuked the wind and the raging of the water, and they ceased, and there came a calm,
25 and He said to them, 'Where is your[P] faith?' and they being afraid did wonder, saying unto one another, 'Who, then, is this, that even the winds He does command, and the water, and they obey Him?'
26 And they sailed down to the region of the Gadarenes, that is over-against Galilee,
27 and He having gone forth upon the land, there met Him a certain man, out of the city, who had demons for a long time, and was not clothed with a garment, and was not abiding in a house, but in the tombs,
28 and having seen Jesus, and having cried out, he fell before Him, and with a loud voice, said, 'What — to me and to You[S], Jesus, Son of God Most High? I beg You[S], may You[S] not afflict me!'
29 For He commanded the unclean spirit to come forth from the man, for many times it had caught him, and he was being bound with chains and fetters — guarded, and breaking apart the bonds he was driven by the demons to the deserts.
30 And Jesus questioned him, saying, 'What is your[S] name?' and he said, 'Legion,' (because many demons were entered into him,)
31 and he was calling on Him, that He may not command them to go away to the abyss,
32 and there was there a herd of many swine feeding in the mountain, and they were calling on Him, that He might allow them to enter into these, and He allowed them,
33 and the demons having gone forth from the man, did enter into the swine, and the herd rushed down the steep to the lake, and were choked.
34 And those feeding [them], having seen what was come to pass, fled, and having gone, told [it] to the city, and to the fields;
35 and they came forth to see what was come to pass, and they came unto Jesus, and found the man sitting, out of whom the demons had gone forth, clothed, and right-minded, at the feet of Jesus, and they were afraid;
36 and those also having seen [it], told them how the demoniac was saved.
37 And the whole multitude of the region of the Gadarenes round about asked Him to go away from them, because they were pressed with great fear, and He having entered into the boat, did turn back.
38 And the man from whom the demons had gone forth was begging of Him to be with Him, and Jesus sent him away, saying,
39 'Turn back to your[S] house, and tell how God did great things to you[S];' and he went away through all the city proclaiming how Jesus did great things to him.
40 And it came to pass, in the turning back of Jesus, the multitude received Him, for they were all looking for Him,
41 and behold, there came a man, whose name [is] Jairus, and he was a chief of the synagogue, and having fallen at the feet of Jesus, was calling on Him to come to his house;
42 because he had an only daughter about twelve years [old], and she was dying. And in His going away, the multitudes were thronging Him,
43 and a woman, having an issue of blood for twelve years, who, having spent all her living on physicians, was not able to be healed by any,
44 having come near behind, touched the fringe of His garment, and presently the issue of her blood stood.
45 And Jesus said, 'Who [is] it that touched Me?' and all denying, Peter and those with him said, 'Master, the multitudes press You[S], and throng [You[S]], and You[S] do say, Who [is] it that touched Me!'
46 And Jesus said, 'Some one did touch Me, for I knew power having gone forth from Me.'
47 And the woman, having seen that she was not hid, trembling, came, and having fallen before Him, declared to Him before all the people for what cause she touched Him, and how she was healed presently;
48 and He said to her, 'Take courage, daughter, your[S] faith has saved you[S], be going on to peace.'
49 While He is yet speaking, there did come a certain one from the chief of the synagogue's [house], saying to Him — 'Your[S] daughter has died, harass not the Teacher;'
50 and Jesus having heard, answered him, saying, 'Be not afraid, only believe, and she shall be saved.'
51 And having come to the house, He allowed no one to go in, except Peter, and James, and John, and the father of the child, and the mother;
52 and they were all weeping, and beating themselves for her, and He said, 'Weep not, she did not die, but does sleep;
53 and they were deriding Him, knowing that she did die;
54 and He having put all forth without, and having taken hold of her hand, called, saying, 'Child, arise;'
55 and her spirit came back, and she arose presently, and He directed that there be given to her to eat;
56 and her parents were amazed, but He charged them to say to no one what was come to pass.

CHAPTER 9

1 And having called together His twelve disciples, He gave them power and authority over all the demons, and to cure sicknesses,

2 and He sent them to proclaim the reign of God, and to heal the ailing.

3 And He said unto them, 'Take nothing for the way, neither staff, nor scrip, nor bread, nor money; neither have two coats each;

4 and into whatever house you[P] may enter, there remain, and from there depart;

5 and as many as may not receive you[P], going forth from that city, shake off even the dust from your[P] feet, for a testimony against them.'

6 And going forth they were going through the several villages, proclaiming good news, and healing everywhere.

7 And Herod the tetrarch heard of all the things being done by Him, and was perplexed, because it was said by certain, that John had been raised out of the dead;

8 and by certain, that Elijah did appear, and by others, that a prophet, one of the ancients, was risen;

9 and Herod said, 'John I did behead, but who is this concerning whom I hear such things?' and he was seeking to see Him.

10 And the apostles having turned back, declared to Him how they did great things, and having taken them, He withdrew by Himself to a desert place of a city called Bethsaida,

11 and the multitudes having known did follow Him, and having received them, He was speaking to them concerning the reign of God, and He cured those having need of service.

12 And the day began to decline, and the twelve having come near, said to Him, 'Send away the multitude, that having gone to the villages and the fields round about, they may lodge and may find provision, because we are in a desert place here.'

13 And He said unto them, 'You[P] give them to eat;' and they said, 'We have no more than five loaves, and two fishes: except, having gone, we may buy victuals for all this people;'

14 for they were about five thousand men. And He said unto His disciples, 'Cause them to recline in companies, in each fifty;'

15 and they did so, and made all to recline;

16 and having taken the five loaves, and the two fishes, having looked up to the heaven, He blessed them, and broke, and was giving to the disciples to set before the multitude;

17 and they did eat, and were all filled, and there was taken up what was over to them of broken pieces, twelve baskets.

18 And it came to pass, as He is praying alone, the disciples were with Him, and He questioned them, saying, 'Who do the multitudes say Me to be?'

19 And they answering said, 'John the Baptist; and others, Elijah; and others, that a prophet, one of the ancients, was risen;'

20 and He said to them, 'And you[P] — who do you[P] say Me to be?' and Peter answering said, 'The Christ of God.'

21 And having charged them, He commanded [them] to say this to no one,

22 saying — 'It is necessary for the Son of Man to suffer many things, and to be rejected by the elders, and chief priests, and scribes, and to be killed, and the third day to be raised.'

23 And He said unto all, 'If any one does will to come after Me, let him disown himself, and take up his cross daily, and follow Me;

24 for whoever may will to save his life, shall lose it, and whoever may lose his life for My sake, he shall save it;

25 for what is a man profited, having gained the whole world, and having lost or having forfeited himself?

26 'For whoever may be ashamed of Me, and of My words, the Son of Man be ashamed of this one shall, when He may come in His glory, and the Father's, and the holy messengers';

27 and I say to you[P], truly, there are certain of those standing here, who shall not taste of death till they may see the reign of God.'

28 And it came to pass, after these words, as it were eight days, that having taken Peter, and John, and James, He went up to the mountain to pray,

29 and it came to pass, in His praying, the appearance of His face became altered, and His garment white — sparkling.

30 And behold, two men were speaking together with Him, who were Moses and Elijah,

31 who having appeared in glory, spoke of His outgoing that He was about to fulfil in Jerusalem,

32 but Peter and those with him were heavy with sleep, and having waked, they saw His glory, and the two men standing with Him.

33 And it came to pass, in their parting from Him, Peter said unto Jesus, 'Master, it is good to us to be here;

and we may make three booths, one for You[S], and one
for Moses, and one for Elijah,' not knowing what he said:
34 and as he was speaking these things, there came a
cloud, and overshadowed them, and they feared in their
entering into the cloud,
35 and a voice came out of the cloud saying, 'This is
My Son — the Beloved; you[P] hear Him;'
36 and when the voice was past, Jesus was found alone;
and they were silent, and declared to no one in those
days anything of what they have seen.
37 And it came to pass on the next day, they having
come down from the mount, there met Him a great
multitude,
38 and behold, a man from the multitude cried out,
saying, 'Teacher, I beg You[S], look upon my son, because
he is my only begotten;
39 and behold, a spirit does take him, and suddenly he
does cry out, and it tears him, with foaming, and it hardly
departs from him, bruising him,
40 and I begged Your[S] disciples that they might cast it
out, and they were not able.'
41 And Jesus answering said, 'O generation,
unsteadfast and perverse, till when shall I be with you[P],
and suffer you[P]? bring your[S] son near here;'
42 and as he is yet coming near, the demon rent him,
and tore [him] sore, and Jesus rebuked the unclean spirit,
and healed the youth, and gave him back to his father.
43 And they were all amazed at the greatness of God,
and while all are wondering at all things that Jesus did,
He said unto His disciples,
44 'Lay you[P] these words to your[P] ears, for the Son of
Man is about to be delivered up to the hands of men.'
45 And they were not knowing this saying, and it was
veiled from them, that they might not perceive it, and
they were afraid to ask Him about this saying.
46 And there entered a reasoning among them, this, Who
may be greater of them?
47 and Jesus having seen the reasoning of their heart,
having taken hold of a child, set him beside Himself,
48 and said to them, 'Whoever may receive this child in
My name, does receive Me, and whoever may receive
Me, does receive Him who sent Me, for he who is least
among you[P] all — he shall be great.'
49 And John answering said, 'Master, we saw a certain
one casting forth the demons in Your[S] name, and we
forbade him, because he does not follow with us;'
50 and Jesus said unto him, 'Forbid not, for he who is
not against us, is for us.'
51 And it came to pass, in the completing of the days of
His being taken up, that He fixed His face to go on to
Jerusalem,
52 and He sent messengers before His face, and having
gone on, they went into a village of Samaritans, to make
ready for Him,
53 and they did not receive Him, because His face was
going on to Jerusalem.
54 And His disciples James and John having seen, said,
'Sir, will You[S] [that] we may command fire to come down
from the heaven, and to consume them, as also Elijah
did?'
55 and having turned, He rebuked them, and said, 'You[P]
have not known of what spirit you[P] are;
56 for the Son of Man did not come to destroy men's
lives, but to save;' and they went on to another village.
57 And it came to pass, as they are going on in the way,
a certain one said unto Him, 'I will follow You[S] wherever
You[S] may go, sir;'
58 and Jesus said to him, 'The foxes have holes, and
the fowls of the heaven places of rest, but the Son of
Man has not where He may recline the head.'
59 And He said unto another, 'Be following me;' and he
said, 'Sir, permit me, having gone away, to bury my father
first;'
60 and Jesus said to him, 'Allow the dead to bury their
own dead, and you[S], having gone away, publish the reign
of God.'
61 And another also said, 'I will follow You[S], sir, but
first permit me to take leave of those in my house;'
62 and Jesus said unto him, 'No one having put his
hand on a plough, and looking back, is fit for the reign
of God.'

CHAPTER 10

1 And after these things, the Lord did appoint also other
seventy, and sent them by twos before His face, to every
city and place where He Himself was about to come,
2 then He said unto them, 'The harvest indeed [is]
abundant, but the workmen few; beg you[P] then the Lord
of the harvest, that He may put forth workmen to His
harvest.
3 'Go away; behold, I send you[P] forth as lambs in the
midst of wolves;
4 carry no bag, no scrip, nor sandals; and salute no one
on the way;
5 and into whatever house you[P] do enter, first say, Peace
to this house;

6 and if indeed there may be there the son of peace, your[P] peace shall rest on it; and if not so, it shall turn back upon you[P].
7 'And in that house remain, eating and drinking the things they have, for worthy [is] the workman of his hire; go not from house to house,
8 and into whatever city you[P] enter, and they may receive you[P], eat the things set before you[P],
9 and heal the ailing in it, and say to them, The reign of God has come near to you[P].
10 'And into whatever city you[P] do enter, and they may not receive you[P], having gone forth to its broad places, say,
11 And the dust that has clung to us, from your[P] city, we do wipe off against you[P], but this you[P] know, that the reign of God has come near to you[P];
12 and I say to you[P], that for Sodom in that day it shall be more tolerable for Sodom than for that city.
13 'Woe to you[S], Chorazin; woe to you[S], Bethsaida; for if the mighty works that were done in you[P] had been done in Tyre and Sidon, long ago, sitting in sackcloth and ashes, they had reformed;
14 but it shall be more tolerable for Tyre and Sidon in the judgment than for you[P].
15 'And you[S], Capernaum, which was exalted unto the heaven, unto hades you[S] shall be brought down.
16 'He who is hearing you[P], does hear Me; and he who is putting you[P] away, does put Me away; and he who is putting Me away, does put away Him who sent Me.'
17 And the seventy turned back with joy, saying, 'Sir, and the demons are being subjected to us in Your[S] name;'
18 and He said to them, 'I was beholding the Adversary, as lightning from the heaven having fallen;
19 behold, I give to you[P] the authority to tread upon serpents and scorpions, and on all the power of the enemy, and nothing by any means shall hurt you[P];
20 but, in this rejoice not, that the spirits are subjected to you[P], but rejoice rather that your[P] names were written in the heavens.'
21 In that hour was Jesus glad in the Spirit, and said, 'I do confess to You[S], Father, Lord of the heaven and of the earth, that You[S] did hide these things from wise men and understanding, and did reveal them to babes; yes, Father, because so it became good pleasure before You[S].
22 'All things were delivered up to Me by My Father, and no one does know who the Son is, except the Father, and who the Father is, except the Son, and he to whom the Son may wish to reveal [Him].'
23 And having turned unto the disciples, He said, by themselves, 'Happy the eyes that are perceiving what you[P] perceive;
24 for I say to you[P], that many prophets and kings did wish to see what you[P] perceive, and did not see, and to hear what you[P] hear, and did not hear.'
25 And behold, a certain lawyer stood up, trying Him, and saying, 'Teacher, having done what, shall I inherit life age-during?'
26 And He said unto him, 'In the law what has been written? how do you[S] read?'
27 And he answering said, 'You[S] shall love the Lord your[S] God out of all your[S] heart, and out of all your[S] soul, and out of all your[S] strength, and out of all your[S] understanding, and your[S] neighbor as yourself[S].'
28 And He said to him, 'Rightly you[S] did answer; this do, and you[S] shall live.'
29 And he, willing to declare himself righteous, said unto Jesus, 'And who is my neighbor?'
30 and Jesus having taken up [the word], said, 'A certain man was going down from Jerusalem to Jericho, and fell among robbers, and having stripped him and inflicted blows, they went away, leaving [him] half dead.
31 'And by a coincidence a certain priest was going down in that way, and having seen him, he passed over on the opposite side;
32 and in like manner also, a Levite, having been about the place, having come and seen, passed over on the opposite side.
33 'But a certain Samaritan, journeying, came along him, and having seen him, he was moved with compassion,
34 and having come near, he bound up his wounds, pouring on oil and wine, and having lifted him up on his own beast, he brought him to an inn, and was careful of him;
35 and on the next day, going forth, taking out two denaries, he gave to the innkeeper, and said to him, Be careful of him, and whatever you[S] may spend more, I, in my coming again, will give back to you[S].
36 'Who, then, of these three, seems to you[S] to have become neighbor of him who fell among the robbers?'
37 and he said, 'He who did the kindness with him,' then Jesus said to him, 'Be going on, and you[S] be doing in like manner.'
38 And it came to pass, in their going on, that He entered into a certain village, and a certain woman, by name Martha, did receive Him into her house,
39 and she had also a sister, called Mary, who also, having seated herself beside the feet of Jesus, was hearing the word,
40 and Martha was distracted about much serving, and having stood by Him, she said, 'Sir, do You[S] not care

that my sister left me alone to serve? say then to her, that she may help along with me.'
41 And Jesus answering said to her, 'Martha, Martha, you[S] are anxious and disquieted about many things,
42 but there is need of one thing, and Mary did choose the good part, that shall not be taken away from her.'

CHAPTER 11

1 And it came to pass, in His being in a certain place praying, as He ceased, a certain one of His disciples said unto Him, 'Sir, teach us to pray, as also John taught his disciples.'
2 And He said to them, 'When you[P] may pray, say you[P]: Our Father who is in the heavens; hallowed be Your[S] name: Your[S] reign come; Your[S] will come to pass, on earth as in heaven also;
3 be giving us our appointed bread daily;
4 and forgive us our sins, for also we ourselves forgive every one indebted to us; and may You[S] not bring us into temptation; but do You[S] deliver us from the evil.'
5 And He said unto them, 'Who of you[P] shall have a friend, and shall go on unto him at midnight, and may say to him, Friend, lend me three loaves,
6 seeing a friend of mine came out of the way unto me, and I have not what I shall set before him,
7 and he from within answering may say, Do not give me trouble, already the door has been shut, and my children with me are in the bed, I am not able, having risen, to give to you[S].
8 'I say to you[P], even if he will not give to him, having risen, because of his being his friend, yet because of his importunity, having risen, he will give him as many as he does need;
9 and I say to you[P], Ask, and it shall be given to you[P]; seek, and you[P] shall find; knock, and it shall be opened to you[P];
10 for every one who is asking does receive; and he who is seeking does find; and to him who is knocking it shall be opened.
11 'And of which of you[P] — the father — if the son shall ask a loaf, will he present a stone to him? and if a fish, will he instead of a fish, present a serpent to him?
12 and if he may ask an egg, will he present a scorpion to him?
13 If, then, you[P], being evil, have known to be giving good gifts to your[P] children, how much more shall the Father who is from heaven give the Holy Spirit to those asking Him!'
14 And He was casting forth a demon, and it was dumb, and it came to pass, the demon having gone forth, the dumb man spoke, and the multitudes wondered,
15 and certain of them said, 'By Beelzeboul, ruler of the demons, does He cast forth the demons;'
16 and others, tempting, were asking a sign out of heaven from Him.
17 And He, knowing their thoughts, said to them, 'Every kingdom having been divided against itself is desolated; and house against house does fall;
18 and if also the Adversary was divided against himself, how shall his kingdom be made to stand? for you[P] say, My casting forth the demons is by Beelzeboul.
19 'But if I by Beelzeboul cast forth the demons — your[P] sons, by whom do they cast forth? because of this they shall be your[P] judges;
20 but if by the finger of God I cast forth the demons, then the reign of God did come unawares upon you[P].
21 'When the armed strong man may keep his hall, are his goods in peace;
22 but when the stronger than he, having come upon [him], may overcome him, he does take away his whole-armor in which he had trusted, and he distributes his spoils;
23 he who is not with Me is against Me, and he who is not gathering with Me does scatter.
24 'When the unclean spirit may go forth from the man it walks through waterless places seeking rest, and not finding, it says, I will turn back to my house from where I came forth;
25 and having come, it finds [it] swept and adorned;
26 then it does go, and take seven other spirits more evil than itself to it, and having entered, they dwell there, and the last of that man becomes worst than the first.'
27 And it came to pass, in His saying these things, a certain woman having lifted up the voice out of the multitude, said to Him, 'Happy the womb that carried You[S], and the paps that You[S] did suck!'
28 And He said, 'Yea, rather, happy those hearing the word of God, and keeping [it]!'
29 And the multitudes crowding together upon Him, He began to say, 'This generation is evil, it does seek after a sign, and a sign shall not be given to it, except the sign of Jonah the prophet,
30 for as Jonah became a sign to the Ninevites, so also shall the Son of Man be to this generation.
31 'A queen of the south shall rise up in the judgment with the men of this generation, and shall condemn them,

because she came from the ends of the earth to hear the wisdom of Solomon; and behold, greater than Solomon here!

32 'Men of Nineveh shall stand up in the judgment with this generation, and shall condemn it, because they reformed at the proclamation of Jonah; and behold, greater than Jonah here!

33 'And no one having lighted a lamp, does put [it] in a secret place, nor under the measure, but on the lamp-stand, that those coming in may behold the light.

34 'The lamp of the body is the eye, when then your^{S} eye may be simple, your^{S} whole body also is lightened; and when it may be evil, your^{S} body also is darkened;

35 take heed, then, for fear that the light that [is] in you^{S} be darkness;

36 if then your^{S} whole body is lightened, not having any part darkened, the whole shall be lightened, as when the lamp by the brightness may give you^{S} light.'

37 And in [His] speaking, a certain Pharisee was asking Him that He might dine with him, and having gone in, he reclined (at meat),

38 and the Pharisee having seen, did wonder that He did not first baptize Himself before the dinner.

39 And the Lord said unto him, 'Now do you^{P}, the Pharisees, make clean the outside of the cup and of the plate, but your^{P} inward part is full of rapine and wickedness;

40 unthinking! did not He who made the outside also make the inside?

41 But what you^{P} have give you^{P} [as] alms, and, behold, all things are clean to you^{P}.

42 'But woe to you^{P}, the Pharisees, because you^{P} tithe the mint, and the rue, and every herb, and you^{P} pass by the judgment, and the love of God; these things it is necessary to do, and those not to be neglecting.

43 'Woe to you^{P}, the Pharisees, because you^{P} love the first seats in the synagogues, and the salutations in the market-places.

44 'Woe to you^{P}, scribes and Pharisees, hypocrites, because you^{P} are as the unseen tombs, and the men walking above have not known.'

45 And one of the lawyers answering, said to Him, 'Teacher, these things saying, You^{S} do insult us also;'

46 and He said, 'And to you^{P}, the lawyers, woe! because you^{P} burden men with burdens grievous to be borne, and you^{P} yourselves^{P} do not touch the burdens with one of your^{P} fingers.

47 'Woe to you^{P}, because you^{P} build the tombs of the prophets, and your^{P} fathers killed them.

48 Then do you^{P} testify, and are well pleased with the works of your^{P} fathers, because they indeed killed them, and you^{P} do build their tombs;

49 because of this also the wisdom of God said: I will send to them prophets, and apostles, and some of them they shall kill and persecute,

50 that the blood of all the prophets, that is being poured forth from the foundation of the world, may be required from this generation;

51 from the blood of Abel unto the blood of Zacharias, who perished between the altar and the house; yes, I say to you^{P}, It shall be required from this generation.

52 'Woe to you^{P}, the lawyers, because you^{P} took away the key of the knowledge; yourselves^{P} you^{P} did not enter; and you^{P} did hinder those coming in.'

53 And in His speaking these things unto them, the scribes and the Pharisees began fearfully to urge and to press Him to speak about many things,

54 laying wait for Him, and seeking to catch something out of His mouth, that they might accuse Him.

CHAPTER 12

1 At which time the myriads of the multitude having been gathered together, so as to tread upon one another, He began to say unto His disciples, first, 'Take heed to yourselves^{P} of the leaven of the Pharisees, which is hypocrisy;

2 and there is nothing covered, that shall not be revealed; and hid, that shall not be known;

3 because whatever you^{P} said in the darkness, shall be heard in the light: and what you^{P} spoke to the ear in the inner-chambers, shall be proclaimed upon the house-tops.

4 'And I say to you^{P}, My friends, be not afraid of those killing the body, and after these things are not having anything over to do;

5 but I will show to you^{P}, whom you^{P} may fear; Fear Him who, after the killing, is having authority to cast to the gehenna; yes, I say to you^{P}, Fear you^{P} Him.

6 'Are not five sparrows sold for two assars? and one of them is not forgotten before God,

7 but even the hairs of your^{P} head have been all numbered; for that reason fear you^{P} not, you^{P} are of more value than many sparrows.

8 'And I say to you^{P}, Every one — whoever may confess with Me before men, the Son of Man also shall confess with him before the messengers of God,

9 and he who has denied Me before men, shall be denied
before the messengers of God,
10 and every one whoever shall say a word to the Son
of Man, it shall be forgiven to him, but to him who did
speak evil to the Holy Spirit, it shall not be forgiven.
11 'And when they bring you^{P} before the synagogues,
and the rulers, and the authorities, be not anxious how
or what you^{P} may reply, or what you^{P} may say,
12 for the Holy Spirit shall teach you^{P} in that hour what
it is necessary for [you^{P}] to say.'
13 And a certain one said to Him, out of the multitude,
'Teacher, say to my brother to divide the inheritance with
me.'
14 And He said to him, 'Man, who set Me a judge or a
divider over you^{P}?'
15 And He said unto them, 'Observe, and beware of the
covetousness, because his life is not in the abundance
of one's goods.'
16 And He spoke a simile unto them, saying, 'Of a certain
rich man the field brought forth well;
17 and he was reasoning within himself, saying, What
shall I do, because I have not where I shall gather
together my fruits?
18 and he said, This I will do, I will take down my
storehouses, and greater ones I will build, and I will
gather together there all my products and my good
things,
19 and I will say to my soul, Soul, you^{S} have many good
things laid up for many years, be resting, eat, drink, be
merry.
20 'And God said to him, Unthinking one! this night
they shall require your^{S} soul from you^{S}, and what things
you^{S} did prepare — to whom shall they be?
21 so [is] he who is treasuring up to himself, and is not
rich toward God.'
22 And He said unto His disciples, 'Because of this, I
say to you^{P}, Be not anxious for your^{P} life, what you^{P}
may eat; nor for the body, what you^{P} may put on;
23 the life is more than the nourishment, and the body
than the clothing.
24 'Consider the ravens, that they sow not, nor reap, to
which there is no barn nor storehouse, and God does
nourish them; how much better are you^{P} than the fowls?
25 and who of you^{P}, being anxious, is able to add to his
age one cubit?
26 If, then, you^{P} are not able for the least — why are
you^{P} anxious for the rest?
27 'Consider the lilies, how do they grow? they labor
not, nor do they spin, and I say to you^{P}, not even
Solomon in all his glory was arrayed as one of these;
28 and if the herbage in the field, that today is, and
tomorrow is cast into an oven, God does so clothe, how
much more you^{P} — you^{P} of little faith?
29 'And you^{P} — seek not what you^{P} may eat, or what
you^{P} may drink, and be not in suspense,
30 for the nations of the world do seek after all these
things, and your^{P} Father has known that you^{P} have need
of these things;
31 but, seek you^{P} the reign of God, and all these things
shall be added to you^{P}.
32 'Fear not, little flock, because your^{P} Father did delight
to give you^{P} the reign;
33 sell your^{P} goods, and give alms, make to yourselves^{P}
bags that become not old, a treasure unfailing in the
heavens, where thief does not come near, nor moth
destroy;
34 for where your^{P} treasure is, there also your heart^{P}
will be.
35 'Let your^{P} loins be girded, and the lamps burning,
36 and you^{P} like to men waiting for their lord, when he
shall return out of the wedding feasts, that he having
come and knocked, immediately they may open to him.
37 'Happy those servants, whom the lord, having come,
shall find watching; truly I say to you^{P}, that he will gird
himself, and will cause them to recline (at meat), and
having come near, will minister to them;
38 and if he may come in the second watch, and in the
third watch he may come, and may find [it] so, happy
are those servants.
39 'And this know, that if the master of the house had
known what hour the thief did come, he would have
watched, and would not have allowed his house to be
broken through;
40 and you^{P}, then, become you^{P} ready, because at the
hour you^{P} think not, the Son of Man does come.'
41 And Peter said to Him, 'Sir, do You^{S} speak this simile
unto us, or also unto all?'
42 And the Lord said, 'Who, then, is the faithful and
prudent steward whom the lord shall set over his
household, to give in season the wheat measure?
43 Happy that servant, whom his lord, having come,
shall find doing so;
44 truly I say to you^{P}, that he will set him over all his
goods.
45 'And if that servant may say in his heart, My lord
does delay to come, and may begin to beat the men-
servants and the maid-servants, to eat also, and to drink,
and to be drunken;

46 the lord of that servant will come in a day in which
he does not look for [him], and in an hour that he does
not know, and will cut him off, and he will appoint his
portion with the unfaithful.
47 'And that servant, who having known his lord's will,
and not having prepared, nor having gone according to
his will, shall be beaten with many stripes,
48 and he who, not having known, and having done
things worthy of stripes, shall be beaten with few; and
to every one to whom much was given, much shall be
required from him; and to whom they did commit much,
more abundantly they will ask of him.
49 ' I came to cast fire to the earth, and what will I if
already it was kindled?
50 but I have a baptism to be baptized with, and how am
I pressed till it may be completed!
51 ' You[P] think that I came to give peace in the earth?
no, I say to you[P], but rather division;
52 for there shall be from this time forth five in one house
divided — three against two, and two against three;
53 a father shall be divided against a son, and a son
against a father, a mother against a daughter, and a
daughter against a mother, a mother-in-law against her
daughter-in-law, and a daughter-in-law against her
mother-in-law.'
54 And He said also to the multitudes, 'When you[P] may
see the cloud rising from the west, immediately you[P] say,
A shower does come, and it is so;
55 and when — a south wind blowing, you[P] say, that
there will be heat, and it is;
56 hypocrites! you[P] have known the face of the earth
and of the heaven to make proof of, but this time — how
do you[P] not make proof of [it]?
57 'And why, also, of yourselves[P], you[P] judge not what
is righteous?
58 for, as you[S] are going away with your[S] opponent to
the ruler, in the way give diligence to be released from
him, for fear that he may drag you[S] unto the judge, and
the judge may deliver you[S] to the officer, and the officer
may cast you[S] into prison;
59 I say to you[S], you[S] may not come forth from there till
you[S] may give back even the last mite.'

CHAPTER 13

1 And there were present certain at that time, telling
Him about the Galileans, whose blood Pilate did mingle
with their sacrifices;
2 and Jesus answering said to them, 'You[P] think that
these Galileans became sinners beyond all the Galileans,
because they have suffered such things?
3 No — I say to you[P], but, if you[P] may not reform, even
all you[P] so shall perish.
4 'Or those eighteen, on whom the tower in Siloam fell,
and killed them; you[P] think that these became debtors
beyond all men who are dwelling in Jerusalem?
5 No — I say to you[P], but, if you[P] may not reform, all
you[P] shall perish in like manner.'
6 And He spoke this simile: 'A certain one had a fig-tree
planted in his vineyard, and he came seeking fruit in it,
and he did not find;
7 and he said unto the vine-dresser, Behold, three years
I come seeking fruit in this fig-tree, and do not find, cut
it off, why also the ground does it render useless?
8 'And he answering said to him, Sir, allow it also this
year, till that I may dig about it, and cast in dung;
9 and if indeed it may bear fruit —; and if not so,
thereafter you[S] shall cut it off.'
10 And He was teaching in one of the synagogues on
the Sabbath,
11 and behold, there was a woman having a spirit of
infirmity eighteen years, and she was bowed together,
and not able to bend back at all,
12 and Jesus having seen her, did call [her] near, and
said to her, 'Woman, you[S] have been loosed from your[S]
infirmity;'
13 and He laid [His] hands on her, and presently she
was set upright, and was glorifying God.
14 And the chief of the synagogue answering — much
displeased that Jesus healed on the Sabbath — said to
the multitude, 'Six days there are in which it is necessary
for [us] to be working; in these, then, coming, be healed,
and not on the Sabbath-day.'
15 Then the Lord answered him and said, 'Hypocrite,
do not each of you[P] loose his ox or ass from the stall on
the Sabbath, and having led away, does water [it]?
16 and this one, being a daughter of Abraham, whom
the Adversary bound, behold, eighteen years, was it not
necessary to be loosed from this bond on the Sabbath-
day?'
17 And He saying these things, all who were opposed
to Him were being ashamed, and all the multitude were
rejoicing over all the glorious things that are being done
by Him.
18 And He said, 'To what is the reign of God like? and
to what shall I liken it?
19 It is like to a grain of mustard, which a man having

taken, did cast into his garden, and it increased, and came to a great tree, and the fowls of the heavens did rest in its branches.'
20 And again He said, 'To what shall I liken the reign of God?
21 It is like leaven, which a woman, having taken, did hide in three measures of meal, till that all was leavened.'
22 And He was going through cities and villages, teaching, and making progress toward Jerusalem;
23 and a certain one said to Him, 'Sir, are those saved few?' and He said unto them,
24 'Be striving to go in through the straight gate, because many, I say to you[P], will seek to go in, and shall not be able;
25 from the time the master of the house may have risen up, and may have shut the door, and you[P] may begin to stand without, and to knock at the door, saying, Lord, lord, open to us, and he answering shall say to you[P], I have not known you[P] from where you are,
26 then you[P] may begin to say, We did eat before you[S], and did drink, and you[S] did teach in our broad places ;
27 and he shall say, I say to you[P], I have not known you[P] from where you[P] are; depart from me, all you[P] workers of the unrighteousness.
28 'There shall be there the weeping and the gnashing of the teeth, when you[P] may see Abraham, and Isaac, and Jacob, and all the prophets, in the reign of God, and yourselves being cast out without;
29 and they shall come from east and west, and from north and south, and shall recline in the reign of God,
30 and behold, there are last who shall be first, and there are first who shall be last.'
31 On that day there came near certain Pharisees, saying to Him, 'Go forth, and be going on from here, for Herod does wish to kill You[S];'
32 and He said to them, 'Having gone, say to this fox, Behold, I cast forth demons, and perfect cures today and tomorrow, and the third [day] I am being perfected;
33 but it is necessary for me today, and tomorrow, and the [day] following, to go on, because it is not possible for a prophet to perish out of Jerusalem.
34 'Jerusalem, Jerusalem, that is killing the prophets, and stoning those sent unto her, how often did I will to gather together your[S] children, as a hen her brood under the wings, and you[P] did not will.
35 'Behold, your[P] house is being left to you[P] desolate, and truly I say to you[P] — you[P] may not see Me, till it may come, when you[P] may say, Blessed [is] He who is coming in the name of the Lord.'

CHAPTER 14

1 And it came to pass, on His going into the house of a certain one of the chiefs of the Pharisees, on a Sabbath, to eat bread, that they were watching Him,
2 and behold, there was a certain dropsical man before Him;
3 and Jesus answering spoke to the lawyers and Pharisees, saying, 'Is it lawful to heal on the Sabbath-day?'
4 and they were silent, and having taken hold of [him], He healed him, and let [him] go;
5 and answering them He said, 'Of which of you[P] shall an ass or ox fall into a pit, and he will not immediately draw it up on the Sabbath-day?'
6 and they were not able to answer Him again unto these things.
7 And He spoke a simile unto those called, marking how they were choosing out the first couches, saying unto them,
8 'When you[S] may be called by any one to marriage-feasts, you[S] may not recline on the first couch, for fear that a more honorable than you[S] may have been called by him,
9 and he who did call you[S] and him having come shall say to you[S], Give to this one place, and then you[S] may begin with shame to occupy the last place.
10 'But, when you[S] may be called, having gone on, recline in the last place, that when he who called you[S] may come, he may say to you[S], Friend, come up higher; then you[S] shall have glory before those reclining with you[S];
11 because every one who is exalting himself shall be humbled, and he who is humbling himself shall be exalted.'
12 And He said also to him who did call Him, 'When you[S] may make a dinner or a supper, be not calling your[S] friends, nor your[S] brethren, nor your[S] kindred, nor rich neighbors, that they may also call you[S] again, and a recompense may come to you[S];
13 but when you[S] may make a feast, be calling poor, maimed, lame, blind,
14 and happy you[S] shall be, because they have not to recompense you[S], for it shall be recompensed to you[S] in the rising again of the righteous.'
15 And one of those reclining with Him, having heard these things, said to Him, 'Happy [is] he who shall eat bread in the reign of God;'

16 and He said to him, 'A certain man made a great supper, and called many,

17 and he sent his servant at the hour of the supper to say to those having been called, Be coming, because now are all things ready.

18 'And they began with one consent all to excuse themselves: The first said to him, A field I bought, and I have need to go forth and see it; I beg of you[S], have me excused.

19 'And another said, Five yoke of oxen I bought, and I go on to prove them; I beg of you[S], have me excused:

20 and another said, A wife I married, and because of this I am not able to come.

21 'And that servant having come, told to his lord these things, then the master of the house, having been angry, said to his servant, Go forth quickly to the broad places and lanes of the city, and the poor, and maimed, and lame, and blind, bring in here.

22 'And the servant said, Sir, it has been done as you[S] did command, and still there is room.

23 'And the lord said unto the servant, Go forth to the ways and hedges, and constrain to come in, that my house may be filled;

24 for I say to you[S], that none of those men who have been called shall taste of my supper.'

25 And there were going on with Him great multitudes, and having turned, He said unto them,

26 'If any one does come unto me, and does not hate his own father, and mother, and wife, and children, and brothers, and sisters, and yet even his own life, he is not able to be My disciple;

27 and whoever does not bear his cross, and come after Me, is not able to be My disciple.

28 'For who of you[P], willing to build a tower, does not first, having sat down, count the expense, whether he have the things for completing?

29 for fear that he having laid a foundation, and not being able to finish, all who are beholding may begin to mock him,

30 saying — This man began to build, and was not able to finish.

31 'Or what king going on to engage with another king in war, does not, having sat down, first consult if he be able with ten thousand to meet him who is coming against him with twenty thousand?

32 and if not so — he being yet a long way off — having sent an embassy, he does ask the things for peace.

33 'So, then, every one of you[P] who does not take leave of all that he himself has, is not able to be My disciple.

34 'The salt [is] good, but if the salt does become tasteless, with what shall it be seasoned?

35 neither is it fit for land nor for manure — they cast it without. He who is having ears to hear — let him hear.'

CHAPTER 15

1 And all the tax-gatherers and the sinners were coming near to Him, to hear Him,

2 and the Pharisees and the scribes were murmuring, saying — This one does receive sinners, and does eat with them.'

3 And He spoke unto them this simile, saying,

4 'What man of you[P] having a hundred sheep, and having lost one out of them, does not leave behind the ninety-nine in the wilderness, and go on after the lost one, till he may find it?

5 and having found, he does lay [it] on his shoulders rejoicing,

6 and having come to the house, he does call together the friends and the neighbors, saying to them, Rejoice with me, because I found my sheep — the lost one.

7 'I say to you[P], that so joy shall be in the heaven over one sinner reforming, rather than over ninety-nine righteous men, who have no need of reformation.

8 'Or what woman having ten drachms, if she may lose one drachm, does not light a lamp, and sweep the house, and seek carefully till that she may find?

9 and having found, she does call together the female friends and the neighbors, saying, Rejoice with me, for I found the drachm that I lost.

10 'So I say to you[P], joy does come before the messengers of God over one sinner reforming.'

11 And He said, 'A certain man had two sons,

12 and the younger of them said to the father, Father, give me the portion of the substance falling to [me], and he divided to them the living.

13 'And not many days after, having gathered all together, the younger son went abroad to a far country, and there he scattered his substance, living riotously;

14 and he having spent all, there came a mighty famine on that country, and himself began to be in want;

15 and having gone on, he joined himself to one of the citizens of that country, and he sent him to the fields to feed swine,

16 and he was desirous to fill his belly from the husks that the swine were eating, and no one was giving to him.

17 'And having come to himself, he said, How many
hirelings of my father have a superabundance of bread,
and I am here perishing with hunger!
18 having risen, I will go on unto my father, and will say
to him, Father, I did sin — to the heaven, and before
you[S],
19 and no more am I worthy to be called your[S] son;
make me as one of your[S] hirelings.
20 'And having risen, he went unto his own father, and
he being yet far distant, his father saw him, and was
moved with compassion, and having ran he fell upon
his neck and kissed him;
21 and the son said to him, Father, I did sin — to the
heaven, and before you[S], and no more am I worthy to be
called your[S] son.
22 'And the father said unto his servants, Bring forth
the first robe, and clothe him, and give a ring for his
hand, and sandals for the feet;
23 and having brought the fatted calf, kill [it], and having
eaten, we may be merry,
24 because this my son was dead, and did live again,
and he was lost, and was found; and they began to be
merry.
25 'And his elder son was in a field, and as, coming, he
drew near to the house, he heard music and dancing,
26 and having called near one of the young men, he
was inquiring what these things might be,
27 and he said to him — Your[S] brother is arrived, and
your[S] father did kill the fatted calf, because he did receive
him back in health.
28 'And he was angry, and would not go in, therefore
his father, having come forth, was entreating him;
29 and he answering said to the father, Behold, so many
years I do serve you[S], and never did I transgress your[S]
command, and you[S] did never give a kid to me, that I
might make merry with my friends;
30 but when your[S] son — this one who did devour your[S]
living with harlots — came, you[S] did kill to him the fatted
calf.
31 'And he said to him, Child, you[S] are always with me,
and all my things are yours[S];
32 but to be merry, and to be glad, it was needful,
because this your[S] brother was dead, and did live again,
he was lost, and was found.'

CHAPTER 16

1 And He said also unto his His disciples, 'A certain
man was rich, who had a steward, and he was accused
to him as scattering his goods;
2 and having called him, he said to him, What [is] this I
hear about you[S]? render the account of your[S]
stewardship, for you[S] may not be steward any longer.
3 'And the steward said in himself, What shall I do,
because my lord does take away the stewardship from
me? I am not able to dig, I am ashamed to beg: —
4 I have known what I shall do, that, when I may be
removed from the stewardship, they may receive me to
their houses.
5 'And having called near each one of his lord's debtors,
he said to the first, How much do you[S] owe to my lord?
6 and he said, A hundred baths of oil; and he said to
him, Take your[S] bill, and having sat down write fifty.
7 'Afterward to another he said, And you[S], how much
do you[S] owe? and he said, A hundred cors of wheat;
and he said to him, Take your[S] bill, and write eighty.
8 'And the lord commended the unrighteous steward
that he did prudently, because the sons of this age are
more prudent than the sons of the light, in respect to
their generation.
9 and I say to you[P], Make friends to yourselves[P] out of
the mammon of unrighteousness, that when you[P] may
fail, they may receive you[P] to the age-during tabernacles.
10 'He who is faithful in the least, [is] also faithful in
much; and he who in the least [is] unrighteous, is also
unrighteous in much;
11 if, then, you[P] became not faithful in the unrighteous
mammon — who will entrust the true to you[P]?
12 and if you[P] became not faithful in the other's —,
who shall give to you[P] your[P] own?
13 'No domestic is able to serve two lords, for either he
will hate the one, and he will love the other; or he will
hold to one, and he will be heedless of the other; you[P]
are not able to serve God and mammon.'
14 And also the Pharisees, being lovers of money, were
hearing all these things, and were deriding Him,
15 and He said to them, 'You[P] are those declaring
yourselves[P] righteous before men, but God does know
your[P] hearts; because that which is high among men,
[is] abomination before God;
16 the law and the prophets [are] till John; since then
the reign of God is proclaimed good news, and every
one does press into it;
17 and it is easier to the heaven and the earth to pass
away, than one tittle of the law to fall.
18 'Every one who is sending away his wife, and
marrying another, does commit adultery; and every one

who is marrying her sent away from a husband does
commit adultery.
19 'And — a certain man was rich, and was clothed in
purple and fine linen, making merry sumptuously every
day,
20 and there was a certain poor man, by name Lazarus,
who was laid at his porch, full of sores,
21 and desiring to be filled from the crumbs that are
falling from the table of the rich man; yes, also the dogs,
coming, were licking his sores.
22 'And it came to pass, that the poor man died, and
that he was carried away by the messengers to the
bosom of Abraham — and the rich man also died, and
was buried;
23 and in the hades having lifted up his eyes, being in
torments, he did see Abraham afar off, and Lazarus in
his bosom,
24 and having cried, he said, Father Abraham, deal kindly
with me, and send Lazarus, that he may dip the tip of his
finger in water, and may cool my tongue, because I am
distressed in this flame.
25 'And Abraham said, Child, remember that you^{S} did
receive — you^{S} — your^{S} good things in your^{S} life, and
Lazarus in like manner the evil things, and now he is
comforted, and you^{S} are distressed;
26 and besides all these things, a great chasm is fixed
between us and you^{S}, so that they who are willing to go
over unto you^{S} from here are not able, nor do they pass
from there through to us.
27 'And he said, I pray you^{S}, then, father, that you^{S} may
send him to the house of my father,
28 for I have five brothers, so that he may thoroughly
testify to them, that they also may not come to this place
of torment.
29 'Abraham said to him, They have Moses and the
prophets, let them hear them;
30 and he said, No, father Abraham, but if any one from
the dead may go unto them, they will reform.
31 And he said to him, If they do not hear Moses and
the prophets, neither will they be persuaded if one may
rise out of the dead.'

CHAPTER 17

1 And He said unto the disciples, 'It is impossible for
the stumbling blocks not to come, but woe [to him]
through whom they come;
2 it is more profitable to him if a weighty millstone is put
round about his neck, and he had been cast into the
sea, than that he may cause one of these little ones to
stumble.
3 'Take heed to yourselves^{P}, and, if your^{S} brother may
sin in regard to you^{S}, rebuke him, and if he may reform,
forgive him,
4 and if seven times in the day he may sin against you^{S},
and seven times in the day may turn back to you^{S}, saying,
I reform; you^{S} shall forgive him.'
5 And the apostles said to the Lord, 'Add faith to us;'
6 and the Lord said, 'If you^{P} had faith as a grain of
mustard, you^{P} would have said to this sycamine, Be
uprooted, and be planted in the sea, and it would have
obeyed you^{P}.
7 'But, who is he of you^{P} — having a servant plowing
or feeding — who, to him having come in out of the field,
will say, Having come near, recline at meat?
8 but will not [rather] say to him, Prepare what I may
sup, and having girded yourself^{S} about, minister to me,
till I eat and drink, and you^{S} shall eat and drink after these
things?
9 Has he favor to that servant because he did the things
directed? I think not.
10 'So also you^{P}, when you^{P} may have done all the things
directed you^{P}, say — We are unprofitable servants,
because that which we owed to do — we have done.'
11 And it came to pass, in His going on to Jerusalem,
that He passed through the midst of Samaria and Galilee,
12 and He entering into a certain village, there met Him
ten leprous men, who stood afar off,
13 and they lifted up the voice, saying, 'Jesus, master,
deal kindly with us;'
14 and having seen [them], He said to them, 'Having
gone on, show yourselves^{P} to the priests;' and it came
to pass, in their going, they were cleansed,
15 and one of them having seen that he was healed did
turn back, with a loud voice glorifying God,
16 and he fell upon [his] face at His feet, giving thanks
to Him, and he was a Samaritan.
17 And Jesus answering said, 'Were not the ten
cleansed, and the nine — where?
18 There were not found who did turn back to give glory
to God, except this alien;'
19 and He said to him, 'Having risen, be going on, your^{S}
faith has saved you^{S}.'
20 And having been questioned by the Pharisees, when
the reign of God does come, He answered them, and said,
'The reign of God does not come with observation;
21 nor shall they say, Behold, here; or behold, there; for

behold, the reign of God is within you[P].'
22 And He said unto His disciples, 'Days will come, when you[P] shall desire to see one of the days of the Son of Man, and you[P] shall not behold [it];
23 and they shall say to you[P], Behold, here; or behold, there; you[P] may not go away, nor follow;
24 for as the lightning that is lightening out of the one [part] under heaven, to the other part under heaven does shine, so shall be also the Son of Man in his day;
25 and first it is necessary for Him to suffer many things, and to be rejected by this generation.
26 'And, as it came to pass in the days of Noah, so shall it be also in the days of the Son of Man;
27 they were eating, they were drinking, they were marrying, they were given in marriage, till the day that Noah entered into the ark, and the deluge came, and destroyed all;
28 in like manner also, as it came to pass in the days of Lot; they were eating, they were drinking, they were buying, they were selling, they were planting, they were building;
29 and on the day Lot went forth from Sodom, He rained fire and brimstone from heaven, and destroyed all.
30 'According to these things it shall be, in the day the Son of Man is revealed;
31 in that day, he who shall be on the house top, and his vessels in the house, let him not come down to take them away; and he in the field, in like manner, let him not turn backward;
32 remember the wife of Lot.
33 Whoever may seek to save his life, shall lose it; and whoever may lose it, shall preserve it.
34 'I say to you[P], In that night, there shall be two men on one couch, the one shall be taken, and the other shall be left;
35 two women shall be grinding at the same place together, the one shall be taken, and the other shall be left;
36 two men shall be in the field, the one shall be taken, and the other left.'
37 And they answering say to Him, 'Where, sir?' and He said to them, 'Where the body [is], there will the eagles be gathered together.'

CHAPTER 18

1 And He spoke also a simile to them, that it is necessary for [us] always to pray, and not to faint,
2 saying, 'A certain judge was in a certain city — he is not God fearing, and he is not regarding man —
3 and a widow was in that city, and she was coming unto him, saying, Do me justice on my opponent,
4 and he would not for a time, but after these things he said in himself, Even if I do not fear God, and do not regard man,
5 yet because this widow does give me trouble, I will do her justice, for fear that, perpetually coming, she may plague me.'
6 And the Lord said, 'Hear you[P] what the unrighteous judge said:
7 and shall not God execute the justice to His choice ones, who are crying unto Him day and night — bearing long in regard to them?
8 I say to you[P], that He will execute the justice to them quickly; but the Son of Man having come, shall he find the faith upon the earth?'
9 And He spoke also unto certain who have been trusting in themselves that they were righteous, and have been despising the rest, this simile:
10 'Two men went up to the temple to pray, the one a Pharisee, and the other a tax-gatherer;
11 the Pharisee having stood by himself, thus prayed: God, I thank You[S] that I am not as the rest of men, rapacious, unrighteous, adulterers, or even as this tax-gatherer;
12 I fast twice in the week, I give tithes of all things — as many as I possess.
13 'And the tax-gatherer, having stood afar off, would not even the eyes lift up to the heaven, but was striking on his breast, saying, God be propitious to me — the sinner!
14 I say to you[P], this one went down declared righteous, to his house, rather than that one: for every one who is exalting himself shall be humbled, and he who is humbling himself shall be exalted.'
15 And they were bringing near also the babes, that He may touch them, and the disciples having seen did rebuke them,
16 and Jesus having called them near, said, 'Allow the little children to come unto Me, and forbid them not, for of such is the reign of God;
17 truly I say to you[P], Whoever may not receive the reign of God as a little child, may not enter into it.'
18 And a certain ruler questioned Him, saying, 'Good teacher, what having done — shall I inherit life age-during?'
19 And Jesus said to him, 'Why do you[S] call me good?

no one [is] good, except One — God;

20 the commands you[S] have known: You[S] may not commit adultery, You[S] may do no murder, You[S] may not steal, You[S] may not bear false witness, Honor your[S] father and your[S] mother.'

21 And he said, 'All these I did keep from my youth;'

22 and having heard these things, Jesus said to him, 'Yet one thing is lacking to you[S]; all things — as many as you[S] have — sell, and distribute to the poor, and you[S] shall have treasure in heaven, and come, be following me;'

23 and he, having heard these things, became very sorrowful, for he was exceeding rich.

24 And Jesus having seen him become very sorrowful, said, 'How hardly shall those having riches enter into the reign of God!

25 for it is easier for a camel to enter through the eye of a needle, than for a rich man to enter into the reign of God.'

26 And those who heard, said, 'And who is able to be saved?'

27 and He said, 'The things impossible with men are possible with God.'

28 And Peter said, 'Behold, we left all, and did follow You[S];'

29 and He said to them, 'Truly I say to you[P], that there is not one who left house, or parents, or brothers, or wife, or children, for the sake of the reign of God,

30 who may not receive back many more in this time, and in the coming age, life age-during.'

31 And having taken the twelve aside, He said unto them, 'Behold, we go up to Jerusalem, and all things shall be completed — that have been written through the prophets — to the Son of Man,

32 for He shall be delivered up to the nations, and shall be mocked, and insulted, and spit upon,

33 and having scourged they shall put Him to death, and on the third day He shall rise again.'

34 And they understood none of these things, and this saying was hid from them, and they were not knowing the things said.

35 And it came to pass, in His coming near to Jericho, a certain blind man was sitting beside the way begging,

36 and having heard a multitude going by, he was inquiring what this may be,

37 and they brought him word that Jesus the Nazarene did pass by,

38 and he cried out, saying, 'Jesus, Son of David, deal kindly with me;'

39 and those going before were rebuking him, that he might be silent, but he was much more crying out, 'Son of David, deal kindly with me.'

40 And Jesus having stood, commanded him to be brought unto Him, and he having come near, He questioned him,

41 saying, 'What will you[S] I shall do to you[S]?' and he said, 'Sir, that I may receive sight.'

42 And Jesus said to him, 'Receive your[S] sight; your[S] faith has saved you[S];'

43 and presently he did receive sight, and was following Him, glorifying God; and all the people, having seen, did give praise to God.

CHAPTER 19

1 And having entered, He was passing through Jericho,

2 and behold, a man, by name called Zaccheus, and he was a chief tax-gatherer, and he was rich,

3 and he was seeking to see Jesus, who He is, and was not able for the multitude, because he was small in stature,

4 and having run forward before, he went up on a sycamore, that he may see Him, because through that [way] He was about to pass by.

5 And as Jesus came up to the place, having looked up, He saw him, and said unto him, 'Zaccheus, having hurried, come down, for today it is necessary for Me to remain in your[S] house;'

6 and he having hurried did come down, and did receive Him rejoicing;

7 and having seen [it], they were all murmuring, saying — ' He went in to lodge with a sinful man!'

8 And Zaccheus having stood, said unto the Lord, 'Behold, the half of my goods, sir, I give to the poor, and if I did take anything by false accusation of any one, I give back fourfold.'

9 And Jesus said unto him — 'Today salvation did come to this house, inasmuch as he also is a son of Abraham;

10 for the Son of Man came to seek and to save the lost.'

11 And while they are hearing these things, having added He spoke a simile, because of His being near to Jerusalem, and of their thinking that the reign of God is about presently to be made known.

12 He said therefore, 'A certain man of birth went on to a far country, to take to himself a kingdom, and to return,

13 and having called ten servants of his own, he gave

to them ten pounds, and said unto them, Do business —till I come;

14 and his citizens were hating him, and did send an embassy after him, saying, We do not wish this one to reign over us.

15 'And it came to pass, on his coming back, having taken the kingdom, that he commanded these servants to be called to him, to whom he gave the money, that he might know what any one had done in business.

16 'And the first came near, saying, Sir, your[S] pound did gain ten pounds;

17 and he said to him, Well done, good servant, because you[S] did become faithful in a very little, be having authority over ten cities.

18 'And the second came, saying, Sir, Your[S] pound made five pounds;

19 and he said also to this one, And you[S], become you[S] over five cities.

20 'And another came, saying, Sir, behold, your[S] pound, that I had lying away in a napkin;

21 for I was afraid of you[S], because you[S] are a strict man; you[S] take up what you[S] did not lay down, and reap what you[S] did not sow.

22 'And he said to him, Out of your[S] mouth I will judge you[S], evil servant: you[S] knew that I am a strict man, taking up what I did not lay down, and reaping what I did not sow!

23 and why did you[S] not give my money to the bank, and I, having come, might have received it with interest?

24 'And to those standing by he said, Take the pound from him, and give to him having the ten pounds —

25 (and they said to him, Sir, he has ten pounds) —

26 for I say to you[P], that to every one having shall be given, and from him not having, also what he has shall be taken from him,

27 but those my enemies, who did not wish me to reign over them, bring here and slay before me.'

28 And having said these things, He went on before, going up to Jerusalem.

29 And it came to pass, as He came near to Bethphage and Bethany, unto the mount called of the Olives, He sent two of His disciples,

30 having said, Go away to the village over-against, in which, entering into, you[P] shall find a colt bound, on which no one of men did ever sit, having loosed it, bring [it];

31 and if any one does question you[P], Why do you[P] loose [it]? thus you[P] shall say to him — The Lord has need of it.'

32 And those sent, having gone away, found according as He said to them,

33 and while they are loosing the colt, its owners said unto them, 'Why loose you[P] the colt?'

34 and they said, 'The Lord has need of it;'

35 and they brought it unto Jesus, and having cast their garments upon the colt, they did set Jesus upon it.

36 And as He is going, they were spreading their garments in the way,

37 and as He is coming near now, at the descent of the mount of the Olives, the whole multitude of the disciples began rejoicing to praise God with a great voice for all the mighty works they had seen,

38 saying, 'blessed [is] He who is coming, a king in the name of the Lord; peace in heaven, and glory in the highest.'

39 And certain of the Pharisees from the multitude said unto Him, 'Teacher, rebuke Your[S] disciples;'

40 and He answering said to them, 'I say to you[P], that, if these shall be silent, the stones will cry out!'

41 And when He came near, having seen the city, He wept over it,

42 saying — 'If you[S] did know, even you[S], at least in this your[S] day, the things for your[S] peace; but now they were hid from your[S] eyes.

43 'Because days shall come upon you[S], and your[S] enemies shall cast a rampart around you[S], and compass you[S] round, and press you[S] on every side,

44 and lay you[S] low, and your[S] children within you[S], and they shall not leave in you[S] a stone upon a stone, because you[S] did not know the time of your[S] inspection.'

45 And having entered into the temple, He began to cast forth those selling in it, and those buying,

46 saying to them, 'It has been written, My house is a house of prayer — but you[P] made it a den of robbers.'

47 And He was teaching daily in the temple, but the chief priests and the scribes were seeking to destroy Him — also the chiefs of the people —

48 and they were not finding what they shall do, for all the people were hanging on Him, hearing Him.

CHAPTER 20

1 And it came to pass, on one of those days, as He is teaching the people in the temple, and proclaiming good news, the chief priests and the scribes, with the elders, came upon [Him],

2 and spoke unto Him, saying, 'Tell us by what authority

You[S] do these things? or who is he that gave to You[S] this authority?'
3 And He answering said unto them, 'I will question you[P] — I also — one thing, and tell me:
4 the baptism of John, from heaven was it, or from men?'
5 And they reasoned with themselves, saying — 'If we may say, From heaven, He will say, Why, then, did you[P] not believe him?
6 and if we may say, From men, all the people will stone us, for they are having been persuaded John to be a prophet.'
7 And they answered, that they knew not from where [it was],
8 and Jesus said to them, 'Neither do I say to you[P] by what authority I do these things.'
9 And He began to speak unto the people this simile: 'A certain man planted a vineyard, and gave it out to husbandmen, and went abroad for a long time,
10 and at the season he sent unto the husbandmen a servant, that they may give to him from the fruit of the vineyard, but the husbandmen having beat him, did send [him] away empty.
11 'And he added to send another servant, and they having beaten and dishonored that one also, did send away empty;
12 and he added to send a third, and this one also, having wounded, they did cast out.
13 'And the owner of the vineyard said, What shall I do? I will send my son — the beloved, perhaps having seen this one, they will do reverence;
14 and having seen him, the husbandmen reasoned among themselves, saying, This is the heir; come, we may kill him, that the inheritance may become ours;
15 and having cast him outside of the vineyard, they killed [him]; what, then, shall the owner of the vineyard do to them?
16 He will come, and destroy these husbandmen, and will give the vineyard to others.' And having heard, they said, 'Let it not be!'
17 and He, having looked upon them, said, 'What, then, is this that has been written: A stone that the builders rejected — this became head of a corner?
18 every one who has fallen on that stone shall be broken, and on whom it may fall, it will crush him to pieces.'
19 And the chief priests and the scribes sought to lay hands on Him in that hour, and they feared the people, for they knew that He spoke this simile against them.
20 And, having watched [Him], they sent forth liers in wait, feigning themselves to be righteous, that they might take hold of His word, to deliver Him up to the rule and to the authority of the governor,
21 and they questioned Him, saying, 'Teacher, we have known that You[S] do say and teach rightly, and do not accept a person, but in truth do teach the way of God;
22 Is it lawful to us to give tribute to Caesar or not?'
23 And He, having perceived their craftiness, said unto them, 'Why do you[P] tempt Me?
24 show Me a denary; it has an image and superscription of whom?' and they answering said, 'Of Caesar:'
25 and He said to them, 'Give back, for that reason, the things of Caesar to Caesar, and the things of God to God;'
26 and they were not able to take hold on His saying before the people, and having wondered at His answer, they were silent.
27 And certain of the Sadducees, who are denying that there is a rising again, having come near, questioned Him,
28 saying, 'Teacher, Moses wrote to us, If any one's brother may die, having a wife, and he may die childless — that his brother may take the wife, and may raise up seed to his brother.
29 'There were, then, seven brothers, and the first having taken a wife, died childless,
30 and the second took the wife, and he died childless,
31 and the third took her, and in like manner also the seven — they left not children, and they died;
32 and last of all died also the woman:
33 in the rising again, then, of which of them does she become wife? — for the seven had her as wife.'
34 And Jesus answering said to them, 'The sons of this age do marry and are given in marriage,
35 but those accounted worthy to obtain that age, and the rising again that is out of the dead, neither marry, nor are they given in marriage;
36 for neither are they able to die any more — for they are like messengers — and they are sons of God, being sons of the rising again.
37 'And that the dead are raised, even Moses showed at the Bush, since he did call the Lord, the God of Abraham, and the God of Isaac, and the God of Jacob;
38 and He is not a God of dead men, but of living, for all live to Him.'
39 And certain of the scribes answering said, 'Teacher, You[S] did say well;'
40 and no more dare they question Him anything.
41 And He said unto them, 'How do they say the Christ to be son of David,

42 and David himself said in the Book of Psalms, The
Lord said to my lord, Sit you[S] on my right hand,
43 till I shall make your[S] enemies your[S] footstool;
44 David, then, does call him lord, and how is he his
son?'
45 And, all the people hearing, He said to His disciples,
46 'Take heed of the scribes, who are wishing to walk in
long robes, and are loving salutations in the markets,
and first seats in the synagogues, and first couches in
the suppers,
47 who devour the houses of the widows, and for a
pretense make long prayers, these shall receive more
abundant judgment.'

CHAPTER 21

1 And having looked up, He saw those who did cast
their gifts to the treasury — rich men,
2 and He saw also a certain poor widow casting there
two mites,
3 and He said, 'Truly I say to you[P], that this poor widow
did cast in more than all;
4 for all these out of their superabundance did cast into
the gifts to God, but this one out of her want, all the
living that she had, did cast in.'
5 And certain saying about the temple, that with goodly
stones and devoted things it has been adorned, He said,
6 'These things that you behold — days will come, in
which there shall not be left a stone upon a stone, that
shall not be thrown down.'
7 And they questioned Him, saying, 'Teacher, when,
then, shall these things be? and what [is] the sign when
these things may be about to happen?'
8 And He said, 'See — you[P] may not be led astray, for
many shall come in My name, saying — I am [He], and
the time has come near; go not on after them then;
9 and when you[P] may hear of wars and uprisings, be
not terrified, for it is necessary for these things to happen
first, but the end [is] not immediately.'
10 Then said He to them, 'Nation shall rise against
nation, and kingdom against kingdom,
11 great shakings also in every place, and famines, and
pestilences, there shall be; fearful things also, and there
shall be great signs from heaven;
12 and before all these, they shall lay their hands on
you[P], and persecute, delivering up to synagogues and
prisons, being brought before kings and governors for
My name's sake;
13 and it shall become to you[P] for a testimony.
14 'Settle, then, to your[P] hearts, not to meditate
beforehand to reply,
15 for I will give to you[P] a mouth and wisdom that all
your[P] opposers shall not be able to refute or resist.
16 'And you[P] shall be delivered up also by parents, and
brothers, and kindred, and friends, and they shall put of
you[P] to death;
17 and you[P] shall be hated by all because of My name —
18 and a hair out of your[P] head shall not perish;
19 in your[P] patience you[P] possess your[P] souls.
20 'And when you[P] may see Jerusalem surrounded by
encampments, then know that her desolation did come
near;
21 then those in Judea, let them flee to the mountains;
and those in her midst, let them depart out; and those in
the countries, let them not come in to her;
22 because these are days of vengeance, to fulfil all
things that have been written.
23 'And woe to those with child, and to those giving
suck, in those days; for there shall be great distress on
the land, and wrath on this people;
24 and they shall fall by the mouth of the sword, and
shall be led captive to all the nations, and Jerusalem shall
be trodden down by nations, till the times of nations be
fulfilled.
25 'And there shall be signs in sun, and moon, and stars,
and on the land [is] distress of nations with perplexity,
sea and billow roaring;
26 men fainting at heart from fear, and expectation of
the things coming on the world, for the powers of the
heavens shall be shaken.
27 'And then they shall see the Son of Man, coming in
a cloud, with power and much glory;
28 and these things beginning to happen bend
yourselves[P] back, and lift up your[P] heads, because your[P]
redemption does draw near.'
29 And He spoke a simile to them: 'See the fig-tree, and
all the trees,
30 when they may now cast forth, having seen, of
yourselves[P] you[P] know that now is the summer near;
31 so also you[P], when you[P] may see these things
happening, you[P] know that the reign of God is near;
32 truly I say to you[P] — This generation may not pass
away till all may have come to pass;
33 the heaven and the earth shall pass away, but My
words may not pass away.
34 'And take heed to yourselves[P], for fear that your[P]
hearts may be weighed down with surfeiting, and

drunkenness, and anxieties of life, and suddenly that day
may come on you[P],
35 for as a snare it shall come on all those dwelling on
the face of all the land,
36 watch you[P], then, in every season, praying that you[P]
may be accounted worthy to escape all these things that
are about to come to pass, and to stand before the Son
of Man.'
37 And He was during the days in the temple teaching,
and during the nights, going forth, He was lodging at
the mount called of Olives;
38 and all the people were coming early unto Him to
hear Him in the temple.

CHAPTER 22

1 And the feast of the unleavened food was coming
near, that is called Passover,
2 and the chief priests and the scribes were seeking
how they may take Him up, for they were afraid of the
people.
3 And the Adversary entered into Judas, who is
surnamed Iscariot, being of the number of the twelve,
4 and he, having gone away, spoke with the chief priests
and the magistrates, how he might deliver Him up to them,
5 and they rejoiced, and covenanted to give him money,
6 and he agreed, and was seeking a favorable season to
deliver Him up to them without tumult.
7 And the day of the unleavened food came, in which it
was necessary for the Passover to be sacrificed,
8 and He sent Peter and John, saying, 'Having gone
on, prepare to us the Passover, that we may eat;'
9 and they said to Him, 'Where will You[S] that we might
prepare?'
10 And He said to them, 'Behold, in your[P] entering into
the city, there shall meet you[P] a man, bearing a pitcher
of water, follow him to the house where he does go in,
11 and you[P] shall say to the master of the house, The
Teacher said to you[P], Where is the guest-chamber where
the Passover I may eat with My disciples?
12 and he shall show you[P] a large upper room furnished,
there make ready;'
13 and they, having gone away, found as He had said
to them, and they made ready the Passover.
14 And when the hour come, He reclined (at meat), and
the twelve apostles with Him,
15 and He said unto them, 'With desire I did desire to
eat this Passover with you[P] before My suffering,
16 for I say to you[P], that no more may I eat of it till it may
be fulfilled in the reign of God.'
17 And having taken a cup, having given thanks, He
said, 'Take this and divide to yourselves[P],
18 for I say to you[P] that I may not drink of the produce
of the vine till the reign of God may come.'
19 And having taken bread, having given thanks, He broke
and gave to them, saying, 'This is My body, that is being
given for you[P], this do you[P] — to remembrance of Me.'
20 In like manner, also, the cup after the supping, saying,
'This cup [is] the new covenant in My blood, that is
being poured forth for you[P].
21 'But, behold, the hand of him delivering Me up [is]
with Me on the table,
22 and indeed the Son of Man does go according to
what has been determined; but woe to that man through
whom He is being delivered up.'
23 And they began to reason among themselves, who
then of them it may be, who is about to do this thing.
24 And there happened also a strife among them — who
of them is accounted to be greater.
25 And He said to them, 'The kings of the nations do
exercise lordship over them, and those exercising
authority upon them are called benefactors;
26 but you[P] [are] not so, but he who is greater among
you[P] — let him be as the younger; and he who is leading,
as he who is ministering;
27 for who is greater? he who is reclining (at meat), or
he who is ministering? is it not he who is reclining (at
meat)? and I — I am in your[P] midst as He who is
ministering.
28 'And you[P] — you[P] are those who have remained
with Me in My temptations,
29 and I appoint to you[P], as My Father did appoint to
Me, a kingdom,
30 that you[P] may eat and may drink at My table, in My
kingdom, and may sit on thrones, judging the twelve
tribes of Israel.'
31 And the Lord said, 'Simon, Simon, behold, the
Adversary did ask you[S] for himself to sift as the wheat,
32 and I begged for you[S], that your[S] faith may not fail;
and you[S], when you[S] did turn, strengthen your[S] brethren.'
33 And he said to Him, 'Sir, I am ready both to go to
prison and to death with You[S];'
34 and He said, 'I say to you[S], Peter, a cock shall not crow
today, before you[S] may disown knowing Me three times.'
35 And He said to them, 'When I sent you[P] without
bag, and scrip, and sandals, did you[P] lack anything?'
and they said, 'Nothing.'

36 Then said He to them, 'But, now, he who is having a bag, let him take [it] up, and in like manner also a scrip; and he who is not having, let him sell his garment, and buy a sword,
37 for I say to you[P], that yet this that has been written it is necessary to be fulfilled in Me: And with lawless ones He was reckoned, for also the things concerning Me have an end.'
38 And they said, 'Sir, behold, here [are] two swords;' and He said to them, 'It is sufficient.'
39 And having gone forth, He went on, according to custom, to the mount of the Olives, and His disciples also followed Him,
40 and having come to the place, He said to them, 'Pray you[P] not to enter into temptation.'
41 And He was withdrawn from them, as it were a stone's cast, and having fallen on the knees He was praying,
42 saying, 'Father, if You[S] be counseling to make this cup pass from Me —; but, not My will, but Yours[S] be done.' —
43 And there appeared to Him a messenger from heaven strengthening Him;
44 and having been in agony, He was more earnestly praying, and His sweat became, as it were, great drops of blood falling upon the ground.
45 And having risen up from the prayer, having come unto the disciples, He found them sleeping from the sorrow,
46 and He said to them, 'Why do you[P] sleep? having risen, pray that you[P] may not enter into temptation.'
47 And while He is speaking, behold, a multitude, and he who is called Judas, one of the twelve, was coming before them, and he came near to Jesus to kiss Him,
48 and Jesus said to him, 'Judas, you[S] do deliver up the Son of Man with a kiss?'
49 And those about Him, having seen what was about to be, said to Him, 'Sir, shall we strike with a sword?'
50 And a certain one of them struck the servant of the chief priest, and took off his right ear,
51 and Jesus answering said, 'Allow you[P] thus far,' and having touched his ear, He healed him.
52 And Jesus said to those having come upon Him — chief priests, and magistrates of the temple, and elders — 'You[P] have come forth as upon a robber, with swords and sticks?
53 while I was with you[P] in the temple daily, you[P] did stretch forth no hands against Me; but this is your[P] hour and the power of the darkness.'
54 And having taken Him, they led and brought Him to the house of the chief priest. And Peter was following afar off,
55 and they having kindled a fire in the midst of the court, and having sat down together, Peter was sitting in the midst of them,
56 and a certain maid having seen him sitting at the light, and having earnestly looked at him, she said, 'And this one was with Him!'
57 and he disowned Him, saying, 'Woman, I have not known Him.'
58 And after a little, another having seen him, said, 'And you[S] are of them!' and Peter said, 'Man, I am not.'
59 And one hour, as it were, having intervened, a certain other was confidently affirming, saying, 'Of a truth this one also was with Him, for he is also a Galilean;'
60 and Peter said, 'Man, I have not known what you[S] say;' and presently, while he is speaking, a cock crowed.
61 And the Lord having turned did look on Peter, and Peter remembered the word of the Lord, how He said to him — 'Before a cock shall crow, you[S] may disown me three times;'
62 and Peter having gone without, wept bitterly.
63 And the men who were holding Jesus were mocking Him, beating [Him];
64 and having blindfolded Him, they were striking Him on the face, and were questioning Him, saying, 'Prophesy who he is who struck You[S]?'
65 and many other things, speaking evilly, they spoke in regard to him.
66 And when it became day there was gathered together the eldership of the people, chief priests also, and scribes, and they led Him up to their own sanhedrim,
67 saying, 'If You[S] be the Christ, tell us.' And He said to them, 'If I may tell you[P], you[P] will not believe;
68 and if I also question [you[P]], you[P] will not answer me or send me away;
69 from this time forth, there shall be the Son of Man sitting on the right hand of the power of God.'
70 And they all said, 'You[S], then, are the Son of God?' and He said unto them, 'You[P] say [it], because I am;'
71 and they said, 'What need have we of testimony yet? for we ourselves did hear [it] from His mouth.'

CHAPTER 23

1 And having risen, the whole multitude of them did lead Him to Pilate,
2 and began to accuse Him, saying, 'This one we found

perverting the nation, and forbidding to give tribute to
Caesar, saying Himself to be Christ a king.'
3 And Pilate questioned Him, saying, 'You[S] are the king
of the Jews?' and He answering him, said, 'You[S] do say
[it].'
4 And Pilate said unto the chief priests, and the
multitude, 'I find no fault in this man;'
5 and they were the more urgent, saying — 'He does
stir up the people, teaching throughout the whole of
Judea — having begun from Galilee — unto this place.'
6 And Pilate having heard of Galilee, questioned if the
man is a Galilean,
7 and having known that He is from the jurisdiction of
Herod, he sent Him back unto Herod, he being also in
Jerusalem in those days.
8 And Herod having seen Jesus did rejoice exceedingly,
for he was wishing for a long [time] to see Him, because
of hearing many things about Him, and he was hoping
to see some sign done by Him,
9 and was questioning Him in many words, and he
answered Him nothing.
10 And the chief priests and the scribes stood
vehemently accusing Him,
11 and Herod with his soldiers having set Him at nothing,
and having mocked, having put around Him gorgeous
apparel, did send Him back to Pilate,
12 and both Pilate and Herod became friends with one
another on that day, for they were at enmity between
themselves before.
13 And Pilate having called together the chief priests,
and the rulers, and the people,
14 said unto them, 'You[P] brought to me this man as
perverting the people, and behold, I having examined
before you[P], found in this man no fault in those things
you[P] bring forward against him;
15 no, nor yet Herod, for I sent you[P] back unto him, and
behold, nothing worthy of death is having been done
by Him;
16 having chastised, therefore, I will release Him,'
17 for it was necessary for him to release to them one at
every feast,
18 and they cried out — the whole multitude — saying,
'Away with this one, and release to us Barabbas,'
19 who had been, because of a certain sedition made in
the city, and murder, cast into prison.
20 Pilate again then — wishing to release Jesus — called
to them,
21 but they were calling out, saying, 'Crucify, crucify
Him.'
22 And he said unto them a third time, 'Why, what evil
did He? no cause of death did I find in Him; having
chastised Him, then, I will release [Him].'
23 And they were pressing with loud voices asking Him
to be crucified, and their voices, and those of the chief
priests, were prevailing,
24 and Pilate gave judgment for their request being done,
25 and he released him who because of sedition and
murder had been cast into the prison, whom they were
asking, and he gave Jesus up to their will.
26 And as they led Him away, having taken hold on
Simon, a certain Cyrenian, coming from the field, they
put on him the cross, to bear [it] behind Jesus.
27 And there was following Him a great multitude of the
people, and of women, who also were beating
themselves and lamenting Him,
28 and Jesus having turned unto them, said, 'Daughters
of Jerusalem, weep not for Me, but you[P] weep for
yourselves[P], and for your[P] children;
29 for, behold, days do come, in which they shall say,
Happy the barren, and wombs that did not bare, and paps
that did not give suck;
30 then they shall begin to say to the mountains, Fall
on us, and to the hills, Cover us; —
31 for, if in the green tree they do these things — in the
dry what may happen?'
32 And there were also others — two evil-doers — with
Him, to be put to death;
33 and when they came to the place that is called Skull,
there they crucified Him and the evil-doers, one on the
right hand and one on the left.
34 And Jesus said, 'Father, forgive them, for they have
not known what they do;' and parting his garments they
cast a lot.
35 And the people were standing, looking on, and the
rulers also were sneering with them, saying, 'Others He
saved, let Him save Himself, if this be the Christ, the
choice one of God.'
36 And mocking Him also were the soldiers, coming near
and offering vinegar to Him,
37 and saying, 'If You[S] be the king of the Jews, save
Yourself[S].'
38 And there was also a superscription written over Him,
in letters of Greek, and Roman, and Hebrew, 'This is the
King of the Jews.'
39 And one of the evil-doers who were hanged, was
speaking evil of Him, saying, 'If You[S] be the Christ, save
Yourself[S] and us.'
40 And the other answering, was rebuking him, saying,

'Do you[S] not even fear God, that you[S] are in the same judgment?
41 and we indeed righteously, for we receive back things worthy of what we did, but this one did nothing out of place;'
42 and he said to Jesus, 'Remember me, Lord, when You[S] may come in Your[S] reign;'
43 and Jesus said to him, 'Truly I say to you[S], Today you[S] shall be with Me in the paradise.'
44 And it was, as it were, the sixth hour, and darkness came over all the land till the ninth hour,
45 and the sun was darkened, and the vail of the sanctuary was rent in the midst,
46 and having cried with a loud voice, Jesus said, 'Father, to Your[S] hands I commit My spirit;' and these things having said, He breathed forth the spirit.
47 And the centurion having seen what was done, did glorify God, saying, 'Really this man was righteous;'
48 and all the multitudes who were come together to this sight, beholding the things that came to pass, striking their breasts did turn back;
49 and all His acquaintances stood afar off, and women who did follow Him from Galilee, beholding these things.
50 And behold, a man, by name Joseph, being a counselor, a man good and righteous,
51 — he was not consenting to their counsel and deed — from Arimathea, a city of the Jews, who also himself was expecting the reign of God,
52 he, having gone near to Pilate, asked the body of Jesus,
53 and having taken it down, he wrapped it in fine linen, and placed it in a tomb carved out, where no one was yet laid.
54 And the day was a preparation, and Sabbath was approaching,
55 and the women also who have come with Him out of Galilee having followed after, beheld the tomb, and how His body was placed,
56 and having turned back, they made ready spices and ointments, and on the Sabbath, indeed, they rested, according to the command.

CHAPTER 24

1 And on the first of the Sabbaths, at early dawn, they came to the tomb, bearing the spices they made ready, and certain [others] with them,
2 and they found the stone having been rolled away from the tomb,
3 and having gone in, they found not the body of the Lord Jesus.
4 And it came to pass, while they are perplexed about this, that behold, two men stood by them in glittering apparel,
5 and on their having become afraid, and having inclined the face to the earth, they said to them, 'Why do you[P] seek the living with the dead?
6 He is not here, but was raised; remember how He spoke to you[P], being yet in Galilee,
7 saying — It is necessary for the Son of Man to be delivered up to the hands of sinful men, and to be crucified, and the third day to rise again.'
8 And they remembered His sayings,
9 and having turned back from the tomb told all these things to the eleven, and to all the rest.
10 And it was the Magdalene Mary, and Joanna, and Mary of James, and the other women with them, who told unto the apostles these things,
11 and their sayings appeared before them as idle talk, and they were not believing them.
12 And Peter having risen, did run to the tomb, and having stooped down he saw the linen clothes lying alone, and he went away to his own home, wondering at that which was come to pass.
13 And, behold, two of them were going on during that day to a village, distant sixty furlongs from Jerusalem, the name of which [is] Emmaus,
14 and they were conversing with one another about all these things that have happened.
15 And it came to pass in their conversing and reasoning together, that Jesus Himself, having come near, was going on with them,
16 and their eyes were held so as not to know Him,
17 and He said unto them, 'What [are] these words that you[P] exchange with one another, walking, and you[P] are sad?'
18 And the one, whose name was Cleopas, answering, said unto him, 'Are You[S] alone such a stranger in Jerusalem, that You[S] have not known the things that came to pass in it in these days?'
19 And He said to them, 'What things?' And they said to Him, 'The things about Jesus of Nazareth, who became a man — a prophet — powerful in deed and word, before God and all the people,
20 how also the chief priests and our rulers did deliver Him up to a judgment of death, and crucified Him;
21 and we were hoping that He it is who is about to

redeem Israel, and also with all these things, this third
day is passing today, since these things happened.
22 'And certain women of ours also astonished us,
coming early to the tomb,
23 and having not found His body, they came, saying
also to have seen an apparition of messengers, who say
He is alive,
24 and certain of those with us went away unto the tomb,
and found as even the women said, and they saw Him
not.'
25 And He said unto them, 'O inconsiderate and slow
in heart, to believe on all that the prophets spoke!
26 Was it not necessary for the Christ to suffer these
things, and to enter into His glory?'
27 and having begun from Moses, and from all the
prophets, He was expounding to them the things about
Himself in all the Writings.
28 And they came near to the village where they were
going, and He made an appearance of going on further,
29 and they constrained Him, saying, 'Remain with us,
for it is toward evening,' and the day did decline, and
He went in to remain with them.
30 And it came to pass, in His reclining (at meat) with
them, having taken the bread, He blessed, and having
broken, He was giving to them,
31 and their eyes were opened, and they recognized
Him, and He became unseen by them.
32 And they said one to another, 'Was not our heart
burning within us, as He was speaking to us in the way,
and as He was opening up the Writings to us?'
33 And they, having risen up the same hour, turned back
to Jerusalem, and found gathered together the eleven,
and those with them,
34 saying — 'The Lord was raised indeed, and was seen
by Simon;'
35 and they were telling the things in the way, and how
He was made known to them in the breaking of the bread,
36 and as they are speaking these things, Jesus Himself
stood in the midst of them, and said to them, 'Peace —
to you[P];'
37 and being amazed, and becoming frightened, they
were thinking themselves to see a spirit.
38 And He said to them, 'Why are you[P] troubled? and
why do reasonings come up in your[P] hearts?
39 see My hands and My feet, that I am He; handle Me
and see, because a spirit has not flesh and bones, as
you[P] see Me having.'
40 And having said this, He showed to them the hands
and the feet,
41 and while they are not believing from the joy, and
wondering, He said to them, 'Have you[P] anything here
to eat?'
42 and they gave to Him part of a broiled fish, and of an
honeycomb,
43 and having taken, He did eat before them,
44 and He said to them, 'These [are] the words that I
spoke unto you[P], being yet with you[P], that it is necessary
for all the things that are written in the Law of Moses,
and the Prophets, and the Psalms, about me to be
fulfilled.'
45 Then He opened up their understanding to
understand the Writings,
46 and He said to them — 'Thus it has been written,
and thus it was necessary for the Christ to suffer, and to
rise out of the dead the third day,
47 and reformation and remission of sins to be
proclaimed in His name to all the nations, beginning from
Jerusalem:
48 and you[P] — you[P] are witnesses of these things.
49 'And, behold, I do send the promise of My Father
upon you[P], but you[P] — abide you[P] in the city of
Jerusalem till you[P] be clothed with power from on high.'
50 And He led them forth without — unto Bethany, and
having lifted up His hands He did bless them,
51 and it came to pass, in His blessing them, He was
parted from them, and was borne up to the heaven;
52 and they, having bowed before Him, did turn back to
Jerusalem with great joy,
53 and were continually in the temple, praising and
blessing God. Amen.

The Gospel according to
JOHN

CHAPTER 1

1 In the beginning was the Word, and the Word was
with God, and the Word was God;
2 this one was in the beginning with God;
3 all things did happen through Him, and without Him
not even one thing happened that had happened.
4 In Him was life, and the life was the light of men,
5 and the light in the darkness did shine, and the
darkness did not perceive it.
6 There came a man — having been sent from God —
whose name [is] John,
7 this one came for testimony, that he might testify about
the Light, that all might believe through him;
8 that one was not the Light, but — that he might testify
about the Light.
9 He was the true Light, which does enlighten every
man, coming to the world;
10 in the world He was, and the world through Him was
made, and the world did not know Him:
11 to His own things He came, and His own people did
not receive Him;
12 but as many as did receive Him to them He gave
authority to become sons of God — to those believing
in His name,
13 who — not of blood nor of a will of flesh, nor of a will
of man but — of God were begotten.
14 And the Word became flesh, and did tabernacle
among us, and we beheld His glory, glory as of an only
begotten of a father, full of grace and truth.
15 John does testify concerning Him, and has cried,
saying, 'This was He of whom I said, He who is coming
after me, has come before me, for He was before me;'
16 and out of His fullness did we all receive, and grace
over-against grace;
17 for the law was given through Moses, the grace and
the truth did come through Jesus Christ;
18 no one has ever seen God; the only begotten Son,
who is on the bosom of the Father — he did declare.
19 And this is the testimony of John, when the Jews
sent the priests and Levites out of Jerusalem, that they
might question him, 'Who are you[S]?'
20 and he confessed and did not deny, and confessed
— 'I am not the Christ.'
21 And they questioned him, 'What then? Are you[S]
Elijah?' and he said, 'I am not.' — 'Are you[S] the prophet?'
and he answered, 'No.'
22 They then said to him, 'Who are you[S], that we may
give an answer to those sending us? what do you[S] say
concerning yourself[S]?'
23 He said, 'I [am] a voice of one crying in the wilderness:
Make straight the way of the Lord, as said Isaiah the
prophet.'
24 And those sent were of the Pharisees,
25 and they questioned him and said to him, 'Why, then,
do you[S] baptize, if you[S] are not the Christ, nor Elijah,
nor the prophet?'
26 John answered them, saying, 'I baptize with water,
but He has stood in midst of you[P] whom you[P] have not
known, this one it is who is coming after me, who has
been before me,
27 of whom I am not worthy that I may loose the cord of
His sandal.'
28 These things came to pass in Bethabara, beyond the
Jordan, where John was baptizing,
29 on the morning John saw Jesus coming unto him,
and said, 'Behold, the Lamb of God, who is taking away
the sin of the world;
30 this is He concerning whom I said, After me does
come a man, who has come before me, because He was
before me:
31 and I knew Him not, but, that He might be made
known to Israel, because of this I came baptizing with
the water.
32 And John testified, saying — 'I have seen the Spirit
coming down, as a dove, out of heaven, and it remained
on Him;
33 and I did not know Him, but He who sent me to baptize
with water, He said to me, On whomsoever you may see
the Spirit coming down, and remaining on Him, this is
He who is baptizing with the Holy Spirit;

34 and I have seen, and have testified, that this is the Son of God.'
35 On the morning, again, John was standing, and two of his disciples,
36 and having looked on Jesus walking, he said, 'Behold, the Lamb of God;'
37 and the two disciples heard him speaking, and they followed Jesus.
38 And Jesus having turned, and having beheld them following, said to them, 'What do you[P] seek?' and they said to them, 'Rabbi, (which is, being interpreted, Teacher,) where do You[S] stay?'
39 He said to them, 'Come and see;' they came, and saw where He did stay, and they remained with Him that day and the hour was about the tenth.
40 Andrew, the brother of Simon Peter, was one of the two who heard from John, and followed Him;
41 this one did first find his own brother Simon, and said to him, 'We have found the Messiah,' (which is, being interpreted, The Anointed,)
42 and he brought him unto Jesus: and having looked upon him, Jesus said, 'You[S] are Simon, the son of Jonas, you[S] shall be called Cephas,' (which is interpreted, A rock.)
43 On the morning, He desired to go forth to Galilee, and He found Philip, and said to him, 'Be following Me.'
44 And Philip was from Bethsaida, of the city of Andrew and Peter;
45 Philip found Nathanael, and said to him, 'Him of whom Moses wrote in the Law, and the prophets, we have found, Jesus the son of Joseph, who [is] from Nazareth;'
46 and Nathanael said to him, 'Is any good thing able to come from Nazareth?' Philip said to him, 'Come and see.'
47 Jesus saw Nathanael coming unto Him, and He said concerning him, 'Behold, truly an Israelite, in whom guile is not;'
48 Nathanael said to him, 'Where do You[S] know me from?' Jesus answered and said to him, 'Before Philip's calling you[S] — you[S] being under the fig-tree — I saw you[S].'
49 Nathanael answered and said to him, 'Rabbi, You[S] are the Son of God, You[S] are the king of Israel.'
50 Jesus answered and said to him, 'Because I said to you[S], I saw you[S] under the fig-tree, you[S] do believe; you[S] shall see greater things than these;'
51 and He said to him, 'Truly, truly, I say to you[S], from now on you[S] shall see the heaven opened, and the messengers of God going up and coming down upon the Son of Man.'

CHAPTER 2

1 And the third day a marriage happened in Cana of Galilee, and the mother of Jesus was there,
2 and Jesus was also called, and His disciples, to the marriage;
3 and wine having run out, the mother of Jesus said unto Him, ' They have no wine;'
4 Jesus said to her, 'What – is it to me and to you[S], woman? My hour is not yet come.'
5 His mother said to the servants, 'Do whatever He may say to you[S].'
6 And there were there six water-jugs of stone, placed according to the purifying of the Jews, each holding two or three measures.
7 Jesus said to them, 'Fill the water-jugs with water;' and they filled them — unto the brim;
8 and He said to them, 'Draw out, now, and bring it to the director of the apartment;' and they brought it.
9 And as the director of the apartment tasted the water become wine, and did not know where it was from, (but the ministrants knew, who have drawn the water,) the director of the feast did call the bridegroom,
10 and said to him, 'Every man, at first sets out the good wine; and when they may have drunk freely, then the inferior; you did keep the good wine till now.'
11 This beginning of the signs did Jesus in Cana of Galilee, and revealed His glory, and His disciples believed in Him;
12 after this He went down to Capernaum, He, and His mother, and His brethren, and His disciples; and there they remained not many days.
13 And the Passover of the Jews was near, and Jesus went up to Jerusalem,
14 and He found in the temple those selling oxen, and sheep, and doves, and the money-changers sitting,
15 and having made a whip of small cords, He put all forth out of the temple, also the sheep, and the oxen; and He poured out the coins of the money-changers, and the tables he overthrew,
16 and to those selling the doves He said, 'Take these things from here; make not the house of My Father a house of merchandise.'
17 And His disciples remembered that it is written, 'The zeal of Your[S] house did eat Me up;'
18 the Jews then answered and said to Him, 'What sign do You[S] show to us — that You[S] do these things?'
19 Jesus answered and said to them, 'Destroy this

sanctuary, and in three days I will raise it up.'
20 The Jews, consequently, said, 'Forty and six years
was this sanctuary in building, and will You[S] raise it up
in three days?'
21 but He spoke concerning the sanctuary of His body;
22 when, then, He was raised out of the dead, His
disciples remembered that He said this to them, and they
believed the Writing, and the word that Jesus said.
23 And as He was in Jerusalem, in the Passover, in the
feast, many believed in His name, beholding His signs
that He was doing;
24 and Jesus Himself was not trusting Himself to them,
because of His knowing all [men],
25 and because He had no need that any should testify
concerning man, for He Himself was knowing what was
in man.

CHAPTER 3

1 And there was a man of the Pharisees, Nicodemus his
name, a ruler of the Jews,
2 this one came unto Him by night, and said to Him,
'Rabbi, we have known that You[S] have come from God
— a teacher, for no one is able to do these signs that
You[S] do, if God may not be with Him.'
3 Jesus answered and said to him, 'Truly, truly, I say to
you[S], If any one may not be born from above, he is not
able to see the reign of God;'
4 Nicodemus said unto Him, 'How is a man able to be
born, being old? is he able to enter into the womb of his
mother a second time, and to be born?'
5 Jesus answered, 'Truly, truly, I say to you[S], If any one
may not be born of water, and the Spirit, he is not able
to enter into the reign of God;
6 that which has been born of the flesh is flesh, and
that which has been born of the Spirit is spirit.
7 'You[S] may not wonder that I said to you[S], It is
necessary for you[S] to be born from above;
8 the Spirit will blow where He desires, and His voice
you[S] do hear, but you[S] have not known from where He
comes, and where He goes; thus is every one who has
been born of the Spirit.'
9 Nicodemus answered and said to him, 'How are these
things able to happen?'
10 Jesus answered and said to him, 'You[S] are the teacher
of Israel — and these things you[S] do not know!
11 'Truly, truly, I say to you[S] – We speak of what we
know, and we testify of what we have seen, and you[P] do
not receive our testimony;
12 if I speak to you[P] of the earthly things, and you[P] do
not believe, how, if I shall speak to you[P] of the heavenly
things, will you[P] believe?
13 and no one has gone up to the heaven, except He
who came down out of the heaven — the Son of Man
who is in the heaven.
14 'And as Moses did lift up the serpent in the
wilderness, so it is necessary for the Son of Man to be
lifted up,
15 that every one who is believing in Him may not perish,
but may have life age-during,
16 for God did so love the world, that He gave His Son
— the only begotten, that every one who is believing in
Him may not perish, but may have life age-during.
17 For God did not send His Son to the world that He
may judge the world, but that the world may be saved
through Him;
18 he who is believing in Him is not judged, but he who
is not believing has been judged already, because he
has not believed in the name of the only begotten Son
of God.
19 'And this is the judgment, that the light had come to
the world, and men did love the darkness rather than
the light, for their works were evil;
20 for every one who is doing wicked things hates the
light, and do not come unto the light, that his works may
not be detected;
21 but he who is doing the truth does come to the light,
that his works may be made known, that they have been
worked in God.'
22 After these things came Jesus and His disciples to
the land of Judea, and there He did stay with them, and
was baptizing;
23 and John was also baptizing in Aenon, near to Salem,
because there were many waters there, and they were
coming and were being baptized —
24 for John was not yet cast into the prison —
25 there arose then a question from the disciples of John
with [some] Jews about purifying,
26 and they came unto John, and said to him, 'Rabbi,
He who was with you[S] beyond the Jordan, to whom you[S]
did testify, behold, this one is baptizing, and all are
coming unto Him.'
27 John answered and said, 'A man is not able to receive
anything, if it has not been given Him from the heaven;
28 you[P] yourselves[P] do testify to me that I said, I am
not the Christ, but, that I am having been sent before
Him;

29 he who is having the bride is bridegroom, and the
friend of the bridegroom, who is standing and hearing
him, with joy does rejoice because of the voice of the
bridegroom; this, then, my joy has been fulfilled.
30 ‘ It is necessary for Him to increase, and me to become
less;
31 He who is coming from above is above all; he who is
from the earth, from the earth he is, and from the earth he
speaks; He who is coming from the heaven is above all.
32 ‘And He does testify of what He has seen and heard,
and none received His testimony;
33 he who is receiving His testimony did seal that God
is true;
34 for He whom God sent speaks the sayings of God;
for God does not give the Spirit by measure;
35 the Father does love the Son, and has given all things
into His hand;
36 he who is believing in the Son, has life age-during;
and he who is not believing the Son, shall not see life,
but the wrath of God does remain upon him.’

CHAPTER 4

1 When therefore the Lord knew that the Pharisees heard
that Jesus did make and baptize more disciples than John,
2 (though indeed Jesus Himself was not baptizing, but
His disciples,)
3 He left Judea and went away again to Galilee,
4 and it was needful for Him to go through Samaria.
5 He came, therefore, to a city of Samaria, called Sychar,
near to the place that Jacob gave to Joseph his son;
6 and there was there a well of Jacob. Jesus
consequently having been weary from the journeying,
was sitting thus on the well; it was as it were the sixth
hour;
7 there came a woman out of Samaria to draw water.
Jesus said to her, ‘Give Me to drink;’
8 for His disciples were gone away to the city, that they
may buy foods;
9 the Samaritan woman consequently said to Him, ‘How
do You[S], being a Jew, ask drink from me, being a
Samaritan woman?’ for Jews have no dealing with
Samaritans.
10 Jesus answered and said to her, ‘If you[S] had known
the gift of God, and who it is who is saying to you[S], Give
Me to drink, you[S] would have asked Him, and He would
have given you[S] living water.’
11 The woman said to Him, ‘Sir, You[S] have not even a
vessel to draw with, and the well is deep; where, then,
have You[S] the living water?
12 Are You[S] greater than our father Jacob, who did give
us the well, and himself did drink out of it, and his sons,
and his cattle?’
13 Jesus answered and said to her, ‘Every one who is
drinking of this water shall thirst again;
14 but whoever may drink of the water that I will give
him, may not thirst — to the age; and the water that I
will give him shall become in him a well of water,
springing up to life age-during.’
15 The woman said unto Him, ‘Sir, give me this water,
that I may not thirst, nor come here to draw.’
16 Jesus said to her, ‘Go, call your[S] husband, and come
here;’
17 the woman answered and said, ‘I have not a husband.’
Jesus said to her, ‘Well did you[S] say — A husband I
have not;
18 for five husbands you[S] have had, and, now, he whom
you[S] have is not your[S] husband; this have you[S] said
truly.’
19 The woman said to Him, ‘Sir, I perceive that You[S] are
a prophet;
20 our fathers in this mountain did worship, and you[P]
— you[P] say that in Jerusalem is the place where it needful
to worship.’
21 Jesus said to her, ‘Woman, believe Me, that there
does come an hour, when neither in this mountain, nor
in Jerusalem, shall you[P] worship the Father;
22 you[P] worship what you[P] have not known; we worship
what we have known, because the salvation is of the
Jews;
23 but, there comes an hour, and it is now, when the
true worshippers will worship the Father in spirit and
truth, for the Father also does seek such to worship Him;
24 God [is] a Spirit, and those worshipping Him, it is
needful to worship in spirit and truth.’
25 The woman said to Him, ‘I have known that Messiah
does come, who is called Christ, when that one may
come, He will tell us all things;’
26 Jesus said to her, ‘I am [He], who am speaking to
you[S].’
27 And upon this came His disciples, and were
wondering that He was speaking with a woman, no one,
however, said, ‘What do You[S] seek?’ or ‘Why do You[S]
speak with her?’
28 The woman then left her water-jug, and went away
to the city, and said to the men,
29 ‘Come, see a man, who told me all things — as many

as I did; is this the Christ?'
30 They went forth for that reason out of the city, and
were coming unto Him.
31 And in the meanwhile His disciples were asking Him,
saying, 'Rabbi, eat;'
32 and He said to them, 'I have food to eat that you[P]
have not known.'
33 The disciples then said one to another, 'Did any one
bring Him anything to eat?'
34 Jesus said to them, 'My food is, that I may do the
will of Him who sent Me, and may finish His work;
35 do not say that it is yet four months, and the harvest
comes; behold, I say to you[P], Lift up your[P] eyes, and
see the fields, that they are white unto harvest already.
36 'And he who is reaping does receive a reward, and
does gather fruit to life age-during, that both he who is
sowing and he who is reaping may rejoice together;
37 for in this the saying is the true one, that one is the
sower and another the reaper.
38 I sent you[P] to reap that on which you[P] have not
labored; others labored, and you[P] have entered into their
labor.
39 And from that city many believed in Him, of the
Samaritans, because of the word of the woman testifying,
— 'He told me all things — as many as I did.'
40 When, then, the Samaritans came unto Him, they were
asking Him to remain with them, and He remained there
two days;
41 and many more did believe because of His word,
42 and said to the woman — 'No more because of your[S]
speaking do we believe; for we ourselves have heard
and known that this is truly the Savior of the world —
the Christ.'
43 And after the two days He went forth from there, and
went away to Galilee,
44 for Jesus Himself testified that a prophet in His own
country shall not have honor;
45 when then, He came to Galilee, the Galileans received
Him, having seen all things that He did in Jerusalem in
the feast — for they also went to the feast.
46 Jesus came, therefore, again to Cana of Galilee, where
He made the water wine, and there was a certain courtier,
whose son was ailing in Capernaum,
47 he, having heard that Jesus is come out of Judea to
Galilee, went away unto Him, and was asking Him that
he may come down and may heal his son, for he was
about to die.
48 Jesus then said unto him, 'If you[P] do not see signs
and wonders, you[P] will not believe.'
49 The courtier said unto Him, 'Sir, come down before
my child die;'
50 Jesus said to him, 'Be going on; your[S] son does live.'
And the man believed the word that Jesus said to him,
and was going on,
51 and he now going down, his servants met him, and
told, saying — 'Your[S] child does live;'
52 he inquired then of them the hour in which he became
better, and they said to him — 'Yesterday at the seventh
hour the fever left him;'
53 then the father knew that [it was] in that hour in which
Jesus said to him — 'Your[S] son does live,' and he himself
believed, and his whole house;
54 this again a second sign did Jesus, having come out
of Judea to Galilee.

CHAPTER 5

1 After these things there was a feast of the Jews, and
Jesus went up to Jerusalem,
2 and there is in Jerusalem by the sheep-[gate] a pool
that is called in Hebrew Bethesda, having five porches,
3 in these were lying a great multitude of the ailing, blind,
lame, withered, waiting for the moving of the water,
4 for a messenger at a set time was going down in the
pool, and was troubling the water, then the first having
gone in after the troubling of the water, became whole
of whatever sickness he was held.
5 and there was a certain man there being in ailment
thirty and eight years,
6 Jesus having seen him lying, and having known that
he is already a long time, He said to him, 'Do you[S] wish
to become whole?'
7 The ailing man answered Him, 'Sir, I have no man,
that, when the water may be troubled, he may put me
into the pool, and while I am coming, another does go
down before me.'
8 Jesus said to him, 'Rise, take up your[S] couch, and be
walking;'
9 and immediately the man became whole, and he took
up his couch, and was walking, and it was a Sabbath on
that day,
10 the Jews then said to him that had been healed, 'It is
a Sabbath; it is not lawful to you[S] to take up the couch.'
11 He answered them, 'He who made me whole — that
one said to me, Take up your[S] couch, and be walking;'
12 they questioned him, then, 'Who is the man who is
saying to you[S], Take up your[S] couch and be walking?'

13 But he that was healed had not known who He is, for Jesus did move away, a multitude being in the place.
14 After these things, Jesus found him in the temple, and said to him, 'Behold, you[S] have become whole; sin no more, for fear that something worse may happen to you[S].'
15 The man went away, and told the Jews that it is Jesus who made him whole,
16 and because of this were the Jews persecuting Jesus, and seeking to kill Him, because these things He was doing on a Sabbath.
17 And Jesus answered them, 'My Father does work until now, and I work;'
18 because of this, then, were the Jews seeking the more to kill Him, because not only was He breaking the Sabbath, but He also called God His own Father, making Himself equal to God.
19 Jesus therefore responded and said to them, 'Truly, truly, I say to you[P], The Son is not able to do anything of Himself, if He may not see the Father doing anything; for whatever things He may do, these also the Son in like manner does;
20 for the Father does love the Son, and does show to Him all things that He Himself does; and He will show Him greater works than these, that you[P] may wonder.
21 'For, as the Father does raise the dead, and does make alive, so also the Son does make alive whom He wills;
22 for neither does the Father judge any one, but all the judgment He has given to the Son,
23 that all may honor the Son according as they honor the Father; he who is not honoring the Son, does not honor the Father who sent Him.
24 'Truly, truly, I say to you[P] — He who is hearing My word, and is believing Him who sent Me, has life age-during, and to judgment he does not come, but has passed out of the death to the life.
25 'Truly, truly, I say to you[P] — There comes an hour, and it is now, when the dead shall hear the voice of the Son of God, and those having heard shall live;
26 for, as the Father has life in Himself, so He gave also to the Son to have life in Himself,
27 and He gave Him authority also to do judgment, because He is Son of Man.
28 'Wonder not at this, because there does come an hour in which all those in the tombs shall hear His voice,
29 and they shall come forth; those who did the good things to a rising again of life, and those who practiced the evil things to a rising again of judgment.
30 'I am not able of Myself to do anything; according as I hear I judge, and My judgment is righteous, because I seek not My own will, but the will of the Father who sent Me.
31 'If I testify concerning Myself, My testimony is not true;
32 there is another who is testifying concerning Me, and I have known that the testimony that he does testify concerning Me is true;
33 you[P] have sent unto John, and he has testified to the truth.
34 'But I do not receive testimony from man, but these things I say that you[P] may be saved;
35 he was the burning and shining lamp, and you[P] did will to be glad, for an hour, in his light.
36 'But I have the testimony greater than John's, for the works that the Father gave Me, that I might finish them, the works themselves that I do, they testify concerning Me, that the Father has sent Me.
37 'And the Father who sent Me Himself has testified concerning Me; you[P] have neither heard His voice at any time, nor have you[P] seen His appearance;
38 and you[P] have not His word remaining in you[P], because whom He sent, Him you[P] do not believe.
39 'You[P] search the Writings, because you[P] think to have life age-during in them, and these are they that are testifying concerning Me;
40 and you[P] do not will to come unto Me, that you[P] may have life;
41 I do not receive glory from man,
42 but I have known you[P], that you[P] have not the love of God in yourselves[P].
43 'I have come in the name of My Father, and you[P] do not receive Me; if another may come in his own name, him you[P] will receive;
44 how are you[P] able — you[P] — to believe, receiving glory from one another, and you[P] seek not the glory that [is] from God alone?
45 'Do not think that I will accuse you[P] unto the Father; there is who is accusing you[P], Moses — in whom you[P] have hoped;
46 for if you[P] were believing Moses, you[P] would have been believing Me, for he wrote concerning Me;
47 but if you[P] believe not his writings, how shall you[P] believe My sayings?'

CHAPTER 6

1 After these things Jesus went away beyond the sea of Galilee (of Tiberias),

2 and there was following Him a great multitude, because
they were seeing His signs that He was doing on the
ailing;
3 and Jesus went up to the mount, and He was sitting
there with His disciples,
4 and the Passover was near, the feast of the Jews.
5 Jesus then having lifted up [His] eyes and having
seen that a great multitude did come to Him, said unto
Philip, 'From where shall we buy loaves, that these may
eat?' —
6 and this he said, trying him, for He Himself had known
what He was about to do.
7 Philip answered Him, 'Two hundred denaries' worth
of loaves are not sufficient to them, that each of them
may receive some little;'
8 one of His disciples — Andrew, the brother of Simon
Peter — said to Him,
9 'There is one little lad here who has five barley loaves,
and two fishes, but these — what are they to so many?'
10 And Jesus said, 'Make the men to sit down;' and
there was much grass in the place, the men then sat
down, in number, as it were, five thousand,
11 and Jesus took the loaves, and having given thanks
He distributed to the disciples, and the disciples to those
reclining, in like manner, also of the little fishes as much
as they wished.
12 And when they were filled, He said to His disciples,
'Gather together the broken pieces that are over, that
nothing may be lost;'
13 they gathered together, consequently, and filled
twelve hand-baskets with broken pieces, from the five
barley loaves that were over to those having eaten.
14 The men, then, having seen the sign that Jesus did,
said — 'This is truly the Prophet, who is coming to the
world;'
15 Jesus, for that reason, having known that they are
about to come, and to take Him by force that they may
make Him king, retired again to the mountain Himself
alone.
16 And when evening came, His disciples went down
to the sea,
17 and having entered into the boat, they were going
over the sea to Capernaum, and darkness had already
come, and Jesus had not come unto them,
18 the sea also — a great wind blowing — was being
raised,
19 having pushed onwards, for that reason, about
twenty-five or thirty furlongs, they behold Jesus walking
on the sea, and coming near to the boat, and they were
afraid;
20 and He said to them, 'I am [He], be not afraid;'
21 they were willing then to receive Him into the boat,
and immediately the boat came unto the land to which
they were going.
22 On the morrow, the multitude that was standing on the
other side of the sea, having seen that there was no other
little boat there except one — that into which His disciples
entered — and that Jesus went not in with His disciples
into the little boat, but His disciples went away alone,
23 (and other little boats came from Tiberias, near the
place where they did eat the bread, the Lord having given
thanks),
24 when for that reason the multitude saw that Jesus is
not there, nor His disciples, they also themselves did
enter into the boats, and came to Capernaum seeking
Jesus;
25 and having found Him on the other side of the sea,
they said to Him, 'Rabbi, when did You[S] come here?'
26 Jesus answered them and said, 'Truly, truly, I say to
you[P], You[P] seek Me, not because you[P] saw signs, but
because you[P] did eat of the loaves, and were satisfied;
27 work not for the food that is perishing, but for the
food that is remaining to life age-during, which the Son
of Man will give to you[P], for Him did the Father seal —
[even] God.'
28 They said for that reason unto Him, 'What may we
do that we may work the works of God?'
29 Jesus answered and said to them, 'This is the work
of God, that you[P] may believe in Him whom He did send.'
30 They said for that reason to Him, 'What sign, then,
do You[S], that we may see and may believe You[S]? what
do You[S] work?
31 our fathers did eat the manna in the wilderness,
according as it is having been written, Bread out of the
heaven He gave them to eat.'
32 Jesus, consequently, said to them, 'Truly, truly, I say
to you[P], Moses did not give you[P] the bread out of the
heaven; but My Father does give you[P] the true bread
out of the heaven;
33 for the bread of God is that which is coming down
out of the heaven, and giving life to the world.'
34 They said, for that reason, unto Him, 'Sir, always
give us this bread.'
35 And Jesus said to them, 'I am the bread of the life; he
who is coming unto Me may not hunger, and he who is
believing in Me may not thirst — at any time;
36 but I said to you[P], that you[P] also have seen Me, and
you[P] believe not;

37 all that the Father does give to Me will come unto Me; and him who is coming unto Me, I may in no wise cast without,
38 because I have come down out of the heaven, not that I may do My will, but the will of Him who sent Me.
39 'And this is the will of the Father who sent Me, that all that He has given to Me I may not lose of it, but may raise it up in the last day;
40 and this is the will of Him who sent Me, that every one who is beholding the Son, and is believing in Him, may have life age-during, and I will raise him up in the last day.'
41 The Jews, for that reason, were murmuring at Him, because He said, 'I am the bread that came down out of the heaven;'
42 and they said, 'Is not this Jesus, the son of Joseph, whose father and mother we have known? how then says this one — Out of the heaven I have come down?'
43 Jesus answered, for that reason, and said to them, 'Murmur not one with another;
44 no one is able to come unto Me, if the Father who sent Me may not draw him, and I will raise him up in the last day;
45 it is having been written in the prophets, And they shall be all taught of God; every one for that reason who heard from the Father, and learned, comes to Me;
46 not that any one has seen the Father, except He who is from God, He has seen the Father.
47 'Truly, truly, I say to you[P], He who is believing in Me, has life age-during;
48 I am the bread of the life;
49 your[P] fathers did eat the manna in the wilderness, and they died;
50 this is the bread that out of the heaven is coming down, that any one may eat of it, and not die.
51 'I am the living bread that came down out of the heaven; if any one may eat of this bread he shall live — to the age; and the bread also that I will give is My flesh, that I will give for the life of the world.'
52 The Jews, consequently, were striving with one another, saying, 'How is this one able to give us [His] flesh to eat?'
53 Jesus, for that reason, said to them, 'Truly, truly, I say to you[P], If you[P] may not eat the flesh of the Son of Man, and may not drink His blood, you[P] have no life in yourselves[P];
54 he who is eating My flesh, and is drinking My blood, has life age-during, and I will raise him up in the last day;
55 for My flesh truly is food, and My blood truly is drink;
56 he who is eating My flesh, and is drinking My blood, does remain in Me, and I in him.
57 'According as the living Father sent Me, and I live because of the Father, he also who is eating Me, even that one shall live because of Me;
58 this is the bread that came down out of the heaven; not as your[P] fathers did eat the manna, and died; he who is eating this bread shall live — to the age.'
59 These things He said in a synagogue, teaching in Capernaum;
60 many, consequently, of His disciples having heard, said, 'This word is hard; who is able to hear it?'
61 And Jesus having known in Himself that His disciples are murmuring about this, said to them, 'Does this stumble you[P]?
62 if then you[P] may behold the Son of Man going up where He was before?
63 the spirit it is that is giving life; the flesh does not profit anything; the sayings that I speak to you[P] are spirit, and they are life;
64 but there are certain of you[P] who do not believe;' for Jesus had known from the beginning who they are who are not believing, and who is he who will deliver Him up,
65 and He said, 'Because of this I have said to you[P] — No one is able to come unto Me, if it may not have been given him from My Father.'
66 From this [time] many of His disciples went away backward, and were no more walking with Him,
67 Jesus, for that reason, said to the twelve, 'Do you[P] also wish to go away?'
68 Simon Peter, for that reason, answered Him, 'Sir, unto whom shall we go? You[S] have sayings of life age-during;
69 and we have believed, and we have known, that You[S] are the Christ, the Son of the living God.'
70 Jesus answered them, 'Did not I choose you[P] — the twelve? and of you[P] — one is a devil.
71 And he spoke of Judas, Simon's [son], Iscariot, for he was about to deliver Him up, being one of the twelve.

CHAPTER 7

1 And Jesus was walking after these things in Galilee, for He did not wish to walk in Judea, because the Jews were seeking to kill Him,
2 and the feast of the Jews was near — that of

tabernacles —
3 His brethren, for that reason, said unto Him, 'Remove
from here, and go away to Judea, that Your[S] disciples
also may behold Your[S] works that You[S] do;
4 for no one does anything in secret, and himself seeks
to be in public; if You[S] do these things — reveal Yourself[S]
to the world;'
5 for not even were His brethren believing in Him.
6 Jesus, for that reason, said to them, 'My time is not
yet present, but your[P] time is always ready;
7 the world is not able to hate you[P], but Me it does hate,
because I testify concerning it that its works are evil.
8 You[P] — go you up to this feast; I do not yet go up to
this feast, because My time has not yet been fulfilled;'
9 and saying these things to them, He remained in
Galilee.
10 And when His brethren went up, then also He Himself
went up to the feast, not obviously, but as in secret;
11 the Jews, for that reason, were seeking Him, in the
feast, and said, 'Where is that one?'
12 and there was much murmuring about Him among
the multitudes, some indeed said — 'He is good;' and
others said, 'No, but He leads astray the multitude;'
13 no one, however, was speaking freely about Him,
through fear of the Jews.
14 And it being now the middle of the feast, Jesus went
up to the temple, and He was teaching,
15 and the Jews were wondering, saying, 'How has this
one known letters — not having learned?'
16 Jesus answered them and said, 'My teaching is not
Mine, but His who sent Me;
17 if any one may will to do His will, he shall know
concerning the teaching, whether it is of God, or — I do
speak from Myself.
18 'He who is speaking from himself does seek his own
glory, but He who is seeking the glory of Him who sent
Him, this one is true, and unrighteousness is not in Him;
19 has not Moses given you[P] the law? and none of you[P]
does the law; why do you[P] seek to kill Me?'
20 The multitude answered and said, 'You[S] have a
demon, who does seek to kill You[S]?'
21 Jesus answered and said to them, 'One work I did,
and you[P] all wonder,
22 because of this, Moses has given you[P] the
circumcision — not that it is of Moses, but of the fathers
— and on a Sabbath you[P] circumcise a man;
23 if a man does receive circumcision on a Sabbath that
the law of Moses may not be broken, are you[P] angry
with Me that I made a man all whole on a Sabbath?
24 judge not according to appearance, but the righteous
judgment judge.'
25 Certain, for that reason, of the Jerusalemites said, 'Is
not this He whom they are seeking to kill?
26 and, behold, He does speak freely, and they say
nothing to Him; did the rulers at all know truly that this
is truly the Christ?
27 but this one — we have known from where He is;
and the Christ, when He does come, no one does know
from where He is.'
28 Jesus cried, for that reason, in the temple, teaching
and saying, 'You[P] have both known Me, and you[P] have
known from where I am; and I have not come of Myself,
but He who sent Me is true, whom you[P] have not known;
29 and I have known Him, because I am from Him, and
He did send Me.'
30 They were seeking, for that reason, to seize Him, and
no one laid the hand on Him, because His hour had not
yet come,
31 and many out of the multitude did believe in Him,
and said — 'The Christ — when He may come — will
He do more signs than these that this one did?'
32 The Pharisees heard the multitude murmuring these
things concerning Him, and the Pharisees and the chief
priests sent officers that they may take Him;
33 Jesus, for that reason, said to them, 'Yet a little time I
am with you[P], and I go away unto Him who sent Me;
34 you[P] will seek Me, and you[P] shall not find; and where
I am, you[P] are not able to come.'
35 The Jews, for that reason, said among themselves,
'Where is this one about to go that we shall not find
Him? — is He about to go to the dispersion of the
Greeks? and to teach the Greeks;
36 what is this word that He said, You[P] will seek Me,
and you[P] shall not find? and, Where I am, you[P] are not
able to come?'
37 And in the last, the great day of the feast, Jesus stood
and cried, saying, 'If any one does thirst, let him come
unto Me and drink;
38 he who is believing in Me, according as the Writing
said, Out of his belly shall flow rivers of living water;'
39 and this He said of the Spirit, which those believing
in Him were about to receive; for not yet was the Holy
Spirit, because Jesus was not yet glorified.
40 Many, consequently out of the multitude, having
heard the word, said, 'This is truly the Prophet;'
41 others said, 'This is the Christ;' and others said,
'Why, does the Christ come out of Galilee?
42 Did not the Writing say, that out of the seed of David,

and from Bethlehem — the village where David was —
the Christ does come?'
43 A division, for that reason, arose among the multitude
because of Him.
44 And certain of them were willing to seize Him, but no
one laid hands on Him;
45 the officers came, for that reason, unto the chief
priests and Pharisees, and they said to them, 'Why did
you[P] not bring Him?'
46 The officers answered, 'Never so spoke man — as
this man.'
47 The Pharisees, consequently, answered them, 'Have
you[P] also been led astray?
48 did any one out of the rulers believe in Him? or out
of the Pharisees?
49 but this multitude, that is not knowing the law, is
accursed.'
50 Nicodemus said unto them — he who came unto
Him by night — being one of them,
51 'Does our law judge the man, if it may not hear from
Him first, and know what He does?'
52 They answered and said to Him, 'Are you[S] also out
of Galilee? search and see, that a prophet out of Galilee
has not risen;'
53 and each one went on to his house, but Jesus went
on to the mount of the Olives.

CHAPTER 8

1 And at dawn He came again to the temple,
2 and all the people were coming unto Him, and having
sat down, He was teaching them;
3 and the scribes and the Pharisees bring unto Him a
woman having been taken in adultery, and having set
her in the midst,
4 they say to Him, 'Teacher, this woman was taken in
the very crime — committing adultery,
5 and in the law, Moses did command us that such be
stoned; You[S], consequently, what do You[S] say?'
6 and this they said, trying Him, that they might have to
accuse Him. And Jesus, having stooped down, with the
finger He was writing on the ground,
7 and when they continued asking Him, having bent
Himself back, He said unto them, 'The sinless of you[P]
— let him cast the first stone at her;'
8 and again having stooped down, He was writing on
the ground,
9 and they having heard, and being convicted by the
conscience, were going forth one by one, having begun
from the elders — unto the last; and Jesus was left alone,
and the woman standing in the midst.
10 And Jesus having bent Himself back, and having
seen no one but the woman, said to her, 'Woman, where
are those — your[S] accusers? did no one pass sentence
upon you[S]?'
11 and she said, 'No one, Sir;' and Jesus said to her,
'Neither do I pass sentence on you[S]; be going on, and
no more sin.'
12 Again, consequently, Jesus spoke to them, saying,
'I am the light of the world; he who is following Me shall
not walk in the darkness, but he shall have the light of
the life.'
13 The Pharisees, for that reason, said to Him, 'You[S] do
testify of Yourself[S], Your[S] testimony is not true;'
14 Jesus answered and said to them, 'And if I testify of
Myself — My testimony is true, because I have known
from where I came, and where I go, and you[P] — you[P]
have not known from where I come, or where I go.
15 'You[P] do judge according to the flesh; I do not judge
any one,
16 and even if I do judge My judgment is true, because
I am not alone, but I and the Father who sent Me;
17 and also in your[P] law it has been written, that the
testimony of two men are true;
18 I am [one] who is testifying of Myself, and the Father
who sent Me does testify of Me.'
19 They said, for that reason, to Him, 'Where is Your
father?' Jesus answered, 'You[P] have neither known Me
nor My Father: if you[P] had known Me, you[P] would have
known My Father also.'
20 These sayings Jesus spoke in the treasury, teaching
in the temple, and no one seized Him, because His hour
had not yet come;
21 consequently said Jesus again to them, 'I go away,
and you[P] will seek Me, and in your[P] sin you[P] shall die;
where I go away, you[P] are not able to come.'
22 The Jews, for that reason, said, 'Will He kill Himself,
because He says, Where I go away, you[P] are not able to
come?'
23 and He said to them, 'You[P] are from beneath, I am
from above; you[P] are of this world, I am not of this world;
24 I said, for that reason, to you[P], that you[P] shall die in
your[P] sins, for if you[P] may not believe that I am [He],
you[P] shall die in your[P] sins.'
25 They said, for that reason, to Him, 'You[S] — who are
You[S]?' and Jesus said to them, 'Even what I did speak of
to you[P] at the beginning;

26 I have many things to speak concerning you[P] and to
judge, but He who sent Me is true, and I — what things
I heard from Him — these I say to the world.'
27 They knew not that He spoke to them of the Father;
28 Jesus, for that reason, said to them, 'When you[P] may
lift up the Son of Man then you[P] will know that I am
[He]; and of Myself I do nothing, but according as My
Father did teach me, these things I speak;
29 and He who sent Me is with Me; the Father did not
leave Me alone, because I always do the things pleasing
to Him.'
30 As He is speaking these things, many believed in
Him;
31 Jesus, for that reason, said unto the Jews who
believed in Him, 'If you[P] may remain in My word, truly
you[P] are My disciples, and you[P] shall know the truth,
32 and the truth shall make you[P] free.'
33 They answered Him, 'We are the seed of Abraham;
and we have been servants to no one at any time; how
do You[S] say — You[P] shall become free?'
34 Jesus answered them, 'Truly, truly, I say to you[P] —
Every one who is committing sin, is a servant of the sin,
35 and the servant does not remain in the house — to
the age, the Son does remain — to the age;
36 if then the Son may make you[P] free, in reality you[P]
shall be free.
37 'I have known that you[P] are seed of Abraham, but
you[P] seek to kill Me, because My word has no place in
you[P];
38 I — do speak that which I have seen with My Father,
and you[P], for that reason, that which you[P] have seen
with your[P] father — you[P] do.'
39 They answered and said to Him, 'Our father is
Abraham;' Jesus said to them, 'If you[P] were children of
Abraham, you[P] would be doing the works of Abraham;
40 and now, you[P] seek to kill Me — a man who has
spoken to you[P] the truth I heard from God; this Abraham
did not;
41 you[P] do the works of your[P] father.' They said, for
that reason, to Him, 'We have not been born of
whoredom; we have one Father — God;'
42 Jesus then said to them, 'If God were your[P] father,
you[P] would be loving Me, for I came forth from God,
and am come; for I have neither come of Myself, but He
sent Me;
43 why do you[P] not know My speech? because you[P]
are not able to hear My word.
44 'You[P] are of a father — the devil, and the desires of
your[P] father you[P] will to do; he was a man-slayer from
the beginning, and he has not stood in the truth, because
there is no truth in him; when one may speak the
falsehood, he speaks of his own, because he is a liar —
also his father.
45 'And because I say the truth, you[P] do not believe
Me.
46 Who of you[P] does convict Me of sin? and if I speak
truth, why do you[P] not believe Me?
47 he who is of God, the sayings of God he does hear;
because of this you[P] do not hear, because you[P] are not
of God.'
48 The Jews, for that reason, answered and said to Him,
'Do we not say well, that You[S] are a Samaritan, and have
a demon?'
49 Jesus answered, 'I have not a demon, but I honor
My Father, and you[P] dishonor Me;
50 and I do not seek My own glory; there is who is
seeking and is judging;
51 truly, truly, I say to you[P], If any one may keep My
word, he may not see death — to the age.'
52 The Jews, consequently, said to Him, 'Now we have
known that You[S] have a demon; Abraham did die, and
the prophets, and You[S] do say, If any one may keep My
word, he shall not taste of death — to the age!
53 Are You[S] greater than our father Abraham, who died?
and the prophets died; whom do You[S] make Yourself[S]?'
54 Jesus answered, 'If I glorify Myself, My glory is
nothing; it is My Father who is glorifying Me, of whom
you[P] say that He is your[P] God;
55 and you[P] have not known Him, and I have known
Him, and if I say that I have not known Him, I shall be
like you[P] — speaking falsely; but I have known Him,
and I keep His word;
56 Abraham, your[P] father, was glad that he might see
My day; and he saw, and did rejoice.'
57 The Jews, for that reason, said unto Him, 'You[S] are
not yet fifty years old, and You[S] have seen Abraham?'
58 Jesus said to them, 'Truly, truly, I say to you[P], Before
Abraham's coming — I am;'
59 they took up, for that reason, stones that they may
cast at Him, but Jesus hid Himself, and went forth out of
the temple, going through the midst of them, and so
passed by.

CHAPTER 9

1 And passing by, He saw a man blind from birth,
2 and His disciples asked Him, saying, 'Rabbi, who did

sin, this one or his parents, that he should be born
blind?'
3 Jesus answered, 'Neither did this one sin nor his parents,
but that the works of God may be revealed in him;
4 it is required of Me to be working the works of Him
who sent Me while it is day; night does come, when no
one is able to work: —
5 when I am in the world, I am a light of the world.'
6 Saying these things, He spat on the ground, and made
clay of the spittle, and rubbed the clay on the eyes of
the blind man, and said to him,
7 'Go away, wash at the pool of Siloam,' which is,
interpreted, Sent he went away, for that reason, and did
wash, and came seeing;
8 the neighbors, consequently, and those seeing him
before, that he was blind, said, 'Is not this he who is
sitting and begging?'
9 others said — 'This is he;' and others — 'He is like to
him;' he himself said, — 'I am [he].'
10 They said, consequently, to him, 'How were your[S]
eyes opened?'
11 he answered and said, 'A man called Jesus made clay,
and rubbed my eyes, and said to me, Go away to the
pool of Siloam, and wash; and having gone away and
having washed, I received sight;'
12 they said, for that reason, to him, 'Where is that one?'
he said, 'I have not known.'
13 They bring him who once [was] blind to the Pharisees,
14 and it was a Sabbath when Jesus made the clay, and
opened his eyes.
15 Again, consequently, the Pharisees also were asking
him how he received sight, and he said to them, ' He did
put clay upon my eyes, and I did wash — and I see.'
16 Of the Pharisees, for that reason, certain said, 'This
man is not from God, because he does not keep the
Sabbath;' others said, 'How is a man — a sinful one —
able to do such signs?' and there was a division among
them.
17 They said to the blind man again, 'You[S] — what do
you[S] say of Him — that He opened your[S] eyes?'
18 and he said — 'He is a prophet.' The Jews, for that
reason, did not believe concerning him that he was blind
and did receive sight, until that they called the parents
of him who received sight,
19 and they asked them, saying, 'Is your[P] son, of whom
you[P] say that he was born blind? how then now does
he see?'
20 His parents answered them and said, 'We have known
that this is our son, and that he was born blind;
21 and how he now sees, we have not known; or who
opened his eyes, we have not known; himself is of age,
ask him; he himself shall speak concerning himself.'
22 These things said his parents, because they were
afraid of the Jews, for already had the Jews agreed
together, that if any one may confess Him — Christ, he
may be put out of the synagogue;
23 because of this his parents said — 'He is of age, ask
him.'
24 They called, for that reason, a second time the man
who was blind, and they said to him, 'Give glory to God,
we have known that this man is a sinner;'
25 he answered, consequently, and said, 'If he be a
sinner — I have not known, one thing I have known,
that, being blind, now I see.'
26 And they said to him again, 'What did He to you[S]?
how did He open your[S] eyes?'
27 He answered them, 'I told you[P] already, and you[P] did
not hear; why do you[P] wish to hear again? do you[P] also
wish to become His disciples?'
28 They reviled him, for that reason, and said, 'You[S] are
His disciple, and we are Moses' disciples;
29 we have known that God had spoken to Moses, but
this one — we have not known from where He is.'
30 The man answered and said to them, 'Why, in this is
a wonderful thing, that you[P] have not known from where
He is, and He opened my eyes!
31 and we have known that God does not hear sinners,
but, if any one may be a worshiper of God, and may do
His will, He does hear him;
32 it was not heard from the age, that any one did open
eyes of one who has been born blind;
33 if this one were not from God, he were not able to do
anything.'
34 They answered and said to him, ' You[S] were born
altogether in sins, and you[S] do teach us!' and they cast
him forth without.
35 Jesus heard that they cast him forth without, and
having found him, He said to him, 'Do you[S] believe in
the Son of God?'
36 he answered and said, 'Who is He, sir, that I may
believe in Him?'
37 And Jesus said to him, 'You[S] have both seen Him,
and He who is speaking with you[S] is He;'
38 and he said, 'I believe, sir,' and bowed before Him.
39 And Jesus said, 'For judgment I did come to this
world, that those not seeing may see, and those seeing
may become blind.'
40 And those of the Pharisees who were with Him heard

these things, and they said to Him, 'Are we also blind?'
41 Jesus said to them, 'If you[P] were blind, you[P] were
not having had sin, but now you[P] say — We see, for
that reason your[P] sin does remain.

CHAPTER 10

1 'Truly, truly, I say to you[P], He who is not entering
through the door to the fold of the sheep, but is going
up from another side, that one is a thief and a robber;
2 and he who is entering through the door is shepherd
of the sheep;
3 to this one the doorkeeper does open, and the sheep
hear his voice, and he does call his own sheep by name,
and does lead them forth;
4 and when he may put forth his own sheep, he goes on
before them, and the sheep follow him, because they
have known his voice;
5 and a stranger they will not follow, but will flee from
him, because they have not known the voice of
strangers.'
6 This similitude spoke Jesus to them, and they knew
not what the things were that He was speaking to them;
7 For that reason Jesus said again to them, 'Truly, truly,
I say to you[P] — I am the door of the sheep;
8 all, as many as came before Me, are thieves and
robbers, but the sheep did not hear them;
9 I am the door, if any one may come in through Me, he
shall be saved, and he shall come in, and go out, and
find pasture.
10 'The thief does not come, except that he may steal,
and kill, and destroy; I came that they may have life,
and may have [it] abundantly.
11 'I am the good shepherd; the good shepherd lays
down his life for the sheep;
12 and the hireling, and not being a shepherd, whose
own the sheep are not, does behold the wolf coming,
and does leave the sheep, and does flee; and the wolf
catches them, and scatters the sheep;
13 and the hireling does flee because he is an hireling,
and is not caring for the sheep.
14 'I am the good shepherd, and I know My [sheep],
and am known by Mine,
15 according as the Father does know Me, and I know
the Father, and I lay down My life for the sheep,
16 and I have other sheep that are not of this fold, these
also it is necessary for me to bring, and My voice they
will hear, and there shall become one flock — one
shepherd.
17 'Because of this does the Father love Me, because I
lay down My life, that again I may take it;
18 no one does take it from Me, but I lay it down of
Myself; I have authority to lay it down, and I have
authority to take it again; this command I received from
My Father.'
19 Consequently, again, there came a division among
the Jews, because of these words,
20 and many of them said, 'He has a demon, and is mad,
why do you[P] hear Him?'
21 others said, 'These sayings are not those of a
demoniac; is a demon able to open blind men's eyes?'
22 And the dedication in Jerusalem came, and it was
winter,
23 and Jesus was walking in the temple, in the porch of
Solomon,
24 the Jews, consequently, came round about Him, and
said to Him, 'Till when do You[S] hold our soul in
suspense? if You[S] are the Christ, tell us freely.'
25 Jesus answered them, 'I told you[P], and you[P] do not
believe; the works that I do in the name of My Father,
these testify concerning Me;
26 but you[P] do not believe, for you[P] are not of My sheep,
27 according as I said to you[P]: My sheep do hear My
voice, and I know them, and they follow Me,
28 and I give to them life age-during, and they shall not
perish — to the age, and no one shall pluck them out of
My hand;
29 My Father, who has given to Me, is greater than all,
and no one is able to pluck out of the hand of My Father;
30 I and the Father are one.'
31 For that reason, again, did the Jews take up stones
that they may stone Him;
32 Jesus answered them, 'Many good works did I show
you[P] from My Father; because of which work of them
do you[P] stone Me?'
33 The Jews answered Him, saying, 'We do not stone
You[S] for a good work, but for speaking evil, and because
You[S], being a man, do make Yourself[S] God.'
34 Jesus answered them, 'Is it not having been written
in your[P] law: I said, you[P] are gods?
35 if He did call them gods unto whom the word of God
came, (and the Writing is not able to be broken,)
36 of Him whom the Father did sanctify, and send to the
world, do you[P] say — You[S] speak evil, because I said, I
am the Son of God?
37 if I do not the works of My Father, do not believe
Me;

38 and if I do, even if you[P] may not believe Me, the
works believe, that you[P] may know and may believe that
the Father [is] in Me, and I in Him.'
39 For that reason they were seeking again to seize Him,
and He went forth out of their hand,
40 and went away again to the other side of the Jordan,
to the place where John was at first baptizing, and
remained there,
41 and many came unto Him, and said — 'John, indeed,
did no sign, and all things, as many as John said about
this one were true;'
42 and many did believe in Him there.

CHAPTER 11

1 And there was a certain one ailing, Lazarus, from
Bethany, of the village of Mary and Martha her sister —
2 and it was Mary who did anoint the Lord with ointment,
and did wipe his feet with her hair, whose brother Lazarus
was ailing —
3 for that reason the sisters sent unto Him, saying, 'Sir,
behold, he whom You[S] do love is ailing;'
4 and Jesus having heard, said, 'This ailment is not unto
death, but for the glory of God, that the Son of God may
be glorified through it.'
5 And Jesus was loving Martha, and her sister, and
Lazarus,
6 when, for that reason, He heard that he is ailing, then
indeed He remained in the place in which He was two
days,
7 then after this, He said to the disciples, 'We may go to
Judea again;'
8 the disciples say to Him, 'Rabbi, now the Jews were
seeking to stone You[S], and again You[S] do go there!'
9 Jesus answered, 'Are there not twelve hours in the
day? if any one may walk in the day, he does not stumble,
because the light of this world he does see;
10 and if any one may walk in the night, he stumbles,
because the light is not in him.'
11 These things He said, and after this He said to them,
'Lazarus our friend has fallen asleep, but I go on that I
may awake him;'
12 for that reason His disciples said, 'Sir, if he has fallen
asleep, he will be saved;'
13 but Jesus had spoken about his death, but they
thought that He spoke about the repose of sleep.
14 Then, for that reason, Jesus said to them freely,
'Lazarus has died;
15 and I rejoice, for your[P] sake, (that you[P] may believe,)
that I was not there; but we may go to him;'
16 consequently said Thomas, who is called Didymus,
to the fellow-disciples, 'We may go — we also, that we
may die with Him,'
17 Jesus, consequently, having come, found him having
been in the tomb four days already.
18 And Bethany was near to Jerusalem, about fifteen
furlongs off,
19 and many of the Jews had come unto Martha and
Mary, that they might comfort them concerning their
brother;
20 Martha, for that reason, when she heard that Jesus
did come, met Him, and Mary kept sitting in the house.
21 Martha, consequently, said unto Jesus, 'Sir, if You[S]
had been here, my brother would not have died;
22 but even now, I have known that whatever You[S] may
ask of God, God will give to You[S];'
23 Jesus said to her, 'Your[S] brother shall rise again.'
24 Martha said to Him, 'I have known that he will rise
again, in the rising again in the last day;'
25 Jesus said to her, 'I am the rising again, and the life;
he who is believing in Me, even if he may die, shall live;
26 and every one who is living and believing in Me shall
not die — to the age;
27 believe you[S] this?' she said to Him, 'Yes, sir, I have
believed that You[S] are the Christ, the Son of God, who is
coming to the world.'
28 And having said these things, she went away, and
called Mary her sister privately, saying, 'The Teacher is
present, and does call you[S];'
29 she, when she heard, rose up quickly, and did come
to Him;
30 and Jesus had not yet come to the village, but was in
the place where Martha met Him;
31 the Jews, consequently, who were with her in the
house, and were comforting her, having seen Mary that
she rose up quickly and went forth, followed her, saying
— 'She does go away to the tomb, that she may weep
there.'
32 Mary, consequently, when she came where Jesus was,
having seen Him, fell at His feet, saying to Him, 'Sir, if
You[S] had been here, my brother would not have died;'
33 Jesus, for that reason, when He saw her weeping,
and the Jews who came with her weeping, did groan in
the spirit, and troubled Himself, and He said,
34 'Where have you[P] laid him?' they say to Him, 'Sir,
come and see;'
35 Jesus wept.

36 The Jews, for that reason, said, 'Behold, how He was
loving him!'
37 and certain of them said, 'Was not this one, who did
open the eyes of the blind man, able to cause that also
this one might not have died?'
38 Jesus, for that reason, again groaning in Himself,
came to the tomb, and it was a cave, and a stone was
lying upon it,
39 Jesus said, 'Take you[P] away the stone;' the sister of
him who had died — Martha — said to Him, 'Sir, already
he stinks, for he is four days dead;'
40 Jesus said to her, 'Said I not to you[S], that if you[S] may
believe, you[S] shall see the glory of God?'
41 They took away, for that reason, the stone where the
dead was laid, and Jesus lifted His eyes upwards, and
said, 'Father, I thank You[S], that You[S] did hear Me;
42 and I knew that You[S] always do hear Me, but, because
of the multitude that is standing by, I said [it], that they
may believe that You[S] did send Me.'
43 And saying these things, He cried out with a loud
voice, 'Lazarus, come forth;'
44 and he who died came forth, being bound feet and
hands with grave-clothes, and his face was bound about
with a napkin; Jesus said to them, 'Loose him, and allow
to go.'
45 Many, for that reason, of the Jews who came unto
Mary, and beheld what Jesus did, believed in Him;
46 but certain of them went away unto the Pharisees,
and told them what Jesus did;
47 the chief priests, for that reason, and the Pharisees,
gathered together a sanhedrim, and said, 'What may we
do? because this man does many signs?
48 if we may leave Him alone thus, all will believe in
Him; and the Romans will come, and will take away both
our place and nation.'
49 and a certain one of them, Caiaphas, being chief priest
of that year, said to them, 'You[P] have not known
anything,
50 nor reason that it is good for us that one man may
die for the people, and not the whole nation perish.'
51 And this he said not of himself, but being chief priest
of that year, he did prophesy that Jesus was about to
die for the nation,
52 and not for the nation only, but that also the children
of God, who have been scattered abroad, He may gather
together into one.
53 From that day, therefore, they took counsel together
that they may kill Him;
54 Jesus, for that reason, was no more freely walking
among the Jews, but went away from there to the region
near the wilderness, to a city called Ephraim, and there
He delayed with His disciples.
55 And the Passover of the Jews was near, and many
went up to Jerusalem out of the country before the
Passover, that they might purify themselves;
56 they were seeking, for that reason, Jesus, and said
one with another, standing in the temple, 'What does
appear to you[P] — that He may not come to the feast?'
57 and both the chief priests and the Pharisees had given
a command, that if any one may know where He is, he
may show [it], so that they may seize Him.

CHAPTER 12

1 Jesus, consequently, six days before the Passover,
came to Bethany, where Lazarus was, who had died,
whom He raised out of the dead;
2 they made, for that reason, to Him a supper there, and
Martha was ministering, and Lazarus was one of those
reclining together (at meat) with Him;
3 Mary, for that reason, having taken a pound of
ointment of spikenard, of great price, anointed the feet
of Jesus and did wipe His feet with her hair, and the
house was filled from the fragrance of the ointment.
4 For that reason one of His disciples said — Judas
Iscariot, of Simon, who is about to deliver Him up —
5 'Why was not this ointment sold for three hundred
denaries, and given to the poor?'
6 and he said this, not because he was caring for the
poor, but because he was a thief, and had the bag, and
what things he was carrying were put in.
7 Jesus, for that reason, said, 'Allow her; she has kept
it for the day of My embalming,
8 for the poor you[P] have always with yourselves[P], and
you[P] have not Me always.'
9 A great multitude, for that reason, of the Jews knew
that He is there, and they came, not because of Jesus
only, but that they may see Lazarus also, whom He raised
out of the dead;
10 and the chief priests took counsel, that they may kill
Lazarus also,
11 because on account of him many of the Jews were
going away, and were believing in Jesus.
12 On the morrow, a great multitude that came to the
feast, having heard that Jesus did come to Jerusalem,
13 took the branches of the palms, and went forth to meet
him, and were crying, 'Hosanna, blessed [is] He who is

coming in the name of the Lord — the king of Israel;'
14 and Jesus having found a young ass did sit upon it,
according as it is written,
15 'Fear not, daughter of Sion, behold, your[S] king does
come, sitting on an ass' colt.'
16 And His disciples did not know these things at the
first, but when Jesus was glorified, then they remembered
that these things were having been written about Him,
and these things they did to Him.
17 The multitude, consequently, who are with Him, were
testifying that He called Lazarus out of the tomb, and
did raise him out of the dead;
18 because of this also did the multitude meet Him,
because they heard of His having done this sign,
19 the Pharisees, for that reason, said among themselves,
'You[P] see that you[P] do not gain anything, behold, the
world did go after Him.'
20 And out of those coming up there were certain Greeks
that they may worship in the feast,
21 these then came near to Philip, who [is] from
Bethsaida of Galilee, and were asking him, saying, 'Sir,
we wish to see Jesus;'
22 Philip came and told Andrew, and again Andrew and
Philip tell Jesus.
23 And Jesus responded to them, saying, 'The hour
has come that the Son of Man may be glorified;
24 truly, truly, I say to you[P], if the grain of the wheat,
having fallen to the earth, may not die, itself remains
alone; and if it may die, it does bear much fruit;
25 he who is loving his life shall lose it, and he who is
hating his life in this world — to life age-during shall
keep it;
26 if any one may minister to Me, let him follow Me, and
where I am, there also My ministrant shall be; and if any
one may minister to Me — the Father will honor him.
27 'Now My soul has been troubled, and what? shall I
say — Father, save Me from this hour? — but because
of this I came to this hour;
28 Father, glorify Your[S] name.' There came, therefore, a
voice out of the heaven, 'I both glorified, and again I
will glorify [it];'
29 the multitude, consequently, having stood and heard,
were saying that there had been thunder; others said,
'A messenger has spoken to Him.'
30 Jesus answered and said, 'Not because of Me has
this voice come, but because of you[P];
31 now is a judgment of this world, now shall the ruler
of this world be cast forth;
32 and I, if I may be lifted up from the earth, will draw all
men unto Myself.'
33 And this he said signifying by what death He was
about to die;
34 the multitude answered Him, 'We heard out of the
law that the Christ does remain — to the age; and how
do You[S] say, That it is necessary for the Son of Man to
be lifted up? who is this — the Son of Man?'
35 Jesus, for that reason, said to them, 'Yet a little time
is the light with you[P]; walk while you[P] have the light,
that darkness may not overtake you[P]; and he who is
walking in the darkness has not known where he goes;
36 while you[P] have the light, believe in the light, that
sons of light you[P] may become.' These things spoke
Jesus, and having gone away, He was hid from them,
37 yet He having done so many signs before them, they
were not believing in Him,
38 that the word of Isaiah the prophet might be fulfilled,
which he said, 'Lord, who gave credence to our report?
and the arm of the Lord — to whom was it revealed?'
39 Because of this they were not able to believe, that
again Isaiah said,
40 'He has blinded their eyes, and hardened their heart,
that they might not see with the eyes, and understand
with the heart, and turn back, and I might heal them;'
41 these things said Isaiah, when he saw His glory, and
spoke of him.
42 Still, however, also did many out of the rulers believe
in Him, but because of the Pharisees they were not
confessing, that they might not be put out of the
synagogue,
43 for they loved the glory of men more than the glory
of God.
44 And Jesus cried and said, 'He who is believing in
Me, does not believe in Me, but in Him who sent Me;
45 and he who is beholding Me, does behold Him who
sent Me;
46 I have come as a light to the world, that every one
who is believing in Me — may not remain in the
darkness;
47 and if any one may hear My sayings, and not believe,
I — I do not judge him, for I came not that I might judge
the world, but that I might save the world.
48 'He who is rejecting Me, and not receiving My
sayings, has one who is judging him, the word that I
spoke, that will judge him in the last day,
49 because I spoke not from Myself, but the Father who
sent Me, He did give Me a command, what I may say,
and what I may speak,
50 and I have known that His command is life age-

during; what, for that reason, I speak, according as the
Father has said to Me, so I speak.'

CHAPTER 13

1 And before the feast of the Passover, Jesus knowing
that His hour had come, that He may remove out of this
world unto the Father, having loved His own who [are]
in the world — to the end He loved them.
2 And supper being come, the devil already having put
[it] into the heart of Judas of Simon, Iscariot, that he
may deliver Him up,
3 Jesus knowing that the Father has given to Him all
things — into [His] hands, and that He came forth from
God, and unto God He goes,
4 did rise from the supper, and did lay down His
garments, and having taken a towel, He girded Himself;
5 afterward He put water into the basin, and began to
wash the feet of His disciples, and to wipe with the towel
with which He was being girded.
6 He came, consequently, unto Simon Peter, and that
one said to Him, 'Sir, You[S] — do You[S] wash my feet?'
7 Jesus answered and said to Him, 'That which I do
you[S] have not known now, but you[S] shall know after
these things;'
8 Peter said to Him, 'You[S] may not wash my feet — to
the age.' Jesus answered him, 'If I may not wash you[S],
you[S] have no part with Me;'
9 Simon Peter said to Him, 'Sir, not my feet only, but
also the hands and the head.'
10 Jesus said to him, 'He who has been bathed has no
need save to wash his feet, but he is clean altogether;
and you[P] are clean, but not all;'
11 for He knew him who is delivering Him up; because
of this He said, 'You[P] are not all clean.'
12 When, consequently, He washed their feet, and took
His garments, having reclined (at meat) again, He said
to them, 'Do you[P] know what I have done to you[P]?
13 you[P] call Me, The Teacher and The Lord, and you[P]
say well, for I am;
14 if then I did wash your[P] feet — the Lord and the
Teacher — you[P] also ought to wash one another's feet.
15 'For an example I gave to you[P], that, according as I
did to you[P], you[P] also may do;
16 truly, truly, I say to you[P], a servant is not greater than
his lord, nor an apostle greater than He who sent him;
17 if these things you[P] have known, happy are you[P], if
you[P] may do them;
18 not concerning you[P] all do I speak; I have known
whom I chose for Myself; but that the Writing may be
fulfilled: He who is eating the bread with me, did lift up
his heel against Me.
19 'From this time I tell you[P], before its coming to pass,
that, when it may come to pass, you[P] may believe that I
am [He];
20 truly, truly, I say to you[P], he who is receiving
whomsoever I may send, does receive Me; and he who
is receiving Me, does receive Him who sent Me.'
21 These things having said, Jesus was troubled in the
spirit, and did testify, and said, 'Truly, truly, I say to you[P],
that one of you[P] will deliver Me up;'
22 the disciples were looking, for that reason, one at
another, doubting concerning whom He spoke.
23 And there was one of His disciples reclining (at meat)
in the bosom of Jesus, whom Jesus was loving;
24 Simon Peter, then, did beckon to this one, to inquire
who He may be concerning whom He spoke,
25 and that one having leant back on the breast of Jesus,
responded to Him, 'Sir, who is it?'
26 Jesus answered, 'That one it is to whom I, having
dipped the morsel, shall give it;' and having dipped the
morsel, He gave [it] to Judas of Simon, Iscariot.
27 And after the morsel, then the Adversary entered
into that one, Jesus, for that reason, said to him, 'What
you[S] do — do quickly;'
28 and none of those reclining at meat knew for what
intent He said this to him,
29 for certain were thinking, since Judas had the bag,
that Jesus said to him, 'Buy what we have need of for
the feast;' or that he may give something to the poor;
30 having received, for that reason, the morsel, that one
immediately went forth, and it was night.
31 When, for that reason, he went forth, Jesus said,
'Now was the Son of Man glorified, and God was
glorified in Him;
32 if God was glorified in Him, God also will glorify Him
in Himself; yes, immediately He will glorify Him.
33 'Little children, yet a little am I with you[P]; you[P] will
seek Me, and, according as I said to the Jews — Where
I go away, you[P] are not able to come, to you[P] also I do
say [it] now.
34 'A new commandment I give to you[P], that you[P] love
one another; according as I did love you[P], that you[P] also
love one another;
35 in this shall all know that you[P] are My disciples, if
you[P] may have love one to another.'
36 Simon Peter said to Him, 'Sir, where do You[S] go away?'

Jesus answered him, 'Where I go away, you[S] are not able
now to follow Me, but afterward you[S] shall follow Me.'
37 Peter said to Him, 'Sir, why am I not able to follow
You[S] now? I will lay down my life for You[S];'
38 Jesus answered him, 'You[S] will lay down your life for
Me! truly, truly, I say to you[S], a cock will not crow till
you[S] may deny Me three times.'

CHAPTER 14

1 'Let not your[P] heart be troubled, believe in God, also
believe in Me;
2 in the house of My Father are many mansions; and if not,
I would have told you[P]; I go on to prepare a place for you[P];
3 and if I go on and prepare a place for you[P], I will come
again, and will receive you[P] unto Myself, that you[P] may
also be where I am;
4 and you[P] have known where I go away, and you[P] have
known the way.'
5 Thomas said to Him, 'Sir, we have not known where
You[S] go away, and how are we able to know the way?'
6 Jesus said to him, 'I am the way, and the truth, and the
life, no one does come unto the Father, if not through Me;
7 if you[P] had known Me, you[P] would have known My
Father also, and from this time you[P] have known Him,
and have seen Him.'
8 Philip said to Him, 'Sir, show the Father to us, and it is
enough for us;'
9 Jesus said to him, 'So long time am I with you[P], and
you[S] have not known Me, Philip? he who has seen Me
has seen the Father; and how do you[S] say, Show the
Father to us?
10 Believe you[S] not that I [am] in the Father, and the
Father is in Me? the sayings that I speak to you[P], I speak
not from Myself, and the Father who is abiding in Me,
Himself does the works;
11 believe Me, that I [am] in the Father, and the Father
in Me; and if not, because of the works themselves,
believe Me.
12 'Truly, truly, I say to you[P], he who is believing in Me,
the works that I do — that one also shall do, and greater
than these he shall do, because I go on to My Father;
13 and whatever you[P] may ask in My name, I will do,
that the Father may be glorified in the Son;
14 if you[P] ask anything in My name I will do [it].
15 'If you[P] love Me, keep My commands,
16 and I will ask the Father, and He will give another
Comforter to you[P], that He may remain with you[P] — to
the age;
17 the Spirit of truth, whom the world is not able to
receive, because it does not behold Him, nor know Him,
and you[P] know Him, because He does remain with you[P],
and shall be in you[P].
18 'I will not leave you[P] bereaved, I come unto you[P];
19 yet a little, and the world does behold Me no more,
and you[P] behold Me, because I live, and you[P] shall live;
20 in that day you[P] shall know that I [am] in My Father,
and you[P] in Me, and I in you[P];
21 he who is having My commands, and is keeping them,
that one it is who is loving Me, and he who is loving Me
shall be loved by My Father, and I will love him, and will
reveal Myself to him.'
22 Judas said to Him, (not the Iscariot), 'Sir, what has
come to pass, that You[S] are about to reveal Yourself[S] to
us, and not to the world?'
23 Jesus answered and said to him, 'If any one may
love Me, he will keep My word, and My Father will love
him, and We will come unto him, and We will make abode
with him;
24 he who is not loving Me, does not keep My words;
and the word that you[P] hear is not Mine, but the Father's
who sent Me.
25 ' I have spoken these things to you[P], remaining with
you[P],
26 and the Comforter, the Holy Spirit, whom the Father
will send in My name, He will teach you[P] all things, and
remind you[P] of all things that I said to you[P].
27 'Peace I leave to you[P]; my peace I give to you[P], not
according as the world does give do I give to you[P]; let
not your[P] heart be troubled, nor let it be afraid;
28 you[P] heard that I said to you[P] — I go away, and I
come unto you[P]; if you[P] did love Me, you[P] would have
rejoiced that I said — I go on to the Father, because My
Father is greater than I.
29 'And now I have said [it] to you[P] before it come to
pass, that when it may come to pass, you[P] may believe;
30 I will no more talk much with you[P], for the ruler of
this world does come, and in Me he has nothing;
31 but that the world may know that I love the Father,
and according as the Father gave Me command so I do;
arise, we may go from here.

CHAPTER 15

1 'I am the true vine, and My Father is the husbandman;
2 every branch in Me not bearing fruit, He does take it

away, and every one bearing fruit, He does cleanse by
pruning it, that it may bear more fruit;
3 already you[P] are clean, because of the word that I
have spoken to you[P];
4 remain in Me, and I in you[P], as the branch is not able
to bear fruit of itself, if it may not remain in the vine, so
neither you[P], if you[P] may not remain in Me.
5 'I am the vine, you[P] the branches; he who is remaining
in Me, and I in him, this one does bear much fruit,
because apart from Me you[P] are not able to do anything;
6 if any one may not remain in Me, he was cast forth
without as the branch, and was withered, and they gather
them, and cast to fire, and they are burned;
7 if you[P] may remain in Me, and My sayings may remain
in you[P], whatever you[P] may wish you[P] shall ask, and it
shall be done to you[P].
8 'In this was My Father glorified, that you[P] may bear
much fruit, and you[P] shall become My disciples.
9 According as the Father did love Me, I also loved
you[P], remain in My love;
10 if you[P] may keep My commandments, you[P] shall
remain in My love, according as I have kept the
commands of My Father, and do remain in His love;
11 these things I have spoken to you[P], that My joy may
remain in you[P], and your[P] joy may be full.
12 'This is My command, that you[P] love one another,
according as I did love you[P];
13 no one has greater love than this, that any one may
lay down his life for his friends;
14 you[P] are my friends, if you[P] may do whatever I
command you[P];
15 no more do I call you[P] servants, because the servant
has not known what his lord does, and I have called
you[P] friends, because all things that I heard from My
Father, I did make known to you[P].
16 'You[P] did not choose out Me, but I chose out you[P],
and did appoint you[P], that you[P] might go away, and might
bear fruit, and your[P] fruit might remain, that whatever
you[P] may ask of the Father in My name, He may give
you[P].
17 'These things I command you[P], that you[P] love one
another;
18 if the world does hate you[P], you[P] know that it has
hated Me before you[P];
19 if you[P] were of the world, the world would have been
loving its own, and because you[P] are not of the world
— but I chose out of the world — because of this the
world hates you[P].
20 'Remember the word that I said to you[P], A servant is
not greater than his lord; if they did persecute Me, they
will persecute you[P] also; if they did keep My word, they
will keep yours[P] also;
21 but they will do all these things to you[P], because of
My name, because they have not known Him who sent
Me;
22 if I had not come and spoken to them, they were not
having sin; but now they have no pretext for their sin.
23 'He who is hating Me, does hate My Father also;
24 if I did not do the works among them that no other
have done, they were not having sin, and now they have
both seen and hated both Me and My Father;
25 but — that the word may be fulfilled that was written
in their law — They hated Me without a cause.
26 'And when the Comforter may come, whom I will
send to you[P] from the Father — the Spirit of truth, who
does come forth from the Father, He will testify of Me;
27 and you[P] also do testify, because you[P] are with Me
from the beginning.

CHAPTER 16

1 ' I have spoken these things to you[P], that you[P] may
not be stumbled,
2 they will put you[P] out of the synagogues; but an hour
does come, that every one who has killed you[P], may think
to offer service unto God;
3 and they will do these things to you[P], because they
did not know the Father, nor Me.
4 'But I have spoken these things to you[P], that when
the hour may come, you[P] may remember them, that I said
[them] to you[P], and I did not say these things to you[P]
from the beginning, because I was with you[P];
5 and now I go away to Him who sent Me, and none of
you[P] does ask Me, Where do You[S] go?
6 but because I have said these things to you[P], the
sorrow has filled your[P] heart.
7 'But I tell you[P] the truth; it is better for you[P] that I go
away, for if I may not go away, the Comforter will not
come unto you[P], and if I go on, I will send Him unto you[P];
8 and having come, He will convict the world concerning
sin, and concerning righteousness, and concerning
judgment;
9 concerning sin indeed, because they do not believe
in Me;
10 and concerning righteousness, because I go away
unto My Father, and no more do you behold Me;
11 and concerning judgment, because the ruler of this

world has been judged.

12 'I have many things to say to you[P] yet, but you[P] are not able to bear [them] now;

13 and when He may come — the Spirit of truth — He will guide you[P] to all the truth, for He will not speak from Himself, but as many things as He will hear He will speak, and He will tell you[P] the coming things;

14 He will glorify Me, because He will take of Mine, and will tell to you[P].

15 'All things, as many as the Father has, are Mine; because of this I said, That He will take of Mine, and will tell to you[P];

16 a little while, and you[P] do not behold Me, and again a little while, and you[P] shall see Me, because I go away unto the Father.'

17 For that reason [some] of His disciples said one to another, 'What is this that He said to us, A little while, and you[P] do not behold Me, and again a little while, and you[P] shall see Me, and, Because I go away unto the Father?'

18 they said then, 'What is this He said — the little while? we have not known what He said.'

19 Jesus, for that reason, knew that they were wishing to ask Him, and He said to them, 'Concerning this do you[P] seek one with another, because I said, A little while, and you[P] do not behold Me, and again a little while, and you[P] shall see Me?

20 truly, truly, I say to you[P], that you[P] shall weep and lament, and the world will rejoice; and you[P] shall be sorrowful, but your[P] sorrow will become joy.

21 'The woman, when she may bear, has sorrow, because her hour did come, and when she may bear the child, no more does she remember the anguish, because of the joy that a man was born to the world.

22 'And you[P], for that reason, now, indeed, have sorrow; and again I will see you[P], and your[P] heart shall rejoice, and no one does take your[P] joy from you[P],

23 and in that day you[P] will question Me nothing; truly, truly, I say to you[P], as many things as you[P] may ask of the Father in My name, He will give you[P];

24 till now you[P] did ask nothing in My name; ask, and you[P] shall receive, that your[P] joy may be full.

25 'These things in similitudes I have spoken to you[P], but there comes an hour when I will speak to you[P] no more in similitudes, but freely of the Father, will tell you[P].

26 'In that day, you[P] will make request in My name, and I do not say to you[P] that I will ask the Father for you[P],

27 for the Father Himself does love you[P], because you[P] have loved Me, and you[P] have believed that I came forth from God;

28 I came forth from the Father, and have come to the world; again I leave the world, and go on unto the Father.'

29 His disciples say to Him, 'Behold, You[S] do speak freely now, and You[S] speak no similitude;

30 now we have known that You[S] have known all things, and have no need that any one do question You[S]; in this we believe that You[S] did come forth from God.'

31 Jesus answered them, 'Now do you[P] believe? behold, there does come an hour,

32 and now it has come, that you[P] may be scattered, each to his own things, and you[P] may leave Me alone, and I am not alone, because the Father is with Me;

33 these things I have spoken to you[P], that you[P] may have peace in Me, in the world you[P] shall have tribulation, but take courage — I have overcome the world.'

CHAPTER 17

1 These things spoke Jesus, and lifted up His eyes to the heaven, and said — 'Father, the hour has come, glorify Your[S] Son, that Your[S] Son also may glorify You[S],

2 according as You[S] did give to Him authority over all flesh, that — all that You[S] have given to Him — He may give to them life age-during;

3 and this is the life age-during, that they may know You[S], the only true God, and Him whom You[S] did send — Jesus Christ;

4 I did glorify You[S] on the earth, I did finish the work that You[S] have given Me, that I may do [it].

5 'And now, glorify Me, You[S] Father, with Yourself[S], with the glory that I had before the world was, with You[S];

6 I did reveal Your[S] name to the men whom You[S] have given to Me out of the world; Yours[S] they were, and to Me You[S] have given them, and Your[S] word they have kept;

7 now they have known that all things, as many as You[S] have given to Me, are from You[S],

8 because the sayings that You[S] have given to Me, I have given to them, and they themselves received, and have known truly, that I came forth from You[S], and they did believe that You[S] did send Me.

9 'I ask in regard to them; I do not ask in regard to the world, but in regard to those whom You[S] have given to Me, because they are Yours[S],

10 and all Mine are Yours[S], and Yours[S] [are] Mine, and I have been glorified in them;

11 and no more am I in the world, and these are in the world, and I come unto You[S]. Holy Father, keep them in Your[S] name, whom You[S] have given to me, that they may be one as We;
12 when I was with them in the world, I was keeping them in Your[S] name; those whom You[S] have given to Me I did guard, and none of them was destroyed, except the son of the destruction, that the Writing may be fulfilled.
13 'And now I come unto You[S], and I speak these things in the world, that they may have My joy fulfilled in themselves;
14 I have given Your[S] word to them, and the world did hate them, because they are not of the world, as I am not of the world;
15 I do not ask that You[S] may take them out of the world, but that You[S] may keep them out of the evil.
16 'Of the world they are not, as I am not of the world;
17 sanctify them in Your[S] truth, Your[S] word is truth;
18 as You[S] did send Me to the world, I also did send them to the world;
19 and for them do I sanctify Myself, that they also themselves may be sanctified in truth.
20 'And I do not ask in regard to these alone, but also in regard to those who shall be believing, through their word, in Me;
21 that they all may be one, as You[S] Father [are] in Me, and I in You[S]; that they also may be one in us, that the world may believe that You[S] did send Me.
22 'And I, the glory that You[S] have given to Me, have given to them, that they may be one as We are one;
23 I in them, and You[S] in Me, that they may be perfected into one, and that the world may know that You[S] did send Me, and did love them as You[S] did love Me.
24 'Father, those whom You[S] have given to Me, I will that where I am they also may be with Me, that they may behold My glory that You[S] did give to Me, because You[S] did love Me before the foundation of the world.
25 'Righteous Father, also the world did not know You[S], and I knew You[S], and these have known that You[S] did send Me,
26 and I made Your[S] name known to them, and will make known, that the love with which You[S] loved Me may be in them, and I in them.'

CHAPTER 18

1 Having said these things, Jesus went forth with His disciples beyond the brook of Kedron, where was a garden, into which He entered, Himself and His disciples,
2 and Judas also, who delivered Him up, had known the place, because many times did Jesus assemble there with His disciples.
3 Judas, for that reason, having taken the band and officers out of the chief priests and Pharisees, did come there with torches and lamps, and weapons;
4 Jesus, for that reason, knowing all things that are coming upon Him, having gone forth, said to them, 'Whom do you[P] seek?'
5 they answered Him, 'Jesus the Nazarene;' Jesus said to them, 'I am [He];' — and Judas who delivered Him up was standing with them; —
6 when, consequently, He said to them — 'I am [He],' they went away backward, and fell to the ground.
7 Again, for that reason, He questioned them, 'Whom do you[P] seek?' and they said, 'Jesus the Nazarene;'
8 Jesus answered, 'I said to you[P] that I am [He]; if, then, you[P] seek Me, allow these to go away;'
9 that the word might be fulfilled that He said — 'Those whom You[S] have given to Me, I did not lose even one of them.'
10 Simon Peter, consequently, having a sword, drew it, and struck the chief priest's servant, and cut off his right ear — and the name of the servant was Malchus —
11 Jesus, for that reason, said to Peter, 'Put the sword into the sheath; the cup that the Father has given to Me, may I not drink it?'
12 The band, consequently, and the captain, and the officers of the Jews, took hold on Jesus, and bound Him,
13 and they led Him away to Annas first, for he was father-in-law of Caiaphas, who was chief priest of that year,
14 and Caiaphas was he who gave counsel to the Jews, that it is good for one man to perish for the people.
15 And following Jesus was Simon Peter, and the other disciple, and that disciple was known to the chief priest, and he entered with Jesus to the hall of the chief priest,
16 and Peter was standing at the door without, for that reason the other disciple who was known to the chief priest went forth, and he spoke to the female keeping the door, and he brought in Peter.
17 Then said the maid keeping the door to Peter, 'Are you[S] also of the disciples of this man?' he said, 'I am not;'
18 and the servants and the officers were standing, having made a fire of coals, because it was cold, and they were warming themselves, and Peter was standing with them, and warming himself.
19 The chief priests, consequently, questioned Jesus

concerning His disciples, and concerning His teaching;
20 Jesus answered him, 'I spoke freely to the world, I
did always teach in a synagogue, and in the temple,
where the Jews do always come together; and in secret
I spoke nothing;
21 why do you[S] question Me? question those having
heard what I spoke to them; behold, these have known
what I said.'
22 And He having said these things, one of the officers
standing by did give Jesus a slap, saying, 'Thus do You[S]
answer the chief priest?'
23 Jesus answered him, 'If I spoke ill, testify concerning
the ill; and if well, why do you[S] strike Me?'
24 Annas then sent Him bound to Caiaphas the chief
priest.
25 And Simon Peter was standing and warming himself,
they said then to him, 'Are you[S] also of His disciples?'
he denied, and said, 'I am not.'
26 One of the servants of the chief priest, being kinsman
of him whose ear Peter cut off, said, 'Did I not see you[S]
in the garden with him?'
27 again, consequently, Peter denied, and immediately
a cock crowed.
28 They led, consequently, Jesus from Caiaphas to the
praetorium, and it was early, and they themselves did
not enter into the praetorium, that they might not be
defiled, but that they might eat the Passover;
29 Pilate, for that reason, went forth unto them, and said,
'What accusation do you[P] bring against this man?'
30 they answered and said to him, 'If He were not an
evil doer, we would not have delivered Him to you[S].'
31 Pilate, for that reason, said to them, 'Take you[P] Him
— you[P] — and judge Him according to your[P] law;' the
Jews, for that reason, said to him, 'It is not lawful to us
to put any one to death;'
32 that the word of Jesus might be fulfilled which He
said, signifying by what death He was about to die.
33 Pilate, for that reason, entered into the praetorium
again, and called Jesus, and said to Him, 'You[S] are the
King of the Jews?'
34 Jesus answered him, 'From yourself[S] do you[S] say
this? or did others say it to you[S] about Me?'
35 Pilate answered, 'Am I a Jew? Your[S] nation, and the
chief priests did deliver You[S] up to me; what did You[S]?'
36 Jesus answered, 'My kingdom is not of this world; if
My kingdom were of this world, My officers would have
struggled that I might not be delivered up to Jews; but
now My kingdom is not from here.'
37 Pilate, for that reason, said to Him, 'Are You[S] then a
king?' Jesus answered, 'You[S] do say [it]; because I am a
king, for this I have been born, and for this I have come
to the world, that I may testify to the truth; every one
who is of the truth, does hear My voice.'
38 Pilate said to Him, 'What is truth?' and having said
this, again he went forth unto the Jews, and said to them,
'I do find no fault in Him;
39 and you[P] have a custom that I shall release to you[P]
one in the Passover; will you[P], for that reason, [that] I
shall release to you[P] the king of the Jews?'
40 for that reason they all cried out again, saying, 'Not
this one — but Barabbas;' and Barabbas was a robber.

CHAPTER 19

1 Then, for that reason, did Pilate take Jesus and scourge
[Him],
2 and the soldiers having braided a crown of thorns,
did place [it] on His head, and a purple garment they
put around Him,
3 and said, 'Hail! the king of the Jews;' and they were
giving Him slaps.
4 Pilate, consequently, again went forth without, and
said to them, 'Behold, I do bring Him to you[P] without,
that you[P] may know that I find no fault in Him;'
5 Jesus, for that reason, came forth without, bearing
the thorny crown and the purple garment; and he said
to them, 'Behold, the man!'
6 When, consequently, the chief priests and the officers
did see Him, they cried out, saying, 'Crucify, crucify;'
Pilate said to them, 'Take you[P] Him — you[P], and crucify;
for I find no fault in Him;'
7 the Jews answered him, 'We have a law, and according to
our law He ought to die, for He made Himself Son of God.'
8 When, for that reason, Pilate heard this word, he was
the more afraid,
9 and entered again to the praetorium, and said to Jesus,
'From where are You[S]?' and Jesus gave him no answer.
10 Pilate, therefore, said to Him, 'You[S] do not speak to
me? have You[S] not known that I have authority to crucify
You[S], and I have authority to release You[S]?'
11 Jesus answered, 'You[S] would have no authority
against Me, if it were not having been given you[S] from
above; because of this, he who is delivering Me up to
you[S] has greater sin.'
12 From this [time] was Pilate seeking to release Him,
and the Jews were crying out, saying, 'If you[S] may
release this one, you[S] are not a friend of Caesar; every

one making himself a king, does speak against Caesar.'
13 Pilate, for that reason, having heard this word, brought Jesus without — and he sat down upon the tribunal — to a place called, 'Pavement,' and in Hebrew, Gabbatha;
14 and it was the preparation of the Passover, and as it were the sixth hour, and he said to the Jews, 'Behold, your[P] king!'
15 and they cried out, 'Take away, take away, crucify Him;' Pilate said to them, ' Shall I crucify your[P] king?' the chief priests answered, 'We have no king except Caesar.'
16 Then, for that reason, he delivered Him up to them, that He may be crucified, and they took Jesus and led [Him] away,
17 and bearing His cross, He went forth to the place called [Place] of a Skull, which is called in Hebrew Golgotha;
18 where they crucified Him, and two others with Him, on this side, and on that side, and Jesus in the midst.
19 And Pilate also wrote a title, and put [it] on the cross, and it was written, 'Jesus the Nazarene, the king of the Jews;'
20 this title, consequently, many of the Jews read, because the place was near to the city where Jesus was crucified, and it was having been written in Hebrew, in Greek, in Roman.
21 The chief priests of the Jews said, for that reason, to Pilate, 'Write not — The king of the Jews, but that one said, I am king of the Jews;'
22 Pilate answered, 'What I have written, I have written.'
23 The soldiers, consequently, when they did crucify Jesus, took His garments, and made four parts, to each soldier a part, also the coat, and the coat was seamless, from the top woven throughout,
24 they said, for that reason, to one another, 'We may not rend it, but cast a lot for it, whose it shall be;' that the Writing might be fulfilled, that is saying, 'They divided My garments to themselves, and upon My raiment they did cast a lot;' the soldiers, for that reason, indeed, did these things.
25 And there stood by the cross of Jesus His mother, and His mother's sister, Mary of Cleopas, and Mary the Magdalene;
26 Jesus, consequently, having seen [His] mother, and the disciple standing by, whom He was loving, He said to His mother, 'Woman, behold, your[S] son;'
27 afterward He said to the disciple, 'Behold, your[S] mother;' and from that hour the disciple took her to his own [home].
28 After this, Jesus knowing that all things now have been finished, that the Writing may be fulfilled, said, 'I thirst;'
29 a vessel, consequently, was placed full of vinegar, and they having filled a sponge with vinegar, and having put [it] around a hyssop stalk, did put [it] to His mouth;
30 when, consequently, Jesus received the vinegar, He said, 'It has been finished;' and having bowed the head, gave up the spirit.
31 The Jews, consequently, that the bodies might not remain on the cross on the sabbath, since it was the preparation, (for that Sabbath day was a great one,) asked of Pilate that their legs may be broken, and they taken away.
32 The soldiers, for that reason, came, and of the first indeed they did break the legs, and of the other who was crucified with Him,
33 and having come to Jesus, when they saw Him already having been dead, they did not break His legs;
34 but one of the soldiers with a spear did pierce His side, and immediately there came forth blood and water;
35 and he who had seen had testified, and his testimony is true, and that one had known that he spoke true things, that you also may believe.
36 For these things came to pass, that the Writing may be fulfilled, 'A bone of Him shall not be broken;'
37 and again another Writing said, 'They shall look to Him whom they did pierce.'
38 And after these things did Joseph of Arimathea — being a disciple of Jesus, but concealed, through the fear of the Jews — ask of Pilate, that he may take away the body of Jesus, and Pilate gave leave; he came, for that reason, and took away the body of Jesus,
39 and Nicodemus also came — who came unto Jesus by night at the first — bearing a mixture of myrrh and aloes, as it were, a hundred pounds.
40 They took, consequently, the body of Jesus, and bound it with linen clothes with the spices, according as it was the custom of the Jews to prepare for burial;
41 and there was a garden in the place where He was crucified, and in the garden a new tomb, in which no one was yet laid;
42 there, for that reason, because of the preparation of the Jews, because the tomb was near, they laid Jesus.

CHAPTER 20

1 And on the first of the Sabbaths, Mary the Magdalene did come early (there being yet darkness) to the tomb, and she saw the stone having been taken away out of

the tomb,
2 she ran, for that reason, and came unto Simon Peter,
and unto the other disciple whom Jesus was loving, and
said to them, 'They took away the Lord out of the tomb,
and we have not known where they laid Him.'
3 Peter, for that reason, went forth, and the other disciple,
and they were coming to the tomb,
4 and the two were running together, and the other
disciple did run forward more quickly than Peter, and
came first to the tomb,
5 and having stooped down, saw the linen clothes lying,
yet, indeed, he entered not.
6 Simon Peter, for that reason, came, following him, and
he entered into the tomb, and beheld the linen clothes
lying,
7 and the napkin that was upon His head, not lying with
the linen clothes, but apart, having been folded up, in
one place;
8 then, consequently, entered also the other disciple
who came first unto the tomb, and he saw, and did
believe;
9 for not yet did they know the Writing, that it was
necessary for Him to rise again out of the dead.
10 The disciples consequently went away again unto
their own friends,
11 and Mary was standing near the tomb, weeping
without; as she was weeping, then, she stooped down
to the tomb, and beheld two messengers in white, sitting,
12 one at the head, and one at the feet, where the body
of Jesus had been laid.
13 And they say to her, 'Woman, why do you[S] weep?'
she said to them, 'Because they took away my Lord, and
I have not known where they laid Him;'
14 and these things having said, she turned backward,
and saw Jesus standing, and she had not known that it
is Jesus.
15 Jesus said to her, 'Woman, why do you[S] weep? whom
do you[S] seek;' she, supposing that He is the gardener,
said to Him, 'Sir, if You[S] did carry Him away, tell me where
You[S] did lay Him, and I will take Him away;'
16 Jesus said to her, 'Mary!' having turned, she said to
Him, 'Rabbouni;' that is to say, 'Teacher.'
17 Jesus said to her, 'Be not touching Me, for I have
not yet ascended unto My Father; and be going on to
My brethren, and say to them, I ascend unto My Father,
and your[P] Father, and to My God, and to your[P] God.'
18 Mary the Magdalene came, telling to the disciples
that she had seen the Lord, and [that] He said these
things to her.
19 It being, consequently, evening, on that day, the first
of the Sabbaths, and the doors having been shut where
the disciples were assembled, through fear of the Jews,
Jesus came and stood in the midst, and said to them,
'Peace to you[P];'
20 and this having said, He showed them His hands
and side; the disciples, for that reason, rejoiced, having
seen the Lord.
21 Jesus, for that reason, said to them again, 'Peace to
you[P]; according as the Father has sent He, I also send
you[P];'
22 and this having said, He breathed on [them], and
said to them, 'Receive the Holy Spirit;
23 if of any you[P] may loose the sins, they are loosed to
them; if of any you[P] may retain, they have been retained.'
24 And Thomas, one of the twelve, who is called
Didymus, was not with them when Jesus came;
25 the other disciples, for that reason, said to him, 'We
have seen the Lord;' and he said to them, 'If I may not
see the mark of the nails in His hands, and may put my
finger to the mark of the nails, and may put my hand to
His side, I will not believe.'
26 And after eight days, again His disciples were within,
and Thomas with them; Jesus came, the doors having
been shut, and He stood in the midst, and said, 'Peace
to you[P]!'
27 then He said to Thomas, 'Bring your[S] finger here,
and see My hands, and bring your[S] hand, and put [it] to
My side, and become not unbelieving, but believing.'
28 And Thomas answered and said to Him, 'My Lord
and my God;'
29 Jesus said to him, 'Because you[S] have seen Me,
Thomas, you[S] have believed; happy those not having
seen, and having believed.'
30 Many indeed, consequently, other signs also did
Jesus before His disciples, that are not written in this
book;
31 and these have been written that you[P] may believe
that Jesus is the Christ, the Son of God, and that
believing you[P] may have life in His name.'

CHAPTER 21

1 After these things did Jesus reveal himself again to
the disciples on the sea of Tiberias, and He did reveal
Himself thus:
2 There were together Simon Peter, and Thomas who is
called Didymus, and Nathanael from Cana of Galilee, and

the [sons] of Zebedee, and two others of His disciples.
3 Simon Peter said to them, 'I go away to fish;' they say
to him, 'We go — we also — with you^{S};' they went forth
and entered into the boat immediately, and on that night
they caught nothing.
4 And morning being now come, Jesus stood at the
shore, yet indeed the disciples did not know that it is
Jesus;
5 Jesus, consequently, said to them, 'Lads, have you^{P}
any meat?'
6 they answered Him, 'No;' and He said to them, 'Cast
the net at the right side of the boat, and you^{P} shall find;'
they cast, for that reason, and no longer were they able
to draw it, from the multitude of the fishes.
7 That disciple, for that reason, whom Jesus was loving
said to Peter, 'It is the Lord!' Simon Peter, for that reason,
having heard that it is the Lord, did gird on the outer
coat, (for he was naked,) and did cast himself into the
sea;
8 and the other disciples came by the little boat, for
they were not far from the land, but as it were about two
hundred cubits off, dragging the net of the fishes;
9 when, for that reason, they came to the land, they
behold a fire of coals lying, and a fish lying on it, and
bread.
10 Jesus said to them, 'Bring you^{P} from the fishes that
you^{P} caught now;'
11 Simon Peter went up, and drew the net up on the
land, full of great fishes, an hundred fifty and three, and
though they were so many, the net was not rent.
12 Jesus said to them, 'Come you^{P}, dine;' and none of
the disciples was venturing to inquire of Him, 'Who are
You^{S}?' knowing that it is the Lord;
13 Jesus, for that reason, did come and take the bread
and give to them, and the fish in like manner;
14 this [is] now a third time Jesus was revealed to His
disciples, having been raised from the dead.
15 When, consequently, they dined, Jesus said to Simon
Peter, 'Simon, [son] of Jonas, do you^{S} love Me more than
these?' he said to Him, 'Yes, Lord; You^{S} have known that
I dearly love You^{S};' He said to him, 'Feed My lambs.'
16 He said to him again, a second time, 'Simon, [son] of
Jonas, do you^{S} love Me?' he said to Him, 'Yes, Lord;
You^{S} have known that I dearly love You^{S};' He said to
him, 'Tend My sheep.'
17 He said to him the third time, 'Simon, [son] of Jonas,
do you^{S} dearly love Me?' Peter was grieved that He said
to him the third time, 'Do you^{S} dearly love Me?' and he
said to Him, 'Lord, You^{S} have known all things; You^{S} do
know that I dearly love You^{S}.' Jesus said to him, 'Feed
My sheep;
18 truly, truly, I say to you^{S}, When you^{S} were younger,
you^{S} were girding yourself^{S} and were walking where you^{S}
did will, but when you^{S} may be old, you^{S} shall stretch
forth your^{S} hands, and another will gird you^{S}, and shall
carry [you^{S}] where you^{S} do not will;'
19 and this He said, signifying by what death he shall
glorify God; and having said this, He said to him, 'Be
following Me.'
20 And Peter having turned about did see the disciple
whom Jesus was loving following, (who also reclined in
the supper on His breast, and said, 'Sir, who is he who
is delivering You^{S} up?')
21 Peter having seen this one, said to Jesus, 'Lord, and
what of this one?'
22 Jesus said to him, 'If I will him to remain till I come,
what — to you^{S}? be you^{S} following Me.' This word, for
that reason, went forth to the brethren that that disciple
would not die,
23 yet Jesus did not say to him, that he would not die,
but, 'If I will him to remain till I come, what — to you^{S}?'
24 this is the disciple who is testifying concerning these
things, and he wrote these things, and we have known
that his testimony is true.
25 And there are also many other things — as many as
Jesus did — which, if they may be written one by one, I
think not even the world itself to have place for the books
written. Amen.

The ACTS of the Apostles

CHAPTER 1

1 The former account, indeed, I made concerning all
things, O Theophilus, that Jesus began both to do and
to teach,
2 till the day in which, having given command, through
the Holy Spirit, to the apostles whom He did choose out,
He was taken up,
3 to whom also He did present himself alive after His
suffering, in many certain proofs, through forty days
being seen by them, and speaking the things concerning
the reign of God.
4 And being assembled together with them, He
commanded them not to depart from Jerusalem, but to
wait for the promise of the Father, which, [He said,] 'You[P]
did hear of Me;
5 because John, indeed, baptized with water, and you[P]
shall be baptized with the Holy Spirit — after not many
days.'
6 They, for that reason, indeed, having come together,
were questioning Him, saying, 'Lord, do You[S] restore the
reign to Israel at this time?'
7 and He said unto them, 'It is not yours[P] to know times
or seasons that the Father did appoint in His own
authority;
8 but you[P] shall receive power at the coming of the Holy
Spirit upon you[P], and you[P] shall be witnesses to Me both
in Jerusalem, and in all Judea, and Samaria, and unto the
end of the earth.'
9 And having said these things — they beholding —
He was taken up, and a cloud did receive Him up from
their sight;
10 and as they were looking steadfastly to the heaven
in His going on, then, behold, two men stood by them
in white apparel,
11 who also said, 'Men, Galileans, why do you[P] stand
gazing into the heaven? this Jesus who was received
up from you[P] into the heaven, shall so come in what
manner you[P] saw Him going on to the heaven.'
12 Then did they return to Jerusalem from the mount
that is called of Olives, that is near Jerusalem, a sabbath's
journey;
13 and when they came in, they went up to the upper
room, where were abiding both Peter, and James, and
John, and Andrew, Philip, and Thomas, Bartholomew,
and Matthew, James, of Alphaeus, and Simon the
Zelotes, and Judas, of James;
14 these all were continuing with one accord in prayer
and supplication, with women, and Mary the mother of
Jesus, and with His brethren.
15 And in these days, Peter having risen up in the midst
of the disciples, said, (the multitude of the names at the
same place also was, as it were, an hundred and twenty,)
16 'Men, brethren, it is necessary for this Writing that it
be fulfilled that beforehand the Holy Spirit spoke through
the mouth of David, concerning Judas, who became
guide to those who took Jesus,
17 because he was numbered among us, and did receive
the share in this ministration,
18 this one, indeed, then, purchased a field out of the
reward of unrighteousness, and falling headlong, burst
asunder in the midst, and all his bowels gushed forth,
19 and it became known to all those dwelling in
Jerusalem, insomuch that that place is called, in their
proper dialect, Aceldama, that is, field of blood,
20 for it has been written in the book of Psalms: Let his
lodging-place become desolate, and let no one be
dwelling in it, and let another take his oversight.
21 'It is necessary, for that reason, of the men who did
go with us during all the time in which the Lord Jesus
went in and went out among us,
22 beginning from the baptism of John, unto the day in
which He was received up from us, one of these to
become with us a witness of his rising again.'
23 And they set two, Joseph called Barsabas, who was
surnamed Justus, and Matthias,
24 and having prayed, they said, 'You[S], Lord, who are
knowing the heart of all, show which one You[S] did
choose of these two
25 to receive the share of this ministration and
apostleship, from which Judas, by transgression, did fall,

to go on to his proper place;'
26 and they gave their lots, and the lot fell upon
Matthias, and he was numbered with the eleven
apostles.

CHAPTER 2

1 And in the day of the Pentecost being fulfilled, they
were all with one desire at the same place,
2 and there came suddenly out of the heaven a sound
as of a bearing violent breath, and it filled all the house
where they were sitting,
3 and there appeared to them divided tongues, as it were
of fire; it sat also upon each one of them,
4 and they were all filled with the Holy Spirit, and began
to speak with other tongues, according as the Spirit was
giving them to declare.
5 And there were dwelling in Jerusalem Jews, devout
men from every nation of those under the heaven,
6 and the rumor of this having come, the multitude came
together, and was confounded, because they were each
one hearing them speaking in his proper dialect,
7 and they were all amazed, and did wonder, saying one
unto another, 'Behold, are not all these who are speaking
Galileans?
8 and how do we hear, each in our proper dialect, in
which we were born?
9 Parthians, and Medes, and Elamites, and those
dwelling in Mesopotamia, in Judea also, and Cappadocia,
Pontus, and Asia,
10 Phrygia also, and Pamphylia, Egypt, and the parts of
Libya, that [are] along Cyrene, and the strangers of
Rome, both Jews and proselytes,
11 Cretes and Arabians, we did hear them speaking the
great things of God in our tongues.'
12 And they were all amazed, and were in doubt, saying
one unto another, 'What would this wish to be?'
13 and others mocking said, — 'They are full of sweet
wine;'
14 and Peter having stood up with the eleven, lifted up
his voice and declared to them, 'Men, Jews! and all those
dwelling in Jerusalem, let this be known to you[P], and
listen to my sayings,
15 for these are not drunken, as you[P] take it up, for it is
the third hour of the day.
16 'But this is that which has been spoken through the
prophet Joel:
17 And it shall be in the last days, said God, I will pour
out of My Spirit upon all flesh, and your[P] sons and your[P]
daughters shall prophesy, and your[P] young men shall
see visions, and your[P] old men shall dream dreams;
18 and also upon My men-servants, and upon My maid-
servants, in those days, I will pour out of My Spirit, and
they shall prophesy;
19 and I will give wonders in the heaven above, and
signs upon the earth beneath — blood, and fire, and
vapor of smoke,
20 the sun shall be turned to darkness, and the moon to
blood, before the coming of the day of the Lord — the
great and illustrious;
21 and it shall be, every one — whoever shall call upon
the name of the Lord, he shall be saved.
22 'Men, Israelites! hear these words, Jesus the
Nazarene, a man approved of God by mighty works
among you[P], and wonders, and signs, that God did
through Him in the midst of you[P], according as also you[P]
yourselves[P] have known;
23 this one, by the determinate counsel and
foreknowledge of God, being given out, having taken
by lawless hands, having crucified — you[P] did slay;
24 whom God did raise up, having loosed the pains of
the death, because it was not possible for Him to be held
by it,
25 for David said in regard to him: I foresaw the Lord
always before me — because He is on my right hand —
that I may not be moved;
26 because of this was my heart cheered, and my tongue
was glad, and yet — my flesh also shall rest on hope,
27 because You[S] will not leave my soul to hades, nor
will You[S] give Your[S] Kind One to see corruption;
28 You[S] did make known to me ways of life, You[S] shall
fill me with joy with Your[S] countenance.
29 'Men, brethren! it is permitted to speak with freedom
unto you[P] concerning the patriarch David, that he both
died and was buried, and his tomb is among us unto
this day;
30 a prophet, for that reason, being, and knowing that
with an oath God did swear to him, out of the fruit of his
loins, according to the flesh, to raise up the Christ, to sit
upon his throne,
31 having foreseen, he did speak concerning the rising
again of the Christ, that his soul was not left to hades,
nor did his flesh see corruption.
32 'God did raise up this Jesus, of which we are all
witnesses;
33 having been exalted at the right hand then of God —
also the promise of the Holy Spirit having received from

the Father — he was shedding this forth, which you[P] now see and hear;
34 for David did not go up to the heavens, and he said himself: The Lord said to my lord, Sit You[S] at My right hand,
35 till I make Your[S] foes Your[S] footstool;
36 assuredly, for that reason, let all the house of Israel know, that did God make him both Lord and Christ — this Jesus whom you[P] did crucify.'
37 And having heard, they were pricked to the heart; they say also to Peter, and to the rest of the apostles, 'What shall we do, men, brethren?'
38 and Peter said unto them, 'Reform, and be baptized each of you[P] on the name of Jesus Christ, to remission of sins, and you[P] shall receive the gift of the Holy Spirit,
39 for the promise is to you[P], and to your[P] children, and to all those afar off, as many as the Lord our God shall call.'
40 Also with many more other words he was testifying and exhorting, saying, 'Be saved from this perverse generation;'
41 then those, indeed, who did gladly receive his word were baptized, and there were added on that day, as it were, three thousand souls,
42 and they were continuing steadfastly in the teaching of the apostles, and the fellowship, and the breaking of the bread, and the prayers.
43 And fear came on every soul, many wonders also and signs were being done through the apostles,
44 and all those believing were at the same place, and had all things common,
45 and the possessions and the goods they were selling, and were parting them to all, according as any one had need.
46 Daily also continuing with one desire in the temple, breaking bread also at every house, they were partaking of food in gladness and simplicity of heart,
47 praising God, and having favor with all the people, and the Lord was adding those being saved every day to the assembly.

CHAPTER 3

1 And Peter and John were going up at the same time to the temple, at the hour of the prayer, the ninth [hour],
2 and a certain man, being lame from the womb of his mother, was being carried, whom they were laying every day at the gate of the temple, called Beautiful, to ask a kindness from those entering into the temple,
3 who, having seen Peter and John about to go into the temple, was begging to receive a kindness.
4 And Peter, having looked steadfastly toward him with John, said, 'Look toward us;'
5 and he was giving heed to them, looking to receive something from them;
6 and Peter said, 'Silver and gold I have none, but what I have, that I give to you[S]; in the name of Jesus Christ of Nazareth, rise up and be walking.'
7 And having seized him by the right hand, he raised [him] up, and presently his feet and ankles were strengthened,
8 and springing up, he stood, and was walking, and did enter with them into the temple, walking and springing, and praising God;
9 and all the people saw him walking and praising God,
10 they were knowing him also that this it was who was sitting at the Beautiful gate of the temple for a kindness, and they were filled with wonder and amazement at what had happened to him.
11 And at the lame man who was healed holding Peter and John, all the people ran together unto them in the porch called Solomon's — greatly amazed,
12 and Peter having seen, answered unto the people, 'Men, Israelites! why wonder you[P] at this? or why look you[P] on us so earnestly, as if by our own power or piety we have made him to walk?
13 'The God of Abraham, and of Isaac, and of Jacob, the God of our fathers, did glorify His child Jesus, whom you[P] delivered up, and denied Him in the presence of Pilate, he having given judgment to release [Him],
14 and you[P] did deny the Holy and Righteous One, and desired a man — a murderer — to be granted to you[P],
15 and you[P] did kill the Prince of the life, whom God did raise out of the dead, of which we are witnesses;
16 and on the faith of His name, this one whom you[P] see and have known, His name made strong, even the faith that [is] through Him did give to him this perfect soundness before you[P] all.
17 'And now, brethren, I have known that you[P] did [it] through ignorance, as also your[P] rulers;
18 and God, what things He had declared before through the mouth of all His prophets, that the Christ should suffer, He did thus fulfil;
19 reform you[P], for that reason, and turn back, for your[P] sins being blotted out, that times of refreshing may come from the presence of the Lord,
20 and He may send Jesus Christ who has been preached

to you[P] before,
21 whom it is necessary for heaven, indeed, to receive
till times of a restitution of all things, of which God spoke
through the mouth of all His holy prophets from the age.
22 'For Moses, indeed, said unto the fathers — The
Lord your[P] God shall raise up a prophet to you[P] out of
your[P] brethren, like to me; you[P] shall hear Him in all
things, as many as He may speak unto you[P];
23 and it shall be, every soul that may not hear that
prophet shall be utterly destroyed out of the people;
24 and also all the prophets from Samuel and those
following in order, as many as spoke, did also foretell of
these days.
25 'You[P] are sons of the prophets, and of the covenant
that God made unto our fathers, saying unto Abraham:
And in your[S] seed shall all the families of the earth be
blessed;
26 to you[P] first, God, having raised up His child Jesus,
did send Him, blessing you[P], in the turning away of each
one from your[P] evil ways.'

CHAPTER 4

1 And as they are speaking unto the people, there came
to them the priests, and the magistrate of the temple,
and the Sadducees —
2 being grieved because of their teaching the people, and
preaching in Jesus the rising again out of the dead —
3 and they laid hands upon them, and did put them in
custody unto the morning, for it was evening already;
4 and many of those hearing the word did believe, and
the number of the men became, as it were, five thousand.
5 And it came to pass upon the morning, there were
gathered together of them the rulers, and elders, and
scribes, to Jerusalem,
6 and Annas the chief priest, and Caiaphas, and John,
and Alexander, and as many as were of the kindred of
the chief priest,
7 and having set them in the midst, they were inquiring,
'In what power, or in what name did you[P] do this?'
8 Then Peter, having been filled with the Holy Spirit,
said unto them: 'Rulers of the people, and elders of Israel,
9 if we today are examined concerning the good deed
to the ailing man, by whom he has been saved,
10 be it known to all of you[P], and to all the people of
Israel, that in the name of Jesus Christ of Nazareth, whom
you[P] did crucify, whom God did raise out of the dead, in
Him has this one stood by before you[P] whole.
11 'This is the stone that was set at nothing by you[P] —
the builders, that became head of a corner;
12 and there is not salvation in any other, for there is no
other name under the heaven that has been given among
men, in which it is necessary for us to be saved.'
13 And beholding the openness of Peter and John, and
having perceived that they are men unlettered and
unrefined, they were wondering — they were taking
knowledge also of them that they had been with Jesus —
14 and seeing the man standing with them who had been
healed, they had nothing to say against [it],
15 and having commanded them to go away out of the
sanhedrim, they took counsel with one another,
16 saying, 'What shall we do to these men? because
that, indeed, a notable sign has been done through them,
to all those dwelling in Jerusalem [is] obvious, and we
are not able to deny [it];
17 but that it may spread no further toward the people,
let us strictly threaten them no more to speak in this name
to any man.'
18 And having called them, they charged them not to
speak at all, nor to teach, in the name of Jesus,
19 and Peter and John answering unto them said,
'Whether it is righteous before God to listen to you[P]
rather than to God, you[P] judge;
20 for we cannot but speak what we did see and hear.'
21 And they having further threatened [them], let them
go, finding nothing how they may punish them, because
of the people, because all were glorifying God for that
which had been done,
22 for above forty years of age was the man upon whom
had been done this sign of the healing.
23 And being let go, they went unto their own friends,
and declared whatever the chief priests and the elders
said unto them,
24 and they having heard, with one harmony did lift up
the voice unto God, and said, 'Lord, You[S] [are] God, who
did make the heaven, and the earth, and the sea, and all
that [are] in them,
25 who, through the mouth of David Your[S] servant, did
say, Why did nations rage, and peoples meditate vain
things?
26 the kings of the earth stood up, and the rulers were
gathered together against the Lord and against His
Christ;
27 for gathered together of a truth against Your[S] holy
child Jesus, whom You[S] did anoint, were both Herod and
Pontius Pilate, with nations and peoples of Israel,
28 to do whatever Your[S] hand and Your[S] counsel did

determine before to come to pass.
29 'And now, Lord, look upon their threatenings, and
grant to Your[S] servants to speak Your[S] word with all
freedom,
30 in the stretching forth of Your[S] hand, for healing, and
signs, and wonders, to come to pass through the name
of Your[S] holy child Jesus.'
31 And they having prayed, the place in which they
were gathered together was shaken, and they were all
filled with the Holy Spirit, and were speaking the word
of God with freedom,
32 and of the multitude of those who did believe the
heart and the soul was one, and not one was saying
that anything of the things he had was his own, but all
things were to them in common.
33 And with great power were the apostles giving the
testimony to the rising again of the Lord Jesus, great
grace also was on them all,
34 for there was not any one among them who did lack,
for as many as were possessors of fields, or houses,
selling [them], were bringing the prices of the thing sold,
35 and were laying them at the feet of the apostles, and
distribution was being made to each according as any
one had need.
36 And Joses, who was surnamed by the apostles
Barnabas — which is, having been interpreted, Son of
Comfort — a Levite, of Cyprus by birth,
37 a field being his, having sold [it], brought the money
and laid [it] at the feet of the apostles.

CHAPTER 5

1 And a certain man, Ananias by name, with Sapphira
his wife, sold a possession,
2 and did keep back of the price — his wife also knowing
— and having brought a certain part, he laid [it] at the
feet of the apostles.
3 And Peter said, 'Ananias, why did the Adversary fill
your[S] heart, for you[S] to lie to the Holy Spirit, and to keep
back of the price of the place?
4 while it remained, did it not remain yours[S]? and having
been sold, was it not in your[S] authority? why [is] it that
you[S] did put this thing in your[S] heart? you[S] did not lie to
men, but to God;'
5 and Ananias hearing these words, having fallen down,
did expire, and great fear came upon all who heard these
things,
6 and having risen, the younger men wound him up,
and having carried forth, they buried [him].
7 And it came to pass, about three hours after, that his
wife, not knowing what had happened, came in,
8 and Peter answered her, 'Tell me if you[S] sold the place
for so much;' and she said, 'Yes, for so much.'
9 And Peter said unto her, 'How was it agreed by you[S],
to tempt the Spirit of the Lord? behold, the feet of those
who did bury your[S] husband [are] at the door, and they
shall carry you[S] forth;'
10 and she fell down presently at his feet, and expired,
and the young men having come in, found her dead, and
having carried forth, they buried [her] by her husband;
11 and great fear came upon all the assembly, and upon
all who heard these things.
12 And through the hands of the apostles came many
signs and wonders among the people, and they were
with one desire all in the porch of Solomon;
13 and of the rest no one was daring to join himself to
them, but the people were magnifying them,
14 (and the more were believers added to the Lord,
multitudes both of men and women,)
15 so as to bring forth the ailing into the broad places,
and to lay [them] upon couches and mats, that at the
coming of Peter, even [his] shadow might overshadow
some one of them;
16 and there were coming together also the people of
the cities round about to Jerusalem, bearing ailing
persons, and those harassed by unclean spirits — who
were all healed.
17 And having risen, the chief priest, and all those with
him — being the sect of the Sadducees — were filled
with zeal,
18 and laid their hands upon the apostles, and did put
them in a public prison;
19 and a messenger of the Lord through the night
opened the doors of the prison, having also brought
them forth, he said,
20 'Go on, and standing, speak in the temple to the
people all the sayings of this life;'
21 and having heard, they did enter at the dawn into
the temple, and were teaching. And the chief priest
having come, and those with him, they called together
the sanhedrim and all the senate of the sons of Israel,
and they sent to the prison to have them brought,
22 and the officers having come, did not find them in
the prison, and having turned back, they told,
23 saying — 'The prison indeed we found shut in all
safety, and the keepers standing without before the
doors, and having opened — within we found no one.'

24 And as the priest, and the magistrate of the temple, and the chief priests, heard these words, they were doubting concerning them to what this would come;
25 and coming near, a certain one told them, saying — ‘Behold, the men whom you[P] did put in the prison are in the temple standing and teaching the people;’
26 then the magistrate having gone away with officers, brought them without violence, for they were fearing the people, for fear that they should be stoned;
27 and having brought them, they set [them] in the sanhedrim, and the chief priest questioned them,
28 saying, ‘Did not we strictly command you[P] not to teach in this name? and behold, you[P] have filled Jerusalem with your[P] teaching, and you[P] intend to bring the blood of this man upon us.’
29 And Peter and the apostles answering, said, ‘It is necessary to obey God, rather than men;
30 and the God of our fathers did raise up Jesus, whom you[P] slew, having hanged upon a tree;
31 this one God, a Prince and a Savior, has exalted with His right hand, to give reformation to Israel, and forgiveness of sins;
32 and we are His witnesses of these sayings, and the Holy Spirit also, whom God gave to those obeying Him.’
33 And they having heard, were cut [to the heart], and were taking counsel to slay them,
34 but a certain one, having risen up in the sanhedrim — a Pharisee, by name Gamaliel, a teacher of law honored by all the people — commanded to put the apostles forth a little,
35 and said unto them, ‘Men, Israelites, take heed to yourselves[P] about these men, what you[P] are about to do,
36 for before these days rose up Theudas, saying, that himself was some one, to whom a number of men did join themselves, as it were four hundred, who was slain, and all, as many as were obeying him, were scattered, and came to nothing.
37 ‘After this one rose up, Judas the Galilean, in the days of the enrolment, and drew away much people after him, and that one perished, and all, as many as were obeying him, were scattered;
38 and now I say to you[P], Refrain from these men, and let them alone, because if this counsel or this work may be of men, it will be overthrown,
39 and if it be of God, you[P] are not able to overthrow it, for fear that perhaps also you[P] be found fighting against God.’
40 And to him they agreed, and having called near the apostles, having beaten [them], they commanded [them] not to speak in the name of Jesus, and let them go;
41 they, indeed, then, departed from the presence of the sanhedrim, rejoicing that for his name they were counted worthy to suffer dishonor,
42 every day also in the temple, and in every house, they were not ceasing teaching and proclaiming good news — Jesus the Christ.

CHAPTER 6

1 And in these days, the disciples multiplying, there came a murmuring of the Hellenists at the Hebrews, because their widows were being overlooked in the daily ministration,
2 and the twelve, having called near the multitude of the disciples, said, ‘It is not pleasing that we, having left the word of God, do minister at tables;
3 look out, for that reason, brethren, seven men of you[P] who are well testified of, full of the Holy Spirit and wisdom, whom we may set over this necessity,
4 and we to prayer, and to the ministration of the word, will give ourselves continually.’
5 And the thing was pleasing before all the multitude, and they did choose Stephen, a man full of faith and the Holy Spirit, and Philip, and Prochorus, and Nicanor, and Timon, and Parmenas, and Nicolaus, a proselyte of Antioch,
6 whom they did set before the apostles, and they, having prayed, laid [their] hands on them.
7 And the word of God did increase, and the number of the disciples did multiply in Jerusalem exceedingly; a great multitude also of the priests were obedient to the faith.
8 And Stephen, full of faith and power, was doing great wonders and signs among the people,
9 and there arose certain of those of the synagogue, called of the Libertines, and Cyrenians, and Alexandrians, and of those from Cilicia, and Asia, disputing with Stephen,
10 and they were not able to resist the wisdom and the spirit with which he was speaking;
11 then they suborned men, saying — ‘We have heard him speaking evil sayings in regard to Moses and God.’
12 They did stir up also the people, and the elders, and the scribes, and having come upon [him], they caught him, and brought [him] to the sanhedrim;
13 they set up also false witnesses, saying, ‘This one

does not cease to speak evil sayings against this holy
place and the law,
14 for we have heard him saying, That this Jesus the
Nazarean shall overthrow this place, and shall change
the customs that Moses delivered to us;'
15 and gazing at him, all those sitting in the sanhedrim
saw his face as it were the face of a messenger.

CHAPTER 7

1 And the chief priest said, 'Are then these things so?'
2 and he said, 'Men, brethren, and fathers, listen: The
God of the glory did appear to our father Abraham, being
in Mesopotamia, before his dwelling in Haran,
3 and He said to him, Go forth out of your[S] land, and
out of your[S] kindred, and come to a land that I shall show
you[S].
4 'Then having come forth out of the land of the
Chaldeans, he dwelt in Haran, and from there, after the
death of his father, He did remove him to this land
wherein you[P] now dwell,
5 and He gave him no inheritance in it, not even a
footstep, and did promise to give it to him for a
possession, and to his seed after him — he having no
child.
6 'And God spoke thus, That his seed shall be
sojourning in a strange land, and they shall cause it to
serve, and shall do it evil four hundred years,
7 and the nation whom they shall serve I will judge,
said God; and after these things they shall come forth
and shall do Me service in this place.
8 'And He gave to him a covenant of circumcision, and
so he fathered Isaac, and did circumcise him on the
eighth day, and Isaac [fathered] Jacob, and Jacob — the
twelve patriarchs;
9 and the patriarchs, having been moved with jealousy,
sold Joseph to Egypt, and God was with him,
10 and did deliver him out of all his tribulations, and
gave him favor and wisdom before Pharaoh king of
Egypt, and he did set him — governor over Egypt and
all his house.
11 'And there came a famine upon all the land of Egypt
and Canaan, and great tribulation, and our fathers were
not finding sustenance,
12 and Jacob having heard that there was corn in Egypt,
sent forth our fathers a first time;
13 and at the second time was Joseph made known to
his brethren, and Joseph's kindred became known to
Pharaoh,
14 and Joseph having sent, did call for his father Jacob,
and all his kindred — with seventy and five souls —
15 and Jacob went down to Egypt, and died, himself
and our fathers,
16 and they were carried over into Sychem, and were
laid in the tomb that Abraham bought for a price in
money from the sons of Emmor, of Sychem.
17 'And according as the time of the promise was
drawing near, which God did swear to Abraham, the
people increased and multiplied in Egypt,
18 till another king rose, who had not known Joseph;
19 this one, having dealt subtly with our kindred, did
evil to our fathers, causing to expose their babes, that
they might not live;
20 in which time Moses was born, and he was fair to
God, and he was brought up three months in the house
of his father;
21 and he having been exposed, the daughter of Pharaoh
took him up, and did rear him for a son to herself;
22 and Moses was taught in all wisdom of the Egyptians,
and he was powerful in words and in works.
23 'And when forty years were fulfilled to him, it came
upon his heart to look after his brethren, the sons of
Israel;
24 and having seen a certain one suffering injustice, he
did defend, and did justice to the oppressed, having
struck the Egyptian;
25 and he was supposing his brethren to understand
that God through his hand did give salvation; and they
did not understand.
26 'On the succeeding day, also, he showed himself to
them as they are striving, and urged them to peace,
saying, Men, you[P] are brethren, why do you[P] injustice
to one another?
27 and he who is doing injustice to the neighbor, did
thrust him away, saying, Who set you[S] a ruler and a judge
over us?
28 do you[S] wish to kill me, as you[S] did kill the Egyptian
yesterday?
29 'And Moses fled at this word, and became a sojourner
in the land of Midian, where he fathered two sons,
30 and forty years having been fulfilled, there appeared
to him in the wilderness of mount Sinai a messenger of
the Lord, in a flame of fire of a bush,
31 and Moses having seen did wonder at the sight;
and he drawing near to behold, there came a voice of
the Lord unto him,
32 I [am] the God of your[S] fathers; the God of Abraham,

and the God of Isaac, and the God of Jacob. 'And Moses
having become terrified, dare not behold,
33 and the Lord said to him, Loose the sandal of your[S]
feet, for the place in which you[S] have stood is holy
ground;
34 seeing I have seen the affliction of My people that
[is] in Egypt, and their groaning I did hear, and came
down to deliver them; and now come, I will send you[S] to
Egypt.
35 'This Moses, whom they did refuse, saying, Who
did set you[S] a ruler and a judge? this one God a ruler
and a redeemer did send, in the hand of a messenger
who appeared to him in the bush;
36 this one did bring them forth, having done wonders
and signs in the land of Egypt, and in the Red Sea, and
in the wilderness forty years;
37 this is the Moses who did say to the sons of Israel:
A prophet shall the Lord your[P] God raise up to you[P] out
of your[P] brethren, like to me, you[P] hear shall him.
38 'This is he who was in the assembly in the wilderness,
with the messenger who is speaking to him in the mount
Sinai, and with our fathers who did receive the living
oracles to give to us;
39 to whom our fathers did not wish to become obedient,
but did thrust away, and turned back to Egypt in their
hearts,
40 saying to Aaron, Make to us gods who shall go on
before us, for this Moses, who brought us forth out of
the land of Egypt, we have not known what has
happened to him.
41 'And they made a calf in those days, and brought a
sacrifice to the idol, and were rejoicing in the works of
their hands,
42 and God did turn, and did give them up to do service
to the host of the heaven, according as it has been
written in the scroll of the prophets: Slain beasts and
sacrifices did you[P] offer to Me forty years in the
wilderness, O house of Israel?
43 and you[P] took up the tabernacle of Moloch, and the
star of your[P] god Remphan — the figures that you[P] made
to bow before them, and I will remove your[P] dwelling
beyond Babylon.
44 'The tabernacle of the testimony was among our
fathers in the wilderness, according as He did direct, who
is speaking to Moses, to make it according to the figure
that he had seen;
45 which also our fathers having in succession received,
did bring in with Joshua, into the possession of the
nations whom God did drive out from the presence of
our fathers, till the days of David,
46 who found favor before God, and requested to find a
tabernacle for the God of Jacob;
47 and Solomon built Him an house.
48 'But the Most High does not dwell in sanctuaries
made with hands, according as the prophet said:
49 The heaven [is] My throne, and the earth My
footstool; what house will you[P] build to Me? said the
Lord, or what [is] the place of My rest?
50 has not My hand made all these things?
51 'You[P] stiff-necked and uncircumcised in heart and in
ears! you[P] do always resist the Holy Spirit; as your[P]
fathers — also you[P];
52 which of the prophets did your[P] fathers not
persecute? and they killed those who declared before
about the coming of the Righteous One, of whom now
you[P] have become betrayers and murderers,
53 who received the law by arrangement of messengers,
and did not keep [it].'
54 And hearing these things, they were cut to the hearts,
and did gnash the teeth at him;
55 and being full of the Holy Spirit, having looked
steadfastly to the heaven, he saw the glory of God, and
Jesus standing on the right hand of God,
56 and he said, 'Behold, I see the heavens having been
opened, and the Son of Man standing on the right hand
of God.'
57 And they, having cried out with a loud voice, stopped
their ears, and did rush upon him with one harmony,
58 and having cast him forth outside of the city, they
were stoning [him] — and the witnesses did put down
their garments at the feet of a young man called Saul —
59 and they were stoning Stephen, calling and saying,
'Lord Jesus, receive my spirit;'
60 and having bowed the knees, he cried with a loud
voice, 'Lord, may you not lay this sin to them;' and
having said this, he fell asleep.

CHAPTER 8

1 And Saul was assenting to his death, and there came
in that day a great persecution upon the assembly in
Jerusalem, all also were scattered abroad in the regions
of Judea and Samaria, except the apostles;
2 and devout men carried away Stephen, and made great
lamentation over him;
3 and Saul was making havoc of the assembly, entering
into every house, and dragging men and women, was

giving them up to prison;
4 they then indeed, having been scattered, went abroad
proclaiming good news — the word.
5 And Philip having gone down to a city of Samaria,
was preaching to them the Christ,
6 the multitudes also were giving heed to the things
spoken by Philip, with one desire, in their hearing and
seeing the signs that he was doing,
7 for unclean spirits came forth from many who were
possessed, crying with a loud voice, and many who have
been paralytic and lame were healed,
8 and there was great joy in that city.
9 And a certain man, by name Simon, was before in the
city using magic, and amazing the nation of Samaria,
saying himself to be a certain great one,
10 to whom they were all giving heed, from small unto
great, saying, 'This one is the great power of God;'
11 and they were giving heed to him, because of his
having for a long time amazed them with deeds of magic.
12 And when they believed Philip, proclaiming good
news, the things concerning the reign of God and the
name of Jesus Christ, they were baptized both men and
women;
13 and Simon also himself did believe, and, having been
baptized, he was continuing with Philip, beholding also
signs and mighty acts being done, he was amazed.
14 And the apostles in Jerusalem having heard that
Samaria had received the word of God, did send unto
them Peter and John,
15 who having come down did pray concerning them,
that they may receive the Holy Spirit, —
16 for as yet he was fallen upon none of them, and they
have been baptized only — to the name of the Lord
Jesus;
17 then were they laying hands on them, and they
received the Holy Spirit.
18 And Simon, having beheld that through the laying
on of the hands of the apostles, the Holy Spirit is given,
brought money before them,
19 saying, 'Give also to me this authority, that on
whomsoever I may lay the hands, he may receive the
Holy Spirit.'
20 And Peter said unto him, 'Your^{S} silver with you^{S} —
may it be to destruction! because you^{S} did think to
possess the gift of God through money;
21 you^{S} have neither part nor lot in this thing, for your^{S}
heart is not right before God;
22 reform, for that reason, from this your^{S} wickedness,
and beg God, if then the purpose of your^{S} heart may be
forgiven you^{S},
23 for in the gall of bitterness, and bond of
unrighteousness, I perceive you^{S} being.'
24 And Simon answering, said, 'You^{P} beg unto the Lord
for me, that nothing may come upon me of the things
you^{P} have spoken.'
25 They indeed, therefore, having testified fully, and
spoken the word of the Lord, did turn back to Jerusalem;
in many villages also of the Samaritans they did proclaim
good news.
26 And a messenger of the Lord spoke unto Philip,
saying, 'Arise, and go on toward the south, on the way
that is going down from Jerusalem to Gaza,' — this is
desert.
27 And having arisen, he went on, and behold, a man of
Ethiopia, a eunuch, a man of rank, of Candace the queen
of the Ethiopians, who was over all her treasure, who
had come to worship to Jerusalem;
28 he was also returning, and is sitting on his chariot,
and he was reading the prophet Isaiah.
29 And the Spirit said to Philip, 'Go near, and be joined
to this chariot;'
30 and Philip having run near, heard him reading the
prophet Isaiah, and said, 'Do you^{S} then know what you^{S}
do read?'
31 and he said, 'Why, how am I able, if some one may
not guide me?' he called Philip also, having come up, to
sit with him.
32 And the contents of the Writing that he was reading
was this: 'He was led as a sheep unto slaughter, and as
a lamb before his shearer dumb, so he does not open
his mouth;
33 in his humiliation his judgment was taken away, and
his generation — who shall declare? because taken from
the earth is his life.'
34 And the eunuch answering Philip said, 'I pray you^{S},
about whom does the prophet say this? about himself,
or about some other one?'
35 and Philip having opened his mouth, and having
begun from this Writing, proclaimed good news to him
— Jesus.
36 And as they were going on the way, they came upon
a certain water, and the eunuch said, 'Behold, water;
what does prevent me to be baptized?'
37 [And Philip said, 'If you^{S} do believe out of all the
heart, it is lawful;' and he answering said, 'I believe Jesus
Christ to be the Son of God;']
38 and he commanded the chariot to stand still, and
they both went down to the water, both Philip and the

eunuch, and he baptized him;
39 and when they came up out of the water, the Spirit of
the Lord caught away Philip, and the eunuch saw him
no more, for he was going on his way rejoicing;
40 and Philip was found at Azotus, and passing through,
he was proclaiming good news to all the cities, till his
coming to Caesarea.

CHAPTER 9

1 And Saul, yet breathing of threatening and slaughter
to the disciples of the Lord, having gone to the chief
priest,
2 did ask from him letters to Damascus, unto the
synagogues, that if he may find any being of the way,
both men and women, he may bring them bound to
Jerusalem.
3 And in the going, he came near to Damascus, and
suddenly there shone round about him a light from the
heaven,
4 and having fallen upon the earth, he heard a voice
saying to him, 'Saul, Saul, why do you^{S} persecute me?'
5 And he said, 'Who are You^{S}, Lord?' and the Lord said,
'I am Jesus whom you^{S} do persecute; hard for you^{S} to
kick at the pricks;'
6 trembling also, and astonished, he said, 'Lord, what
do You^{S} wish me to do?' and the Lord [said] unto him,
'Arise, and enter into the city, and it shall be told you^{S}
what it is necessary for you^{S} to do.'
7 And the men who are journeying with him stood
speechless, hearing indeed the voice but seeing no one,
8 and Saul arose from the earth, and his eyes having
been opened, he beheld no one, and leading him by the
hand they brought him to Damascus,
9 and he was three days without seeing, and he did
neither eat nor drink.
10 And there was a certain disciple in Damascus, by
name Ananias, and the Lord said unto him in a vision,
'Ananias;' and he said, 'Behold me, Lord;'
11 and the Lord [said] unto him, 'Having risen, go on
unto the street that is called Straight, and seek in the
house of Judas, [one] by name Saul of Tarsus, for,
behold, he does pray,
12 and he saw in a vision a man, by name Ananias,
coming in, and putting a hand on him, that he may see
again.'
13 And Ananias answered, 'Lord, I have heard from
many about this man, how many evils he did to Your^{S}
saints in Jerusalem,
14 and here he has authority from the chief priests, to
bind all those calling on Your^{S} name.'
15 And the Lord said unto him, 'Be going on, because a
choice vessel to Me is this one, to bear My name before
nations and kings — the sons also of Israel;
16 for I will show him how many things it is necessary
for him to suffer for My name.'
17 And Ananias went away, and did enter into the house,
and having put upon him [his] hands, said, 'Saul, brother,
the Lord has sent me — Jesus who did appear to you^{S}
in the way in which you^{S} were coming — that you^{S} may
see again, and may be filled with the Holy Spirit.'
18 And immediately there fell from his eyes as it were
scales, he saw again also presently, and having risen,
was baptized,
19 and having received nourishment, was strengthened,
and Saul was with the disciples in Damascus certain
days,
20 and immediately in the synagogues he was preaching
the Christ, that he is the Son of God.
21 And all those hearing were amazed, and said, 'Is not
this he who laid waste in Jerusalem those calling on this
name, and had come here to this intent, that he might
bring them bound to the chief priests?'
22 And Saul was still more strengthened, and he was
confounding the Jews dwelling in Damascus, proving
that this is the Christ.
23 And when many days were fulfilled, the Jews took
counsel together to kill him,
24 and their counsel against [him] was known to Saul;
they were also watching the gates both day and night,
that they may kill him,
25 and the disciples having taken him, by night did let
him down by the wall, letting down in a basket.
26 And Saul, having come to Jerusalem, did try to join
himself to the disciples, and they were all afraid of him,
not believing that he is a disciple,
27 and Barnabas having taken him, brought [him] unto
the apostles, and did declare to them how in the way he
saw the Lord, and that he spoke to him, and how in
Damascus he was speaking boldly in the name of Jesus.
28 And he was with them, coming in and going out in
Jerusalem,
29 and speaking boldly in the name of the Lord Jesus,
he was both speaking and disputing with the Hellenists,
and they were taking in hand to kill him,
30 and the brethren having known, brought him down
to Caesarea, and sent him forth to Tarsus.

31 Then, indeed, the assemblies throughout all Judea,
and Galilee, and Samaria, had peace, being built up, and,
going on in the fear of the Lord, and in the comfort of
the Holy Spirit, they were multiplied.
32 And it came to pass that Peter passing throughout
all [quarters], came down also unto the saints who were
dwelling at Lydda,
33 and he found there a certain man, Aeneas by name
— for eight years laid upon a couch — who was
paralytic,
34 and Peter said to him, 'Aeneas, Jesus the Christ does
heal you[S]; arise and spread for yourself[S];' and
immediately he rose,
35 and all those dwelling at Lydda, and Saron saw him,
and did turn to the Lord.
36 And in Joppa there was a certain female disciple, by
name Tabitha, (which interpreted, is called Dorcas,) this
woman was full of good works and kind acts that she
was doing;
37 and it came to pass in those days she, having ailed,
died, and having bathed her, they laid her in an upper
chamber,
38 and Lydda being near to Joppa, the disciples having
heard that Peter is in that [place], sent two men unto
him, calling on him not to delay to come through unto
them.
39 And Peter having risen, went with them, whom having
come, they brought into the upper chamber, and all the
widows stood by him weeping, and showing coats and
garments, as many as Dorcas was making while she was
with them.
40 And Peter having put them all forth without, having
bowed the knees, did pray, and having turned unto the
body said, 'Tabitha, arise;' and she opened her eyes,
and having seen Peter, she sat up,
41 and having given her [his] hand, he lifted her up,
and having called the saints and the widows, he
presented her alive,
42 and it became known throughout all Joppa, and many
believed on the Lord;
43 and it came to pass, that he remained many days in
Joppa, with a certain one, Simon a tanner.

CHAPTER 10

1 And there was a certain man in Caesarea, by name
Cornelius, a centurion from a band called Italian,
2 pious, and fearing God with all his house, doing also
many kind acts to the people, and begging God always,
3 he saw in a vision plainly, as it were the ninth hour of
the day, a messenger of God coming in unto him, and
saying to him, 'Cornelius;'
4 and he having looked earnestly on him, and becoming
afraid, said, 'What is it, Lord?' And he said to him, 'Your[S]
prayers and your[S] kind acts came up for a memorial
before God,
5 and now send men to Joppa, and send for a certain
one Simon, who is surnamed Peter,
6 this one does lodge with a certain Simon a tanner,
whose house is by the sea; this one shall speak to you[S]
what it is necessary for you[S] to do.'
7 And when the messenger who is speaking to Cornelius
went away, having called two of his domestics, and a
pious soldier of those waiting on him continually,
8 and having declared to them all things, he sent them
to Joppa.
9 And on the morning, as these are proceeding on the
way, and are drawing near to the city, Peter went up upon
the house-top to pray, about the sixth hour,
10 and he became very hungry, and wished to eat; and
they making ready, there a trance fell upon him,
11 and he did behold the heaven opened, and
descending unto him a certain vessel, as a great sheet,
bound at the four corners, and let down upon the earth,
12 in which were all the four-footed beasts of the earth,
and the wild beasts, and the creeping things, and the
fowls of the heaven,
13 and there came a voice unto him: 'Having risen, Peter,
slay and eat.'
14 And Peter said, 'Not so, Lord; because at no time did
I eat anything common or unclean;'
15 and [there is] a voice again a second time unto him:
'What God did cleanse, you[S], you[S] declare not common;'
16 and this was done thrice, and again was the vessel
received up to the heaven.
17 And as Peter was perplexed in himself what the vision
that he saw might be, then, behold, the men who have
been sent from Cornelius, having made inquiry for the
house of Simon, stood at the gate,
18 and having called, they were asking if Simon, who is
surnamed Peter, does lodge here?
19 And Peter thinking about the vision, the Spirit said
to him, 'Behold, three men do seek you[S];
20 but having risen, go down and go on with them,
doubting nothing, because I have sent them;'
21 and Peter having come down unto the men who have
been sent from Cornelius unto him, said, 'Behold, I am

he whom you[P] seek, what [is] the cause for which you[P] are present?'
22 And they said, 'Cornelius, a centurion, a man righteous and fearing God, well testified to, also, by all the nation of the Jews, was divinely warned by a holy messenger to send for you[S], to his house, and to hear sayings from you[S].'
23 Having called them in, therefore, he lodged them, and on the morning Peter went forth with them, and certain of the brethren from Joppa went with him,
24 and on the morning they did enter into Caesarea; and Cornelius was waiting for them, having called together his kindred and near friends,
25 and as it came that Peter entered in, Cornelius having met him, having fallen at [his] feet, did bow before [him];
26 and Peter raised him, saying, 'Stand up; I myself am a man also;'
27 and talking with him he went in, and did find many having come together.
28 And he said unto them, 'You[P] know how it is unlawful for a man, a Jew, to keep company with, or to come unto, one of another race, but God did show to me to call no man common or unclean;
29 therefore also without gainsaying I came, having been sent for; I ask, therefore, for what matter did you[P] send for me?'
30 And Cornelius said, 'Four days ago till this hour, I was fasting, and [at] the ninth hour praying in my house, and, behold, a man stood before me in bright clothing,
31 and he said, Cornelius, your[S] prayer was heard, and your[S] kind acts were remembered before God;
32 send, for that reason, to Joppa, and call for Simon, who is surnamed Peter; this one does lodge in the house of Simon a tanner, by the sea, who having come, shall speak to you[S];
33 at once, therefore, I sent to you[S]; you[S] also did do well, having come; now, for that cause, are we all present before God to hear all things that have been commanded you[S] by God.'
34 And Peter having opened his mouth, said, 'Of a truth, I perceive that God is no respecter of persons,
35 but in every nation he who is fearing Him, and is working righteousness, is acceptable to Him;
36 the word that he sent to the sons of Israel, proclaiming good news — peace through Jesus Christ (this one is Lord of all,)
37 you[P] — you[P] have known; — the word that came throughout all Judea, having begun from Galilee, after the baptism that John preached;
38 Jesus who [is] from Nazareth — how God did anoint Him with the Holy Spirit and power; who went through, doing good, and healing all those oppressed by the devil, because God was with Him;
39 and we — we are witnesses of all things that He did, both in the country of the Jews, and in Jerusalem, — whom they did slay, having hanged upon a tree.
40 'This one God did raise up the third day, and gave Him to become obvious,
41 not to all the people, but to witnesses, to those having been chosen before by God — to us who did eat with [Him], and did drink with Him, after His rising out of the dead;
42 and He commanded us to preach to the people, and to testify fully that it is He who has been ordained judge of living and dead by God —
43 to this one do all the prophets testify, that through His name every one that is believing in him does receive remission of sins.'
44 While Peter is yet speaking these sayings, the Holy spirit fell upon all those hearing the word,
45 and those of the circumcision believing were astonished — as many as came with Peter — because also upon the nations the gift of the Holy Spirit had been poured out,
46 for they were hearing them speaking with tongues and magnifying God.
47 Then answered Peter, ' Is any one able to forbid the water, that these may not be baptized, who the Holy Spirit did receive — even as also we?'
48 he commanded them also to be baptized in the name of the Lord; then they begged him to remain certain days.

CHAPTER 11

1 And the apostles and the brethren who are in Judea heard that also the nations did receive the word of God,
2 and when Peter came up to Jerusalem, those of the circumcision were contending with him,
3 saying — ' You[S] did go in unto uncircumcised men, and did eat with them!'
4 And Peter having begun, did expound to them in order saying,
5 'I was in the city of Joppa praying, and I saw in a trance a vision, a certain vessel coming down, as a great sheet by four corners being let down out of the heaven, and it came unto me;
6 at which having looked steadfastly, I was considering,

and I saw the four-footed beasts of the earth, and the
wild beasts, and the creeping things, and the fowls of
heaven;
7 and I heard a voice saying to me, Having risen, Peter,
slay and eat;
8 and I said, Not so, Lord; because anything common
or unclean has at no time entered into my mouth;
9 and a voice did answer me a second time out of the
heaven, What God did cleanse, you[S] — declare you[S] not
common.
10 'And this happened three times, and again was all
drawn up to the heaven,
11 and, behold, immediately, three men stood at the
house in which I was, having been sent from Caesarea
unto me,
12 and the Spirit said to me to go with them, doubting
nothing, and these six brethren also went with me, and
we did enter into the house of the man,
13 he declared also to us how he saw the messenger in
his house standing, and saying to him, Send men to
Joppa, and call for Simon, who is surnamed Peter,
14 who shall speak sayings by which you[S] shall be
saved, you[S] and all your[S] house.
15 'And in my beginning to speak, the Holy Spirit did
fall upon them, even as also upon us in the beginning,
16 and I remembered the saying of the Lord, how He
said, John indeed did baptize with water, and you[P] shall
be baptized with the Holy Spirit;
17 if then the equal gift God did give to them as also to
us, having believed upon the Lord Jesus Christ, I — how
was I able to withstand God?'
18 And they, having heard these things, were silent,
and were glorifying God, saying, 'Then, indeed, God did
give the reformation to life to the nations also.'
19 Those, indeed, therefore, having been scattered
abroad, from the tribulation that came after Stephen, went
through unto Phenice, and Cyprus, and Antioch,
speaking the word to none except to Jews only;
20 and there were certain of them men of Cyprus and
Cyrene, who having entered into Antioch, were speaking
unto the Hellenists, proclaiming good news — the Lord
Jesus,
21 and the hand of the Lord was with them, a great
number also, having believed, did turn unto the Lord.
22 And the account was heard in the ears of the
assembly that [is] in Jerusalem concerning them, and
they sent forth Barnabas to go through unto Antioch,
23 who, having come, and having seen the grace of God,
was glad, and was exhorting all with purpose of heart to
cling to the Lord,
24 because he was a good man, and full of the Holy
Spirit, and of faith, and a great multitude was added to
the Lord.
25 And Barnabas went forth to Tarsus, to seek for Saul,
26 and having found him, he brought him to Antioch,
and it came to pass that they did assemble together in
the assembly a whole year, and taught a great multitude,
the disciples also were divinely called Christians first in
Antioch.
27 And in those days there came from Jerusalem
prophets to Antioch,
28 and one of them, by name Agabus, having stood up,
did signify through the Spirit a great famine is about to
be throughout all the world — which also came to pass
in the time of Claudius Caesar —
29 and the disciples, according as any one was
prospering, determined each of them to send for
ministration to the brethren dwelling in Judea,
30 which also they did, having sent unto the elders by
the hand of Barnabas and Saul.

CHAPTER 12

1 And about that time, Herod the king put forth his
hands, to do evil to certain of those of the assembly,
2 and he killed James, the brother of John, with the
sword,
3 and having seen that it is pleasing to the Jews, he
added to lay hold of Peter also — and they were the
days of the unleavened food —
4 whom also having seized, he did put in prison, having
delivered [him] to four quaternions of soldiers to guard
him, intending after the Passover to bring him forth to
the people.
5 Peter, therefore, indeed, was kept in the prison, and
fervent prayer was being made by the assembly unto
God for him,
6 and when Herod was about to bring him forth, the
same night was Peter sleeping between two soldiers,
having been bound with two chains, guards also before
the door were keeping the prison,
7 and behold, a messenger of the Lord stood by, and a
light shone in the buildings, and having struck Peter on
the side, he raised him up, saying, 'Rise in a hurry,' and
his chains fell from off [his] hands.
8 The messenger also said to him, 'Gird yourself[S], and
bind on your[S] sandals;' and he did so; and he said to

him, 'Put your[S] garment round and be following me;'
9 and having gone forth, he was following him, and he
knew not that it is true that which is done through the
messenger, and was thinking he saw a vision,
10 and having passed through a first ward, and a second,
they came unto the iron gate that is leading to the city,
which of its own desire did open to them, and having
gone forth, they went on through one street, and
immediately the messenger departed from him.
11 And Peter having come to himself, said, 'Now I have
known of a truth that the Lord did sent forth His
messenger, and did deliver me out of the hand of Herod,
and all the expectation of the people of the Jews;'
12 also, having considered, he came unto the house of
Mary, the mother of John, who is surnamed Mark, where
there were many thronged together and praying.
13 And Peter having knocked at the door of the porch,
there came a damsel to listen, by name Rhoda,
14 and having known the voice of Peter, from the joy
she did not open the porch, but having run in, told of
the standing of Peter before the porch,
15 and they said unto her, 'You[S] are mad;' and she was
confidently affirming [it] to be so, and they said, 'It is
his messenger;'
16 and Peter was continuing knocking, and having
opened, they saw him, and were astonished,
17 and having beckoned to them with the hand to be
silent, he declared to them how the Lord brought him
out of the prison, and he said, 'Declare to James and to
the brethren these things;' and having gone forth, he
went on to another place.
18 And day having come, there was not a little stir among
the soldiers what then was become of Peter,
19 and Herod having sought for him, and not having
found, having examined the guards, did command [them]
to be led away to punishment, and having gone down
from Judea to Caesarea, he was abiding [there].
20 And Herod was highly displeased with the Tyrians
and Sidonians, and with one desire they came unto him,
and having made a friend of Blastus, who [is] over the
bed-chambers of the king, they were asking peace,
because of their country being nourished from the
king's;
21 and on a set day, Herod having arrayed himself in
kingly apparel, and having sat down upon the tribunal,
was making an oration unto them,
22 and the populace were shouting, 'The voice of a god,
and not of a man;'
23 and presently there a messenger of the Lord struck
him, because he did not give the glory to God, and
having been eaten of worms, he expired.
24 And the word of God did grow and did multiply,
25 and Barnabas and Saul did turn back out of Jerusalem,
having fulfilled the ministration, having taken also with
[them] John, who was surnamed Mark.

CHAPTER 13

1 And there were certain in Antioch, in the assembly
there, prophets and teachers; both Barnabas, and
Simeon who is called Niger, and Lucius the Cyrenian,
Manaen also — Herod the tetrarch's foster-brother —
and Saul;
2 and in their ministering to the Lord and fasting, the
Holy Spirit said, 'Separate you[P] to me both Barnabas
and Saul to the work to which I have called them,'
3 then having fasted, and having prayed, and having
laid the hands on them, they sent [them] away.
4 These, indeed, then, having been sent forth by the
Holy Spirit, went down to Seleucia, there also they sailed
to Cyprus,
5 and having come unto Salamis, they declared the word
of God in the synagogues of the Jews, and they had
also John [as] a ministrant;
6 and having gone through the island unto Paphos, they
found a certain magician, a false prophet, a Jew, whose
name [is] Bar-Jesus;
7 who was with the proconsul Sergius Paulus, an
intelligent man; this one having called for Barnabas and
Saul, did desire to hear the word of God,
8 and there withstood them Elymas the magician — for
so is his name interpreted — seeking to pervert the
proconsul from the faith.
9 And Saul — who also [is] Paul — having been filled
with the Holy Spirit, and having looked steadfastly on
him,
10 said, 'O full of all guile, and all lack of restraint, son
of a devil, enemy of all righteousness, will you[S] not cease
perverting the right ways of the Lord?
11 and now, behold, a hand of the Lord [is] upon you[S],
and you[S] shall be blind, not seeing the sun for a season;'
and presently there fell upon him a mist and darkness,
and he, going about, was seeking some to lead [him] by
the hand;
12 then the proconsul having seen what had come to
pass, did believe, being astonished at the teaching of
the Lord.

13 And those about Paul having set sail from Paphos,
came to Perga of Pamphylia, and John having departed
from them, did turn back to Jerusalem,
14 and they having gone through from Perga, came to
Antioch of Pisidia, and having gone into the synagogue
on the Sabbath-day, they sat down,
15 and after the reading of the law and of the prophets,
the chief men of the synagogue sent unto them, saying,
'Men, brethren, if there be a word of exhortation in you[P]
unto the people — say on.'
16 And Paul having risen, and having beckoned with
the hand, said, 'Men, Israelites, and those fearing God,
listen:
17 the God of this people Israel did choose our fathers,
and the people He did exalt in their sojourning in the
land of Egypt, and with an high arm did He bring them
out of it;
18 and about a period of forty years He did allow their
manners in the wilderness,
19 and having destroyed seven nations in the land of
Canaan, He did divide their land by lot to them.
20 'And after these things, about four hundred and fifty
years, He gave judges — till Samuel the prophet;
21 and thereafter they asked for a king, and God did
give to them Saul, son of Kish, a man of the tribe of
Benjamin, for forty years;
22 and having removed him, He did raise up to them
David for king, to whom also having testified, he said, I
found David, the [son] of Jesse, a man according to My
heart, who shall do all My will.
23 'Of this one's seed God, according to promise, did
raise to Israel a Savior — Jesus,
24 John having first preached, before His coming, a
baptism of reformation to all the people of Israel;
25 and as John was fulfilling the course, he said, Whom
do you[P] suppose me to be? I am not [He], but, behold,
He does come after me, of whom I am not worthy to loose
the sandal of [His] feet.
26 'Men, brethren, sons of the race of Abraham, and
those among you[P] fearing God, to you[P] was the word of
this salvation sent,
27 for those dwelling in Jerusalem, and their chiefs, this
one not having known, also the voices of the prophets,
which every Sabbath are being read — having judged
[Him] — did fulfil,
28 and having found no cause of death, they did ask of
Pilate that He should be slain,
29 and when they did complete all the things written
about Him, having taken [Him] down from the tree, they
laid Him in a tomb;
30 and God did raise Him out of the dead,
31 and He was seen for many days of those who did
come up with Him from Galilee to Jerusalem, who are His
witnesses unto the people.
32 'And we do proclaim good news to you[P] — that the
promise made unto the fathers,
33 God has in full completed this to us their children,
having raised up Jesus, as also in the second Psalm it
has been written, You[S] are My Son — I have begotten
You[S] today.
34 'And that He did raise Him up out of the dead, no
more to return to corruption, He has said thus — I will
give the faithful kindnesses of David to you[P];
35 for what reason also in another [place] He said, You[S]
shall not give Your[S] kind One to see corruption,
36 for David, indeed, his own generation having served
by the will of God, did fall asleep, and was added unto
his fathers, and saw corruption,
37 but He whom God did raise up, did not see corruption.
38 'Let it therefore be known to you[P], men, brethren,
that through this one is the forgiveness of sins declared
to you[P],
39 and from all things from which you[P] were not able in
the law of Moses to be declared righteous, in this one
every one who is believing is declared righteous;
40 see, for that reason, it may not come upon you[P] that
has been spoken in the prophets:
41 See, you[P] despisers, and wonder, and perish, because
a work I — I do work in your[P] days, a work in which
you[P] may not believe, though any one may declare [it]
to you[P].'
42 And having gone forth out of the synagogue of the
Jews, the nations were calling upon [them] that on the
next Sabbath these sayings may be spoken to them,
43 and the synagogue having been dismissed, many of
the Jews and of the devout proselytes did follow Paul
and Barnabas, who, speaking to them, were persuading
them to remain in the grace of God.
44 And on the coming Sabbath, almost all the city was
gathered together to hear the word of God,
45 and the Jews having seen the multitudes, were filled
with zeal, and did contradict the things spoken by Paul
— contradicting and speaking evil.
46 And speaking boldly, Paul and Barnabas said, 'To
you[P] it was necessary that first the word of God be
spoken, and seeing you[P] do thrust it away, and do not
judge yourselves[P] worthy of the life age-during, behold,
we do turn to the nations;

47 for so has the Lord commanded us: I have set You[S]
for a light of nations — for Your[S] being for salvation
unto the end of the earth.'
48 And the nations hearing were glad, and were
glorifying the word of the Lord, and did believe — as
many as were appointed to life age-during;
49 and the word of the Lord was spread abroad through
all the region.
50 And the Jews stirred up the devout and honorable
women, and the first men of the city, and did raise
persecution against Paul and Barnabas, and did put them
out from their borders;
51 and they having shaken off the dust of their feet
against them, came to Iconium,
52 and the disciples were filled with joy and the Holy
Spirit.

CHAPTER 14

1 And it came to pass in Iconium, that they did enter
together into the synagogue of the Jews, and spoke, so
that there believed a great multitude both of Jews and
Greeks;
2 and the unbelieving Jews did stir up and made evil
the souls of the nations against the brethren;
3 long time, indeed, for that reason, did they abide
speaking boldly in the Lord, who is testifying to the word
of His grace, and granting signs and wonders to come
to pass through their hands.
4 And the multitude of the city was divided, and some
were with the Jews, and some with the apostles,
5 and when there was a purpose both of the nations
and of the Jews with their rulers to use [them]
despitefully, and to stone them,
6 they having become aware, did flee to the cities of
Lycaonia, Lystra, and Derbe, and to the region round about,
7 and there they were proclaiming good news.
8 And a certain man in Lystra, impotent in the feet, was
sitting, being lame from the womb of his mother — who
never had walked,
9 this one was hearing Paul speaking, who, having
steadfastly beheld him, and having seen that he had faith
to be saved,
10 said with a loud voice, 'Stand up on your[S] feet
upright;' and he was springing and walking,
11 and the multitudes having seen what Paul did, did lift
up their voice, in the speech of Lycaonia, saying, 'The
gods, having become like men, did come down unto us;'
12 they were calling also Barnabas Zeus, and Paul
Hermes, since he was the leader in speaking.
13 And the priest of the Zeus that is before their city,
having brought oxen and garlands unto the porches,
with the multitudes did wish to sacrifice,
14 and having heard, the apostles Barnabas and Paul,
having rent their garments, did spring into the multitude,
crying
15 and saying, 'Men, why do you[P] these things? and
we are men like-affected with you[P], proclaiming good
news to you[P], to turn from these vanities unto the living
God, who made the heaven, and the earth, and the sea,
and all the things in them;
16 who in the past generations did allow all the nations
to go on in their ways,
17 though, indeed, He did not leave himself without
witness, doing good — from heaven giving rains to us,
and fruitful seasons, filling our hearts with food and
gladness;'
18 and these things saying, scarcely did they restrain
the multitudes from sacrificing to them.
19 And there came there, from Antioch and Iconium,
Jews, and they having persuaded the multitudes, and
having stoned Paul, drew him outside of the city, having
supposed him to be dead;
20 and the disciples having surrounded him, having
risen he entered into the city, and on the next morning
he went forth with Barnabas to Derbe.
21 Having proclaimed good news also to that city, and
having discipled many, they turned back to Lystra, and
Iconium, and Antioch,
22 confirming the souls of the disciples, exhorting to
remain in the faith, and that through many tribulations it
is necessary for us to enter into the reign of God,
23 and having appointed to them by vote elders in every
assembly, having prayed with fastings, they commended
them to the Lord in whom they had believed.
24 And having passed through Pisidia, they came to
Pamphylia,
25 and having spoken in Perga the word, they went
down to Attalia,
26 and from there did sail to Antioch, where they had
been given by the grace of God for the work that they
fulfilled;
27 and having come and gathered together the assembly,
they declared as many things as God did with them, and
that He did open a door of faith to the nations;
28 and they abode there not a little time with the
disciples.

CHAPTER 15

1 And certain having come down from Judea, were
teaching the brethren — 'If you[P] be not circumcised after
the custom of Moses, you[P] are not able to be saved;'
2 there having been, for that reason, not a little
dissension and disputation to Paul and Barnabas with
them, they arranged for Paul and Barnabas, and certain
others of them, to go up unto the apostles and elders to
Jerusalem about this question,
3 they indeed, then, having been sent forward by the
assembly, were passing through Phenice and Samaria,
declaring the conversion of the nations, and they were
causing great joy to all the brethren.
4 And having come to Jerusalem, they were received
by the assembly, and the apostles, and the elders, they
declared also as many things as God did with them;
5 and there rose up certain of those of the sect of the
Pharisees who believed, saying — 'It is necessary to
circumcise them, to command them also to keep the law
of Moses.'
6 And there were gathered together the apostles and
the elders, to see about this matter,
7 and there having been much disputing, Peter having
risen up said unto them, 'Men, brethren, you[P] know that
from former days, God among us did make choice,
through my mouth, for the nations to hear the word of
the good news, and to believe;
8 and the heart-knowing God did bare them testimony,
having given to them the Holy Spirit, even as also to us,
9 and did put no difference also between us and them,
by the faith having purified their hearts;
10 now, therefore, why do you[P] tempt God, to put a yoke
upon the neck of the disciples, which neither our fathers
nor we were able to bear?
11 but, through the grace of the Lord Jesus Christ, we
believe to be saved, even as also they.'
12 And all the multitude did keep silence, and were
listening to Barnabas and Paul, declaring as many signs
and wonders as God did among the nations through
them;
13 and after they are silent, James answered, saying,
'Men, brethren, listen to me;
14 Simeon did declare how at first God did look after to
take out of the nations a people for His name,
15 and to this agree the words of the prophets, as it had
been written:
16 After these things I will turn back, and I will build
again the tabernacle of David, that is fallen down, and
its ruins I will build again, and will set it upright —
17 that the residue of men may seek after the Lord, and
all the nations, upon whom My name has been called,
said the Lord, who is doing all these things.
18 'Known from the ages to God are all His works;
19 for what reason I judge: not to trouble those who
from the nations do turn back to God,
20 but to write to them to abstain from the pollutions of
the idols, and the whoredom, and the strangled thing;
and the blood;
21 for Moses from former generations has those
preaching him in every city — being read in the
synagogues every Sabbath.'
22 Then it seemed good to the apostles and the elders,
with the whole assembly, chosen men out of themselves
to send to Antioch with Paul and Barnabas — Judas
surnamed Barsabas, and Silas, leading men among the
brethren —
23 having written through their hand thus: 'The
apostles, and the elders, and the brethren, to those in
Antioch, and Syria, and Cilicia, brethren, who [are] of
the nations, greeting;
24 seeing we have heard that certain having gone forth
from us did trouble you[P] with words, subverting your[P]
souls, saying to be circumcised and to keep the law, to
whom we did give no charge,
25 it seemed good to us, having come together with
one desire, chosen men to send unto you[P], with our
beloved Barnabas and Paul —
26 men who have given up their lives for the name of
our Lord Jesus Christ —
27 we have sent, for that reason, Judas and Silas, and
they by word are telling the same things.
28 'For it seemed good to the Holy Spirit, and to us, to
lay no more burden upon you[P], except these necessary
things:
29 to abstain from things offered to idols, and blood,
and a strangled thing, and whoredom; from which
keeping yourselves[P], you[P] shall do well; be strong!'
30 They then, indeed, having been let go, went to
Antioch, and having brought the multitude together, did
deliver the epistle,
31 and they having read, did rejoice for the consolation;
32 Judas also and Silas, being themselves also prophets,
through much discourse did exhort the brethren, and
confirm,
33 and having passed some time, they were let go with
peace from the brethren unto the apostles;

34 and it seemed good to Silas to remain there still.
35 And Paul and Barnabas continued in Antioch,
teaching and proclaiming good news — with many
others also — the word of the Lord;
36 and after certain days, Paul said unto Barnabas,
'Having turned back again, we may look after our
brethren, in every city in which we have preached the
word of the Lord — how they are.'
37 And Barnabas counseled to take with [them] John
called Mark,
38 and Paul was not thinking it good to take him with
them who withdrew from them from Pamphylia, and did
not go with them to the work;
39 there came, for that reason, a sharp contention, so
that they were parted from one another, and Barnabas
having taken Mark, did sail to Cyprus,
40 and Paul having chosen Silas, went forth, having
been given up to the grace of God by the brethren;
41 and he went through Syria and Cilicia, confirming
the assemblies.

CHAPTER 16

1 And he came to Derbe and Lystra, and behold, a certain
disciple was there, by name Timotheus son of a certain
woman, a believing Jewess, but of a father, a Greek,
2 who was well testified to by the brethren in Lystra
and Iconium;
3 this one did Paul wish to go forth with him, and having
taken [him], he circumcised him, because of the Jews
who are in those places, for they all knew his father —
that he was a Greek.
4 And as they were going on through the cities, they
were delivering to them the decrees to keep, that have
been judged by the apostles and the elders who [are] in
Jerusalem,
5 then, indeed, were the assemblies established in the
faith, and were abounding in number every day;
6 and having gone through Phrygia and the region of
Galatia, having been forbidden by the Holy Spirit to
speak the word in Asia,
7 having gone toward Mysia, they were trying to go on
toward Bithynia, and the Spirit did not allow them,
8 and having passed by Mysia, they came down to
Troas.
9 And a vision through the night appeared to Paul — a
certain man of Macedonia was standing, calling upon
him, and saying, 'Having passed through to Macedonia,
help us;' —
10 and when he saw the vision, immediately we
endeavored to go forth to Macedonia, assuredly
gathering that the Lord had called us to preach good
news to them,
11 having set sail, therefore, from Troas, we came with a
straight course to Samothracia, on the morning also to
Neapolis,
12 from there also to Philippi, which is a principal city of
the part of Macedonia — a colony. And we were in this
city abiding certain days,
13 on the Sabbath-day also we went forth outside of
the city, by a river, where there used to be prayer, and
having sat down, we were speaking to the women who
came together,
14 and a certain woman, by name Lydia, a seller of purple,
of the city of Thyatira, worshipping God, was hearing,
whose heart the Lord did open to attend to the things
spoken by Paul;
15 and when she was baptized, and her household, she
did call upon us, saying, 'If you[P] have judged me to be
faithful to the Lord, having entered into my house,
remain;' and she constrained us.
16 And it came to pass in our going on to prayer, a certain
maid, having a spirit of Python, did meet us, who brought
much employment to her masters by soothsaying,
17 she having followed Paul and us, was crying, saying,
'These men are servants of the Most High God, who
declare to us a way of salvation;'
18 and she was doing this for many days, but Paul
having been grieved, and having turned, said to the
spirit, 'I command you[S], in the name of Jesus Christ, to
come forth from her;' and it came forth the same hour.
19 And her masters having seen that the hope of their
employment was gone, having caught Paul and Silas,
drew [them] to the market-place, unto the rulers,
20 and having brought them to the magistrates, they
said, 'These men do exceedingly trouble our city, being
Jews;
21 and they proclaim customs that are not lawful for us
to receive nor to do, being Romans.'
22 And the multitude rose up together against them,
and the magistrates having torn their garments from
them, were commanding to beat [them] with rods,
23 many blows also having laid upon them, they cast
them to prison, having given charge to the jailor to keep
them safely,
24 who such a charge having received, did put them to
the inner prison, and their feet made fast in the stocks.

25 And at midnight Paul and Silas praying, were singing hymns to God, and the prisoners were hearing them,
26 and suddenly a great earthquake came, so that the foundations of the prison were shaken, opened also presently were all the doors, and of all — the bands were loosed;
27 and the jailor having come out of sleep, and having seen the doors of the prison open, having drawn a sword, was about to kill himself, supposing the prisoners to be fled,
28 and Paul cried out with a loud voice, saying, 'You[S] may not do yourself[S] any harm, for we are all here.'
29 And, having asked for a light, he sprang in, and trembling he fell down before Paul and Silas,
30 and having brought them forth, said, 'Sirs, what must I do — that I may be saved?'
31 and they said, 'Believe on the Lord Jesus Christ, and you[S] shall be saved — you[S] and your[S] house;'
32 and they spoke to him the word of the Lord, and to all those in his household;
33 and having taken them, in that hour of the night, he did bathe [them] from the blows, and was baptized, himself and all his presently,
34 having brought them also into his house, he set food before [them], and was glad with all the household, he having believed in God.
35 And day having come, the magistrates sent the rod-bearers, saying, 'Let those men go;'
36 and the jailor told these words unto Paul — 'The magistrates have sent, that you[P] may be let go; now, therefore, having gone forth go on in peace;'
37 and Paul said to them, 'Having beaten us publicly uncondemned — men, Romans being — they did cast [us] to prison, and now privately do they cast us forth! why no! but having come themselves, let them bring us forth.'
38 And the rod-bearers told to the magistrates these sayings, and they were afraid, having heard that they are Romans,
39 and having come, they begged them, and having brought [them] forth, they were asking [them] to go forth from the city;
40 and they, having gone forth out of the prison, entered into [the house of] Lydia, and having seen the brethren, they comforted them, and went forth.

CHAPTER 17

1 And having passed through Amphipolis, and Apollonia, they came to Thessalonica, where was the synagogue of the Jews,
2 and according to the custom of Paul, he went in unto them, and for three Sabbaths he was reasoning with them from the Writings,
3 opening and alleging, 'That it was necessary for the Christ to suffer, and to rise again out of the dead, and that this is the Christ — Jesus whom I proclaim to you[P].'
4 And certain of them did believe, and attached themselves to Paul and to Silas, also of the worshipping Greeks a great multitude, also not a few of the principal women.
5 And the unbelieving Jews, having been moved with envy, and having taken to them certain evil men of the loungers, and having made a crowd, were setting the city in an uproar; having assailed also the house of Jason, they were seeking them to bring [them] to the populace,
6 and not having found them, they drew Jason and certain brethren unto the city rulers, calling aloud — 'These, having put the world in commotion, are also here present,
7 whom Jason has received; and these all do contrary to the decrees of Caesar, saying another to be king — Jesus.'
8 And they troubled the multitude and the city rulers, hearing these things,
9 and having taking security from Jason and the rest, they let them go.
10 And the brethren immediately, through the night, sent forth both Paul and Silas to Berea, who having come, went to the synagogue of the Jews;
11 and these were more noble than those in Thessalonica, they received the word with all readiness of mind, every day examining the Writings whether those things were so;
12 many, indeed, therefore, of them did believe, and not a few of the honorable Greek women and men.
13 And when the Jews from Thessalonica knew that also in Berea was the word of God declared by Paul, they came there also, agitating the multitudes;
14 and then immediately the brethren sent forth Paul, to go on as it were to the sea, but both Silas and Timothy were remaining there.
15 And those conducting Paul, brought him unto Athens, and having received a command unto Silas and Timotheus that with all speed they may come unto him, they departed;
16 and Paul waiting for them in Athens, his spirit was stirred in him, beholding the city wholly given to idolatry,

17 for that reason, indeed, he was reasoning in the
synagogue with the Jews, and with the worshipping
persons, and in the market-place every day with those
who met with him.
18 And certain of the Epicurean and of the Stoic
philosophers, were meeting together to see him, and
some were saying, 'What would this seed picker wish
to say?' and others, ' He does seem to be an announcer
of strange demons;' because Jesus and the rising again
he did proclaim to them as good news,
19 having also taken him, unto the Areopagus they
brought [him], saying, 'Are we able to know what [is]
this new teaching that is spoken by you[S],
20 for you[S] do bring certain strange things to our ears?
we wish, then, to know what these things would wish to
be;'
21 and all Athenians, and the strangers sojourning, for
nothing else were at leisure but to say something, and
to hear some newer thing.
22 And Paul, having stood in the midst of the
Areopagus, said, 'Men, Athenians, in all things I
perceive you[P] as over-religious;
23 for passing through and contemplating your[P] objects
of worship, I found also an erection on which had been
inscribed: To God — unknown; whom, for that reason
— not knowing — you[P] do worship, this One I announce
to you[P].
24 'God, who did make the world, and all things in it,
this One, of heaven and of earth being Lord, does not
dwell in temples made with hands ,
25 neither is He served by the hands of men — needing
anything, He giving to all life, and breath, and all things;
26 He made also of one blood every nation of men, to
dwell upon all the face of the earth — having ordained
times before appointed, and the bounds of their
dwellings —
27 to seek the Lord, if perhaps they did feel after Him
and find, — though, indeed, He is not far from each one
of us,
28 for we live in Him, and move, and are; as also certain
of your[P] poets have said: For of Him also we are
offspring.
29 'Being, for that reason, offspring of God, we ought
not to think the Godhead to be like to gold, or silver, or
stone, graving of art and device of man;
30 the times, indeed, for that reason, of the ignorance
God having overlooked, does now command all men
everywhere to reform,
31 because He did set a day in which He is about to
judge the world in righteousness, by a man whom He
did ordain, having given assurance to all, having raised
him out of the dead.'
32 And having heard of a rising again of the dead, some,
indeed, were mocking, but others said, 'We will hear you[S]
again concerning this;'
33 and so Paul went forth from the midst of them,
34 and certain men having adhered to him, did believe,
among whom [is] also Dionysius the Areopagite, and a
woman, by name Damaris, and others with them.

CHAPTER 18

1 And after these things, Paul having departed out of
Athens, came to Corinth,
2 and having found a certain Jew, by name Aquilas, of
Pontus by birth, lately come from Italy, and Priscilla his
wife — because of Claudius having directed all the Jews
to depart out of Rome — he came to them,
3 and because of being of the same craft, he did remain
with them, and was working, for they were tent-makers
as to craft;
4 and he was reasoning in the synagogue every
Sabbath, persuading both Jews and Greeks.
5 And when both Silas and Timotheus came down from
Macedonia, Paul was pressed in the Spirit, testifying
fully to the Jews Jesus the Christ;
6 and on their resisting and speaking evil, having shaken
[his] garments, he said unto them, 'Your[P] blood [is] upon
your[P] head — I am clean; from this time on I will go on
to the nations.'
7 And having departed from there, he went to the house
of a certain one, by name Justus, a worshipper of God,
whose house was adjoining the synagogue,
8 and Crispus, the ruler of the synagogue did believe in
the Lord with all his house, and many of the Corinthians
hearing were believing, and they were being baptized.
9 And the Lord said through a vision in the night to
Paul, 'Be not afraid, but be speaking and you[S] may be
not silent;
10 because I am with you[S], and no one shall set on you[S]
to do you[S] evil; because I have much people in this city;'
11 and he continued a year and six months, teaching
among them the word of God.
12 And Gallio being proconsul of Achaia, the Jews made
a rush with one desire upon Paul, and brought him unto
the tribunal,
13 saying — 'Against the law this one does persuade

men to worship God;'

14 and Paul being about to open [his] mouth, Gallio said unto the Jews, 'If, indeed, then, it was anything unrighteous, or an act of wicked lack of restraint, O Jews, according to reason I had borne with you[P],

15 but if it is a question concerning words and names, and of your[P] law, look you[P] yourselves[P] [to it], for a judge of these things I do not wish to be,'

16 and he drove them from the tribunal;

17 and all the Greeks having taken Sosthenes, the chief man of the synagogue, were beating [him] before the tribunal, and not even for these things was Gallio caring.

18 And Paul having remained yet a good many days, having taken leave of the brethren, was sailing to Syria — and with him [are] Priscilla and Aquilas — having shaved [his] head in Cenchera, for he had a vow;

19 and he came down to Ephesus, and did leave them there, and he himself having entered into the synagogue did reason with the Jews:

20 and they having requested [him] to remain a longer time with them, he did not consent,

21 but took leave of them, saying, 'It is necessary for me by all means to keep the coming feast at Jerusalem, and again I will return unto you[P] — God willing.' And he sailed from Ephesus,

22 and having come down to Caesarea, having gone up, and having saluted the assembly, he went down to Antioch.

23 And having made some stay he went forth, going through in order the region of Galatia and Phrygia, strengthening all the disciples.

24 And a certain Jew, Apollos by name, an Alexandrian by birth, a man of eloquence, being mighty in the Writings, came to Ephesus,

25 this one was instructed in the way of the Lord, and being fervent in the Spirit, was speaking and teaching exactly the things about the Lord, knowing only the baptism of John;

26 this one also began to speak boldly in the synagogue, and Aquilas and Priscilla having heard of him, took him to [them], and did more exactly expound to him the way of God,

27 and he being minded to go through into Achaia, the brethren wrote to the disciples, having exhorted them to receive him, who having come, did help them much who have believed through the grace,

28 for he was powerfully refuting the Jews publicly, showing through the Writings Jesus to be the Christ.

CHAPTER 19

1 And it came to pass, in Apollos' being in Corinth, Paul having gone through the upper parts, came to Ephesus, and having found certain disciples,

2 he said unto them, 'Did you[P] receive the Holy Spirit — having believed?' and they said unto him, 'But we did not even hear whether there is any Holy Spirit;'

3 and he said unto them, 'To what, then, were you[P] baptized?' and they said, 'To John's baptism.'

4 And Paul said, 'John, indeed, did baptize with a baptism of reformation, saying to the people that they should believe in him who is coming after him — that is, in the Christ — Jesus;'

5 and they, having heard, were baptized — to the name of the Lord Jesus,

6 and Paul having laid [his] hands on them, the Holy Spirit came upon them, they were speaking also with tongues, and prophesying,

7 and all the men were, as it were, twelve.

8 And having gone into the synagogue, he was speaking boldly for three months, reasoning and persuading the things concerning the reign of God,

9 and when certain were hardened and were disbelieving, speaking evil of the way before the multitude, having departed from them, he did separate the disciples, every day reasoning in the school of a certain Tyrannus.

10 And this happened for two years so that all those dwelling in Asia did hear the word of the Lord Jesus, both Jews and Greeks,

11 mighty works also — not common — was God working through the hands of Paul,

12 so that even handkerchiefs or aprons from his body were brought unto the ailing, and the sicknesses departed from them; the evil spirits also went forth from them.

13 And certain of the wandering exorcist Jews, took upon [them] to name the name of the Lord Jesus over those having the evil spirits, saying, 'We command you[P] by Jesus, whom Paul does preach;'

14 and there were certain — seven sons of Sceva, a Jew, a chief priest — who are doing this thing;

15 and the evil spirit, answering, said, 'Jesus I know, and Paul I am acquainted with; and you[P] — who are you[P]?'

16 And the man, in whom was the evil spirit, leaping upon them, and having overcome them, prevailed against them, so that naked and wounded they did flee out of

that house,
17 and this became known to all, both Jews and Greeks,
who are dwelling at Ephesus, and fear fell upon them all,
and the name of the Lord Jesus was being magnified,
18 many also of those who did believe were coming,
confessing and declaring their acts,
19 and many of those who had practiced the curious
arts, having brought the books together, were burning
[them] before all; and they reckoned together the prices
of them, and found [it] five myriads of silverlings;
20 so powerfully was the word of God increasing and
prevailing.
21 And when these things were fulfilled, Paul purposed
in the Spirit, having gone through Macedonia and
Achaia, to go on to Jerusalem, saying — 'After my being
there, it is necessary for me also to see Rome;'
22 and having sent to Macedonia two of those
ministering to him — Timotheus and Erastus — he
himself stayed a time in Asia.
23 And there came, at that time, not a little stir about the
way,
24 for a certain one, Demetrius by name, a worker in
silver, making silver sanctuaries of Artemis, was bringing
to the artificers not a little gain,
25 whom, having brought in a crowd together, and those
who did work about such things, he said, 'Men, you[P]
know that by this work we have our wealth;
26 and you[P] see and hear, that not only at Ephesus, but
almost in all Asia, this Paul, having persuaded, did turn
away a great multitude, saying, that they who are made
by hands are not gods;
27 and not only is this department in danger of coming
into disregard for us, but also, that the temple of the
great goddess Artemis is to be reckoned for nothing,
and also her greatness is about to be brought down,
whom all Asia and the world does worship.'
28 And they having heard, and having become full of
wrath, were crying out, saying, 'Great [is] the Artemis
of the Ephesians!'
29 and the whole city was filled with confusion, they
rushed also with one desire into the theater, having
caught Gaius and Aristarchus, Macedonians, Paul's
fellow-travelers.
30 And on Paul's purposing to enter in unto the
populace, the disciples were not allowing him,
31 and certain also of the chief men of Asia, being his
friends, having sent unto him, were entreating him not
to venture himself into the theater.
32 Some indeed, for that reason, were calling out one
thing, and some another, for the assembly was confused,
and the greater part did not know for what they were
come together;
33 and out of the multitude they put forward Alexander
— the Jews thrusting him forward — and Alexander
having beckoned with the hand, wished to make defense
to the populace,
34 and having known that he is a Jew, one voice came
out of all, for about two hours, crying, 'Great [is] the
Artemis of the Ephesians!'
35 And the public clerk having quieted the multitude,
said, 'Men, Ephesians, why, who is the man that does
not know that the city of the Ephesians is a devotee of
the great goddess Artemis, and of that which fell down
from Zeus?
36 these things, then, not being to be denied, it is
necessary for you[P] to be quiet, and to do nothing rashly.
37 'For you[P] brought these men, who are neither temple-
robbers nor speaking evil of your[P] goddess;
38 if indeed, therefore, Demetrius and the artificers with
him have a matter with any one, court [days] are held,
and there are proconsuls; let them accuse one another.
39 'And if you[P] seek after anything concerning other
matters, in the legal assembly it shall be determined;
40 for we are also in peril of being accused of
insurrection in regard to this day, there being no
occasion by which we shall be able to give an account
of this concourse;'
41 and these things having said, he dismissed the
assembly.

CHAPTER 20

1 And after the ceasing of the tumult, Paul having called
near the disciples, and having embraced [them], went
forth to go on to Macedonia;
2 and having gone through those parts, and having
exhorted them with many words, he came to Greece;
3 having made also three months' [stay] — a counsel
of the Jews having been against him — being about to
set forth to Syria, there came [to him] a resolution of
returning through Macedonia.
4 And there were accompanying him unto Asia, Sopater
of Berea, and of Thessalonians Aristarchus and
Secundus, and Gaius of Derbe, and Timotheus, and of
Asiatics Tychicus and Trophimus;
5 these, having gone before, did remain for us in Troas,
6 and we sailed, after the days of the unleavened food,

from Philippi, and came unto them to Troas in five days,
where we abode seven days.
7 And on the first of the week, the disciples having been
gathered together to break bread, Paul was discoursing
to them, about to depart on the morning, he was also
continuing the discourse till midnight,
8 and there were many lamps in the upper chamber where
they were gathered together,
9 and there was sitting a certain youth, by name
Eutychus, upon the window — being borne down by a
deep sleep, Paul discoursing long — he having sunk
down from the sleep, fell down from the third story, and
was lifted up dead.
10 And Paul, having gone down, fell upon him, and
having embraced [him], said, 'Make no tumult, for his
life is in him;'
11 and having come up, and having broken bread, and
having tasted, for a long time also having talked — till
daylight, so he went forth,
12 and they brought up the lad alive, and were comforted
in no ordinary measure.
13 And we having gone before unto the ship, did sail to
Assos, from there intending to take in Paul, for so he
had arranged, intending himself to go on foot;
14 and when he met with us at Assos, having taken him
up, we came to Mitylene,
15 and from there having sailed, on the morning we came
over-against Chios, and the next day we arrived at
Samos, and having remained in Trogyllium, on the
following day we came to Miletus,
16 for Paul decided to sail past Ephesus, that there may
not be to him a loss of time in Asia, for he hurried, if it
were possible for him, to be at Jerusalem on the day of
the Pentecost.
17 And from Miletus, having sent to Ephesus, he called
for the elders of the assembly,
18 and when they were come unto him, he said to them,
'You[P] — you[P] know from the first day in which I came to
Asia, how I was with you[P] at all times;
19 serving the Lord with all humility, and many tears,
and temptations, that befell me in the counsels of the
Jews against [me];
20 how I did keep back nothing of what things are
profitable, not to declare to you[P], and to teach you[P]
publicly, and in every house,
21 testifying fully both to Jews and Greeks, reformation
toward God, and faith toward our Lord Jesus Christ.
22 'And now, behold, I — bound in the Spirit — go on
to Jerusalem, not knowing the things that shall befall
me in it,
23 save that the Holy Spirit in every city does testify
fully, saying, that bonds and tribulations remain for me;
24 but I make account of none of these, neither do I count
my life precious to myself, so that I finish my course with
joy, and the ministration that I received from the Lord
Jesus, to testify fully the good news of the grace of God.
25 'And now, behold, I have known that no more shall
you[P] see my face, — you[P] all among whom I did go
preaching the reign of God;
26 why I take you[P] to witness this day, that I [am] clear
from the blood of all,
27 for I did not keep back from declaring to you[P] all the
counsel of God.
28 'Take heed, for that reason, to yourselves[P], and to all
the flock, among which the Holy Spirit made you[P]
overseers, to feed the assembly of God that He acquired
through His own blood,
29 for I have known this, that there shall enter in, after
my departing, grievous wolves unto you[P], not sparing
the flock,
30 and of your[P] own selves there shall arise men,
speaking perverse things, to draw away the disciples
after them.
31 'For that reason, watch, remembering that three years,
night and day, I did not cease warning each one with tears;
32 and now, I commend you[P], brethren, to God, and to
the word of His grace, that is able to build up, and to
give you[P] an inheritance among all those sanctified.
33 'The silver or gold or garments of no one did I covet;
34 and you[P] yourselves[P] know that to my necessities,
and to those who were with me, these hands did minister;
35 all things I did show you[P], that, thus laboring, it is
necessary for [us] to partake with the ailing, to be mindful
also of the words of the Lord Jesus, that He Himself said,
It is more blessed to give than to receive.'
36 And these things having said, having bowed his
knees, with them all, he did pray,
37 and there came a great weeping to all, and having
fallen upon the neck of Paul, they were kissing him,
38 sorrowing most of all for the word that he had said
— that they are about no more to see his face; and they
were accompanying him to the ship.

CHAPTER 21

1 And it came to pass, at our sailing, having been parted
from them, having run direct, we came to Coos, and the

succeeding [day] to Rhodes, and from there to Patara,
2 and having found a ship passing over to Phenicia, having gone on board, we sailed,
3 and having discovered Cyprus, and having left it on the left, we were sailing to Syria, and did land at Tyre, for there was the ship discharging the lading.
4 And having found out the disciples, we tarried there seven days, and they said to Paul, through the Spirit, not to go up to Jerusalem;
5 but when it came that we completed the days, having gone forth, we went on, all bringing us on the way, with women and children, unto the outside of the city, and having bowed the knees upon the shore, we prayed,
6 and having embraced one another, we embarked in the ship, and they returned to their own friends.
7 And we, having finished the course, from Tyre came down to Ptolemais, and having saluted the brethren, we remained one day with them;
8 and on the morning Paul and his company having gone forth, we came to Caesarea, and having entered into the house of Philip the evangelist — who is of the seven — we remained with him,
9 and this one had four daughters, virgins, prophesying.
10 And we remaining many more days, there came down a certain one from Judea, a prophet, by name Agabus,
11 and he having come unto us, and having taken up the girdle of Paul, having bound also his own hands and feet, said, 'Thus says the Holy Spirit, The man whose this girdle is — so shall the Jews in Jerusalem bind, and they shall deliver [him] up to the hands of nations.'
12 And when we heard these things, we called upon [him] — both we, and those of that place — not to go up to Jerusalem,
13 and Paul answered, 'What do you[P] — weeping, and crushing mine heart? for I am ready, not only to be bound, but also to die at Jerusalem, for the name of the Lord Jesus;'
14 and he not being persuaded, we were silent, saying, 'The will of the Lord be done.'
15 And after these days, having taken [our] vessels, we were going up to Jerusalem,
16 and there went also of the disciples from Caesarea with us, bringing with them him with whom we may lodge, a certain Mnason of Cyprus, an aged disciple.
17 And we having come to Jerusalem, the brethren did gladly receive us,
18 and on the morning Paul was going in with us unto James, all the elders also came,
19 and having saluted them, he was declaring, one by one, each of the things God did among the nations through his ministration,
20 and they having heard, were glorifying the Lord. They said also to him, 'You[S] see, brother, how many myriads there are of Jews who have believed, and all are zealous of the law,
21 and they are instructed concerning you[S], that you[S] do teach apostasy from Moses to all Jews among the nations, saying — Not to circumcise the children, nor to walk after the customs;
22 what then is it? certainly it is necessary for the multitude to come together, for they will hear that you[S] have come.
23 'This, for that reason, do that we say to you[S]: We have four men having a vow on themselves,
24 these having taken, be purified with them, and be at expense with them, that they may shave the head, and all may know that the things of which they have been instructed concerning you[S] are nothing, but you[S] do walk — yourself[S] also — the law keeping.
25 'And concerning those of the nations who have believed, we have written, having given judgment, that they observe no such thing, except to keep themselves both from idol-sacrifices, and blood, and a strangled thing, and whoredom.'
26 Then Paul, having taken the men, on the following day, with them having purified himself, was entering into the temple, announcing the fulfillment of the days of the purification, till the offering was offered for each one of them.
27 And, as the seven days were about to be fully ended, the Jews from Asia having beheld him in the temple, were stirring up all the multitude, and they laid hands upon him,
28 crying out, 'Men, Israelites, help! this is the man who, against the people, and the law, and this place, all everywhere is teaching; and further, also, he brought Greeks into the temple, and has defiled this holy place;'
29 for they had seen before Trophimus, the Ephesian, in the city with him, whom they were supposing that Paul brought into the temple.
30 All the city also was moved and there was a running together of the people, and having laid hold on Paul, they were drawing him out of the temple, and immediately were the doors shut,
31 and they seeking to kill him, a rumor came to the chief captain of the band that all Jerusalem had been thrown into confusion,
32 who, at once, having taken soldiers and centurions,

ran down upon them, and they having seen the chief captain and the soldiers, did leave off beating Paul.
33 Then the chief captain, having come near, took him, and commanded [him] to be bound with two chains, and was inquiring who he may be, and what it is he had been doing,
34 and some were crying out one thing, and some another, among the multitude, and not being able to know the certainty because of the tumult, he commanded him to be carried to the castle,
35 and when he came upon the steps, it happened he was borne by the soldiers, because of the violence of the multitude,
36 for the crowd of the people was following after, crying, 'Away with him.'
37 And Paul being about to be led into the castle, said to the chief captain, 'Is it permitted to me to say anything unto you[S]?' and he said, ' You[S] do know Greek?
38 are you not, then, the Egyptian who before these days made an uprising, and did lead the four thousand men of the assassins into the desert?'
39 And Paul said, 'I, indeed, am a man, a Jew, of Tarsus of Cilicia, a citizen of no mean city; and I beg you[S], allow me to speak unto the people.'
40 And he having given him leave, Paul having stood upon the stairs, did beckon with the hand to the people, and there having been a great silence, he spoke unto them in the Hebrew dialect, saying:

CHAPTER 22

1 'Men, brethren, and fathers, hear my defense now unto you[P];' —
2 and they having heard that he was speaking to them in the Hebrew dialect, gave the more silence, and he said, —
3 'I, indeed, am a man, a Jew, having been born in Tarsus of Cilicia, and brought up in this city at the feet of Gamaliel, having been taught according to the exactitude of a law of the fathers, being zealous of God, as all you[P] are today.
4 'And I persecuted this way unto death, binding and delivering up to prisons both men and women,
5 as also the chief priest do testify to me, and all the eldership; from whom also having received letters unto the brethren, to Damascus, I was going on, to bring also those there bound to Jerusalem that they might be punished,
6 and it came to pass, in my going on and coming near to Damascus, about noon, suddenly out of the heaven there shone a great light round about me,
7 I fell also to the ground, and I heard a voice saying to me, Saul, Saul, why do you[S] persecute me?
8 'And I answered, Who are You[S], Lord? and He said unto me, I am Jesus the Nazarene whom you[S] do persecute —
9 and they who are with me did see the light, and became afraid, and they heard not of the voice Him who is speaking to me —
10 and I said, What shall I do, Lord? and the Lord said unto me, Having risen, go on to Damascus, and there it shall be told you[S] concerning all things that have been appointed for you[S] to do.
11 'And when I did not see from the glory of that light, being led by the hand by those who are with me, I came to Damascus,
12 and a certain one, Ananias, a pious man according to the law, being testified to by all the Jews dwelling [there],
13 having come unto me and stood by [me], said to me, Saul, brother, look up; and I did look up to him the same hour;
14 and he said, The God of our fathers did choose you[S] beforehand to know His will, and to see the Righteous One, and to hear a voice out of His mouth,
15 because you[S] shall be his witness unto all men of what you[S] have seen and heard;
16 and now, why delay you[S]? having risen, baptize yourself[S], and wash away your[S] sins, calling upon the name of the Lord.
17 'And it came to pass when I returned to Jerusalem, and while I was praying in the temple, I came into a trance,
18 and I saw Him saying to me, Hurry and go forth in haste out of Jerusalem, because they will not receive your[S] testimony concerning me;
19 and I said, Lord, they — they know that I was imprisoning and was scourging in every synagogue those believing on You[S];
20 and when the blood of Your[S] witness Stephen was being poured forth, I also was standing by and assenting to his death, and keeping the garments of those putting him to death;
21 and He said unto me, Go, because I will send you[S] to nations far off.'
22 And they were hearing him unto this word, and they lifted up their voice, saying, 'Away from the earth with such an one; for it is not fit for him to live.'

23 And they crying out and casting up their garments, and throwing dust into the air,
24 the chief captain commanded him to be brought into the castle, saying, ‘ Let him be examined by scourges;’ that he might know for what cause they were crying so against him.
25 And as he was stretching him with the thongs, Paul said unto the centurion who was standing by, ‘Is it lawful to you[P] to scourge a man, a Roman, uncondemned ;’
26 and the centurion having heard, having gone near to the chief captain, told, saying, ‘Take heed what you[S] are about to do, for this man is a Roman;’
27 and the chief captain having come near, said to him, ‘Tell me, are you[S] a Roman?’ and he said, ‘Yes;’
28 and the chief captain answered, ‘I, with a great sum, did obtain this citizenship;’ but Paul said, ‘But I have been even born [so].’
29 Immediately, therefore, they departed from him who are about to examine him, and the chief captain also was afraid, having learned that he is a Roman, and because he had bound him,
30 and on the morning, intending to know the certainty why he is accused by the Jews, he did loose him from the bonds, and commanded the chief priests and all their sanhedrim to come, and having brought down Paul, he set [him] before them.

CHAPTER 23

1 And Paul having earnestly beheld the sanhedrim, said, ‘Men, brethren, I in all good conscience have lived to God unto this day;’
2 and the chief priest Ananias commanded those standing by him to strike him on the mouth,
3 then Paul said unto him, ‘God is about to strike you[S], you[S] whitewashed wall, and you[S] — you[S] do sit judging me according to the law, and, violating law, do order me to be struck!’
4 And those who stood by said, ‘You[S] do revile the chief priest of God?’
5 and Paul said, ‘I did not know, brethren, that he is chief priest: for it has been written, Of the ruler of your[S] people you[S] shall not speak evil;’
6 and Paul having known that the one part are Sadducees, and the other Pharisees, cried out in the sanhedrim, ‘Men, brethren, I am a Pharisee — son of a Pharisee — I am judged concerning hope and rising again of dead men.’
7 And he having spoken this, there came a dissension of the Pharisees and of the Sadducees, and the crowd was divided,
8 for Sadducees, indeed, say there is no rising again, nor messenger, nor spirit, but Pharisees confess both.
9 And there came a great cry, and the scribes of the Pharisees’ part having arisen, were striving, saying, ‘No evil do we find in this man; and if a spirit spoke to him, or a messenger, we may not fight against God;’
10 and a great dissension having come, the chief captain having been afraid that Paul may be pulled to pieces by them, commanded the soldiery, having gone down, to take him by force out of the midst of them, and to bring [him] to the castle.
11 And on the following night, the Lord having stood by him, said, ‘Take courage, Paul, for as you[S] did fully testify the things concerning me at Jerusalem, so it is necessary for you[S] to testify also at Rome.’
12 And day having come, certain of the Jews having made a concourse, did anathematize themselves, saying neither to eat nor to drink till they may kill Paul;
13 and they were more than forty who made this conspiracy by oath,
14 who having come near to the chief priests and to the elders said, ‘With an anathema we did anathematize ourselves — to taste nothing till we have killed Paul;
15 now, for that reason, you[P], signify you[P] to the chief captain, with the sanhedrim, that tomorrow he may bring him down unto you[P], as being about to know more exactly the things concerning him; and we, before his coming near, are ready to put him to death.’
16 And the son of Paul’s sister having heard of the lying in wait, having gone and entered into the castle, told Paul,
17 and Paul having called near one of the centurions, said, ‘Lead this young man unto the chief captain, for he has something to tell him.’
18 He indeed, then, having taken him, brought him unto the chief captain, and said, ‘The prisoner Paul, having called me near, asked [me] to bring this young man unto you[S], having something to say to you[S].’
19 And the chief captain having taken him by the hand, and having withdrawn by themselves, inquired, ‘What is that which you[S] have to tell me?’
20 and he said — ‘The Jews agreed to request you[S], that tomorrow you[S] may bring down Paul to the sanhedrim, as being about to enquire something more exactly concerning him;
21 you[S], for that reason, may you[S] not yield to them, for

there lie in wait for him more than forty men of them, who did anathematize themselves — not to eat nor to drink till they kill him, and now they are ready, waiting for the promise from you[S].'
22 The chief captain, then, indeed, let the young man go, having charged [him] to tell no one, 'that you[S] did show these things unto me;'
23 and having called near a certain two of the centurions, he said, 'Make ready two hundred soldiers, that they may go on unto Caesarea, and seventy horsemen, and two hundred spearmen, from the third hour of the night;
24 also provide beasts, that, having set Paul on, they may bring him safe unto Felix the governor;'
25 he having written a letter after this description:
26 'Claudius Lysias, to the most noble governor Felix, hail:
27 This man having been taken by the Jews, and being about to be killed by them — having come with the soldiery, I rescued him, having learned that he is a Roman;
28 and, intending to know the cause for which they were accusing him, I brought him down to their sanhedrim,
29 whom I found accused concerning questions of their law, and having no accusation worthy of death or bonds;
30 and a plot having been intimated to me against this man — about to be of the Jews — at once I sent unto you[S], having given command also to the accusers to say the things against him before you[S]; be strong.'
31 Then, indeed, the soldiers according to that directed them, having taken up Paul, brought him through the night to Antipatris,
32 and on the morning, having allowed the horsemen to go on with him, they returned to the castle;
33 those having entered into Caesarea, and delivered the letter to the governor, did also present Paul to him.
34 And the governor having read [it], and inquired of what province he is, and understood that [he is] from Cilicia;
35 'I will hear you[S] — said he — when your[S] accusers also may have come;' he also commanded him to be kept in the praetorium of Herod.

CHAPTER 24

1 And after five days came down the chief priest Ananias, with the elders, and a certain orator — Tertullus, and they made known to the governor [the things] against Paul;
2 and he having been called, Tertullus began to accuse [him], saying, 'Much peace enjoying through you[S], and worthy deeds being done to this nation through your[S] forethought,
3 always, also, and everywhere we receive it, most noble Felix, with all thankfulness;
4 and that I may not be further tedious to you[S], I pray you[S] to hear us concisely in your[S] gentleness;
5 for having found this man a pestilence, and moving a dissension to all the Jews through the world — a ringleader also of the sect of the Nazarenes —
6 who also did try to profane the temple, whom also we took, and according to our law did wish to judge,
7 and Lysias the chief captain having come near, with much violence, did take away out of our hands,
8 having commanded his accusers to come to you[S], from whom you[S] may be able, yourself[S] having examined, to know concerning all these things of which we accuse him;'
9 and the Jews also agreed, professing these things to be so.
10 And Paul answered — the governor having beckoned to him to speak — 'Knowing [that] for many years you[S] have been a judge to this nation, the more cheerfully I do answer the things concerning myself;
11 you[S] being able to know that it is not more than twelve days to me since I went up to worship in Jerusalem,
12 and neither in the temple did they find me reasoning with any one, or making a dissension of the multitude, nor in the synagogues, nor in the city;
13 nor are they able to prove against me the things concerning which they now accuse me.
14 'And I confess this to you[S], that, according to the way that they call a sect, so I serve the God of the fathers, believing all things that in the law and the prophets have been written,
15 having hope toward God, which they themselves also wait for, [that] there is about to be a rising again of the dead, both of righteous and unrighteous;
16 and in this I do exercise myself, to have a conscience void of offence toward God and men always.
17 'And after many years I came, about to do kind acts to my nation, and offerings,
18 in which certain Jews from Asia did find me purified in the temple, not with multitude, nor with tumult,
19 whom it is necessary to be present before you[S], and to accuse, if they had anything against me,
20 or let these same say if they found any unrighteousness in me in my standing before the sanhedrim,

21 except concerning this one voice, in which I cried,
standing among them — Concerning a rising again of
the dead I am judged today by you[P].'
22 And having heard these things, Felix delayed them
— having known more exactly of the things concerning
the way — saying, 'When Lysias the chief captain may
come down, I will know fully the things concerning
you[P];'
23 having given also a direction to the centurion to keep
Paul, to let [him] also have liberty, and to forbid none of
his own friends to minister or to come near to him.
24 And after certain days, Felix having come with
Drusilla his wife, being a Jewess, he sent for Paul, and
heard him concerning the faith toward Christ,
25 and he reasoning concerning righteousness, and
temperance, and the judgment that is about to be, Felix,
having become afraid, answered, 'For the present be
going, and having got time, I will call for you[S];'
26 and at the same time also hoping that money shall be
given to him by Paul, that he may release him, for that
reason, also sending for him the oftener, he was
conversing with him;
27 and two years having been fulfilled, Felix received a
successor, Porcius Festus; Felix also willing to lay a favor
on the Jews, left Paul bound.

CHAPTER 25

1 Festus, therefore, having come into the province, after
three days went up to Jerusalem from Caesarea,
2 and the chief priest and the principal men of the Jews
made known to him [the things] against Paul, and were
calling on him,
3 asking favor against him, that he may send for him to
Jerusalem, making an ambush to put him to death in the
way.
4 Then, indeed, Festus answered that Paul is kept in
Caesarea, and himself is about speedily to go on there,
5 'For that reason those able among you[P] — said he —
having come down together, if there be anything in this
man — let them accuse him;'
6 and having delayed among them more than ten days,
having gone down to Caesarea, on the morning having
sat upon the tribunal, he commanded Paul to be brought;
7 and he having come, there stood round about the Jews
who have come down from Jerusalem — many and
weighty charges they are bringing against Paul, which
they were not able to prove,
8 he making defense — 'Neither in regard to the law of
the Jews, nor in regard to the temple, nor in regard to
Caesar — did I commit any sin.'
9 And Festus willing to lay on the Jews a favor,
answering Paul, said, 'Are you[S] willing, having gone up
to Jerusalem, there to be judged before me concerning
these things?'
10 and Paul said, 'At the tribunal of Caesar I am standing,
where it is necessary for me to be judged; I did no
unrighteousness to Jews, as you[S] do also very well
know;
11 for if indeed I am unrighteous, and anything worthy
of death have done, I deprecate not to die; and if there
is none of the things of which these accuse me, no one
is able to make a favor of me to them; to Caesar I appeal!'
12 then Festus, having communed with the council,
answered, 'To Caesar you have appealed; to Caesar you[S]
shall go.'
13 And certain days having passed, Agrippa the king,
and Bernice, came down to Caesarea saluting Festus,
14 and as they were continuing there more days, Festus
submitted to the king the things concerning Paul, saying,
'There is a certain man, left by Felix, a prisoner,
15 about whom, in my being at Jerusalem, the chief
priests and the elders of the Jews laid information, asking
a decision against him,
16 unto whom I answered, that it is not a custom of
Romans to make a favor of any man to die, before that
he who is accused may have the accusers face to face,
and may receive place of defense in regard to the charge
laid against [him].
17 'They, therefore, having come together — I, making
no delay, on the succeeding [day] having sat upon the
tribunal, did command the man to be brought,
18 concerning whom the accusers, having stood up,
were bringing against [him] no accusation of the things
I was thinking of,
19 but certain questions concerning their own religion
they had against him, and concerning a certain Jesus
who was dead, whom Paul affirmed to be alive;
20 and I, doubting in regard to the question concerning
this, said, If he would wish to go on to Jerusalem, and
there to be judged concerning these things —
21 but Paul having appealed to be kept to the hearing
of Sebastus, I did command him to be kept till I might
send him unto Caesar.'
22 And Agrippa said unto Festus, 'I was wishing also
myself to hear the man;' and he said, 'Tomorrow you[S]
shall hear him;'

23 on the morning, for that reason — on the coming of Agrippa and Bernice with much display, and they having entered into the audience chamber, with the chief captains also, and the principal men of the city, and Festus having ordered — Paul was brought forth.
24 And Festus said, 'King Agrippa, and all men who are present with us, you[P] see this one, about whom all the multitude of the Jews did deal with me, both in Jerusalem and here, crying out, He ought not to live any longer;
25 and I, having found him to have done nothing worthy of death, and he also himself having appealed to Sebastus, I decided to send him,
26 concerning whom I have no certain thing to write to [my] lord, for what reason I brought him forth before you[P], and specially before you[S], king Agrippa, that the examination having been made, I may have something to write;
27 for it does seem to me irrational, sending a prisoner, not also to signify the charges against him.'

CHAPTER 26

1 And Agrippa said unto Paul, 'It is permitted to you[S] to speak for yourself[S];' then Paul having stretched forth the hand, was making a defense:
2 'Concerning all things of which I am accused by Jews, king Agrippa, I have thought myself happy, being about to make a defense before you[S] today,
3 especially knowing you[S] to be acquainted with all things — both customs and questions — among Jews; wherefore, I beg you[S], to patiently hear me.
4 'The manner of my life then, indeed, from youth — which from the beginning was among my nation, in Jerusalem — all the Jews do know ,
5 knowing me before from the first, (if they may be willing to testify,) that after the most exact sect of our worship, I lived a Pharisee;
6 and now for the hope of the promise made to the fathers by God, I have stood judged,
7 to which our twelve tribes, intently serving night and day, do hope to come, concerning which hope I am accused, king Agrippa, by the Jews;
8 why is it judged incredible with you[P], if God does raise the dead?
9 'I, indeed, for that reason, thought with myself, that against the name of Jesus of Nazareth it is necessary for [me] to do many things,
10 which also I did in Jerusalem, and many of the saints I did shut up in prison, having received the authority from the chief priests; they also being put to death, I gave my vote against them,
11 and in every synagogue, often punishing them, I was constraining [them] to speak evil, being also exceedingly mad against them, I was also persecuting [them] even unto strange cities.
12 'In which things, also, going on to Damascus — with authority and commission from the chief priests —
13 at midday, I saw in the way, O king, out of heaven, above the brightness of the sun, shining round about me a light — and those going on with me;
14 and we all having fallen to the earth, I heard a voice speaking unto me, and saying in the Hebrew dialect, Saul, Saul, why do you[S] persecute Me? hard for you[S] to kick against pricks!
15 'And I said, Who are You[S], Lord? and He said, I am Jesus whom you[S] do persecute;
16 but rise, and stand upon your[S] feet, for for this I appeared to you[S], to appoint you an officer and a witness both of the things you[S] did see, and of the things [in which] I will appear to you[S],
17 delivering you[S] from the people, and the nations, to whom now I send you[S],
18 to open their eyes, to turn [them] from darkness to light, and [from] the authority of the Adversary unto God, for their receiving forgiveness of sins, and a lot among those having been sanctified, by faith that [is] toward me.
19 'On which, king Agrippa, I was not disobedient to the heavenly vision,
20 but to those in Damascus first, and to those in Jerusalem, to all the region also of Judea, and to the nations, I was preaching to reform, and to turn back unto God, doing works worthy of reformation;
21 because of these things the Jews — having caught me in the temple — were endeavoring to kill [me].
22 'Having obtained, for this cause, help from God, till this day, I have stood witnessing both to small and to great, saying nothing besides the things that both the prophets and Moses spoke of as about to come,
23 that the Christ is to suffer, whether first by a rising from the dead, he is about to proclaim light to the people and to the nations.'
24 And, he thus making a defense, Festus with a loud voice said, 'You[S] are mad, Paul; much learning does turn you[S] mad;'
25 and he said, 'I am not mad, most noble Festus, but of the sayings I speak forth truth and soberness ;

26 for the king does know concerning these things,
before whom also I speak boldly, for none of these
things, I am persuaded, are hidden from him; for this
thing has not been done in a corner;
27 do you[S] believe, king Agrippa, the prophets? I have
known that you[S] do believe!'
28 And Agrippa said unto Paul, 'In a little you[S] do
persuade me to become a Christian!'
29 and Paul said, 'I would have wished to God, both in
a little, and in much, not only you[S], but also all those
hearing me today, to become such as I also am — except
these bonds.'
30 And, he having spoken these things, the king rose
up, and the governor, Bernice also, and those sitting with
them,
31 and having withdrawn, they were speaking unto one
another, saying — 'This man does nothing worthy of
death or of bonds;'
32 and Agrippa said to Festus, 'This man might have
been released if he had not appealed to Caesar.'

CHAPTER 27

1 And when our sailing to Italy was determined, they
were delivering up both Paul and certain others,
prisoners, to a centurion, by name Julius, of the band of
Sebastus,
2 and having embarked in a ship of Adramyttium, we,
being about to sail by the coasts of Asia, did set sail,
there being with us Aristarchus, a Macedonian of
Thessalonica,
3 on the next [day] also we touched at Sidon, and Julius,
courteously treating Paul, did permit [him], having gone
on unto friends, to receive [their] care.
4 And from there, having set sail, we sailed under
Cyprus, because of the winds being contrary,
5 and having sailed over the sea over-against Cilicia
and Pamphylia, we came to Myria of Lycia,
6 and there the centurion having found a ship of
Alexandria, sailing to Italy, did put us into it,
7 and having sailed slowly many days, and with
difficulty coming over-against Cnidus, the wind not
allowing us, we sailed under Crete, over-against
Salmone,
8 and hardly passing it, we came to a certain place called
'Fair Havens,' near to which was the city [of] Lasaea.
9 And much time being spent, and the sailing being now
dangerous — because of the fast also being already past
— Paul was admonishing,
10 saying to them, 'Men, I perceive that with hurt, and
much damage, not only of the lading and of the ship,
but also of our lives — the voyage is about to be;'
11 but the centurion gave more credence to the pilot
and to the shipowner than to the things spoken by Paul;
12 and the haven being inconvenient to winter in, the
more part gave counsel to sail from there also, if by any
means they might be able, having attained to Phenice,
[there] to winter, [which is] a haven of Crete, looking to
the south-west and north-west,
13 and a south wind blowing softly, having thought
they had obtained [their] purpose, having lifted anchor,
they sailed close by Crete,
14 and not long after there arose against it a tumultuous
wind, that is called Euroclydon,
15 and the ship being caught, and not being able to
bear up against the wind, having given [her] up, we were
borne on,
16 and having run under a certain little isle, called Clauda,
we were hardly able to become masters of the boat,
17 which having taken up, they were using helps,
supporting the ship, and fearing that they may fall on
the quicksand, having let down the mast — so were
borne on.
18 And we, being exceedingly tempest-tossed, the
succeeding [day] they were making a clearing,
19 and on the third [day] with our own hands the tackling
of the ship we cast out,
20 and neither sun nor stars appearing for more days,
and not a little tempest lying upon us, thereafter all hope
was taken away of our being saved.
21 And there having been long fasting, then Paul having
stood in the midst of them, said, 'It is necessary for
[you[P]], indeed, O men — having listened to me — not
to set sail from Crete, and to save this hurt and damage;
22 and now I urge you[P] to be of good cheer, for there
shall be no loss of life among you[P] — but of the ship;
23 for there stood by me this night a messenger of God
— whose I am, and whom I serve —
24 saying, Be not afraid Paul; it is necessary for you[S] to
stand before Caesar; and, behold, God has granted to
you[S] all those sailing with you[S];
25 for that reason be of good cheer, men! for I believe
God, that so it shall be, even as it has been spoken to me,
26 and it is necessary for us to be cast on a certain
island.'
27 And when the fourteenth night came — we being
borne up and down in the Adria — toward the middle of

the night the sailors were supposing that some country
drew near to them;
28 and having sounded they found twenty fathoms,
and having gone a little farther, and again having
sounded, they found fifteen fathoms,
29 and fearing that we may fall on rough places, having
cast four anchors out of the stern, they were wishing
day to come.
30 And the sailors seeking to flee out of the ship, and
having let down the boat to the sea, in pretense as [if]
out of the foreship they are about to cast anchors,
31 Paul said to the centurion and to the soldiers, 'If
these do not remain in the ship — you[P] are not able to
be saved;'
32 then the soldiers did cut off the ropes of the boat,
and allowed it to fall off.
33 And till the day was about to be, Paul was calling
upon all to partake of nourishment, saying, 'Fourteen
days today, waiting, you[P] continue fasting, having taken
nothing,
34 for that reason I call upon you[P] to take nourishment,
for this is for your[P] safety, for of not one of you[P] shall a
hair from the head fall;'
35 and having said these things, and having taken bread,
he gave thanks to God before all, and having broken
[it], he began to eat;
36 and all having become of good cheer, also took food
themselves,
37 (and we were — all the souls in the ship — two
hundred, seventy and six),
38 and having eaten sufficient nourishment, they were
lightening the ship, casting forth the wheat into the sea.
39 And when the day came, they were not discerning
the land, but a certain creek were perceiving having a
beach, into which they took counsel, if possible, to thrust
forward the ship,
40 and the anchors having taken up, they were
committing [it] to the sea, at the same time — having
loosed the bands of the rudders, and having hoisted up
the mainsail to the wind — they were making for the
shore,
41 and having fallen into a place of two seas, they ran
the ship aground, and the fore-part, indeed, having stuck
fast, did remain immoveable, but the hinder-part was
broken by the violence of the waves.
42 And the soldiers' counsel was that they should kill
the prisoners, for fear that any one having swam out
should escape,
43 but the centurion, wishing to save Paul, hindered
them from the counsel, and did command those able to
swim, having cast themselves out first — to get unto
the land,
44 and the rest, some indeed upon boards, and some
upon certain things of the ship; and thus it came to pass
that all came safe unto the land.

CHAPTER 28

1 And having been saved, then they knew that the island
is called Melita,
2 and the foreigners were showing us no ordinary
kindness, for having kindled a fire, they received us all,
because of the pressing rain, and because of the cold;
3 but Paul having gathered together a quantity of sticks,
and having laid [them] upon the fire, a viper — having
come out of the heat — did fasten on his hand.
4 And when the foreigners saw the beast hanging from
his hand, they said unto one another, 'Certainly this man
is a murderer, whom, having been saved out of the sea,
the justice did not allow to live;'
5 he then, indeed, having shaken off the beast into the
fire, suffered no evil,
6 and they were expecting him to be about to be inflamed,
or to fall down suddenly dead, and they, expecting [it] a
long time, and seeing nothing uncommon happening to
him, changing [their] minds, said he was a god.
7 And in the neighborhood of that place were lands of
the principal man of the island, by name Publius, who,
having received us, three days did courteously lodge
[us];
8 and it came to pass, the father of Publius with feverish
heats and dysentery pressed, was laid, unto whom Paul
having entered, and having prayed, having laid [his]
hands on him, healed him;
9 this, consequently, being done, the others also in the
island having infirmities were coming and were healed;
10 who also with many honors did honor us, and we
setting sail — they were lading [us] with the things that
were necessary.
11 And after three months, we set sail in a ship (that
had wintered in the isle) of Alexandria, with the sign
Dioscuri,
12 and having landed at Syracuse, we remained three
days,
13 from there having gone round, we came to Rhegium,
and after one day, a south wind having sprung up, the
second [day] we came to Puteoli;

14 where, having found brethren, we were called upon
to remain with them seven days, and thus we came to
Rome;
15 and from there, the brethren having heard the things
concerning us, came forth to meet us, unto Appii Forum,
and Three Taverns — whom Paul having seen, having
given thanks to God, took courage.
16 And when we came to Rome, the centurion delivered
up the prisoners to the captain of the barrack, but Paul
was allowed to remain by himself, with the soldier
guarding him.
17 And it came to pass after three days, Paul called
together those who are the principal men of the Jews,
and they having come together, he said unto them: 'Men,
brethren, I — having done nothing contrary to the
people, or to the customs of the fathers — a prisoner
from Jerusalem, was delivered up to the hands of the
Romans;
18 who, having examined me, were wishing to release
[me], because of their being no cause of death in me,
19 and the Jews having spoken against [it], I was
constrained to appeal unto Caesar — not as having
anything to accuse my nation of;
20 for this cause, consequently, I called for you[P] to see
and to speak with [you[P]], for because of the hope of
Israel I am bound with this chain.'
21 And they said unto him, 'We did neither receive
letters concerning you[S] from Judea, nor did any one who
came of the brethren declare or speak any evil
concerning you[S],
22 and we think it good to hear from you[S] what you[S] do
think, for, indeed, concerning this sect it is known to us
that everywhere it is spoken against;'
23 and having appointed him a day, they came, more of
them unto him, to the lodging, to whom he was
expounding, testifying fully the reign of God, persuading
them also of the things concerning Jesus, both from the
law of Moses, and the prophets, from morning till evening,
24 and, some, indeed, were believing the things spoken,
and some were not believing.
25 And not being agreed with one another, they were
going away, Paul having spoken one word — 'Well did
the Holy Spirit speak through Isaiah the prophet unto
our fathers,
26 saying, Go on unto this people and say, With hearing
you[P] shall hear, and you[P] shall not understand, and
seeing you[P] shall see, and you[P] shall not perceive,
27 for the heart of this people was made gross, and with
the ears they heard heavily, and their eyes they did close,
for fear that they may see with the eyes, and with the
heart may understand, and be turned back, and I may
heal them.
28 'Be it known, therefore, to you[P], that the salvation of
God was sent to the nations, these also will hear it;'
29 and he having said these things, the Jews went away,
having much disputation among themselves;
30 and Paul remained an entire two years in his own
hired [house], and was receiving all those coming in unto
him,
31 preaching the reign of God, and teaching the things
concerning the Lord Jesus Christ with all boldness —
unforbidden.

The Epistle of Paul the Apostle to the
ROMANS

CHAPTER 1

1 Paul, a servant of Jesus Christ, a called apostle, having
been separated to the good news of God —
2 which He announced before through His prophets in
holy writings —
3 concerning His Son, (who is come of the seed of David
according to the flesh,
4 who is marked out Son of God in power, according to
the Spirit of sanctification, by the rising again from the
dead,) Jesus Christ our Lord;
5 through whom we did receive grace and apostleship,
for obedience of faith among all the nations, in behalf of
his name;
6 among whom are you[P] also, the called of Jesus Christ;
7 to all who are in Rome, beloved of God, called saints;
Grace to you[P], and peace, from God our Father, and [from]
the Lord Jesus Christ!
8 first, indeed, I thank my God through Jesus Christ for
you[P] all, that your[P] faith is proclaimed in the whole world;
9 for God is my witness, whom I serve in my spirit in the
good news of His Son, how unceasingly I make mention
of you[P],
10 always begging in my prayers, if by any means now
at length I shall have a prosperous journey, by the will
of God, to come unto you[P],
11 for I long to see you[P], that I may impart to you[P] some
spiritual gift, that you[P] may be established;
12 and that is, that I may be comforted together among you[P],
through the faith in one another, both yours[P] and mine.
13 And I do not wish you[P] to be ignorant, brethren, that
many times I did purpose to come unto you[P] — and was
hindered till the present time — that I might have some
fruit among you[P] also, even as also among the other
nations.
14 Both to Greeks and to foreigners, both to wise and
to thoughtless, I am a debtor,
15 so, as much as in me is, I am ready also to proclaim
good news to you[P] who [are] in Rome,
16 for I am not ashamed of the good news of the Christ,
for it is the power of God to salvation to every one who
is believing, both to Jew first, and to Greek.
17 For the righteousness of God in it is revealed from
faith to faith, according as it has been written, 'And the
righteous one shall live by faith,'
18 for revealed is the wrath of God from heaven upon
all impiety and unrighteousness of men, holding down
the truth in unrighteousness.
19 Because that which is known of God is revealed
among them, for God did reveal [it] to them,
20 for the invisible things of Him from the creation of
the world, by the things made being understood, are
plainly seen, both His eternal power and Godhead — to
their being inexcusable;
21 because, having known God they did not glorify
[Him] as God, nor gave thanks, but were made vain in
their reasonings, and their unintelligent heart was
darkened,
22 professing to be wise, they were made fools,
23 and changed the glory of the incorruptible God into
the likeness of an image of corruptible man, and of fowls,
and of quadrupeds, and of reptiles.
24 For what reason also God did give them up, in the
desires of their hearts, to uncleanness, to dishonor their
bodies among themselves;
25 who did change the truth of God into a falsehood,
and did honor and serve the creature rather than the
Creator, who is blessed to the ages. Amen.
26 Because of this did God give them up to dishonorable
affections, for even their females did change the natural
use into that against nature;
27 and in like manner also the males having left the
natural use of the female, did burn in their longing toward
one another; males with males working shame, and the
recompense of their error that was fit, receiving in
themselves.
28 And, according as they did not approve of having
God in knowledge, God gave them up to a disapproved
mind, to do the things not seemly;
29 having been filled with all unrighteousness,
whoredom, wickedness, covetousness, malice; full of

envy, murder, strife, deceit, evil dispositions; whisperers,
30 evil-speakers, God-haters, insulting, proud, boasters,
inventors of evil things, disobedient to parents,
31 unintelligent, faithless, without natural affection,
implacable, unmerciful;
32 who having known the righteous judgment of God
— that those practicing such things are worthy of death
— not only do them, but also have delight with those
practicing them.

CHAPTER 2

1 For that reason, you[S] are inexcusable, O man — every
one who is judging — for in that in which you[S] do judge
the other, you[S] do condemn yourself[S], for you[S] who are
judging do practice the same things,
2 and we have known that the judgment of God is
according to truth, upon those practicing such things.
3 And do you[S] think this, O man, who are judging those
who are practicing such things, and are doing them, that
you[S] shall escape the judgment of God?
4 or do you[S] despise the riches of His goodness, and
forbearance, and long-suffering? — not knowing that
the goodness of God does lead you[S] to reformation!
5 but, according to your[S] hardness and impenitent heart,
you[S] do treasure up to yourself[S] wrath, in a day of wrath
and of the revelation of the righteous judgment of God,
6 who shall render to each according to his works;
7 to those, indeed, who in continuance of a good work,
do seek glory, and honor, and incorruptibility — life age-
during;
8 and to those contentious, and disobedient, indeed, to
the truth, and obeying the unrighteousness —
indignation and wrath,
9 tribulation and distress, upon every soul of man that
is working the evil, both of Jew first, and of Greek;
10 and glory, and honor, and peace, to every one who
is working the good, both to Jew first, and to Greek.
11 For there is no acceptance of faces with God,
12 for as many as did sin without law, shall perish
without law also, and as many as did sin in law, shall be
judged through law,
13 for not the hearers of the law [are] righteous before God,
but the doers of the law shall be declared righteous: —
14 For, when nations that have not a law, by nature may
do the things of the law, these not having a law — are a
law to themselves;
15 who do show the work of the law written in their
hearts, their conscience also witnessing with them, and
between one another the thoughts accusing or else
defending,
16 in the day when God shall judge the secrets of men,
according to my good news, through Jesus Christ.
17 Behold, you[S] are named a Jew, and do rest upon the
law, and do boast in God,
18 and do know the will, and do approve the distinctions,
being instructed out of the law,
19 and has confidence that you[S] yourself[S] are a leader
of blind ones, a light of those in darkness,
20 an instructor of foolish ones, a teacher of babes, having
the form of the knowledge and of the truth in the law.
21 You[S], then, who are teaching another, do you[S] not
teach yourself[S]?
22 you[S] who are preaching not to steal, do you[S] steal?
you[S] who are saying not to commit adultery, do you[S]
commit adultery? you[S] who are abhorring the idols, do
you[S] rob temples?
23 you[S] who do boast in the law, do you[S] dishonor God
through the transgression of the law?
24 for because of you[P] the name of God is evil spoken
of among the nations, according as it has been written.
25 For circumcision, indeed, does profit, if you[S] may
practice law, but if you[S] may be a transgressor of law,
your[S] circumcision has become uncircumcision.
26 If, for that reason the uncircumcision may keep the
righteousness of the law, shall not his uncircumcision
be reckoned for circumcision?
27 and the uncircumcision, by nature, fulfilling the law,
shall judge you[S] who, through letter and circumcision,
[are] a transgressor of law.
28 For he is not a Jew who is [so] outwardly, neither [is]
circumcision that which is outward in flesh;
29 but a Jew [is] he who is [so] inwardly, and
circumcision [is] of the heart, in spirit, not in letter, of
which the praise is not of men, but of God.

CHAPTER 3

1 What, then, [is] the superiority of the Jew? or what
the profit of the circumcision?
2 much in every way; for first, indeed, that they were
entrusted with the oracles of God;
3 for what, if certain were faithless? shall their
faithlessness make useless the faithfulness of God?
4 let it not be! and let God become true, and every man
false, according as it has been written, 'That You[S] may

be declared righteous in Your[S] words, and may overcome
in Your[S] being judged.'
5 And, if God's righteousness does establish our
unrighteousness, what shall we say? is God who is
inflicting the wrath unrighteous? (after the manner of a
man I speak)
6 let it not be! since how shall God judge the world?
7 for if the truth of God in my falsehood did more abound
to His glory, why yet am I also as a sinner judged?
8 and not, as we are evil spoken of, and as certain affirm
us to say — 'We may do the evil things, that the good
ones may come?' whose judgment is righteous.
9 What, then? are we better? not at all! for we did before
charge both Jews and Greeks with being all under sin,
10 according as it has been written — 'There is none
righteous, not even one;
11 There is none who is understanding, there is none
who is seeking after God.
12 All did go out of the way, together they became
unprofitable, there is none doing good, there is not even
one.
13 A sepulchre opened [is] their throat; with their tongues
they used deceit; poison of asps [is] under their lips.
14 Whose mouth is full of cursing and bitterness.
15 Swift [are] their feet to shed blood.
16 Ruin and misery [are] in their ways.
17 And they did not know a way of peace.
18 There is no fear of God before their eyes.'
19 And we have known that as many things as the law
said, it does speak to those in the law, that every mouth
may be stopped, and all the world may come under
judgment to God;
20 for what reason shall no flesh be declared righteous
before Him by works of law, for through law is a
knowledge of sin.
21 And now has the righteousness of God been revealed
apart from law, testified to by the law and the prophets,
22 and the righteousness of God [is] through the faith
of Jesus Christ to all, and upon all those believing, —
for there is no difference,
23 for all did sin, and are come short of the glory of God —
24 being declared righteous freely by His grace through
the redemption that [is] in Christ Jesus,
25 whom God did set forth a mercy seat, through the
faith in his blood, for the showing forth of His
righteousness, because of the passing over of the
bygone sins in the forbearance of God —
26 for the showing forth of His righteousness in the
present time, for His being righteous, and declaring him
righteous who [is] of the faith of Jesus.
27 Where then [is] the boasting? it was excluded; by
what law? of works? no, but by a law of faith:
28 for that reason do we reckon a man to be declared
righteous by faith, apart from works of law.
29 [Is He] the God of Jews only, and not also of nations?
30 yes, also of nations; since one [is] God who shall
declare righteous the circumcision by faith, and the
uncircumcision through the faith.
31 Do we then make law useless through the faith? let it
not be! yes, we do establish law.

CHAPTER 4

1 What, then, shall we say Abraham our father, to have
found, according to flesh?
2 for if Abraham by works was declared righteous, he
has to boast — but not before god;
3 for what does the writing say? 'And Abraham did
believe God, and it was reckoned to him — to
righteousness;'
4 and to him who is working, the reward is not reckoned
of grace, but of debt;
5 and to him who is not working, and is believing upon
Him who is declaring the impious righteous, his faith is
reckoned — to righteousness:
6 even as David also does speak of the happiness of
the man to whom God does reckon righteousness apart
from works:
7 'Happy they whose lawless acts were forgiven, and
whose sins were covered;
8 happy the man to whom the Lord may not reckon sin.'
9 [Is] this happiness, then, upon the circumcision, or
also upon the uncircumcision — for we say that the faith
was reckoned to Abraham — to righteousness?
10 how then was it reckoned? he being in circumcision,
or in uncircumcision? not in circumcision, but in
uncircumcision;
11 and he did receive a sign of circumcision, a seal of
the righteousness of the faith in the uncircumcision, for
his being father of all those believing through
uncircumcision, for the righteousness also being
reckoned to them,
12 and father of circumcision to those not of
circumcision only, but who also walk in the steps of the
faith, that [is] in the uncircumcision of our father
Abraham.
13 For the promise to Abraham, or to his seed, of his

being heir of the world, [is] not through law but through
the righteousness of faith;
14 for if they who are of law [are] heirs, the faith has
been made void, and the promise has been made useless;
15 for the law does work wrath; for where law is not,
neither [is] transgression.
16 Because of this [it is] of faith, that [it may be]
according to grace, for the promise being sure to all the
seed, not to that which [is] of the law only, but also to
that which [is] of the faith of Abraham,
17 who is father of us all (according as it has been written
— 'A father of many nations I have set you[S],') before
Him whom he did believe — God, who is quickening the
dead, and is calling the things that be not as being.
18 Who, against hope in hope did believe, for his
becoming father of many nations according to that
spoken: 'So shall your[S] seed be;'
19 and not having been weak in the faith, he did not
consider his own body, already become dead, (being about
a hundred years old,) and the deadness of Sarah's womb,
20 and did not stagger in unbelief at the promise of God,
but was strengthened in faith, having given glory to God,
21 and having been fully persuaded that what He has
promised He is able also to do:
22 for what reason also it was reckoned to him to
righteousness.
23 And it was not written on his account alone, that it
was reckoned to him,
24 but also on ours, to whom it is about to be reckoned
— to us believing on Him who did raise up Jesus our
Lord out of the dead,
25 who was delivered up because of our offenses, and
was raised up because of our being declared righteous.

CHAPTER 5

1 Having been declared righteous, then, by faith, we
have peace toward God through our Lord Jesus Christ,
2 through whom also we have the access by the faith
into this grace in which we have stood, and we boast
on the hope of the glory of God.
3 And not only [so], but we also boast in the tribulations,
knowing that the tribulation does work endurance;
4 and the endurance, experience; and the experience,
hope;
5 and the hope does not make ashamed, because the
love of God has been poured forth in our hearts through
the Holy Spirit that has been given to us.
6 For in our being still ailing, Christ in due time did die
for the impious;
7 for scarcely will any one die for a righteous man, for
perhaps some one also does dare to die for the good
man;
8 and God does commend His own love to us, that, in
our being still sinners, Christ did die for us;
9 much more, then, having been declared righteous now
in his blood, we shall be saved through him from the wrath;
10 for if, being enemies, we have been reconciled to
God through the death of His Son, much more, having
been reconciled, we shall be saved in his life.
11 And not only [so], but we are also boasting in God,
through our Lord Jesus Christ, through whom now we
did receive the reconciliation;
12 because of this, even as through one man the sin did
enter into the world, and through the sin the death; and
thus to all men the death did pass through, for that all
did sin;
13 for till law sin was in the world: and sin is not reckoned
when there is not law;
14 but the death did reign from Adam till Moses, even
upon those not having sinned in the likeness of Adam's
transgression, who is a type of him who is coming.
15 But, not as the offense so also [is] the free gift; for if
by the offense of the one the many did die, much more
did the grace of God, and the free gift in grace of the one
man Jesus Christ, abound to the many;
16 and not as through one who did sin [is] the free gift,
for the judgment indeed [is] of one to condemnation,
but the gift [is] of many offenses to a declaration of
'Righteous,'
17 for if by the offense of the one the death did reign
through the one, much more those, who the abundance
of the grace and of the free gift of the righteousness are
receiving, shall reign in life through the one — Jesus
Christ.
18 So, then, as through one offense to all men [it is] to
condemnation, so also through one declaration of
'Righteous' [it is] to all men to justification of life;
19 for as through the disobedience of the one man, the
many were constituted sinners: so also through the
obedience of the one, shall the many be constituted
righteous.
20 And law came in, that the offense might abound, and
where the sin did abound, the grace did overabound,
21 that even as the sin did reign in the death, so also
the grace may reign, through righteousness, to life age-
during, through Jesus Christ our Lord.

CHAPTER 6

1 What, then, shall we say? shall we continue in the sin
that the grace may abound?
2 let it not be! we who died to the sin — how shall we
still live in it?
3 are you[P] ignorant that we, as many as were baptized
to Christ Jesus, were baptized to his death?
4 we were buried together, then, with him through the
baptism to the death, that even as Christ was raised up
out of the dead through the glory of the Father, so also
we might walk in newness of life.
5 For, if we have become planted together to the likeness
of his death, [so] also we shall be of the rising again;
6 this knowing, that our old man was crucified with [him],
that the body of the sin may be made useless, for our no
longer serving the sin;
7 for he who has died has been set free from the sin.
8 And if we died with Christ, we believe that we also
shall live with him,
9 knowing that Christ, having been raised up out of the
dead, does no more die, death has no more lordship over
him;
10 for in that he died, to the sin he died once, and in
that he lives, he lives to God;
11 so also you[P], reckon yourselves[P] to be dead indeed
to the sin, and living to God in Jesus Christ our Lord.
12 Let not then the sin reign in your[P] mortal body, to
obey it in its desires;
13 neither present you[P] your[P] members instruments of
unrighteousness to the sin, but present yourselves[P] to
God as living out of the dead, and your[P] members
instruments of righteousness to God;
14 for sin shall not have lordship over you[P], for you[P]
are not under law, but under grace.
15 What then? shall we sin because we are not under
law but under grace? let it not be!
16 have you[P] not known that to whom you[P] present
yourselves[P] servants for obedience, you[P] are servants
to him to whom you[P] obey, whether of sin to death, or
of obedience to righteousness?
17 and thanks to God, that you[P] were servants of the
sin, and — were obedient from the heart to the form of
teaching to which you[P] were delivered up;
18 and having been freed from the sin, you[P] became
servants to the righteousness.
19 In the manner of men I speak, because of the
weakness of your[P] flesh, for even as you[P] did present
your[P] members servants to the uncleanness and to the
lawlessness — to the lawlessness, so now present your[P]
members servants to the righteousness — to
sanctification,
20 for when you[P] were servants of the sin, you[P] were
free from the righteousness,
21 what fruit, for that reason, were you[P] having then, in
the things of which you[P] are now ashamed? for the end
of those [is] death.
22 And now, having been freed from the sin, and having
become servants to God, you[P] have your[P] fruit — to
sanctification, and the end life age-during;
23 for the wages of the sin [is] death, and the gift of
God [is] life age-during in Christ Jesus our Lord.

CHAPTER 7

1 Are you[P] ignorant, brethren — for I speak to those
knowing law — that the law has lordship over the man
as long as he lives?
2 for the married woman to the living husband has been
bound by law, and if the husband may die, she has been
free from the law of the husband;
3 so, then, the husband being alive, she shall be called
an adulteress if she may become another man's; and if
the husband may die, she is free from the law, so as not
to be an adulteress, having become another man's.
4 So that, my brethren, you[P] also were made dead to the
law through the body of the Christ, for your[P] becoming
another's, who was raised up out of the dead, that we
might bear fruit to God;
5 for when we were in the flesh, the passions of the
sins, that [are] through the law, were working in our
members, to bear fruit to the death;
6 and now we have ceased from the law, that being dead
in which we were held, so that we may serve in newness
of spirit, and not in oldness of letter.
7 What, then, shall we say? the law [is] sin? let it not
be! but the sin I did not know except through law, for
also the covetousness I had not known if the law had
not said:
8 'You[S] shall not covet;' and the sin having received an
opportunity, through the command, did work in me all
covetousness — for apart from law sin is dead.
9 And I was alive apart from law once, and the command
having come, the sin revived, and I died;
10 and the command that [is] for life, for death this was
found by me;

11 for the sin, having received an opportunity, through
the command, did deceive me, and through it did slay
[me];
12 so that the law, indeed, [is] holy, and the command
holy, and righteous, and good.
13 That which is good then, to me has it become death?
let it not be! but the sin, that it might appear sin, through
the good, working death to me, that the sin might become
exceeding sinful through the command,
14 for we have known that the law is spiritual, and I am
fleshly, sold by the sin;
15 for that which I work, I do not acknowledge; for not
what I will, this I practice, but what I hate, this I do.
16 And if what I do not will, this I do, I consent to the
law that [it is] good,
17 and now it is no longer I that work it, but the sin
dwelling in me,
18 for I have known that there does not dwell in me,
that is, in my flesh, good: for to will is present with me,
and to work that which is right I do not find,
19 for the good that I will, I do not; but the evil that I do
not will, this I practice.
20 And if what I do not will, this I do, it is no longer I
that work it, but the sin that is dwelling in me.
21 I find, then, the law, that when I desire to do what is
right, with me the evil is present,
22 for I delight in the law of God according to the inward
man,
23 and I behold another law in my members, warring
against the law of my mind, and bringing me into
captivity to the law of the sin that [is] in my members.
24 A wretched man I [am]! who shall deliver me out of
the body of this death?
25 I thank God — through Jesus Christ our Lord; so
then, I myself indeed with the mind do serve the law of
God, and with the flesh, the law of sin.

CHAPTER 8

1 There is, then, now no condemnation to those in Christ
Jesus, who walk not according to the flesh, but
according to the Spirit;
2 for the law of the Spirit of the life in Christ Jesus did
set me free from the law of the sin and of the death;
3 for what the law was not able to do, in that it was
weak through the flesh, God, having sent His own Son
in the likeness of sinful flesh, and for sin, did condemn
the sin in the flesh,
4 that the righteousness of the law may be fulfilled in
us, who do not walk according to the flesh, but according
to the Spirit.
5 For those who are according to the flesh, do mind the
things of the flesh; and those according to the Spirit,
the things of the Spirit;
6 for the mind of the flesh [is] death, and the mind of
the Spirit — life and peace;
7 because the mind of the flesh [is] enmity to God, for it
does not subject itself to the law of God,
8 for neither is it able; and those who are in the flesh are
not able to please God.
9 And you[P] are not in the flesh, but in the Spirit, if indeed
the Spirit of God does dwell in you[P]; and if any one has
not the Spirit of Christ — this one is not His;
10 and if Christ [is] in you[P], the body, indeed, [is] dead
because of sin, and the Spirit [is] life because of
righteousness,
11 and if the Spirit of Him who did raise up Jesus out of
the dead does dwell in you[P], He who did raise up the
Christ out of the dead shall quicken also your[P] dying
bodies, through His Spirit dwelling in you[P].
12 So, then, brethren, we are debtors, not to the flesh,
to live according to the flesh;
13 for if you[P] do live according to the flesh, you[P] are
about to die; and if, by the Spirit, you[P] put the deeds of
the body to death, you[P] shall live;
14 for as many as are led by the Spirit of God, these are
the sons of God;
15 for you[P] did not receive a spirit of bondage again for
fear, but you[P] did receive a spirit of adoption in which
we cry, 'Abba — Father.'
16 The Spirit himself does testify with our spirit, that
we are children of God;
17 and if children, also heirs, heirs, indeed, of God, and
heirs together of Christ — if, indeed, we suffer together,
that we may also be glorified together.
18 For I reckon that the sufferings of the present time
[are] not worthy [to be compared] with the glory about
to be revealed in us;
19 for the earnest looking out of the creation does expect
the revelation of the sons of God;
20 for to vanity was the creation made subject — not of
its will, but because of Him who did subject [it] — in
hope,
21 that also the creation itself shall be set free from the
servitude of the corruption to the liberty of the glory of
the children of God;
22 for we have known that all the creation does groan

together, and does travail in pain together till now.
23 And not only [so], but also we ourselves, having the first-fruit of the Spirit, we also ourselves do groan in ourselves, expecting adoption — the redemption of our body;
24 for in hope we were saved, and hope beheld is not hope; for what any one does behold, why also does he hope for [it]?
25 and if we hope for what we do not behold, through continuance we expect [it].
26 And, in like manner also, the Spirit does help our weaknesses; for, what we may pray for, as it is necessary for [us], we have not known, but the Spirit himself does make intercession for us with groanings unutterable,
27 and He who is searching the hearts has known what [is] the mind of the Spirit, because according to God he does intercede for saints.
28 And we have known that to those loving God all things do work together for good, to those who are called according to purpose;
29 because whom He did foreknow, He also did fore-appoint, conformed to the image of His Son, that he might be first-born among many brethren;
30 and whom He did fore-appoint, these also He did call; and whom He did call, these also He declared righteous; and whom He declared righteous, these also He did glorify.
31 What, then, shall we say unto these things? if God [is] for us, who [is] against us?
32 He who indeed did not spare His own Son, but did deliver Him up for us all, how shall He not also with Him grant to us all things ?
33 Who shall lay a charge against the choice ones of God? God [is] He that is declaring righteous,
34 who [is] he that is condemning? Christ [is] He that died, yes, rather also, was raised up; who is also on the right hand of God — who also does intercede for us.
35 Who shall separate us from the love of the Christ? tribulation, or distress, or persecution, or famine, or nakedness, or peril, or sword?
36 (according as it has been written — 'For Your[S] sake we are put to death all the day long, we were reckoned as sheep of slaughter,')
37 but in all these we more than conquer, through him who loved us;
38 for I am persuaded that neither death, nor life, nor messengers, nor principalities, nor powers, nor things present,
39 nor things about to be, nor height, nor depth, nor any other created thing, shall be able to separate us from the love of God, that [is] in Christ Jesus our Lord.

CHAPTER 9

1 Truth I say in Christ, I lie not, my conscience bearing testimony with me in the Holy Spirit,
2 that I have great grief and unceasing pain in my heart —
3 for I was wishing, I myself, to be curse from the Christ — for my brethren, my kindred, according to the flesh,
4 who are Israelites, whose [is] the adoption, and the glory, and the covenants, and the lawgiving, and the service, and the promises,
5 whose [are] the fathers, and of whom [is] the Christ, according to the flesh, who is over all, God blessed to the ages. Amen.
6 And it is not possible that the word of God has failed; for not all who [are] of Israel are these Israel;
7 nor because they are seed of Abraham [are] all children, but — 'in Isaac shall a seed be called to you[S];'
8 that is, the children of the flesh — these [are] not children of God; but the children of the promise are reckoned for seed;
9 for the word of promise [is] this; 'According to this time I will come, and there shall be to Sarah a son.'
10 And not only [so], but also Rebecca, having conceived by one — Isaac our father —
11 (for they being not yet born, neither having done anything good or evil, that the purpose of God, according to choice, might remain; not of works, but of Him who is calling,) it was said to her —
12 'The greater shall serve the less;'
13 according as it has been written, 'Jacob I did love, and Esau I did hate.'
14 What, then, shall we say? unrighteousness [is] with God? let it not be!
15 for to Moses He said, 'I will do kindness to whom I do kindness, and I will have compassion on whom I have compassion;'
16 so, then — not of him who is willing, nor of him who is running, but of God who is doing kindness:
17 for the Writing said to Pharaoh — 'For this very thing I did raise you[S] up, that I might show in you[S] My power, and that My name might be declared in all the land;'
18 so, then, to whom He wills, He does kindness, and to whom He wills, He does harden.
19 You[S] will say, then, to me, 'Why yet does He find fault? for who has resisted His counsel?'

20 nay, but, O man, who are you[S] that are answering
again to God? shall the thing formed say to Him who
did form [it], Why did you[S] make me thus?
21 has not the potter authority over the clay, out of the
same lump to make the one vessel to honor, and the one
to dishonor?
22 And if God, willing to show the wrath and to make
known His power, did endure, in much long suffering,
vessels of wrath fitted for destruction,
23 and that He might make known the riches of His glory
on vessels of kindness, that He before prepared for glory,
whom also He did call — us —
24 not only out of Jews, but also out of nations,
25 as also in Hosea He said, 'I will call what [is] not My
people — My people; and her not beloved — Beloved,
26 and it shall be — in the place where it was said to
them, You[P] [are] not My people; there they shall be called
sons of the living God.'
27 And Isaiah does cry concerning Israel, 'If the number
of the sons of Israel may be as the sand of the sea, the
remnant shall be saved;
28 for a matter He is finishing, and is cutting short in
righteousness, because a matter cut short will the Lord
do upon the land.
29 and according as Isaiah said before, 'Except the Lord
of Sabaoth did leave to us a seed, as Sodom we had
become, and as Gomorrah we had been made like.'
30 What, then, shall we say? that nations who are not
pursuing righteousness did attain to righteousness, and
righteousness that [is] of faith,
31 and Israel, pursuing a law of righteousness, at a law
of righteousness did not arrive;
32 for what reason? because — not by faith, but as by
works of law; for they did stumble at the stone of
stumbling,
33 according as it has been written, 'Behold, I place in
Sion a stone of stumbling and a rock of offense; and
every one who is believing thereon shall not be
ashamed.'

CHAPTER 10

1 Brethren, the pleasure indeed of my heart, and my
supplication that [is] to God for Israel, is — for salvation;
2 for I bear them testimony that they have a zeal of God,
but not according to knowledge,
3 for not knowing the righteousness of God, and their
own righteousness seeking to establish, they did not
submit to the righteousness of God.
4 For Christ is an end of law for righteousness to every
one who is believing,
5 for Moses does describe the righteousness that [is]
of the law, that, 'The man who did them shall live in them,'
6 and the righteousness of faith does thus speak: 'You[S]
may not say in your[S] heart, Who shall go up to the
heaven,' that is, Christ to bring down?
7 or, 'Who shall go down to the abyss,' that is, Christ
out of the dead to bring up.
8 But what does it say? 'Near you[S] is the saying — in
your[S] mouth, and in your[S] heart:' that is, the saying of
the faith, that we preach;
9 that if you[S] may confess with your[S] mouth the Lord
Jesus, and may believe in your[S] heart that God did raise
him out of the dead, you[S] shall be saved,
10 for with the heart does [one] believe to righteousness,
and with the mouth is confession made to salvation;
11 for the Writing said, 'Every one who is believing on
him shall not be ashamed,'
12 for there is no difference between Jew and Greek, for
the same Lord of all [is] rich to all those calling upon
Him,
13 for every one — whoever shall call upon the name of
the Lord, he shall be saved.'
14 How then shall they call upon [him] in whom they
did not believe? and how shall they believe [on him] of
whom they did not hear? and how shall they hear apart
from one preaching?
15 and how shall they preach, if they may not be sent?
according as it has been written, 'How beautiful the feet
of those proclaiming good tidings of peace, of those
proclaiming good tidings of the good things!'
16 But they were not all obedient to the good tidings,
for Isaiah said, 'Lord, who did give credence to our
report?'
17 so then the faith [is] by a report, and the report
through a saying of God,
18 but I say, Did they not hear? yes, indeed — 'to all
the earth their voice went forth, and their sayings to the
ends of the habitable world.'
19 But I say, Did not Israel know? first Moses said, 'I
will provoke you[P] to jealousy by [that which is] not a
nation; by an unintelligent nation I will anger you[P],'
20 and Isaiah is very bold, and said, 'I was found by
those not seeking Me; I became known to those not
inquiring after Me;'
21 and unto Israel He said, 'All the day I did stretch out
My hands unto a people unbelieving and gainsaying.'

CHAPTER 11

1 I say, then, Did God cast away His people? let it not
be! for I also am an Israelite, of the seed of Abraham, of
the tribe of Benjamin:
2 God did not cast away His people whom He knew
before; have you[P] not known — in Elijah — what the
Writing said? how he does plead with God concerning
Israel, saying,
3 'Lord, Your[S] prophets they did kill, and Your[S] altars
they dug down, and I was left alone, and they seek my
life;'
4 but what said the divine answer to him? 'I left to Myself
seven thousand men, who did not bow a knee to Baal.'
5 So then also in the present time a remnant according
to the choice of grace there has been;
6 and if by grace, no more of works, otherwise the grace
becomes no more grace; and if of works, it is no more
grace, otherwise the work is no more work.
7 What then? What Israel does seek after, this it did not
obtain, and the chosen did obtain, and the rest were
hardened,
8 according as it has been written, 'God gave to them a
spirit of deep sleep, eyes not to see, and ears not to
hear,' — unto this very day,
9 and David said, 'Let their table become for a snare,
and for a trap, and for a stumbling-block, and for a
recompense to them;
10 let their eyes be darkened — not to behold, and their
back do You[S] always bow down.'
11 I say, then, Did they stumble that they might fall? let
it not be! but by their fall the salvation [is] to the nations,
to arouse them to jealousy;
12 and if the fall of them [is] the riches of a world, and
the diminution of them the riches of nations, how much
more the fullness of them?
13 For to you[P] I speak — to the nations — inasmuch as
I am indeed an apostle of nations, I do glorify my
ministration;
14 if by any means I shall arouse mine own flesh to
jealousy, and shall save some of them,
15 for if the casting away of them [is] a reconciliation of
the world, what the reception — if not life out of the
dead?
16 and if the first-fruit [is] holy, the lump also; and if the
root [is] holy, the branches also.
17 And if certain of the branches were broken off, and
you[S], being a wild olive tree, were grafted in among them,
and did become a fellow-partaker of the root and of the
fatness of the olive tree —
18 do not boast against the branches; and if you[S] do
boast, you[S] do not bear the root, but the root you[S]!
19 You[S] will say, then, 'The branches were broken off,
that I might be grafted in;' right!
20 by unbelief they were broken off, and you[S] have
stood by faith; be not high-minded, but be fearing;
21 for if God did not spare the natural branches — fear
that perhaps He also shall not spare you[S].
22 Behold, then, goodness and severity of God — upon
those indeed who fell, severity; and upon you[S],
goodness, if you[S] may remain in the goodness,
otherwise, you[S] also shall be cut off.
23 And those also, if they may not remain in unbelief,
shall be grafted in, for God is able again to graft them in;
24 for if you[S], out of the olive tree, wild by nature, were
cut out, and, contrary to nature, were grafted into a good
olive tree, how much rather shall they, who [are]
according to nature, be grafted into their own olive tree?
25 For I do not wish you[P] to be ignorant, brethren, of
this secret — that you[P] may not be wise in your[P] own
conceits — that hardness in part to Israel has happened
till the fullness of the nations may come in;
26 and so all Israel shall be saved, according as it has
been written, 'There shall come forth out of Sion he who
is delivering, and he shall turn away impiety from Jacob,
27 and this to them [is] the covenant from Me, when I
may take away their sins.'
28 As regards, indeed, the good tidings, [they are]
enemies on your[P] account; and as regards the choice —
beloved on account of the fathers;
29 for unrepented of [are] the gifts and the calling of
God;
30 for as you[P] also once did not believe in God, and
now did find kindness by the unbelief of these:
31 so also these now did not believe, that in your[P]
kindness they also may find kindness;
32 for God did shut up together the whole to unbelief,
that to the whole He might do kindness.
33 O depth of riches, and wisdom and knowledge of
God! how unsearchable His judgments, and untraceable
His ways!
34 for who did know the mind of the Lord? or who did
become His counselor?
35 or who did first give to Him, and it shall be given
back to him again?
36 because of Him, and through Him, and to Him [are]
the all things; to Him [is] the glory — to the ages. Amen.

CHAPTER 12

1 I call upon you[P], for that reason, brethren, through the compassions of God, to present your[P] bodies a sacrifice — living, sanctified, acceptable to God — your[P] intelligent service;
2 and be not conformed to this age, but be transformed by the renewing of your[P] mind, for your[P] proving what [is] the will of God — the good, and acceptable, and perfect.
3 For I say, through the grace that was given to me, to every one who is among you[P], not to think above what it is necessary to think; but to think so as to think wisely, as to each God did deal a measure of faith,
4 for as in one body we have many members, and all the members have not the same office,
5 so we, the many, one body are in Christ, and members each one of one another.
6 And having gifts, different according to the grace that was given to us; whether prophecy — 'According to the proportion of faith!'
7 or ministration — 'In the ministration!' or he who is teaching — 'In the teaching!'
8 or he who is exhorting — 'In the exhortation!' he who is sharing — 'In simplicity!' he who is leading — 'In diligence?' he who is doing kindness — 'In cheerfulness.'
9 The love unfeigned: abhorring the evil; adhering to the good;
10 in the love of brethren, to one another kindly affectioned: in the honor going before one another;
11 not slothful in the diligence; fervent in the spirit; serving the Lord;
12 rejoicing in the hope; enduring in the tribulation; persevering in the prayer;
13 communicating to the necessities of the saints; pursuing the hospitality.
14 Bless those persecuting you[P]; bless, and not curse;
15 to rejoice with the rejoicing, and to weep with the weeping,
16 of the same mind one toward another, not minding the high things, but with the lowly going along; become not wise in your[P] own conceit;
17 giving back to no one evil for evil; providing right things before all men.
18 If possible — so far as in you[P] — with all men being in peace;
19 not avenging yourselves[P], beloved, but give place to the wrath, for it has been written, 'Vengeance [is] Mine,
20 I will recompense again, said the Lord;' if, then, your[S] enemy does hunger, feed him; if he does thirst, give him drink; for this doing, you[S] shall heap coals of fire upon his head;
21 Be not overcome by the evil, but overcome, in the good, the evil.

CHAPTER 13

1 Let every soul be subject to the higher authorities, for there is no authority except from God, and the existing authorities are appointed by God,
2 so that he who is setting himself against the authority, has resisted against God's ordinance; and those resisting, shall receive judgment to themselves.
3 For those ruling are not a terror to the good works, but to the evil; and do you[S] wish not to be afraid of the authority? be doing that which is good, and you[S] shall have praise from it,
4 for it is a ministrant of God to you[S] for good; and if that which is evil you[S] may do, be fearing, for not in vain does it bear the sword; for it is a ministrant of God, an avenger for wrath to him who is doing that which is evil.
5 For what reason it is necessary to be subject, not only because of the wrath, but also because of the conscience,
6 for because of this also pay you[P] tribute; for they are servants of God, on this very thing attending continually;
7 render, for that reason, to all [their] dues; to whom tribute, the tribute; to whom custom, the custom; to whom fear, the fear; to whom honor, the honor.
8 To no one owe anything, except to love one another; for he who is loving the other — law he has fulfilled,
9 for, 'You[S] shall not commit adultery, You[S] shall do no murder, You[S] shall not steal, You[S] shall not bear false testimony, You[S] shall not covet;' and if there is any other command, in this word it is summed up, in this: 'You[S] shall love your[S] neighbor as yourself[S];'
10 the love to the neighbor does work no ill; the love, for that reason, [is] the fullness of law.
11 And this, knowing the time, that for us, the hour already [is] to be aroused out of sleep, for now nearer [is] our salvation than when we did believe;
12 the night did advance, and the day came near; let us

lay aside, for that reason, the works of the darkness, and
let us put on the armor of the light;
13 as in day-time, let us walk becomingly; not in
revellings and drunkennesses, not in chamberings and
lasciviousnesses, not in strife and emulation;
14 but put you[P] on the Lord Jesus Christ, and for the
flesh take no forethought — for desires.

CHAPTER 14

1 And him who is weak in the faith receive you[P] — not
to determinations of reasonings;
2 one does believe that he may eat all things — and he
who is weak does eat herbs;
3 let not him who is eating despise him who is not eating:
and let not him who is not eating judge him who is eating,
for God did receive him.
4 You[S] — who are you[S] that are judging another's
domestic? to his own master he does stand or fall; and
he shall be made to stand, for God is able to make him
stand.
5 One does judge one day above another, and another
does judge every day [alike]; let each be fully assured
in his own mind.
6 He who is regarding the day, he does regard [it] to the
Lord, and he who is not regarding the day, he does not
regard [it] to the Lord. He who is eating, he does eat to
the Lord, for he does give thanks to God; and he who is
not eating, he does not eat to the Lord, and does give
thanks to God.
7 For none of us does live to himself, and none does die
to himself;
8 for both, if we may live, we live to the Lord; if also we
may die, we die to the Lord; both then if we may live,
also if we may die, we are the Lord's;
9 for because of this Christ both died and rose again,
and lived again, that both of dead and of living he may
be Lord.
10 And you[S], why do you[S] judge your[S] brother? or again,
you[S], why do you[S] set your[S] brother at nothing? for we
shall all stand at the tribunal of the Christ;
11 for it has been written, 'I live! said the Lord – every
knee shall bow to Me, and every tongue shall confess
to God;'
12 so, then, each of us shall give reckoning concerning
himself to God;
13 no longer, for that reason, may we judge one another,
but this judge you[P] rather, not to put a stumbling-stone
before the brother, or an offense.
14 I have known, and am persuaded, in the Lord Jesus,
that nothing [is] unclean of itself, except to him who is
reckoning anything to be unclean — to that one [it is]
unclean;
15 and if through victuals your[S] brother is grieved, no
more do you[S] walk according to love; do not with your[S]
victuals destroy that one for whom Christ died.
16 Let not, then, your[P] good be evil spoken of,
17 for the reign of God is not eating and drinking, but
righteousness, and peace, and joy in the Holy Spirit;
18 for he who is serving the Christ in these things, [is]
acceptable to God and approved of men.
19 So, then, may we pursue the things of peace, and the
things of building up one another;
20 cast not down the work of God for the sake of
victuals; all things, indeed, [are] pure, but evil [is] to the
man who is eating through stumbling.
21 Right [it is] not to eat flesh, nor to drink wine, nor to
[do anything] in which your[S] brother does stumble, or
is made to fall, or is weak.
22 You[S] have faith! to yourself[S] have [it] before God;
happy is he who is not judging himself in what he does
approve,
23 and he who is making a difference, if he may eat, has
been condemned, because [it is] not of faith; and all that
[is] not of faith is sin.

CHAPTER 15

1 And we ought — we who are strong — to bear the
infirmities of the weak, and not to please ourselves;
2 for let each one of us please the neighbor for good,
unto edification,
3 for even the Christ did not please himself, but,
according as it has been written, 'The reproaches of
those reproaching You[S] fell upon Me;'
4 for, as many things as were written before, were written
before for our instruction, that through the endurance,
and the exhortation of the Writings, we might have the
hope.
5 And may the God of the endurance, and of the
exhortation, give to you[P] to have the same mind toward
one another, according to Christ Jesus;
6 that with one desire — with one mouth — you[P] may
glorify the God and Father of our Lord Jesus Christ;
7 for what reason receive you[P] one another, according
as also the Christ did receive us, to the glory of God.

8 And I say Jesus Christ to have become a ministrant of
circumcision for the truth of God, to confirm the promises
to the fathers,
9 and the nations for kindness to glorify God, according
as it has been written, 'Because of this I will confess to
You[S] among nations, and I will sing praise to Your[S] name,'
10 and again it said, 'Rejoice you[P] nations, with His
people;'
11 and again, 'Praise the Lord, all you[P] nations; and
glorify Him, all you[P] peoples;'
12 and again, Isaiah said, 'There shall be the root of
Jesse, and he who is rising to rule nations — upon him
shall nations hope;'
13 and the God of the hope shall fill you[P] with all joy
and peace in the believing, for your[P] abounding in the
hope in power of the Holy Spirit.
14 And I am persuaded, my brethren — I myself also —
concerning you[P], that you[P] yourselves[P] also are full of
goodness, having been filled with all knowledge, able
also to admonish one another;
15 and the more boldly I did write to you[P], brethren, in
part, as putting you[P] in mind, because of the grace that
is given to me by God,
16 for my being a servant of Jesus Christ to the nations,
acting as priest in the good news of God, that the offering
up of the nations may become acceptable, sanctified by
the Holy Spirit.
17 I have, then, a boasting in Christ Jesus, in the things
pertaining to God,
18 for I will not dare to speak anything of the things
that Christ did not work through me, to obedience of
nations, by word and deed,
19 in power of signs and wonders, in power of the Spirit
of God; so that I, from Jerusalem, and in a circle as far as
Illyricum, have fully preached the good news of the
Christ;
20 and so counting it honor to proclaim good news, not
where Christ was named — that I might not build upon
another's foundation —
21 but according as it has been written, 'To whom it
was not told concerning him, they shall see; and they
who have not heard, shall understand.'
22 For what reason, also, I was hindered many times
from coming unto you[P],
23 and now, no longer having place in these parts, and
having a longing to come unto you[P] for many years,
24 when I may go on to Spain I will come unto you[P], for I
hope in going through, to see you[P], and by you[P] to be set
forward from there, if of you[P] first, in part, I shall be filled.
25 And, now, I go on to Jerusalem, ministering to the
saints;
26 for it pleased Macedonia and Achaia well to make a
certain contribution for the poor of the saints who [are]
in Jerusalem;
27 for it pleased well, and they are their debtors, for if
the nations did participate in their spiritual things, they
ought also, in the fleshly things, to minister to them.
28 This, then, having finished, and having sealed this
fruit to them, I will return through you[P], to Spain;
29 and I have known that coming unto you[P] — I shall
come in the fullness of the blessing of the good news of
Christ.
30 And I call upon you[P], brethren, through our Lord
Jesus Christ, and through the love of the Spirit, to strive
together with me in the prayers for me unto God,
31 that I may be delivered from those not believing in
Judea, and that my ministration, that [is] for Jerusalem,
may become acceptable to the saints;
32 that in joy I may come unto you[P], through the will of
God, and may be refreshed with you[P],
33 and the God of the peace [be] with you[P] all. Amen.

CHAPTER 16

1 And I commend you[P] to Phebe our sister — being a
ministrant of the assembly that [is] in Cenchrea —
2 that you[P] may receive her in the Lord, as does become
saints, and may assist her in whatever matter she may
have need of you[P] — for she also became a leader of
many, and of myself.
3 Salute Priscilla and Aquilas, my fellow-workmen in
Christ Jesus —
4 who did lay down their own neck for my life, to whom
not only I give thanks, but also all the assemblies of the
nations —
5 and the assembly at their house; salute Epaenetus,
my beloved, who is first-fruit of Achaia to Christ.
6 Salute Mary, who did labor much for us;
7 salute Andronicus and Junias, my kindred, and my
fellow-captives, who are of note among the apostles,
who also have been in Christ before me.
8 Salute Amplias, my beloved in the Lord;
9 salute Arbanus, our fellow-workman in Christ, and
Stachys, my beloved;
10 salute Apelles, the approved in Christ; salute those
of the [household] of Aristobulus;
11 salute Herodion, my kinsman; salute those of the

[household] of Narcissus, who are in the Lord;
12 salute Tryphaena, and Tryphosa, who are laboring
in the Lord; salute Persis, the beloved, who did labor
much in the Lord.
13 Salute Rufus, the choice one in the Lord, and his
mother and mine,
14 salute Asyncritus, Phlegon, Hermas, Patrobas,
Hermes, and the brethren with them;
15 salute Philologus, and Julias, Nereus, and his sister,
and Olympas, and all the saints with them;
16 salute one another in a holy kiss; the assemblies of
Christ do salute you[P].
17 And I call upon you[P], brethren, to mark those who
the divisions and the stumbling-blocks, contrary to the
teaching that you[P] did learn, are causing, and turn you[P]
away from them;
18 for such do not serve our Lord Jesus Christ, but their
own belly; and through the good word and fair speech
they deceive the hearts of the harmless,
19 for your[P] obedience did reach to all; I rejoice, for that
reason, as regards you[P], and I wish you[P] to be wise,
indeed, as to the good, and harmless as to the evil;
20 and the God of the peace shall bruise the Adversary
under your[P] feet quickly; the grace of our Lord Jesus
Christ [be] with you[P]. Amen!
21 Salute you[P] do Timotheus, my fellow-workman, and
Lucius, and Jason, and Sosipater, my kindred;
22 I Tertius salute you[P] (who wrote the letter) in the
Lord;
23 Gaius does salute you[P], my host, and of the whole
assembly; Erastus does salute you[P], the steward of the
city, and Quartus the brother,
24 the grace of our Lord Jesus Christ [be] with you[P] all.
Amen.
25 And to Him who is able to establish you[P], according
to my good news, and the preaching of Jesus Christ,
according to the revelation of the secret, in the times of
the ages having been kept silent,
26 and now having been made known, also, through
prophetic writings, according to a command of the age-
during God, having been made known to all the nations
for obedience of faith —
27 to the only wise God, through Jesus Christ, to him
[be] glory to the ages. Amen.

The FIRST Epistle Of Paul The Apostle To The
CORINTHIANS

CHAPTER 1

1 Paul, a called apostle of Jesus Christ, through the will
of God, and Sosthenes the brother,
2 to the assembly of God that is in Corinth, to those
sanctified in Christ Jesus, called saints, with all those
calling upon the name of our Lord Jesus Christ in every
place — both theirs and ours:
3 Grace to you[P] and peace from God our Father and the
Lord Jesus Christ!
4 I give thanks to my God always concerning you[P] for
the grace of God that was given to you[P] in Christ Jesus,
5 that you[P] were enriched in him in every thing, in all
discourse and all knowledge,
6 according as the testimony of the Christ was confirmed
in you[P],
7 so that you[P] are not behind in any gift, waiting for the
revelation of our Lord Jesus Christ,
8 who also shall confirm you[P] unto the end —
unblamable in the day of our Lord Jesus Christ;
9 faithful [is] God, through whom you[P] were called to
the fellowship of His Son Jesus Christ our Lord.
10 And I call upon you[P], brethren, through the name of
our Lord Jesus Christ, that you[P] may all say the same
thing, and there may not be divisions among you[P], and
you[P] may be perfected in the same mind, and in the same
judgment,
11 for it was signified to me concerning you[P], my brethren,
by those of Chloe, that contentions are among you[P];
12 and I say this, that each one of you[P] said, 'I, indeed,
am of Paul' — 'and I of Apollos,' — 'and I of Cephas,'
— 'and I of Christ.'
13 Has the Christ been divided? was Paul crucified for
you[P]? or were you[P] baptized to the name of Paul;
14 I give thanks to God that I did baptize no one of
you[P], except Crispus and Gaius —
15 that no one may say that I did baptize to my own name;
16 and I did baptize also Stephanas' household —
further, I have not known if I did baptize any other.
17 For Christ did not send me to baptize, but — to
proclaim good news; not in wisdom of discourse, that
the cross of the Christ may not be made of none effect;
18 for the word of the cross is foolishness to those
indeed perishing, and to us — those being saved — it
is the power of God,
19 for it has been written, 'I will destroy the wisdom of
the wise, and I will bring to nothing the intelligence of
the intelligent;'
20 where [is] the wise? where the scribe? where a
disputer of this age? did not God make the wisdom of
this world foolish?
21 for, seeing in the wisdom of God the world through
the wisdom knew not God, it did please God through
the foolishness of the preaching to save those believing.
22 Since also Jews ask a sign, and Greeks seek wisdom,
23 also we — we preach Christ crucified, to Jews, indeed,
a stumbling-block, and to Greeks foolishness,
24 and to those called — both Jews and Greeks — Christ
the power of God, and the wisdom of God,
25 because the foolishness of God is wiser than men,
and the weakness of God is stronger than men;
26 for see your[P] calling, brethren, that not many [are] wise
according to the flesh, not many mighty, not many noble;
27 but God did choose the foolish things of the world, that
He may put the wise to shame; and God did choose the weak
things of the world that He may put to shame the strong;
28 and the base things of the world, and the things
despised did God choose, and the things that are not,
that He may make useless the things that are —
29 that no flesh may glory before Him;
30 and of Him you[P] — you[P] are in Christ Jesus, who
became to us wisdom from God, righteousness also, and
sanctification, and redemption,
31 that, according as it has been written, 'He who is
glorying — let him glory in the Lord.'

CHAPTER 2

1 And I, having come unto you[P], brethren, came — not
in superiority of discourse or wisdom — declaring to

you[P] the testimony of God,
2 for I decided not to know any thing among you[P], except
Jesus Christ, and him crucified;
3 and I, in weakness, and in fear, and in much trembling,
was with you[P];
4 and my word and my preaching was not in persuasive
words of human wisdom, but in demonstration of the
Spirit and of power —
5 that your[P] faith may not be in the wisdom of men, but
in the power of God.
6 And we speak wisdom among the perfect, and wisdom
not of this age, nor of the rulers of this age — of those
becoming useless,
7 but we speak the hidden wisdom of God in a secret,
that God foreordained before the ages to our glory,
8 which no one of the rulers of this age did know, for if
they had known, they would not have crucified the Lord
of the glory;
9 but, according as it has been written, 'What eye did not
see, and ear did not hear, and came not up upon the heart
of man, what God did prepare for those loving Him —'
10 but God did reveal [them] through His Spirit to us,
for the Spirit does search all things, even the depths of
God,
11 for who of men has known the things of the man,
except the spirit of the man that [is] in him? so also no
one has known the things of God, except the Spirit of
God.
12 And we did not receive the spirit of the world, but
the Spirit that [is] of God, that we may know the things
conferred on us by God,
13 which things also we speak, not in words taught by
human wisdom, but in those taught by the Holy Spirit,
spiritual things comparing with spiritual things,
14 and the natural man does not receive the things of
the Spirit of God, for to him they are foolishness, and he
is not able to know [them], because they are discerned
spiritually;
15 and he who is spiritual, does discern indeed all things,
and he himself is discerned by no one;
16 for who did know the mind of the Lord that he shall
instruct Him? and we — we have the mind of Christ.

CHAPTER 3

1 And I, brethren, was not able to speak to you[P] as to
spiritual, but as to fleshly — as to babes in Christ;
2 I fed you[P] with milk, and not with meat, for you[P] were
not yet able, but not even now are you[P] able yet,
3 for you[P] are fleshly yet, for where [there is] among
you[P] envying, and strife, and divisions, are you[P] not
fleshly, and do walk in the manner of men?
4 for when one may say, 'I, indeed, am of Paul;' and
another, 'I — of Apollos;' are you[P] not fleshly?
5 Who, then, is Paul, and who Apollos, but ministrants
through whom you[P] did believe, and to each as the Lord
gave?
6 I planted, Apollos watered, but God was giving
growth;
7 so that neither is he who is planting anything, nor he
who is watering, but He who is giving growth — God;
8 and he who is planting and he who is watering are
one, and each shall receive his own reward, according
to his own labor,
9 for we are fellow-workmen of God; God's tillage, you[P]
are God's building.
10 According to the grace of God that was given to me,
as a wise master-builder, I have laid a foundation, and
another does build on [it],
11 for no one is able to lay other foundation except that
which is laid, which is Jesus the Christ;
12 and if any one does build upon this foundation gold,
silver, precious stones, wood, hay, straw —
13 of each the work shall become revealed, for the day
shall declare [it], because it is revealed in fire, and the
work of each, what kind it is, the fire shall prove;
14 if the work of any one does remain that he built on
[it], a wage he shall receive;
15 if the work of any is burned up, he shall suffer loss;
and himself shall be saved, but so as through fire.
16 have you[P] not known that you[P] are a sanctuary of
God, and the Spirit of God does dwell in you[P]?
17 if any one does waste the sanctuary of God, God
shall waste him; for the sanctuary of God is holy, the
which you[P] are.
18 Let no one deceive himself; if any one does seem to
be wise among you[P] in this age — let him become a fool,
that he may become wise,
19 for the wisdom of this world is foolishness with God,
for it has been written, 'Who is taking the wise in their
craftiness;'
20 and again, 'The Lord does know the reasonings of
the wise, that they are vain.'
21 So then, let no one glory in men, for all things are
yours[P],
22 whether Paul, or Apollos, or Cephas, or the world, or
life, or death, or things present, or things about to be —

all are yours[P],
23 and you[P] [are] Christ's, and Christ [is] God's.

CHAPTER 4

1 Let a man so reckon us as officers of Christ, and
stewards of the secrets of God,
2 and as to the rest, it is required in the stewards that
one may be found faithful,
3 and to me it is for a very little thing that I may be
judged by you[P], or by man's day, but I do not judge even
myself,
4 for to myself I have been conscious of nothing, but
not in this have I been declared right — and he who is
discerning me is the Lord:
5 so, then, judge you[P] nothing before the time, till the Lord
may come, who will both bring to light the hidden things of
the darkness, and will reveal the counsels of the hearts,
and then the praise shall come to each from God.
6 And these things, brethren, I did transfer to myself
and to Apollos because of you[P], that in us you may learn
not to think above that which has been written, that you[P]
may not be puffed up one for one against the other,
7 for who does make you[S] to differ? and what have you[S],
that you[S] did not receive? and if you[S] did also receive,
why do you[S] glory as not having received?
8 Already you[P] are having been filled, already you[P] were
rich, you[P] did reign apart from us, and I would also you[P]
did reign, that we also may reign together with you[P],
9 for I think that God did set us forth the last apostles
— as appointed to death, because we became a spectacle
to the world, and messengers, and men;
10 we [are] fools because of Christ, and you[P] wise in
Christ; we [are] ailing, and you[P] strong; you[P] glorious,
and we dishonored;
11 unto the present hour we both hunger, and thirst,
and are naked, and are buffeted, and wander about,
12 and labor, working with [our] own hands; being
reviled, we bless; being persecuted, we suffer;
13 being spoken evil of, we entreat; we did become as
filth of the world — an outcast of all things — till now.
14 Not [as] putting you[P] to shame do I write these things,
but I do admonish as my beloved children,
15 for if you[P] may have a myriad of child-conductors in
Christ, yet not many fathers; for in Christ Jesus, through
the good news, I — I did beget you[P];
16 I call upon you[P], for that reason, become you[P]
followers of me;
17 because of this I sent to you[P] Timotheus, who is my
child, beloved and faithful in the Lord, who shall remind
you[P] of my ways in Christ, according as I teach
everywhere in every assembly.
18 And as if I were not coming unto you[P] certain were
puffed up;
19 but I will come quickly unto you[P], if the Lord may
will, and I will know not the word of those puffed up,
but the power;
20 for the reign of God is not in word, but in power?
21 what do you[P] wish? shall I come unto you[P] with a
rod, or in love, with a spirit also of meekness?

CHAPTER 5

1 Whoredom is actually heard of among you[P], and such
whoredom as is not even named among the nations —
as that one has the wife of the father! —
2 and you[P] are having been puffed up, and did not rather
mourn, that he who did this work may be removed out
of the midst of you[P],
3 for I indeed, as being absent as to the body, and
present as to the spirit, have already judged, as being
present, him who so worked this thing:
4 in the name of our Lord Jesus Christ — you[P] being
gathered together, also my spirit — with the power of
our Lord Jesus Christ,
5 to deliver up such a one to the Adversary for the
destruction of the flesh, that the spirit may be saved in
the day of the Lord Jesus.
6 Not good [is] your[P] glorying; have you[P] not known
that a little leaven does leaven the whole lump?
7 cleanse out, for that reason, the old leaven, that you[P]
may be a new lump, according as you[P] are unleavened,
for also our Passover was sacrificed for us — Christ,
8 so that we may keep the feast, not with old leaven,
nor with the leaven of evil and wickedness, but with
unleavened food of sincerity and truth.
9 I did write to you[P] in the epistle, not to keep company
with whoremongers —
10 and certainly not with the whoremongers of this
world, or with the covetous, or extortioners, or idolaters,
seeing you[P] ought then to go forth out of the world —
11 and now, I did write to you[P] not to keep company
with [him], if any one, being named a brother, may be a
whoremonger, or covetous, or an idolater, or a railer, or
a drunkard, or an extortioner — not even to eat together
with such a one;

12 for what have I also to judge those without? do you[P] not judge those within?
13 and God does judge those without; and you[P] put away the evil from among yourselves[P].

CHAPTER 6

1 Dare any one of you[P], having a matter with the other, go to be judged before the unrighteous, and not before the saints?
2 have you[P] not known that the saints shall judge the world? and if by you[P] the world is judged, are you[P] unworthy of the smaller judgments?
3 have you[P] not known that we shall judge messengers? why not then the things of life?
4 of the things of life, indeed, then, if you[P] may have judgment, those despised in the assembly — you[P] cause these to sit;
5 I speak unto your[P] shame: so there is not one wise man among you[P], not even one, who shall be able to discern in the midst of his brethren!
6 but brother with brother does go to be judged, and this before unbelievers!
7 Already, indeed, then, there is altogether a fault among you[P], that you[P] have judgments with one another; rather why do you[P] not allow injustice? rather why be you[P] not defrauded?
8 but you[P] — you[P] do injustice, and you[P] defraud, and these — brethren!
9 have you[P] not known that the unrighteous shall not inherit the reign of God? be not led astray; neither whoremongers, nor idolaters, nor adulterers, nor effeminate, nor sodomites,
10 nor thieves, nor covetous, nor drunkards, nor revilers, nor extortioners, shall inherit the reign of God.
11 And certain of you[P] were these! but you[P] were washed, but you[P] were sanctified, but you[P] were declared righteous, in the name of the Lord Jesus, and in the Spirit of our God.
12 All things are lawful to me, but all things are not profitable; all things are lawful to me, but I — I will not be under authority by any;
13 the meats [are] for the belly, and the belly for the meats. And God shall make useless both this and these; and the body [is] not for whoredom, but for the Lord, and the Lord for the body;
14 and God did both raise the Lord , and will raise us up through His power.
15 Have you[P] not known that your[P] bodies are members of Christ? having taken, then, the members of the Christ, shall I make [them] members of an harlot? let it be not!
16 have you[P] not known that he who is joined to the harlot is one body? 'for they shall be — said He — the two for one flesh.'
17 And he who is joined to the Lord is one spirit;
18 flee the whoredom; every sin — whatever a man may commit — is without the body, and he who is committing whoredom, does sin against his own body.
19 Have you[P] not known that your[P] body is a sanctuary of the Holy Spirit in you[P], which you[P] have from God? and you[P] are not your[P] own,
20 for you[P] were bought with a price; glorify, then, God in your[P] body and in your[P] spirit, which are God's.

CHAPTER 7

1 And concerning the things of which you[P] wrote to me: [it is] good for a man not to touch a woman,
2 and because of the whoredom let each man have his own wife, and let each woman have her proper husband;
3 let the husband render to the wife the due benevolence, and in like manner also the wife to the husband;
4 the wife has not authority over her own body, but the husband; and, in like manner also, the husband has not authority over his own body, but the wife.
5 Defraud not one another, except by consent for a time, that you[P] may be free for fasting and prayer, and again may come together, that the Adversary may not tempt you[P] because of your[P] incontinence;
6 and this I say by way of concurrence — not of command,
7 for I wish all men to be even as I myself [am]; but each has his own gift of God, one indeed thus, and one thus.
8 And I say to the unmarried and to the widows: it is good for them if they may remain even as I [am];
9 and if they have not continence — let them marry, for it is better to marry than to burn;
10 and to the married I announce — not I, but the Lord — let not a wife separate from a husband:
11 but and if she may separate, let her remain unmarried, or let her be reconciled to the husband, and let not a husband send away a wife.
12 And to the rest I speak — not the Lord — if any brother has a wife unbelieving, and she is pleased to dwell with him, let him not send her away;

13 and a woman who has a husband unbelieving, and
he is pleased to dwell with her, let her not send him away;
14 for the unbelieving husband has been sanctified in
the wife, and the unbelieving wife has been sanctified
in the husband; otherwise your children are unclean, but
now they are holy.
15 And, if the unbelieving does separate himself — let
him separate himself: the brother or the sister is not under
servitude in such [cases], and God has called us in
peace;
16 for what, have you[S] known, O wife, whether you[S]
shall save the husband? or what, have you[S] known, O
husband, whether you[S] shall save the wife?
17 if not, as God did distribute to each, as the Lord has
called each — so let him walk; and thus do I direct in all
the assemblies:
18 being circumcised — was any one called? let him
not become uncircumcised; was any one called in
uncircumcision? let him not be circumcised;
19 the circumcision is nothing, and the uncircumcision
is nothing — but a keeping of the commands of God.
20 Each in the calling in which he was called — let him
remain in this;
21 a servant — were you[S] called? be not anxious; but if
also you[S] are able to become free — use [it] rather;
22 for he who [is] in the Lord — having been called a
servant — is the Lord's freedman: in like manner also he
the freeman, having been called, is servant of Christ:
23 you[P] were bought with a price, become not servants
of men;
24 each, in that in which he was called, brethren, in this
let him remain with God.
25 And concerning the virgins, I have not a command
of the Lord; and I give judgment as having obtained
kindness from the Lord to be faithful:
26 I suppose, for that reason, this to be good because
of the present necessity, that [it is] good for a man that
the matter be thus: —
27 Have you[S] been bound to a wife? seek not to be
loosed; have you[S] been loosed from a wife? seek not a
wife.
28 But and if you[S] may marry, you[S] did not sin; and if
the virgin may marry, she did not sin; and such shall
have tribulation in the flesh: and I spare you[P].
29 And this I say, brethren, the time from now on is
having been shortened — that both those having wives
may be as not having;
30 and those weeping, as not weeping; and those
rejoicing, as not rejoicing; and those buying, as not
possessing;
31 and those using this world, as not using [it] up; for
passing away is the fashion of this world.
32 And I wish you[P] to be without anxiety; the unmarried
is anxious for the things of the Lord, how he shall please
the Lord;
33 and the married is anxious for the things of the world,
how he shall please the wife.
34 The wife and the virgin have been distinguished: the
unmarried is anxious for the things of the Lord, that she
may be holy both in body and in spirit, and the married
is anxious for the things of the world, how she shall
please the husband.
35 And this I say for your[P] own profit: not that I may
cast a noose upon you[P], but for the seemliness and
devotedness to the Lord, undistractedly,
36 and if any one does think [it] to be unseemly to his
virgin, if she may be beyond the bloom of age, and it
ought so to be, let him do what he wills; he does not sin
— let him marry.
37 And he who has stood steadfast in the heart — not
having necessity — and has authority over his own will,
and this he has determined in his heart — to keep his
own virgin — does well;
38 so that both he who is giving in marriage does well,
and he who is not giving in marriage does better.
39 A wife has been bound by law as long time as her
husband may live, and if her husband may sleep, she is
free to be married to whom she will — only in the Lord;
40 and she is happier if she may so remain — according
to my judgment; and I think I also have the Spirit of God.

CHAPTER 8

1 And concerning the things sacrificed to idols, we have
known that we all have knowledge: knowledge puffs up,
but love builds up;
2 and if any one does think to know anything, he has
not yet known anything according as it is necessary for
[him] to know;
3 and if any one does love God, this one has been known
by Him.
4 Concerning then the eating of the things sacrificed to
idols, we have known that an idol [is] nothing in the
world, and that there is no other God except one;
5 for even if there are those called gods, whether in
heaven, whether upon earth — as there are gods many
and lords many —

6 yet to us [is] one God, the Father, of whom [are] the all things, and we to Him; and one Lord, Jesus Christ, through whom [are] the all things, and we through Him;

7 but the knowledge [is] not in all men, and certain with conscience of the idol, till now, do eat [it] as a thing sacrificed to an idol, and their conscience, being weak, is defiled.

8 But victuals do not commend us to God, for neither if we may eat are we in advance; nor if we may not eat, are we behind;

9 but see, for fear that this privilege of yours[P] may become a stumbling-block to the infirm,

10 for if any one may see you[S] that have knowledge in an idol's temple reclining at meat — shall not his conscience — he being infirm — be emboldened to eat the things sacrificed to idols,

11 and the brother who is infirm shall perish by your[S] knowledge, because of whom Christ died?

12 and thus sinning in regard to the brethren, and striking their weak conscience — you[P] sin in regard to Christ;

13 for what reason, if victuals cause my brother to stumble, I may eat no flesh — to the age — that I may not cause my brother to stumble.

CHAPTER 9

1 Am I not an apostle? am I not free? Have I not seen Jesus Christ our Lord? are you[P] not my work in the Lord?

2 if to others I am not an apostle — yet doubtless to you[P] I am; for you[P] are the seal of my apostleship in the Lord.

3 My defense to those who examine me in this;

4 have we not authority to eat and to drink?

5 have we not authority a sister — a wife — to lead about, as also the other apostles, and the brethren of the Lord, and Cephas?

6 or only I and Barnabas, have we not authority — not to work?

7 who does serve as a soldier at his own charges at any time? who does plant a vineyard, and does not eat of its fruit? or who does feed a flock, and does not eat of the milk of the flock?

8 Do I speak these things according to man? or does not also the law say these things?

9 for in the law of Moses it has been written, 'you[S] shall not muzzle an ox treading out corn;' does God care for the oxen?

10 or because of us by all means does He say [it]? yes, because of us it was written, because in hope ought the plower to plow, and he who is treading [ought] of his hope to partake in hope.

11 If we did sow to you[P] the spiritual things — [is it] great if we do reap your[P] fleshly things?

12 if others do partake of the authority over you[P] — not we more? but we did not use this authority, but we bear all things, that we may give no hindrance to the good news of the Christ.

13 Have you[P] not known that those working about the things of the temple — do eat of the temple, and those waiting at the altar — with the altar are partakers?

14 so also did the Lord direct to those proclaiming the good news: to live of the good news.

15 And I have used none of these things; neither did I write these things that it may be so done in my case, for [it is] good for me rather to die, than that any one may make my glorying void;

16 for if I may proclaim good news, it is no glorying for me, is laid upon me for necessity, and woe is to me if I may not proclaim good news;

17 for if I willing do this, I have a reward; and if unwillingly — with a stewardship I have been entrusted!

18 What, then, is my reward? — that proclaiming good news, without charge I shall make the good news of the Christ, not to abuse my authority in the good news;

19 for being free from all men, I made myself servant to all men, that the more I might gain;

20 and I became to the Jews as a Jew, that Jews I might gain; to those under law as under law, that those under law I might gain;

21 to those without law, as without law — (not being without law to God, but within law to Christ) — that I might gain those without law;

22 I became to the infirm as infirm, that the infirm I might gain; I have become all things to all men, that by all means I may save some.

23 And I do this because of the good news, that I may become a fellow-partaker of it;

24 have you[P] not known that those running in a race — all indeed run, but one does receive the prize? so run you[P], that you[P] may obtain;

25 and every one who is striving, is in all things temperate; these, indeed, then, that they may receive a corruptible crown, but we an incorruptible;

26 I, for that reason, thus run, not as uncertainly, thus I fight, as not beating air;

27 but I chastise my body, and bring [it] into servitude,

for fear that by any means, having preached to others — I myself may become disapproved.

CHAPTER 10

1 And I do not wish you[P] to be ignorant, brethren, that all our fathers were under the cloud, and all passed through the sea,
2 and all were baptized to Moses in the cloud, and in the sea;
3 and all did eat the same spiritual food,
4 and all did drink the same spiritual drink, for they were drinking of a spiritual rock following them, and the rock was the Christ;
5 but God was not well pleased in the most of them, for they were strewn in the wilderness,
6 and those things became types of us, for our not passionately desiring evil things, as also these did desire.
7 Neither become you[P] idolaters, as certain of them, as it has been written, 'The people sat down to eat and to drink, and stood up to play;'
8 neither may we commit whoredom, as certain of them did commit whoredom, and there fell twenty-three thousand in one day;
9 neither may we tempt the Christ, as also certain of them did tempt, and by the serpents did perish;
10 neither murmur you[P], as also some of them did murmur, and did perish by the destroyer.
11 And all these things as types did happen to those persons, and they were written for our admonition, to whom the end of the ages did come,
12 so that he who is thinking to stand — let him observe, for fear that he fall.
13 No temptation has taken you[P] — except human; and God is faithful, who will not allow you[P] to be tempted above what you[P] are able, but He will make, with the temptation, also the outlet, for your[P] being able to bear [it].
14 For what reason, my beloved, flee from the idolatry;
15 I speak as to wise men – you[P] judge what I say:
16 The cup of the blessing that we bless — is it not the fellowship of the blood of the Christ? the bread that we break — is it not the fellowship of the body of the Christ?
17 because one bread, one body, are we the many — for we all do partake of the one bread.
18 See Israel according to the flesh! are not those eating the sacrifices in the fellowship of the altar?
19 what then do I say? that an idol is anything? or that a sacrifice offered to an idol is anything? —
20 [no,] but that the things that the nations sacrifice — they sacrifice to demons and not to God; and I do not wish you[P] to come into the fellowship of the demons.
21 You[P] are not able to drink the cup of the Lord, and the cup of demons; you[P] are not able to partake of the table of the Lord, and of the table of demons;
22 do we arouse the Lord to jealousy? are we stronger than He?
23 All things are lawful to me, but all things are not profitable; all things are lawful to me, but all things do not build up;
24 let no one seek his own — but each another's.
25 Whatever is sold in the meat-market you[P] eat, not inquiring, because of the conscience,
26 for the earth [is] the Lord's, and its fullness;
27 and if any one of the unbelieving do call you[P], and you[P] wish to go, eat all that is set before you[P], nothing inquiring, because of the conscience;
28 and if any one may say to you[P], 'This is a thing sacrificed to an idol,' — do not eat, because of that one who showed [it], and of the conscience, for the earth [is] the Lord's and its fullness:
29 and conscience, I say, not of yourself[S], but of the other, for why [is it] that my liberty is judged by another's conscience?
30 and if I thankfully do partake, why am I evil spoken of, for that for which I give thanks?
31 Whether, then, you[P] eat, or drink, or do anything, do all to the glory of God;
32 become offenseless, both to Jews and Greeks, and to the assembly of God;
33 as I also do please all in all things, not seeking my own profit, but that of many — that they may be saved.

CHAPTER 11

1 You[P] become followers of me, as I also [am] of Christ.
2 And I praise you[P], brethren, that you[P] remember me in all things, and according as I did deliver to you[P], you[P] keep the deliverances,
3 and I wish you[P] to know that the head of every man is the Christ, and the head of a woman is the husband, and the head of Christ is God.
4 Every man praying or prophesying, having the head covered, does dishonor his head,
5 and every woman praying or prophesying with the head uncovered, does dishonor her own head, for it is

one and the same thing with her being shaven,
6 for if a woman is not covered — then let her be shorn,
and if [it is] a shame for a woman to be shorn or shaven
— let her be covered;
7 for a man, indeed, ought not to cover the head, being
the image and glory of God, and a woman is the glory of
a man,
8 for a man is not of a woman, but a woman [is] of a
man,
9 for a man also was not created because of the woman,
but a woman because of the man;
10 because of this the woman ought to have [a token
of] authority upon the head, because of the messengers;
11 but neither [is] a man apart from a woman, nor a
woman apart from a man, in the Lord,
12 for as the woman [is] of the man, so also the man [is]
through the woman, and the all things [are] of God.
13 You[P] judge in your[P] own selves; is it seemly for a
woman to pray to God uncovered?
14 does not even nature itself teach you[P], that if a man
indeed have long hair, it is a dishonor to him?
15 and a woman, if she have long hair, a glory it is to
her, because the hair has been given to her instead of a
covering;
16 and if any one does think to be contentious, we have
no such custom, neither the assemblies of God.
17 And this declaring, I give no praise, because not for
the better, but you[P] come together for the worse;
18 for first, indeed, you[P] coming together in an assembly, I
hear of divisions being among you[P], and partly I believe [it],
19 for it is necessary for sects also to be among you[P],
that those approved may become revealed among you[P];
20 you[P], then, coming together at the same place — it is
not to eat the Lord's supper;
21 for each his own supper does take before in the
eating, and one is hungry, and another is drunk;
22 why, have you[P] not houses to eat and to drink in? or
do you[P] despise the assembly of God, and shame those
not having? what may I say to you[P]? shall I praise you[P]
in this? I do not praise!
23 For I — I received from the Lord that which also I did
deliver to you[P], that the Lord Jesus in the night in which
He was delivered up, took bread,
24 and having given thanks, He broke, and said, 'Take
you[P], eat you[P], this is my body, that is being broken for
you[P]; this do you[P] — to the remembrance of me.'
25 In like manner also the cup after the supping, saying,
'This cup is the new covenant in my blood; this do you[P], as
often as you[P] may drink [it] — to the remembrance of me;'
26 for as often as you[P] may eat this bread, and may
drink this cup, you[P] do show forth the death of the Lord
— till He may come;
27 so that whoever may eat this bread or may drink the
cup of the Lord unworthily, he shall be guilty of the body
and blood of the Lord:
28 and let a man be proving himself, and so let him eat
of the bread, and let him drink of the cup;
29 for he who is eating and drinking unworthily, he does
eat and drink judgment to himself — not discerning the
body of the Lord.
30 Because of this, among you[P] many [are] weak and
sickly, and many do sleep;
31 for if we were discerning ourselves, we would not be
being judged,
32 and being judged by the Lord, we are chastened,
that we may not be condemned with the world;
33 so then, my brethren, coming together to eat, you[P]
wait for one another;
34 and if any one is hungry, let him eat at home, that
you[P] may not come to judgment together; and the rest,
whenever I may come, I shall arrange.

CHAPTER 12

1 And concerning the spiritual things, brethren, I do
not wish you[P] to be ignorant;
2 you[P] have known that you[P] were nations, unto the
dumb idols — as you[P] were led — being carried away;
3 for what reason, I give you[P] to understand that no
one, speaking in the Spirit of God, said Jesus [is] cursed,
and no one is able to say Jesus [is] Lord, except in the
Holy Spirit.
4 And there are diversities of gifts, and the same Spirit;
5 and there are diversities of ministrations, and the same
Lord;
6 and there are diversities of workings, and it is the same
God — who is working the all in all.
7 And to each has been given the manifestation of the
Spirit for profit;
8 for through the Spirit a word of wisdom has been given
to one, and to another a word of knowledge, according
to the same Spirit;
9 and to another faith in the same Spirit, and to another
gifts of healings in the same Spirit;
10 and to another in-workings of mighty deeds; and to
another prophecy; and to another discernings of spirits;
and to another [various] kinds of tongues; and to

another interpretation of tongues:
11 and the one and the same Spirit does work all these, dividing to each severally as he intended.
12 For, even as the body is one, and has many members, and all the members of the one body, being many, are one body, so also [is] the Christ,
13 for also we all were baptized to one body in one Spirit, whether Jews or Greeks, whether servants or freemen, and all were made to drink into one Spirit,
14 for also the body is not one member, but many;
15 if the foot may say, 'Because I am not a hand, I am not of the body;' it is not, because of this, not of the body;
16 and if the ear may say, 'Because I am not an eye, I am not of the body;' it is not, because of this, not of the body?
17 If the whole body [were] an eye, where the hearing? if the whole hearing, where the smelling?
18 and now, God did set the members each one of them in the body, according as He willed,
19 and if all were one member, where the body?
20 and now, indeed, [are] many members, and one body;
21 and an eye is not able to say to the hand, 'I have no need of you[S];' nor again the head to the feet, 'I have no need of you[P].'
22 But much more the members of the body which seem to be more infirm are necessary,
23 and those that we think to be less honorable of the body, around these we put more abundant honor, and our unseemly things have seemliness more abundant,
24 and our seemly things have no need; but God did temper the body together, to the lacking part having given more abundant honor,
25 that there may be no division in the body, but that the members may have the same anxiety for one another,
26 and whether one member does suffer, all the members do suffer with [it], or one member is glorified, all the members do rejoice with [it];
27 and you[P] are the body of Christ, and members in particular.
28 And some, indeed, did God set in the assembly, first apostles, secondly prophets, thirdly teachers, afterwards powers, afterwards gifts of healings, helpings, governings, various kinds of tongues;
29 [are] all apostles? [are] all prophets? [are] all teachers? [are] all powers?
30 have all gifts of healings? do all speak with tongues? do all interpret?
31 and earnestly desire the better gifts; and yet do I show to you[P] a far excelling way:

CHAPTER 13

1 If I speak with the tongues of men and of messengers, and have not love, I have become brass sounding, or a cymbal tinkling;
2 and if I have prophecy, and know all the secrets, and all the knowledge, and if I have all the faith, so as to remove mountains, and have not love, I am nothing;
3 and if I give away all my goods to feed others, and if I give up my body that I may be burned, and have not love, I am profited nothing.
4 The love is long-suffering, it is kind, the love does not envy, the love does not brag about itself, is not puffed up,
5 does not act unseemly, does not seek its own things, is not provoked, does not impute evil,
6 rejoices not over the unrighteousness, and rejoices with the truth;
7 it bears all things, it believes all, it hopes all, it endures all.
8 The love does never fail; and whether [there be] prophecies, they shall become useless; whether tongues, they shall cease; whether knowledge, it shall become useless;
9 for in part we know, and in part we prophecy;
10 and when that which is perfect may come, then that which [is] in part shall become useless.
11 When I was a babe, I was speaking as a babe, I was thinking as a babe, I was reasoning as a babe, and when I have become a man, I have made useless the things of the babe;
12 for we see now through a mirror obscurely, and then face to face; now I know in part, and then I shall fully know, as also I was known;
13 and now there does remain faith, hope, love — these three; and the greatest of these [is] love.

CHAPTER 14

1 Pursue the love, and earnestly seek the spiritual things, and rather that you[P] may prophecy,
2 for he who is speaking in an [unknown] tongue — to men he does not speak, but to God, for no one does listen, and in spirit he does speak secrets;
3 and he who is prophesying to men does speak

edification, and exhortation, and comfort;
4 he who is speaking in an [unknown] tongue, does
edify himself, and he who is prophesying, does edify an
assembly;
5 and I wish you[P] all to speak with tongues, and more
that you[P] may prophecy, for greater is he who is
prophesying than he who is speaking with tongues,
except one may interpret, that the assembly may receive
edification.
6 And now, brethren, if I may come unto you[P] speaking
tongues, what shall I profit you[P], except I shall speak to
you[P] either in revelation, or in knowledge, or in
prophesying, or in teaching?
7 yet the things without life giving sound — whether
pipe or harp — if they may not give a difference in the
sounds, how shall be known that which is piped or that
which is harped?
8 for if also a trumpet may give an uncertain sound,
who shall prepare himself for battle?
9 so also you[P], if through the tongue, you[P] may not
give speech easily understood — how shall that which
is spoken be known? for you[P] shall be speaking to air.
10 There are, it may be, so many kinds of voices in the
world, and none of them is unmeaning,
11 if, then, I do not know the power of the voice, I shall
be to him who is speaking a foreigner, and he who is
speaking, is to me a foreigner;
12 so also you[P], since you[P] are earnestly desirous of
spiritual gifts, seek for the building up of the assembly
that you[P] may abound;
13 for what reason he who is speaking in an [unknown]
tongue — let him pray that he may interpret;
14 for if I pray in an [unknown] tongue, my spirit does
pray, and my understanding is unfruitful.
15 What then is it? I will pray with the spirit, and I will
pray also with the understanding; I will sing psalms with
the spirit, and I will sing psalms also with the
understanding;
16 since, if you[S] may bless with the spirit, he who is
filling the place of the unlearned, how shall he say the
Amen at your[S] giving of thanks, since he has not known
what you[S] do say?
17 for you[S], indeed, do give thanks well, but the other is
not built up!
18 I give thanks to my God — more than you[P] all with
tongues speaking —
19 but in an assembly I wish to speak five words through
my understanding, that others also I may instruct, rather
than myriads of words in an [unknown] tongue.
20 Brethren, become not children in the understanding,
but be you[P] babes in the evil, and become you[P] perfect
in the understanding;
21 in the law it has been written, that, 'With other
tongues and with other lips I will speak to this people,
and not even so will they hear Me, said the Lord;'
22 so that the tongues are for a sign, not to the believing,
but to the unbelieving; and the prophesy [is] not for the
unbelieving, but for the believing,
23 If, for that reason, the whole assembly may come
together, to the same place, and all may speak with
tongues, and there may come in unlearned or
unbelievers, will they not say that you[P] are mad?
24 and if all may prophecy, and any one may come in,
an unbeliever or unlearned, he is convicted by all, he is
discerned by all,
25 and so the secrets of his heart become revealed, and
so having fallen upon [his] face, he will bow before God,
declaring that God really is among you[P].
26 What then is it, brethren? whenever you[P] may come
together, each of you[P] has a psalm, has a teaching, has
a tongue, has a revelation, has an interpretation? let all
things be for building up;
27 if any one do speak an [unknown] tongue, by two,
or at the most, by three, and in turn, and let one interpret;
28 and if there may be no interpreter, let him be silent in
an assembly, and let him speak to himself, and to God.
29 And prophets — let two or three speak, and let the
others discern,
30 and if to another sitting [anything] may be revealed,
let the first be silent;
31 for you[P] are able, one by one, all to prophesy, that all
may learn, and all may be exhorted,
32 and the spiritual gift of prophets are subject to
prophets,
33 for God is not [a God] of tumult, but of peace, as in
all the assemblies of the saints.
34 Your[P] women in the assemblies let them be silent, for
it has not been permitted to them to speak, but to be
subject, as also the law said;
35 and if they wish to learn anything, let them question
their own husbands at home, for it is a shame to women
to speak in an assembly.
36 From you[P] did the word of God come forth? or to
you[P] alone did it come?
37 if any one does think to be a prophet, or spiritual, let
him acknowledge the things that I write to you[P] — that
they are commands of the Lord;
38 and if any one is ignorant — let him be ignorant;

39 so that, brethren, earnestly desire to prophesy, and do not forbid to speak with tongues;
40 let all things be done decently and in order.

CHAPTER 15

1 And I make known to you[P], brethren, the good news that I proclaimed to you[P], which also you[P] did receive, in which also you[P] have stood,
2 through which also you[P] are being saved, in what words I proclaimed good news to you[P], if you[P] hold fast, except you[P] did believe in vain,
3 for I delivered to you[P] first, what also I did receive, that Christ died for our sins, according to the Writings,
4 and that He was buried, and that He has risen on the third day, according to the Writings,
5 and that He appeared to Cephas, then to the twelve,
6 afterwards He appeared to above five hundred brethren at once, of whom the greater part remain till now, and certain also did fall asleep;
7 afterwards He appeared to James, then to all the apostles.
8 And last of all — as to the untimely birth — He appeared also to me,
9 for I am the least of the apostles, who am not worthy to be called an apostle, because I did persecute the assembly of God,
10 and by the grace of God I am what I am, and His grace that [is] towards me came not in vain, but more abundantly did I labor than they all, yet not I, but the grace of God that [is] with me;
11 whether, then, I or they, so we preach, and so you[P] did believe.
12 And if Christ is preached, that out of the dead He has risen, how say certain among you[P], that there is no rising again of dead persons?
13 and if there be no rising again of dead persons, neither has Christ risen;
14 and if Christ has not risen, then void [is] our preaching, and void also your faith,
15 and we also are found false witnesses of God, because we did testify of God that He raised up the Christ, whom He did not raise if then dead persons do not rise;
16 for if dead persons do not rise, neither has Christ risen,
17 and if Christ has not risen, vain is your[P] faith, you[P] are yet in your[P] sins;
18 then, also, those having fallen asleep in Christ did perish;
19 if in this life we have hope in Christ only, of all men we are most to be pitied.
20 And now, Christ has risen out of the dead — He became the first-fruits of those sleeping,
21 for since through man [is] the death, also through man [is] a rising again of the dead,
22 for even as in Adam all die, so also in the Christ all shall be made alive,
23 and each in his proper order, a first-fruit Christ, afterwards those who are the Christ's, in His presence,
24 then — the end, when He may deliver up the reign to God, even the Father, when He may have made all rule useless, and all authority and power —
25 for it is necessary for Him to reign till He may have put all the enemies under His feet —
26 the last enemy is done away — death;
27 for He did put all things under His feet, and, when one may say that all things have been subjected, [it is] evident that He who did subject the all things to Him is excepted,
28 and when the all things may be subjected to Him, then the Son also Himself shall be subject to Him, who did subject to Him the all things, that God may be the all in all.
29 Seeing what shall they do who are baptized for the dead, if the dead do not rise at all? why also are they baptized for the dead?
30 why also do we stand in peril every hour?
31 Every day do I die, by the glorying of you[P] that I have in Christ Jesus our Lord:
32 if after the manner of a man with wild beasts I fought in Ephesus, what the advantage to me if the dead do not rise? let us eat and drink, for to-morrow we die!
33 Be not led astray; evil communications corrupt good manners;
34 awake up, as is right, and sin not; for certain have an ignorance of God; for shame to you[P] I say [it].
35 But some one will say, 'How do the dead rise?
36 unwise! you[S] — what you[S] do sow is not quickened except it may die;
37 and that which you[S] do sow, you[S] do not sow the body that shall be, but bare grain, it may be of wheat, or of some one of the others,
38 and God does give to it a body according as He willed, and to each of the seeds its proper body.
39 All flesh [is] not the same flesh, but there is one flesh of men, and another flesh of beasts, and another of

fishes, and another of birds;
40 and [there are] heavenly bodies, and earthly bodies;
but one [is] the glory of the heavenly, and another that
of the earthly;
41 one glory of sun, and another glory of moon, and
another glory of stars, for star from star does differ in
glory.
42 So also [is] the rising again of the dead: it is sown in
corruption, it is raised in incorruption;
43 it is sown in dishonor, it is raised in glory; it is sown
in weakness, it is raised in power;
44 it is sown a natural body, it is raised a spiritual body;
there is a natural body, and there is a spiritual body;
45 so also it has been written, 'The first man Adam
became a living creature,' the last Adam [is] for a life-
giving spirit,
46 but that which is spiritual [is] not first, but that which
[was] natural, afterwards that which [is] spiritual.
47 The first man [is] out of the earth, earthy; the second
man [is] the Lord out of heaven;
48 as [is] the earthy, such [are] also the earthy; and as
[is] the heavenly, such [are] also the heavenly;
49 and, according as we did bear the image of the earthy,
we shall bear also the image of the heavenly.
50 And this I say, brethren, that flesh and blood is not
able to inherit the reign of God, nor does the corruption
inherit the incorruption;
51 behold, I tell you[P] a secret; we indeed shall not all
sleep, and we all shall be changed;
52 in a moment, in the twinkling of an eye, in the last
trumpet, for it shall sound, and the dead shall be raised
incorruptible, and we — we shall be changed:
53 for it is necessary for this corruptible to put on
incorruption, and this mortal to put on immortality;
54 and when this corruptible may have put on
incorruption, and this mortal may have put on
immortality, then shall be brought to pass the word that
has been written, 'The Death was swallowed up — to
victory;
55 where, O Death, your[S] sting? where, O Hades, your[S]
victory?'
56 and the sting of the death [is] the sin, and the power
of the sin the law;
57 and to God — thanks, to Him who is giving us the
victory through our Lord Jesus Christ;
58 so that, my brethren beloved, become you[P] steadfast,
unmovable, abounding in the work of the Lord at all
times, knowing that your[P] labor is not vain in the Lord.

CHAPTER 16

1 And concerning the collection that [is] for the saints,
as I directed to the assemblies of Galatia, so also you[P]
— do you[P];
2 on every first [day] of the week, let each one of you[P]
lay by him, treasuring up whatever he may have
prospered, that when I may come then collections may
not be made;
3 and whenever I may come, whomsoever you[P] may
approve, through letters, these I will send to carry your[P]
favor to Jerusalem;
4 and if it be meet for me also to go, they shall go with
me.
5 And I will come unto you[P], when I pass through
Macedonia — for I do pass through Macedonia —
6 and with you[P], it may be, I will abide, or even winter,
that you[P] may send me forward wheresoever I go,
7 for I do not wish to see you[P] now in the passing, but
I hope to remain a certain time with you[P], if the Lord may
permit;
8 and I will remain in Ephesus till the Pentecost,
9 for a door has been opened to me — great and effectual
— and withstanders [are] many.
10 And if Timotheus may come, see that he may become
without fear with you[P], for he does work the work of the
Lord, even as I,
11 no one, then, may despise him; and send you[P] him
forward in peace, that he may come to me, for I expect
him with the brethren;
12 and concerning Apollos our brother, much I did
entreat him that he may come unto you[P] with the
brethren, and it was not at all [his] will that he may come
now, and he will come when he may find convenient.
13 Watch you[P], stand in the faith; be men, be strong;
14 let all your[P] things be done in love.
15 And I entreat you[P], brethren, you[P] have known the
household of Stephanas, that it is the first-fruit of Achaia,
and they did set themselves to the ministration to the
saints —
16 that you[P] also be subject to such, and to every one
who is working with [us] and laboring;
17 and I rejoice over the presence of Stephanas, and
Fortunatus, and Achaicus, because these did fill up the
lack of you[P];
18 for they did refresh my spirit and yours[P];
acknowledge you[P], for that reason, those who [are] such.

19 Salute you^{P} do the assemblies of Asia; Aquilas and
Priscilla do salute you^{P} much in the Lord, with the
assembly in their house;
20 all the brethren do salute you^{P}; salute you^{P} one
another in an holy kiss.

21 The salutation of [me] Paul with my hand;
22 if any one does not love the Lord Jesus Christ — let
him be cursed! The Lord has come!
23 The grace of the Lord Jesus Christ [is] with you^{P};
24 my love [is] with you^{P} all in Christ Jesus. Amen.

The SECOND Epistle Of Paul The Apostle To The
CORINTHIANS

CHAPTER 1

1 Paul, an apostle of Jesus Christ, through the will of
God, and Timotheus the brother, to the assembly of God
that is in Corinth, with all the saints who are in all Achaia:
2 Grace to you[P] and peace from God our Father, and the
Lord Jesus Christ!
3 Blessed [is] God, even the Father of our Lord Jesus
Christ, the Father of the mercies, and God of all comfort,
4 who is comforting us in all our tribulation, for our being
able to comfort those in any tribulation through the
comfort with which we are comforted ourselves by God;
5 because, as the sufferings of the Christ do abound to
us, so through the Christ does our comfort abound also;
6 and whether we be in tribulation, [it is] for your[P]
comfort and salvation, that is worked in the enduring of
the same sufferings that we also suffer; whether we are
comforted, [it is] for your[P] comfort and salvation;
7 and our hope [is] steadfast for you[P], knowing that
even as you[P] are partakers of the sufferings — so also
of the comfort.
8 For we do not wish you[P] to be ignorant, brethren, of
our tribulation that happened to us in Asia, that we were
exceedingly burdened above [our] power, so that we
despaired even of life;
9 but we ourselves have had the sentence of the death
in ourselves , that we may not be trusting on ourselves,
but on God, who is raising the dead,
10 who did deliver us out of so great a death, and does
deliver, in whom we have hoped that even yet He will
deliver;
11 you[P] working together also by your[P] supplication
for us, that the gift to us through many persons, through
many may be thankfully acknowledged for us.
12 For our glorying is this: the testimony of our
conscience, that in simplicity and sincerity of God, not
in fleshly wisdom, but in the grace of God, we did
conduct ourselves in the world, and more abundantly
toward you[P];
13 for no other things do we write to you[P], but what
you[P] either do read or also acknowledge, and I hope that
also you[P] shall acknowledge unto the end,
14 according as also you[P] did acknowledge us in part,
that we are your[P] glory, even as also you[P] [are] ours, in
the day of the Lord Jesus;
15 and in this confidence I was purposing to come unto
you[P] before, that a second favor you[P] might have,
16 and to pass through you[P] to Macedonia, and again
from Macedonia to come unto you[P], and to be sent
forward to Judea by you[P].
17 This, for that reason, counseling, did I then use the
lightness; or the things that I counsel, according to the
flesh do I counsel, that it may be with me Yes, yes, and
No, no?
18 and God [is] faithful, that our word unto you[P] became
not Yes and No,
19 for the Son of God, Jesus Christ, having been
preached among you[P] through us — through me and
Silvanus and Timotheus — did not become Yes and No,
but in Him it has become Yes;
20 for as many as [are] promises of God, in Him [are] the
Yes, and in Him the Amen, for glory to God through us;
21 and He who is confirming you[P] into Christ with us,
and did anoint us, [is] God,
22 who also sealed us, and gave the earnest of the Spirit
in our hearts.
23 And I do call upon my soul for a witness on God,
that sparing you[P], I came not yet to Corinth;
24 not that we are lords over your[P] faith, but we are
workers together with your[P] joy, for you[P] stand by the
faith.

CHAPTER 2

1 And I decided this to myself, not to come in sorrow
unto you[P] again,
2 for if I make you[P] sorry, then who is he who is making
me glad, except he who is made sorry by me?
3 and I wrote to you[P] this same thing, that having come,
I may not have sorrow from them of whom it is necessary

for me to have joy, having confidence in you[P] all, that
my joy is of you all,
4 for out of much tribulation and pressure of heart I
wrote to you[P] through many tears, not that you[P] might
be made sorry, but that you[P] might know the love that I
have more abundantly toward you[P].
5 And if any one has caused sorrow, he has not caused
sorrow to me, but in part, that I may not burden you[P] all;
6 sufficient to such a one is this punishment, that [is]
by the more part,
7 so that, on the contrary, [it is] rather for you[P] to forgive
and to comfort, for fear that by over abundant sorrow
such a one may be swallowed up;
8 for what reason, I call upon you[P] to confirm love to
him,
9 for, for this also did I write, that I might know the proof
of you[P], whether you[P] are obedient in regard to all things.
10 And to whom you[P] forgive anything — I also; for I
also, if I have forgiven anything, to whom I have forgiven
[it], because of you[P] — in the person of Christ — [I
forgive it,]
11 that we may not be over-reached by the Adversary,
for we are not ignorant of his devices.
12 And having come to Troas for the good news of the
Christ, and a door having been opened to me in the Lord,
13 I have not had rest to my spirit, on my not finding
Titus my brother, but having taken leave of them, I went
forth to Macedonia;
14 and to God [are] thanks, who at all times is leading
us in triumph in the Christ, and the fragrance of His
knowledge He is revealing in every place through us,
15 because we are a sweet fragrance of Christ to God, in
those being saved, and in those being lost;
16 to the one, indeed, a fragrance of death to death, and
to the other, a fragrance of life to life; and who is
sufficient for these things?
17 for we are not as the many, adulterating the word of
God, but as of sincerity — but as of God; in the presence
of God, in Christ we do speak.

CHAPTER 3

1 Do we begin again to recommend ourselves, except
we need, as some, letters of recommendation unto you[P],
or from you[P]?
2 you[P] are our letter, having been written in our hearts,
known and read by all men,
3 made known that you[P] are a letter of Christ ministered
by us, written not with ink, but with the Spirit of the
living God, not in the tablets of stone, but in fleshy
tablets of the heart,
4 and such trust we have through the Christ toward
God,
5 not that we are sufficient of ourselves to think
anything, as of ourselves, but our sufficiency [is] of God,
6 who also made us sufficient [to be] ministrants of a
new covenant, not of letter, but of spirit; for the letter
does kill, and the spirit does make alive.
7 and if the ministration of the death, in letters, engraved
in stones, came in glory, so that the sons of Israel were
not able to look steadfastly to the face of Moses,
because of the glory of his face — which was being made
useless,
8 how shall the ministration of the Spirit not be more in
glory?
9 for if the ministration of the condemnation [is] glory,
much more does the ministration of the righteousness
abound in glory;
10 for also even that which has been glorious, has not
been glorious — in this respect, because of the superior
glory;
11 for if that which is being made useless [is] through
glory, much more that which is remaining [is] in glory.
12 Having, then, such hope, we use much freedom of
speech,
13 and [are] not as Moses, who was putting a veil upon
his own face, for the sons of Israel not steadfastly to
look to the end of that which is being made useless,
14 but their minds were hardened, for unto this day the
same veil at the reading of the Old Covenant does remain
unwithdrawn — which is being made useless in Christ —
15 but till today, when Moses is read, a veil does lie
upon their heart,
16 and whenever they may turn unto the Lord, the veil
is taken away.
17 And the Lord is the Spirit; and where the Spirit of the
Lord [is], there [is] liberty;
18 and we all, with unveiled face, beholding the glory
of the Lord in a mirror, are being transformed to the same
image, from glory to glory, even as by the Spirit of the
Lord.

CHAPTER 4

1 Because of this, having this ministration, according
as we did receive kindness, we do not faint,

2 but did renounce the hidden things of shame for
ourselves, not walking in craftiness, nor deceitfully using
the word of God, but by the manifestation of the truth
recommending ourselves unto every conscience of men,
before God;
3 and if also our good news is veiled, it is veiled in those
perishing,
4 in whom the god of this age did blind the minds of the
unbelieving, that there does not shine forth to them the
enlightening of the good news of the glory of the Christ,
who is the image of God;
5 for we do not preach ourselves, but Christ Jesus —
Lord, and ourselves your[P] servants because of Jesus;
6 because [it is] God who said, Out of darkness light
[is] to shine, who did shine in our hearts, for the
enlightening of the knowledge of the glory of God in
the face of Jesus Christ.
7 And we have this treasure in earthen vessels, that the
excellency of the power may be of God, and not of us;
8 being in tribulation on every side, but not restricted;
perplexed, but not in despair;
9 persecuted, but not forsaken; cast down, but not
destroyed;
10 at all times the dying of the Lord Jesus bearing about
in the body, that the life also of Jesus in our body may
be revealed,
11 for always are we who are living delivered up to death
because of Jesus, that the life also of Jesus may be
revealed in our dying flesh,
12 so that, the death indeed does work in us, and the
life in you[P].
13 And having the same spirit of the faith, according to
that which has been written, 'I believed, for that reason
I did speak;' we also do believe, for that reason also do
we speak;
14 knowing that He who did raise up the Lord Jesus,
shall raise us up also through Jesus, and shall present
with you[P],
15 for the all things [are] because of you[P], that the grace
having been multiplied, because of the thanksgiving of
the more, may abound to the glory of God;
16 for what reason, we faint not, but if also our outward
man does decay, yet the inward is renewed day by day;
17 for the momentary light matter of our tribulation, more
and more exceedingly an age-during weight of glory does
work out for us —
18 we not looking to the things seen, but to the things
not seen; for the things seen [are] temporary, but the
things not seen [are] age-during.

CHAPTER 5

1 For we have known that if our earthly house of the
tabernacle may be thrown down, we have a building from
God, an house not made with hands — age-during — in
the heavens,
2 for also in this we groan, earnestly desiring to clothe
ourselves with our dwelling that is from heaven,
3 if so be that, having clothed ourselves, we shall not
be found naked,
4 for we also who are in the tabernacle do groan, being
burdened, seeing we wish not to unclothe ourselves,
but to clothe ourselves, that the mortal may be
swallowed up of the life.
5 And He who did work us to this self-same thing [is]
God, who also did give the earnest of the Spirit to us;
6 having courage, then, at all times, and knowing that
being at home in the body, we are away from home from
the Lord, —
7 for we walk through faith, not through sight —
8 we have courage, and are well pleased rather to be
away from the home of the body, and to be at home with
the Lord.
9 For what reason also we are ambitious, whether at
home or away from home, to be well pleasing to him,
10 it is necessary for all of us to be revealed before the
tribunal of the Christ, that each one may receive the
things [done] through the body, in reference to the
things that he did, whether good or evil;
11 having known, for that reason, the fear of the Lord,
we persuade men, and we are revealed to God, and I hope
also in your[P] consciences to have been revealed;
12 for not again do we recommend ourselves to you[P],
but we are giving occasion to you[P] of glorifying in our
behalf, that you[P] may have [something] in reference to
those glorifying in face and not in heart;
13 for whether we were beside ourselves, [it was] to
God; whether we be of sound mind — [it is] to you[P],
14 for the love of the Christ does constrain us, having
judged thus: that if one for all died, then the whole died,
15 and he died for all, that those living, no more may
live to themselves, but to him who died for them, and
was raised again.
16 So that we from this time on have known no one
according to the flesh, and even if we have known Christ
according to the flesh, yet now we know him no more;
17 so that if any one [is] in Christ — [he is] a new
creature; the old things did pass away, behold, the all

things have become new.
18 And the all things [are] of God, who reconciled us to
Himself through Jesus Christ, and did give to us the
ministration of the reconciliation,
19 how that God was in Christ — a world reconciling to
Himself, not reckoning their trespasses to them; and
having put the word of the reconciliation in us,
20 in behalf of Christ, then, we are ambassadors, as if
God were calling through us, we beg, in behalf of Christ,
'Be you[P] reconciled to God;'
21 for Him who did not know sin, He did make sin in our
behalf, that we may become the righteousness of God
in him.

CHAPTER 6

1 And working together also we call upon [you[P]] that
you[P] receive not the grace of God in vain—
2 for He said, 'In an acceptable time I did hear you[S], and
in a day of salvation I did help you[S], behold, now [is] a
well-accepted time; behold, now, a day of salvation,' —
3 in nothing giving any cause of offence, that the
ministration may be not blamed,
4 but recommending ourselves in everything as God's
ministrants; in much patience, in tribulations, in
necessities, in distresses,
5 in stripes, in imprisonments, in insurrections, in labors,
in watchings, in fastings,
6 in pureness, in knowledge, in long-suffering, in
kindness, in the Holy Spirit, in love unfeigned,
7 in the word of truth, in the power of God, through the
armor of the righteousness, on the right and on the left,
8 through glory and dishonor, through evil report and
good report, as leading astray, and true;
9 as unknown, and recognized; as dying, and behold,
we live; as chastened, and not put to death;
10 as sorrowful, and always rejoicing; as poor, and
making many rich; as having nothing, and possessing
all things.
11 Our mouth has been open unto you[P], O Corinthians,
our heart has been enlarged!
12 you[P] are not restricted in us, and you[P] are restricted
in your[P] [own] bowels,
13 and [as] a recompense of the same kind, (I say [it] as
to children,) be you[P] enlarged — also you[P]!
14 Become not yoked with others — unbelievers, for
what partaking [is there] to righteousness and
lawlessness?
15 and what fellowship to light with darkness? and what
concord to Christ with Belial? or what part to a believer
with an unbeliever?
16 and what agreement to the sanctuary of God with
idols? for you[P] are a sanctuary of the living God,
according as God said — 'I will dwell in them, and will
walk among [them], and I will be their God, and they shall
be My people,
17 for what reason, come you[P] forth out of the midst of
them, and be separated, said the Lord, and do not touch
an unclean thing, and I — I will receive you[P],
18 and I will be to you[P] for a Father, and you[P] — you[P]
shall be to Me for sons and daughters, said the Lord
Almighty.'

CHAPTER 7

1 Having, then, these promises, beloved, may we cleanse
ourselves from every pollution of flesh and spirit,
perfecting sanctification in the fear of God;
2 receive us; we did wrong no one ; we did waste no
one; we did defraud no one;
3 not to condemn you[P] do I say [it], for I have said before
that in our hearts you[P] are to die with and to live with;
4 great [is] my freedom of speech unto you[P], great my
glory on your[P] behalf; I have been filled with the comfort,
I overabound with the joy on all our tribulation,
5 for also we, having come to Macedonia, no relaxation
has our flesh had, but on every side we are in tribulation,
without [are] fightings, within — fears;
6 but He who is comforting the cast-down — God —
He did comfort us in the presence of Titus;
7 and not only in his presence, but also in the comfort
with which he was comforted over you[P], declaring to us
your[P] longing desire, your[P] lamentation, your[P] zeal for
me, so that the more I did rejoice,
8 because even if I made you[P] sorry in the letter, I do
not repent — if even I did repent — for I perceive that
the letter, even if for an hour, did make you[P] sorry.
9 I do rejoice now, not that you[P] were made sorry, but
that you[P] were made sorry to reformation, for you[P] were
made sorry toward God, that in nothing you[P] might
receive damage from us;
10 for the sorrow toward God not to be repented of does
work reformation to salvation, and the sorrow of the
world does work death,
11 for, behold, this same thing — your[P] being made sorry
toward God — how it does work much diligence in you[P]!

but defense, but displeasure, but fear, but longing desire, but zeal, but revenge; in every thing you[P] did approve yourselves[P] to be pure in the matter.

12 If, then, I also wrote to you[P] — not for his cause who did wrong, nor for his cause who did suffer wrong, but for our diligence in your[P] behalf being revealed unto you[P] before God —

13 because of this we have been comforted in your[P] comfort, and more abundantly the more did we rejoice in the joy of Titus, that his spirit has been refreshed from you[P] all;

14 because if I have boasted to him anything in your[P] behalf, I was not put to shame; but as all things we did speak to you[P] in truth, so also our boasting before Titus became truth,

15 and his tender affection is more abundantly toward you[P], remembering the obedience of you[P] all, how with fear and trembling you[P] did receive him;

16 I rejoice, for that reason, that in everything I have courage in you[P].

CHAPTER 8

1 And we make known to you[P], brethren, the grace of God, that has been given in the assemblies of Macedonia,

2 because in much trial of tribulation the abundance of their joy, and their deep poverty, did abound to the riches of their liberality;

3 because, according to [their] power, I testify, and above [their] power, they were willing of themselves,

4 with much entreaty calling on us to receive the favor and the fellowship of the ministration to the saints,

5 and not according as we expected, but they did give themselves first to the Lord, and to us, through the will of God,

6 so that we exhorted Titus, that, according as he did begin before, so also he may finish to you[P] also this favor,

7 but even as you[P] do abound in every thing, in faith, and word, and knowledge, and all diligence, and in your[P] love to us, that also you[P] may abound in this grace;

8 not according to command do I speak, but because of the diligence of others, and of your[P] love proving the genuineness,

9 for you[P] know the grace of our Lord Jesus Christ, that He became poor because of you[P] — being rich, that you[P] by that poverty may become rich.

10 and I do give an opinion in this: for this [is] expedient to you[P], who not only to do, but also to will, did begin before — a year ago,

11 and now also finish doing [it], that even as [there is] the readiness of the will, so also the finishing, out of that which you[P] have,

12 for if the willing mind is present, according to that which any one may have it is well-accepted, not according to that which he has not;

13 for not that release for others, and you[P] pressured, [do I speak,]

14 but by equality, at the present time your[P] abundance — for their want, that also their abundance may be for your[P] want, that there may be equality,

15 according as it has been written, 'He who [did gather] much, had nothing over; and he who [did gather] little, had no lack.'

16 And thanks to God, who is putting the same diligence for you[P] in the heart of Titus,

17 because indeed the exhortation he accepted, and being more diligent, of his own accord he went forth unto you[P],

18 and we sent with him the brother, whose praise in the good news [is] through all the assemblies,

19 and not only so, but who was also appointed by vote by the assemblies, our fellow-traveler, that is ministered by us with this favor, unto the glory of the same Lord, and your[P] willing mind;

20 avoiding this, for fear that any one may blame us in this abundance that is ministered by us,

21 providing right things, not only before the Lord, but also before men;

22 and we sent with them our brother, whom we proved in many things many times being diligent, and now much more diligent, by the great confidence that is toward you[P],

23 whether — about Titus — my partner and towards you[P] fellow-worker, whether — our brethren, apostles of assemblies — glory of Christ;

24 the showing as a result of your[P] love, and of our boasting on your[P] behalf, to them show you[P], even in the face of the assemblies.

CHAPTER 9

1 For, indeed, concerning the ministration that [is] for the saints, it is superfluous for me to write to you[P],

2 for I have known your[P] readiness of mind, which I

boast of to Macedonians in your[P] behalf, that Achaia has been prepared a year ago, and the zeal of you[P] did stir up the more part,
3 and I sent the brethren, that our boasting on your[P] behalf may not be made vain in this respect; that, according as I said, you[P] may be ready,
4 for fear that if Macedonians may come with me, and find you[P] unprepared, we — we may be put to shame (that we say not — you[P]) in this same confidence of boasting.
5 For that reason, I thought [it] necessary to exhort the brethren, that they may go before to you[P], and may make up before your[P] formerly announced blessing, that this be ready, as a blessing, and not as covetousness.
6 And this: He who is sowing sparingly, also shall reap sparingly; and he who is sowing in blessings, also shall reap in blessings;
7 each one, according as he does purpose in heart, not out of sorrow or out of necessity, for God does love a cheerful giver,
8 and God [is] able to cause all grace to abound to you[P], that always having all sufficiency in every thing, you[P] may abound to every good work,
9 (according as it has been written, 'He dispersed abroad, he gave to the poor, his righteousness does remain to the age,')
10 and may He who is supplying seed to the sower, and bread for food, supply and multiply your[P] sown seed, and increase the fruits of your[P] righteousness,
11 in every thing being enriched to all liberality, which does work through us thanksgiving to God,
12 because the ministration of this service not only is supplying the wants of the saints, but is also abounding through many thanksgivings to God,
13 through the proof of this ministration glorifying God for the subjection of your[P] confession to the good news of the Christ, and [for] the liberality of the fellowship to them and to all,
14 and by their supplication in your[P] behalf, longing after you[P] because of the exceeding grace of God upon you[P];
15 thanks also to God for His unspeakable gift!

CHAPTER 10

1 And I, Paul, myself, do call upon you[P] — through the meekness and gentleness of the Christ — who in presence, indeed [am] humble among you[P], and being absent, have courage toward you[P],
2 and I beg [you[P]], that, being present, I may not have courage, with the confidence with which I reckon to be bold against certain reckoning us as walking according to the flesh;
3 for walking in the flesh, not according to the flesh do we war,
4 for the weapons of our warfare [are] not fleshly, but powerful to God for bringing down of strongholds,
5 bringing down reasonings, and every high thing lifted up against the knowledge of God, and bringing into captivity every thought to the obedience of the Christ,
6 and being in readiness to avenge every disobedience, whenever your[P] obedience may be fulfilled.
7 The things in presence do you[P] see? if any one has trusted in himself to be Christ's, this let him reckon again from himself, that according as he is Christ's, so also we [are] Christ's;
8 for even if also anything I shall boast more abundantly concerning our authority, that the Lord gave us for building up, and not for casting you[P] down, I shall not be ashamed;
9 that I may not seem as if I would terrify you[P] through the letters,
10 'because the letters indeed — said one — [are] weighty and strong, and the bodily presence weak, and the speech despicable.'
11 This one — let him reckon thus: that such as we are in word, through letters, being absent, such also, being present, [we are] in deed.
12 For we do not make bold to rank or to compare ourselves with certain of those commending themselves, but they, among themselves measuring themselves, and comparing themselves with themselves, are not wise,
13 and we in regard to the unmeasured things will not boast ourselves, but after the measure of the line that the God of measure did appoint to us — to reach even unto you[P];
14 for not as not reaching to you[P] do we stretch ourselves overmuch, for even did we come unto you[P] in the good news of the Christ,
15 not boasting of the things not measured, in other men's labors, and having hope — your[P] faith increasing — to be enlarged in you[P], according to our line — into abundance,
16 to proclaim good news in the [places] beyond you[P], not in another's line in regard to the things made ready, to boast;
17 and he who is boasting — let him boast in the Lord;

18 for not he who is commending himself is approved, but he whom the Lord does commend.

CHAPTER 11

1 O that you[P] were bearing with me a little of the folly, but you[P] also do bear with me:
2 for I am zealous for you[P] with zeal of God, for I did betroth you[P] to one husband, a pure virgin, to present to Christ,
3 and I fear, that, as the serpent did beguile Eve in his subtlety, so your[P] minds may be corrupted from the simplicity that [is] in the Christ;
4 for if, indeed, he who is coming does preach another Jesus whom we did not preach, or another Spirit you[P] receive which you[P] did not receive, or other good news which you[P] did not accept — well were you[P] bearing [it],
5 for I reckon that I have been nothing behind the very chiefest apostles,
6 and even if unlearned in word — yet not in knowledge, but in every thing we were made known in all things to you[P].
7 The sin did I do — humbling myself that you[P] might be exalted, because I did proclaim freely the good news of God to you[P]?
8 other assemblies I did rob, having taken wages, for your[P] ministration;
9 and being present with you[P], and having been in want, I was chargeable to no one, for my lack did the brethren supply — having come from Macedonia — and in everything burdenless to you[P] I did keep myself, and will keep.
10 The truth of Christ is in me, because this boasting shall not be stopped in regard to me in the regions of Achaia;
11 for what reason? because I do not love you[P]? God has known!
12 and what I do, I also will do, that I may cut off the occasion of those wishing an occasion, that in that which they boast they may be found according as we also;
13 for those such [are] false apostles, deceitful workers, transforming themselves into apostles of Christ,
14 and no wonder — for even the Adversary does transform himself into a messenger of light;
15 no great thing, then, if also his ministrants do transform themselves as ministrants of righteousness — whose end shall be according to their works.
16 Again I say, may no one think me to be a fool; and if otherwise, even as a fool receive me, that I also may boast a little.
17 That which I speak, I speak not according to the Lord, but as in foolishness, in this the confidence of boasting;
18 since many boast according to the flesh, I also will boast:
19 for gladly do you[P] bear with the fools — being wise,
20 for you[P] bear, if any one is bringing you[P] under bondage, if any one does devour, if any one does take away, if any one does exalt himself, if any one does strike you[P] on the face;
21 I speak in reference to dishonor, how that we were weak, and in whatever any one is bold — in foolishness I say [it] — I also am bold.
22 Hebrews are they? I also! Israelites are they? I also! seed of Abraham are they? I also!
23 ministrants of Christ are they? — I speak as beside myself — I more; in labors more abundantly, in stripes above measure, in prisons more frequently, in deaths many times;
24 from Jews five times forty [stripes] save one I did receive;
25 three times was I beaten with rods, once was I stoned, three times was I shipwrecked, a night and a day in the deep I have passed;
26 journeyings many times, perils of rivers, perils of robbers, perils from kindred, perils from nations, perils in city, perils in wilderness, perils in sea, perils among false brethren;
27 in laboriousness and painfulness, in watchings many times, in hunger and thirst, in fastings many times, in cold and nakedness;
28 apart from the things without — the crowding upon me that is daily — the care of all the assemblies.
29 Who is infirm, and I am not infirm? who is stumbled, and I am not fired;
30 if it is necessary for [me] to boast, I will boast of the things of my infirmity;
31 the God and Father of our Lord Jesus Christ — who is blessed to the ages — has known that I do not lie! —
32 In Damascus the ethnarch of Aretas the king was watching the city of the Damascenes, wishing to seize me,
33 and I was let down through a window in a rope basket, through the wall, and fled out of his hands.

CHAPTER 12

1 To boast, really, is not profitable for me, for I will come to visions and revelations of the Lord.

2 I have known a man in Christ, fourteen years ago —
whether in the body I have not known, whether out of
the body I have not known, God has known — such an
one being caught away unto the third heaven;
3 and I have known such a man — whether in the body,
whether out of the body, I have not known, God has
known, —
4 that he was caught away to the paradise, and heard
unutterable sayings, that it is not possible for man to
speak.
5 I will boast of such an one, and I will not boast of
myself, except in my infirmities,
6 for if I may wish to boast, I shall not be a fool, for truth
I will say; but I forebear, for fear that any one in regard
to me may think anything above what he does see me,
or does hear anything of me;
7 and that by the exceeding greatness of the revelations
I might not be exalted overmuch, there was given to me
a thorn in the flesh, a messenger of the Adversary, that
he might buffet me, that I might not be exalted overmuch.
8 Concerning this thing did I call upon the Lord three
times, that it might depart from me,
9 and He said to me, 'Sufficient for you[S] is My grace,
for My power is perfected in infirmity;' most gladly, for
that reason, will I rather boast in my infirmities, that the
power of the Christ may rest on me:
10 for what reason I am well pleased in infirmities, in
damages, in necessities, in persecutions, in distresses
— for Christ; for whenever I am infirm, then I am
powerful;
11 I have become a fool — boasting; you[P] — you[P] did
compel me; for I ought to have been commended by
you[P], for in nothing was I behind the very chiefest
apostles — even if I am nothing.
12 The signs, indeed, of the apostle were worked among
you[P] in all patience, in signs, and wonders, and mighty
deeds,
13 for what is there in which you[P] were inferior to the
rest of the assemblies, except that I myself was not a
burden to you[P]? forgive me this injustice!
14 Behold, a third time I am ready to come unto you[P],
and I will not be a burden to you[P], for I seek not yours[P],
but you[P], for the children ought not to lay up for the
parents, but the parents for the children,
15 and I most gladly will spend and be entirely spent
for your[P] souls, even if, more abundantly loving you[P], I
am loved less.
16 And be it [so], I — I did not burden you[P], but being
crafty, with guile I did take you[P];
17 any one of those whom I have sent unto you[P] — did
I take advantage of you[P] by him?
18 I entreated Titus, and did send with [him] the brother;
did Titus take advantage of you[P]? did we not walk in
the same spirit? — did we not in the same steps?
19 Again, think you[P] that we are making defense to
you[P]? We do speak before God in Christ; and the all
things, beloved, [are] for your[P] up-building,
20 for I fear that, having come, I may find you[P] not such
as I wish, and I — I may be found by you[P] such as you[P]
do not wish, for fear that there be strifes, envyings,
wraths, revelries, evil-speakings, whisperings, puffings
up, insurrections,
21 for fear that again having come, my God may humble
me in regard to you[P], and I may mourn many of those
having sinned before, and not having reformed
concerning the uncleanness, and whoredom, and
lasciviousness, that they did practice.

CHAPTER 13

1 This third time do I come unto you[P]; on the mouth of
two witnesses or three shall every saying be established;
2 I have said before, and I say [it] before, as being
present, the second time, and being absent, now, do I
write to those having sinned before, and to all the rest,
that if I come again, I will not spare,
3 since you[P] seek a proof of the Christ speaking in me,
who is not infirm to you[P], but is powerful in you[P],
4 for even if he was crucified from infirmity, yet he does
live from the power of God; for we also are weak in him, but
we shall live with him from the power of God toward you[P].
5 You[P] try your[P] own selves, if you[P] are in the faith;
you[P] prove your[P] own selves; do you[P] not know your[P]
own selves, that Jesus Christ is in you[P], if you[P] be not in
some respect disapproved of?
6 and I hope that you[P] shall know that we — we are not
disapproved of;
7 and I pray before God that you[P] do no evil, not that
we may appear approved, but that you[P] may do that
which is right, and we may be as disapproved;
8 for we are not able to do anything against the truth,
but for the truth;
9 for we rejoice when we may be infirm, and you[P] may
be powerful; and this also we pray for — your[P]
perfection!
10 because of this, these things — being absent — I
write, that being present, I may not treat [any] sharply,

according to the authority that the Lord did give me for
building up, and not for casting down.
11 From this time forth, brethren, rejoice; be made
perfect, be comforted, be of the same mind, be at peace,
and the God of the love and peace shall be with you[P];
12 salute one another in an holy kiss;
13 all the saints do salute you[P];
14 the grace of the Lord Jesus Christ, and the love of
God, and the fellowship of the Holy Spirit, [is] with you[P]
all! Amen.

The Epistle Of Paul The Apostle To The
GALATIANS

CHAPTER 1

1 Paul, an apostle — not from men, nor through man,
but through Jesus Christ, and God the Father, who did
raise him out of the dead —
2 and all the brethren with me, to the assemblies of
Galatia:
3 Grace to you[P], and peace from God the Father, and our
Lord Jesus Christ,
4 who did give Himself for our sins, that He might deliver
us out of the present evil age, according to the will of
God even our Father,
5 to whom [is] the glory to the ages of the ages. Amen.
6 I wonder that you[P] are so quickly removed from Him
who did call you[P] in the grace of Christ to another good
news;
7 that is not another, except there be certain who are
troubling you[P], and wishing to pervert the good news
of the Christ;
8 but even if we or a messenger out of heaven may
proclaim good news to you[P] different from what we did
proclaim to you[P] — let him be cursed!
9 as we have said before, and now say again, If any one
may proclaim good news to you[P] different from what
you[P] did receive — let him be cursed!
10 for now do I persuade men, or God? or do I seek to
please men? for if yet I did please men — I should not
be Christ's servant.
11 And I make known to you[P], brethren, the good news
that were proclaimed by me, that it is not according to
man,
12 for neither did I receive it from man, nor was I taught
[it], but through a revelation of Jesus Christ,
13 for you[P] did hear of my behavior once in Judaism,
that I was exceedingly persecuting the assembly of God,
and wasting it,
14 and I was advancing in Judaism above many equals
in age in mine own race, being more abundantly zealous
of my fathers' deliverances,
15 and when God was well pleased — having separated
me from the womb of my mother, and having called [me]
through His grace —
16 to reveal His Son in me, that I might proclaim Him
good news among the nations, immediately I conferred
not with flesh and blood,
17 nor did I go up to Jerusalem unto those who were
apostles before me, but I went away to Arabia, and again
returned to Damascus,
18 then, after three years I went up to Jerusalem to
enquire about Peter, and remained with him fifteen days,
19 and I did not see other of the apostles, except James,
the brother of the Lord.
20 And the things that I write to you[P], behold, before
God — I lie not;
21 then I came to the regions of Syria and of Cilicia,
22 and was unknown by face to the assemblies of Judea,
that [are] in Christ,
23 and only they were hearing, that 'he who is
persecuting us then, does now proclaim good news —
the faith that then he was wasting;'
24 and they were glorifying God in me.

CHAPTER 2

1 Then, after fourteen years again I went up to Jerusalem
with Barnabas, having taken with me also Titus;
2 and I went up by revelation, and did submit to them
the good news that I preach among the nations, and
privately to those esteemed, for fear that in vain I might
run or did run;
3 but not even Titus, who [is] with me, being a Greek,
was compelled to be circumcised —
4 and [that] because of the false brethren brought in
unawares, who did come in privily to spy out our liberty
that we have in Christ Jesus, that they might bring us
under bondage,
5 to whom not even for an hour we gave place by
subjection, that the truth of the good news might remain
to you[P].
6 And from those who were esteemed to be something

— whatever they were then, it makes no difference to me — God accepts not the face of man, for — those esteemed did add nothing to me,
7 but, on the contrary, having seen that I have been entrusted with the good news of the uncircumcision, as Peter with [that] of the circumcision,
8 for He who did work with Peter to the apostleship of the circumcision, did work also in me in regard to the nations,
9 and having known the grace that was given to me, James, and Cephas, and John, who were esteemed to be pillars, they did give to me a right hand of fellowship, and to Barnabas, that we to the nations, and they [may go] to the circumcision,
10 only, that we should be mindful of the poor, which also I was diligent — this very thing — to do.
11 And when Peter came to Antioch, to the face I stood up against him, because he was blameworthy,
12 for before the coming of certain from James, he was eating with the nations, and when they came, he was withdrawing and separating himself, fearing those of the circumcision,
13 and dissemble with him also did the other Jews, so that also Barnabas was carried away by their dissimulation.
14 But when I saw that they are not walking uprightly to the truth of the good news, I said to Peter before all, 'If you[S], being a Jew, do live in the manner of the nations, and not in the manner of the Jews, how do you[S] compel the nations to Judaize?
15 we by nature Jews, and not sinners of the nations,
16 having known also that a man is not declared righteous by works of law, if not through the faith of Jesus Christ, also we did believe in Christ Jesus, that we might be declared righteous by the faith of Christ, and not by works of law, for what reason shall no flesh be declared righteous by works of law.'
17 And if, seeking to be declared righteous in Christ, we ourselves also were found sinners, [is] then Christ a ministrant of sin? let it not be!
18 for if the things I threw down, I build these up again, I set myself forth a transgressor;
19 for I through law, did die, that I may live to God;
20 I have been crucified with Christ, and I do live no more, and Christ does live in me; and that which I now live in the flesh — I live in the faith of the Son of God, who did love me and did give himself for me;
21 I do not make void the grace of God, for if righteousness [be] through law — then Christ died in vain.

CHAPTER 3

1 O thoughtless Galatians, who did bewitch you[P], not to obey the truth — before whose eyes Jesus Christ crucified was described before among you[P]?
2 this only do I wish to learn from you[P] — did you[P] receive the Spirit by works of law, or by the hearing of faith?
3 so thoughtless are you[P]! having begun in the Spirit, now do you[P] end in the flesh?
4 so many things did you[P] suffer in vain! if, indeed, even in vain.
5 He, for that reason, who is supplying the Spirit to you[P], and working mighty acts among you[P] — [is it] by works of law or by the hearing of faith?
6 according as Abraham did believe God, and it was reckoned to him — to righteousness;
7 know you[P], then, that those of faith — these are sons of Abraham,
8 and the Writing having foreseen that by faith God does declare righteous the nations, did proclaim to Abraham before the good news —
9 'Blessed shall be all the nations in you[S];' so that those of faith are blessed with the faithful Abraham,
10 for as many as are of works of law are under a curse, for it has been written, 'Cursed [is] every one who is not remaining in all things that have been written in the Book of the Law — to do them,'
11 and that in law no one is declared righteous with God, is evident, because 'The righteous shall live by faith;'
12 and the law is not by faith, but — 'The man who did them shall live in them.'
13 Christ did redeem us from the curse of the law, having become a curse for us, for it has been written, 'Cursed is every one who is hanging on a tree,'
14 that the blessing of Abraham may come to the nations in Christ Jesus, that we may receive the promise of the Spirit through the faith.
15 Brethren, as a man I say [it], no one does make void or does add to even a confirmed covenant of man,
16 and to Abraham were the promises spoken, and to his seed; He does not say, 'And to seeds,' as of many, but as of one, 'And to your[S] seed,' which is Christ;
17 and this I say, A covenant confirmed before by God to Christ, the law, that came four hundred and thirty years after, does not set aside, to make void the promise,
18 for if the inheritance [be] by law, [it is] no more by

promise, but God did grant [it] to Abraham through
promise.
19 Why, then, the law? it was added on account of the
transgressions, till the seed might come to which the
promise had been made, having been set in order
through messengers in the hand of a mediator —
20 and the mediator is not of one, and God is one —
21 the law, then, [is] against the promises of God? — let
it not be! for if a law was given that was able to make
alive, truly there would have been the righteousness by
law,
22 but the Writing did shut up the whole under sin, that
the promise by faith of Jesus Christ may be given to
those believing.
23 And before the coming of the faith, we were being
kept under law, shut up to the faith about to be revealed,
24 so that the law became our child-conductor — to
Christ, that by faith we may be declared righteous,
25 and the faith having come, we are under a child-
conductor no more,
26 for you[P] are all sons of God through the faith in Christ
Jesus,
27 for as many as were baptized to Christ did put on
Christ;
28 there is not here Jew or Greek, there is not here
servant nor freeman, there is not here male and female,
for all you[P] are one in Christ Jesus;
29 and if you[P] [are] of Christ then you[P] are seed of
Abraham, and according to promise — heirs.

CHAPTER 4

1 And I say, so long time as the heir is a babe, he differs
nothing from a servant — being lord of all,
2 but is under tutors and stewards till the time appointed
of the father,
3 so also we, when we were babes, were in servitude
under the elements of the world,
4 and when the fullness of time did come, God sent forth
His Son, come of a woman, come under law,
5 that he may redeem those under law, that we may
receive the adoption of sons;
6 and because you[P] are sons, God did send forth the
spirit of His Son into your[P] hearts, crying, 'Abba,
Father!'
7 so that you[S] are no more a servant, but a son, and if a
son, also an heir of God through Christ.
8 But then, indeed, not having known God, you[P] were
in servitude to those not by nature gods,
9 and now, having known God — and rather being
known by God — how turn you[P] again unto the weak
and poor elements to which you[P] desire to be in servitude
anew?
10 you[P] observe days, and months, and times, and years!
11 I am afraid of you[P], for fear that I did labor in vain
toward you[P].
12 Become as I [am] — because I also [am] as your[P]
brethren, I beg you[P]; you[P] did no hurt to me,
13 and you[P] have known that through infirmity of the
flesh I did proclaim good news to you[P] at the first,
14 and you[P] did not despise nor reject my trial that [is]
in my flesh, but you[P] did receive me as a messenger of
God — as Christ Jesus;
15 what then was your[P] happiness? for I testify to you[P],
that if possible, your[P] eyes having plucked out, you[P]
would have given to me;
16 so that have I become your enemy, being true to
you[P]?
17 they are zealous for you[P] — [yet] not well, but they
wish to shut us out, that you[P] may be zealous for them;
18 and [it is] good to be zealously regarded, in what is
good, at all times, and not only in my being present with
you[P];
19 my little children, of whom again I travail in birth, till
Christ may be formed in you[P],
20 and I was wishing to be present with you[P] now, and
to change my voice, because I am in doubt about you[P].
21 Tell me, you[P] who are willing to be under law, do
you[P] not hear the law?
22 for it has been written, that Abraham had two sons,
one by the maid-servant, and one by the free-woman,
23 but he who [is] of the maid-servant, has been
according to flesh, and he who [is] of the free-woman,
through the promise;
24 which things are allegorized, for these are the two
covenants: one, indeed, from mount Sinai, to bringing
forth servitude, which is Hagar;
25 for this Hagar is mount Sinai in Arabia, and does
correspond to the Jerusalem that now [is], and is in
servitude with her children,
26 and the Jerusalem above is the free-woman, which is
mother of us all,
27 for it has been written, 'Rejoice, O barren, who are
not bearing; break forth and cry, you[S] who are not
travailing, because many [are] the children of the
desolate — more than of her having the husband.'
28 And we, brethren, as Isaac, are children of promise,

29 but as then he who was born according to the flesh
did persecute him according to the spirit, so also now;
30 but what said the Writing? 'Cast forth the maid-
servant and her son, for the son of the maid-servant may
not be heir with the son of the free-woman;'
31 then, brethren, we are not a maid-servant's children,
but the free-woman's.

CHAPTER 5

1 In the freedom, then, with which Christ did make you[P]
free — stand you[P], and be not held fast again by a yoke
of servitude;
2 behold, I Paul do say to you[P], that if you[P] be
circumcised, Christ shall profit you[P] nothing;
3 and I testify again to every man circumcised, that he
is a debtor to do the whole law;
4 you[P] were freed from the Christ, you[P] who are declared
righteous in law; you[P] fell away from the grace;
5 for we by the Spirit, by faith, do wait for a hope of
righteousness,
6 for in Christ Jesus neither circumcision serves
anything, nor uncircumcision, but faith working through
love.
7 You[P] were running well; who did hinder you[P] — not
to obey the truth?
8 the obedience [is] not of him who is calling you[P]!
9 a little leaven does leaven the whole lump;
10 I have confidence in regard to you[P] in the Lord, that
you[P] will be none otherwise minded; and he who is
troubling you[P] shall bear the judgment, whoever he may
be.
11 And I, brethren, if I yet preach uncircumcision, why
yet am I persecuted? then has the stumbling-block of
the cross been done away;
12 O that even they who are unsettling you[P] would cut
themselves off!
13 For you[P] — you[P] were called to freedom, brethren,
only not the freedom for an occasion to the flesh, but
serve you[P] one another through the love,
14 for all the law is fulfilled in one word — in this: 'You[S]
shall love your[S] neighbor as yourself[S];'
15 and if you[P] do bite and devour one another, see —
that you[P] may not be consumed by one another.
16 And I say: In the Spirit walk you[P], and you[P] may not
complete the desire of the flesh;
17 for the flesh does desire contrary to the Spirit, and
the Spirit contrary to the flesh, and these are opposed
one to another, that the things that you[P] may will —
these you[P] may not do;
18 and if you[P] are led by the Spirit, you[P] are not under
law.
19 And revealed also are the works of the flesh, which
are: Adultery, whoredom, uncleanness, lasciviousness,
20 idolatry, witchcraft, hatred, strifes, emulations,
wraths, rivalries, dissensions, sects,
21 envyings, murders, drunkennesses, revellings, and
such like, of which I tell you[P] before, as I also said before,
that those doing such things shall not inherit the reign
of God.
22 And the fruit of the Spirit is: Love, joy, peace, long-
suffering, kindness, goodness, faith,
23 meekness, temperance: against such there is no law;
24 and those who are Christ's, the flesh did crucify with
the affections, and the desires;
25 if we may live in the Spirit, also we may walk in the
Spirit;
26 let us not become vain-glorious — provoking one
another, envying one another!

CHAPTER 6

1 Brethren, if a man also may be overtaken in any
trespass, you[P] who [are] spiritual restore such a one in
a spirit of meekness, considering yourself[S] — for fear
that you[S] may be tempted also;
2 bear you[P] the burdens of one another, and so fill up
the law of the Christ,
3 for if any one does think [himself] to be something —
being nothing — he does deceive himself;
4 and let each one prove his own work, and then he
shall have the glorying in regard to himself alone , and
not in regard to the other,
5 for each one shall bear his own burden.
6 And let him who is instructed in the word share with
him who is instructing — in all good things.
7 Be not led astray; God is not mocked; for what a man
may sow — that also he shall reap,
8 because he who is sowing to his own flesh, of the
flesh shall reap corruption; and he who is sowing to the
Spirit, of the Spirit shall reap life age-during;
9 and in the doing good we may not be faint-hearted,
for at the proper time we shall reap — not desponding;
10 for that reason, then, as we have opportunity, may
we work the good to all, and especially unto those of
the household of the faith.

11 You[P] see how I have written to you[P] in large letters
with my own hand;
12 as many as are willing to make a good appearance in
the flesh, these constrain you[P] to be circumcised — only
that they may not be persecuted for the cross of the
Christ,
13 for neither do those circumcised keep the law
themselves, but they wish you[P] to be circumcised, that
they may glory in your[P] flesh.
14 And for me, let it not be — to glory, except in the
cross of our Lord Jesus Christ, through which the world
has been crucified to me, and I to the world;
15 for in Christ Jesus neither circumcision serves
anything, nor uncircumcision, but a new creation;
16 and as many as do walk by this rule — peace upon
them, and kindness, and on the Israel of God!
17 From this time forth, let no one give me trouble, for I
do bear the scars of the Lord Jesus in my body.
18 The grace of our Lord Jesus Christ [is] with your[P]
spirit, brethren! Amen.

The Epistle Of Paul The Apostle To The
EPHESIANS

CHAPTER 1

1 Paul, an apostle of Jesus Christ through the will of God, to the saints who are in Ephesus, and to the faithful in Christ Jesus:
2 Grace to you[P], and peace from God our Father, and the Lord Jesus Christ!
3 Blessed [is] the God and Father of our Lord Jesus Christ, who did bless us in every spiritual blessing in the heavenly places in Christ,
4 according as He did choose us in him before the foundation of the world, for our being holy and unblemished before Him, in love,
5 having foreordained us to the adoption of sons through Jesus Christ to Himself, according to the good pleasure of His will,
6 to the praise of the glory of His grace, in which He did make us accepted in the beloved,
7 in whom we have the redemption through His blood, the remission of the trespasses, according to the riches of His grace,
8 in which He did abound toward us in all wisdom and prudence,
9 having made known to us the secret of His will, according to His good pleasure, that He purposed in Himself,
10 in regard to the dispensation of the fullness of the times, to bring the whole in the Christ into one, both the things in the heavens, and the things upon the earth — in Him;
11 in whom also we did obtain an inheritance, being foreordained according to the purpose of Him who is working the all things according to the counsel of His will,
12 for our being to the praise of His glory, [even] those who did first hope in the Christ,
13 in whom you[P] also, having heard the word of the truth — the good news of your[P] salvation — in whom also having believed, you[P] were sealed with the Holy Spirit of the promise,
14 which is an earnest of our inheritance, to the redemption of the acquired possession, to the praise of His glory.
15 Because of this I also, having heard of your[P] faith in the Lord Jesus, and the love to all the saints,
16 do not cease giving thanks for you[P], making mention of you[P] in my prayers,
17 that the God of our Lord Jesus Christ, the Father of the glory, may give to you[P] a spirit of wisdom and revelation in the recognition of him,
18 the eyes of your[P] understanding being enlightened, for your[P] knowing what is the hope of His calling, and what the riches of the glory of His inheritance in the saints,
19 and what the exceeding greatness of His power to us who are believing, according to the working of the power of His might,
20 which He worked in the Christ, having raised Him out of the dead, and did set [Him] at His right hand in the heavenly [places],
21 far above all principality, and authority, and might, and lordship, and every name named, not only in this age, but also in the coming one;
22 and He did put all things under His feet, and did give Him — head over all things to the assembly,
23 which is His body, the fullness of Him who is filling the all in all,

CHAPTER 2

1 Also you[P] — being dead in the trespasses and the sins,
2 in which once you[P] did walk according to the age of this world, according to the ruler of the authority of the air, of the spirit that is now working in the sons of disobedience,
3 among whom also we all did walk once in the desires of our flesh, doing the wishes of the flesh and of the thoughts, and were by nature children of wrath — as also the others,
4 and God, being rich in kindness, because of His great love with which He loved us,
5 even being dead in the trespasses, did make us to live

together with the Christ, (you[P] are having been saved
by grace,)
6 and did raise [us] up together, and did seat [us]
together in the heavenly [places] in Christ Jesus,
7 that He might show, in the ages that are coming, the
exceeding riches of His grace in kindness toward us in
Christ Jesus,
8 for you[P] are having been saved by grace, through
faith, and this not of you[P] — the gift of God,
9 not of works, that no one may boast;
10 for we are workmanship of Him, created in Christ
Jesus to good works, which God did prepare before, that
we may walk in them.
11 For what reason, remember, that you[P] [were] once
the nations in the flesh, who are called Uncircumcision
by that called Circumcision in the flesh made by hands,
12 that you[P] were at that time apart from Christ, having
been alienated from the commonwealth of Israel, and
strangers to the covenants of the promise, having no
hope, and without God, in the world;
13 and now, in Christ Jesus, you[P] being once afar off
became near in the blood of the Christ,
14 for he is our peace, who did make both one, and did
break down the middle wall of the enclosure,
15 the enmity in his flesh, having done away the law of
the commands in ordinances, that the two he might
create into one new man in himself, making peace,
16 and might reconcile both in one body to God through
the cross, having slain the enmity in it,
17 and having come, he did proclaim good news —
peace to you[P] — the far-off and the near,
18 because we have the access through him — we both
— in one Spirit unto the Father.
19 Then, for that reason, you[P] are no more strangers
and foreigners, but fellow-citizens of the saints, and of
the household of God,
20 being built upon the foundation of the apostles and
prophets, Jesus Christ himself being chief corner-[stone],
21 in whom all the building fitly framed together does
increase to an holy sanctuary in the Lord,
22 in whom also you[P] are built together, for a habitation
of God in the Spirit.

CHAPTER 3

1 For this cause, I Paul, the prisoner of Christ Jesus for
you[P] the nations,
2 if, indeed, you[P] did hear of the dispensation of the
grace of God that was given to me in regard to you[P],
3 that by revelation He made known to me the secret,
according as I wrote before in few [words] —
4 in regard to which you[P] are able, reading [it], to
understand my knowledge in the secret of the Christ,
5 which in other generations was not made known to
the sons of men, as it was now revealed to His holy
apostles and prophets in the Spirit —
6 that the nations be fellow-heirs, and of the same body,
and partakers of His promise in the Christ, through the
good news,
7 of which I became a ministrant, according to the gift
of the grace of God that was given to me, according to
the working of His power;
8 to me — the less than the least of all the saints — was
given this grace, to proclaim good news among the
nations — the untraceable riches of the Christ,
9 and to cause all to see what [is] the fellowship of the
secret that has been hid from the ages in God, who did
create the all things by Jesus Christ,
10 that there might be made known now to the
principalities and the authorities in the heavenly [places],
through the assembly, the many kinds of wisdom of God,
11 according to a purpose of the ages, which He made
in Christ Jesus our Lord,
12 in whom we have the freedom and the access in
confidence through the faith of Him,
13 for what reason, I ask [you[P]] not to faint in my
tribulations for you[P], which is your[P] glory.
14 For this cause I bow my knees unto the Father of our
Lord Jesus Christ,
15 of whom the whole family in the heavens and on
earth is named,
16 that He may give to you[P], according to the riches of
His glory, with might to be strengthened through His
Spirit, in regard to the inner man,
17 that the Christ may dwell in your[P] hearts through the
faith, in love having been rooted and founded,
18 that you[P] may be in strength to comprehend, with all
the saints, what [is] the breadth, and length, and depth,
and height,
19 to know also the love of the Christ that is exceeding
the knowledge, that you[P] may be filled — to all the
fullness of God;
20 and to Him who is able above all things to do
exceeding abundantly what we ask or think, according
to the power that is working in us,
21 to Him [is] the glory in the assembly in Christ Jesus,
to all the generations of the age of the ages. Amen.

CHAPTER 4

1 Call upon you[P], then, do I — the prisoner of the Lord
— to walk worthily of the calling with which you[P] were
called,
2 with all lowliness and meekness, with long-suffering,
forbearing one another in love,
3 being diligent to keep the unity of the Spirit in the
bond of the peace;
4 one body and one Spirit, according as also you[P] were
called in one hope of your[P] calling;
5 one Lord, one faith, one baptism,
6 one God and Father of all, who [is] over all, and through
all, and in you[P] all,
7 and to each one of you[P] was given the grace, according
to the measure of the gift of Christ,
8 for what reason, he said, 'Having gone up on high he
led captivity captive, and gave gifts to men,' —
9 and that, He went up, what is it except that He also
went down first to the lower parts of the earth?
10 He who went down is the same also who went up far
above all the heavens, that He may fill all things —
11 and He gave some [as] apostles, and some [as]
prophets, and some [as] proclaimers of good news, and
some [as] shepherds and teachers,
12 unto the perfecting of the saints, for a work of
ministration, for a building up of the body of the Christ,
13 till we may all come to the unity of the faith and of
the recognition of the Son of God, to a perfect man, to a
measure of stature of the fullness of the Christ,
14 that we may no more be babes, tossed and borne
about by every wind of the teaching, in the sleight of
men, in craftiness, unto the artifice of leading astray,
15 and, being true in love, we may increase to Him [in]
all things, who is the head — the Christ;
16 from whom the whole body, being fitly joined together
and united, through the supply of every joint, according
to the working in the measure of each single part, the
increase of the body does make for the building up of
itself in love.
17 This, then, I say, and I testify in the Lord; you[P] are
no more to walk, as also the other nations walk, in the
vanity of their mind,
18 being darkened in the understanding, being alienated
from the life of God, because of the ignorance that is in
them, because of the hardness of their heart,
19 who, having ceased to feel, did give themselves up
to the lasciviousness, for the working of all uncleanness
in greediness;
20 and you[P] did not so learn the Christ,
21 if so be you[P] did hear Him, and in Him were taught,
as truth is in Jesus;
22 you[P] are to put off concerning the former behavior
the old man, that is corrupt according to the desires of
the deceit,
23 and to be renewed in the spirit of your[P] mind,
24 and to put on the new man, which, according to God,
was created in righteousness and kindness of the truth.
25 For what reason, putting away the lying, speak truth
each with his neighbor, because we are members one of
another;
26 be angry and do not sin; let not the sun go down
upon your[P] wrath,
27 neither give place to the devil;
28 whoso is stealing let him no more steal, but rather let
him labor, working the thing that is good with the hands,
that he may have to impart to him having need.
29 Let no corrupt word go forth out of your[P] mouth, but
what is good unto the needful building up, that it may
give grace to the hearers;
30 and make not the Holy Spirit of God sorrowful, in
which you[P] were sealed to a day of redemption.
31 Let all bitterness, and wrath, and anger, and clamor,
and evil-speaking, be put away from you[P], with all malice,
32 and become kind one to another, tender-hearted,
forgiving one another, according as also God in Christ
did forgive you[P].

CHAPTER 5

1 Become, then, followers of God, as children beloved,
2 and walk in love, as also the Christ did love us, and
did give Himself for us, an offering and a sacrifice to
God for an odor of a sweet smell,
3 and whoredom, and all uncleanness, or covetousness,
let it not even be named among you[P], as becomes saints;
4 also filthiness, and foolish talking, or jesting, — the
things not fit — but rather thanksgiving;
5 for this you[P] know, that every whoremonger, or
unclean, or covetous person, who is an idolater, has no
inheritance in the reign of the Christ and God.
6 Let no one deceive you[P] with vain words, for because
of these things comes the anger of God upon the sons
of the disobedience,
7 become not, then, partakers with them,
8 for you[P] were once darkness, and now light in the

Lord; walk you[P] as children of light,
9 for the fruit of the Spirit [is] in all goodness, and
righteousness, and truth,
10 proving what is well-pleasing to the Lord,
11 and have no fellowship with the unfruitful works of
the darkness and rather even convict,
12 for it is a shame even to speak of the things done in
secret by them,
13 and all the things reproved by the light are revealed,
for everything that is revealed is light;
14 for what reason he said, 'Arouse yourself[S], you[S] who
are sleeping, and arise out of the dead, and the Christ
shall shine upon you[S].'
15 See, then, how exactly you[P] walk, not as unwise, but
as wise,
16 redeeming the time, because the days are evil;
17 because of this become not fools, but —
understanding what [is] the will of the Lord,
18 and be not drunk with wine, in which is dissoluteness,
but be filled in the Spirit,
19 speaking to yourselves[P] in psalms and hymns and
spiritual songs, singing and making melody in your[P]
heart to the Lord,
20 giving thanks always for all things, in the name of
our Lord Jesus Christ, to the God and Father;
21 subjecting yourselves[P] to one another in the fear of
God.
22 The wives! subject yourselves[P] to your[P] own
husbands, as to the Lord,
23 because the husband is head of the wife, as also the
Christ [is] head of the assembly, and he is savior of the
body,
24 but even as the assembly is subject to Christ, so
also [are] the wives to their own husbands in everything.
25 The husbands! love your[P] own wives, as also the
Christ did love the assembly, and did give Himself for it,
26 that He might sanctify it, having cleansed [it] with
the bathing of the water in the saying,
27 that He might present it to Himself the assembly in
glory, not having spot or wrinkle, or any of such things,
but that it may be holy and unblemished;
28 so ought the husbands to love their own wives as
their own bodies: he who is loving his own wife — he
does love himself;
29 for no one ever did hate his own flesh, but does
nourish and cherish it, as also the Lord — the assembly,
30 because we are members of his body, of his flesh,
and of his bones;
31 'for this cause shall a man leave his father and mother,
and shall be joined to his wife, and they shall be — the
two — for one flesh;'
32 this secret is great, and I speak in regard to Christ
and to the assembly;
33 but you[P] also, every one in particular — let each so
love his own wife as himself, and the wife — that she
may reverence the husband.

CHAPTER 6

1 The children! obey your[P] parents in the Lord, for this
is righteous;
2 honor your[S] father and mother,
3 which is the first command with a promise, 'That it
may be well with you[S], and you[S] may live a long time
upon the land.'
4 And the fathers! provoke not your[P] children, but
nourish them in the instruction and admonition of the
Lord.
5 The servants! obey the masters according to the flesh
with fear and trembling, in the simplicity of your[P] heart,
as to the Christ;
6 not with eye-service as men-pleasers, but as servants
of the Christ, doing the will of God out of soul,
7 with good-will serving, as to the Lord, and not to men,
8 having known that whatever good thing each one may
do, this he shall receive from the Lord, whether servant
or freeman.
9 And the masters! do you[P] the same things unto them,
letting threatening alone, having known that also your[P]
Master is in the heavens, and acceptance of persons is
not with him.
10 As to the rest, my brethren, be strong in the Lord,
and in the power of his might;
11 put on the whole armor of God, for your[P] being able
to stand against the wiles of the devil,
12 because we have not the wrestling with blood and
flesh, but with the principalities, with the authorities, with
the world-rulers of the darkness of this age, with the
spiritual things of the evil in the heavenly places;
13 because of this take you[P] up the whole armor of God,
that you[P] may be able to resist in the day of the evil, and
all things having done — to stand.
14 Stand, for that reason, having your[P] loins girt about
in truth, and having put on the breastplate of the
righteousness,
15 and having the feet shod in the preparation of the
good-news of the peace;

16 above all, having taken up the shield of the faith, in
which you[P] shall be able to quench all the fiery darts of
the evil one,
17 and receive the helmet of the salvation, and the sword
of the Spirit, which is the saying of God,
18 through all prayer and supplication praying at all
times in the Spirit, and in regard to this same, watching
in all perseverance and supplication for all the saints —
19 and in behalf of me, that to me may be given a word
in the opening of my mouth, in freedom, to make known
the secret of the good news,
20 for which I am an ambassador in a chain, that in it I
may speak freely — as it is necessary for me to speak.
21 And that you[P] may know — you[P] also — the things
concerning me — what I do, Tychicus, the beloved
brother and faithful ministrant in the Lord, shall make
known all things to you[P],
22 whom I did send unto you[P] for this very thing, that
you[P] might know the things concerning us, and that he
might comfort your[P] hearts.
23 Peace to the brethren, and love, with faith, from God
the Father, and the Lord Jesus Christ!
24 The grace with all those loving our Lord Jesus Christ
— undecayingly! Amen.

The Epistle Of Paul The Apostle To The

PHILIPPIANS

CHAPTER 1

1 Paul and Timotheus, servants of Jesus Christ, to all the saints in Christ Jesus who are in Philippi, with overseers and ministrants;

2 Grace to you[P], and peace from God our Father, and the Lord Jesus Christ.

3 I give thanks to my God upon all the remembrance of you[P],

4 always, in every supplication of mine for you[P] all, making the supplication with joy,

5 for your[P] contribution to the good news from the first day till now,

6 having been confident of this very thing, that He who did begin a good work in you[P], will perform [it] till a day of Jesus Christ,

7 according as it is righteous for me to think this in behalf of you[P] all, because of my having you[P] in the heart, both in my bonds, and [in] the defense and confirmation of the good news, all of you[P] being fellow-partakers of grace with me.

8 For God is my witness, how I long for you[P] all in the bowels of Jesus Christ,

9 and this I pray, that your[P] love may abound yet more and more in full knowledge, and all judgment,

10 for your[P] proving the things that differ, that you[P] may be pure and offenseless — to a day of Christ,

11 being filled with the fruit of righteousness, that [is] through Jesus Christ, to the glory and praise of God.

12 And I wish you[P] to know, brethren, that the things concerning me, have come rather to an advancement of the good news,

13 so that my bonds have become revealed in Christ in the whole praetorium, and to the other places — all,

14 and the greater part of the brethren in the Lord, having confidence by my bonds, are more abundantly bold — to speak the word fearlessly.

15 Certain, indeed, even through envy and contention, and certain also through good-will, do preach the Christ;

16 the one, indeed, do proclaim the Christ of rivalry, not purely, supposing to add affliction to my bonds,

17 and the other out of love, having known that I am set for defense of the good news:

18 what then? in every way, whether in pretense or in truth, Christ is proclaimed — and in this I rejoice, yes, and shall rejoice.

19 For I have known that this shall fall out to me for salvation, through your[P] supplication, and the supply of the Spirit of Christ Jesus,

20 according to my earnest expectation and hope, that I shall be ashamed in nothing, and in all freedom, as always, also now Christ shall be magnified in my body, whether through life or through death,

21 for to me to live [is] Christ, and to die gain.

22 And if to live in the flesh [is] to me a fruit of work, then what shall I choose? I know not;

23 for I am pressed by the two, having the desire to depart, and to be with Christ, for it is far better,

24 and to remain in the flesh is more necessary on your[P] account,

25 and of this being persuaded, I have known that I shall remain and continue with you[P] all, to your[P] advancement and joy of the faith,

26 that your[P] boasting may abound in Christ Jesus in me through my presence again to you[P].

27 Only conduct you[P] yourselves[P] worthily of the good news of the Christ, that, whether having come and seen you[P], whether being absent I may hear of the things concerning you[P], that you[P] stand fast in one spirit, with one soul, striving together for the faith of the good news,

28 and not terrified in anything by those opposing, which to them indeed is a token of destruction, and to you[P] of salvation, and that from God;

29 because it was granted to you[P], on behalf of Christ, not only to believe in him, but also to suffer on behalf of him;

30 the same conflict having, such as you[P] saw in me, and now hear of in me.

CHAPTER 2

1 If, then, any exhortation [is] in Christ, if any comfort

of love, if any fellowship of spirit, if any bowels and
mercies,
2 fulfil you[P] my joy, that you[P] may mind the same thing
— having the same love — of one soul — minding the
one thing,
3 nothing in rivalry or vain-glory, but in humility of mind
counting one another more excellent than yourselves[P] —
4 you[P] not each to your[P] own look, but each also to the
things of others.
5 For, let this mind be in you[P] that [is] also in Christ
Jesus,
6 who, being in the form of God, thought [it] not robbery
to be equal to God,
7 but did empty himself, having taken the form of a
servant, having been made in the likeness of men,
8 and in fashion having been found as a man, he
humbled himself, having become obedient unto death
— death even of a cross,
9 for what reason, also, God did highly exalt him, and
gave to him a name that [is] above every name,
10 that in the name of Jesus every knee may bow — of
heavenlies, and earthlies, and what are under the earth —
11 and every tongue may confess that Jesus Christ [is]
Lord, to the glory of God the Father.
12 So that, my beloved, as you[P] always obey, not as
only in my presence, but now much more in my absence,
work out your[P] own salvation with fear and trembling,
13 for it is God who is working in you[P] both to will and
to work for His good pleasure.
14 Do all things without murmurings and reasonings,
15 that you[P] may become blameless and harmless,
children of God, unblemished in the midst of a crooked
and perverse generation, among whom you[P] do appear
as luminaries in the world,
16 holding forth the word of life, for rejoicing to me in
regard to a day of Christ, that I did not run in vain, nor
did I labor in vain;
17 but if also I am poured forth upon the sacrifice and
service of your[P] faith, I rejoice and joy with you[P] all,
18 because of this do you[P] also rejoice and joy with me.
19 And I hope, in the Lord Jesus, to send Timotheus to
you[P] quickly, that I also may be of good spirit, having
known the things concerning you[P],
20 for I have no one like-minded, who will care for the
things concerning you[P] sincerely,
21 for the whole seek their own things, not the things
of the Christ Jesus,
22 and the proof of him you[P] know, that as a child
[serves] a father, he did serve with me in regard to the
good news;
23 him, indeed, for that reason, I hope to send, when I
may see through the things concerning me —
immediately;
24 and I trust in the Lord that I myself also shall quickly
come.
25 And I thought [it] necessary Epaphroditus — my
brother, and fellow-workman, and fellow-soldier, and
your[P] apostle and servant to my need — to send unto
you[P],
26 seeing he was longing after you[P] all, and in heaviness,
because you[P] heard that he ailed,
27 for he also ailed near to death, but God did deal kindly
with him, and not with him only, but also with me, that I
might not have sorrow upon sorrow.
28 The more eagerly, for that reason, I did send him,
that having seen him again you[P] may rejoice, and I may
be the less sorrowful;
29 receive him, for that reason, in the Lord, with all joy,
and hold such in honor,
30 because he drew near to death on account of the
work of the Christ, having hazarded the life that he might
fill up your[P] deficiency of service unto me.

CHAPTER 3

1 As to the rest, my brethren, rejoice in the Lord; to
write the same things to you[P] indeed is not tiresome to
me, and for you[P] [is] sure;
2 look to the dogs, look to the evil-workers, look to the
concision;
3 for we are the circumcision, who are serving God by
the Spirit, and glorying in Christ Jesus, and having no
trust in flesh,
4 though I also have [cause of] trust in flesh. If any
other one does think to have trust in flesh, I more;
5 circumcision on the eighth day! of the race of Israel!
of the tribe of Benjamin! a Hebrew of Hebrews! a Pharisee
according to law!
6 according to zeal persecuting the assembly! becoming
blameless according to righteousness that is in law!
7 But what things were to me gains, these I have
counted, because of the Christ, loss;
8 yes, indeed, and I count all things to be loss, because
of the excellency of the knowledge of Christ Jesus my
Lord, because of whom I suffered loss of the all things,
and do count them to be refuse, that I may gain Christ,
and be found in him,

9 not having my righteousness, which [is] of law, but that which [is] through faith of Christ — the righteousness that is of God by the faith,
10 to know him, and the power of his rising again, and the fellowship of his sufferings, being conformed to his death,
11 if anyhow I may attain to the rising again of the dead.
12 Not that I did already obtain, or have been already perfected; but I pursue, if also I may lay hold of that for which also I was laid hold of by the Christ Jesus;
13 brethren, I do not reckon myself to have laid hold; and one thing — forgetting the things behind indeed, and stretching forth to the things before —
14 I pursue to the mark for the prize of the high calling of God in Christ Jesus.
15 As many, for that reason, as [are] perfect — let us think this, and if you[P] think otherwise [in] anything, this also shall God reveal to you[P],
16 but to what we have come — walk by the same rule, think the same thing;
17 become followers together of me, brethren, and observe those thus walking, according as you[P] have us — a pattern;
18 for many walk of whom I told you[P] many times — and now also weeping tell — the enemies of the cross of the Christ!
19 whose end [is] destruction, whose god [is] the belly, and whose glory [is] in their shame, who are minding the things on earth.
20 For our citizenship is in the heavens, from where also we await a Savior — the Lord Jesus Christ —
21 who shall transform the body of our humiliation to its becoming conformed to the body of his glory, according to the working of his power, even to subject the all things to himself.

CHAPTER 4

1 So then, my brethren, beloved and longed for, my joy and crown, so stand you[P] in the Lord, beloved.
2 I exhort Euodia, and I exhort Syntyche, to be of the same mind in the Lord;
3 and I ask also you[S], genuine yoke-fellow, be assisting those women who did strive along with me in the good news, with Clement also, and the others, my fellow-workers, whose names [are] in the book of life.
4 Rejoice in the Lord always; again I will say, rejoice;
5 let your[P] forbearance be known to all men; the Lord [is] near;
6 be anxious for nothing, but by prayer in everything, and by supplication, with thanksgiving, let your[P] requests be made known unto God;
7 and the peace of God, that is surpassing all understanding, shall guard your[P] hearts and your[P] thoughts in Christ Jesus.
8 As to the rest, brethren, as many things as are true, as many as [are] grave, as many as [are] righteous, as many as [are] pure, as many as [are] lovely, as many as [are] of good report, if any worthiness, and if any praise, think upon these things;
9 the things that also you[P] did learn, and receive, and hear, and saw in me, those do, and the God of the peace shall be with you[P].
10 And I rejoiced in the Lord greatly, that now at length you[P] flourished again in caring for me, for which also you[P] were caring, and lacked opportunity;
11 not that I say [it] in respect of want, for I did learn in the things in which I am — to be content;
12 I have known both to be abased, and I have known to abound; I have been initiated in everything and in all things, both to be full and to be hungry, both to abound and to be in want.
13 I have strength for all things, in Christ's strengthening me;
14 but you[P] did well, having communicated with my tribulation;
15 and you[P] have known, even you[P] Philippians, that in the beginning of the good news when I went forth from Macedonia, no assembly did communicate with me in regard to giving and receiving except you[P] only;
16 because also in Thessalonica, both once and again you[P] sent to my need;
17 not that I seek after the gift, but I seek after the fruit that is overflowing to your[P] account;
18 and I have all things, and abound; I am filled, having received from Epaphroditus the things from you[P] — an odor of a sweet smell — a sacrifice acceptable, well-pleasing to God:
19 and my God shall supply all your[P] need, according to His riches in glory in Christ Jesus;
20 and to God, even our Father, [is] the glory — to the ages of the ages. Amen.
21 Salute you[P] every saint in Christ Jesus; the brethren with me salute you[P] there;
22 all the saints salute you[P] there, and specially those of Caesar's house;
23 the grace of our Lord Jesus Christ [is] with you[P] all. Amen.

The Epistle Of Paul The Apostle To The
COLOSSIANS

CHAPTER 1

1 Paul, an apostle of Jesus Christ through the will of God, and Timotheus the brother,
2 to the saints in Colossae, and to the faithful brethren in Christ: Grace to you[P], and peace from God our Father, and the Lord Jesus Christ!
3 We give thanks to the God and Father of our Lord Jesus Christ, always praying for you[P],
4 having heard of your[P] faith in Christ Jesus, and of the love that [is] to all the saints,
5 because of the hope that is laid up for you[P] in the heavens, which you[P] heard of before in the word of the truth of the good news,
6 which is present to you[P], as also in all the world, and is bearing fruit, as also in you[P], from the day in which you[P] heard, and knew the grace of God in truth;
7 as you[P] also learned from Epaphras, our beloved fellow-servant, who is a faithful ministrant of the Christ for you[P],
8 who also did declare to us your[P] love in the Spirit.
9 Because of this, we also, from the day in which we heard, do not cease praying for you[P], and asking that you[P] may be filled with the full knowledge of His will in all wisdom and spiritual understanding,
10 to your[P] walking worthily of the Lord to all pleasing, in every good work being fruitful, and increasing to the knowledge of God,
11 in all might being made mighty according to the power of His glory, to all endurance and long-suffering with joy.
12 Giving thanks to the Father who did make us meet for the participation of the inheritance of the saints in the light,
13 who did rescue us out of the authority of the darkness, and did translate [us] into the reign of the Son of His love,
14 in whom we have the redemption through His blood, the forgiveness of the sins,
15 who is the image of the invisible God, first-born of all creation,
16 because in Him were the all things created, those in the heavens, and those upon the earth, those visible, and those invisible, whether thrones, whether lordships, whether principalities, whether authorities; all things through Him, and for Him, have been created,
17 and Himself is before all, and the all things in Him have consisted.
18 And Himself is the head of the body — the assembly — who is a beginning, a first-born out of the dead, that He might become in all [things] — Himself — first,
19 because in Him it did please all the fullness to tabernacle,
20 and through Him to reconcile the all things to Himself — having made peace through the blood of His cross — through Him, whether the things upon the earth, whether the things in the heavens.
21 And you[P] — once being alienated, and enemies in the mind, in the evil works, yet now did He reconcile,
22 in the body of His flesh through the death, to present you[P] holy, and unblemished, and unblameable before Himself,
23 if also you[P] remain in the faith, being founded and settled, and not moved away from the hope of the good news, which you[P] heard, which was preached in all the creation that [is] under the heaven, of which I became — I Paul — a ministrant.
24 I now rejoice in my sufferings for you[P], and do fill up the things lacking of the tribulations of the Christ in my flesh for His body, which is the assembly,
25 of which I — I did become a ministrant according to the dispensation of God, that was given to me for you[P], to fulfil the word of God,
26 the secret that has been hid from the ages and from the generations, but now was revealed to his saints,
27 to whom God did will to make known what [is] the riches of the glory of this secret among the nations — which is Christ in you[P], the hope of the glory,
28 whom we proclaim, warning every man, and teaching every man, in all wisdom, that we may present every man perfect in Christ Jesus,

29 for which also I labor, striving according to His
working that is working in power in me.

CHAPTER 2

1 For I wish you[P] to know how great a conflict I have
for you[P] and those in Laodicea, and as many as have
not seen my face in the flesh,
2 that their hearts may be comforted, being united in
love, and to all riches of the full assurance of the
understanding, to the full knowledge of the secret of
the God and Father, and of the Christ,
3 in whom are all the treasures of the wisdom and the
knowledge hid,
4 and this I say, that no one may beguile you[P] in enticing
words,
5 for if even in the flesh I am absent — yet in the spirit
I am with you[P], joying and beholding your[P] order, and
the steadfastness of your[P] faith in regard to Christ;
6 as, then, you[P] did receive Christ Jesus the Lord, you[P]
walk in Him,
7 being rooted and built up in Him, and confirmed in the
faith, as you[P] were taught — abounding in thanksgiving
in it.
8 See that no one shall be carrying you[P] away as spoil
through the philosophy and vain deceit, according to
the deliverance of men, according to the rudiments of
the world, and not according to Christ,
9 because in Him does tabernacle all the fullness of the
Godhead bodily,
10 and you[P] are made full in Him, who is the head of all
principality and authority,
11 in whom also you[P] were circumcised with a
circumcision not made with hands, in the putting off of
the body of the sins of the flesh in the circumcision of
the Christ,
12 being buried with Him in the baptism, in which also
you[P] rose with [Him] through the faith of the working of
God, who did raise Him out of the dead.
13 And you[P] — being dead in the trespasses and the
uncircumcision of your[P] flesh — He made alive together
with Him, having forgiven you[P] all the trespasses,
14 having blotted out the handwriting in the ordinances
that is against us, that was contrary to us, and He has
taken it out of the way, having nailed it to the cross;
15 having stripped the principalities and the authorities,
He made a show of them openly — having triumphed
over them in it.
16 Let no one, then, judge you[P] in eating or in drinking,
or in respect of a feast, or of a new moon, or of Sabbaths,
17 which are a shadow of the coming things, and the
body [is] of the Christ;
18 let no one beguile you[P] of your[P] prize, delighting in
humble-mindedness and [in] worship of the messengers,
intruding into the things he has not seen, being vainly
puffed up by the mind of his flesh,
19 and not holding the head, from which all the body —
through the joints and bands gathering supply, and
being knit together — may increase with the increase of
God.
20 If, then, you[P] did die with the Christ from the
rudiments of the world, why, as living in the world, are
you[P] subject to ordinances?
21 — you[S] may not touch, nor taste, nor handle —
22 which are all for destruction with the using, after the
commands and teachings of men,
23 which are, indeed, having a matter of wisdom in will-
worship, and humble-mindedness, and neglecting of
body — not in any honor, unto a satisfying of the flesh.

CHAPTER 3

1 If, then, you[P] were raised with the Christ, seek you[P]
the things above, where the Christ is, on the right hand
of God seated,
2 mind you[P] the things above, not the things upon the
earth,
3 for you[P] did die, and your[P] life has been hid with the
Christ in God;
4 when the Christ — our life — may be revealed, then
also we shall be revealed in glory with Him.
5 Put to death, then, your[P] members that [are] upon the
earth — whoredom, uncleanness, passion, evil desire,
and the covetousness, which is idolatry —
6 because of which things comes the anger of God upon
the sons of the disobedience,
7 in which also you[P] — you[P] did walk once, when you[P]
lived in them;
8 but now put off, even you[P], the whole — anger, wrath,
malice, evil-speaking, filthy talking — out of your[P]
mouth.
9 Lie not one to another, having put off the old man
with his practices,
10 and having put on the new, which is renewed in regard
to knowledge, after the image of Him who did create him;
11 where there is not Greek and Jew, circumcision and

uncircumcision, foreigner, Scythian, servant, freeman —
but the all and in all — Christ.
12 Put on, for that reason, as choice ones of God, holy
and beloved, bowels of mercies, kindness, humble-
mindedness, meekness, long-suffering,
13 forbearing one another, and forgiving each other, if
any one may have a quarrel with any one, as also the
Christ did forgive you[P] — so also you[P];
14 and above all these things, [have] love, which is a
bond of the perfection,
15 and let the peace of God rule in your[P] hearts, to which
also you[P] were called in one body, and become thankful.
16 Let the word of Christ dwell in you[P] richly, in all
wisdom, teaching and admonishing each other, in
psalms, and hymns, and spiritual songs, in grace singing
in your[P] hearts to the Lord;
17 and all, whatever you[P] may do in word or in work,
[do] all things in the name of the Lord Jesus — giving
thanks to the God and Father, through Him.
18 The wives! be subject to your[P] own husbands, as is
fit in the Lord;
19 the husbands! love your[P] wives, and be not bitter
with them;
20 the children! obey the parents in all things, for this is
well-pleasing to the Lord;
21 the fathers! vex not your[P] children, for fear that they
be discouraged.
22 The servants! obey in all things those who are
masters according to the flesh, not in eye-service as men-
pleasers, but in simplicity of heart, fearing God;
23 and all, whatever you[P] may do — out of soul work
— as to the Lord, and not to men,
24 having known that you[P] shall receive the recompense
of the inheritance from the Lord — for the Lord Christ
you[P] serve;
25 and he who is doing unrighteously shall receive what
he did unrighteously, and there is no acceptance of
persons.

CHAPTER 4

1 The masters! you[P] give that which is righteous and
equal to the servants, having known that you[P] also have
a Master in the heavens.
2 You[P] continue in the prayer , watching in it in
thanksgiving;
3 praying at the same time also for us, that God may
open to us a door for the word, to speak the secret of
the Christ, because of which also I have been bound,
4 that I may reveal it, as it is necessary for me to speak;
5 you[P] walk in wisdom toward those without, the time
forestalling;
6 your[P] word always in grace — with salt being
seasoned — to know how it is necessary for you[P] to
answer each one.
7 All the things concerning me shall Tychicus make
known to you[P] — the beloved brother, and faithful
ministrant, and fellow-servant in the Lord —
8 whom I did send unto you[P] for this very thing, that he
might know the things concerning you[P], and might
comfort your[P] hearts,
9 with Onesimus the faithful and beloved brother, who
is of you[P]; all things that [are] here shall they make
known to you[P].
10 Salute you[P] does Aristarchus, my fellow-captive, and
Marcus, the nephew of Barnabas, (concerning whom
you[P] did receive commands — receive him if he may
come unto you[P],)
11 and Jesus who is called Justus, who are of the
circumcision: these only [are] fellow-workers for the
reign of God who did become a comfort to me.
12 Salute you[P] does Epaphras, who [is] of you[P], a servant
of Christ, always striving for you[P] in the prayers, that
you[P] may stand perfect and made full in all the will of
God,
13 for I do testify to him, that he has much zeal for you[P],
and those in Laodicea, and those in Hierapolis.
14 Salute you[P] does Lukas, the beloved physician, and
Demas;
15 those in Laodicea salute you[P] — brethren, and
Nymphas, and the assembly in his house;
16 and when the epistle may be read with you[P], cause
that it may be read also in the assembly of the
Laodiceans, and that you[P] also may read the [epistle]
from Laodicea;
17 and say to Archippus, 'See to the ministration that
you[S] did receive in the Lord, that you[S] may fulfil it.'
18 The salutation by the hand of me, Paul; remember
my bonds; the grace [is] with you[P]. Amen.

The FIRST Epistle Of Paul The Apostle To The
THESSALONIANS

CHAPTER 1

1 Paul, and Silvanus, and Timotheus, to the assembly
of Thessalonians in God the Father, and the Lord Jesus
Christ: Grace to you[P], and peace, from God our Father,
and the Lord Jesus Christ!
2 We give thanks to God always for you[P] all, making
mention of you[P] in our prayers,
3 unceasingly remembering of you[P] the work of the faith,
and the labor of the love, and the endurance of the hope,
of our Lord Jesus Christ, in the presence of our God and
Father,
4 having known, beloved brethren, by God, your[P]
election,
5 because our good news did not come to you[P] in word
only, but also in power, and in the Holy Spirit, and in
much assurance, even as you[P] have known of what sort
we became among you[P] because of you[P],
6 and you[P] — you[P] did become imitators of us, and of
the Lord, having received the word in much tribulation,
with joy of the Holy Spirit,
7 so that you[P] became patterns to all those believing in
Macedonia and Achaia,
8 for from you[P] has sounded forth the word of the Lord,
not only in Macedonia and Achaia, but also your[P] faith
toward God did go forth in every place, so that we have
no need to say anything,
9 for they themselves do declare concerning us what
entrance we had unto you[P], and how you[P] did turn from
the idols unto God, to serve a living and true God,
10 and to wait for His Son from the heavens, whom He
did raise out of the dead — Jesus, who is rescuing us
from the anger that is coming.

CHAPTER 2

1 For yourselves[P] have known, brethren, our entrance
in unto you[P], that it did not become vain,
2 but having both suffered before, and having been
injuriously treated (as you[P] have known) in Philippi, we
were bold in our God to speak unto you[P] the good news
of God in much conflict,
3 for our exhortation [is] not out of deceit, nor out of
uncleanness, nor in guile,
4 but as we have been approved by God to be entrusted
with the good news, so we speak, not as pleasing men,
but God, who is proving our hearts,
5 for at no time did we come with speech of flattery, (as
you[P] have known,) nor in a pretext for covetousness,
(God [is] witness!)
6 nor seeking glory of men, neither from you[P] nor from
others, being able to be burdensome, as Christ's
apostles.
7 But we became gentle in your[P] midst, as a nurse may
cherish her own children,
8 so being desirous of you[P], we are well-pleased to impart
to you[P] not only the good news of God, but also our own
souls, because you[P] have become beloved to us,
9 for you[P] remember, brethren, our labor and travail, for,
night and day working not to be a burden upon any of
you[P], we did preach to you[P] the good news of God;
10 you[P] [are] witnesses — God also — how we became
kindly and righteously, and blamelessly to you[P] who
believe,
11 even as you[P] have known, how each one of you[P], as
a father his own children, we are exhorting you[P], and
comforting, and testifying,
12 for your[P] walking worthily of God, who is calling you[P]
to His own reign and glory.
13 Because of this also, we — we do give thanks to
God continually, that, having received the word of
hearing of God from us, you[P] accepted, not the word of
man, but as it is truly, the word of God, who also does
work in you[P] who believe;
14 for you[P] became imitators, brethren, of the assemblies
of God that are in Judea in Christ Jesus, because such
things you[P] suffered, even you[P], from your[P] own
countrymen, as also they from the Jews,
15 who did put to death both the Lord Jesus and their
own prophets, and did persecute us, and they are not

pleasing God, and [are] contrary to all men,
16 forbidding us to speak to the nations that they might
be saved, to fill up their sins always, but the anger did
come upon them — to the end!
17 And we, brethren, having been taken from you[P] for
the space of an hour — in presence, not in heart — did
hasten the more abundantly to see your[P] face in much
desire,
18 for what reason we wished to come unto you[P], (I
indeed Paul,) both once and again, and the Adversary
did hinder us;
19 for what [is] our hope, or joy, or crown of rejoicing?
are not even you[P] before our Lord Jesus Christ in His
presence?
20 for you[P] are our glory and joy.

CHAPTER 3

1 For what reason no longer forbearing, we thought
good to be left in Athens alone,
2 and did send Timotheus — our brother, and a
ministrant of God, and our fellow-workman in the good
news of the Christ — to establish you[P], and to comfort
you[P] concerning your[P] faith,
3 that no one be moved in these tribulations, for
yourselves[P] have known that we are set for this,
4 for even when we were with you[P], we said to you[P]
beforehand, that we are about to suffer tribulation, as
also it did come to pass, and you[P] have known [it];
5 because of this also, I, no longer forbearing, did send
to know your[P] faith, for fear that he who is tempting did
tempt you[P], and our labor might be in vain.
6 And now Timotheus having come unto us from you[P],
and having declared good news of your[P] faith and love
to us, and that you[P] have a good remembrance of us
always, desiring much to see us, as we also [to see] you[P],
7 because of this we were comforted, brethren, over
you[P], in all our tribulation and necessity, through your[P]
faith,
8 because now we live, if you[P] may stand fast in the
Lord;
9 for what thanks are we able to recompense to God for
you[P], for all the joy with which we do joy because of
you[P] in the presence of our God?
10 exceedingly begging night and day, that we might
see your[P] face, and perfect the things lacking in your[P]
faith.
11 And our God and Father Himself, and our Lord Jesus
Christ, direct our way unto you[P],
12 and the Lord cause you[P] to increase and to abound
in the love to one another, and to all, even as we also to
you[P],
13 to the establishing your[P] hearts blameless in
sanctification before our God and Father, in the presence
of our Lord Jesus Christ with all His saints.

CHAPTER 4

1 As to the rest, then, brethren, we request you[P], and
call upon you[P] in the Lord Jesus, as you[P] did receive
from us how it is necessary for you[P] to walk and to please
God, that you[P] may abound the more,
2 for you[P] have known what commands we gave you[P]
through the Lord Jesus,
3 for this is the will of God — your[P] sanctification; that
you[P] abstain from the whoredom,
4 that each of you[P] know his own vessel to possess in
sanctification and honor,
5 not in the affection of desire, as also the nations that
were not knowing God,
6 that no one go beyond and defraud his brother in the
matter, because the Lord [is] an avenger of all these, as
also we spoke before to you[P] and testified,
7 for God did not call us on uncleanness, but in
sanctification;
8 he, for that reason, who is despising — does not
despise man, but God, who also did give His Holy Spirit
to us.
9 And concerning the brotherly love, you[P] have no need
of [my] writing to you[P], for you[P] yourselves[P] are God-
taught to love one another,
10 for you[P] do it also to all the brethren who [are] in all
Macedonia; and we call upon you[P], brethren, to abound
still more,
11 and to study to be quiet, and to do your[P] own
business, and to work with your[P] own hands, as we did
command you[P],
12 that you[P] may walk becomingly unto those without,
and may have lack of nothing.
13 And I do not wish you[P] to be ignorant, brethren,
concerning those who have fallen asleep, that you[P] may
not sorrow, as also the rest who have not hope,
14 for if we believe that Jesus died and rose again, so also
God He will bring those asleep through Jesus with Him,
15 for this we say to you[P] in the word of the Lord, that
we who are living — who do remain over to the presence

of the Lord — may not precede those asleep,
16 because the Lord Himself, in a shout, in the voice of
a chief-messenger, and in the trump of God, shall come
down from heaven, and the dead in Christ shall rise first,
17 then we who are living, who are remaining over,
together with them shall be caught away in clouds to
meet the Lord in air, and so we shall be always with the
Lord;
18 so, then, comfort you[P] one another in these words.

CHAPTER 5

1 And concerning the times and the seasons, brethren,
you[P] have no need of my writing to you[P],
2 for yourselves[P] have known thoroughly that the day
of the Lord does so come as a thief in the night,
3 for when they may say, Peace and surety, then sudden
destruction does stand by them, as the travail [does]
her who is with child, and they shall not escape;
4 and you[P], brethren, are not in darkness, that the day
may catch you[P] as a thief;
5 all you[P] are sons of light, and sons of day; we are not
of night, nor of darkness,
6 so, then, we may not sleep as also the others, but
watch and be sober,
7 for those sleeping, by night do sleep, and those making
themselves drunk, by night are drunken,
8 and we, being of the day — let us be sober, putting
on a breastplate of faith and love, and an helmet — a
hope of salvation,
9 because God did not appoint us to anger, but to the
acquiring of salvation through our Lord Jesus Christ,
10 who did die for us, that whether we wake — whether
we sleep — together we may live with Him;
11 for what reason, comfort you[P] one another, and build
you[P] up, one the one, as also you[P] do.
12 And we ask you[P], brethren, to know those laboring
among you[P], and leading you[P] in the Lord, and
admonishing you[P],
13 and to esteem them very abundantly in love, because
of their work; be at peace among yourselves[P];
14 and we exhort you[P], brethren, admonish the
disorderly, comfort the feeble-minded, support the infirm,
be patient unto all;
15 see no one may render evil for evil to any one, but
always pursue you[P] that which is good, both to one
another and to all;
16 always rejoice you[P];
17 continually pray you[P];
18 give thanks in every thing, for this [is] the will of
God in Christ Jesus in regard to you[P].
19 Quench not the Spirit;
20 despise not prophesyings;
21 prove all things; hold fast that which is good;
22 abstain you[P] from all appearance of evil;
23 and the God of the peace Himself sanctify you[P]
wholly, and may your[P] whole spirit, and soul, and body,
be preserved unblameably in the presence of our Lord
Jesus Christ;
24 steadfast is He who is calling you[P], who also will do
[it].
25 Brethren, pray for us;
26 salute all the brethren in an holy kiss;
27 I charge you[P] [by] the Lord, that the letter be read to
all the holy brethren;
28 the grace of our Lord Jesus Christ [is] with you[P]!
Amen.

The SECOND Epistle Of Paul The Apostle To The THESSALONIANS

CHAPTER 1

1 Paul, and Silvanus, and Timotheus, to the assembly of Thessalonians in God our Father, and the Lord Jesus Christ:

2 Grace to you[P], and peace, from God our Father, and the Lord Jesus Christ!

3 We ought to give thanks to God always for you[P], brethren, as it is meet, because your[P] faith does increase greatly, and the love of each one of you[P] all does abound, to one another;

4 so that we ourselves do glory in you[P] in the assemblies of God, for your[P] endurance and faith in all your[P] persecutions and tribulations that you[P] bear;

5 a token of the righteous judgment of God, for your[P] being counted worthy of the reign of God, for which also you[P] suffer,

6 since [it is] a righteous thing with God to give back to those troubling you[P] — trouble,

7 and to you[P] who are troubled — rest with us in the revelation of the Lord Jesus from heaven, with messengers of His power,

8 in flaming fire, giving vengeance to those not knowing God, and to those not obeying the good news of our Lord Jesus Christ;

9 who shall suffer justice — age-during destruction — from the face of the Lord, and from the glory of His strength,

10 when He may come to be glorified in His saints, and to be wondered at in all those believing — because our testimony was believed among you[P] — in that day;

11 for which also we do pray always for you[P], that our God may count you[P] worthy of the calling, and may fulfill all the good pleasure of goodness, and the work of the faith in power,

12 that the name of our Lord Jesus Christ may be glorified in you[P], and you[P] in Him, according to the grace of our God and Lord Jesus Christ.

CHAPTER 2

1 And we ask you[P], brethren, in regard to the presence of our Lord Jesus Christ, and of our gathering together unto Him,

2 that you[P] be not quickly shaken in mind, nor be troubled, neither through spirit, neither through word, neither through letters as through us, as that the day of Christ has arrived;

3 let not any one deceive you[P] in any manner, because — if the falling away may not come first, and the man of sin be revealed — the son of the destruction,

4 who is opposing and is raising himself up above all called God or worshipped, so that he has sat down in the sanctuary of God as God, showing himself off that he is God — [the day does not come].

5 Do you[P] not remember that, being yet with you[P], these things I said to you[P]?

6 and now, you[P] have known what is keeping down, for his being revealed in his own time,

7 for the secret of the lawlessness does already work, only he who is keeping down now [will hinder] — till he may be out of the way,

8 and then shall the Lawless One be revealed, whom the Lord shall consume with the spirit of His mouth, and shall destroy with the manifestation of His presence,

9 [him,] whose presence is according to the working of the Adversary, in all power, and signs, and lying wonders,

10 and in all deceitfulness of the unrighteousness in those perishing, because they did not receive the love of the truth for their being saved,

11 and because of this shall God send to them a working of delusion, for their believing the lie,

12 that they may be judged — all who did not believe the truth, but were well pleased in the unrighteousness.

13 And we — we ought to give thanks to God always for you[P], brethren, beloved by the Lord, that God did choose you[P] from the beginning to salvation, in sanctification of the Spirit, and belief of the truth,

14 to which He did call you[P] through our good news, to the acquiring of the glory of our Lord Jesus Christ;
15 so, then, brethren, stand you[P] fast, and hold the deliverances that you[P] were taught, whether through word, whether through our letter;
16 and may our Lord Jesus Christ Himself, and our God and Father, who did love us, and did give comfort age-during, and good hope in grace,
17 comfort your[P] hearts, and establish you[P] in every good word and work.

CHAPTER 3

1 As to the rest, pray you[P], brethren, concerning us, that the word of the Lord may run and may be glorified, as also with you[P],
2 and that we may be delivered from the unreasonable and evil men, for the faith [is] not of all;
3 and steadfast is the Lord, who shall establish you[P], and shall guard [you[P]] from the evil;
4 and we have confidence in the Lord touching you[P], that the things that we command you[P], you[P] both do and will do;
5 and the Lord direct your[P] hearts to the love of God, and to the endurance of the Christ.
6 And we command you[P], brethren, in the name of our Lord Jesus Christ, to withdraw yourselves[P] from every brother walking disorderly, and not after the deliverance that you[P] received from us,
7 for yourselves[P] have known how it is necessary for [you[P]] to imitate us, because we did not act disorderly among you[P];
8 nor did we eat bread of any one for nothing, but in labor and in travail, night and day working, not to be chargeable to any of you[P];
9 not because we have not authority, but that we might give ourselves a pattern to you[P], to imitate us;
10 for even when we were with you[P], this we did command you[P], that if any one is not willing to work, neither let him eat,
11 for we hear of certain walking disorderly among you[P], nothing working, but over working,
12 and such we command and exhort through our Lord Jesus Christ, that with quietness working, they may eat their own bread;
13 and you[P], brethren, may you[P] not be weary doing well,
14 and if any one do not obey our word through the letter, you[P] note this one, and have no company with him, that he may be ashamed,
15 and count [him] not as an enemy, but you[P] admonish [him] as a brother;
16 and may the Lord of the peace Himself give to you[P] the peace always in every way; the Lord [is] with you[P] all!
17 The salutation by the hand of me, Paul, which is a sign in every letter; thus I write;
18 the grace of our Lord Jesus Christ [is] with you[P] all! Amen.

The FIRST Epistle Of Paul The Apostle To
TIMOTHY

CHAPTER 1

1 Paul, an apostle of Jesus Christ, according to a command of God our Savior, and of the Lord Jesus Christ our hope,
2 to Timotheus — genuine child in faith: Grace, kindness, peace, from God our Father, and Christ Jesus our Lord,
3 according as I did exhort you[S] to remain in Ephesus — I going on to Macedonia — that you[S] might charge certain not to teach any other thing,
4 nor to give heed to fables and endless genealogies, that cause questions rather than the building up of God that is in faith: —
5 And the end of the charge is love out of a pure heart, and of a good conscience, and of faith unfeigned,
6 from which certain, having swerved, did turn aside to vain discourse,
7 willing to be teachers of law, not understanding either the things they say, nor concerning what they claim,
8 and we have known that the law [is] good, if any one may use it lawfully;
9 having known this, that law is not set for a righteous man, but for lawless and insubordinate persons, ungodly and sinners, impious and profane, parricides and matricides, men-slayers,
10 whoremongers, sodomites, men-stealers, liars, perjured persons, and if there be any other thing that is adverse to sound doctrine,
11 according to the good news of the glory of the blessed God, with which I was entrusted.
12 And I give thanks to Him who enabled me — Christ Jesus our Lord — that He did reckon me steadfast, having put [me] to the ministration,
13 who before was speaking evil, and persecuting, and insulting, but I found kindness, because, being ignorant, I did [it] in unbelief,
14 and exceedingly abound did the grace of our Lord, with faith and love that [is] in Christ Jesus:
15 steadfast [is] the word, and worthy of all acceptation, that Christ Jesus came to the world to save sinners — I am first of whom;
16 but because of this I found kindness, that Jesus Christ might show forth in me first all long-suffering, for a pattern of those about to believe on Him to life age-during:
17 and to the King of the ages, the incorruptible, invisible, only wise God, [is] honor and glory — to the ages of the ages! Amen.
18 I commit this charge to you[S], child Timotheus, according to the prophesies that went before upon you[S], that you[S] may war the good warfare in them,
19 having faith and a good conscience, which certain having thrust away, did make shipwreck concerning the faith,
20 of whom are Hymenaeus and Alexander, whom I did deliver to the Adversary, that they might be instructed not to speak evil.

CHAPTER 2

1 I exhort, then, first of all, there be made supplications, prayers, intercessions, thanksgivings, for all men:
2 for kings, and all who are in authority, that a quiet and peaceable life we may lead in all piety and gravity,
3 for this [is] right and acceptable before God our Savior,
4 who does will all men to be saved, and to come to the full knowledge of the truth;
5 for one [is] God, one also [is] mediator of God and of men, the man Christ Jesus,
6 who did give Himself a ransom for all — the testimony in its own times —
7 in regard to which I was set a preacher and apostle — truth I say in Christ, I do not lie — a teacher of nations, in faith and truth.
8 I wish, for that reason, that men pray in every place, lifting up kind hands, apart from anger and reasoning;
9 in like manner also the women, in becoming apparel, to adorn themselves with modesty and sobriety, not in braided hair, or gold, or pearls, or garments of great price,
10 but — which becomes women professing godly piety

— through good works.
11 Let a woman in quietness learn in all subjection,
12 and I do not allow a woman to teach, nor to rule a husband, but to be in quietness,
13 for Adam was first formed, then Eve,
14 and Adam was not deceived, but the woman, having been deceived, into transgression came,
15 and she shall be saved through the child-bearing, if they remain in faith, and love, and sanctification, with sobriety.

CHAPTER 3

1 Steadfast [is] the word: If any one does long for the oversight, he desires a right work;
2 it is necessary, for that reason, the overseer to be blameless, a husband of one wife, vigilant, sober, decent, a friend of strangers, apt to teach,
3 not given to wine, not a striker, not given to filthy lucre, but gentle, not contentious, not a lover of money,
4 leading his own house well, having children in subjection with all gravity,
5 (and if any one has not known [how] to lead his own house, how shall he take care of an assembly of God?)
6 not a new convert, for fear that having been puffed up he may fall to a judgment of the devil;
7 and it is necessary for him also to have a good testimony from those without, that he may not fall into reproach and a snare of the devil.
8 Ministrants — in like manner grave, not double-tongued, not given to much wine, not given to filthy lucre,
9 having the secret of the faith in a pure conscience,
10 and let these also first be proved, then let them minister, being unblameable.
11 Women — in like manner grave, not false accusers, vigilant, faithful in all things.
12 Ministrants — let them be husbands of one wife; leading the children well, and their own houses,
13 for those who did minister well do acquire a good step to themselves, and much boldness in faith that [is] in Christ Jesus.
14 These things I write to you[S], hoping to come unto you[S] soon,
15 and if I delay, that you[S] may know how it is necessary for [you[S]] to conduct yourself[S] in the house of God, which is an assembly of the living God — a pillar and foundation of the truth,
16 and, confessedly, great is the secret of piety — God was revealed in flesh, declared righteous in spirit, seen by messengers, preached among nations, believed on in the world, taken up in glory!

CHAPTER 4

1 And the Spirit expressly speaks, that in latter times shall certain fall away from the faith, giving heed to seducing spirits and teachings of demons,
2 speaking lies in hypocrisy, being seared in their own conscience,
3 forbidding to marry — to abstain from meats that God created to be received with thanksgiving by those believing and acknowledging the truth,
4 because every creature of God [is] good, and nothing [is] to be rejected, being received with thanksgiving,
5 for it is sanctified through the word of God and intercession.
6 Placing these things before the brethren, you[S] shall be a good ministrant of Jesus Christ, being nourished by the words of the faith, and of the good teaching, which you[S] did follow after,
7 and reject you[S] the profane and reject old women's fables, and exercise yourself[S] unto piety,
8 for the bodily exercise is unto little profit, and the piety is profitable to all things, a promise having of the life that now is, and of that which is coming;
9 steadfast [is] the word, and worthy of all acceptation;
10 for we both labor for this and are reproached, because we hope on the living God, who is Savior of all men — especially of those believing.
11 Charge these things, and teach;
12 let no one despise your youth, but become you[S] a pattern of those believing in word, in behavior, in love, in spirit, in faith, in purity;
13 till I come, give heed to the reading, to the exhortation, to the teaching;
14 be not careless of the gift in you[S], that was given you[S] through prophecy, with laying on of the hands of the eldership;
15 be careful of these things; be in these things, that your[S] advancement may be revealed in all things;
16 take heed to yourself[S], and to the teaching; remain in them, for doing this thing, both you[S] shall save yourself[S], and those hearing you[S].

CHAPTER 5

1 You[S] may not rebuke an aged person, but be entreating as a father; younger persons as brethren;

2 aged women as mothers, younger ones as sisters — in all purity;

3 honor widows who are really widows;

4 and if any widow have children or grandchildren, let them learn first to show piety to their own house, and to give back a recompense to the parents, for this is right and acceptable before God.

5 And she who is really a widow and desolate, has hoped upon God, and does remain in the supplications and in the prayers night and day,

6 and she who is given to luxury, living — has died;

7 and charge these things, that they may be blameless;

8 and if any one for his own — and especially for those of the household — does not provide, he has denied the faith, and he is worse than an unbeliever.

9 A widow — let her not be enrolled under sixty years of age, having been a wife of one husband,

10 being testified to in good works: if she brought up children, if she entertained strangers, if she washed saints' feet, if she relieved those in tribulation, if she followed after every good work;

11 and be refusing younger widows, for when they may revel against the Christ, they wish to marry,

12 having judgment, because they did cast away the first faith,

13 and at the same time also, they learn [to be] idle, going about the houses; and not only idle, but also tattlers and busybodies, speaking the things they ought not;

14 I wish, for that reason, younger ones to marry, to bear children, to be mistress of the house, to give no occasion to the opposer to reviling;

15 for already certain did turn aside after the Adversary.

16 If any believing man or believing woman have widows, let them relieve them, and let not the assembly be burdened, that it may relieve those really widows.

17 The well-leading elders let them be counted worthy of double honor, especially those laboring in word and teaching,

18 for the Writing said, ' You[S] shall not muzzle an ox treading out,' and 'Worthy [is] the workman of his reward.'

19 Receive not an accusation against an elder, except upon two or three witnesses.

20 Those sinning, reprove before all, that the others also may have fear;

21 I testify fully, before God and the Lord Jesus Christ, and the choice messengers, that you[S] may keep these things, without forejudging, doing nothing by partiality.

22 Be laying hands quickly on no one, nor be having fellowship with sins of others; be keeping yourself[S] pure;

23 no longer be drinking water, but be using a little wine, because of your[S] stomach and of your[S] often infirmities;

24 the sins of certain men are revealed beforehand, leading before to judgment, and certain also they follow after;

25 in like manner also the right works are revealed beforehand, and those that are otherwise are not able to be hid.

CHAPTER 6

1 As many as are servants under a yoke, let them reckon their own masters worthy of all honor, that the name of God and the teaching may not be spoken evil of;

2 and those having believing masters, let them not slight [them], because they are brethren, but rather let them serve, because they are steadfast and beloved, who are partaking of the benefit. These things be teaching and exhorting;

3 if any one be teaching otherwise, and do not consent to sound words — those of our Lord Jesus Christ — and to the teaching according to piety,

4 he is proud, knowing nothing, but doting about questions and word-striving, out of which does come envy, strife, evil-speakings, evil-surmisings,

5 wranglings of men wholly corrupted in mind, and destitute of the truth, supposing the piety to be gain; depart from such;

6 but it is great gain — the piety with contentment;

7 for we did bring nothing into the world — [it is] revealed that we are able to carry nothing out;

8 but having food and raiment — we shall suffice ourselves with these;

9 and those wishing to be rich, do fall into temptation and a snare, and many desires, foolish and hurtful, that sink men into ruin and destruction,

10 for a root of all the evils is the love of money, which certain longing for did go astray from the faith, and did pierce themselves through with many sorrows;

11 and you[S], O man of God, flee these things, and pursue righteousness, piety, faith, love, endurance, meekness;

12 be striving the good strife of the faith, be laying hold
on the life age-during, to which also you[S] were called,
and did profess the right profession before many
witnesses.
13 I charge you[S], before God, who is making all things
alive, and of Christ Jesus, who did testify the right
profession before Pontius Pilate,
14 that you[S] keep the command unspotted, unblameable,
till the manifestation of our Lord Jesus Christ,
15 which in His own times He shall show — the blessed
and only potentate, the King of the kings and Lord of
the lords,
16 who only is having immortality, dwelling in light
unapproachable, whom no one of men did see, nor is able
to see, to whom [is] honor and might age-during! Amen.
17 Charge you[S] those rich in the present age not to be
high-minded, nor to hope in the uncertainty of riches,
but in the living God, who is giving to us all things richly
for enjoyment; —
18 to do good, to be rich in good works, to be ready to
impart, willing to communicate,
19 treasuring up to themselves a right foundation for the
time to come, that they may lay hold on the life age-during.
20 O Timotheus, guard you[S] the thing entrusted,
avoiding the profane vain-words and opposition of the
falsely-named knowledge,
21 which certain professing — did swerve concerning
the faith; the grace [is] with you[S]. Amen.

The SECOND Epistle Of Paul The Apostle To
TIMOTHY

CHAPTER 1

1 Paul, an apostle of Jesus Christ, through the will of God, according to a promise of life that [is] in Christ Jesus,
2 to Timotheus, beloved child: Grace, kindness, peace, from God the Father, and Christ Jesus our Lord!
3 I am thankful to God, whom I serve from ancestors in a pure conscience, that unceasingly I have remembrance concerning you[S] in my supplications night and day,
4 desiring greatly to see you[S], being mindful of your[S] tears, that I may be filled with joy,
5 taking remembrance of the unfeigned faith that is in you[S], that dwelt first in your[S] grandmother Lois, and your[S] mother Eunice, and I am persuaded that also in you[S].
6 For which cause I remind you[S] to stir up the gift of God that is in you[S] through the putting on of my hands,
7 for God did not give us a spirit of fear, but of power, and of love, and of a sound mind;
8 for that reason you[S] may not be ashamed of the testimony of our Lord, nor of me his prisoner, but do you[S] suffer evil along with the good news according to the power of God,
9 who did save us, and did call with an holy calling, not according to our works, but according to His own purpose and grace, that was given to us in Christ Jesus, before the times of the ages,
10 and was made known now through the manifestation of our Savior Jesus Christ, who indeed did abolish death, and did enlighten life and immortality through the good news,
11 to which I was placed a preacher and an apostle, and a teacher of nations,
12 for which cause also I suffer these things, but I am not ashamed, for I have known in whom I have believed, and have been persuaded that he is able to guard that which I have committed to him — to that day.
13 Hold you[S] the pattern of sound words, which you[S] did hear from me, in faith and love that [is] in Christ Jesus;
14 guard you[S] the good thing committed through the Holy Spirit that is dwelling in us;
15 you[S] have known this, that they did turn from me — all those in Asia, of whom are Phygellus and Hermogenes;
16 may the Lord give kindness to the house of Onesiphorus, because many times he did refresh me, and was not ashamed of my chain,
17 but being in Rome, very diligently he sought me, and found;
18 may the Lord give to him to find kindness from the Lord in that day; and you[S] do very well know how many things in Ephesus he did minister.

CHAPTER 2

1 You[S], for that reason, my child, be strong in the grace that [is] in Christ Jesus,
2 and the things that you[S] did hear from me through many witnesses, be committing these things to steadfast men, who shall be sufficient to teach others also;
3 you[S], for that reason, suffer evil as a good soldier of Jesus Christ;
4 no one serving as a soldier did entangle himself with the affairs of life, that he may please him who did enlist him;
5 and if also any one may strive, he is not crowned, except he may strive lawfully;
6 it is necessary for the laboring husbandman to partake first of the fruits;
7 be considering what things I say, for the Lord give understanding in all things to you[S].
8 Remember Jesus Christ, raised out of the dead, of the seed of David, according to my good news,
9 in which I suffer evil — unto bonds, as an evil-doer, but the word of God has not been bound;
10 because of this do I endure all things, because of the choice ones, that they also may obtain salvation that [is] in Christ Jesus, with glory age-during.

11 Steadfast [is] the word: For if we died together — we also shall live together;
12 if we do endure together — we shall also reign together; if we deny [Him], He also shall deny us;
13 if we are not steadfast, He remains steadfast; He is not able to deny Himself.
14 Remind [them] of these things, testifying fully before the Lord — not to strive about words to nothing profitable, but to the subversion of those hearing;
15 be diligent to present yourself[S] approved to God — a workman irreproachable, rightly dividing the word of the truth;
16 and stand aloof from the profane vain talkings, for they will advance to more impiety,
17 and their word will have pasture as a gangrene, of whom is Hymenaeus and Philetus,
18 who did swerve concerning the truth, saying the rising again to have already been, and do overthrow the faith of some;
19 sure, nevertheless, has the foundation of God stood, having this seal, 'The Lord has known those who are His,' and 'Let him depart from unrighteousness — every one who is naming the name of Christ.'
20 And in a great house there are not only vessels of gold and of silver, but also of wood and of earth, and some to honor, and some to dishonor:
21 if, then, any one may cleanse himself from these, he shall be a vessel to honor, sanctified and profitable to the master — having been prepared to every good work,
22 and flee you[S] the youthful lusts, and pursue righteousness, faith, love, peace, with those calling upon the Lord out of a pure heart;
23 and be avoiding the foolish and uninstructed questions, having known that they produce strife,
24 and it is necessary for a servant of the Lord not to strive, but to be gentle unto all, apt to teach, patient under evil,
25 in meekness instructing those opposing — if perhaps God may give to them repentance to an acknowledging of the truth,
26 and they may awake out of the devil's snare, having been caught by him at his will.

CHAPTER 3

1 And this know you[S], that in the last days there shall come perilous times,
2 for men shall be lovers of themselves, lovers of money, boasters, proud, evil-speakers, disobedient to parents, unthankful, unkind,
3 without natural affection, implacable, false accusers, incontinent, fierce, not lovers of those who are good,
4 traitors, heady, lofty, lovers of pleasure more than lovers of God,
5 having a form of piety, and its power having denied; and be turning away from these,
6 for of these there are those coming into the houses and leading the silly women captive, laden with sins, led away with various desires,
7 always learning, and never able to come to a knowledge of truth,
8 and, even as Jannes and Jambres stood against Moses, so also these do stand against the truth, men corrupted in mind, disapproved concerning the faith;
9 but they shall not advance any further, for their folly shall be revealed to all, as theirs also did become.
10 And you[S] — you[S] have followed after my teaching, manner of life, purpose, faith, long-suffering, love, endurance,
11 the persecutions, the afflictions, that befell me in Antioch, in Iconium, in Lystra; what persecutions I endured, and the Lord did deliver me out of all,
12 and all also who will to live piously in Christ Jesus shall be persecuted,
13 and evil men and impostors shall advance to the worse, leading astray and being led astray.
14 And you[S] — be remaining in the things which you[S] did learn and were entrusted with, having known from whom you[S] did learn,
15 and because you[S] have known the Holy Writings from a babe, which are able to make you[S] wise — to salvation, through faith that [is] in Christ Jesus;
16 every Writing [is] God-breathed, and profitable for teaching, for conviction, for setting aright, for instruction that [is] in righteousness,
17 that the man of God may be fitted — for every good work having been completed.

CHAPTER 4

1 I do fully testify, then, before God, and the Lord Jesus Christ, who is about to judge living and dead at his manifestation and his reign —
2 preach the word; be earnest in season, out of season, convict, rebuke, exhort, in all long-suffering and teaching,

3 for there shall be a season when they will not allow
the sound teaching, but according to their own desires
they shall heap up teachers to themselves — itching in
the hearing,
4 and indeed, they shall turn away the hearing from the
truth, and they shall be turned aside to the fables.
5 And you^{S} — watch in all things; suffer evil; do the
work of one proclaiming good news; make full assurance
of your^{S} ministration,
6 for I am already being poured out, and the time of my
release has arrived;
7 I have striven the good strife, I have finished the
course, I have kept the faith,
8 from this time forth there is laid up for me the crown of
the righteousness that the Lord — the Righteous Judge
— shall give to me in that day, and not only to me, but
also to all those loving his manifestation.
9 Be diligent to come unto me quickly,
10 for Demas forsook me, having loved the present age,
and went on to Thessalonica, Crescens to Galatia, Titus
to Dalmatia,
11 Lukas only is with me; having taken Markus, bring
with yourself^{S}, for he is profitable to me for ministration;
12 and I sent Tychicus to Ephesus;
13 the cloak that I left in Troas with Carpus, coming,
bring you^{S} and the books — especially the parchments.
14 Alexander the coppersmith did me much evil; may
the Lord repay to him according to his works,
15 of whom also do you^{S} beware, for greatly has he stood
against our words;
16 in my first defense no one stood with me, but all
forsook me, (may it not be reckoned to them!)
17 and the Lord stood by me, and did strengthen me,
that through me the preaching might be fully assured,
and all the nations might hear, and I was freed out of the
mouth of a lion,
18 and the Lord shall free me from every evil work, and
shall save [me] — to his heavenly kingdom; to whom
[is] the glory to the ages of the ages! Amen.
19 Salute Prisca and Aquilas, and Onesiphorus'
household;
20 Erastus did remain in Corinth, and I left Trophimus in
Miletus infirm;
21 be diligent to come before winter. Eubulus salute does
you^{S}, and Pudens, and Linus, and Claudia, and all the
brethren.
22 The Lord Jesus Christ [is] with your^{S} spirit; the grace
[is] with you^{S}! Amen.

The Epistle Of Paul The Apostle To
TITUS

CHAPTER 1

1 Paul, a servant of God, and an apostle of Jesus Christ,
according to the faith of the choice ones of God, and an
acknowledging of truth that [is] according to piety,
2 upon hope of life age-during, which God, who does
not lie, did promise before times of ages,
3 (and He made known His word in proper times,) in
preaching, which I was entrusted with, according to a
charge of God our Savior,
4 to Titus — true child according to a common faith:
Grace, kindness, peace, from God the Father, and the
Lord Jesus Christ our Savior!
5 I left you[S] in Crete for this cause, that you[S] may arrange
the things lacking, and may set down elders in every
city, as I did appoint to you[S];
6 if any one is blameless, a husband of one wife, having
steadfast children, not under accusation of riotous living
or insubordinate —
7 for it is necessary for the overseer to be blameless, as
God's steward, not self-pleased, nor irascible, not given
to wine, not a striker, not given to filthy lucre;
8 but a lover of strangers, a lover of good men, sober-
minded, righteous, kind, self-controlled,
9 holding — according to the teaching — to the
steadfast word, that he may be able to exhort in the
sound teaching also, and to convict the gainsayers;
10 for there are many both insubordinate, vain-talkers,
and mind-deceivers — especially they of the
circumcision —
11 whose mouth it is necessary to stop, who do overturn
whole households, teaching things that are not
necessary, for filthy lucre's sake.
12 A certain one of them, a prophet of their own, said —
'Cretans! always liars, evil beasts, lazy bellies!'
13 this testimony is true; for which cause convict them
sharply, that they may be sound in the faith,
14 not giving heed to Jewish fables and commands of
men, turning themselves away from the truth;
15 all things, indeed, [are] pure to the pure, and to the
defiled and unsteadfast nothing [is] pure, but even the
mind and the conscience [are] defiled of them;
16 they profess to know God, and they deny [Him] in
the works, being abominable, and disobedient, and
disapproved unto every good work.

CHAPTER 2

1 And you[S] — be speaking what does become the sound
teaching;
2 aged men to be temperate, grave, sober, sound in the
faith, in the love, in the endurance;
3 aged women, in like manner, in deportment as does
become sacred persons, not false accusers, not enslaved
to much wine, teachers of good things,
4 that they may make the young women sober-minded,
to be lovers of [their] husbands, lovers of [their] children,
5 sober, pure, keepers of [their own] houses, good,
subject to their own husbands, that the word of God
may not be spoken evil of.
6 Be exhorting the younger men, in like manner, to be
sober-minded;
7 yourself[S] showing a pattern of good works concerning
all things; in the teaching uncorruptedness, gravity,
incorruptibility,
8 discourse sound, irreprehensible, that he who is of
the contrary part may be ashamed, having nothing evil
to say concerning you[S].
9 Servants – [are] to be subject to their own masters, to
be well-pleasing in all things, not gainsaying,
10 not purloining, but showing all good steadfastness,
that they may adorn the teaching of God our Savior in
all things.
11 For the saving grace of God was made known to all
men,
12 teaching us, that denying the impiety and the worldly
desires, we may live in the present age soberly and
righteously and piously,
13 waiting for the blessed hope and manifestation of
the glory of our great God and Savior Jesus Christ,

14 who did give himself for us, that he might ransom us
from all lawlessness, and might purify a peculiar people
to himself, zealous of good works;
15 be speaking these things, and exhorting, and
convicting, with all charge; let no one despise you[S]!

CHAPTER 3

1 Remind them to be subject to principalities and
authorities, to obey rule, to be ready unto every good
work,
2 to speak evil of no one, not to be quarrelsome —
gentle, showing all meekness to all men,
3 for we were once — also we — thoughtless,
disobedient, led astray, serving desires and varied
pleasures, in malice and envy living, odious — hating
one another;
4 and when the kindness and the love of God our Savior
did appear to men
5 (not by works that [are] in righteousness that we did
but according to His kindness,) He did save us, through
a bathing of regeneration, and a renewing of the Holy
Spirit,
6 which He poured richly upon us, through Jesus Christ
our Savior,
7 that having been declared righteous by His grace, we
may become heirs according to the hope of life age-
during.
8 Steadfast [is] the word; and concerning these things I
counsel you[S] to affirm fully, that they may be thoughtful,
to be leading in good works — who have believed God;
these are the good and profitable things to men,
9 and foolish questions, and genealogies, and
contentions, and strivings about law, stand away from
— for they are unprofitable and vain.
10 A sectarian man, be rejecting after a first and second
admonition,
11 having known that he who [is] such has been
subverted, and does sin, being self-condemned.
12 When I shall send Artemas unto you[S], or Tychicus,
be diligent to come to Nicopolis unto me, for I have
determined to winter there.
13 Bring Zenas the lawyer and Apollos diligently on
their way, that nothing may be lacking to them,
14 and let them learn — ours also — to be leading in
good works to the necessary uses, that they may not be
unfruitful.
15 All those with me do salute you[S]; salute those loving
us in faith; the grace [is] with you[P] all!

The Epistle Of Paul The Apostle To
PHILEMON

1 Paul, a prisoner of Christ Jesus, and Timotheus the
brother, to Philemon our beloved and fellow-worker,
2 and Apphia the beloved, and Archippus our fellow-
soldier, and the assembly in your house:
3 Grace to you[P], and peace, from God our Father, and
the Lord Jesus Christ!
4 I give thanks to my God, always making mention of
you[S] in my prayers,
5 hearing of your[S] love and faith that you[S] have unto
the Lord Jesus and toward all the saints,
6 that the fellowship of your[S] faith may become working
in the full knowledge of every good thing that [is] in
you[S] toward Christ Jesus;
7 for we have much joy and comfort in your[S] love,
because the bowels of the saints have been refreshed
through you[S], brother.
8 Wherefore, having much boldness in Christ to
command you[S] that which is fit —
9 because of the love I rather entreat, being such an one
as Paul the aged, and now also a prisoner of Jesus Christ;
10 I entreat you[S] concerning my child — whom I did
beget in my bonds — Onesimus,
11 who once was unprofitable to you[S], and now is
profitable to me and to you[S],
12 whom I did send again, and him (that is, my own
bowels) you[S] receive,
13 whom I did wish to retain to myself, that in your[S]
behalf he might minister to me in the bonds of the good
news,
14 and apart from your[S] mind I willed to do nothing,
that your[S] good deed may not be as of necessity, but of
willingness,
15 for perhaps because of this he did depart for an hour,
that age-duringly you[S] may have him,
16 no more as a servant, but above a servant — a
beloved brother, especially to me, and how much more
to you[S], both in the flesh and in the Lord!
17 If, then, you[S] have fellowship with me, receive him
as me,
18 and if he did hurt to you[S], or does owe anything, be
reckoning this to me;
19 I, Paul did write with my hand, I — I will repay; that I
may not say that also yourself[S], besides, you[S] do owe
to me.
20 Yes, brother, may I have profit of you[S] in the Lord;
refresh my bowels in the Lord;
21 I did write to you[S] having been confident in your[S]
obedience, having also known that above what I may
say you[S] will do;
22 and at the same time also prepare a lodging for me,
for I hope that through your[P] prayers I shall be granted
to you[P].
23 Epaphras does salute you[S], (my fellow-captive in
Christ Jesus,)
24 Markus, Aristarchus, Demas, Lukas, my fellow-
workmen!
25 The grace of our Lord Jesus Christ [is] with your[P]
spirit! Amen.

The Epistle Of Paul The Apostle To The

HEBREWS

CHAPTER 1

1 In many parts, and many ways, God of old having
spoken to the fathers in the prophets,
2 did speak to us in a Son in these last days, whom He
appointed heir of all things, through whom also He did
make the ages;
3 who being the brightness of the glory, and the impress
of His subsistence, bearing up also the all things by the
saying of His might — having made a cleansing of our
sins through Himself, sat down at the right hand of the
greatness in the highest,
4 having become so much better than the messengers,
as He did inherit a more excellent name than they.
5 For to which of the messengers said He ever, 'You[S]
are My Son — I have begotten you[S] today?' and again,
'I will be to him for a father, and he shall be to Me for a
son?'
6 and when again He may bring in the first-born to the
world, He said, 'And let them bow before him — all
messengers of God;'
7 and unto the messengers, indeed, He said, 'Who is
making His messengers spirits, and His ministers a flame
of fire;'
8 and unto the Son: 'Your[S] throne, O God, [is] to the age
of the age; a scepter of righteousness [is] the scepter of
Your[S] reign;
9 You[S] did love righteousness, and did hate lawlessness;
because of this did He anoint You[S] — God, your God —
with oil of gladness above Your[S] partners;'
10 and, 'You[S], at the beginning, Lord, did found the
earth, and the heavens are a work of Your[S] hands;
11 these shall perish, and You[S] do remain, and all, as a
garment, shall become old,
12 and You[S] shall roll them together as a mantle, and
they shall be changed, and You[S] are the same, and Your[S]
years shall not fail.'
13 And unto which of the messengers said He ever, 'Sit
at My right hand, till I may make your[S] enemies your[S]
footstool?'
14 are they not all spirits of service — for ministration
being sent forth because of those about to inherit
salvation?

CHAPTER 2

1 Because of this it is necessary for [us] to take heed
more abundantly to the things heard, for fear that we
may glide aside,
2 for if the word being spoken through messengers did
become steadfast, and every transgression and
disobedience did receive a just recompense,
3 how shall we escape, having neglected so great
salvation? which a beginning receiving — to be spoken
through the Lord — by those having heard was
confirmed to us,
4 God also bearing joint-witness both with signs and
wonders, and various powers, and distributions of the
Holy Spirit, according to His will.
5 For He did not subject the coming world to
messengers, concerning which we speak,
6 and one in a certain place did testify fully, saying,
'What is man, that You[S] are mindful of him, or a son of
man, that You[S] do look after him?
7 You[S] did make him some little less than messengers,
with glory and honor You[S] did crown Him, and did set
Him over the works of Your[S] hands,
8 You[S] did put all things in subjection under His feet,'
for in the subjecting the all things to Him, He did leave
nothing unsubjected to Him, and now not yet do we see
the all things subjected to Him,
9 and Him who was made some little less than
messengers we see — Jesus — because of the suffering
of the death, having been crowned with glory and honor,
that by the grace of God He might taste of death for every
one.
10 For it was becoming to Him, because of whom [are]
the all things, and through whom [are] the all things,
bringing many sons to glory, the author of their salvation
through sufferings to make perfect,

11 for both He who is sanctifying and those sanctified
[are] all of one, for which cause He is not ashamed to
call them brethren,
12 saying, 'I will declare Your[S] name to my brethren, in
the midst of an assembly I will sing praise to You[S];' and
again, 'I will be trusting on Him;'
13 and again, 'Behold I and the children that God did
give to me.'
14 Seeing, then, the children have partaken of flesh and
blood, He Himself also in like manner did take part of
the same, that through death He might destroy him
having the power of death — that is, the devil —
15 and might deliver those, whoever, with fear of death,
throughout all their life, were subjects of bondage,
16 for, doubtless, it does not lay hold of messengers,
but it lays hold of seed of Abraham,
17 for what reason it did be appropriate for Him in all
things to be made like to the brethren, that He might
become a kind and steadfast chief-priest in the things
with God, to make propitiation for the sins of the people,
18 for in that He suffered, being tempted Himself, He is
able to help those who are tempted.

CHAPTER 3

1 For what reason, holy brethren, partakers of a heavenly
calling, consider the apostle and chief priest of our
profession, Christ Jesus,
2 being steadfast to Him who did appoint Him, as also
Moses in all his house,
3 for this one has been counted worthy of more glory
than Moses , inasmuch as he who does build it has more
honor than the house,
4 for every house is built by some one, and He who did
build the all things [is] God,
5 and Moses indeed [was] steadfast in all his house, as
an attendant, for a testimony of those things that were
to be spoken,
6 and Christ, as a Son over His house, whose house are
we, if we hold fast the boldness and the rejoicing of the
hope unto the end.
7 For what reason, (as the Holy Spirit said, 'Today, if
you[P] may hear His voice —
8 you[P] may not harden your[P] hearts, as in the
provocation, in the day of the temptation in the
wilderness,
9 in which your[P] fathers did tempt Me , they did prove
Me, and saw My works forty years;
10 for what reason I was grieved with that generation,
and said, Always do they go astray in heart, and these
have not known My ways;
11 so I swore in My anger, If they shall enter into My
rest—!')
12 See, brethren, for fear that there shall be in any of
you[P] an evil heart of unbelief in the falling away from
the living God,
13 but exhort you[P] one another every day, while the
Today is called, that none of you[P] may be hardened by
the deceitfulness of the sin,
14 for we have become partakers of the Christ, if we
may hold fast the beginning of the confidence unto the
end,
15 in its being said, 'Today, if you[P] may hear His voice,
you[P] may not harden your[P] hearts, as in the
provocation,'
16 for certain having heard did provoke, but not all who
did come out of Egypt through Moses;
17 but with whom was He grieved forty years? was it
not with those who did sin, whose carcasses fell in the
wilderness?
18 and to whom did He swear that they shall not enter
into His rest, except to those who did not believe? —
19 and we see that they were not able to enter in because
of unbelief.

CHAPTER 4

1 We may fear, then, that a promise being left of entering
into His rest, any one of you[P] may seem to have come
short,
2 for we also are having good news proclaimed, even
as they, but the word heard did not profit them, not being
mixed with faith in those who heard,
3 for we do enter into the rest — we who did believe, as
He said, 'So I swore in My anger, If they shall enter into
My rest—;' and yet the works were done from the
foundation of the world,
4 for He spoke in a certain place concerning the seventh
[day] thus: 'And God did rest in the seventh day from
all His works;'
5 and in this [place] again, 'If they shall enter into My
rest—;'
6 since then, it remains for certain to enter into it, and
those who did first hear good news entered not in
because of unbelief —
7 again He does limit a certain day, 'Today,' (in David

saying, after so long a time,) as it has been said, 'Today,
if you[P] may hear His voice, you[P] may not harden your[P]
hearts,'
8 for if Joshua had given them rest, He would not have
spoken concerning another day after these things;
9 there does remain, then, a sabbatic rest to the people
of God,
10 for he who did enter into his rest, he also rested from
his works, as God from His own.
11 May we be diligent, then, to enter into that rest, that
no one may fall in the same example of the unbelief,
12 for the reckoning of God is living, and working, and
sharp above every two-edged sword, and piercing unto
the dividing asunder both of soul and spirit, of joints
also and marrow, and a discerner of thoughts and intents
of the heart;
13 and there is not a created thing not revealed before
Him, but all things [are] naked and open to His eyes —
with whom is our reckoning.
14 Having, then, a great chief priest passed through the
heavens — Jesus the Son of God — may we hold fast
the profession,
15 for we have not a chief priest unable to sympathize
with our infirmities, but [one] tempted in all things in
like manner — apart from sin;
16 we may come near, then, with freedom, to the throne
of the grace, that we may receive kindness, and find
grace — for seasonable help.

CHAPTER 5

1 For every chief priest — taken out of men — is set in
things [pertaining] to God in behalf of men, that he may
offer both gifts and sacrifices for sins,
2 able to be gentle to those ignorant and going astray,
since himself also is compassed with infirmity;
3 and because of this infirmity he ought, as for the
people, to offer for sins so also for himself;
4 and no one does take the honor to himself, but he
who is called by God, as also Aaron:
5 so also the Christ did not glorify Himself to become
chief priest, but He who spoke unto him: 'You[S] are My
Son, I have begotten You[S] today;'
6 as also in another [place] He said, 'You[S] [are] a priest
— to the age, according to the order of Melchisedek;'
7 who in the days of His flesh having offered up both
prayers and supplications unto Him who was able to
save Him from death — with strong crying and tears —
and having been heard in respect to that which He
feared,
8 through being a Son, did learn by the things which
He suffered — the obedience,
9 and having been made perfect, He did become to all
those obeying him a cause of salvation age-during,
10 having been addressed by God a chief priest,
according to the order of Melchisedek,
11 concerning whom we have much discourse and of
hard explanation to say, since you[P] have become dull of
hearing,
12 for even owing to be teachers, because of the time,
again you[P] have need that one teach you[P] what [are]
the elements of the beginning of the oracles of God, and
you[P] have become having need of milk, and not of strong
food,
13 for every one who is partaking of milk [is] unskilled
in the word of righteousness — for he is an infant,
14 and the strong food is of perfect men, who because
of the use are having the senses exercised, unto the
discernment both of good and of evil.

CHAPTER 6

1 For what reason, having left the word of the beginning
of the Christ, we may advance unto the perfection, not
again a foundation laying of reformation from dead
works, and of faith on God,
2 of the teaching of baptisms, of laying on of hands
also, of rising again of the dead also, and of judgment
age-during,
3 and this we will do, if God may permit,
4 for [it is] impossible for those once enlightened, having
tasted also of the heavenly gift, and having became
partakers of the Holy Spirit,
5 and did taste the good saying of God, the powers
also of the coming age,
6 and having fallen away, to again renew [them] to
reformation, having crucified again the Son of God to
themselves, and exposed to public shame.
7 For earth, that is drinking in the rain many times coming
upon it, and is bringing forth herbs fit for those because
of whom also it is dressed, does partake of blessing from
God,
8 and that which is bearing thorns and briers [is]
disapproved of, and near to cursing, whose end [is] for
burning;
9 and we are persuaded, concerning you[P], beloved, the

things that are better, and accompanying salvation,
though even thus we speak,
10 for God is not unrighteous to forget your[P] work, and
the labor of the love, that you[P] showed to His name,
having ministered to the saints and ministering;
11 and we desire each one of you[P] to show the same
diligence, unto the full assurance of the hope unto the
end,
12 that you[P] may not become slothful, but followers of
those who are inheriting the promises through faith and
patient endurance.
13 For to Abraham God, having made promise, seeing
He was able to swear by no greater, did swear by Himself,
14 saying, 'Blessing indeed I will bless you[S], and
multiplying I will multiply you[S];'
15 and so, having patiently endured, he did obtain the
promise;
16 for men indeed do swear by the greater, and an end
of all controversy to them for confirmation [is] the oath,
17 in which God, more abundantly willing to show to
the heirs of the promise the immutability of his counsel,
did interpose by an oath,
18 that through two immutable things, in which [it is]
impossible for God to lie, we who did flee for refuge to
lay hold on the hope set before [us] may have a strong
comfort,
19 which we have, as an anchor of the soul, both sure
and steadfast, and entering into that within the veil,
20 where a forerunner for us did enter — Jesus, having
become chief priest after the order of Melchisedek — to
the age.

CHAPTER 7

1 For this Melchisedek, king of Salem, priest of God
Most High, who did meet Abraham turning back from
the slaughter of the kings, and did bless him,
2 to whom also did Abraham divide a tenth of all, (first,
indeed, being interpreted, 'King of righteousness,' and
then also, King of Salem, which is, King of Peace,)
3 without father, without mother, without genealogy,
having neither beginning of days nor end of life, and
being made like to the Son of God, does remain a priest
continually.
4 And see how great this one [is], to whom also Abraham
the patriarch did give out a tenth of the best of the spoils,
5 and those, indeed, out of the sons of Levi receiving
the priesthood, a command have to take tithes from the
people according to the law, that is, their brethren, even
though they came forth out of the loins of Abraham;
6 and he who was not reckoned by genealogy of them,
received tithes from Abraham, and he has blessed him
having the promises,
7 and apart from all controversy, the less is blessed by
the better —
8 and here, indeed, men who die do receive tithes, and
there [he], who is testified to that he was living,
9 and so to speak, through Abraham even Levi who is
receiving tithes, has paid tithes,
10 for he was yet in the loins of the father when
Melchisedek met him.
11 If indeed, then, perfection were through the Levitical
priesthood — for the people under it had received law
— what further need, according to the order of
Melchisedek, for another priest to arise, and not to be
called according to the order of Aaron?
12 for the priesthood being changed, of necessity also,
a change of the law does come,
13 for He of whom these things are said has had part in
another tribe, of whom no one gave attendance at the
altar,
14 for [it is] evident that our Lord has arisen out of Judah,
in regard to which tribe Moses spoke nothing
concerning priesthood.
15 And it is yet more abundantly most evident, if
according to the similitude of Melchisedek there does
arise another priest,
16 who came not according to the law of a fleshly
command, but according to the power of an endless life,
17 for He does testify — 'You[S] [are] a priest — to the
age, according to the order of Melchisedek;'
18 for a disannulling indeed does come of the command
going before because of its weakness, and
unprofitableness,
19 (for did the law perfect nothing) and the bringing in
of a better hope, through which we draw near to God.
20 And inasmuch as [it is] not apart from oath, (for those
indeed are become priests apart from oath,
21 and He with an oath through Him who is saying unto
him, 'The Lord swore, and will not repent, You[S] [are] a
priest — to the age, according to the order of
Melchisedek;')
22 by so much has Jesus become surety of a better
covenant,
23 and those indeed who have become priests are many,
because by death they are hindered from remaining;
24 and He, because of His remaining — to the age, has

the priesthood not transient,

25 from where also He is able to save to the very end, those coming through Him unto God — ever living to make intercession for them.

26 For such a chief priest did become us — kind, harmless, undefiled, separate from the sinners, and become higher than the heavens,

27 who has no necessity daily, as the chief priests, first to offer up sacrifice for his own sins, then for those of the people; for this he did once, having offered up himself;

28 for the law does appoint men chief priests, having infirmity, but the word of the oath that [is] after the law [appoints] the Son — to the age having been perfected.

CHAPTER 8

1 And the sum concerning the things spoken of [is]: we have such a chief priest, who did sit down at the right hand of the throne of the greatness in the heavens,

2 a servant of the holy places, and of the true tabernacle, which the Lord did set up, and not man,

3 for every chief priest is appointed to offer both gifts and sacrifices, by reason of which [it is] necessary for this one to have also something that he may offer;

4 for if, indeed, he were upon earth, he would not be a priest — (there being the priests who are offering according to the law, the gifts,

5 who do serve unto an example and shadow of the heavenly things, as Moses had been divinely warned, being about to construct the tabernacle, for 'See (said He) you[S] may make all things according to the pattern that was shown to you[S] in the mount;') —

6 and now He has obtained a more excellent service, how much also is He mediator of a better covenant, which has been sanctioned on better promises,

7 for if that first were faultless, a place would not have been sought for a second.

8 For finding fault, He said to them, 'Behold, days come, says the Lord, and I will complete with the house of Israel, and with the house of Judah, a new covenant,

9 not according to the covenant that I made with their fathers, in the day of My taking [them] by their hand, to bring them out of the land of Egypt — because they did not remain in My covenant, and I did not regard them, said the Lord, —

10 because this [is] the covenant that I will make with the house of Israel, after those days, said the Lord, giving My laws into their mind, and I will write them upon their hearts, and I will be to them for a God, and they shall be to Me for a people;

11 and they shall not teach each his neighbor, and each his brother, saying, Know you[S] the Lord, because they shall all know Me from the small one of them unto the great one of them,

12 because I will be merciful to their unrighteousness, and their sins and their lawlessnesses I will remember no more;' —

13 in the saying 'new,' He has made the first old, and what does become obsolete and is old [is] near disappearing.

CHAPTER 9

1 It had, indeed, then (even the first tabernacle) ordinances of service, also a worldly sanctuary,

2 for a tabernacle was prepared, the first, in which was both the lamp-stand, and the table, and the bread of the presence — which is called 'Holy;'

3 and after the second veil a tabernacle that is called 'Holy of holies,'

4 having a golden censer, and the ark of the covenant overlaid all round about with gold, in which [is] the golden pot having the manna, and the rod of Aaron that budded, and the tables of the covenant,

5 and over it cherubim of the glory, overshadowing the mercy-seat, concerning which we are not now to speak particularly.

6 And these things having been thus prepared, into the first tabernacle, indeed, at all times the priests do go in, performing the services,

7 and into the second, once in the year, only the chief priest, not apart from blood, which he does offer for himself and the errors of the people,

8 the Holy Spirit evidencing this that the way of the holy [places] has not yet been revealed, the first tabernacle having yet a standing;

9 which [is] a simile in regard to the present time, in which both gifts and sacrifices are offered, which are not able, in regard to conscience, to make perfect him who is serving,

10 only in victuals, and drinks, and different baptisms, and fleshly ordinances — till the time of reformation imposed upon [them].

11 And Christ being come, chief priest of the coming good things, through the greater and more perfect

tabernacle not made with hands — that is, not of this creation —

12 neither through blood of goats and calves, but through His own blood, did enter in into the holy places once, having obtained age-during redemption;

13 for if the blood of bulls, and goats, and ashes of an heifer, sprinkling those defiled, does sanctify to the purifying of the flesh,

14 how much more shall the blood of the Christ (who through the age-during Spirit did offer Himself unblemished to God) purify your[P] conscience from dead works to serve the living God?

15 And because of this, He is mediator of a new covenant, that, death having come, for redemption of the transgressions under the first covenant, those called may receive the promise of the age-during inheritance,

16 for where a covenant [is], the death of the covenant-victim is necessary to come in,

17 for a covenant over dead victims [is] steadfast, since it is no force at all when the covenant-victim lives,

18 from which not even the first has been initiated apart from blood,

19 for every command having been spoken, according to law, by Moses, to all the people, having taken the blood of the calves and goats, with water, and scarlet wool, and hyssop, he did sprinkle both the book itself and all the people,

20 saying, 'This [is] the blood of the covenant that God enjoined unto you[P],'

21 and both the tabernacle and all the vessels of the service he did sprinkle with blood in like manner,

22 and with blood almost all things are purified according to the law, and apart from blood-shedding forgiveness does not come.

23 [It is] necessary, for that reason, the pattern indeed of the things in the heavens to be purified with these, and the heavenly things themselves with better sacrifices than these;

24 for the Christ enter did not into holy places made with hands — figures of the true — but into the heaven itself, now to be revealed in the presence of God for us;

25 nor that He may offer Himself many times, even as the chief priest does enter into the holy places every year with blood of others;

26 since it had been necessary for Him to suffer many times from the foundation of the world, but now once, at the full end of the ages, for putting away of sin through his sacrifice, He has been revealed;

27 and as it is laid up to men once to die, and after this — judgment,

28 so also the Christ, having been offered once to bear the sins of many, shall appear a second time, apart from a sin-offering, to those waiting for him — to salvation!

CHAPTER 10

1 For the law having a shadow of the coming good things — not the very image of the matters, every year, by the same sacrifices that they offer continually, is never able to make those coming near perfect,

2 since, would they not have ceased to be offered, because of those serving having no more conscience of sins, having been purified once?

3 but in those [sacrifices] is a remembrance of sins every year,

4 for it is impossible for blood of bulls and goats to take away sins.

5 For what reason, coming into the world, He said, 'Sacrifice and offering You[S] did not will, and You[S] did prepare a body for Me,

6 in burnt-offerings, and concerning sin-offerings, You[S] did not delight,

7 then I said, Behold, I come, (in a volume of the book it has been written concerning me,) to do, O God, Your[S] will;'

8 saying above — 'Sacrifice, and offering, and burnt-offerings, and concerning sin-offering You[S] did not will, nor delight in,' — which are offered according to the law —

9 then He said, 'Behold, I come to do, O God, Your[S] will;' He does take away the first that He may establish the second;

10 in the which will we are having been sanctified through the offering of the body of Jesus Christ once,

11 and every priest, indeed, has stood daily serving, and the same sacrifices offering many times, that are never able to take away sins.

12 And He, having offered one sacrifice for sin — to the end, did sit down on the right hand of God, —

13 as to the rest, expecting till He may place His enemies [as] His footstool,

14 for by one offering He has perfected those sanctified to the end;

15 and the Holy Spirit does testify to us also, for after that He has said before,

16 'This [is] the covenant that I will make with them after those days, said the Lord, giving My laws on their

hearts, and I will write them upon their minds,'
17 and ' I will remember their sins and their lawlessness
no more;'
18 and where forgiveness of these [is], there is no more
offering for sin.
19 Having, for that reason, brethren, boldness for the
entrance into the holy places, in the blood of Jesus,
20 which way He did initiate for us — new and living,
through the veil, that is, His flesh —
21 and a high priest over the house of God,
22 may we draw near with a true heart, in full assurance
of faith, having the hearts sprinkled from an evil
conscience, and having the body bathed with pure
water;
23 may we hold fast the unwavering profession of the
hope, (for faithful [is] He who did promise),
24 and may we consider one another to provoke to love
and to good works,
25 not forsaking the assembling of ourselves together,
as a custom of certain [is], but exhorting, and so much
the more as you[P] see the day coming near.
26 For we — willfully sinning after the receiving the full
knowledge of the truth — no more does there remain a
sacrifice for sins,
27 but a certain fearful looking for of judgment, and fiery
zeal, about to devour the opposers;
28 any one who did set a law of Moses at nothing, apart
from mercies, by two or three witnesses, does die,
29 of how much sorer punishment shall he be counted
worthy who did trample on the Son of God, and did count
the blood of the covenant a common thing, in which he
was sanctified, and did despite to the Spirit of the grace?
30 for we have known Him who is saying, 'Vengeance
[is] Mine, I will recompense, says the Lord;' and again,
'The Lord shall judge His people;' —
31 fearful [is] the falling into the hands of a living God.
32 And call to your[P] remembrance the former days, in
which, having been enlightened, you[P] did endure much
conflict of sufferings,
33 partly both with reproaches and tribulations being
made spectacles, and partly having become partners of
those so living,
34 for also you[P] sympathized with my bonds, and you[P]
did receive the robbery of your[P] goods with joy, knowing
that you[P] have in yourselves[P] a better substance in the
heavens, and an enduring one.
35 You[P] may not cast away, then, your[P] boldness, which
has great recompense of reward,
36 for you[P] have need of patience, that the will of God
having done, you[P] may receive the promise,
37 for yet a very very little, He who is coming will come,
and will not tarry;
38 and 'the righteous shall live by faith,' and 'if he may
draw back, My soul has no pleasure in him,'
39 and we are not of those drawing back to destruction,
but of those believing to a preserving of soul.

CHAPTER 11

1 And faith is a confidence of things hoped for, a
conviction of matters not seen,
2 for in this were the elders testified of;
3 by faith we understand the ages to have been prepared
by a saying of God, in regard to the things seen not
having come out of things appearing;
4 by faith did Abel offer a better sacrifice to God than
Cain, through which he was testified to be righteous,
God testifying of his gifts, and through it, he being dead,
does yet speak.
5 By faith Enoch was translated — not to see death,
and was not found, because God did translate him; for
before his translation he had been testified to — that he
had pleased God well,
6 and apart from faith it is impossible to please well, for
it is necessary for him who is coming to God to believe
that He is, and to those seeking Him He becomes a
rewarder.
7 By faith Noah, having been divinely warned
concerning the things not yet seen, having feared, did
prepare an ark to the salvation of his house, through
which he did condemn the world, and according to faith
he became heir of the righteousness.
8 By faith Abraham, being called, did obey, to go forth
to the place that he was about to receive for an
inheritance, and he went forth, not knowing where he
did go;
9 by faith he did sojourn in the land of the promise as a
strange country, having dwelt with Isaac and Jacob in
tabernacles, fellow-heirs of the same promise,
10 for he was looking for the city having the foundations,
whose artificer and constructor [is] God.
11 By faith also Sarah herself did receive power to
conceive seed, and she bare after the time of life, seeing
she did judge Him who did promise faithful;
12 for what reason, also from one were begotten — and
that of one who had become dead — as the stars of the
heaven in multitude, and as sand that [is] by the sea-

shore — the innumerable.
13 All these died in faith, not having received the
promises, but having seen them from afar, and having
been persuaded, and having saluted [them], and having
confessed that they are strangers and sojourners upon
the earth,
14 for those saying such things make known that they
seek a country;
15 and if, indeed, they had been mindful of that from
which they came forth, they might have had an
opportunity to return,
16 but now they long for a better, that is, an heavenly,
for what reason God is not ashamed of them, to be called
their God, for He did prepare for them a city.
17 By faith Abraham had offered up Isaac, being tried,
and he did offer up the only begotten who did receive
the promises,
18 of whom it was said — 'In Isaac shall a seed be called
to you[S];'
19 reckoning that God is able to raise up even out of the
dead, from where also in a figure he did receive [him].
20 By faith, concerning coming things, Isaac did bless
Jacob and Esau;
21 by faith Jacob dying — did bless each of the sons of
Joseph, and did bow down upon the top of his staff;
22 by faith, Joseph dying, did make mention concerning
the outgoing of the sons of Israel, and did give command
concerning his bones.
23 By faith Moses, having been born, was hid three
months by his parents, because they saw the child
comely, and were not afraid of the decree of the king;
24 by faith Moses, having become great, did refuse to
be called a son of the daughter of Pharaoh,
25 having chosen rather to be afflicted with the people
of God, than to have sin's pleasure for a season,
26 having reckoned the reproach of the Christ greater
wealth than the treasures in Egypt, for he did look to
the recompense of reward;
27 by faith he left Egypt behind, not having been afraid
of the wrath of the king, for, as seeing the Invisible One
— he endured;
28 by faith he kept the Passover, and the sprinkling of
the blood, that He who is destroying the first-born might
not touch them.
29 By faith they did pass through the Red Sea as through
dry land, which the Egyptians having received a trial of,
were swallowed up;
30 by faith the walls of Jericho did fall, having been
surrounded for seven days;
31 by faith Rahab the harlot did not perish with those
who disbelieved, having received the spies with peace.
32 And what shall I yet say? for the time will fail me
recounting about Gideon, Barak also, and Samson, and
Jephthah, David also, and Samuel, and the prophets,
33 who did subdue kingdoms through faith, worked
righteousness, obtained promises, stopped mouths of
lions,
34 quenched the power of fire, escaped the mouth of
the sword, were made powerful out of infirmities, became
strong in battle, caused camps of the aliens to give way.
35 Women received their dead by a rising again, and
others were tortured, not accepting the redemption, that
they might receive a better rising again,
36 and others did receive trial of mockings and
scourgings, and yet of bonds and imprisonment;
37 they were stoned, they were sawn apart, they were
tried; they died in the killing of the sword; they went
about in sheepskins, in goatskins — being destitute,
afflicted, injuriously treated,
38 of whom the world was not worthy; in deserts
wandering, and [in] mountains, and [in] caves, and [in]
the holes of the earth;
39 and these all, having been testified to through the
faith, did not receive the promise,
40 God having provided something better for us, that
apart from us they might not be made perfect.

CHAPTER 12

1 For that reason, we also having so great a cloud of
witnesses set around us, having put off every weight,
and the closely besetting sin, through endurance may
we run the contest that is set before us,
2 looking to the author and perfecter of faith — Jesus,
who, over-against the joy set before him — did endure
a cross, having despised shame, did sit down on the
right hand also of the throne of God;
3 for consider again Him who endured such gainsaying
from the sinners to Himself, that you[P] may not be wearied
in your[P] souls — being faint.
4 Not yet did you[P] resist unto blood — striving with
the sin;
5 and you[P] have forgotten the exhortation that does
speak fully with you[P] as with sons, 'My son, be not
despising chastening of the Lord, nor be faint, being
reproved by Him,
6 for whom the Lord does love He does chasten, and

He chastises every son whom He receives;'
7 if you endure chastening, as to sons God bears Himself
to you[P], for who is a son whom a father does not
chasten?
8 and if you[P] are apart from chastening, of which all
have become partakers, then you[P] are bastards, and not
sons.
9 Then, indeed, we have had fathers of our flesh,
chastising [us], and we were reverencing [them]; shall
we not much rather be subject to the Father of the spirits,
and live?
10 for they, indeed, for a few days, according to what
seemed good to them, were chastening, but He for profit,
to be partakers of His separation;
11 and all chastening for the present, indeed, does not
seem to be of joy, but of sorrow, yet afterward the
peaceable fruit of righteousness to those exercised
through it — it does yield.
12 For what reason, set you[P] up the hanging-down
hands and the loosened knees;
13 and make straight paths for your[P] feet, that that which
is lame may not be turned aside, but rather be healed;
14 pursue peace with all, and the separation, apart from
which no one shall see the Lord,
15 looking diligently over for fear that any one be failing
of the grace of God, for fear that any root of bitterness
springing up may give trouble, and through this many
may be defiled;
16 for fear that any one be a fornicator, or a profane
person, as Esau, who did sell his birthright in exchange
for one morsel of food,
17 for you[P] know that also afterwards, wishing to inherit
the blessing, he was disapproved of, for he found not a
place of reformation, though having sought it with tears.
18 For you[P] came not near to the mount touched and
scorched with fire, and to blackness, and darkness, and
tempest,
19 and a sound of a trumpet, and a voice of sayings,
which those having heard did entreat that a word might
not be added to them,
20 for they were not bearing that which is commanded,
'And if a beast may touch the mountain, it shall be
stoned, or with an arrow shot through,'
21 and, (so terrible was the sight,) Moses said, 'I am
exceedingly fearful, and trembling.'
22 But, you[P] came to Mount Zion, and to a city of the
living God, to the heavenly Jerusalem, and to myriads
of messengers,
23 to the company and assembly of the first-born
enrolled in heaven, and to God the judge of all, and to
spirits of righteous men made perfect,
24 and to a mediator of a new covenant — Jesus, and to
blood of sprinkling, speaking better things than that of
Abel!
25 See, may you[P] not refuse Him who is speaking, for if
those did not escape who refused Him who was divinely
speaking upon earth — much less we who do turn away
from Him who [speaks] from heaven,
26 whose voice the earth shook then, and now has He
promised, saying, 'Yet once — I shake not only the earth,
but also the heaven;'
27 and this — 'Yet once' — does make evident the
removal of the things shaken, as of things having been
made, that the things not shaken may remain;
28 for what reason, receiving a kingdom that cannot be
shaken, may we have grace, through which we may serve
God well-pleasingly, with reverence and religious fear;
29 for also our God [is] a consuming fire.

CHAPTER 13

1 Let brotherly love remain;
2 be not forgetful of the hospitality, for through this
certain did entertain messengers unawares;
3 be mindful of those in bonds, as having been bound
with them, of those maltreated, as also yourselves[P] being
in the body;
4 honorable [is] the marriage in all, and the bed undefiled,
and God shall judge whoremongers and adulterers.
5 The behavior without covetousness, being content
with the things present, for He has said, 'No, I will not
leave, no, nor forsake you[S],'
6 so that we do boldly say, 'The Lord [is] a helper to
me, and I will not fear what man shall do to me.'
7 Be mindful of those leading you[P], who did speak the
word of God to you[P], whose faith — considering the
issue of the behavior — be imitating,
8 Jesus Christ the same yesterday and today, and to
the ages;
9 be not carried about with various and strange
teachings, for [it is] good that the heart be confirmed by
grace, not with meats, in which they who were occupied
were not profited;
10 we have an altar, of which they who are serving the
tabernacle have no authority to eat,
11 for of those beasts whose blood is brought for sin
into the holy places through the chief priest — of these

the bodies are burned without the camp.
12 For what reason, also Jesus — that He might sanctify
the people through [His] own blood — did suffer without
the gate;
13 now, then, may we go forth unto Him without the
camp, bearing His reproach;
14 for we have not here an abiding city, but we seek the
coming one;
15 through Him, then, we may offer up a sacrifice of
praise always to God, that is, the fruit of lips, giving
thanks to His name;
16 and of doing good, and of fellowship, be not forgetful,
for God is well-pleased with such sacrifices.
17 Be obedient to those leading you[P], and be subject,
for these do watch for your[P] souls, as about to give
account, that they may do this with joy, and not sighing,
for this [is] unprofitable to you[P].
18 Pray for us, for we trust that we have a good
conscience, willing to behave well in all things,
19 and more abundantly do I call upon [you[P]] to do
this, that I may be restored to you[P] more quickly.
20 And the God of the peace, who did bring up the great
shepherd of the sheep out of the dead — in the blood
of an age-during covenant — our Lord Jesus,
21 make you[P] perfect in every good work to do His will,
doing in you[P] that which is well-pleasing before Him,
through Jesus Christ, to whom [is] the glory — to the
ages of the ages! Amen.
22 And I entreat you[P], brethren, allow the word of the
exhortation, for also I have written to you[P] through few
words.
23 Know you[P] that the brother Timotheus is released,
with whom, if he may come more shortly, I will see you[P].
24 Salute all those leading you[P], and all the saints; those
from Italy do salute you[P]:
25 the grace [is] with you[P] all! Amen.

The Epistle Of
JAMES

CHAPTER 1

1 James, of God and of the Lord Jesus Christ a servant,
to the Twelve Tribes who are in the dispersion: Hail!
2 Count [it] all joy, my brethren, when you^P may fall into
various temptations;
3 knowing that the proof of your^P faith does work
endurance,
4 and let the endurance have a perfect work, that you^P
may be perfect and entire — lacking in nothing;
5 and if any of you^P do lack wisdom, let him ask from
God, who is giving to all liberally, and not reproaching,
and it shall be given to him;
6 and let him ask in faith, doubting nothing, for he who
is doubting has been like a wave of the sea, driven by
wind and tossed,
7 for let that man not suppose that he shall receive
anything from the Lord —
8 a two-souled man [is] unstable in all his ways.
9 And let the brother who is low rejoice in his exaltation,
10 and the rich in his becoming low, because he shall
pass away as a flower of grass;
11 for the sun did rise with the burning heat, and did
wither the grass, and the flower of it fell, and the grace
of its appearance did perish, so also the rich in his way
shall fade away!
12 Happy the man who does endure temptation,
because, becoming approved, he shall receive the crown
of the life, which the Lord did promise to those loving
Him.
13 Let no one say, being tempted — 'I am tempted from
God,' for God is not tempted of evil, and Himself does
tempt no one,
14 and each one is tempted, being led away and enticed
by his own desires,
15 afterward the desire having conceived, does give
birth to sin, and the sin having been perfected, does
bring forth death.
16 Be not led astray, my beloved brethren;
17 every good giving, and every perfect gift is from
above, coming down from the Father of the lights, with
whom is no variation, or shadow of turning;
18 having counseled, He did produce us with a word of
truth, for our being a certain first-fruit of His creatures.
19 So then, my beloved brethren, let every man be swift
to hear, slow to speak, slow to anger,
20 for the wrath of a man does not work the
righteousness of God;
21 for what reason having put aside all filthiness and
superabundance of evil, be receiving the engrafted word
in meekness, that is able to save your^P souls;
22 and become you^P doers of the word, and not hearers
only, deceiving yourselves^P,
23 because, if any one is a hearer of the word and not a
doer, this one has been like to a man viewing his natural
face in a mirror,
24 for he did view himself, and has gone away, and
immediately he did forget of what kind he was;
25 and he who did look into the perfect law — that of
liberty, and did continue there, this one — not becoming
a forgetful hearer, but a doer of work — this one shall be
happy in his doing.
26 If any one does think to be religious among you^P,
not bridling his tongue, but deceiving his heart, of this
one the religion [is];
27 religion pure and undefiled with the God and Father
is this, to look after orphans and widows in their
tribulation — to keep himself unspotted from the world.

CHAPTER 2

1 My brethren, hold not, in respect of persons, the faith
of the glory of our Lord Jesus Christ,
2 for if there may come into your^P synagogue a man
with gold ring, in gay raiment, and there may come in
also a poor man in vile raiment,
3 and you^P may look upon him bearing the gay raiment,
and may say to him, 'You^S — sit you^S here well,' and to
the poor man may say, 'You^S — stand you^S there, or, Sit
you^S here under my footstool,' —

4 you[P] did not judge fully in yourselves[P], and did become
ill-reasoning judges.
5 Listen, my beloved brethren, did not God choose the
poor of this world, rich in faith, and heirs of the reign
that He promised to those loving Him?
6 and you[P] did dishonor the poor one; do not the rich
oppress you[P] and themselves draw you[P] to judgment-
seats;
7 do they not themselves speak evil of the good name
that was called upon you[P]?
8 If, indeed, you[P] complete royal law, according to the
Writing, 'You[S] shall love your[S] neighbor as yourself[S],'
— you[P] do well;
9 and if you[P] accept persons, you[P] do work sin, being
convicted by the law as transgressors;
10 for whoever shall keep the whole law, and shall
stumble in one [point], he has become guilty of all;
11 for He who is saying, 'You[S] may not commit adultery,'
said also, 'You[S] may do no murder;' and if you[S] shall not
commit adultery, and shall commit murder, you[S] have
become a transgressor of law;
12 so you[P] speak and so do, as about to be judged by a
law of liberty,
13 for the judgment without kindness [is] to him not
having done kindness, and exult does kindness over
judgment.
14 What [is] the profit, my brethren, if faith, any one
may speak of having, and he may not have works? is
that faith able to save him?
15 and if a brother or sister may be naked, and may be
destitute of the daily food,
16 and any one of you[P] may say to them, 'Depart you[P]
in peace, be warmed, and be filled,' and may not give to
them the things needful for the body, what [is] the profit?
17 so also the faith, if it may not have works, is dead by
itself.
18 But say may some one, You[S] have faith, and I have
works, show me your[S] faith out of your[S] works, and I
will show you[S] out of my works my faith:
19 you[S] — you[S] do believe that God is one; you[S] do
well, and the demons believe, and they shudder!
20 And do you[S] wish to know, O vain man, that the faith
apart from the works is dead?
21 Abraham our father — was not he declared righteous
out of works, having brought up Isaac his son upon the
altar?
22 do you[S] see that the faith was working with his works,
and out of the works the faith was perfected?
23 and fulfilled was the Writing that is saying, 'And
Abraham did believe God, and it was reckoned to him
— to righteousness;' and, he was called 'Friend of God'.
24 You[P] see, then, that out of works is man declared
righteous, and not out of faith only;
25 and in like manner also Rahab the harlot — was she
not declared righteous out of works, having received
the messengers, and by having sent forth another way?
26 for as the body apart from the spirit is dead, so also
the faith apart from the works is dead.

CHAPTER 3

1 Become not many teachers, my brethren, having
known that greater judgment we shall receive,
2 for we all make many stumbles; if any one does not
stumble in word, this one [is] a perfect man, able to bridle
also the whole body;
3 behold, the bits we put into the mouths of the horses
for their obeying us, and their whole body we turn about;
4 behold, also the ships, being so great, and by fierce
winds being driven, are led about by a very small helm,
wheresoever the impulse of the helmsman does counsel,
5 so also the tongue is a little member, and does boast
greatly; behold, a little fire how it does kindle much
wood!
6 and the tongue [is] a fire, the world of the
unrighteousness, so the tongue is set in our members,
which is spotting our whole body, and is setting on fire
the course of nature, and is set on fire by the gehenna.
7 For every nature, both of beasts and of fowls, both of
creeping things and things of the sea, is subdued, and
has been subdued, by the human nature,
8 and no one of men is able to subdue the tongue, [it is]
an unruly evil, full of deadly poison,
9 with it we do bless the God and Father, and with it we
do curse the men made according to the similitude of
God;
10 out of the same mouth does come forth blessing and
cursing; it does not need, my brethren, these things so
to happen;
11 does the fountain pour forth the sweet and the bitter
out of the same opening?
12 is a fig-tree able, my brethren, to make olives? or a
vine figs? so no fountain [is able] to make salt and sweet
water.
13 Who [is] wise and intelligent among you[P]? let him
show his works out of the good behavior in meekness
of wisdom,

14 and if you[P] have bitter zeal, and rivalry in your[P] heart, glory not, nor lie against the truth;

15 this wisdom is not descending from above, but earthly, physical, demon-like,

16 for where zeal and rivalry [are], there is insurrection and every evil matter;

17 and the wisdom from above, first, indeed, is pure, then peaceable, gentle, easily entreated, full of kindness and good fruits, uncontentious, and unhypocritical: —

18 and the fruit of the righteousness in peace is sown to those making peace.

CHAPTER 4

1 From where [are] wars and fightings among you[P]? not from there — out of your[P] passions, that are as soldiers in your[P] members?

2 you[P] desire, and you[P] have not; you[P] murder, and are zealous, and are not able to attain; you[P] fight and war, and you[P] have not, because of your[P] not asking;

3 you[P] ask, and you[P] receive not, because you[P] ask evilly, that in your[P] pleasures you may spend [it].

4 Adulterers and adulteresses! have you[P] not known that friendship of the world is enmity with God? whoever, then, may counsel to be a friend of the world, he is set an enemy of God.

5 Do you[P] think that emptily the Writing says, ' The spirit that did dwell in us earnestly desires to envy,'

6 and greater grace he does give, for what reason he says, 'God does set Himself up against proud ones, and He does give grace to lowly ones?'

7 be subject, then, to God; stand up against the devil, and he will flee from you[P];

8 draw near to God, and He will draw near to you[P]; cleanse hands, you[P] sinners! and purify hearts, you[P] two-souled!

9 be exceeding afflicted, and mourn, and weep, let your[P] laughter be turned to mourning, and the joy to heaviness;

10 be made low before the Lord, and He shall exalt you[P].

11 Speak not one against another, brethren; he who is speaking against a brother, and is judging his brother, does speak against law, and does judge law, and if you[S] do judge law, you[S] are not a doer of law but a judge;

12 one is the lawgiver, who is able to save and to destroy; you[S] — who are you[S] that does judge the other?

13 Go, now, you[P] who are saying, 'Today and tomorrow we will go on to such a city, and will pass there one year, and traffic, and make gain;'

14 who do not know the thing of the morrow; for what is your[P] life? for it is a vapor that is appearing for a little, and then is vanishing;

15 instead of your[P] saying, 'If the Lord may will, we shall live, and do this or that;'

16 and now you[P] glory in your[P] pride; all such glorying is evil;

17 to him, then, knowing to do good, and not doing, it is sin to him.

CHAPTER 5

1 Go, now, you[P] rich! weep, howling over your[P] miseries that are coming upon [you[P]];

2 your[P] riches have rotted, and your[P] garments have become moth-eaten;

3 your[P] gold and silver have rotted, and the rust of them shall be for a testimony to you[P], and shall eat your[P] flesh as fire. You[P] made treasure in the last days!

4 behold, the reward of the workmen, of those who in-gathered your fields, which has been fraudulently kept back by you[P] — does cry out, and the exclamations of those who did reap have entered into the ears of the Lord of Sabaoth;

5 you[P] did live in luxury upon the earth, and were wanton; you[P] did nourish your[P] hearts, as in a day of slaughter;

6 you[P] did condemn — you[P] did murder the righteous one, he does not resist you[P].

7 Be patient, then, brethren, till the presence of the Lord; behold, the husbandman does expect the precious fruit of the earth, being patient for it, till he may receive rain — early and latter;

8 be patient, you[P] also; establish your[P] hearts, because the presence of the Lord has drawn near;

9 murmur not against one another, brethren, that you[P] may not be condemned; behold, the Judge has stood before the door.

10 Take you[P] an example of the suffering of evil, my brethren, and of the patience, the prophets who did speak in the name of the Lord;

11 behold, we call happy those who are enduring; you[P] heard of the endurance of Job, and you[P] have seen the end of the Lord, that very compassionate is the Lord, and pitying.

12 And before all things, my brethren, do not swear, neither by the heaven, neither by the earth, neither by any other oath, and let your[P] Yes be Yes, and the No,

No; that you[P] may not fall under judgment.
13 Does any one suffer evil among you[P]? let him pray;
is any of good cheer? let him sing psalms;
14 is any infirm among you[P]? let him call for the elders
of the assembly, and let them pray over him, having
anointed him with oil, in the name of the Lord,
15 and the prayer of the faith shall save the distressed
one, and the Lord shall raise him up, and if he may have
committed sins, they shall be forgiven to him.
16 Be confessing to one another the trespasses, and be
praying for one another, that you[P] may be healed; very
strong is a working supplication of a righteous man;
17 Elijah was a man like affected as we, and with prayer
he did pray — not to rain, and it did not rain upon the
land three years and six months;
18 and again he did pray, and the heaven did give rain,
and the land did bring forth her fruit.
19 Brethren, if any among you[P] may go astray from the
truth, and any one may turn him back,
20 let him know that he who did turn back a sinner from
the straying of his way shall save a soul from death,
and shall cover a multitude of sins.

The FIRST Epistle Of
PETER

CHAPTER 1

1 Peter, an apostle of Jesus Christ, to the choice
sojourners of the dispersion of Pontus, Galatia,
Cappadocia, Asia, and Bithynia,
2 according to a foreknowledge of God the Father, in
sanctification of the Spirit, to obedience and sprinkling
of the blood of Jesus Christ: Grace to you[P] and peace be
multiplied!
3 Blessed [is] the God and Father of our Lord Jesus
Christ, who, according to the abundance of His kindness
did beget us again to a living hope, through the rising
again of Jesus Christ out of the dead,
4 to an inheritance incorruptible, and undefiled, and
unfading, reserved in the heavens for you[P],
5 who, are being guarded in the power of God, through
faith, unto salvation, ready to be revealed in the last time,
6 in which you[P] are glad, a little now, if it be necessary,
being made to sorrow in various trials,
7 that the proof of your[P] faith — much more precious
than of gold that is perishing, and being approved
through fire — may be found to praise, and honor, and
glory, in the revelation of Jesus Christ,
8 whom, not having seen, you[P] love, in whom, now not
seeing and believing, you[P] are glad with joy unspeakable
and glorified,
9 receiving the end of your[P] faith — salvation of souls;
10 concerning which salvation prophets did seek out
and search out, who did prophecy concerning the grace
toward you[P],
11 searching in regard to what or what manner of time
the Spirit of Christ that was revealing in them, testifying
beforehand the sufferings of Christ and the glory after
these,
12 to whom it was revealed, that not to themselves, but
they were ministering these to us, which now were told
to you[P] (through those who did proclaim good news to
you[P],) in the Holy Spirit sent from heaven, to which
things messengers do desire to bend looking.
13 For what reason having girded up the loins of your[P]
mind, being sober, hope perfectly upon the grace that is
being brought to you[P] in the revelation of Jesus Christ,
14 as obedient children, not fashioning yourselves[P] to
the former desires in your[P] ignorance,
15 but according as He who did call you[P] [is] holy, you[P]
also, become holy in all behavior,
16 because it has been written, 'Become you[P] holy,
because I am holy;'
17 and if you[P] do call on the Father, who without
acceptance of persons is judging according to the work
of each, pass you[P] the time of your[P] sojourn in fear,
18 having known that, not with corruptible things —
silver or gold — were you[P] redeemed from your[P] foolish
behavior delivered by fathers,
19 but with precious blood, as of a lamb unblemished
and unspotted — Christ's —
20 foreknown, indeed, before the foundation of the
world, and revealed in the last times because of you[P],
21 who do believe in God through Him, who did raise
out of the dead, and did give glory to Him, so that your[P]
faith and hope may be in God.
22 Your[P] souls having purified in the obedience of the
truth through the Spirit to brotherly love unfeigned, love
you[P] one another earnestly out of a pure heart,
23 being begotten again, not out of corruptible seed,
but incorruptible, through a word of God — living and
remaining — to the age;
24 because all flesh [is] as grass, and all glory of man as
flower of grass; the grass did wither, and the flower of it
fell away,
25 and the saying of the Lord does remain — to the
age; and this is the saying that was proclaimed good
news to you[P].

CHAPTER 2

1 Having put aside, then, all evil, and all guile, and
hypocrisies, and envyings, and all evil speakings,
2 as new-born babes desire you[P] the word's pure milk,
that you[P] may grow in it,

3 if so be you^P did taste that the Lord [is] gracious,
4 to whom coming — a living stone — by men, indeed, having been disapproved of, but with God choice, precious,
5 and you^P yourselves^P, as living stones, are built up, a spiritual house, a holy priesthood, to offer up spiritual sacrifices acceptable to God through Jesus Christ.
6 For what reason, also, it is contained in the Writing: 'Behold, I lay in Zion a chief corner-stone, choice, precious, and he who is believing on him may not be put to shame;'
7 to you^P, then, who are believing [is] the preciousness; and to the unbelieving, a stone that the builders disapproved of, this one did become for the head of a corner,
8 and a stone of stumbling and a rock of offence — who are stumbling at the word, being unbelieving, — to which also they were set;
9 and you^P [are] a choice race, a royal priesthood, a holy nation, a people acquired, that you^P may show forth the excellences of Him who did call you^P out of darkness to His wondrous light;
10 who [were] once not a people, and [are] now the people of God; who had not found kindness, and now have found kindness.
11 Beloved, I call upon [you^P], as strangers and sojourners, to keep from the fleshly desires, that war against the soul,
12 having your^P behavior right among the nations, that in that which they speak against you^P as evil-doers, having beheld of the good works, they may glorify God in a day of inspection.
13 Be subject, then, to every human creation, because of the Lord, whether to a king, as the highest,
14 whether to governors, as to those sent through him, for punishment, indeed, of evil-doers, and a praise of those doing good;
15 because, so is the will of God, doing good, to put to silence the ignorance of the foolish men;
16 as free, and not having the freedom as the cloak of the evil, but as servants of God;
17 give you^P honor to all; love you^P the brotherhood; fear you^P God; honor you^P the king.
18 The domestics! be subjecting yourselves^P in all fear to the masters, not only to the good and gentle, but also to the cross;
19 for this [is] gracious, if because of conscience toward God any one does endure sorrows, suffering unrighteously;
20 for what renown [is it], if sinning and being buffeted, you^P do endure [it]? but if, doing good and suffering [for it], you^P do endure, this [is] gracious with God,
21 for you^P were called to this, because Christ also did suffer for you^P, leaving to you^P an example, that you^P may follow His steps,
22 who did not commit sin, nor was guile found in His mouth,
23 who being reviled — was not reviling again, suffering — was not threatening, and was committing Himself to Him who is judging righteously,
24 who Himself did bear our sins in His body, upon the tree, that having died to the sins, we may live to the righteousness; by whose stripes you^P were healed,
25 for you^P were as sheep going astray, but you^P turned back now to the shepherd and overseer of your^P souls.

CHAPTER 3

1 In like manner, the wives, be you^P subject to your^P own husbands, that even if certain are disobedient to the word, through the conversation of the wives, without the word, they may be won,
2 having beheld your^P pure behavior in fear,
3 whose adorning — let it not be that which is outward, of plaiting of hair, and of putting around of things of gold, or of putting on of garments,
4 but — the hidden man of the heart, in the incorruptible thing of the meek and quiet spirit, which is, before God, of great price,
5 for thus once also the holy women who did hope on God, were adorning themselves, being subject to their own husbands,
6 as Sarah was obedient to Abraham, calling him 'sir,' of whom you^P did become daughters, doing good, and not fearing any terror.
7 The husbands, in like manner, dwelling with [them], according to knowledge, as to a weaker vessel — to the wife — imparting honor, as also being heirs together of the grace of life, that your^P prayers be not hindered.
8 And finally, being all of one mind, having fellow-feeling, loving as brethren, compassionate, courteous,
9 not giving back evil for evil, or railing for railing, and on the contrary, blessing, having known that you^P were called to this, that you^P may inherit a blessing;
10 for 'he who is willing to love life, and to see good days, let him guard his tongue from evil, and his lips — not to speak guile;

11 let him turn aside from evil, and do good, let him seek peace and pursue it;
12 because the eyes of the Lord [are] upon the righteous, and His ears — to their supplication, and the face of the Lord [is] upon those doing evil;'
13 and who [is] he who will be doing you evil, if you[P] may become imitators of Him who is good?
14 but if you[P] also should suffer because of righteousness, happy [are you[P]]! and be not afraid of their fear, nor be troubled,
15 and sanctify the Lord God in your[P] hearts. And [be] ready always for defense to every one who is asking of you[P] an account concerning the hope that [is] in you[P], with meekness and fear;
16 having a good conscience, that in that in which they speak against you[P] as evil-doers, they may be ashamed who are traducing your[P] good behavior in Christ;
17 for [it is] better doing good, if the will of God will it, to suffer, than doing evil;
18 because also Christ once did suffer for sin — righteous for unrighteous — that he might lead us to God, having been put to death indeed, in the flesh, and having been made alive in the spirit,
19 in which also having gone he did preach to the spirits in prison,
20 who sometime disbelieved, when once the long-suffering of God did wait, in days of Noah — being preparing an ark — in which few, that is, eight souls, were saved through water;
21 also to which an antitype does now save us — baptism, (not a putting away of the filth of flesh, but the question of a good conscience in regard to God,) through the rising again of Jesus Christ,
22 who is at the right hand of God, having gone on to heaven — messengers, and authorities, and powers, having been subjected to Him.

CHAPTER 4

1 Christ, then, having suffered for us in the flesh, you[P] also with the same mind arm yourselves[P], because He who did suffer in the flesh has done with sin,
2 no more in the desires of men, but in the will of God, to live the rest of the time in the flesh;
3 for sufficient to us [is] the past time of life to have worked the will of the nations, having walked in lasciviousnesses, desires, excesses of wines, revellings, drinking-bouts, and unlawful idolatries,
4 in which they think it strange — your[P] not running with them to the same excess of dissoluteness, speaking evil,
5 who shall give an account to Him who is ready to judge living and dead,
6 for for this was good news proclaimed also to dead men, that they may be judged, indeed, according to men in the flesh, and may live according to God in the spirit.
7 And the end of all things has come near; be sober-minded, then, and watch unto the prayers,
8 and, before all things, having the earnest love to one another, because the love shall cover a multitude of sins;
9 hospitable to one another, without murmuring;
10 each, according as he received a gift, ministering it to one another, as good stewards of the varied grace of God;
11 if any one does speak — 'as oracles of God;' if any one does minister — 'as of the ability which God does supply;' that God may be glorified in all things through Jesus Christ, to whom is the glory and the power — to the ages of the ages. Amen.
12 Beloved, think it not strange at the fiery suffering among you[P] that is coming to try you[P], as if a strange thing were happening to you[P],
13 but, according as you[P] have fellowship with the sufferings of the Christ, rejoice you[P], that also you[P] may rejoice, exulting, in the revelation of his glory;
14 if you[P] be reproached in the name of Christ — happy [are you[P]], because the Spirit of glory and of God does rest upon you[P]; in regard, indeed, to them, He is evil-spoken of, and in regard to you[P], He is glorified;
15 for let none of you[P] suffer as a murderer, or thief, or evil-doer, or as an inspector into other men's matters;
16 and if as a Christian, let him not be ashamed; and let him glorify God in this respect;
17 because it is the time of the beginning of the judgment from the house of God, and if first from us, what the end of those disobedient to the good news of God?
18 And if the righteous man is scarcely saved, the ungodly and sinner — where shall he appear?
19 so that also those suffering according to the will of god, as to a steadfast Creator, let them commit their own souls in good doing.

CHAPTER 5

1 Elders who [are] among you[P], I exhort, who [am] a fellow-elder, and a witness of the sufferings of the Christ,

and a partaker of the glory about to be revealed,
2 feed the flock of God that [is] among you[P], overseeing
not constrainedly, but willingly, neither for filthy lucre,
but of a ready mind,
3 neither as exercising lordship over the heritages, but
becoming patterns of the flock,
4 and at the manifestation of the chief Shepherd, you[P]
shall receive the unfading crown of glory.
5 In like manner, you[P] younger, be subject to elders, and
all subjecting yourselves[P] to one another; clothe
yourselves[P] with humble-mindedness, because God does
resist the proud, but He does give grace to the humble;
6 be humbled, then, under the powerful hand of God,
that He may exalt you[P] in good time,
7 having cast all your[P] care upon Him, because He cares
for you[P].
8 Be sober, vigilant, because your[P] opponent the devil,
as a roaring lion, does walk about, seeking whom he may
swallow up,
9 whom resist, steadfast in the faith, having known the
same sufferings to be accomplished to your[P]
brotherhood in the world.
10 And the God of all grace, who did call you[P] to His
age-during glory in Christ Jesus, having suffered a little,
Himself make you[P] perfect, establish, strengthen, settle
[you[P]];
11 to Him [is] the glory, and the power — to the ages
and the ages! Amen.
12 Through Silvanus, the faithful brother to you[P], as I
reckon, through few [words] I did write, exhorting and
testifying this to be the true grace of God in which you[P]
have stood.
13 The [assembly] jointly elected in Babylon does salute
you[P], and Markus my son.
14 Salute you[P] one another in a kiss of love; peace to
you[P] all who [are] in Christ Jesus! Amen.

The SECOND Epistle Of
PETER

CHAPTER 1

1 Simeon Peter, a servant and an apostle of Jesus Christ, to those who did obtain a like precious faith with us in the righteousness of our God and Savior Jesus Christ:
2 Grace to you[P], and peace be multiplied in the acknowledgment of God and of Jesus our Lord!
3 As His divine power (the things pertaining unto life and piety) has given all things to us, through the acknowledgment of Him who did call us through glory and worthiness,
4 through which the most great and precious promises have been given to us, that through these you[P] may become partakers of a divine nature, having escaped from the corruption in the world in desires.
5 And this same also — having brought in all diligence besides, supplied in your[P] faith the worthiness, and in the worthiness the knowledge,
6 and in the knowledge the temperance, and in the temperance the endurance, and in the endurance the piety,
7 and in the piety the brotherly kindness, and in the brotherly kindness the love;
8 for these things being to you[P] and abounding, do make [you[P]] neither inert nor unfruitful in regard to the acknowledging of our Lord Jesus Christ,
9 for he with whom these things are not present is blind, dim-sighted, having become forgetful of the cleansing of his old sins;
10 for what reason, the rather, brethren, be diligent to make your[P] calling and choice steadfast, for doing these things, you[P] may never stumble,
11 for so, richly shall be supplied to you[P] the entrance into the age-during reign of our Lord and Savior Jesus Christ.
12 For what reason, I will not be careless always to remind you[P] concerning these things, though, having known them, and having been established in the present truth,
13 and I think right, so long as I am in this tabernacle, to stir you[P] up in reminding [you[P]],
14 having known that soon is the laying aside of my tabernacle, even as also our Lord Jesus Christ did show to me,
15 and I will be diligent that also you[P] have at every time, after my outgoing, power to make to yourselves[P] the remembrance of these things.
16 For, not having followed out skillfully devised fables, we did make known to you[P] the power and presence of our Lord Jesus Christ, but having become eye-witnesses of his majesty —
17 for having received honor and glory from God the Father, such a voice being borne to Him by the excellent glory: 'This is My Son — the beloved, in whom I was well pleased;'
18 and this voice we — we did hear, borne out of heaven, being with Him in the holy mount.
19 And we have the prophetic word more firm, to which we do well giving heed, as to a lamp shining in a dark place, till day may dawn, and a morning star may arise — in your[P] hearts;
20 this first knowing, that no prophecy of the Writing does come of private exposition,
21 for not by will of man did prophecy ever come, but borne on by the Holy Spirit, holy men of God spoke.

CHAPTER 2

1 And there did come also false prophets among the people, as also among you[P] there shall be false teachers, who shall bring in besides destructive sects, and denying the Master who bought them, bringing to themselves quick destruction,
2 and many shall follow out their destructive ways, because of whom the way of the truth shall be evil spoken of,
3 and in covetousness, with molded words, they shall make merchandise of you[P], whose judgment of old is not idle, and their destruction does not slumber.
4 For if God did not spare messengers who sinned, but

with chains of thick gloom, having cast [them] down to Tartarus, did deliver [them] to judgment, having been reserved,
5 and did not spare the old world, but the eighth person, Noah, a preacher of righteousness, did keep, having brought a flood on the world of the impious,
6 and having turned the cities of Sodom and Gomorrah to ashes, did condemn with an overthrow, an example to those about to be impious having set [them];
7 and righteous Lot, worn down by the conduct in lasciviousness of the impious, He did rescue,
8 for in seeing and hearing, the righteous man, dwelling among them, day by day the righteous soul was harassing with unlawful works.
9 The Lord has known to rescue pious ones out of temptation, and unrighteous ones to a day of judgment, being punished, to keep,
10 and chiefly those going behind the flesh in desire of uncleanness, and despising lordship; presumptuous, self-complacent, they are not afraid to speak evil of dignities,
11 whereas messengers, being greater in strength and power, do not bear an evil speaking judgment against them before the Lord;
12 and these, as irrational natural beasts, made to be caught and destroyed — in what things they are ignorant of, speaking evil — in their destruction shall be destroyed,
13 about to receive a reward of unrighteousness, counting the luxury in the day pleasures, spots and blemishes, luxuriating in their deceits, feasting with you[P],
14 having eyes full of adultery, and unable to cease from sin, enticing unstable souls, having an heart exercised in covetousnesses, children of a curse,
15 having forsaken a right way, they did go astray, having followed in the way of Balaam the [son] of Bosor, who did love a reward of unrighteousness,
16 and had a rebuke of his own iniquity — a dumb ass, having spoken in man's voice, did forbid the madness of the prophet.
17 These are wells without water, and clouds driven by a tempest, to whom the thick gloom of the darkness to the age has been kept;
18 for overswellings speaking of vanity, they do entice in desires of the flesh — lasciviousnesses, those who had truly escaped from those conducting themselves in error,
19 promising liberty to them, themselves being servants of the corruption, for by whom any one has been overcome, to this one also he has been brought to servitude,
20 for, if having escaped from the pollutions of the world, in the acknowledging of the Lord and Savior Jesus Christ, and being entangled by these again, they have been overcome, the last things has become worse to them than the first,
21 for it were better to them not to have acknowledged the way of the righteousness, than having acknowledged [it], to turn back from the holy command delivered to them,
22 and that of the true similitude has happened to them; 'A dog did turn back upon his own vomit,' and, 'A sow having bathed herself — to rolling in mire.'

CHAPTER 3

1 This, now, beloved, I write a second letter to you[P], in both which I stir up your[P] pure mind in reminding [you[P]],
2 to be mindful of the sayings said by the holy prophets before, and of the command of us the apostles of the Lord and Savior,
3 this first knowing, that there shall come in the latter end of the days scoffers, going on according to their own desires,
4 and saying, 'Where is the promise of His presence? for since the fathers did fall asleep, all things so remain from the beginning of the creation;'
5 for this is willingly unobserved by them, that the heavens were of old, and the earth out of water and through water standing together by the word of God,
6 through which the then world, having been deluged by water, was destroyed;
7 and the present heavens and the earth, are treasured by the same word, being kept for fire to a day of judgment and destruction of the impious men.
8 And this one thing let not be unobserved by you[P], beloved, that one day with the Lord [is] as a thousand years, and a thousand years as one day;
9 the Lord is not slow in regard to the promise, as certain count slowness, but is long-suffering to us, not counseling any to be lost but all to pass on to reformation,
10 and it will come — the day of the Lord — as a thief in the night, in which the heavens will pass away with a rushing noise, and the elements be dissolved with burning heat, and earth and the works in it shall be burnt up.

11 All these, then, being dissolved, what kind of persons
does it necessitate you^{P} to be in holy behaviors and
pious acts?
12 waiting for and hasting to the presence of the day of
God, by which the heavens, being on fire, shall be
dissolved, and the elements shall melt with burning heat;
13 and we do wait for new heavens and a new earth
according to His promise, in which righteousness does
dwell;
14 for what reason, beloved, these things waiting for,
be diligent, spotless and unblameable, to be found in
peace by Him,
15 and count you the long-suffering of our Lord
salvation, according as also our beloved brother Paul
— according to the wisdom given to him — did write to
you^{P},
16 as also in all the epistles, speaking in them concerning
these things, among which things are certain hard to be
understood, which the untaught and unstable do wrest,
as also the other Writings, unto their own destruction.
17 You^{P}, then, beloved, knowing before, take heed, for
fear that, together with the error of the impious being
led away, you^{P} may fall from your^{P} own steadfastness,
18 and increase you^{P} in grace, and in the knowledge of
our Lord and Savior Jesus Christ; to him [is] the glory
both now, and to the day of the age! Amen.

The FIRST Epistle Of
JOHN

CHAPTER 1

1 That which was from the beginning, that which we have heard, that which we have seen with our eyes, that which we did behold, and our hands did handle, concerning the Word of the Life —
2 and the Life was revealed, and we have seen, and do testify, and declare to you[P] the Life, the age-during, which was with the Father, and was shown to us —
3 that which we have seen and heard we declare to you[P], that you[P] may also have fellowship with us, and our fellowship [is] with the Father, and with His Son Jesus Christ;
4 and we write these things to you[P], that your[P] joy may be full.
5 And this is the message that we have heard from Him, and announce to you[P], that God is light, and darkness is not at all in Him;
6 if we may say — 'we have fellowship with Him,' and may walk in the darkness — we lie, and do not the truth;
7 and if we may walk in the light, as He is in the light — we have fellowship one with another, and the blood of Jesus Christ His Son does cleanse us from every sin;
8 if we may say — 'we have not sin,' we lead ourselves astray, and the truth is not in us;
9 if we may confess our sins, He is steadfast and righteous that He may forgive us the sins, and may cleanse us from every unrighteousness;
10 if we may say — 'we have not sinned,' we make Him a liar , and His word is not in us.

CHAPTER 2

1 My little children, I write these things to you[P], that you may not sin[P]: and if any one may sin, we have an advocate with the Father, Jesus Christ, a righteous one,
2 and he — he is an atoning sacrifice for our sins, and not only for ours , but also for the whole world,
3 and in this we know that we have known him, if his commands we may keep;
4 he who is saying, 'I have known him,' and is not keeping his command, he is a liar, and the truth is not in him;
5 and whoever may keep his word, truly the love of God has been perfected in him; in this we know that we are in him.
6 He who is saying he does remain in him, should also himself walk as according he walked.
7 Brethren, I write not a new command to you[P], but an old command, that you[P] had from the beginning — the old command is the word that you[P] heard from the beginning;
8 again, I write to you[P] a new command, which thing is true in him and in you[P], because the darkness does pass away, and the true light does now shine;
9 he who is saying, he is in the light, and is hating his brother, he is in the darkness till now;
10 he who is loving his brother, he does remain in the light, and there is not a stumbling-block in him;
11 and he who is hating his brother, he is in the darkness, and he does walk in the darkness, and he has not known where he does go, because the darkness did blind his eyes.
12 I write to you[P], little children, because the sins have been forgiven you[P] through his name;
13 I write to you[P], fathers, because you[P] have known him who [is] from the beginning; I write to you[P], young men, because you[P] have overcome the evil. I write to you[P], little youths, because you[P] have known the Father:
14 I did write to you[P], fathers, because you[P] have known him who [is] from the beginning; I did write to you[P], young men, because you[P] are strong, and the word of God does remain in you[P], and you[P] have overcome the evil.
15 Love you[P] not the world, nor the things in the world; if any one does love the world, the love of the Father is not in him,
16 because all that [is] in the world — the desire of the flesh, and the desire of the eyes, and the boastful showiness of the life — is not of the Father, but of the world,

17 and the world does pass away, and the desire of it,
and he who is doing the will of God, he does remain —
to the age.
18 Little youths, it is the last hour; and even as you[P] heard
that the antichrist does come, even now antichrists have
become many — when we know that it is the last hour;
19 they went forth out of us, but they were not of us,
for if they had been of us, they would have remained
with us; but — that they might be plainly shown that
they are not all of us.
20 And you[P] have an anointing from the Holy One, and
have known all things;
21 I did not write to you[P] because you[P] have not known
the truth, but because you[P] have known it, and because
no lie is of the truth.
22 Who is the liar, except he who is denying that Jesus
is the Christ? this one is the antichrist who is denying
the Father and the Son;
23 every one who is denying the Son, neither has he
the Father, [he who is confessing the Son has the Father
also.]
24 You[P], then, that which you[P] heard from the beginning,
let it remain in you[P]; if that which you[P] did hear from the
beginning may remain in you[P], you[P] also shall remain in
the Son and in the Father,
25 and this is the promise that He did promise us — the
life the age-during.
26 I did write these things to you[P] concerning those
leading you[P] astray;
27 and you[P], the anointing that you[P] did receive from
him, it does remain in you[P], and you[P] have no need that
any one may teach you[P], but as the same anointing does
teach you[P] concerning all, and is true, and is not a lie,
and even as was taught you[P], you[P] shall remain in him.
28 And now, little children, remain in him, that when he
may be made known, we may have boldness, and may
not be ashamed before him, in his presence;
29 if you[P] know that he is righteous, you[P] know that
every one doing the righteousness, has been begotten
of him.

CHAPTER 3

1 You[P] see what love the Father has given to us, that we
may be called children of God; because of this the world
does not know us, because it did not know Him;
2 beloved, now, we are children of God, and it was not
yet made known what we shall be, and we have known
that if he may be made known, we shall be like him,
because we shall see him as he is;
3 and every one who is having this hope on him, does
purify himself, even as he is pure.
4 Every one who is doing the sin, he also does do the
lawlessness, and the sin is the lawlessness,
5 and you[P] have known that he was made known that
he may take away our sins, and sin is not in him;
6 every one who is remaining in him does not sin; every
one who is sinning, has not seen him, nor known him.
7 Little children, let no one lead you[P] astray; he who is
doing the righteousness is righteous, even as he is
righteous,
8 he who is doing the sin, he is of the devil, because the
devil did sin from the beginning; the Son of God was
made known for this, that he may break up the works of
the devil;
9 every one who has been begotten of God, he does
not sin, because his seed does remain in him, and he is
not able to sin, because he has been begotten of God.
10 In this are the children of God obvious, and the
children of the devil; every one who is not doing
righteousness, is not of God, and he who is not loving
his brother,
11 because this is the message that you[P] did hear from
the beginning, that we may love one another,
12 not as Cain – he was of the evil one, and he did slay
his brother, and why did he slay him? because his works
were evil, and those of his brother righteous.
13 Do not wonder, my brethren, if the world does hate
you[P];
14 we — we have known that we have passed out of
the death to the life, because we love the brethren; he
who is not loving the brother does remain in the death.
15 Every one who is hating his brother – he is a man-
killer, and you[P] have known that no man-killer has life
age-during remaining in him,
16 in this we have known the love, because he did lay
down his life for us, and we ought to lay down the lives
for the brethren;
17 and whoever may have the goods of the world, and may
view his brother having need, and may shut up his bowels
from him — how does the love of God remain in him?
18 My little children, may we not love in word nor in
tongue, but in word and in truth!
19 and in this we know that we are of the truth, and
before Him we shall assure our hearts,
20 because if our heart may condemn – because God is
greater than our heart, and He does know all things.

21 Beloved, if our heart may not condemn us, we have boldness toward God,

22 and whatever we may ask, we receive from Him, because we keep His commands, and we do the things pleasing before Him,

23 and this is His command, that we may believe in the name of His Son Jesus Christ, and may love one another, even as He did give command to us,

24 and he who is keeping His commands, he does remain in Him, and He in him; and in this we know that He does remain in us, from the Spirit that He gave us.

CHAPTER 4

1 Beloved, believe not every spirit, but prove the spirits, if they are of God, because many false prophets have gone forth to the world;

2 in this you[P] know the Spirit of God; every spirit that does confess Jesus Christ having come in the flesh, it is of God,

3 and every spirit that does not confess Jesus Christ having come in the flesh, it is not of God; and this is that of the antichrist, which you[P] heard that it does come, and now it is already in the world.

4 You[P] – you[P] are of God, little children, and you[P] have overcome them; because greater is He who [is] in you[P], than he who is in the world.

5 They – they are of the world; because of this they speak from the world, and the world does hear them;

6 we – we are of God; he who is knowing God does hear us; he who is not of God, does not hear us; from this we know the spirit of the truth, and the spirit of the error.

7 Beloved, may we love one another, because the love is of God, and every one who is loving, he has been begotten of God, and does know God;

8 he who is not loving did not know God, because God is love.

9 In this the love of God was made known in us, because His Son — the only begotten – God has sent to the world, that we may live through him;

10 in this is the love, not that we loved God, but that He did love us, and did send His Son a propitiation for our sins.

11 Beloved, if God did so love us, we should also love one another;

12 no one has ever seen God; if we may love one another, God does remain in us, and His love is having been perfected in us;

13 in this we know that we do remain in Him, and He in us, because He has given us of His Spirit.

14 And we — we have seen and do testify, that the Father has sent the Son — Savior of the world;

15 whoever may confess that Jesus is the Son of God, God does remain in him, and he in God;

16 and we — we have known and believed the love, that God has in us; God is love, and he who is remaining in the love, he does remain in God, and God in him.

17 In this has been the love with us made perfect, that boldness we may have in the day of the judgment, because even as He is, we — we also are in this world;

18 fear is not in the love, but the perfect love does cast out the fear, because the fear has punishment, and he who is fearing has not been made perfect in the love;

19 we — we love him, because He — He first loved us;

20 if any one may say — 'I love God,' and his brother he may hate, he is a liar; for he who is not loving his brother whom he has seen, how is he able to love God, whom has not seen?

21 and this [is] the command we have from Him, that he who is loving God, may also love his brother.

CHAPTER 5

1 Every one who is believing that Jesus is the Christ, he has been begotten of God, and every one who is loving Him who did beget, does also love him who is begotten of Him:

2 in this we know that we love the children of God, when we may love God, and His commands may keep;

3 for this is the love of God, that we may keep His commands, and His commands are not burdensome;

4 because every one who is begotten of God does overcome the world, and this is the victory that did overcome the world — our faith;

5 who is he who is overcoming the world, if not he who is believing that Jesus is the Son of God?

6 This one is he who did come through water and blood — Jesus the Christ, not in the water only, but in the water and the blood; and it is the Spirit that is testifying, because the Spirit is the truth,

7 because three are who are testifying [in the heaven, the Father, the Word, and the Holy Spirit, and these — the three — are one;

8 and three are who are testifying in the earth], the Spirit, and the water, and the blood, and the three are into the one.

9 If we receive the testimony of men, the testimony of

God is greater, because this is the testimony of God that
He has testified concerning His Son.
10 He who is believing in the Son of God, has the
testimony in himself; he who is not believing God, has
made Him a liar, because he has not believed in the
testimony that God has testified concerning His Son;
11 and this is the testimony, that God did give to us life
age-during, and this — the life — is in His Son;
12 he who is having the Son, has the life; he who is not
having the Son of God – he has not the life.
13 I did write these things to you[P] who are believing in
the name of the Son of God, that you[P] may know that
you[P] have life age-during, and that you[P] may believe in
the name of the Son of God.
14 And this is the boldness that we have toward Him,
that if anything we may ask according to his will, He
does hear us,
15 and if we have known that He does hear us, whatever
we may ask, we have known that we have the requests
that we have requested from Him.
16 If any one may see his brother sinning a sin not unto
death, he shall ask, and He shall give to him life to those
sinning not unto death; there is sin to death, not
concerning it do I speak that he may beg;
17 all unrighteousness is sin, and there is sin not unto
death.
18 We have known that every one who has been
begotten of God does not sin, but he who was begotten
of God does keep himself, and the evil one does not
touch him;
19 we have known that we are of God, and the whole
world in the evil does lie;
20 and we have known that the Son of God is come, and
has given us a mind, that we may know Him who is true,
and we are in Him who is true, in His Son Jesus Christ;
this one is the true God and the life age-during!
21 Little children, guard yourselves[P] from the idols!
Amen.

The SECOND Epistle Of
JOHN

1 The Elder to the choice Kyria, and to her children,
whom I love in truth, and not I only, but also all those
having known the truth,
2 because of the truth that is remaining in us, and shall
be with us to the age,
3 there shall be with you[P] grace, kindness, peace, from
God the Father, and from the Lord Jesus Christ, the Son
of the Father, in truth and love.
4 I rejoiced exceedingly that I have found of your[S]
children walking in truth, even as a command we did
receive from the Father;
5 and now I beg you[S], Kyria, not as writing to you[S] a
new command, but which we had from the beginning,
that we may love one another,
6 and this is the love, that we may walk according to
His commands; this is the command, even as you[P] did
hear from the beginning, that in it you[P] may walk,
7 because many leading astray did enter into the world,
who are not confessing Jesus Christ coming in flesh;
this one is he who is leading astray, and the antichrist.
8 See to yourselves[P] that you[P] may not lose the things
that we worked, but may receive a full reward;
9 every one who is transgressing, and is not remaining
in the teaching of the Christ, has not God; he who is
remaining in the teaching of the Christ, this one has both
the Father and the Son;
10 if any one does come unto you[P], and does not bear
this teaching, receive him not into the house, and say
not to him, 'Hail!'
11 for he who is saying to him, 'Hail,' has fellowship
with his evil works.
12 Having many things to write to you[P], I did not intend
through paper and ink, but I hope to come unto you[P],
and speak mouth to mouth, that our joy may be full;
13 the children of your[S] choice sister do salute you[S].
Amen.

The THIRD Epistle Of
JOHN

1 The Elder to Gaius the beloved, whom I love in truth!
2 beloved, I desire you^{S} to prosper concerning all things,
and to be in health, even as your^{S} soul does prosper,
3 for I rejoiced exceedingly, brethren coming and
testifying of the truth in you^{S}, even as you^{S} do walk in
truth;
4 I have no joy greater than these things, that I may
hear of my children walking in truth.
5 Beloved, faithfully do you^{S} do whatever you^{S} may work
to the brethren and to the strangers,
6 who did testify of your^{S} love before an assembly, whom
you^{S} will do well, having sent forward worthily of God,
7 because for [His] name they went forth, receiving
nothing from the nations;
8 we, then, ought to receive such, that we may become
fellow-workers to the truth.
9 I did write to the assembly, but he who is loving the first
place among them — Diotrephes — does not receive us;
10 because of this, if I may come, I will cause him to
remember his works that he does, with evil words prating
against us; and not content with these, neither does he
himself receive the brethren, and he does forbid those
intending, and he does cast out of the assembly.
11 Beloved, be you^{S} not following that which is evil,
but that which is good; he who is doing good, he is of
God, and he who is doing evil has not seen God;
12 testimony has been given by all to Demtrius, and by
the truth itself, and we also — we do testify, and you^{P}
have known that our testimony is true.
13 I had many things to write, but I do not wish through
ink and pen to write to you^{S},
14 and I hope straightway to see you^{S}, and mouth to
mouth we shall speak. Peace to you^{S}! the friends do
salute you^{S}; be saluting the friends by name.

The Epistle Of
JUDE

1 Judas, of Jesus Christ a servant, and brother of James,
to those sanctified in God the Father, and in Jesus Christ
kept — called,
2 kindness to you[P], and peace, and love, be multiplied!
3 Beloved, using all diligence to write to you[P] concerning
the common salvation, I had necessity to write to you[P],
exhorting to agonize for the faith once delivered to the saints,
4 for there did come in certain men unobserved, long
ago having been written beforehand to this judgment,
impious, perverting the grace of our God to
lasciviousness, and denying our only Master, God, and
Lord — Jesus Christ,
5 and I intend to remind you[P], you[P] knowing this once,
that the Lord, having saved a people out of the land of
Egypt, again did destroy those who did not believe;
6 messengers also, those who did not keep their own
principality, but did leave their proper dwelling, to a
judgment of a great day, in bonds everlasting, He has
kept under darkness,
7 as Sodom and Gomorrah, and the cities around them,
in like manner to these, having given themselves to
whoredom, and gone after other flesh, have been set
before — an example, of fire age-during, justice suffering.
8 In like manner, nevertheless, those dreaming indeed
do defile the flesh also, and they put away lordship, and
they speak evil of dignities,
9 yet Michael, the chief messenger, when, contending
with the devil, he was disputing about the body of
Moses, did not dare to bring up an evil-speaking
judgment, but said, 'The Lord rebuke you[S]!'
10 and these, as many things indeed as they have not
known, they speak evil of; and as many things as
naturally (as the irrational beasts) they understand, they
are corrupted in these;
11 woe to them! because they did go on in the way of
Cain, and for reward they did rush to the deceit of
Balaam, and they did perish in the gainsaying of Korah.
12 These are in your[P] love-feasts craggy rocks; feasting
together with you[P], shepherding themselves without
fear; clouds without water, by winds carried about; trees
autumnal, without fruit, twice dead, rooted up;
13 wild waves of a sea, foaming out their own shames;
stars going astray, to whom the gloom of the darkness
to the age has been kept.
14 And the seventh from Adam – Enoch —did prophesy
to these also saying, 'Behold, the Lord did come in His
saintly myriads,
15 to do judgment against all, and to convict all their
impious ones, concerning all their works of impiety that
they did impiously, and concerning all the stiff things
that impious sinners did speak against Him.'
16 These are murmurers, repiners; walking according to
their desires, and their mouth does speak great swellings,
giving admiration to persons for the sake of profit;
17 and you[P], beloved, remember you[P] the sayings
spoken before by the apostles of our Lord Jesus Christ:
18 that they said to you[P], that in the last time there shall
be scoffers, going on after their own desires of impieties,
19 these are those setting themselves apart, natural men,
not having the Spirit.
20 And you[P], beloved, building yourselves[P] up on your[P]
most holy faith, praying in the Holy Spirit,
21 yourselves[P] in the love of God keep you[P], waiting for
the kindness of our Lord Jesus Christ — to life age-
during;
22 and be kind to some, judging thoroughly,
23 and some in fear save you[P], out of the fire snatching,
hating even the coat spotted from the flesh.
24 And to Him who is able to guard you[P] not stumbling,
and to set [you[P]] in the presence of His glory
unblemished, in gladness,
25 to the only wise God our Savior, [is] glory and
greatness, power and authority, both now and to all the
ages! Amen.

The REVELATION Of JESUS CHRIST

CHAPTER 1

1 A revelation of Jesus Christ, that God gave to Him, to show to His servants what things it is necessary to come to pass quickly; and he did signify [it], having sent through His messenger to His servant John,
2 who did testify the word of God, and the testimony of Jesus Christ, as many things also as he did see.
3 Happy is he who is reading, and those hearing, the words of the prophecy, and keeping the things written in it — for the time is near!
4 John to the seven assemblies that [are] in Asia: Grace to you[P], and peace, from Him who is, and who was, and who is coming, and from the Seven Spirits that are before His throne,
5 and from Jesus Christ, the faithful witness, the first-born out of the dead, and the ruler of the kings of the earth; to Him who did love us, and did bathe us from our sins in His blood,
6 and did make us kings and priests to His God and Father, to Him [is] the glory and the power to the ages of the ages! Amen.
7 Behold, He does come with the clouds, and every eye shall see Him, even those who did pierce Him, and all the tribes of the land shall wail because of Him. Yes! Amen!
8 'I am the Alpha and the Omega, beginning and end, says the Lord, who is, and who was, and who is coming — the Almighty.'
9 I, John, who also [am] your[P] brother, and fellow-partner in the tribulation, and in the reign and endurance, of Jesus Christ, was in the isle that is called Patmos, because of the word of God, and because of the testimony of Jesus Christ;
10 I was in the Spirit on the Lord's-day, and I heard behind me a great voice, as of a trumpet, saying,
11 'I am the Alpha and the Omega, the First and the Last;' and, 'What you[S] do see, write in a scroll, and send to the seven assemblies that [are] in Asia; to Ephesus, and to Smyrna, and to Pergamos, and to Thyatira, and to Sardis, and to Philadelphia, and to Laodicea.'
12 And I did turn to see the voice that did speak with me, and having turned, I saw seven golden lamp-stands,
13 and in the midst of the seven lamp-stands, [one] like to a son of man, clothed to the foot, and girt round at the breast with a golden girdle,
14 and His head and hairs white, as if white wool — as snow, and His eyes as a flame of fire;
15 and His feet like to fine brass, as having been fired in a furnace, and His voice as a sound of many waters,
16 and having seven stars in His right hand, and a sharp two-edged sword is proceeding out of His mouth, and His countenance [is] as the sun shining in its might.
17 And when I saw Him, I did fall at His feet as dead, and He placed His right hand upon me, saying to me, 'Be not afraid; I am the First and the Last,
18 and He who is living, and I did become dead, and, behold, I am living to the ages of the ages. Amen! and I have the keys of the hades and of the death.
19 'Write the things that you[S] have seen, and the things that are, and the things that are about to come after these things;
20 the secret of the seven stars that you[S] have seen upon My right hand, and the seven golden lamp-stands: the seven stars are messengers of the seven assemblies, and the seven lamp-stands that you[S] have seen are seven assemblies.

CHAPTER 2

1 'To the messenger of the Ephesian assembly write: These things says He who is holding the seven stars in His right hand, who is walking in the midst of the seven lamp-stands — the golden:
2 I have known your[S] works, and your[S] labor, and your[S] endurance, and that you[S] are not able to bear evil ones, and that you[S] have tried those saying themselves to be apostles and are not, and have found them liars,
3 and you[S] did bear, and have endurance, and have toiled because of My name, and have not been weary.

4 'But I have against you[S]: That you[S] did leave your[S] first love!
5 remember, then, from where you[S] have fallen, and reform, and do the first works; and if not, I come to you[S] quickly, and will remove your lamp-stand from its place — if you[S] may not reform;
6 but this you[S] have, that you[S] do hate the works of the Nicolaitans, that I also hate.
7 He who is having an ear — let him hear what the Spirit says to the assemblies: To him who is overcoming — I will give to him to eat of the tree of life that is in the midst of the paradise of God.
8 'And to the messenger of the assembly of the Smyrneans write: These things says the First and the Last, who did become dead and did live;
9 I have known your[S] works, and tribulation, and poverty — yet you[S] are rich — and the evil-speaking of those saying themselves to be Jews, and are not, but [are] a synagogue of the Adversary.
10 'Be not afraid of the things that you[S] are about to suffer; behold, the devil is about to cast of you[P] to prison, that you[P] may be tried, and you[P] shall have tribulation ten days; become you[S] faithful unto death, and I will give to you[S] the crown of the life.
11 He who is having an ear — let him hear what the Spirit says to the assemblies: He who is overcoming may not be injured of the second death.
12 'And to the messenger of the assembly in Pergamos write: These things says He who is having the sharp two-edged sword:
13 I have known your[S] works, and where you[S] do dwell — where the throne of the Adversary [is] — and you[S] do hold fast My name, and you[S] did not deny My faith, even in the days in which Antipas [was] My faithful witness, who was put to death beside you[P], where the Adversary does dwell.
14 'But I have a few things against you[S]: That you[S] have there those holding the teaching of Balaam, who did teach Balak to cast a stumbling-block before the sons of Israel, to eat idol-sacrifices, and to commit whoredom;
15 so have you[S], even you[S], those holding the teaching of the Nicolaitans — which thing I hate.
16 'Reform! and if not, I come to you[S] quickly, and will fight against them with the sword of My mouth.
17 He who is having an ear — let him hear what the Spirit says to the assemblies: To him who is overcoming, I will give to him to eat from the hidden manna, and will give to him a white stone, and upon the stone a new name written, that no one knew except him who is receiving [it].
18 'And to the messenger of the assembly of Thyatira write: These things says the Son of God, who is having His eyes as a flame of fire, and His feet like to fine brass;
19 I have known your[S] works, and love, and ministration, and faith, and your[S] endurance, and your[S] works — and the last [are] more than the first.
20 'But I have a few things against you[S]: That you[S] do suffer the woman Jezebel, who is calling herself a prophetess, to teach, and to lead astray, my servants to commit whoredom, and to eat idol-sacrifices;
21 and I did give to her a time that she might reform from her whoredom, and she did not reform;
22 behold, I will cast her into a couch, and those committing adultery with her into great tribulation — if they may not repent of their works,
23 and I will kill her children in death, and all the assemblies shall know that I am He who is searching reins and hearts; and I will give to you[P] — to each — according to your[P] works.
24 'And to you[P] I say, and to the rest who are in Thyatira, as many as have not this teaching, and who did not know the depths of the Adversary, as they say; I will not put upon you[P] other burden;
25 but that which you[P] have — hold you[P], till I may come;
26 and he who is overcoming, and who is keeping my works unto the end, I will give authority over the nations to him,
27 and he shall rule them with a rod of iron — they shall be broken as the vessels of the potter — as I also have received from My Father;
28 and I will give to him the morning star.
29 He who is having an ear — let him hear what the Spirit says to the assemblies.

CHAPTER 3

1 And to the messenger of the assembly in Sardis write: These things says He who is having the Seven Spirits of God, and the seven stars: I have known your[S] works, and that you[S] have the name that you[S] do live, and you[S] are dead;
2 become watching, and strengthen the rest of the things that are about to die, for I have not found your[S] works fulfilled before God.
3 'Remember, then, how you[S] have received, and heard, and be keeping, and reform: if, then, you[S] may not watch,

I will come upon you[S] as a thief, and you[S] may not know
what hour I will come upon you[S].
4 You[S] have a few names even in Sardis who did not
defile their garments, and they shall walk with me in
white, because they are worthy.
5 He who is overcoming — this one — shall be arrayed
in white garments, and I will not blot out his name from
the scroll of the life, and I will confess his name before
My Father, and before His messengers.
6 He who is having an ear — let him hear what the Spirit
says to the assemblies.
7 'And to the messenger of the assembly in Philadelphia
write: These things says He who is holy, He who is true,
He who is having the key of David, He who is opening
and no one does shut, and He shuts and no one does
open!
8 I have known your[S] works; behold, I have set before
you[S] a door — opened, and no one is able to shut it,
because you[S] have a little power, and did keep my word,
and did not deny my name;
9 behold, I make of the synagogue of the Adversary
those saying themselves to be Jews, and are not, but do
lie; behold, I will make them that they may come and
bow before your[S] feet, and may know that I loved you[S].
10 'Because you[S] did keep the word of My endurance, I
also will keep you[S] from the hour of the trial that is about
to come upon all the world, to try those dwelling upon
the earth.
11 Behold, I come quickly, be holding fast that which
you[S] have, that no one may receive your[S] crown.
12 He who is overcoming — I will make him a pillar in
the sanctuary of My God, and without he may not go
any more, and I will write upon him the name of My God,
and the name of the city of My God, the new Jerusalem,
that does come down out of the heaven from My God
— also My new name.
13 He who is having an ear — let him hear what the
Spirit says to the assemblies.
14 'And to the messenger of the assembly of the
Laodiceans write: These things says the Amen, the
witness — the faithful and true — the chief of the
creation of God;
15 I have known your[S] works, that you[S] are neither cold
nor hot; I would you[S] were cold or hot.
16 So — because you[S] are lukewarm, and neither cold
nor hot, I am about to vomit you[S] out of My mouth;
17 because you[S] say — I am rich, and have grown rich,
and have need of nothing, and have not known that you[S]
are the wretched, and miserable, and poor, and blind,
and naked,
18 I counsel you[S] to buy from me gold fired by fire, that
you[S] may be rich, and white garments that you[S] may be
arrayed, and the shame of your[S] nakedness may not be
revealed, and anoint your[S] eyes with eye-salve, that you[S]
may see.
19 'As many as I love, I do convict and chasten; be
zealous, then, and reform;
20 behold, I have stood at the door, and I knock; if any
one may hear My voice, and may open the door, I will
come in unto him, and will sup with him, and he with Me.
21 He who is overcoming — I will give to him to sit with
me in my throne, as I also did overcome and did sit down
with My Father in His throne.
22 He who is having an ear — let him hear what the
Spirit says to the assemblies.'

CHAPTER 4

1 After these things I saw, and behold, a door opened
in the heaven, and the first voice that I heard [is] as of a
trumpet speaking with me, saying, 'Come up here, and I
will show you[S] what it is necessary to come to pass after
these things;'
2 and immediately I was in the Spirit, and behold, a
throne was set in the heaven, and upon the throne is
[one] sitting,
3 and He who is sitting was in sight like a stone, jasper
and sardine: and a rainbow was round the throne in sight
like an emerald.
4 And around the throne [are] thrones twenty and four,
and upon the thrones I saw the twenty and four elders
sitting, clothed in white garments, and they had crowns
of gold upon their heads;
5 and lightnings do proceed out of the throne, and
thunders, and voices; and seven lamps of fire are
burning before the throne, which are the Seven Spirits
of God,
6 and before the throne [is] a sea of glass like to crystal,
and in the midst of the throne, and round the throne,
[are] four living creatures, full of eyes before and behind;
7 and the first living creature [is] like a lion, and the
second living creature [is] like a calf, and the third living
creature has the face as a man, and the fourth living
creature [is] like an eagle flying.
8 And the four living creatures, each by itself severally,
had six wings, around and within [are] full of eyes, and
they have not rest day and night, saying, 'Holy, holy,

holy, Lord God Almighty, who was, and who is, and who
is coming;'
9 and when the living creatures do give glory, and honor,
and thanks, to Him who is sitting upon the throne, who
is living to the ages of the ages,
10 the twenty and four elders do fall down before Him
who is sitting upon the throne, and bow before Him who
is living to the ages of the ages, and they cast their
crowns before the throne, saying,
11 'Worthy are You[S], O Lord, to receive the glory, and
the honor, and the power, because You[S] — You[S] did
create the all things, and because of Your[S] will are they,
and they were created.'

CHAPTER 5

1 And I saw upon the right hand of Him who is sitting
upon the throne a scroll, written within and on the back,
sealed with seven seals;
2 and I saw a strong messenger crying with a great voice,
'Who is worthy to open the scroll and to loose the seals
of it?'
3 and no one was able in the heaven, nor upon the earth,
nor under the earth, to open the scroll, nor to behold it.
4 And I was weeping much, because no one was found
worthy to open and to read the scroll, nor to behold it,
5 and one of the elders says to me, 'Weep not; behold,
the Lion did overcome, who is of the tribe of Judah, the
root of David, to open the scroll, and to loose the seven
seals of it;
6 and I saw, and behold, in the midst of the throne, and
of the four living creatures, and in the midst of the elders,
a Lamb has stood as it had been slain, having seven
horns and seven eyes, which are the Seven Spirits of
God, which are sent to all the earth,
7 and He came and took the scroll out of the right hand
of Him who is sitting upon the throne.
8 And when He took the scroll, the four living creatures
and the twenty-four elders fell before the Lamb, having
each one harps and golden vials full of perfumes, which
are the prayers of the saints,
9 and they sing a new song, saying, 'Worthy are You[S]
to take the scroll, and to open the seals of it, because
You[S] were slain, and did redeem us to God in Your[S] blood,
out of every tribe, and tongue, and people, and nation,
10 and did make us kings and priests to our God, and
we shall reign upon the earth.'
11 And I saw, and I heard the voice of many messengers
round the throne, and the living creatures, and the elders
— and the number of them was myriads of myriads, and
thousands of thousands —
12 saying with a great voice, 'Worthy is the Lamb that
was slain to receive the power, and riches, and wisdom,
and strength, and honor, and glory, and blessing!'
13 and every creature that is in the heaven, and in the
earth, and under the earth, and the things that are upon
the sea, and the all things in them, I heard saying, 'To
Him who is sitting upon the throne, and to the Lamb,
[is] the blessing, and the honor, and the glory, and the
might — to the ages of the ages!'
14 and the four living creatures said, 'Amen!' and the
twenty-four elders fell down and they bow before Him
who is living to the ages of the ages.

CHAPTER 6

1 And I saw when the Lamb opened one of the seals,
and I heard one of the four living creatures saying, as it
were a voice of thunder, 'Come and behold!'
2 and I saw, and behold, a white horse, and he who is
sitting upon it is having a bow, and there was given to
him a crown, and he went forth overcoming, and that he
may overcome.
3 And when He opened the second seal, I heard the
second living creature saying, 'Come and behold!'
4 and there went forth another horse — red, and to him
who is sitting upon it, there was given to him to take the
peace from the land, and that they may slay one another,
and there was given to him a great sword.
5 And when He opened the third seal, I heard the third
living creature saying, 'Come and behold!' and I saw,
and behold, a black horse, and he who is sitting upon it
is having a balance in his hand,
6 and I heard a voice in the midst of the four living
creatures saying, 'A measure of wheat for a denary, and
three measures of barley for a denary,' and 'The oil and
the wine you may not injure.'
7 And when He opened the fourth seal, I heard the voice
of the fourth living creature saying, 'Come and behold!'
8 and I saw, and behold, a pale horse, and he who is
sitting upon him — his name is Death, and Hades does
follow with him, and there was given to them authority
to kill, (over the fourth part of the land,) with sword, and
with hunger, and with death, and by the beasts of the
land.
9 And when He opened the fifth seal, I saw under the

altar the souls of those slain because of the word of God,
and because of the testimony that they held,
10 and they were crying with a great voice, saying, 'Till
when, O Master, the Holy and the True, did You[S] not
judge and take vengeance of our blood from those
dwelling upon the land?'
11 and there was given white robes to each one, and it
was said to them that they may rest themselves yet a
little time, till may be fulfilled also their fellow-servants
and their brethren, who are about to be killed — even as
they.
12 And I saw when He opened the sixth seal, and behold,
a great earthquake came, and the sun became black as
sackcloth of hair, and the moon became as blood,
13 and the stars of the heaven fell to the earth — as a
fig-tree does cast her winter figs, by a great wind being
shaken —
14 and heaven departed as a scroll rolled up, and every
mountain and island — they were moved out of their
places;
15 and the kings of the earth, and the great men, and
the rich, and the chiefs of thousands, and the mighty,
and every servant, and every freeman, hid themselves
in the dens, and in the rocks of the mountains,
16 and they say to the mountains and to the rocks, 'Fall
upon us, and hide us from the face of Him who is sitting
upon the throne, and from the anger of the Lamb,'
17 because the great day of His anger did come, and
who is able to stand?

CHAPTER 7

1 And after these things I saw four messengers, standing
upon the four corners of the land, holding the four winds
of the land, that the wind may not blow upon the land,
nor upon the sea, nor upon any tree;
2 and I saw another messenger going up from the rising
of the sun, having a seal of the living God, and he did
cry with a great voice to the four messengers, to whom
it was given to injure the land and the sea, saying,
3 'Do not injure the land, nor the sea, nor the trees, till
we may seal the servants of our God upon their
foreheads.'
4 And I heard the number of those sealed, (one hundred
and forty four thousands were sealed out of all the tribes
of the sons of Israel):
5 twelve thousand of the tribe of Judah were sealed;
twelve thousand of the tribe of Reuben were sealed;
twelve thousand of the tribe of Gad were sealed;
6 twelve thousand of the tribe of Asher were sealed;
twelve thousand of the tribe of Naphtali were sealed;
twelve thousand of the tribe of Manasseh were sealed;
7 twelve thousand of the tribe of Simeon were sealed;
twelve thousand of the tribe of Levi were sealed; twelve
thousand of the tribe of Issachar were sealed;
8 twelve thousand of the tribe of Zebulun were sealed;
twelve thousand of the tribe of Joseph were sealed;
twelve thousand of the tribe of Benjamin were sealed.
9 After these things I saw, and behold, a great multitude,
which no one was able to number, out of all nations,
and tribes, and peoples, and tongues, standing before
the throne, and before the Lamb, arrayed in white robes,
and palms in their hands,
10 and crying with a great voice, saying, 'The salvation
[is] to Him who is sitting upon the throne — to our God,
and to the Lamb!'
11 And all the messengers stood around the throne,
and the elders and the four living creatures, and they
fell upon their face, and bowed before God,
12 saying, 'Amen! the blessing, and the glory, and the
wisdom, and the thanksgiving, and the honor, and the
power, and the strength, [are] to our God — to the ages
of the ages! Amen!'
13 And one of the elders did answer, saying to me,
'These, who have been arrayed with the white robes —
who are they, and from where came they?'
14 and I have said to him, 'Sir, you have known;' and he
said to me, 'These are those who are coming out of the
great tribulation, and they did wash their robes, and they
made their robes white in the blood of the Lamb;
15 because of this are they before the throne of God,
and they do service to Him day and night in His
sanctuary, and He who is sitting upon the throne shall
tabernacle over them;
16 they shall not hunger any more, nor may the sun fall
upon them, nor any heat,
17 because the Lamb that [is] in the midst of the throne
shall feed them, and shall lead them unto living fountains
of waters, and God shall wipe away every tear from their
eyes.'

CHAPTER 8

1 And when He opened the seventh seal, there came
silence in the heaven about half-an-hour,
2 and I saw the seven messengers who have stood

before God, and there were given to them seven
trumpets,
3 and another messenger did come, and he stood at the
altar, having a golden censer, and there was given to
him much perfume, that he may give [it] to the prayers
of all the saints upon the golden altar that [is] before
the throne,
4 and the smoke of the perfumes did go up to the prayers
of the saints out of the hand of the messenger, before
God;
5 and the messenger took the censer, and did fill it out
of the fire of the altar, and did cast [it] to the earth, and
there came voices, and thunders, and lightnings, and
an earthquake.
6 And the seven messengers who are having the seven
trumpets did prepare themselves that they may sound;
7 and the first messenger did sound, and there came
hail and fire, mingled with blood, and it was cast to the
land, and the third of the trees was burnt up, and all the
green grass was burnt up.
8 And the second messenger did sound, and as it were
a great mountain with fire burning was cast into the sea,
and the third of the sea became blood,
9 and the third of the creatures that [are] in the sea did
die, those having life, and the third of the ships were
destroyed.
10 And the third messenger did sound, and there fell a
great star out of the heaven, burning as a lamp, and it
did fall upon the third of the rivers, and upon the
fountains of waters,
11 and the name of the star is called Wormwood, and
the third of the waters does become wormwood, and
many of the men did die of the waters, because they
were made bitter.
12 And the fourth messenger did sound, and destroyed
was the third of the sun, and the third of the moon, and
the third of the stars, that darkened may be the third of
them, and that the day may not shine — the third of it,
and the night in like manner.
13 And I saw, and I heard one messenger, flying in the
mid-heaven, saying with a great voice, 'Woe, woe, woe,
to those dwelling upon the land from the rest of the
voices of the trumpet of the three messengers who are
about to sound.'

CHAPTER 9

1 And the fifth messenger did sound, and I saw a star
out of the heaven having fallen to the earth, and there
was given to it the key of the pit of the abyss,
2 and he did open the pit of the abyss, and there came
up a smoke out of the pit as smoke of a great furnace,
and darkened was the sun and the air, from the smoke of
the pit.
3 And out of the smoke came forth locusts to the earth,
and there was given to them authority, as scorpions of
the earth have authority,
4 and it was said to them that they may not injure the
grass of the earth, nor any green thing, nor any tree, but
— only the men who have not the seal of God upon
their foreheads,
5 and it was given to them that they may not kill them,
but that they may be tormented five months, and their
torment [is] as the torment of a scorpion, when it may
strike a man;
6 and in those days shall men seek the death, and they
shall not find it, and they shall desire to die, and the
death shall flee from them.
7 And the likenesses of the locusts [are] like to horses
made ready to battle, and upon their heads as crowns
like gold, and their faces as faces of men,
8 and they had hair as hair of women, and their teeth
were as [those] of lions,
9 and they had breastplates as breastplates of iron, and
the noise of their wings [is] as the noise of chariots of
many horses running to battle;
10 and they have tails like to scorpions, and stings were
in their tails; and their authority [is] to injure men five
months;
11 and they have over them a king — the messenger of
the abyss — a name [is] to him in Hebrew, Abaddon,
and in the Greek he has a name, Apollyon.
12 The first woe did go forth, behold, there come yet
two woes after these things.
13 And the sixth messenger did sound, and I heard a
voice out of the four horns of the altar of gold that is
before God,
14 saying to the sixth messenger who had the trumpet,
'Loose the four messengers who are bound at the great
river Euphrates;'
15 and loosed were the four messengers, who have been
made ready for the hour, and day, and month, and year,
that they may kill the third of men;
16 and the number of the forces of the horsemen [is]
two myriads of myriads, and I heard the number of them.
17 And thus I saw the horses in the vision, and those
sitting upon them, having breastplates of fire, and

jacinth, and brimstone; and the heads of the horses [are]
as heads of lions, and out of their mouths proceeds fire,
and smoke, and brimstone;
18 by these three were the third of men killed, from the
fire, and from the smoke, and from the brimstone, that is
proceeding out of their mouth,
19 for their authorities are in their mouth, and in their
tails, for their tails [are] like serpents, having heads, and
with them they do injure;
20 and the rest of men, who were not killed in these
plagues, neither did reform from the works of their hands,
that they may not bow before the demons, and idols,
those of gold, and those of silver, and those of brass,
and those of stone, and those of wood, that are neither
able to see, nor to hear, nor to walk,
21 yes they did not reform from their murders, nor from
their sorceries, nor from their whoredoms, nor from their
thefts.

CHAPTER 10

1 And I saw another strong messenger coming down
out of the heaven, arrayed with a cloud, and a rainbow
upon the head, and his face as the sun, and his feet as
pillars of fire,
2 and he had in his hand a little scroll opened, and he
did place his right foot upon the sea, and the left upon
the land,
3 and he cried with a great voice, as a lion does roar,
and when he cried, the seven thunders did speak out
their voices;
4 and when the seven thunders spoke their voices, I
was about to write, and I heard a voice out of the heaven
saying to me, 'Seal the things that the seven thunders
spoke,' and, 'You[S] may not write these things.'
5 And the messenger whom I saw standing upon the
sea, and upon the land, did lift up his hand to the heaven,
6 and did swear in Him who does live to the ages of the
ages, who did create the heaven and the things in it,
and the land and the things in it, and the sea and the
things in it — that time shall not be yet,
7 but in the days of the voice of the seventh messenger,
when he may be about to sound, and the secret of God
may be finished, as He did declare to His own servants,
to the prophets.
8 And the voice that I heard out of the heaven is again
speaking with me, and saying, 'Go, take the little scroll
that is open in the hand of the messenger who has been
standing upon the sea, and upon the land:'
9 and I went away unto the messenger, saying to him,
'Give me the little scroll;' and he says to me, 'Take, and
eat it up, and it shall make your[S] belly bitter, but in your[S]
mouth it shall be sweet — as honey.'
10 And I took the little scroll out of the hand of the
messenger, and did eat it up, and it was as honey in my
mouth — sweet, and when I did eat it — my belly was
made bitter;
11 and he says to me, 'It is necessary for you[S] again to
prophesy about peoples, and nations, and tongues, and
kings — many.'

CHAPTER 11

1 And there was given to me a reed like to a rod, and the
messenger stood, saying, 'Rise, and measure the
sanctuary of God, and the altar, and those worshipping
in it;
2 and leave out the court that is without the sanctuary,
and you[S] may not measure it, because it was given to
the nations, and they shall tread down the holy city
forty-two months;
3 and I will give to My two witnesses, and they shall
prophesy days, a thousand, two hundred, sixty, arrayed
with sackcloth;
4 these are the two olive [trees], and the two lamp-stands
that do stand before the God of the earth;
5 and if any one may will to injure them, fire does proceed
out of their mouth, and does devour their enemies, and
if any one may will to injure them, thus it is necessary
for him to be killed.
6 These have authority to shut the heaven, that it may
not rain rain in the days of their prophecy, and authority
they have over the waters to turn them to blood, and to
afflict the land with every plague, as often as they may
will.
7 'And when they may finish their testimony, the beast
that is coming up out of the abyss shall make war with
them, and overcome them, and kill them,
8 and their dead bodies [are] upon the broad-place of
the great city (that is called spiritually Sodom, and Egypt,
where also our Lord was crucified,)
9 and they shall behold — they of the peoples, and
tribes, and tongues, and nations — their dead bodies
three days and a half, and their dead bodies they shall
not allow to be put into tombs,
10 and those dwelling upon the land shall rejoice over

them, and shall make merry, and they shall send gifts to
one another, because these — the two prophets — did
torment those dwelling upon the land.'
11 And after the three days and a half, a spirit of life
from God did enter into them, and they stood upon their
feet, and great fear fell upon those beholding them,
12 and they heard a great voice out of the heaven saying
to them, 'Come up here;' and they went up to the heaven
in the cloud, and their enemies beheld them;
13 and in that hour came a great earthquake, and the
tenth of the city did fall, and killed in the earthquake
were names of men — seven thousands, and the rest
became affrighted, and they gave glory to the God of
the heaven.
14 The second woe did go forth, behold, the third woe
does come quickly.
15 And the seventh messenger did sound, and there
came great voices in the heaven, saying, 'The kingdoms
of the world did become [those] of our Lord and of His
Christ, and he shall reign to the ages of the ages!'
16 and the twenty and four elders, who before God are
sitting upon their thrones, did fall upon their faces, and
did bow before God,
17 saying, 'We give thanks to You[S], O Lord God, the
Almighty, who are, and who was, and who are coming,
because You[S] have taken Your[S] great power and did
reign;
18 and the nations were angry, and Your[S] anger did come,
and the time of the dead, to be judged, and to give the
reward to Your[S] servants, to the prophets, and to the
saints, and to those fearing Your[S] name, to the small and
to the great, and to destroy those who are destroying
the land.'
19 And the sanctuary of God was opened in the heaven,
and there was seen the ark of His covenant in His
sanctuary, and there did come lightnings, and voices,
and thunders, and an earthquake, and great hail.

CHAPTER 12

1 And a great sign was seen in the heaven, a woman
arrayed with the sun, and the moon under her feet, and
upon her head a crown of twelve stars,
2 and being with child she does cry out, travailing and
pained to bring forth.
3 And there was seen another sign in the heaven, and,
behold, a great red dragon, having seven heads and ten
horns, and upon his head seven diadems,
4 and his tail does draw the third of the stars of the
heaven, and he did cast them to the earth; and the dragon
did stand before the woman who is about to bring forth,
that when she may bring forth, he may devour her child;
5 and she brought forth a male child, who is about to
rule all the nations with a rod of iron, and her child was
caught away unto God and His throne,
6 and the woman did flee to the wilderness, where she
has a place made ready from God, that there they may
nourish her — days a thousand, two hundred, sixty.
7 And there came war in the heaven; Michael and his
messengers did war against the dragon, and the dragon
did war, and his messengers,
8 and they did not prevail, nor was their place found
any more in the heaven;
9 and the great dragon was cast forth — the old serpent,
who is called 'Devil,' and 'the Adversary,' who is leading
astray the whole world — he was cast forth to the earth,
and his messengers were cast forth with him.
10 And I heard a great voice saying in the heaven, 'Now
did come the salvation, and the power, and the reign, of
our God, and the authority of His Christ, because cast
down was the accuser of our brethren, who is accusing
them before our God day and night;
11 and they did overcome him because of the blood of
the Lamb, and because of the word of their testimony,
and they did not love their life — unto death;
12 because of this be glad, you[P] heavens, and those
who do tabernacle in them; woe to those inhabiting the
land and the sea, because the Devil did go down unto
you[P], having great wrath, having known that he has little
time.'
13 And when the dragon saw that he was cast forth to
the earth, he pursued the woman who did bring forth
the male,
14 and there were given to the woman two wings of the
great eagle, that she may fly to the wilderness, to her
place, where she is nourished a time, and times, and half
a time, from the face of the serpent;
15 and the serpent did cast forth after the woman, out
of his mouth, water as a river, that he may cause her to
be carried away by the river,
16 and the land did help the woman, and the land did
open its mouth and did swallow up the river, that the
dragon did cast forth out of his mouth;
17 and the dragon was angry against the woman, and
went away to make war with the rest of her seed, those
keeping the commands of God, and having the testimony
of Jesus Christ.

CHAPTER 13

1 And I stood upon the sand of the sea, and I saw a beast coming up out of the sea, having seven heads and ten horns, and upon its horns ten diadems, and upon its heads a name of evil speaking,

2 and the beast that I saw was like to a leopard, and its feet as of a bear, and its mouth as the mouth of a lion, and the dragon did give to it his power, and his throne, and great authority.

3 And I saw one of its heads as slain to death, and its deadly stroke was healed, and all the earth did wonder after the beast,

4 and they did bow before the dragon who did give authority to the beast, and they did bow before the beast, saying, 'Who [is] like to the beast? who is able to war with it?'

5 And there was given to it a mouth speaking great things, and evil-speakings, and there was given to it authority to make war forty-two months,

6 and it did open its mouth for evil-speaking toward God, to speak evil of His name, and of His tabernacle, and of those who in the heaven tabernacle,

7 and there was given to it to make war with the saints, and to overcome them, and there was given to it authority over every tribe, and tongue, and nation.

8 And all who are dwelling upon the land shall bow before it, whose names have not been written in the scroll of the life of the Lamb slain from the foundation of the world;

9 if any one has an ear — let him hear:

10 if any one does gather a captivity, he does go away into captivity; if any one does kill by sword, it is necessary for him to be killed by sword; here is the endurance and the faith of the saints.

11 And I saw another beast coming up out of the land, and it had two horns, like a lamb, and it was speaking as a dragon,

12 and all the authority of the first beast does it do before it, and it makes the land and those dwelling in it that they shall bow before the first beast, whose deadly stroke was healed,

13 and it does great signs, that also it may make fire to come down from the heaven to the earth before men,

14 and it leads astray those dwelling on the land, because of the signs that were given it to do before the beast, saying to those dwelling upon the land to make an image to the beast that has the stroke of the sword and did live,

15 and there was given to it to give a spirit to the image of the beast, that also the image of the beast may speak, and [that] it may cause as many as shall not bow before the image of the beast, that they may be killed.

16 And it makes all, the small, and the great, and the rich, and the poor, and the freemen, and the servants, that it may give to them a mark upon their right hand or upon their foreheads,

17 and that no one may be able to buy, or to sell, except he who is having the mark, or the name of the beast, or the number of his name.

18 Here is the wisdom! He who is having the understanding, let him count the number of the beast, for the number of a man it is, and its number [is] six hundred and sixty six.

CHAPTER 14

1 And I saw, and behold, a Lamb having stood upon the mount Sion, and with Him an hundred forty-four thousands, having the name of His Father written upon their foreheads;

2 and I heard a voice out of the heaven, as a voice of many waters, and as a voice of great thunder, and I heard a voice of harpers harping with their harps,

3 and they sing, as it were, a new song before the throne, and before the four living creatures, and the elders, and no one was able to learn the song except the hundred forty-four thousands, who have been bought from the earth;

4 these are they who were not defiled with women, for they are virgin; these are they who are following the Lamb wheresoever he may go; these were bought from among men — a first-fruit to God and to the Lamb —

5 and in their mouth there was not found guile, for they are unblemished before the throne of God.

6 And I saw another messenger flying in mid-heaven, having good news age-during to proclaim to those dwelling upon the earth, and to every nation, and tribe, and tongue, and people,

7 saying in a great voice, 'Fear you[P] God, and give glory to Him, because the hour of His judgment did come, and bow you[P] before Him who did make the heaven, and the land, and sea, and fountains of waters.'

8 And another messenger did follow, saying, 'Fall, fall, did Babylon, the great city, because of the wine of the wrath of her whoredom she has given to all nations to drink.'

9 And a third messenger did follow them, saying in a

great voice, 'If any one does bow before the beast, and
his image, and does receive a mark upon his forehead,
or upon his hand,
10 he also shall drink of the wine of the wrath of God,
that has been mingled unmixed in the cup of His anger,
and he shall be tormented in fire and brimstone before
the holy messengers, and before the Lamb,
11 and the smoke of their torment does go up to ages of
ages; and they have no rest day and night, who are
bowing before the beast and his image, also if any does
receive the mark of his name.
12 Here is endurance of the saints: here [are] those
keeping the commands of God, and the faith of Jesus.'
13 And I heard a voice out of the heaven saying to me,
'Write: Happy are the dead who are dying in the Lord
from this time!' 'Yes, (says the Spirit,) That they may
rest from their labors — and their works do follow them!'
14 And I saw, and behold, a white cloud, and upon the
cloud [one] sitting like to a son of man, having upon his
head a golden crown, and in his hand a sharp sickle;
15 and another messenger did come forth out of the
sanctuary crying in a great voice to him who is sitting
upon the cloud, 'Send forth your[S] sickle and reap,
because the hour of reaping has come to you[S], because
the harvest of the earth has been ripe;'
16 and he who is sitting upon the cloud did put forth
his sickle upon the earth, and the earth was reaped.
17 And another messenger did come forth out of the
sanctuary that [is] in the heaven, having — he also — a
sharp sickle,
18 and another messenger did come forth out from the
altar, having authority over the fire, and he called with a
great cry to him having the sharp sickle, saying, 'Send
forth your[S] sharp sickle, and gather the clusters of the
vine of the earth, because her grapes have come to
perfection;'
19 and the messenger did put forth his sickle to the earth,
and did gather the vine of the earth, and did cast [it] to
the great wine-press of the wrath of God;
20 and trodden was the wine-press outside of the city,
and blood did come forth out of the wine-press — unto
the bridles of the horses, a thousand, six hundred
furlongs.

CHAPTER 15

1 And I saw another sign in the heaven, great and
wonderful, seven messengers having the seven last
plagues, because in these was completed the wrath of
God,
2 and I saw as a sea of glass mingled with fire, and those
who do gain the victory over the beast, and his image,
and his mark, [and] the number of his name, standing by
the sea of the glass, having harps of God,
3 and they sing the song of Moses, servant of God,
and the song of the Lamb, saying, 'Great and wonderful
[are] Your[S] works, O Lord God, the Almighty, righteous
and true [are] Your[S] ways, O King of saints,
4 who may not fear You[S], O Lord, and glorify Your[S] name?
because You[S] alone [are] kind, because all the nations
shall come and bow before You[S], because Your[S] righteous
acts were revealed.'
5 And after these things I saw, and behold, opened was
the sanctuary of the tabernacle of the testimony in the
heaven;
6 and the seven messengers having the seven plagues
did come forth, out of the sanctuary, clothed in linen,
pure and shining, and girded round the breasts with
golden girdles:
7 and one of the four living creatures did give to the
seven messengers seven golden vials, full of the wrath
of God, who is living to the ages of the ages;
8 and the sanctuary was filled with smoke from the glory
of God, and from His power, and no one was able to
enter into the sanctuary till the seven plagues of the
seven messengers may be finished.

CHAPTER 16

1 And I heard a great voice out of the sanctuary saying
to the seven messengers, 'Go away, and pour out the
vials of the wrath of God to the earth;'
2 and the first did go away, and did pour out his vial
upon the land, and there came a sore — bad and grievous
— to men, those having the mark of the beast, and those
bowing to his image.
3 And the second messenger did pour out his vial to
the sea, and there came blood as of [one] dead, and every
living soul died in the sea.
4 And the third messenger did pour out his vial to the
rivers, and to the fountains of the waters, and there came
blood,
5 and I heard the messenger of the waters, saying,
'righteous, O Lord, are You[S], who are, and who was, and
who shall be, because these things You[S] did judge,
6 because they did pour out blood of saints and

prophets, and to them You[S] did give blood to drink, for
they are worthy;'
7 and I heard another out of the altar, saying, 'Yes, Lord
God, the Almighty, true and righteous [are] Your[S]
judgments.'
8 And the fourth messenger did pour out his vial upon
the sun, and there was given to him to scorch men with
fire,
9 and men were scorched with great heat, and they did
speak evil of the name of God, who has authority over
these plagues, and they did not reform — to give to Him
glory.
10 And the fifth messenger did pour out his vial upon
the throne of the beast, and his kingdom did become
darkened, and they were gnawing their tongues from the
pain,
11 and they did speak evil of the God of the heaven,
from their pains, and from their sores, and they did not
reform from their works.
12 And the sixth messenger did pour out his vial upon
the great river, the Euphrates, and its water was dried
up, that the way of the kings who are from the rising of
the sun may be made ready;
13 and I saw [come] out of the mouth of the dragon,
and out of the mouth of the beast, and out of the mouth
of the false prophet, three unclean spirits like frogs —
14 for they are spirits of demons, doing signs — which
go forth unto the kings of the earth, and of the whole
world, to bring them together to the battle of that great
day of God the Almighty; —
15 'behold, I do come as a thief; happy [is] he who is
watching, and keeping his garments, that he may not
walk naked, and they may see his unseemliness,' —
16 and they did bring them together to the place that is
called in Hebrew Armageddon.
17 And the seventh messenger did pour out his vial to
the air, and there came forth a great voice from the
sanctuary of the heaven, from the throne, saying, 'It has
come!'
18 and there came voices, and thunders, and lightnings;
and a great earthquake came, such as came not since
men came upon the earth, so mighty an earthquake —
so great!
19 And it came — the great city — into three parts, and
the cities of the nations did fall, and Babylon the great
was remembered before God, to give the cup of the wine
of the wrath of His anger to her,
20 and every island did flee away, and mountains were
not found,
21 and great hail (as of talent weight) did come down
out of the heaven upon men, and men did speak evil of
God because of the plague of the hail, because its plague
is very great.

CHAPTER 17

1 And there came one of the seven messengers, who
were having the seven vials, and he spoke with me,
saying to me, 'Come, I will show to you[S] the judgment
of the great whore, who is sitting upon the many waters,
2 with whom the kings of the earth did commit
whoredom; and those inhabiting the earth were made
drunk from the wine of her whoredom;'
3 and he carried me away to a wilderness in the Spirit,
and I saw a woman sitting upon a scarlet-colored beast,
full of names of evil-speaking, having seven heads and
ten horns,
4 and the woman was arrayed with purple and scarlet-
color, and gilded with gold, and precious stone, and
pearls, having a golden cup in her hand full of
abominations and uncleanness of her whoredom,
5 and upon her forehead was a name written: 'Secret,
Babylon the Great, the Mother of the Whores, and the
Abominations of the earth.'
6 And I saw the woman drunken from the blood of the
saints, and from the blood of the witnesses of Jesus,
and I did wonder — having seen her — with great
wonder;
7 and the messenger said to me, 'For what reason did
you[S] wonder? I — I will tell you[S] the secret of the woman
and of the beast that [is] carrying her, which has the
seven heads and the ten horns.
8 'The beast that you did see: it was, and it is not; and
it is about to come up out of the abyss, and to go away
to destruction, and those dwelling upon the earth shall
wonder, whose names have not been written upon the
scroll of the life from the foundation of the world,
beholding the beast that was, and is not, although it is.
9 'Here [is] the mind that is having wisdom; the seven heads
are seven mountains, upon which the woman does sit,
10 and there are seven kings, the five did fall, and the
one is, the other did not yet come, and when he may
come, it is necessary for him to remain a little time;
11 and the beast that was, and is not, he also is eighth,
and he is out of the seven, and he does go away to
destruction.
12 'And the ten horns that you[S] saw, are ten kings, who

did not yet receive a kingdom, but do receive authority
as kings the same hour with the beast,
13 these have one mind, and they shall give over their
own power and authority to the beast;
14 these shall make war with the Lamb, and the Lamb
shall overcome them, because he is Lord of lords, and
King of kings, and those with him are called, and choice,
and steadfast.'
15 And he says to me, 'The waters that you[S] did see,
where the whore does sit, are peoples, and multitudes,
and nations, and tongues;'
16 and the ten horns that you[S] did see upon the beast,
these shall hate the whore, and shall make her desolate
and naked, and shall eat her flesh, and shall burn her in
fire,
17 for God did give into their hearts to do its mind, and
to make one mind, and to give their kingdom to the beast
till the sayings of God may be complete,
18 and the woman that you[S] did see is the great city
that is having reign over the kings of the land.'

CHAPTER 18

1 And after these things I saw another messenger
coming down out of the heaven, having great authority,
and the earth was lightened from his glory,
2 and he did cry in might — a great voice, saying, 'Fall,
fall did Babylon the great, and she became a habitation
of demons, and a hold of every unclean spirit, and a hold
of every unclean and hateful bird,
3 because all the nations have drunk of the wine of the
wrath of her whoredom, and the kings of the earth did
commit whoredom with her, and merchants of the earth
were made rich from the power of her revel.
4 And I heard another voice out of the heaven, saying,
'Come forth out of her, My people, that you[P] may not
partake with her sins, and that you[P] may not receive of
her plagues,
5 because her sins did follow — unto the heaven, and
God did remember her unrighteousness.
6 Render to her as also she did render to you[P], and
double to her doubles according to her works; in the
cup that she did mingle to her double mingle.
7 'As much as she did glorify herself and did revel, give
to her so much torment and sorrow, because in her heart
she says, I sit a queen, and I am not a widow, and I shall
not see sorrow;
8 because of this, in one day, shall come her plagues,
death, and sorrow, and famine; and she shall be utterly
burned in fire, because strong [is] the Lord God who is
judging her;
9 and weep over her, and strike themselves for her, shall
the kings of the earth, who did commit whoredom with
her and did revel, when they may see the smoke of her
burning,
10 having stood from afar because of the fear of her
torment, saying, Woe, woe, the great city! Babylon, the
strong city! because your[S] judgment did come in one
hour.
11 'And the merchants of the earth shall weep and
sorrow over her, because no one does buy their lading
any more;
12 lading of gold, and silver, and precious stone, and
pearl, and fine linen, and purple, and silk, and scarlet,
and all thyine wood, and every vessel of ivory, and every
vessel of most precious wood, and brass, and iron, and
marble,
13 and cinnamon, and odors, and ointment, and
frankincense, and wine, and oil, and fine flour, and wheat,
and cattle, and sheep, and of horses, and of chariots,
and of bodies and souls of men.
14 'And the fruits of the desire of your[S] soul did go
away from you[S], and all things — the dainty and the
bright — did go away from you[S], and may you[S] find them
no more at all.
15 The merchants of these things, who were made rich
by her, shall stand far off because of the fear of her
torment, weeping, and sorrowing,
16 and saying, Woe, woe, the great city, that was arrayed
with fine linen, and purple, and scarlet, and gilded in
gold, and precious stone, and pearls — because so much
riches were made waste in one hour!
17 'And every shipmaster, and all the company upon
the ships, and sailors, and as many as work the sea,
stood far off,
18 and were crying, seeing the smoke of her burning,
saying, What [city is] like to the great city?
19 and they did cast dust upon their heads, and were
crying out, weeping and sorrowing, saying, Woe, woe,
the great city! in which all having ships in the sea were
made rich, out of her costliness — for in one hour was
she made waste.
20 'Be glad over her, O heaven, and you[P] holy apostles
and prophets, because God did judge your[P] judgment
of her!'
21 And one strong messenger did take up a stone as a
great millstone, and did cast [it] to the sea, saying, 'Thus

shall Babylon be cast with violence, the great city, and may not be found any more at all;

22 and voice of harpers, and musicians, and pipers, and trumpeters, may not be heard at all in you[S] any more; and any artisan of any art may not be found at all in you[S] any more; and noise of a millstone may not be heard at all in you[S] any more;

23 and light of a lamp may not shine at all in you[S] any more; and voice of bridegroom and of bride may not be heard at all in you[S] any more; because your[S] merchants were the great ones of the earth, because all the nations were led astray in your[S] sorcery ,

24 and blood of prophets and of saints was found in her, and of all those who have been slain on the earth.'

CHAPTER 19

1 And after these things I heard a great voice of a great multitude in the heaven, saying, 'Alleluia! the salvation, and the glory, and the honor, and the power, [is] to the Lord our God;

2 because true and righteous [are] His judgments, because He did judge the great whore who did corrupt the earth in her whoredom, and He did avenge the blood of His servants at her hand;'

3 and a second time they said, 'Alleluia;' and her smoke does come up — to the ages of the ages!

4 And fall down did the elders — the twenty and four — and the four living creatures, and they did bow before God who is sitting upon the throne, saying, 'Amen, Alleluia.'

5 And a voice out of the throne did come forth, saying, 'Praise our God, all you[P] His servants, and those fearing Him, both the small and the great;'

6 and I heard as the voice of a great multitude, and as the voice of many waters, and as the voice of mighty thunderings, saying, 'Alleluia! because the Lord God — the Almighty did reign!

7 may we rejoice and exult, and give the glory to Him, because the marriage of the Lamb did come, and his wife did make herself ready;

8 and there was given to her that she may be arrayed with fine linen, pure and shining, for the fine linen is the righteous acts of the saints.'

9 And he says to me, 'Write: Happy [are] they who have been called to the supper of the marriage of the Lamb;' and he says to me, 'These [are] the true words of God;'

10 and I fell before his feet, to bow before him, and he says to me, 'See — not! I am fellow servant of you[S], and of your[S] brethren, those having the testimony of Jesus; bow before God, for the testimony of Jesus is the spirit of the prophecy.'

11 And I saw the heaven having been opened, and behold, a white horse, and He who is sitting upon it is called Faithful and True, and He does judge and war in righteousness,

12 and His eyes [are] as a flame of fire, and upon His head [are] many diadems — having a name written that no one has known, except Himself,

13 and He is arrayed with a garment covered with blood, and His name is called, The Word of God.

14 And the armies in the heaven were following Him upon white horses, clothed in fine linen — white and pure;

15 and out of His mouth does proceed a sharp sword, that with it He may destroy the nations, and He shall rule them with a rod of iron, and He does tread the press of the wine of the wrath and the anger of God the Almighty,

16 and He has upon the garment and upon His thigh the name written, 'King of kings, and Lord of lords.'

17 And I saw one messenger standing in the sun, and he cried, a great voice, saying to all the birds that are flying in mid-heaven, 'Come and be gathered together to the supper of the great God,

18 that you[P] may eat flesh of kings, and flesh of chiefs of thousands, and flesh of strong men, and flesh of horses, and of those sitting on them, and the flesh of all — freemen and servants — both small and great.'

19 And I saw the beast, and the kings of the earth, and their armies, having been gathered together to make war with Him who is sitting upon the horse, and with His army;

20 and the beast was taken, and with him the false prophet who did the signs before him, in which he led astray those who did receive the mark of the beast, and those who did bow before his image; they were cast living — the two — to the lake of the fire, that is burning with brimstone;

21 and the rest were killed with the sword of Him who is sitting on the horse, which [sword] is proceeding out of His mouth, and all the birds were filled out of their flesh.

CHAPTER 20

1 And I saw a messenger coming down out of the heaven, having the key of the abyss, and a great chain

over his hand,
2 and he laid hold on the dragon, the old serpent, who
is Devil and Adversary, and did bind him a thousand
years,
3 and he cast him to the abyss, and did shut him up,
and put a seal upon him, that he may not lead astray the
nations any more, till the thousand years may be
finished; and after these it is necessary for him to be
loosed a little time.
4 And I saw thrones, and they sat upon them, and
judgment was given to them, and the souls of those who
have been beheaded because of the testimony of Jesus,
and because of the word of God, and who did not bow
before the beast, nor his image, and did not receive the
mark upon their forehead and upon their hand, and they
did live and reign with Christ the thousand years;
5 and the rest of the dead did not live again till the
thousand years may be finished; this [is] the first rising
again.
6 Happy and holy [is] he who is having part in the first
rising again; the second death has not authority over
these, but they shall be priests of God and of the Christ,
and shall reign with him a thousand years.
7 And when the thousand years may be finished, the
Adversary shall be loosed out of his prison,
8 and he shall go forth to lead the nations astray, that
are in the four corners of the earth — Gog and Magog
— to gather them together to war, of whom the number
[is] as the sand of the sea;
9 and they did go up over the breadth of the land, and
did surround the camp of the saints, and the beloved
city, and there came down fire from God out of the
heaven, and devoured them;
10 and the Devil, who is leading them astray, was cast
into the lake of fire and brimstone, where [are] the beast
and the false prophet, and they shall be tormented day
and night — to the ages of the ages.
11 And I saw a great white throne, and Him who is sitting
upon it, from whose face the earth and the heaven did
flee away, and place was not found for them;
12 and I saw the dead, small and great, standing before
God, and scrolls were opened, and another scroll was
opened, which is that of the life, and the dead were
judged out of the things written in the scrolls —
according to their works;
13 and the sea did give up those dead in it, and the
death and the hades did give up the dead in them, and
they were judged, each one according to their works;
14 and the death and the hades were cast to the lake of
the fire — this [is] the second death;
15 and if any one was not found written in the scroll of
the life, he was cast to the lake of the fire.

CHAPTER 21

1 And I saw a new heaven and a new earth, for the first
heaven and the first earth did pass away, and the sea is
not any more;
2 and I, John, saw the holy city — new Jerusalem —
coming down from God out of the heaven, made ready
as a bride adorned for her husband;
3 and I heard a great voice out of the heaven, saying,
'Behold, the tabernacle of God [is] with men, and He will
tabernacle with them, and they shall be His peoples, and
God Himself shall be with them — their God,
4 and God shall wipe away every tear from their eyes,
and the death shall not be any more, nor sorrow, nor
crying, nor shall there be any more pain, because the
first things did go away.'
5 And He who is sitting upon the throne said, 'Behold,
I make all things new; and He says to me, 'Write, because
these words are true and steadfast;'
6 and He said to me, 'It has been done! I am the Alpha
and the Omega, the Beginning and the End; I, to him
who is thirsting, will give of the fountain of the water of
the life freely;
7 he who is overcoming shall inherit all things, and I
will be to him — a God, and he shall be to me — the son,
8 and to fearful, and unsteadfast, and abominable, and
murderers, and whoremongers, and sorcerers, and
idolaters, and all the liars, their part [is] in the lake that
is burning with fire and brimstone, which is a second
death.'
9 And there came unto me one of the seven messengers,
who have the seven vials that are full of the seven last
plagues, and he spoke with me, saying, 'Come, I will
show you[S] the bride of the Lamb — the wife,'
10 and he carried me away in the Spirit to a mountain
great and high, and did show to me the great city, the
holy Jerusalem, coming down out of the heaven from
God,
11 having the glory of God, and her light [is] like a stone
most precious, as a jasper stone clear as crystal,
12 having also a wall great and high, having twelve
gates, and at the gates twelve messengers, and names
written thereon, which are [those] of the twelve tribes
of the sons of Israel,

13 three gates at the east, three gates at the north, three
gates at the south, three gates at the west;
14 and the wall of the city had twelve foundations, and
names of the twelve apostles of the Lamb in them.
15 And he who is speaking with me had a golden reed,
that he may measure the city, and its gates, and its wall;
16 and the city lies square, and the length of it is as
great as the breadth; and he did measure the city with
the reed — twelve thousand furlongs; the length, and
the breadth, and the height, of it are equal;
17 and he measured its wall, an hundred forty-four
cubits, the measure of a man, that is, of the messenger;
18 and the building of its wall was jasper, and the city
[is] pure gold — like to pure glass;
19 and the foundations of the wall of the city have been
adorned with every precious stone; the first foundation
jasper; the second, sapphire; the third, chalcedony; the
fourth, emerald;
20 the fifth, sardonyx; the sixth, sardius; the seventh,
chrysolite; the eighth, beryl; the ninth, topaz; the tenth,
chrysoprasus; the eleventh, jacinth; the twelfth,
amethyst.
21 And the twelve gates [are] twelve pearls, each one
of the several gates was of one pearl; and the broad-
place of the city [is] pure gold — as transparent glass.
22 And I did not see a sanctuary in it, for the Lord God,
the Almighty, is its sanctuary, and the Lamb,
23 and the city has no need of the sun, nor of the moon,
that they may shine in it; for the glory of God did lighten
it, and the lamp of it [is] the Lamb;
24 and the nations of the saved shall walk in its light,
and the kings of the earth do bring their glory and honor
into it,
25 and its gates shall not at all be shut by day, for there
shall not be night;
26 and they shall bring the glory and the honor of the
nations into it;
27 and there may not at all enter into it any thing defiling
and doing abomination, and a lie, but — those written
in the scroll of the life of the Lamb.

CHAPTER 22

1 And he showed me a pure river of water of life, bright
as crystal, going forth out of the throne of God and of
the Lamb:
2 in the midst of its broad place, and of the river on this
side and on that, [is] a tree of life, yielding twelve fruits,
in each several month rendering its fruits, and the leaves
of the tree [are] for the service of the nations;
3 and there shall not be any curse any more, and the
throne of God and of the Lamb shall be in it, and His
servants shall serve Him,
4 and they shall see His face, and His name [is] upon
their foreheads,
5 and there shall not be night, and they have no need of
a lamp and light of a sun, because the Lord God does
give them light, and they shall reign — to the ages of
the ages.
6 And he said to me, ‘These words [are] steadfast and
true, and the Lord God of the holy prophets did send
His messenger to show to His servants the things that
it is necessary to come quickly:
7 Behold, I come quickly; happy [is] he who is keeping
the words of the prophecy of this scroll.’
8 And I, John, am he who is seeing these things and
hearing, and when I heard and beheld, I fell down to
bow before the feet of the messenger who is showing
me these things;
9 and he says to me, ‘See — not; for I am fellow-servant
of you[S], and of your[S] brethren the prophets, and of those
keeping the words of this scroll; bow before God.’
10 And he says to me, ‘You[S] may not seal the words of
the prophecy of this scroll, because the time is near;
11 he who is unrighteous — let him be unrighteous still,
and he who is filthy — let him be filthy still, and he who
is righteous — let him be declared righteous still, and
he who is sanctified — let him be sanctified still:
12 And behold, I come quickly, and my reward [is] with
me, to render to each as his work shall be;
13 I am the Alpha and the Omega — the Beginning and
End — the First and the Last.
14 ‘Happy are those doing His commands that the
authority unto the tree of the life shall be theirs, and
they may enter into the city by the gates;
15 and without [are] the dogs, and the sorcerers, and
the whoremongers, and the murderers, and the idolaters,
and every one who is loving and is doing a lie.
16 ‘I, Jesus did send My messenger to testify to you[P]
these things concerning the assemblies; I am the root
and the offspring of David, the bright and morning star!
17 And the Spirit and the Bride say, Come; and he who
is hearing — let him say, Come; and he who is thirsting
— let him come; and he who is willing — let him take the
water of life freely.
18 ‘For I testify to every one hearing the words of the
prophecy of this scroll, if any one may add unto these,

God shall add to him the plagues that have been written
in this scroll,
19 and if any one may take away from the words of the
scroll of this prophecy, God shall take away his part from
the scroll of the life, and out of the holy city, and the
things that have been written in this scroll;'
20 he says — who is testifying these things — 'Yes, I
come quickly!' Amen! Yes, be coming, Lord Jesus!
21 The grace of our Lord Jesus Christ [is] with you[P] all.
Amen.

End of the

New Testament

The Book Of
Psalms

Psalm 1

1 O the happiness of that one, who has not walked in the counsel of the wicked. And has not stood in the way of sinners, and has not sat in the seat of scorners;
2 But — his delight [is] in the law of Jehovah, and he does meditate in His law by day and by night:
3 And he has been as a tree, planted by rivulets of water, that gives its fruit in its season, and its leaf does not wither, and he causes all that he does to prosper.
4 Not so the wicked: but — that wind drives away as chaff!
5 For that reason the wicked rise not in judgment, nor sinners in the company of the righteous,
6 For Jehovah is knowing the way of the righteous, and the way of the wicked is lost!

Psalm 2

1 Why have nations tumultuously assembled? And do peoples meditate vanity?
2 Kings of the earth do station themselves, and princes have been united together, against Jehovah, and against His Messiah:
3 'Let us draw off Their cords, and cast Their thick bands from us.'
4 He who is sitting in the heavens does laugh, the Lord does mock at them.
5 Then does He speak unto them in His anger, and in His wrath He does trouble them:
6 'And I — I have anointed My King, Upon Zion — My holy hill.'
7 I declare concerning a statute: Jehovah said unto me, ' You[S] [are] My Son, I have brought you[S] forth today.
8 Ask of Me and I give nations — your[S] inheritance, and your[S] possession — the ends of earth.
9 You[S] do rule them with a scepter of iron, You[S] do crush them as a vessel of a potter.'
10 And now, O kings, act wisely, be instructed, O judges of earth,
11 Serve you[P] Jehovah with fear, and rejoice with trembling.
12 Kiss the Chosen One, for fear that He be angry, and you[P] lose the way, when His anger burns but a little, O the happiness of all trusting in Him!

Psalm 3

1 A Psalm of David, in his fleeing from the face of Absalom his son. Jehovah, how my distresses have multiplied! Many are rising up against me.
2 Many are saying of my soul, 'There is no salvation for him in God.' Selah.
3 And You[S], O Jehovah, [are] a shield for me, my honor, and lifter up of my head.
4 My voice [is] unto Jehovah: I call: and He answers me from his holy hill, Selah.
5 I — I have lain down, and I sleep, I have waked, for Jehovah sustains me.
6 I am not afraid of myriads of people, that they have set round about against me.
7 Rise, O Jehovah! save me, my God. Because You[S] have struck all my enemies [on] the cheek. You[S] have broken the teeth of the wicked.
8 Of Jehovah [is] this salvation; Your[S] blessing [is] on Your[S] people! Selah.

Psalm 4

1 To the Overseer with Stringed Instruments. — A Psalm of David. In my calling You[S] answer me, O God of my righteousness. In adversity You[S] gave enlargement to me; favor me, and hear my prayer.
2 Sons of men! till when [is] my glory for shame? You[P] love a vain thing, you[P] seek a lie. Selah.
3 And know you[P] that Jehovah has separated a saintly one to Himself. Jehovah hears in my calling to Him.
4 'Tremble you[P], and do not sin;' say you[P] [thus] in

your[P] heart on your[P] bed, and be you[P] silent. Selah.
5 Sacrifice you[P] sacrifices of righteousness, and trust you[P] unto Jehovah.
6 Many are saying, 'Who does show us good?' lift the light of Your[S] face on us, O Jehovah,
7 You[S] have given joy in my heart, from the time their corn and their wine have been multiplied.
8 In peace together I lie down and sleep, for You[S], O Jehovah, alone, do cause me to dwell in confidence!

Psalm 5

1 To the Overseer, 'Concerning the Inheritances.' — A Psalm of David. Hear my sayings, O Jehovah, consider my meditation.
2 Be attentive to the voice of my cry, my king and my God, for I pray habitually unto You[S].
3 Jehovah, [at] morning You[S] hear my voice, [at] morning I set in array for You[S], and I look out.
4 For You[S] [are] not a God desiring wickedness, evil inhabits You[S] not.
5 The boastful station not themselves before Your[S] eyes: You[S] have hated all working iniquity.
6 You[S] destroy those speaking lies, Jehovah does abominate a man of blood and deceit.
7 And I, in the abundance of Your[S] kindness, I enter Your[S] house, I bow myself toward Your[S] holy temple in Your[S] fear.
8 O Jehovah, lead me in Your[S] righteousness, because of those observing me, make straight Your[S] way before me,
9 For there is no stability in their mouth. Their heart [is] mischiefs, an open grave [is] their throat, they make their tongue smooth.
10 Declare them guilty, O God, let them fall from their own counsels, drive them away in the abundance of their transgressions, because they have rebelled against You[S].
11 And all trusting in You[S] do rejoice, they sing to the age, and You[S] cover them over, and those loving Your[S] name exult in You[S].
12 For You[S] bless the righteous, O Jehovah, as a buckler does compass him with favor!

Psalm 6

1 To the Overseer with stringed instruments, on the octave. — A Psalm of David. O Jehovah, reprove me not in Your[S] anger, nor chastise me in Your[S] fury.
2 Favor me, O Jehovah, for I [am] weak, heal me, O Jehovah, for my bones have been troubled,
3 And my soul has been troubled greatly, and You[S], O Jehovah, till when?
4 Turn back, O Jehovah, draw out my soul, save me for Your[S] kindness' sake.
5 For there is not Your[S] memorial in death, in Sheol, who does give thanks to You[S]?
6 I have been weary with my sighing, I meditate through all the night [on] my bed, I waste my couch with my tear.
7 My eye is old from provocation, it is old because of all my adversaries,
8 Turn from me all you[P] workers of iniquity, for Jehovah heard the voice of my weeping,
9 Jehovah has heard my supplication, Jehovah receives my prayer.
10 All my enemies are ashamed and troubled greatly, they turn back — ashamed [in] a moment!

Psalm 7

1 'The Erring One,' by David, that he sung to Jehovah concerning the words of Cush a Benjamite. O Jehovah, my God, I have trusted in You[S], save me from all my pursuers, and deliver me.
2 For fear that he tear my soul as a lion, rending, and there is no deliverer.
3 O Jehovah, my God, if I have done this, if there is iniquity in my hands,
4 If I have done my well-wisher evil, and draw my adversary without cause,
5 an enemy pursues my soul, and overtakes, and treads down my life to the earth, and places my honor in the dust. Selah.
6 Rise, O Jehovah, in Your[S] anger, be lifted up at the wrath of my adversaries, and awake You[S] for me: You[S] have commanded judgment:
7 And a company of peoples compass You[S], and over it You[S] turn back on high,
8 Jehovah does judge the peoples; judge me, O Jehovah, according to my righteousness, and according to my integrity on me,
9 Let, I pray You[S] be ended the evil of the wicked, and establish You[S] the righteous, and a trier of hearts and reins is the righteous God.
10 My shield [is] on God, Savior of the upright in heart!
11 God [is] a righteous judge, and He is not angry at all times.

12 If [one] turn not, He sharpens His sword , He has
trodden His bow — He prepares it,
13 Yes, for him He has prepared instruments of death,
He makes His arrows for burning pursuers.
14 Behold, he travails [with] iniquity, and he has
conceived perverseness, and has brought forth
falsehood.
15 A pit he has prepared, and he digs it, and he falls into
a ditch he makes.
16 His perverseness does return on his head, and his
violence comes down on his crown.
17 I thank Jehovah, according to His righteousness,
and praise the name of Jehovah Most High!

Psalm 8

1 To the Overseer, 'On the Gittith.' A Psalm of David.
Jehovah, our Lord, How honorable Your[S] name in all the
earth! Who sets Your[S] honor on the heavens.
2 From the mouths of infants and sucklings You[S] have
founded strength, because of Your[S] adversaries, to still
an enemy and a self-avenger.
3 For I see Your[S] heavens, a work of Your[S] fingers, moon
and stars that You[S] did establish.
4 What [is] man that You[S] remember him? The son of
man that You[S] inspect him?
5 And cause him to lack a little of Godhead, and compass
him with honor and majesty.
6 You[S] do cause him to rule over the works of Your[S]
hands, You[S] have placed all under his feet.
7 Sheep and oxen, all of them, and also beasts of the
field,
8 Bird of the heavens, and fish of the sea, passing
through the paths of the seas!
9 Jehovah, our Lord, how honorable Your[S] name in all
the earth!

Psalm 9

1 To the Overseer, 'On the Death of Labben.' — A Psalm
of David. I confess, O Jehovah, with all my heart, I
recount all Your[S] wonders,
2 I rejoice and exult in You[S], I praise Your[S] Name, O Most
High.
3 In my enemies turning backward, they stumble and
perish from Your[S] face.
4 For You[S] have done my judgment and my right. You[S]
have sat on a throne, a judge of righteousness.
5 You[S] have rebuked nations, You[S] have destroyed the
wicked, You[S] have blotted out their name to the age and
for ever.
6 O you[S] Enemy, destructions have been finished for
ever, as to cities you[S] have plucked up, their memorial
has perished with them.
7 And Jehovah abides to the age, He is preparing His
throne for judgment.
8 And He judges the world in righteousness, He judges
the peoples in uprightness.
9 And Jehovah is a tower for the bruised, a tower for
times of adversity.
10 They who do know Your[S] name trust in You[S], for You[S]
have not forsaken those seeking You[S], O Jehovah.
11 Sing you[P] praise to Jehovah, inhabiting Zion, declare
you[P] His acts among the peoples,
12 for He has remembered them who is seeking for blood,
He has not forgotten the cry of the afflicted.
13 Favor me, O Jehovah, see my affliction by those
hating me, You[S] who lifts me up from the gates of death,
14 So that I recount all Your[S] praise, in the gates of the
daughter of Zion. I rejoice on Your[S] salvation.
15 Nations have sunk in a pit they made, their foot has
been captured in a net that they hid.
16 Jehovah has been known, He has done judgment,
the wicked has been snared by a work of His hands.
Meditation. Selah.
17 The wicked do turn back to Sheol, all nations
forgetting God.
18 For the needy is not forgotten for ever, the hope of
the humble lost to the age.
19 Rise, O Jehovah, let not man be strong, let nations
be judged before Your[S] face.
20 Appoint, O Jehovah, a director to them, let nations
know they [are] men! Selah.

Psalm 10

1 Why, Jehovah, do You[S] stand at a distance? You[S] do
hide in times of adversity,
2 through the pride of the wicked, is the poor inflamed,
they are caught in devices that they devised.
3 Because the wicked has boasted of the desire of his
soul, and he has blessed a dishonest gainer, he has
despised Jehovah.
4 The wicked according to the height of his face, inquires
not. 'God is not!' [are] all his devices.

5 His ways do pain at all times, Your[S] judgments [are] on high before him, all his adversaries — he puffs at them.
6 He has said in his heart, 'I am not moved,' to generation and generation not in evil.
7 His mouth is full of oaths, and deceits, and fraud: under his tongue [is] perverseness and iniquity,
8 He does sit in an ambush of the villages, he does slay the innocent in secret places. His eyes watch secretly for the afflicted,
9 He lies in wait in a secret place, as a lion in a covert. He lies in wait to catch the poor, he catches the poor, drawing him into his net.
10 He is bruised — he bows down, The afflicted has fallen by his mighty ones.
11 He said in his heart, 'God has forgotten, He has hid His face, He has never seen.'
12 Arise, O Jehovah! O God, lift up Your[S] hand! Forget not the humble.
13 For what reason has the wicked despised God? He has said in his heart, 'It is not required.'
14 You[S] have seen, for You[S] behold perverseness and anger; by giving into Your[S] hand, the afflicted does leave [it] on You[S], You[S] have been a helper of the fatherless.
15 Break the arm of the wicked and the evil, seek out his wickedness, find none;
16 Jehovah [is] king to the age, and for ever, the nations have perished out of His land!
17 You[S] have heard the desire of the humble, O Jehovah. You[S] prepare their heart; You[S] cause Your[S] ear to attend,
18 To judge the fatherless and bruised: He adds no more to oppress — man of the earth!

Psalm 11

1 To the Overseer. — By David. In Jehovah I trusted, how say you[P] to my soul, 'They moved [to] Your[S] mountain for the bird?
2 For behold, the wicked tread a bow, they have prepared their arrow on the string, to shoot in darkness at the upright in heart.
3 When the foundations are destroyed, the righteous — what has he done?
4 'Jehovah [is] in his holy temple: Jehovah — His throne [is] in the heavens. His eyes see — His eyelids try the sons of men.
5 Jehovah try for the righteous. And the wicked and the lover of violence, has His soul hated,
6 He pours snares, fire, and brimstone on the wicked, and a horrible wind [is] the portion of their cup.
7 For righteous [is] Jehovah, He has loved righteousness, His countenance does see the upright!'

Psalm 12

1 To the Overseer, on the octave. — A Psalm of David. Save, Jehovah, for the saintly has failed, for the steadfast have ceased from the sons of men:
2 they speak vanity each with his neighbour, lip of flattery! They speak with heart and heart.
3 Jehovah does cut off all lips of flattery, a tongue speaking great things,
4 who said, 'By our tongue we do mightily: Our lips [are] our own; who [is] lord over us?'
5 Because of the spoiling of the poor, because of the groaning of the needy, now do I arise, says Jehovah, I set in safety [him who] does breathe for it.
6 Sayings of Jehovah [are] pure sayings; silver tried in a furnace of earth refined sevenfold.
7 You[S], O Jehovah, do preserve them, You[S] keep us from this generation to the age.
8 Around the wicked walk continually, according as vileness is exalted by sons of men!

Psalm 13

1 To the Overseer. — A Psalm of David. Till when, O Jehovah, do You[S] forget me? — for ever? Till when do You[S] hide Your[S] face from me?
2 Till when do I set counsels in my soul? Sorrow in my heart daily? Till when is my enemy exalted over me?
3 Look attentively; answer me, O Jehovah, my God, enlighten my eyes, for fear that I sleep in death,
4 for fear that my enemy say, 'I overcame him,' My adversaries joy when I am moved.
5 And I, I have trusted in Your[S] kindness, my heart does rejoice in Your[S] salvation.
6 I do sing to Jehovah, for He has conferred benefits upon me!

Psalm 14

1 To the Overseer. — By David. A fool has said in his heart, 'God is not;' they have done corruptly, they have

done abominable actions, there is not a doer of good.

2 Jehovah has looked from the heavens on the sons of men, to see if there is a wise one — seeking God.

3 The whole have turned aside, together they have been filthy: there is not a doer of good, not even one.

4 Have all working iniquity not known? Those consuming my people have eaten bread, they have not called Jehovah.

5 There they have feared a fear, for God [is] in the generation of the righteous.

6 You^{P} cause the counsel of the poor to stink, Because Jehovah [is] his refuge.

7 'Who does give the salvation of Israel from Zion? When Jehovah does turn back [to] a captivity of His people, Jacob does rejoice — Israel is glad!

Psalm 15

1 A Psalm of David. Jehovah, who does stay in Your^{S} tent? Who does dwell in Your^{S} holy hill?

2 He who is walking uprightly, and working righteousness, and speaking truth in his heart.

3 He has not slandered by his tongue, he has not done evil to his friend; and he has not lifted up reproach against his neighbor.

4 A rejected one [is] despised in his eyes, and he does honor those fearing Jehovah. He has sworn to suffer evil, and changes not;

5 he has not given his silver in usury, and has not taken a bribe against the innocent; whoso is doing these is not moved to the age!

Psalm 16

1 A Secret Treasure of David. Preserve me, O God, for I did trust in You^{S}.

2 You^{S} have said to Jehovah, 'You^{S} [are] My Lord;' my good [is] not for your^{S} own sake;

3 For the holy ones who [are] in the land, And the honorable, all my delight [is] in them.

4 Multiplied are their griefs, [who] have hastened backward; I pour not out their libations of blood, nor do I take up their names on my lips.

5 Jehovah [is] the portion of my share, and of my cup, You^{S} — You^{S} do uphold my lot.

6 Lines have fallen to me in pleasant places, yes, a beauteous inheritance [is] for me.

7 I bless Jehovah who has counseled me; also my reins instruct me [in] the nights.

8 I did place Jehovah before me continually, because — at my right hand I am not moved.

9 For that reason has my heart been glad, and my honor does rejoice, also my flesh dwells confidently:

10 For You^{S} do not leave my soul to Sheol, nor gives Your^{S} saintly one to see corruption.

11 You^{S} cause me to know the path of life; fullness of joys [is] with Your^{S} presence, pleasant things by Your^{S} right hand for ever!

Psalm 17

1 A Prayer of David. Hear, O Jehovah, righteousness, attend my cry, give ear [to] my prayer, without lips of deceit.

2 My judgment does go out from before You^{S}; Your^{S} eyes do see uprightly.

3 You^{S} have proved my heart, You^{S} have inspected by night, You^{S} have tried me, You^{S} find nothing; my thoughts pass not over my mouth.

4 As to doings of man, through a word of Your^{S} lips I have observed the paths of a destroyer;

5 To uphold my goings in Your^{S} paths, my steps have not slid.

6 I — I called You^{S}, for You^{S} do answer me, O God, incline Your^{S} ear to me, hear my speech.

7 Separate wonderfully Your^{S} kindness, O Savior of the confiding, by Your^{S} right hand, from withstanders.

8 Keep me as the apple, the daughter of the eye; You^{S} do hide me in shadow of Your^{S} wings.

9 From the face of the wicked who spoiled me. My enemies in soul go round against me.

10 Their fat they have closed up, their mouths have spoken with pride:

11 'Our steps now have compassed [him];' they set their eyes to turn aside in the land.

12 His likeness desirous to tear as a lion, as a young lion dwelling in secret places.

13 Arise, O Jehovah, go before his face, cause him to bend. Deliver my soul from the wicked, Your^{S} sword,

14 from men, Your^{S} hand, O Jehovah, from men of the world, their portion [is] in life, and [with] Your^{S} hidden things You^{S} fill their belly, they are satisfied [with] sons; and have left their abundance to their sucklings.

15 I — in righteousness, I see Your^{S} face; I am satisfied, in awaking, [with] Your^{S} form!

Psalm 18

1 To the Overseer. — By a servant of Jehovah, by David, who has spoken the words of this song to Jehovah in the day Jehovah delivered him from the hand of all his enemies, and from the hand of Saul, and he said: — I love You[S], O Jehovah, my strength.
2 Jehovah [is] my rock, and my bulwark, and my deliverer, My God [is] my rock, I trust in Him: my shield, and a horn of my salvation, my high tower.
3 The 'Praised One' I call Jehovah, and I am saved from my enemies.
4 Cords of death have compassed me, and streams of the worthless make me afraid.
5 Cords of Sheol have surrounded me, snares of death have been before me.
6 In my adversity I call Jehovah, and I cry unto my God. He hears my voice from His temple, and My cry before Him comes into His ears.
7 And the earth does shake and tremble, and foundations of hills are troubled, and they shake — because He has wrath.
8 Smoke has gone up by His nostrils, and fire from His mouth consumes, coals have been kindled by it.
9 And He inclines the heavens, and comes down, and thick darkness [is] under His feet.
10 And He rides on a cherub, and does fly, and He flies on wings of wind.
11 He makes darkness His secret place, round about Him His tabernacle, darkness of waters, thick clouds of the skies.
12 From the brightness over-against Him His thick clouds have passed on, hail and coals of fire.
13 And Jehovah does thunder in the heavens, and the Most High gives forth His voice, hail and coals of fire.
14 And He sends His arrows and scatters them, and much lightning, and crushes them.
15 And seen are the streams of waters, and revealed are foundations of the earth. From Your[S] rebuke, O Jehovah, from the breath of the spirit of Your[S] anger.
16 He sends from above — He takes me, He draws me out of many waters.
17 He delivers me from my strong enemy, and from those hating me, for they have been stronger than I.
18 They go before me in a day of my calamity and Jehovah is for a support to me.
19 And He brings me forth to a large place, He draws me out, because He delighted in me.
20 Jehovah does recompense me according to my righteousness, according to the cleanness of my hands, He does return to me.
21 For I have kept the ways of Jehovah, and have not done wickedly against my God.
22 For all His judgments [are] before me, and I turn not His statutes from me.
23 And I am perfect with him, and I keep myself from my iniquity.
24 And Jehovah does return to me, according to my righteousness, according to the cleanness of my hands, over-against his eyes.
25 With the kind You[S] show Yourself[S] kind, with a perfect man shows Yourself[S] perfect.
26 With the pure You[S] show Yourself[S] pure, and with the perverse shows Yourself[S] a wrestler,
27 For You[S] save a poor people, and cause the eyes of the high to fall.
28 For You[S] — You[S] light my lamp, Jehovah my God enlightens my darkness.
29 For by You[S] I run — a troop! And by my God I leap a wall.
30 God! perfect [is] His way, the saying of Jehovah is tried, He [is] a shield to all those trusting in Him.
31 For who [is] God besides Jehovah? And who [is] a rock save our God?
32 God! who is girding me [with] strength, and He make my way perfect.
33 Making my feet like hinds, and on my high places causes me to stand.
34 Teaching my hands for battle, and a bow of brass was brought down by my arms.
35 And You[S] give the shield of Your[S] salvation to me, and Your[S] right hand does support me, and Your[S] lowliness makes me great.
36 You[S] enlarge my step under me, and my ankles have not slid.
37 I pursue my enemies, and overtake them, and turn back not till they are consumed.
38 I strike them, and they are not able to rise, they fall under my feet,
39 And You[S] gird me [with] strength for battle, cause my withstanders to bow under me.
40 As to my enemies — You[S] have given the neck to me, as to those hating me — I cut them off.
41 They cry, and there is no savior, on Jehovah, and He does not answer them.
42 And I beat them as dust before wind, I empty them out as mire of the streets.

43 You[S] do deliver me from the strivings of the people, You[S] place me for a head of nations, a people I have not known do serve me.
44 At the hearing of the ear they listen to me, sons of a stranger pretend obedience to me,
45 sons of a stranger fade away, and are slain out of their close places.
46 Jehovah lives — and blessed [is] my rock, and exalted is the God of my salvation.
47 God — who is giving vengeance to me, and He subdues peoples under me,
48 my deliverer from my enemies, You[S] raise me above my withstanders, do deliver me from a man of violence.
49 For that reason I confess You[S] among nations, O Jehovah, and I sing praise to Your[S] name,
50 Magnifying the salvation of His king, and doing kindness to His anointed, To David, and to his seed — unto the age!

Psalm 19

1 To the Overseer. — A Psalm of David. The heavens [are] recounting the honor of God, and the expanse [is] declaring the work of His hands.
2 Day to day utters speech, and night to night shows knowledge.
3 There is no speech, and there are no words. Their voice has not been heard.
4 Their line has gone forth into all the earth, and to the end of the world their sayings, for the sun He placed a tent in them,
5 And he, as a bridegroom, goes out from his covering, He rejoices as a mighty one to run the path.
6 From the end of the heavens [is] his going out, and his revolution [is] unto their ends, and nothing is hid from his heat.
7 The law of Jehovah [is] perfect, refreshing the soul, the testimonies of Jehovah [are] steadfast, making wise the simple,
8 The precepts of Jehovah [are] upright, rejoicing the heart, the command of Jehovah [is] pure, enlightening the eyes,
9 The fear of Jehovah [is] clean, standing to the age, the judgments of Jehovah [are] true, they have been righteous — together.
10 They are more desirable than gold, yes, than much fine gold; and sweeter than honey, even liquid honey of the comb.
11 Also — Your[S] servant is warned by them, 'In keeping them [is] a great reward.'
12 Errors! who does understand? From hidden ones declare me innocent,
13 Also — from presumptuous ones keep back Your[S] servant, let them not rule over me, then am I perfect, and declared innocent of much transgression,
14 let the sayings of my mouth, and the meditation of my heart, be for a pleasing thing before You[S], O Jehovah, my rock, and my redeemer!

Psalm 20

1 To the Overseer. — A Psalm of David. Jehovah does answer you[S], in a day of adversity, the name of the God of Jacob does set you[S] on high,
2 He does send your[S] help from the sanctuary, and does support you[S] from Zion,
3 He does remember all your[S] presents, and does reduce your[S] burnt-offering to ashes. Selah.
4 He does give to you[S] according to your[S] heart, and does fulfill all your[S] counsel.
5 We sing of your[S] salvation, and set up a banner in the name of our God. Jehovah does fulfill all your[S] requests.
6 Now I have known that Jehovah has saved His anointed, He answers him from His holy heavens, with the saving might of His right hand.
7 Some of chariots, and some of horses, and we make mention of the name of Jehovah our God.
8 They — they have bowed and have fallen, and we have risen and station ourselves upright.
9 O Jehovah, save the king, He does answer us in the day we call!

Psalm 21

1 To the Overseer. — A Psalm of David. Jehovah, the king joyful is in Your[S] strength, how greatly he rejoices in Your[S] salvation.
2 You[S] gave to him the desire of his heart, and You[S] have not withheld the request of his lips. Selah.
3 For You[S] put blessings of goodness before him, You[S] set a crown of fine gold on his head.
4 He has asked life from You[S], You[S] have given to him — length of days, age-during — and for ever.
5 Great [is] his honor in Your[S] salvation, You[S] place honor and majesty on him.

6 For You[S] make him blessings for ever, You[S] do cause him to rejoice with joy, by Your[S] countenance.
7 For the king is trusting in Jehovah, and he is not moved in the kindness of the Most High.
8 You[S] hand comes to all Your[S] enemies, Your[S] right hand does find Your[S] haters.
9 You[S] make them as a furnace of fire, at the time of Your[S] presence. Jehovah in His anger does swallow them, and fire does devour them.
10 You[S] destroy their fruit from earth, and their seed from the sons of men.
11 For they stretched out evil against You[S], they devised a wicked device, they prevail not,
12 for You[S] make them a butt, when You[S] prepare Your[S] strings against their faces.
13 Be You[S] exalted, O Jehovah in, Your[S] strength, we sing and we praise Your[S] might!

Psalm 22

1 To the Overseer, on 'The Hind of the Morning.' — A Psalm of David. My God, my God, why have You[S] forsaken me? Far from my salvation, the words of my roaring?
2 My God, I call by day, and You[S] answer not, and by night, and there is no silence to me.
3 And You[S] [are] holy, sitting — the Praise of Israel.
4 Our fathers did trust in You[S] — they trusted, and You[S] do deliver them.
5 They cried unto You[S], and were delivered, they trusted in You[S], and were not ashamed.
6 And I [am] a worm, and no man, a reproach of man, and despised of the people.
7 All beholding me do mock at me, they make free with the lip — shake the head,
8 'Roll unto Jehovah, He does deliver him, He does deliver him, for he delighted in him.'
9 For you[S] [is] He bringing me forth from the womb, causing me to trust, on the breasts of my mother.
10 I have been cast on You[S] from the womb, from the belly of my mother You[S] [are] my God.
11 Be not far from me, for adversity is near, for there is no helper.
12 Many bulls have surrounded me, mighty ones of Bashan have compassed me,
13 They have opened their mouth against me, a lion tearing and roaring.
14 I have been poured out as waters, and all my bones have separated themselves, my heart has been like wax, it is melted in the midst of my bowels.
15 My power is dried up as an earthen vessel, and my tongue is cleaving to my jaws.
16 And You[S] appointed me to the dust of death, for dogs have surrounded me, a company of evil doers have compassed me, piercing my hands and my feet.
17 I count all my bones — they look expectingly, they look upon me,
18 they apportion my garments to themselves, and they cause a lot to fall for my clothing.
19 And You[S], O Jehovah, be not far off, O my strength, hurry to help me.
20 Deliver my soul from the sword, my only one from the paw of a dog.
21 Save me from the mouth of a lion: — and — from the horns of the high places You[S] have answered me!
22 I declare Your[S] name to my brethren, I praise You[S] in the midst of the assembly.
23 You[P] who fear Jehovah, praise you[P] Him, all the seed of Jacob, honor you[P] Him, and be afraid of Him, all you[P] seed of Israel.
24 For He has not despised, nor abominated, the affliction of the afflicted, nor has He hidden His face from him, and in his crying unto Him He hears.
25 My praise of You[S] [is] in the great assembly. I complete my vows before His fearers.
26 The humble do eat and are satisfied, those seeking Him do praise Jehovah, your[P] heart does live for ever.
27 Remember and return unto Jehovah, do all ends of the earth, and bow themselves before You[S], do all families of the nations,
28 for to Jehovah [is] the kingdom, and He is ruling among nations.
29 And the fat ones of earth have eaten, and they bow themselves, bow before Him do all going down to dust, and he [who] has not revived his soul.
30 A seed does serve Him, it is declared of the Lord to the generation.
31 They come and declare His righteousness, to a people that is borne, that He has made!

Psalm 23

1 A Psalm of David. Jehovah [is] my shepherd, I do not lack,
2 He causes me to lie down in pastures of tender grass, He does lead me by quiet waters.

3 He refreshes my soul, He leads me in paths of righteousness, for His name's sake,
4 Also — when I walk in a valley of death-shade, I fear no evil, for You[S] [are] with me, Your[S] rod and Your[S] staff — they comfort me.
5 You[S] arrange a table before me, over-against my adversaries, You[S] have anointed my head with oil, my cup is full!
6 Only — goodness and kindness pursue me, all the days of my life, and my dwelling [is] in the house of Jehovah, for a length of days!

Psalm 24

1 A Psalm of David. To Jehovah [is] the earth and its fullness, the world and the inhabitants in it.
2 For He has founded it on the seas, and He does establish it on the floods.
3 Who goes up into the hill of Jehovah? And who rises up in His holy place?
4 The clean of hands, and pure of heart, who has not lifted up his soul to vanity, nor has sworn to deceit.
5 He bears away a blessing from Jehovah, righteousness from the God of his salvation.
6 This [is] a generation of those seeking Him. Seeking Your[S] face, O Jacob! Selah.
7 Lift up, O gates, your[P] heads, and be lifted up, O doors age-during, and the king of glory does come in!
8 Who [is] this — 'the king of glory?' Jehovah — strong and mighty, Jehovah, the mighty in battle.
9 Lift up, O gates, your[P] heads, and be lifted up, O doors age-during, and the king of glory does come in!
10 Who [is] He — this 'king of glory?' Jehovah of hosts — He [is] the king of glory! Selah.

Psalm 25

1 By David. Unto You[S], O Jehovah, I lift up my soul.
2 My God, I have trusted in You[S], let me not be ashamed, let not my enemies exult over me.
3 Also let none waiting on You[S] be ashamed, let the treacherous dealers be ashamed without cause.
4 Your[S] ways, O Jehovah, cause me to know, Your[S] paths teach You[S] me.
5 Cause me to tread in Your[S] truth, and teach me, for You[S] [are] the God of my salvation, I have waited near You[S] all the day.
6 Remember Your[S] mercies, O Jehovah, and Your[S] kindnesses, for they [are] from the age.
7 Sins of my youth, and my transgressions, do not You[S] remember. According to Your[S] kindness be mindful of me, for Your[S] goodness' sake, O Jehovah.
8 Good and upright [is] Jehovah, for that reason He directs sinners in the way.
9 He causes the humble to tread in judgment, and teaches the humble His way.
10 All the paths of Jehovah [are] kindness and truth, to those keeping His covenant, and His testimonies.
11 For Your[S] name's sake, O Jehovah, You[S] have pardoned my iniquity, for it [is] great.
12 Who [is] this — the man fearing Jehovah? He directs him in the way He does choose.
13 His soul does remain in good, and his seed does possess the land.
14 The secret of Jehovah [is] for those fearing Him, and His covenant — to cause them to know.
15 My eyes [are] continually unto Jehovah, for He brings my feet out from a net.
16 Turn You[S] unto me, and favor me, for I [am] lonely and afflicted.
17 The distresses of my heart have enlarged themselves, bring me out from my distresses.
18 See my affliction and my misery, and bear with all my sins.
19 See my enemies, for they have been many, and they have hated me with violent hatred.
20 Keep my soul, and deliver me, let me not be ashamed, for I trusted in You[S].
21 Integrity and uprightness do keep me, for I have waited [on] You[S].
22 Redeem Israel, O God, from all his distresses!

Psalm 26

1 By David. Judge me, O Jehovah, for I have walked in my integrity, and I have trusted in Jehovah, I slide not.
2 Try me, O Jehovah, and prove me, purified [are] my reins and my heart.
3 For Your[S] kindness [is] before my eyes, and I have walked habitually in Your[S] truth.
4 I have not sat with vain men, and I enter not with dissemblers.
5 I have hated the assembly of evil doers, and I sit not with the wicked.
6 I wash my hands in innocency, and I compass Your[S]

altar, O Jehovah.
7 To sound with a voice of confession, and to recount all Your[S] wonders.
8 Jehovah, I have loved the habitation of Your[S] house, and the place of the tabernacle of Your[S] honor.
9 Do not gather my soul with sinners, and my life with men of blood,
10 in whose hand [is] a wicked device, and their right hand [is] full of bribes.
11 And I, I walk in my integrity, redeem me, and favor me.
12 My foot has stood in uprightness, I bless Jehovah in assemblies!

Psalm 27

1 By David. Jehovah [is] my light and my salvation, whom do I fear? Jehovah [is] the strength of my life, of whom am I afraid?
2 When evil doers come near to me to eat my flesh, my adversaries and my enemies to me, they have stumbled and fallen.
3 Though a host does encamp against me, my heart does not fear, though war rises up against me, in this I [am] confident.
4 One [thing] I asked of Jehovah — it I seek. My dwelling in the house of Jehovah, all the days of my life, to look on the pleasantness of Jehovah, and to inquire in His temple.
5 For He hides me in a tabernacle in the day of evil, He hides me in a secret place of His tent, he raises me up on a rock.
6 And now, lifted up is my head, above my enemies — my surrounders, and I sacrifice sacrifices of shouting in His tent, I sing, yes, I sing praise to Jehovah.
7 Hear, O Jehovah, my voice — I call, and favor me, and answer me.
8 My heart said to You[S] ‘They sought my face, Your[S] face, O Jehovah, I seek.’
9 Hide not Your[S] face from me, turn Your[S] servant not aside in anger, You[S] have been my help. Leave me not, nor forsake me, O God of my salvation.
10 When my father and my mother have forsaken me, then does Jehovah gather me.
11 Show me, O Jehovah, Your[S] way, and lead me in a path of uprightness, for the sake of my beholders.
12 Give me not to the will of my adversaries, for false witnesses have risen against me, and they breathe out violence to me.
13 I had not believed to look on the goodness of Jehovah in the land of the living!
14 Look unto Jehovah — be strong, and He does strengthen your[S] heart, yes, look unto Jehovah!

Psalm 28

1 By David. Unto You, O Jehovah, I call, my rock, be not silent to me! For fear that You[S] be silent to me, and I have been compared with those going down to the pit.
2 Hear the voice of my supplications, in my crying unto You[S], in my lifting up my hands toward Your[S] holy oracle.
3 Draw me not with the wicked, and with workers of iniquity, speaking peace with their neighbors, and evil in their heart.
4 Give to them according to their acting, and according to the evil of their doings. Give to them according to the work of their hands. Return their deed to them.
5 For they attend not to the doing of Jehovah, and unto the work of His hands. He throws them down, and does not build them up.
6 Blessed [is] Jehovah, for He has heard the voice of my supplications.
7 Jehovah [is] my strength, and my shield, my heart trusted in Him, and I have been helped. And my heart exults, and I thank Him with my song.
8 Jehovah [is] strength to him, yes, He [is] the strength of the salvation of His anointed.
9 Save Your[S] people, and bless Your[S] inheritance, and feed them, and carry them to the age!

Psalm 29

1 A Psalm of David. Ascribe to Jehovah, you[P] sons of the mighty, ascribe honor and strength to Jehovah.
2 Ascribe the honor of His name to Jehovah, bow yourselves[P] to Jehovah, in the beauty of holiness.
3 The voice of Jehovah [is] on the waters, the God of glory has thundered, Jehovah [is] on many waters.
4 The voice of Jehovah [is] with power, the voice of Jehovah [is] with majesty,
5 the voice of Jehovah [is] shattering cedars, yes, Jehovah shatters the cedars of Lebanon.
6 And He causes them to skip as a calf, Lebanon and Sirion as a son of Reems,
7 the voice of Jehovah is hewing fiery flames,

8 the voice of Jehovah pains a wilderness, Jehovah pains the wilderness of Kadesh.
9 The voice of Jehovah pains the oaks, and makes bare the forests, and in His temple every one says, 'Glory.'
10 Jehovah has sat on the deluge, and Jehovah sits king — to the age,
11 Jehovah gives strength to his people, Jehovah blesses His people with peace!

Psalm 30

1 A Psalm. — A song of the dedication of the house of David. I exalt You[S], O Jehovah, for You[S] have drawn me up, and have not let my enemies rejoice over me.
2 Jehovah my God, I have cried to You[S], and You[S] do heal me.
3 Jehovah, You[S] have brought my soul up from Sheol, You[S] have kept me alive, from going down [to] the pit.
4 Sing praise to Jehovah, you[P] His saints, and give thanks at the remembrance of His holiness,
5 for — a moment [is] in His anger, Life [is] in His good-will, at evening remains weeping, and at morning singing.
6 And I — I have said in my ease, 'I am not moved — to the age.
7 O Jehovah, in Your[S] good pleasure, You[S] have caused strength to remain for my mountain,' You[S] have hidden Your[S] face — I have been troubled.
8 Unto You[S], O Jehovah, I call, and unto Jehovah I make supplication.
9 'What gain [is] in my blood? In my going down unto corruption? Does dust thank You[S]? does it declare Your[S] truth?
10 Hear, O Jehovah, and favor me, O Jehovah, be a helper to me.'
11 You[S] have turned my mourning to dancing for me, You[S] have loosed my sackcloth, and girded me [with] joy.
12 So that honor does praise You[S], and is not silent, O Jehovah, my God, to the age I thank You[S]!

Psalm 31

1 To the Overseer. — A Psalm of David. In You[S], O Jehovah, I have trusted, let me not be ashamed to the age, deliver me in Your[S] righteousness.
2 Incline Your[S] ear unto me hastily, deliver me, be to me for a strong rock, for a house of bulwarks to save me.
3 For You[S] [are] my rock and my bulwark, for Your[S] name's sake lead me and tend me.
4 Bring me out from the net that they hid for me, for You[S] [are] my strength.
5 I commit my spirit into Your[S] hand, You[S] have redeemed me, Jehovah God of truth.
6 I have hated the observers of lying vanities, and I have been confident toward Jehovah.
7 I rejoice, and am glad in Your[S] kindness, in that You[S] have seen my affliction, You[S] have known my soul in adversities.
8 And You[S] have not shut me up, into the hand of an enemy, You[S] have caused my feet to stand in a broad place.
9 Favor me, O Jehovah, for distress [is] to me, my eye, my soul, and my body have become old by provocation.
10 For my life has been consumed in sorrow and my years in sighing. My strength has been feeble because of my iniquity, and my bones have become old.
11 Among all my adversaries I have been a reproach, and to my neighbors exceedingly, and a fear to my acquaintances, those seeing me without — fled from me.
12 I have been forgotten as dead out of mind, I have been as a perishing vessel.
13 For I have heard an evil account of many, fear [is] round about. In their being united against me, they have devised to take my life,
14 And I on You[S] — I have trusted, O Jehovah, I have said, 'You[S] [are] my God.'
15 In Your[S] hand [are] my times, deliver me from the hand of my enemies, and from my pursuers.
16 Cause Your[S] face to shine on Your[S] servant, save me in Your[S] kindness.
17 O Jehovah, let me not be ashamed, for I have called You[S], let the wicked be ashamed, let them become silent to Sheol.
18 Let lips of falsehood become dumb, that are speaking against the righteous, ancient sayings, in pride and contempt.
19 How abundant is Your[S] goodness, that You[S] have laid up for those fearing You[S],
20 You[S] have worked for those trusting in You[S], before sons of men. You[S] hide them in the secret place of Your[S] presence, from artifices of man, You[S] conceal them in a tabernacle, from the strife of tongues.
21 Blessed [is] Jehovah, for He has made marvelous His kindness to me in a city of bulwarks.
22 And I — I have said in my haste, 'I have been cut off from before Your[S] eyes,' but You[S] have heard the voice

of my supplications, in my crying unto You[S].
23 Love Jehovah, all you[P] His saints, Jehovah is keeping
the faithful, and recompensing a proud doer abundantly.
24 Be strong, and He strengthens your[P] heart, all you[P]
who are waiting for Jehovah!

Psalm 32

1 By David. — An Instruction. O the happiness of him
whose transgression [is] forgiven, whose sin is covered.
2 O the happiness of a man, to whom Jehovah imputes
not iniquity, and in whose spirit there is no deceit.
3 When I have kept silence, my bones have become
old, through my roaring all the day.
4 When by day and by night Your[S] hand is heavy upon
me, my moisture has been changed into the droughts of
summer. Selah.
5 I cause You[S] to know my sin, and I have not covered
my iniquity. I have said, 'I confess concerning My
transgressions to Jehovah,' and You[S] — You[S] have taken
away, the iniquity of my sin. Selah.
6 Every saintly one does pray to You[S] for this, as to find
the time. Surely at an overflowing of many waters, they
come not unto him.
7 You[S] [are] a hiding-place for me, You[S] do keep me from
distress, [with] songs of deliverance do compass me.
Selah.
8 I cause you[S] to act wisely, and direct you[S] in the way
that you[S] go, I cause my eye to take counsel concerning
you[S].
9 Be you[P] not as a horse — as a mule, without
understanding, with bridle and bit, its ornaments, to curb,
not to come near unto you[S].
10 Many [are] the pains of the wicked; as to him who is
trusting in Jehovah, kindness does compass him.
11 Be glad in Jehovah, and rejoice, you[P] righteous, and
sing, all you[P] upright of heart!

Psalm 33

1 Sing, you[P] righteous, in Jehovah, for upright ones
praise [is] comely.
2 Give you[P] thanks to Jehovah with a harp, with psaltery
of ten strings sing praise to Him,
3 Sing you[P] a new song to Him, play skillfully with
shouting.
4 For upright [is] the word of Jehovah, and all His work
[is] in faithfulness.
5 Loving righteousness and judgment, the earth is full
of the kindness of Jehovah.
6 By the word of Jehovah the heavens have been made,
and all their host by the breath of His mouth.
7 Gathering the waters of the sea as a heap, putting the
depths in treasuries.
8 All the earth are afraid of Jehovah, all the inhabitants
of the world are afraid of Him.
9 For He has said, and it is, He has commanded, and it
stands.
10 Jehovah made void the counsel of nations, He
disallowed the thoughts of the peoples.
11 The counsel of Jehovah stands to the age, the
thoughts of His heart to all generations.
12 O the happiness of the nation whose God [is]
Jehovah, of the people He did choose, for an inheritance
to Him.
13 has Jehovah looked from the heavens, He has seen
all the sons of men.
14 From the fixed place of His dwelling, He looked unto
all inhabitants of the earth;
15 who is forming their hearts together, who is attending
unto all their works.
16 The king is not saved by the multitude of a force. A
mighty man is not delivered, by abundance of power.
17 A false thing [is] the horse for safety, and by the
abundance of his strength He does not deliver.
18 Behold, the eye of Jehovah [is] to those fearing Him,
to those waiting for His kindness,
19 to deliver their soul from death, and to keep them
alive in famine.
20 Our soul has waited for Jehovah, He [is] our help
and our shield,
21 For our heart does rejoice in Him, for we have trusted
in His holy name.
22 Let Your[S] kindness, O Jehovah, be upon us, as we
have waited for You[S]!

Psalm 34

1 By David, in his changing his behavior before
Abimelech, and he drives him away, and he goes. I do
bless Jehovah at all times, continually His praise [is] in
my mouth.
2 My soul boast does herself in Jehovah, the humble
do hear and rejoice.
3 Ascribe you[P] greatness to Jehovah with me, and we

exalt His name together.
4 I sought Jehovah, and He answered me, and did deliver
me from all my fears.
5 They looked expectingly unto Him, and they became
bright, and their faces are not ashamed.
6 This poor [one] called, and Jehovah heard, and saved
him from all his distresses.
7 A messenger of Jehovah is encamping, round about
those who fear Him, and He arms them.
8 Taste you[P] and see that Jehovah [is] good, O the
happiness of the man who trusts in Him.
9 Fear Jehovah, you[P] His holy ones, for there is no lack
to those fearing Him.
10 Young lions have lacked and been hungry, and those
seeking Jehovah lack not any good,
11 Come you[P], children, listen to me, I do teach you[P] the
fear of Jehovah.
12 Who [is] the man that is desiring life? Loving days
to see good?
13 Keep your[S] tongue from evil, and your[S] lips from
speaking deceit.
14 Turn aside from evil and do good, seek peace and
pursue it.
15 The eyes of Jehovah [are] unto the righteous, and
His ears unto their cry.
16 (The face of Jehovah [is] on doers of evil, to cut off
their memorial from earth.)
17 They cried, and Jehovah heard, and delivered them
from all their distresses.
18 Jehovah [is] near to the broken of heart, and He saves
the bruised of spirit.
19 Many [are] the evils of the righteous, Jehovah does
deliver him out of them all.
20 He is keeping all his bones, not one of them has been
broken.
21 Evil does put the wicked to death, and those hating
the righteous are desolate.
22 Jehovah redeems the soul of His servants, and none
trusting in Him are desolate!

Psalm 35

1 By David. Strive, Jehovah, with my strivers, fight with
my fighters,
2 Take hold of shield and buckler, and rise for my help,
3 And draw out spear and lance, to meet my pursuers.
Say to my soul, 'I [am] your[S] salvation.'
4 They are ashamed and blush, those seeking my soul,
turned backward and confounded, those devising my
evil.
5 They are as chaff before wind, and a messenger of
Jehovah driving away.
6 Their way is darkness and slipperiness, and a
messenger of Jehovah their pursuer.
7 For without cause they hid their netpit for me, without
cause they dug for my soul.
8 Desolation does meet him — he knows not, and his net
that he hid catches him, for desolation he falls into it.
9 And my soul is joyful in Jehovah, it rejoices in His
salvation.
10 All my bones say, 'Jehovah, who is like You[S],
delivering the poor from the stronger than he, and the
poor and needy from his plunderer.'
11 Violent witnesses rise up, they ask me that which I
have not known.
12 They pay me evil for good, bereaving my soul,
13 And I — in their sickness my clothing [is] sackcloth,
I have humbled my soul with fastings, and my prayer
returns unto my bosom.
14 As [if] a friend, as [if] my brother, I walked habitually,
as a mourner for a mother, I have bowed down mourning.
15 And — in my halting they have rejoiced, and have
been gathered together, gathered against me were the
afflicters, and I have not known, they have rent, and they
have not ceased;
16 with profane ones, mockers in feasts, gnashing their
teeth against me.
17 Lord, how long do You[S] behold? Keep back my soul
from their desolations, my only one from young lions.
18 I thank You[S] in a great assembly, I praise You[S] among
a mighty people.
19 My enemies rejoice not over me [with] falsehood,
those hating me without cause wink the eye.
20 For they speak not peace, and against the quiet of
the land, they devise deceitful words,
21 And they enlarge their mouth against me, they said,
'Aha, aha, our eye has seen.'
22 You[S] have seen, O Jehovah, be not silent, O Lord —
be not far from me,
23 Stir up, and wake to my judgment, my God, and my
Lord, to my plea.
24 Judge me according to Your righteousness, O
Jehovah my God, and they do not rejoice over me.
25 They do not say in their heart, 'Aha, our desire.' They
do not say, 'We swallowed him up.'
26 They are ashamed and confounded together, who
are rejoicing at my evil. They put on shame and

confusion, who are magnifying themselves against me.
27 They sing and rejoice, who are desiring my righteousness, and they say continually, 'Jehovah is magnified, who is desiring the peace of His servant.'
28 And my tongue utters Your[S] righteousness, all the day Your[S] praise!

Psalm 36

1 To the Overseer. — By a servant of Jehovah, by David. The transgression of the wicked is affirming within my heart, 'Fear of God is not before his eyes,
2 for he made [it] smooth to himself in his eyes, to find his iniquity to be hated.
3 The words of his mouth [are] iniquity and deceit, he ceased to act prudently — to do good.
4 He devises iniquity on his bed, he stations himself on a way not good, he does not refuse evil.'
5 O Jehovah, Your[S] kindness [is] in the heavens, Your[S] faithfulness [is] unto the clouds.
6 Your[S] righteousness [is] as mountains of God, Your[S] judgments [are] a great deep. You[S] save man and beast, O Jehovah.
7 How precious [is] Your[S] kindness, O God, and the sons of men do trust in the shadow of Your[S] wings.
8 They are filled from the fatness of Your[S] house, and You[S] do cause them to drink the stream of Your[S] delights.
9 For with You[S] [is] a fountain of life, in Your[S] light we see light.
10 Draw out Your[S] kindness to those knowing You[S], and Your[S] righteousness to the upright of heart.
11 Let not a foot of pride meet me, and let not a hand of the wicked move me.
12 There have workers of iniquity fallen, they have been overthrown, and have not been able to arise!

Psalm 37

1 By David. Do not fret because of evil doers, be not envious against doers of iniquity,
2 for they are cut off speedily as grass, and do fade as the greenness of the tender grass.
3 Trust in Jehovah, and do good, dwell [in] the land, and enjoy faithfulness,
4 And delight yourself[S] on Jehovah, and He gives to you[S] the petitions of your heart.
5 Roll on Jehovah your[S] way, and trust upon Him, and He works,
6 and has brought out your[S] righteousness as light, and your[S] judgment as noon-day.
7 Be silent for Jehovah, and stay yourself[S] for Him, do not fret because of him who is making his way prosperous, because of a man doing wicked devices.
8 Desist from anger, and forsake fury, fret not yourself[S] only to do evil.
9 For evil doers are cut off, as to those waiting on Jehovah, they possess the land.
10 And yet a little, and the wicked is not, and you[S] have considered his place, and it is not.
11 And the humble do possess the land, and they have delighted themselves in the abundance of peace.
12 The wicked is devising against the righteous, and gnashing his teeth against him.
13 The Lord does laugh at him, for He has seen that his day comes.
14 The wicked have opened a sword, and they have trodden their bow, to cause the poor and needy to fall, to slaughter the upright of the way.
15 Their sword does enter into their own heart, and their bows are broken.
16 Better [is] the little of the righteous, than the wicked store of many.
17 For the arms of the wicked are broken, and Jehovah is sustaining the righteous.
18 Jehovah knows the days of the perfect, and their inheritance is — to the age.
19 They are not ashamed in a time of evil, and they are satisfied in days of famine.
20 But the wicked perish, and the enemies of Jehovah, as the preciousness of lambs, have been consumed, they have been consumed in smoke.
21 The wicked is borrowing and repays not, and the righteous is gracious and giving.
22 For His blessed ones do possess the land, and His reviled ones are cut off.
23 From Jehovah [are] the steps of a man, they have been prepared, and he desires his way.
24 When he falls, he is not cast down, for Jehovah is sustaining his hand.
25 I have been young, I have also become old, and I have not seen the righteous forsaken, and his seed seeking bread.
26 All the day he is gracious and lending, and his seed [is] for a blessing.
27 Turn aside from evil, and do good, and dwell to the age.

28 For Jehovah is loving judgment, and He does not forsake His saintly ones, they have been kept to the age, and the seed of the wicked is cut off.
29 The righteous possess the land, and they dwell on it for ever.
30 The mouth of the righteous utters wisdom, and his tongue speaks judgment.
31 The law of his God [is] his heart, his steps do not slide.
32 The wicked is watching for the righteous, and is seeking to put him to death.
33 Jehovah does not leave him in his hand, nor condemn him in his being judged.
34 Look unto Jehovah, and keep His way, and He does exalt you[S] to possess the land, in the wicked being cut off — you[S] see!
35 I have seen the wicked terrible, and spreading as a green native plant,
36 and he passes away, and behold, he is not, and I seek him, and he is not found!
37 Observe the perfect, and see the upright, for the latter end of each [is] peace.
38 And transgressors were destroyed together, the latter end of the wicked was cut off.
39 And the salvation of the righteous [is] from Jehovah, their strong place in a time of adversity.
40 And Jehovah does help them and deliver them, He delivers them from the wicked, and saves them, because they trusted in Him!

Psalm 38

1 A Psalm of David, 'To cause to remember.' Jehovah, in Your[S] wrath reprove me not, nor chastise me in Your[S] fury.
2 For Your[S] arrows have come down on me, and You[S] let down Your[S] hand upon me.
3 Soundness is not in my flesh, because of Your[S] indignation, peace is not in my bones because of my sin.
4 For my iniquities have passed over my head, as a heavy burden — too heavy for me.
5 Stunk — my wounds have become corrupt, because of my folly.
6 I have been bent down, I have been bowed down — unto excess, all the day I have gone mourning.
7 For my flanks have been full of drought, and soundness is not in my flesh.
8 I have been feeble and afflicted — unto excess, I have roared from disquietude of heart.
9 Lord, all my desire [is] before You[S], and my sighing from You[S] has not been hid.
10 My heart [is] panting, my power has forsaken me, and the light of my eyes, even they are not with me.
11 My lovers and my friends stand over-against my plague. And my neighbors have stood afar off.
12 And those seeking my soul lay a snare, and those seeking my evil have spoken mischievous things, and they do meditate deceits all the day.
13 And I, as deaf, hear not. And as a dumb one who opens not his mouth.
14 Yea, I am as a man who hears not, and in his mouth are no reproofs.
15 Because for You[S], O Jehovah, I have waited, You[S] do answer, O Lord my God.
16 When I said, 'For fear that they rejoice over me, in the slipping of my foot against me they magnified themselves.
17 For I am ready to halt, and my pain [is] before me continually.
18 For I declare my iniquity, I am sorry for my sin.
19 And my enemies [are] lively, they have been strong, and those hating me without cause, have been multiplied.
20 And those paying evil for good accuse me, because of my pursuing good.
21 Do not forsake me, O Jehovah, my God, be not far from me,
22 Hurry to help me, O Lord, my salvation!

Psalm 39

1 To the Overseer, to Jeduthun. — A Psalm of David. I have said, 'I observe my ways, against sinning with my tongue, I keep a curb for my mouth, while the wicked [is] before me.'
2 I was dumb [with] silence, I kept silent from good, and my pain is excited.
3 Hot [is] my heart within me, the fire does burn in my meditating, I have spoken with my tongue.
4 'Cause me to know, O Jehovah, my end, and the measure of my days — what it [is],' I know how frail I [am].
5 Behold, You[S] have made my days handbreadths, and my age [is] as nothing before You[S], only, all vanity [is] every man set up. Selah.
6 Only, in an image does each walk habitually, only, [in]

vain, they are disquieted, he heaps up and knows not who gathers them.
7 And, now, what have I expected? O Lord, my hope — it [is] of You[S].
8 Deliver me from all my transgressions, make me not a reproach of the fool.
9 I have been dumb, I open not my mouth, because You[S] — You[S] have done [it].
10 Turn aside Your[S] stroke from off me, I have been consumed from the striving of Your[S] hand.
11 With reproofs against iniquity, You[S] have corrected man, and does waste his desirableness as a moth, only, vanity [is] every man. Selah.
12 Hear my prayer, O Jehovah, and give ear [to] my cry, be not silent unto my tear, for I [am] a guest with You[S], a settler like all my fathers.
13 Look from me, and I brighten up before I go and am not!

Psalm 40

1 To the Overseer. — A Psalm of David. I have diligently expected Jehovah, and He inclines to me, and hears my cry,
2 and He does cause me to come up from a pit of desolation — from mire of mud, and He raises up my feet on a rock, He is establishing my steps.
3 And He puts a new song in my mouth, 'Praise to our God.' Many do see and fear, and trust in Jehovah.
4 O the happiness of the man who has made Jehovah his trust, and has not turned unto the proud, and those turning aside to lies.
5 You[S] have done much, Jehovah my God; Your[S] wonders and Your[S] thoughts toward us, there is none to arrange unto You[S], I declare and speak: they have been more than to be numbered.
6 You[S] have not desired sacrifice and present, You[S] have prepared ears for me, You[S] have not asked burnt and sin-offering.
7 Then said I, 'Behold, I have come,' it is written of me in the roll of the book,
8 to do Your[S] pleasure, my God, I have delighted, and Your[S] law [is] within my heart.
9 I have proclaimed tidings of righteousness in the great assembly, behold, I restrain not my lips, O Jehovah, You[S] have known.
10 I have not concealed Your[S] righteousness in the midst of my heart, I have told Your[S] faithfulness and Your[S] salvation, I have not hidden Your[S] kindness and Your[S] truth, to the great assembly.
11 You[S], O Jehovah, restrain not Your[S] mercies from me, Your[S] kindness and Your[S] truth do continually keep me.
12 For evils innumerable have compassed me, my iniquities have overtaken me, and I have not been able to see; they have been more than the hairs of my head, and my heart has forsaken me.
13 Be pleased, O Jehovah, to deliver me, O Jehovah, for my help make haste.
14 They are ashamed and confounded together, who are seeking my soul to destroy it, they are turned backward, and are ashamed, who are desiring my evil.
15 They are desolate because of their shame, who are saying to me, 'Aha, aha.'
16 All seeking You[S] rejoice and are glad in You[S], those loving Your[S] salvation say continually, 'Jehovah is magnified.'
17 And I [am] poor and needy, the Lord does devise for me. You[S] [are] my help and my deliverer, O my God, delay You[S] not.

Psalm 41

1 To the Overseer. — A Psalm of David. O the happiness of him who is acting wisely unto the poor, Jehovah does deliver him in a day of evil.
2 Jehovah does preserve him and revive him, he is happy in the land, and You[S] give him not into the will of his enemies.
3 Jehovah supports on a couch of sickness, You[S] have turned all his bed in his weakness.
4 I — I said, 'O Jehovah, favor me, heal my soul, for I did sin against You[S],'
5 My enemies say evil of me: when he dies — his name has perished!
6 And if he came to see — he speaks vanity, his heart gathers iniquity to itself, he goes out — he speaks at the street.
7 All hating me whisper together against me, against me they devise evil to me:
8 A thing of Belial is poured out on him, and because he lay down he rises not again.
9 Even my ally, in whom I trusted, one eating my bread, made great the heel against me,
10 And You[S], Jehovah, favor me, and cause me to rise, and I give recompense to them.
11 By this I have known, that You[S] have delighted in

me, because my enemy shouts not over me.
12 As to me, in my integrity, You[S] have taken hold upon me, and cause me to stand before You[S] to the age.
13 Blessed [is] Jehovah, God of Israel, from the age — and unto the age. Amen and Amen.

Psalm 42

1 To the Overseer. — An Instruction. By sons of Korah. As a hart does pant for streams of water, so my soul pants toward You[S], O God.
2 My soul thirsted for God, for the living God, when do I enter and see the face of God?
3 My tear has been bread to me day and night, in their saying unto me all the day, 'Where [is] your[S] God?'
4 These I remember, and pour out my soul in me, for I pass over into the booth, I go softly with them unto the house of God, with the voice of singing and confession, the multitude keeping feast!
5 What! bow you yourself[S], O my soul? Yes, are you[S] troubled within me? Wait for God, for still I confess Him: the salvation of my countenance — My God!
6 My soul does bow itself in me, for that reason I remember You[S] from the land of Jordan, and of the Hermons, from the hill Mizar.
7 Deep unto deep is calling at the noise of Your[S] water-spouts, all Your[S] breakers and Your[S] billows passed over me.
8 By day Jehovah commands His kindness, and by night a song [is] with me, a prayer of my life to the God.
9 I say to God my rock, 'Why have You[S] forgotten me? Why go I mourning in the oppression of an enemy?
10 My adversaries have reproached me with a sword in my bones, in their saying unto me all the day, 'Where [is] your[S] God?'
11 What! bow you yourself[S], O my soul? And what! are you[S] troubled within me? Wait for God, for still I confess Him, the salvation of my countenance, and my God!

Psalm 43

1 Judge me, O God, and plead my cause against a nation not pious, You[S] do deliver me from a man of deceit and perverseness,
2 For You[S] [are] the God of my strength. Why have You[S] cast me off? Why do I go mourning up and down, in the oppression of an enemy?
3 Send forth Your[S] light and Your[S] truth, they — they lead me, they bring me in, unto Your[S] holy hill, and unto Your[S] tabernacles.
4 And I go in unto the altar of God, unto God, the joy of my rejoicing. And I thank You[S] with a harp, O God, my God.
5 What! bow you[S] yourself[S], O my soul? And what! are you[S] troubled within me? Wait for God, for still I confess Him, the salvation of my countenance, and my God!

Psalm 44

1 To the Overseer. — By sons of Korah. An Instruction. O God, with our ears we have heard, our fathers have recounted to us, the work You[S] did work in their days, in the days of old.
2 You[S], [with] Your[S] hand, has dispossessed nations. And You[S] do plant them. You[S] afflict peoples, and sends them away.
3 For, they possessed the land not by their sword, and their arm gave not salvation to them, but Your[S] right hand, and Your[S] arm, and the light of Your[S] countenance, because You[S] had accepted them.
4 You[S] [are] He, my king, O God, command the deliverances of Jacob.
5 By You[S] we do push our adversaries, by Your[S] name tread down our withstanders,
6 for, I do not trust in my bow, and my sword does not save me.
7 For You[S] have saved us from our adversaries, and You[S] have put to shame those hating us.
8 We have boasted all the day in God, and we thank Your[S] name to the age. Selah.
9 You[S] have cast off in anger and cause us to blush, and go not forth with our hosts.
10 You[S] cause us to turn backward from an adversary, and those hating us, have spoiled for themselves.
11 You[S] make us food like sheep, and You[S] have scattered us among nations.
12 You[S] sell Your[S] people — without wealth, and have not become great by their price.
13 You[S] make us a reproach to our neighbors, a scorn and a reproach to our surrounders.
14 You[S] make us a simile among nations, a shaking of the head among peoples.
15 My confusion [is] before me all the day, and the shame of my face has covered me.
16 Because of the voice of a reproacher and reviler, because of an enemy and a self-avenger.
17 All this met us, and we did not forget You[S], nor have

we dealt falsely in Your^{S} covenant.
18 We turn not backward our heart, nor does our step
turn aside from Your^{S} path.
19 But You^{S} have afflicted us in a place of dragons, and
do cover us over with death-shade.
20 If we have forgotten the name of our God, and spread
our hands to a strange God,
21 Does not God search this out? For He knows the
secrets of the heart.
22 Surely, for Your^{S} sake we have been slain all the day,
reckoned as sheep of the slaughter.
23 Stir up — why do You^{S} sleep, O Lord? Awake, cast
us not off for ever.
24 Why Your^{S} face hides You^{S}? You^{S} forget our afflictions
and our oppression,
25 for our soul has bowed to the dust, our belly has
cleaved to the earth.
26 Arise, a help to us, and ransom us for Your^{S} kindness'
sake.

Psalm 45

1 To the Overseer. — 'On the Lilies.' — By sons of
Korah. — An Instruction. — A song of loves. My heart
has composed a good thing, I am telling my works to a
king, my tongue [is] the pen of a speedy writer.
2 You^{S} have been beautified above the sons of men,
grace has been poured into your^{S} lips, for that reason
has God blessed you^{S} to the age.
3 Gird Your^{S} sword upon the thigh, O mighty, Your^{S} glory
and Your^{S} majesty!
4 As to Your^{S} majesty — prosper! — ride! Because of
truth, and meekness — righteousness, and Your^{S} right
hand shows You^{S} fearful things.
5 Your^{S} arrows [are] sharp, — peoples fall under You^{S}
— in the heart of the enemies of the king.
6 Your^{S} throne, O God, [is] age-during, and for ever, a
scepter of uprightness [is] the scepter of Your^{S} kingdom.
7 You^{S} have loved righteousness and hates wickedness,
for that reason God, your^{S} God, has anointed you^{S}, oil
of joy above your^{S} companions.
8 Myrrh and aloes, cassia! all your^{S} garments, out of palaces
of ivory stringed instruments have made you^{S} glad.
9 Daughters of kings [are] among your^{S} precious ones, a
queen has stood at your^{S} right hand, in pure gold of Ophir.
10 Listen, O daughter, and see, incline your^{S} ear, and
forget your^{S} people, and your^{S} father's house,
11 And the king does desire your^{S} beauty, because he
[is] your^{S} lord — bow yourself^{S} to him,
12 And the daughter of Tyre with a present, the rich of
the people do appease your^{S} face.
13 All glory [is] the daughter of the king within, of gold-
embroidered work [is] her clothing.
14 She is brought to the king in various colors, virgins
— after her — her companions, are brought to you^{S}.
15 They are brought with joy and gladness, they come
into the palace of the king.
16 Instead of your^{S} fathers are your^{S} sons, you^{S} do
appoint them for princes in all the earth.
17 I make mention of Your^{S} name in all generations, for
that reason do peoples praise You^{S}, to the age, and for
ever!

Psalm 46

1 To the Overseer. — By sons of Korah. 'For the Virgins.'
— A song. God [is] a refuge and strength to us, found
most surely a help in adversities.
2 For that reason we fear not in the changing of earth,
and in the slipping of mountains into the heart of the seas.
3 Roar — troubled are its waters, mountains they shake
in its pride. Selah.
4 A river — its rivulets rejoice the city of God, Your holy
place of the tabernacles of the Most High.
5 God [is] in her midst — she is not moved, God does
help her at the turn of the morn!
6 Troubled have been nations, moved have been
kingdoms, He has given forth with His voice, earth melts.
7 Jehovah of Hosts [is] with us, a tower for us [is] the
God of Jacob. Selah.
8 Come you^{P}, see the works of Jehovah, who has done
astonishing things in the earth,
9 Causing wars to cease, unto the end of the earth, he
breaks the bow, and the spear He has cut asunder, He
does burn chariots with fire.
10 Desist, and know that I [am] God, I am exalted among
nations, I am exalted in the earth.
11 Jehovah of hosts [is] with us, a tower for us [is] the
God of Jacob! Selah.

Psalm 47

1 To the Overseer. — By sons of Korah. A Psalm. All
you^{P} peoples, clap the hand, shout to God with a voice
of singing,

2 For Jehovah Most High [is] fearful, a great king over all the earth.
3 He leads peoples under us, and nations under our feet.
4 He does choose for us our inheritance, the excellency of Jacob that He loves. Selah.
5 God has gone up with a shout, Jehovah with the sound of a trumpet.
6 Praise God — praise — give praise to our king, praise.
7 For king of all the earth [is] God, give praise, O understanding one.
8 God has reigned over nations, God has sat on His holy throne,
9 Nobles of peoples have been gathered, [with] the people of the God of Abraham, for to God [are] the shields of earth, greatly has He been exalted!

Psalm 48

1 A Song, a Psalm, by sons of Korah. Great [is] Jehovah, and praised greatly, in the city of our God — His holy hill.
2 Beautiful [for] elevation, a joy of all the land, [is] Mount Zion, the sides of the north, the city of a great king.
3 God in her high places is known for a tower.
4 For, behold, the kings met, they passed by together,
5 They have seen — so they have marvelled, they have been troubled, they were hurried away.
6 Trembling has seized them there, pain, as of a travailing woman.
7 You[S] shatter ships of Tarshish by an east wind.
8 As we have heard, so we have seen, in the city of Jehovah of hosts, in the city of our God, God does establish her — to the age. Selah.
9 We have thought, O God, of Your[S] kindness, in the midst of Your[S] temple,
10 As [is] Your[S] name, O God, so [is] Your[S] praise, over the ends of the earth, righteousness has filled Your[S] right hand.
11 Mount Zion does rejoice, the daughters of Judah are joyful, for the sake of Your[S] judgments.
12 Compass Zion, and go round her, count her towers,
13 Set your[P] heart to her bulwark, consider her high places, so that you[P] recount to a later generation,
14 That this God [is] our God — to the age and for ever, He — He does lead us over death!

Psalm 49

1 To the Overseer. — By sons of Korah. A Psalm. Hear this, all you[P] peoples, give ear, all you[P] inhabitants of the world.
2 Both low and high, rich and needy together.
3 My mouth speaks wise things, and the meditations of my heart [are] things of understanding.
4 I incline my ear to a simile, I open my riddle with a harp:
5 Why do I fear in days of evil? The iniquity of my usurpers does compass me.
6 Those trusting on their wealth, and in the multitude of their riches, do show themselves foolish.
7 A brother does ransom no one at all, he does not give his atonement to God.
8 And precious [is] the redemption of their soul, and it has ceased — to the age.
9 And still he lives for ever, he sees not the pit.
10 For he sees wise men die, together the foolish and brutish perish, and have left their wealth to others.
11 Their heart [is]: their houses [are] to the age, their tabernacles to all generations. They proclaimed their names over the lands.
12 And man does not remain in honor, he has been like the beasts, they have been cut off.
13 This their way [is] folly for them, and their posterity are pleased with their sayings. Selah.
14 They have set themselves as sheep for Sheol, death does afflict them, and the upright rule over them in the morning, and their form [is] for consumption. Sheol [is] a dwelling for him.
15 Only, God does ransom my soul from the hand of Sheol, for He does receive me. Selah.
16 Fear not, when one makes wealth, when the honor of his house is abundant,
17 for he receives nothing at his death, his honor goes not down after him.
18 For in his life he blesses his soul, (and they praise you[S] when you[S] do well for yourself[S].)
19 It comes to the generation of his fathers, for ever they see not the light.
20 Man in honor, who understands not, has been like the beasts, they have been cut off!

Psalm 50

1 A Psalm of Asaph. The God of gods — Jehovah — has spoken, and He calls to the earth from the rising of the sun unto its going in.
2 From Zion, the perfection of beauty, God shone.
3 Our God comes, and is not silent, fire does devour

before Him, and round about him it has been very tempestuous.

4 He does call unto the heavens from above, and unto the earth, to judge His people.

5 Gather you^{P} My saints to Me, making covenant with Me over a sacrifice.

6 And the heavens declare His righteousness, for God Himself [is] judge. Selah.

7 Hear, O My people, and I speak, O Israel, and I testify against you^{S}, God, I [am] your God.

8 Not do I reprove you^{S} for your^{S} sacrifices, yes, your^{S} burnt-offerings [are] before Me continually.

9 I take not a bullock from your^{S} house, he-goats from your^{S} folds.

10 For every beast of the forest [is] Mine, the cattle on the hills of oxen.

11 I have known every fowl of the mountains, and the wild beast of the field [is] with Me.

12 If I am hungry I tell not to you^{S}, for Mine [is] the world and its fullness.

13 Do I eat the flesh of bulls, and drink the blood of he-goats?

14 Sacrifice confession to God, and complete your^{S} vows to the Most High.

15 And call Me in a day of adversity, I deliver you^{S}, and you^{S} honor Me.

16 And to the wicked God has said: What to you^{S} — to recount My statutes? That you^{S} lift up My covenant on your^{S} mouth?

17 Yes, you^{S} have hated instruction, and do cast My words behind you^{S}.

18 If you^{S} have seen a thief, then you^{S} are pleased with him, and your^{S} portion [is] with adulterers.

19 You^{S} have sent forth your^{S} mouth with evil, and your^{S} tongue joins deceit together,

20 you^{S} sit, you^{S} speak against your^{S} brother, give slander against a son of your^{S} mother.

21 You^{S} did these, and I kept silent, you^{S} have thought that I am like you^{S}, I reprove you^{S}, and set in array before your^{S} eyes.

22 Understand this, I pray you^{P}, you^{P} who are forgetting God, for fear that I tear, and there is no deliverer.

23 He who is sacrificing praise honors Me, as to him who makes a way, I cause him to look on the salvation of God!

Psalm 51

1 To the Overseer. — A Psalm of David, in the coming of Nathan the prophet in unto him, when he had gone in unto Bath-Sheba. Favor me, O God, according to Your^{S} kindness, according to the abundance of Your^{S} mercies, blot out my transgressions.

2 Thoroughly wash me from my iniquity, and cleanse me from my sin,

3 for I do know my transgressions, and my sin [is] before me continually.

4 Against You^{S}, You^{S} only, I have sinned, and done the evil thing in Your^{S} eyes, so that You^{S} are righteous in Your^{S} words, You^{S} are pure in Your^{S} judging.

5 Behold, I have been brought forth in iniquity, and my mother did conceive me in sin.

6 Behold, You^{S} have desired truth in the inward parts, and You^{S} caused me to know wisdom in the hidden part.

7 You^{S} cleanse me with hyssop and I am clean, wash me, and I am whiter than snow.

8 You^{S} cause me to hear joy and gladness, You^{S} make bones You^{S} have bruised joyful.

9 Hide Your^{S} face from my sin. And blot out all my iniquities.

10 Prepare for me a clean heart, O God, and renew a right spirit within me.

11 Cast me not forth from Your^{S} presence, and take not Your^{S} Holy Spirit from me.

12 Restore to me the joy of Your^{S} salvation, and a willing spirit does sustain me.

13 I teach transgressors Your^{S} ways, and sinners do return unto You^{S}.

14 Deliver me from blood, O God, God of my salvation, my tongue sings of Your^{S} righteousness.

15 O Lord, You^{S} do open my lips, and my mouth declares Your^{S} praise.

16 For You^{S} desire not sacrifice, or I give [it], You^{S} accept not burnt-offering.

17 The sacrifices of God [are] a broken spirit, a heart broken and bruised, O God, You^{S} do not despise.

18 Do good in Your good pleasure with Zion, You^{S} do build the walls of Jerusalem.

19 Then You^{S} desire sacrifices of righteousness, burnt-offering, and whole burnt-offering, then they offer bullocks on Your^{S} altar!

Psalm 52

1 To the Overseer. — An instruction, by David, in the coming in of Doeg the Edomite, and he declares to Saul, and says to him, 'David came in unto the house of

Ahimelech.' What, boasts you[S] in evil, O mighty one? The kindness of God [is] all the day.

2 Your[S] tongue does devise mischiefs, like a sharp razor, working deceit.

3 You[S] have loved evil rather than good, lying, than speaking righteousness. Selah.

4 You[S] have loved all devouring words, O you[S] deceitful tongue.

5 Also — God does break you[S] down for ever, takes you[S], and pulls you[S] out of the tent, and He has uprooted you[S] out of the land of the living. Selah.

6 And the righteous see, and fear, and laugh at him.

7 'Behold, the man who makes not God his strong place, and trusts in the abundance of his riches, he is strong in his mischiefs.'

8 And I, as a green olive in the house of God, I have trusted in the kindness of God, to the age and for ever,

9 I thank You[S] to the age, because You[S] have done [it], and I wait [on] Your[S] name for [it is] good before Your[S] saints!

Psalm 53

1 To the Overseer. — 'On a disease.' — An instruction, by David. A fool said in his heart, 'There is no God.' They have done corruptly, yes, they have done abominable iniquity, there is none doing good.

2 God looked on the sons of men from the heavens, to see if there be an understanding one, [one] seeking God.

3 Every one went back, together they became filthy, there is none doing good — not even one.

4 Have not workers of iniquity known, those eating my people have eaten bread, they have not called God.

5 There they feared a fear — there was no fear, for God has scattered the bones of him who is encamping against you[S], you[S] have put to shame, for God has despised them.

6 Who does give the salvation of Israel from Zion? When God turns back [to] a captivity of His people, Jacob does rejoice — Israel is glad!

Psalm 54

1 To the Overseer with stringed instruments. — An instruction, by David, in the coming in of the Ziphim, and they say to Saul, 'Is not David hiding himself with us?' O God, save me by Your[S] name, and judge me by Your[S] might.

2 O God, hear my prayer, give ear to the sayings of my mouth,

3 for strangers have risen up against me and terrible ones have sought my soul, they have not set God before them. Selah.

4 Behold, God [is] a helper to me, the Lord [is] with those supporting my soul,

5 the evil thing does turn back to my enemies, cut them off in Your[S] truth.

6 With a free will-offering I sacrifice to You[S], I thank Your[S] name, O Jehovah, for [it is] good,

7 for, He delivered me from all adversity, and my eye has looked on my enemies!

Psalm 55

1 To the Overseer with stringed instruments. — An instruction, by David. Give ear, O God, [to] my prayer, and hide not from my supplication.

2 Attend to me, and answer me, I mourn in my meditation, and make a noise,

3 because of the voice of an enemy, because of the oppression of the wicked, for they cause sorrow to move against me, and in anger they hate me.

4 My heart is pained within me, and terrors of death have fallen on me.

5 Fear and trembling come in to me, and horror does cover me.

6 And I say, 'Who does give to me a wing as a dove? I fly away and rest,

7 behold, I move far off, I lodge in a wilderness. Selah.

8 I hurry escape for myself, from a rushing wind, from a whirlwind.

9 Swallow up, O Lord, divide their tongue, for I saw violence and strife in a city.

10 By day and by night they go round it, on its walls. Both iniquity and perverseness [are] in its midst,

11 Mischiefs [are] in its midst. Fraud and deceit depart not from its street.

12 For an enemy reproaches me not, or I bear [it], he who is hating me has not magnified himself against me, or I hide from him.

13 But you[S], a man — as mine equal, my familiar friend, and my acquaintance.

14 When together we sweeten counsel, we walk in company into the house of God.

15 Desolations [are] upon them, they go down [to] Sheol

— alive, for wickedness [is] in their dwelling, in their midst.
16 I — I call to God, and Jehovah saves me.
17 Evening, and morning, and noon, I meditate, and make a noise, and He hears my voice,
18 He has ransomed my soul in peace from him who is near to me, for with the multitude they were with me.
19 God does hear and afflict them, and He sits of old. Selah. Because they have no changes, and fear not God,
20 he has sent forth his hands against his well-wishers, he has polluted his covenant.
21 His mouth has been sweeter than honey, and his heart [is] war! His words have been softer than oil, and they [are] drawn [swords].
22 Cast on Jehovah that which He has given you^{S}, and He does sustain you^{S}, He does not allow for ever the moving of the righteous.
23 And You, O God, do bring them down to a pit of destruction, men of blood and deceit reach not to half their days, and I — I do trust in You^{S}!

Psalm 56

1 To the Overseer. — 'On the Dumb Dove far off.' — A secret treasure of David, in the Philistines' taking hold of him in Gath. Favor me, O God, for man swallowed me up, he oppresses me all the day fighting,
2 my enemies have swallowed up all the day, for many [are] fighting against me, O most High,
3 the day I am afraid I am confident toward You^{S}.
4 In God I praise His word, I have trusted in God, I fear not what flesh does to me.
5 All the day they wrest my words, all their thoughts concerning me [are] for evil,
6 they assemble, they hide, they watch my heels, when they have expected my soul.
7 They escape by iniquity, the peoples put down in anger, O God.
8 You^{S} have counted my wandering, You^{S} — You^{S} place my tear in Your^{S} bottle, are they not in Your^{S} book?
9 Then do turn back my enemies in the day I call. This I have known, that God [is] for me.
10 In God I praise the word, In Jehovah I praise the word.
11 In God I trusted, I fear not what man does to me,
12 Your^{S} vows, O God, [are] on me, I repay thank-offerings to You^{S}.
13 For You^{S} have delivered my soul from death, do You^{S} not my feet from falling? To walk habitually before God in the light of the living!

Psalm 57

1 To the Overseer. — 'Destroy not.' — A secret treasure of David, in his fleeing from the face of Saul into a cave. Favor me, O God, favor me, for my soul is trusting in You^{S}, and I trust in the shadow of Your^{S} wings, until the calamities pass over.
2 I call to God Most High, to God [who] is perfecting for me.
3 He sends from the heaven, and saves me, He reproached — who is panting after me. Selah. God sends forth His kindness and His truth.
4 My soul [is] in the midst of lions, I lie down [among] flames — sons of men, their teeth [are] a spear and arrows, and their tongue a sharp sword.
5 Be You^{S} exalted above the heavens, O God, Your^{S} honor above all the earth.
6 They have prepared a net for my steps, my soul has bowed down, they have dug a pit before me, they have fallen into its midst. Selah.
7 Prepared is my heart, O God, prepared is my heart, I sing and praise.
8 Awake, my honor, awake, psaltery and harp, I awake the morning dawn.
9 I thank You^{S} among the peoples, O Lord, I praise You^{S} among the nations.
10 For Your^{S} kindness [is] great unto the heavens, and Your^{S} truth unto the clouds.
11 Be You^{S} exalted above the heavens, O God. Your^{S} honor above all the earth!

Psalm 58

1 To the Overseer. — 'Destroy not.' — A secret treasure, by David. Is it true, O dumb one, you^{P} speak righteously? You^{P} judge uprightly, O sons of men?
2 You^{P} work iniquities even in heart, in the land you^{P} ponder the violence of your^{P} hands.
3 The wicked have been estranged from the womb, they have erred from the belly, speaking lies.
4 Their poison [is] as poison of a serpent, as a deaf asp shutting its ear,
5 Which listens not to the voice of whisperers, a most skilful charmer of charms.
6 O God, break their teeth in their mouth, break down

the jaw-teeth of young lions, O Jehovah.
7 They are melted as waters, they go up and down for themselves, his arrow proceeds as they cut themselves off.
8 He goes on as a snail that melts, [as] an untimely birth of a woman, they have not seen the sun.
9 Before your[P] pots discern the bramble, He whirls away the raw as well as the heated.
10 The righteous rejoices that he has seen vengeance, he washes his steps in the blood of the wicked.
11 And man says: 'Surely fruit [is] for the righteous: surely there is a God judging in the earth!'

Psalm 59

1 To the Overseer. — 'Destroy not,' by David. — A secret treasure, in Saul's sending, and they watch the house to put him to death. Deliver me from my enemies, O my God, set me on high from my withstanders.
2 Deliver me from workers of iniquity, and save me from men of blood.
3 For, behold, they laid wait for my soul, strong ones are assembled against me, not my transgression nor my sin, O Jehovah.
4 Without punishment they run and prepare themselves, stir up to meet me, and see.
5 And You[S], Jehovah, God of Hosts, God of Israel, awake to inspect all the nations. Favor not any treacherous dealers of iniquity. Selah.
6 They turn back at evening, they make a noise like a dog, and go round about the city.
7 Behold, they belch out with their mouths, swords [are] in their lips, for 'Who hears?'
8 And You[S], O Jehovah do laugh at them, You[S] do mock at all the nations.
9 O my Strength, I take heed unto You[S], for God [is] my tower — the God of my kindness.
10 God does go before me, He causes me to look on my enemies.
11 Slay them not, for fear that my people forget, shake them by Your[S] strength, and bring them down, O Lord our shield.
12 The sin of their mouth [is] a word of their lips, and they are captured in their pride, and they recount from the curse and lying.
13 Consume in fury, consume and they are not, and they know that God is ruling in Jacob, to the ends of the earth. Selah.
14 And they turn back at evening, they make a noise like a dog, and they go round about the city.
15 They — they wander for food, if they are not satisfied — then they murmur.
16 And I — I sing [of] Your[S] strength, and I sing at morn [of] Your[S] kindness, for You[S] have been a tower to me, and a refuge for me in a day of adversity.
17 O my Strength, I sing praise unto You[S], for God [is] my tower, the God of my kindness!

Psalm 60

1 To the Overseer. — 'Concerning the Lily of Testimony,' a secret treasure of David, to teach, in his striving with Aram-Naharaim, and with Aram-Zobah, and Joab turns back and struck Edom in the valley of Salt — twelve thousand. O God, You[S] had cast us off, You[S] had broken us — had been angry! — You[S] do turn back to us.
2 You[S] have caused the land to tremble, You[S] have broken it, heal its breaches, for it has moved.
3 You[S] have shown Your[S] people a hard thing, You[S] have caused us to drink wine of trembling.
4 You[S] have given a banner to those fearing You[S]. To be lifted up as a banner because of truth. Selah.
5 That Your[S] beloved ones may be drawn out, save [with] Your[S] right hand, and answer us.
6 God has spoken in His holiness: I exult — I distribute Shechem, and I measure the valley of Succoth,
7 Gilead [is] mine, and Manasseh [is] mine, and Ephraim [is] the strength of my head, Judah [is] my lawgiver,
8 Moab [is] my pot for washing, over Edom I cast my shoe, shout, concerning me, O Philistia.
9 Who does bring me [to] a city of bulwarks? Who has led me unto Edom?
10 Is it not You[S], O God? Have You[S] cast us off? And do You[S] not go forth, O God, with our hosts!
11 Give to us help from adversity, and vain [is] the deliverance of man.
12 We do mightily in God, and He treads down our adversaries!

Psalm 61

1 To the Overseer, on stringed instruments. — By David. Hear, O God, my loud cry, attend to my prayer.
2 From the end of the land I call unto You[S], in the feebleness of my heart, You[S] do lead me into a rock higher than I.

3 For You^S have been a refuge for me, a tower of strength because of the enemy.
4 I stay in Your^S tent to the ages, I trust in the secret place of Your^S wings. Selah.
5 For You^S, O God, have listened to my vows, You^S have appointed the inheritance of those fearing Your^S name.
6 You^S add days to the days of the king, his years as generation and generation.
7 He dwells to the age before God, appoint kindness and truth — they keep him.
8 So do I praise Your^S name for ever, when I pay my vows day by day!

Psalm 62

1 To the Overseer, for Jeduthun. — A Psalm of David. Only — toward God [is] my soul silent, from Him [is] my salvation.
2 Only — He [is] my rock, and my salvation, my tower, I am not much moved.
3 Till when do you^P devise mischief against a man? You^P are destroyed all of you^P, as a wall inclined, a hedge that is cast down.
4 Only — from his excellency they have consulted to drive away, they enjoy a lie, they bless with their mouth, and revile with their heart. Selah.
5 Only — for God, be silent, O my soul, for my hope [is] from Him.
6 Only — He [is] my rock and my salvation, my tower, I am not moved.
7 On God [is] my salvation, and my honor, the rock of my strength, my refuge [is] in God.
8 Trust in Him at all times, O people, pour forth your heart before Him, God [is] a refuge for us. Selah.
9 Only — the low [are] vanity, the high a lie. In balances to go up they [are] lighter than vanity.
10 Trust not in oppression, and become not vain in robbery, wealth — when it increases — set not the heart.
11 Once has God spoken, twice I heard this, that 'strength [is] with God.'
12 And with You^S, O Lord, [is] kindness, for You^S do recompense to each, according to his work!

Psalm 63

1 A Psalm of David, in his being in the wilderness of Judah. O God, You^S [are] my God, earnestly do I seek You^S, my soul has thirsted for You^S, my flesh has longed for You^S, in a land dry and weary, without waters.
2 So I have seen You^S in the sanctuary, to behold Your^S strength and Your^S honor.
3 Because Your^S kindness [is] better than life, my lips do praise You^S.
4 So I bless You^S in my life, I lift up my hands in Your^S name.
5 As [with] milk and fatness is my soul satisfied, and my mouth does praise [with] singing lips.
6 If I have remembered You^S on my couch, in the watches — I meditate on You^S.
7 For You^S have been a help to me, and I sing in the shadow of Your^S wings.
8 My soul has been faithful after You^S, Your^S right hand has taken hold on me.
9 And they who for desolation seek my soul, go in to the lower parts of the earth.
10 They cause him to run on the edge of the sword, they are a portion for foxes.
11 And the king does rejoice in God, every one swearing by Him does boast himself, but stopped is the mouth of those speaking lies!

Psalm 64

1 To the Overseer. — A Psalm of David. Hear, O God, my voice, in my meditation, You^S keep my life from the fear of an enemy,
2 hide me from the secret counsel of evil doers, from the tumult of workers of iniquity.
3 Who sharpened their tongue as a sword, they directed their arrow — a bitter word.
4 To shoot the perfect in secret places, suddenly they shoot him, and fear not.
5 They strengthen an evil thing for themselves, they recount of the hiding of snares, they have said, 'Who does look at it?'
6 They search out perverse things, 'We perfected a searching search,' and the inward part of man, and the heart [are] deep.
7 And God does shoot them [with] an arrow, their wounds have been sudden,
8 And they cause him to stumble, against them [is] their own tongue, every looker on them flees away.
9 And all men fear, and declare the work of God, and they have considered His deed wisely.
10 The righteous does rejoice in Jehovah, and has

trusted in Him, and all the upright of heart do boast themselves!

Psalm 65

1 To the Overseer. — A Psalm of David. A Song. To You[S], silence — praise, O God, [is] in Zion, and a vow is completed to You[S].
2 Hearer of prayer, all flesh comes to You[S].
3 Matters of iniquities were mightier than I, our transgressions — You[S] do cover them.
4 O the happiness of [him whom] You[S] choose, and draw near, he inhabits Your[S] courts, we are satisfied with the goodness of Your[S] house, Your[S] holy temple.
5 By fearful things You[S] answer us in righteousness, O God of our salvation, the confidence of all far off ends of earth and sea.
6 Establishing mountains by His power, He has been girded with might,
7 restraining the noise of seas, the noise of their billows, and the multitude of the peoples.
8 And the inhabitants of the uttermost parts are afraid from Your[S] signs, You[S] cause the outgoings of morning and evening to sing.
9 You[S] have inspected the earth, and water it, You[S] make it very rich, the rivulet of God [is] full of water, You[S] prepare their corn, when thus You[S] do prepare it,
10 Its ridges have been filled, its furrow has been deepened, You[S] do soften it with showers, You[S] bless its springing up.
11 You[S] have crowned the year of Your[S] goodness, and Your[S] paths drop fatness.
12 The pastures of a wilderness do drop, and You[S] gird on joy of the heights.
13 Lambs have clothed the flock, and valleys are covered with corn, they shout — yes, they sing!

Psalm 66

1 To the Overseer. — A Song, a Psalm. Shout you[P] to God, all the earth.
2 Praise you[P] the honor of His name, make you[P] His praise honorable.
3 Say to God, 'How fearful [are] Your[S] works, by the abundance of Your[S] strength, Your[S] enemies pretend obedience to You[S].
4 All the earth do bow to You[S], they sing praise to You[S], they praise Your[S] name.' Selah.
5 Come you[P], and see the works of God, fearful acts toward the sons of men.
6 He has turned a sea to dry land, they pass over on foot through a river, there do we rejoice in Him.
7 Ruling by His might to the age, His eyes do watch among the nations, the lawless exalt not themselves. Selah.
8 Bless, you[P] peoples, our God, and sound the voice of His praise,
9 Who has placed our soul in life, and allowed not our feet to be moved.
10 For You[S] have tried us, O God, You[S] have refined us as the refining of silver.
11 You[S] have brought us into a net, You[S] have placed pressure on our loins.
12 You[S] have caused man to ride at our head. We have entered into fire and into water, and You[S] bring us out to a watered place.
13 I enter Your[S] house with burnt-offerings, I complete my vows to You[S],
14 For my lips were opened, and my mouth spoke in my distress:
15 ' I offer burnt-offerings of fatlings to You[S], with perfume of rams, I prepare a bullock with he-goats.' Selah.
16 Come, hear, all you[P] who fear God, and I recount what he did for my soul.
17 I have called unto Him [with] my mouth, and exaltation [is] under my tongue.
18 Iniquity, if I have seen in my heart, the Lord does not hear.
19 But God has heard, He has attended to the voice of my prayer.
20 Blessed [is] God, who has not turned aside my prayer, and His loving-kindness, from me!

Psalm 67

1 To the Overseer, with stringed instruments. — A Psalm, a Song. God does favor us and bless us, does cause His face to shine with us. Selah.
2 For the knowledge of Your[S] way in earth, among all nations of Your[S] salvation.
3 Peoples do praise You[S], O God, peoples do praise You[S], all of them.
4 Nations do rejoice and sing, for You[S] judge peoples uprightly, and comfort peoples on earth. Selah.
5 Peoples do confess You[S], O God, peoples do confess

You^{S} — all of them.

6 Earth has given her increase, God does bless us — our God,

7 God does bless us, and all ends of earth fear Him!

Psalm 68

1 To the Overseer. — A Psalm, a song of David. God does rise — scattered are His enemies! And those hating Him flee from His face.

2 You^{S} drive away as the driving away of smoke, as the melting of wax before fire, the wicked perish at the presence of God.

3 And the righteous rejoice, they exult before God, and they joy with gladness.

4 Sing you^{P} to God — praise His name, raise up a highway for Him who is riding in deserts, in Jah [is] His name, and exult before Him.

5 Father of the fatherless, and judge of the widows, [is] God in His holy habitation.

6 God — causing the lonely to dwell at home, bringing bound ones out into prosperity, only — the lawless have inhabited a dry place.

7 O God, in Your^{S} going forth before Your^{S} people, in Your^{S} stepping through the wilderness, Selah.

8 The earth has shaken, yes, the heavens have dropped before God, this Sinai — before God, the God of Israel.

9 You^{S} shake out a shower of free-will gifts, O God. Your inheritance, when it has been weary, You^{S} have established it.

10 Your^{S} company have dwelt in it, You^{S} prepare for the poor in Your^{S} goodness, O God.

11 The Lord does give the saying, the female proclaimers [are] a numerous host.

12 Kings of hosts flee utterly away, and a female inhabitant of the house apportions spoil.

13 Though you^{P} do lie between two boundaries, wings of a dove covered with silver, and her wings with yellow gold.

14 When the Mighty spreads kings in it, it does snow in Salmon.

15 A hill of God [is] the hill of Bashan, a hill of heights [is] the hill of Bashan.

16 Why do you^{P} envy, O high hills, the hill God has desired for His seat? Jehovah also does tabernacle for ever.

17 The chariots of God [are] myriads, thousands of changes, the Lord [is] among them, in Sinai, in the sanctuary.

18 You^{S} have ascended on high, You^{S} have taken captivity captive, You^{S} have taken gifts for men, that even the lawless may rest, O Jah God.

19 Blessed [is] the Lord, day by day He lays on us. God Himself [is] our salvation. Selah.

20 God Himself [is] to us a God for deliverances, and Jehovah Lord has the outgoings of death.

21 Only — God does strike the head of His enemies, the hairy crown of a habitual walker in his guilt.

22 The Lord said: 'From Bashan I bring back, I bring back from the depths of the sea.

23 So that you^{S} dash your^{S} foot in blood, [in the blood of] enemies — the tongue of Your^{S} dogs.'

24 They have seen Your^{S} goings, O God, goings of my God, my king, in the sanctuary.

25 Singers have been before, behind [are] players on instruments, in the midst virgins playing with timbrels.

26 You^{P} in assemblies bless God, the Lord — from the fountain of Israel.

27 There [is] little Benjamin their ruler, heads of Judah their defense, heads of Zebulun — heads of Naphtali.

28 Your^{S} God has commanded your^{S} strength, be strong, O God, this You^{S} have worked for us.

29 Because of Your^{S} temple at Jerusalem, kings do bring a present to You^{S}.

30 Rebuke a beast of the reeds, a company of bulls, with calves of the peoples, each humbling himself with pieces of silver, You^{S} scatter peoples delighting in conflicts.

31 Fat ones do come out of Egypt, Cush causes her hands to run to God.

32 Kingdoms of the earth, sing you^{P} to God, praise you^{P} the Lord. Selah.

33 To him who is riding on the heavens of the heavens of old, behold, He gives a strong voice with His voice.

34 Ascribe you^{P} strength to God, His excellency [is] over Israel, and His strength in the clouds.

35 Fearful, O God, out of Your^{S} sanctuaries, the God of Israel Himself, giving strength and might to the people. Blessed [is] God!

Psalm 69

1 To the Overseer. — 'On the Lilies,' by David. Save me, O God, for waters have come unto the soul.

2 I have sunk in deep mire, and there is no standing, I have come into the depths of the waters, and a flood has overflown me.

3 I have been wearied with my calling, my throat has

been burnt, my eyes have been consumed, waiting for
my God.
4 Those hating me without cause have been more than the
hairs of my head, mighty have been my destroyers, my lying
enemies, that which I took not away — I bring back.
5 O God, You[S] — You[S] have known concerning my
overturn, and my desolations have not been hid from You[S].
6 Let not those waiting on You[S] be ashamed because of
me, O Lord, Jehovah of Hosts, let not those seeking You[S]
blush because of me, O God of Israel.
7 For I have borne reproach because of You[S], shame
has covered my face.
8 I have been a stranger to my brother, and a foreigner
to sons of my mother.
9 For zeal for Your[S] house has consumed me, and the
reproaches of Your[S] reproachers have fallen upon me.
10 And I weep in the fasting of my soul, and it is for a
reproach to me.
11 And I make my clothing sackcloth, and I am for a
simile to them.
12 Those sitting at the gate meditate concerning me,
and those drinking strong drink, play on instruments.
13 And I — my prayer [is] to You[S], O Jehovah, a time of
good pleasure, O God, in the abundance of Your[S]
kindness, answer me in the truth of Your[S] salvation.
14 Deliver me from the mire, and let me not sink, let me
be delivered from those hating me, and from deep places
of waters.
15 Let not a flood of waters overflow me, nor let the deep
swallow me up, nor let the pit shut her mouth upon me.
16 Answer me, O Jehovah, for Your[S] kindness [is] good,
turn You[S] unto me according to the abundance Of Your[S]
mercies,
17 And hide not Your[S] face from Your[S] servant, for I am
in distress — hurry, answer me.
18 Be near unto my soul — redeem it, ransom me
because of my enemies.
19 You[S] — You[S] have known my reproach, and my
shame, and my blushing, before You[S] [are] all my
adversaries.
20 Reproach has broken my heart, and I am sick, and I
look for a bemoaner, and there is none, and for
comforters, and I have found none.
21 And they give gall for my food, and cause me to
drink vinegar for my thirst.
22 Their table is for a snare before them, and for a
recompense — for a trap.
23 Darkened are their eyes from seeing, and You[S] shake
their loins continually.
24 Pour Your[S] indignation upon them, and the fierceness
of Your[S] anger does seize them.
25 Their tower is desolated, there is no dweller in their
tents.
26 For they have pursued him You[S] have afflicted, and
recount of the pain of Your[S] pierced ones.
27 Give punishment for their iniquity, and they enter
not into Your[S] righteousness.
28 They are blotted out of the book of life, and are not
written with the righteous.
29 And I [am] afflicted and pained, Your[S] salvation, O
God, does set me on high.
30 I praise the name of God with a song, and I magnify
Him with thanksgiving,
31 And it is better to Jehovah than an ox, a bullock —
horned — hoofed.
32 The humble have seen — they rejoice, you[P] who
seek God — and your[P] heart lives.
33 For Jehovah listens unto the needy, and He has not
despised His bound ones.
34 The heavens and earth do praise Him, seas, and every
moving thing in them.
35 For God does save Zion, and does build the cities of
Judah, and they have dwelt there, and possess it.
36 And the seed of His servants inherit it, and those
loving His name dwell in it!

Psalm 70

1 To the Overseer, by David. — 'To cause to remember.'
O God, to deliver me, O Jehovah, for my help, hurry.
2 Let them who are seeking my soul be ashamed and
confounded, let them who are desiring my evil be turned
backward and blush.
3 Let them turn back because of their shame, who are
saying, 'Aha, aha.'
4 Let all those seeking You[S] joy and be glad in You[S], and
let those loving Your[S] salvation say continually, 'God is
magnified.'
5 And I [am] poor and needy, O God, hurry to me, You[S]
[are] my help and my deliverer, O Jehovah, delay You[S]
not!

Psalm 71

1 In You[S], O Jehovah, I have trusted, let me not be
ashamed to the age.

2 You^S do deliver me in Your^S righteousness, and do cause me to escape, incline Your^S ear unto me, and save me.

3 Be to me for a rock — a habitation, to go in continually, You^S have given command to save me, for You^S [are] my rock and my bulwark.

4 O my God, cause me to escape from the hand of the wicked, from the hand of the perverse and violent.

5 For You^S [are] my hope, O Lord Jehovah, my trust from my youth.

6 I have been supported from the womb by You^S, You^S do cut me out from my mother's bowels, my praise [is] in You^S continually.

7 I have been as a wonder to many, and You^S [are] my strong refuge.

8 My mouth is filled [with] Your^S praise, all the day [with] Your^S beauty.

9 Cast me not off at the time of old age, forsake me not according to the consumption of my power.

10 For my enemies have spoken against me, and those watching my soul have taken counsel together,

11 Saying, 'God has forsaken him, pursue and catch him, for there is no deliverer.'

12 O God, be not far from me, O my God, act swiftly for my help.

13 They are ashamed, they are consumed, who are opposing my soul, they are covered [with] reproach and blushing, who are seeking my evil,

14 And I continually do wait with hope, and have added unto all Your^S praise.

15 My mouth recounts Your^S righteousness, Your^S salvation all the day, for I have not known the numbers.

16 I come in the might of the Lord Jehovah, I mention Your^S righteousness — Yours^S only.

17 God, You^S have taught me from my youth, and until this time I declare Your^S wonders.

18 And also unto old age and gray hairs, O God, forsake me not, till I declare Your^S strength to a generation, Your^S might to every one that comes.

19 And Your^S righteousness, O God, [is] unto the heights, because You^S have done great things, O God, who [is] like You^S?

20 Because You^S have showed me many and sad distresses, You^S turn back — You^S revive me, and from the depths of the earth, You^S turn back — You^S bring me up.

21 You^S do increase my greatness, and You^S surround — You^S comfort me,

22 I also thank You^S with a vessel of psaltery, Your^S truth, O my God, I sing to You^S with a harp, O Holy One of Israel,

23 My lips cry aloud when I sing praise to You^S, and my soul that You^S have redeemed,

24 My tongue also utters all the day Your^S righteousness, because ashamed — because confounded, have been those seeking my evil!

Psalm 72

1 By Solomon. O God, give Your^S judgments to the king, and Your^S righteousness to the king's son.

2 He judges Your^S people with righteousness, and Your^S poor with judgment.

3 The mountains bear peace to the people, and the heights by righteousness.

4 He judges the poor of the people, gives deliverance to the sons of the needy, and bruises the oppressor.

5 They fear You^S with the sun, and before the moon, generation — generations.

6 He comes down as rain on mown grass, as showers — sprinkling the earth.

7 The righteous does flourish in his days, and abundance of peace till the moon is not.

8 And he rules from sea unto sea, and from the river unto the ends of earth.

9 The inhabitants of the dry places do bow before him, and his enemies lick the dust.

10 Kings of Tarshish and of the isles send back a present. Kings of Sheba and Seba bring near a reward.

11 And all kings do bow themselves to him, all nations do serve him,

12 For he delivers the needy who cry, and the poor when he has no helper,

13 He has pity on the poor and needy, and he saves the souls of the needy,

14 He redeems their soul from fraud and from violence, and precious is their blood in his eyes.

15 And he lives, and gives to him of the gold of Sheba, and prays for him continually, all the day he does bless him.

16 There is a handful of corn in the earth, on the top of mountains, like Lebanon does shake its fruit, and they flourish out of the city as the herb of the earth.

17 His name is to the age, before the sun is his name continued, and they bless themselves in him, all nations do pronounce him happy.

18 Blessed is Jehovah God, God of Israel, He alone is

doing wonders,
19 And blessed [is] the Name of His honor to the age, and the whole earth is filled [with] His honor. Amen, and amen!
20 The prayers of David son of Jesse have been ended.

Psalm 73

1 A Psalm of Asaph. Only — God [is] good to Israel, to the clean of heart. And I — as a little thing, my feet have been turned aside,
2 as nothing, my steps have slipped, for I have been envious of the boastful,
3 I see the peace of the wicked, that there are no bands at their death,
4 And their might [is] firm.
5 They are not in the misery of mortals, and they are not plagued with common men.
6 For that reason has pride encircled them, violence covers them as a dress.
7 Their eye has come out from fat. The imaginations of the heart transgressed;
8 They do corruptly, and they speak in the wickedness of oppression, they speak from on high.
9 They have set their mouth in the heavens, and their tongue walks in the earth.
10 For that reason do His people return here, and waters of fullness are wrung out to them.
11 And they have said, 'How has God known? And is there knowledge in the Most High?'
12 Behold, these [are] the wicked and easy ones of the age, they have increased strength.
13 Only — a vain thing! I have purified my heart, and I wash my hands in innocency,
14 And I am plagued all the day, and my reproof [is] every morning.
15 If I have said, 'I recount thus,' behold, I have deceived a generation of Your[S] sons.
16 And I think to know this, it [is] perverseness in my eyes,
17 till I come in to the sanctuaries of God, I attend to their latter end.
18 Only, You[S] do set them in slippery places, You[S] have caused them to fall to desolations.
19 How have they become a desolation as in a moment, they have been ended — consumed from terrors.
20 Awakening as from a dream, O Lord, in awaking, You[S] despise their image.
21 For my heart does show itself violent, and my reins prick themselves,
22 And I am brutish, and do not know. I have been a beast with You[S].
23 And I [am] continually with You[S], You[S] have laid hold on my right hand.
24 With Your[S] counsel You[S] do lead me, and do receive me after honor.
25 Whom have I in the heavens? And with You[S] I have desired none in earth.
26 My flesh and my heart has been consumed, the rock of my heart and my portion [is] God to the age.
27 For, behold, those far from You[S] do perish, You[S] have cut off every one, who is going a whoring from You[S].
28 And I — nearness of God to me [is] good, I have placed my refuge in the Lord Jehovah, to recount all Your[S] works!

Psalm 74

1 An Instruction of Asaph. Why, O God, have You[S] cast off for ever? Your[S] anger smokes against the flock of Your[S] pasture.
2 Remember Your[S] company. You did[S] purchase of old, You[S] did redeem the rod of Your[S] inheritance, this mount Zion — You[S] did dwell in it.
3 Lift up Your[S] steps to the perpetual desolations, everything the enemy did wickedly in the sanctuary.
4 Your[S] adversaries have roared, in the midst of Your[S] meeting-places, they have set their banners as standards.
5 He is known as one bringing in axes against a thicket of wood on high.
6 And now, they break down its carvings together with axe and hatchet,
7 They have sent fire into Your[S] sanctuary, they polluted the tabernacle of Your[S] name to the earth,
8 They said in their hearts, 'Let us oppress them together,' they did burn all the meeting-places of God in the land.
9 We have not seen our banners, there is no more a prophet, nor with us is one knowing how long.
10 Till when, O God, does an adversary reproach? Does an enemy despise Your[S] name for ever?
11 Why do You[S] turn back Your[S] hand, even Your[S] right hand? Remove [it] from the midst of Your[S] bosom.
12 And God [is] my king of old, working salvation in the midst of the earth.

13 You^{S} have broken a sea-[monster] by Your^{S} strength, You^{S} have shattered heads of dragons by the waters,
14 You^{S} have broken the heads of leviathan, You^{S} make him food, for the people of the dry places.
15 You^{S} have adhered a fountain and a stream, You^{S} have dried up perennial flowings.
16 Yours^{S} [is] the day, also Yours^{S} [is] the night, You^{S} have prepared a light giver — the sun.
17 You^{S} have set up all the borders of earth, summer and winter You^{S} have formed them.
18 Remember this — an enemy reproached Jehovah, and a foolish people have despised Your^{S} name.
19 Give not up to a company, the soul of Your^{S} turtle-dove, forget not the company of Your^{S} poor ones for ever.
20 Look attentively to the covenant, for the dark places of earth, have been full of habitations of violence.
21 Let not the oppressed turn back ashamed, let the poor and needy praise Your name,
22 Arise, O God, plead Your^{S} plea, remember Your^{S} reproach from a fool all the day.
23 Forget not the voice of Your^{S} adversaries, the noise of Your^{S} withstanders is going up continually!

Psalm 75

1 To the Overseer. — 'Destroy not.' — A Psalm of Asaph. — A Song. We have given thanks to You^{S}, O God, we have given thanks, and near [is] Your^{S} name, they have recounted Your^{S} wonders.
2 When I receive an appointment, I — I do judge uprightly.
3 Melted is the earth and all its inhabitants, I — I have pondered its pillars. Selah.
4 I have said to the boastful, 'Be not boastful,' and to the wicked, 'Raise not up a horn.'
5 Raise not up your^{P} horn on high, (you^{P} speak with a stiff neck.)
6 for not from the east, or from the west, nor from the wilderness — [is] elevation.
7 But God [is] judge, this He makes low — and this He lifts up.
8 For a cup [is] in the hand of Jehovah, and the wine has foamed, it is full of mixture, and He pours out of it, wring out only its dregs, and drink, do all the wicked of the earth,
9 And I — I declare [it] to the age, I sing praise to the God of Jacob.
10 And I cut off all horns of the wicked, exalted are the horns of the righteous!

Psalm 76

1 To the Overseer with stringed instruments. — A Psalm of Asaph. — A Song. In Judah [is] God known, in Israel His name [is] great.
2 And His tabernacle is in Salem, and His habitation in Zion.
3 There He has shattered arrows of a bow, shield, and sword, and battle. Selah.
4 You^{S} [are] bright, honorable above hills of prey.
5 The mighty of heart have spoiled themselves, they have slept their sleep, and none of the men of might found their hands.
6 From Your^{S} rebuke, O God of Jacob, both rider and horse have been fast asleep.
7 You^{S}, fearful [are] You^{S}, and who does stand before You^{S}, since You^{S} have been angry!
8 From heaven You^{S} have sounded judgment, Earth has feared, and has been still,
9 In the rising of God to judgment, to save all the humble of earth. Selah.
10 For the fierceness of man praises You^{S}, You^{S} gird on the remnant of fierceness.
11 Vow and complete to Jehovah your^{P} God, all you^{P} surrounding him. They bring presents to the Fearful One.
12 He does gather the spirit of leaders, fearful to the kings of earth!

Psalm 77

1 To the Overseer, for Jeduthun. — A Psalm of Asaph. My voice [is] to God, and I cry, my voice [is] to God, and He has given ear unto me.
2 I sought the Lord in a day of my distress, my hand by night has been spread out, and it does not cease, my soul has refused to be comforted.
3 I remember God, and make a noise, I meditate, and feeble is my spirit. Selah.
4 You^{S} have taken hold of the watches of my eyes, I have been moved, and I speak not.
5 I have reckoned the days of old, the years of the ages.
6 I remember my music in the night, I meditate with my heart, and my spirit does search diligently:
7 Does the Lord cast off to the ages? Does He add to be

pleased no more?
8 Has His kindness ceased for ever? The saying failed
to all generations?
9 Has God forgotten [His] favors? Has He shut up His
mercies in anger? Selah.
10 And I say: 'My weakness is, the changes of the right
hand of the Most High.'
11 I mention the doings of Jah, for I remember Your[S]
wonders of old,
12 And I have meditated on all Your[S] working, and I talk
concerning Your[S] doings.
13 O God, in holiness [is] Your[S] way, who [is] a great
god like God?
14 You[S] [are] the God doing wonders. You[S] have made
Your[S] strength known among the peoples,
15 You[S] have redeemed Your[S] people with strength, the
sons of Jacob and Joseph. Selah.
16 The waters have seen You[S], O God, the waters have
seen You[S], they are afraid — also depths are troubled.
17 Thick clouds have poured out waters, the skies have
given forth a noise, also — Your[S] arrows go up and
down.
18 The voice of Your[S] thunder [is] in the spheres,
lightnings have lightened the world, the earth has
trembled, yes, it shakes.
19 In the sea [is] Your[S] way, and Your[S] paths [are] in
many waters, and Your[S] tracks have not been known.
20 You[S] have led Your[S] people as a flock, by the hand of
Moses and Aaron!

Psalm 78

1 An Instruction of Asaph. Give ear, O my people, to
my law, incline your[P] ear to sayings of my mouth.
2 I open my mouth with a simile, I bring forth hidden
things of old,
3 That we have heard and do know, and our fathers
have recounted to us.
4 We do not hide from their sons, recounting to a later
generation praises of Jehovah, and His strength, and
His wonders that He has done.
5 And He raises up a testimony in Jacob, and has placed
a law in Israel, that He commanded our fathers, to make
them known to their sons.
6 So that a later generation does know, sons who are
born, do rise and recount to their sons,
7 and place their confidence in God, and forget not the
doings of God, but keep His commands.
8 And they are not like their fathers, a generation
apostate and rebellious, a generation! it has not prepared
its heart, nor [is] its spirit steadfast with God.
9 Sons of Ephraim — armed bearers of bow, have turned
in a day of conflict.
10 They have not kept the covenant of God, and they
have refused to walk in His law,
11 and they forget His doings, and His wonders that He
showed them.
12 He has done wonders before their fathers, in the land
of Egypt — the field of Zoan.
13 He divided a sea, and caused them to pass over, yes,
He causes waters to stand as a heap.
14 And leads them with a cloud by day, and all the night
with a light of fire.
15 He split rocks in a wilderness, and gives drink — as
the great deep.
16 And brings out streams from a rock, and causes
waters to come down as rivers.
17 And still they add to sin against Him, to provoke the
Most High in the dry place.
18 And they try God in their heart, to ask food for their
lust.
19 And they speak against God — they said: 'Is God
able to array a table in a wilderness?'
20 Behold, He has struck a rock, and waters flow, yes,
streams overflow. 'Also — [is] He able to give bread?
Does He prepare flesh for His people?'
21 For that reason has Jehovah heard, and He showed
Himself angry, and fire has been kindled against Jacob,
and anger also has gone up against Israel,
22 for they have not believed in God, nor have they
trusted in His salvation.
23 And He commands clouds from above, yes, He has
opened doors of the heavens.
24 And He rains manna on them to eat, yes, He has
given corn of heaven to them.
25 Each has eaten food of the Mighty, He sent venison
to them to satiety.
26 He causes an east wind to journey in the heavens,
and leads a south wind by His strength,
27 And He rains flesh as dust on them, and as sand of
the seas — winged fowl,
28 And causes [it] to fall in the midst of His camp, round
about His tabernacles.
29 And they eat, and are greatly satisfied, and He brings
their desire to them.
30 They have not been estranged from their desire, yet
[is] their food in their mouth,

31 and the anger of God has gone up against them, and
He slays among their fat ones, and He caused youths of
Israel to bend.
32 With all this they have sinned again, and have not
believed in His wonders.
33 And He consumes their days in vanity, and their years
in trouble.
34 If He slew them, then they sought Him, and turned
back, and sought God earnestly,
35 and they remember that God [is] their rock, and God
Most High their redeemer.
36 And — they deceive Him with their mouth, and do
lie to Him with their tongue,
37 and their heart has not been right with Him, and they
have not been steadfast in His covenant.
38 And He — the Merciful One, pardons iniquity, and
destroys not, and has often turned back His anger, and
wakes not up all His fury.
39 And He remembers that they [are] flesh, a wind going
on — and it returns not.
40 How often do they provoke Him in the wilderness,
grieve Him in the desolate place?
41 Yes, they turn back, and try God, and have limited
the Holy One of Israel.
42 They have not remembered His hand the day He
ransomed them from the adversary.
43 When He set His signs in Egypt, and His wonders in
the field of Zoan,
44 and He turns their streams to blood, and they drink
not their floods.
45 He sends the beetle among them, and it consumes
them, and the frog, and it destroys them,
46 And gives their increase to the caterpillar, and their
labor to the locust.
47 He destroys their vine with hail, and their sycamores
with frost,
48 and delivers up their beasts to the hail, and their
cattle to the burning flames.
49 He sends the fury of His anger on them, wrath, and
indignation, and distress — a discharge of evil
messengers.
50 He ponders a path for His anger, He kept not back
their soul from death, yes, He delivered up their life to
the pestilence.
51 And He strikes every first-born in Egypt, the first-
fruit of the strong in tents of Ham.
52 And causes His people to journey as a flock, and
guides them as a drove in a wilderness,
53 and He leads them confidently, and they have not
been afraid, and their enemies have covered the sea.
54 And He brings them in unto the border of His
sanctuary, this mountain His right hand had got,
55 And casts out nations from before them, and causes
them to fall in the line of inheritance, and causes the
tribes of Israel to dwell in their tents,
56 and they tempt and provoke God Most High, and
have not kept His testimonies.
57 And they turn back, and deal treacherously like their
fathers, they have been turned like a deceitful bow,
58 and make Him angry with their high places, and make
Him zealous with their graven images,
59 God has heard, and shows Himself angry. And kicks
exceedingly against Israel.
60 And He leaves the tabernacle of Shiloh, the tent He
had placed among men,
61 and He gives His strength to captivity, and His beauty
into the hand of an adversary,
62 and delivers His people up to the sword, and showed
Himself angry with His inheritance.
63 Fire has consumed His young men, and His virgins
have not been praised.
64 His priests have fallen by the sword, and their widows
weep not.
65 And the Lord wakes as a sleeper, as a mighty one
crying aloud from wine.
66 And He strikes His adversaries backward, He has
put a age-during reproach on them,
67 and He kicks against the tent of Joseph, and has not
fixed on the tribe of Ephraim.
68 And He chooses the tribe of Judah, with mount Zion
that He loved,
69 And builds His sanctuary as a high place, like the
earth, He founded it to the age.
70 And He fixes on David His servant, and takes him
from the folds of a flock,
71 He has brought him in from behind suckling ones, to
rule over Jacob His people, and over Israel His
inheritance.
72 And he rules them according to the integrity of his
heart, and leads them by the skillfulness of his hands!

Psalm 79

1 A Psalm of Asaph. O God, nations have come into
Your[S] inheritance, they have defiled Your[S] holy temple,
they made Jerusalem become heaps,
2 they gave the dead bodies of Your[S] servants food for

the fowls of the heavens, the flesh of Your[S] saints for
the wild beast of the earth.
3 They have shed their blood as water round about
Jerusalem, and there is none burying.
4 We have been a reproach to our neighbors, a scorn
and a derision to our surrounders.
5 Till when, O Jehovah? Are You[S] angry for ever? Your[S]
jealousy does burn as fire.
6 Pour Your[S] fury on the nations who have not known
You[S], and on kingdoms that have not called in Your[S]
name.
7 For [one] has devoured Jacob, and they have made
his habitation desolate.
8 Remember not for us the iniquities of forefathers, hurry,
let Your[S] mercies go before us, for we have been very
weak.
9 Help us, O God of our salvation, because of the honor
of Your[S] name, and deliver us, and cover over our sins,
for Your[S] name's sake.
10 Why do the nations say, 'Where [is] their God?' Let
be known among the nations before our eyes, the
vengeance of the blood of Your[S] servants that is shed.
11 Let the groaning of the prisoner come in before You[S],
according to the greatness of Your[S] arm, leave You[S] the
sons of death.
12 And turn You[S] back to our neighbors, sevenfold unto
their bosom, their reproach, wherewith they reproached
You[S], O Lord.
13 And we, Your[S] people, and the flock of Your[S] pasture,
we give thanks to You[S] to the age, we recount Your[S]
praise to all generations!

Psalm 80

1 To the Overseer. — 'On the Lilies.' A testimony of
Asaph. — A Psalm. Shepherd of Israel, give ear, leading
Joseph as a flock, inhabiting the cherubs — shine forth,
2 Before Ephraim, and Benjamin, and Manasseh, wake
up Your[S] might, and come for our salvation.
3 O God, cause us to turn back, and cause Your[S] face to
shine, and we are saved.
4 Jehovah, God of Hosts, till when? You[S] have burned
against the prayer of Your[S] people.
5 You[S] have caused them to eat bread of tears, and cause
them to drink with tears a third time.
6 You[S] make us a strife to our neighbors, and our enemies
mock at it.
7 God of Hosts, turn us back, and cause Your[S] face to
shine, and we are saved.
8 You[S] do bring a vine out of Egypt, You[S] do cast out
nations, and plant it.
9 You[S] have looked before it, and do root it, and it fills
the land,
10 hills have been covered [with] its shadow, and its
boughs [are] cedars of God.
11 It sends forth its branches unto the sea, and its
sucklings unto the river.
12 Why have You[S] broken down its hedges, and all
passing by the way have plucked it?
13 A boar out of the forest does waste it, and a wild
beast of the fields consumes it.
14 God of Hosts, turn back, we beg You[S], look from
heaven, and see, and inspect this vine,
15 and the root that Your[S] right hand planted, and the
branch You[S] made strong for You[S],
16 burnt with fire — cut down, they perish from the
rebuke of Your[S] face.
17 Let Your[S] hand be on the man of Your[S] right hand, on
the son of man You[S] have strengthened for Yourself[S].
18 And we do not go back from You[S], You[S] do revive us,
and we call in Your[S] name.
19 O Jehovah, God of Hosts, turn us back, cause Your[S]
face to shine, and we are saved!

Psalm 81

1 To the Overseer. — 'On the Gittith.' By Asaph. Cry
aloud to God our strength, shout to the God of Jacob.
2 Lift up a song, and give out a timbrel, a pleasant harp
with psaltery.
3 Blow a trumpet in the month, in the new moon, at the
day of our festival,
4 for it [is] a statute to Israel, an ordinance of the God of
Jacob.
5 He has placed it a testimony on Joseph, in his going
forth over the land of Egypt. A lip, I have not known —
I hear.
6 I turned aside his shoulder from the burden, his hands
pass over from the basket.
7 In distress you[S] have called and I deliver you[S], I answer
you[S] in the secret place of thunder, I try you[S] by the
waters of Meribah. Selah.
8 Hear, O My people, and I testify to you[S], O Israel, if
you[S] do listen to me:
9 There is not a strange god in you[S], and you[S] bow not
yourself[S] to a strange god.

10 I [am] Jehovah your[S] God, who brings you[S] up out of the land of Egypt. Enlarge your[S] mouth, and I fill it.
11 But, My people listened not to My voice, and Israel has not consented to Me.
12 And I send them away in the enmity of their heart, they walk in their own counsels.
13 O that My people were listening to Me, Israel would walk in My ways.
14 As a little thing I cause their enemies to bow, and I turn back My hand against their adversaries,
15 those hating Jehovah pretend obedience to Him, but their time is — to the age.
16 He causes him to eat of the fat of wheat, and I satisfy you[S] [with] honey from a rock!

Psalm 82

1 — A Psalm of Asaph. God has stood in the company of God, in the midst God does judge.
2 Till when do you[P] judge perversely? And lift up the face of the wicked? Selah.
3 Judge you[P] the weak and fatherless, declare righteous the afflicted and the poor.
4 Let the weak and needy escape, deliver them from the hand of the wicked.
5 They knew not, nor do they understand, they walk in darkness habitually, moved are all the foundations of earth.
6 I — I have said, 'Gods you[P] [are], and sons of the Most High — all of you[P],
7 But as man you[P] die, and you[P] fall as one of the heads,
8 Rise, O God, judge the earth, for You[S] have inheritance among all the nations!

Psalm 83

1 A Song, — A Psalm of Asaph. O God, let there be no silence to You[S], be not silent, nor be quiet, O God.
2 For, behold, Your[S] enemies do roar, and those hating You[S] have lifted up the head,
3 they take crafty counsel against Your[S] people, and consult against Your[S] hidden ones.
4 They have said, 'Come, and we cut them off from [being] a nation, and the name of Israel is not remembered any more.'
5 For they consulted in heart together, they make a covenant against You[S],
6 Tents of Edom, and Ishmaelites, Moab, and the Hagarenes,
7 Gebal, and Ammon, and Amalek, Philistia with inhabitants of Tyre,
8 Asshur also is joined with them, they have been an arm to sons of Lot. Selah.
9 Do to them as [to] Midian, as [to] Sisera, as [to] Jabin, at the stream Kishon.
10 They were destroyed at Endor, they were dung for the ground!
11 Make their nobles as Oreb and as Zeeb, and all their princes as Zebah and Zalmunna,
12 Who have said, 'Let us occupy the comely places of God for ourselves.'
13 O my God, make them as a rolling thing, as stubble before wind.
14 As a fire does burn a forest, and as a flame sets hills on fire,
15 So do You[S] pursue them with Your[S] whirlwind, and with Your[S] hurricane trouble them.
16 Fill their faces [with] shame, and they seek Your[S] name, O Jehovah.
17 They are ashamed and troubled for ever, yes, they are confounded and lost.
18 And they know that You[S] — (Your[S] name [is] Jehovah — by Yourself[S],) [are] the Most High over all the earth!

Psalm 84

1 To the Overseer. — 'On the Gittith By sons of Korah.' — A Psalm. How beloved Your[S] tabernacles, Jehovah of Hosts!
2 My soul desired, yes, it has also been consumed, for the courts of Jehovah, my heart and my flesh cry aloud unto the living God,
3 (Even a sparrow has found a house, and a swallow a nest for herself, where she has placed her brood,) Your[S] altars, O Jehovah of Hosts, my king and my God.
4 O the happiness of those inhabiting Your[S] house, yet do they praise You[S]. Selah.
5 O the happiness of a man whose strength is in You[S], highways [are] in their heart.
6 Those passing through a valley of weeping, do make it a fountain, blessings also cover the director.
7 They go from strength unto strength, he appears unto God in Zion.
8 O Jehovah, God of Hosts, hear my prayer, give ear, O God of Jacob. Selah.

9 Our shield, see, O God, and behold the face of Your^{S}
anointed,
10 For good [is] a day in Your courts, O Teacher! I have
chosen rather to be at the threshold, in the house of my
God, than to dwell in tents of wickedness.
11 For Jehovah God [is] a sun and a shield, Jehovah
does give grace and honor. He withholds not good to
those walking in uprightness.
12 Jehovah of Hosts! O the happiness of a man trusting
in You^{S}.

Psalm 85

1 To the Overseer. — By sons of Korah. A Psalm. You^{S}
have accepted, O Jehovah, Your^{S} land, You^{S} have turned
[to] the captivity of Jacob.
2 You^{S} have borne away the iniquity of Your^{S} people,
You^{S} have covered all their sin. Selah.
3 You^{S} have gathered up all Your^{S} wrath, You^{S} have
turned back from the fierceness of Your^{S} anger.
4 Turn back [to] us, O God of our salvation, and make
Your^{S} anger with us void.
5 Are You^{S} angry against us to the age? Do You^{S} draw
out Your^{S} anger to generation and generation?
6 Do You^{S} not turn back? You^{S} revive us, and Your^{S}
people do rejoice in You^{S}.
7 Show us, O Jehovah, Your^{S} kindness, and You^{S} do
give Your^{S} salvation to us.
8 I hear what God Jehovah speaks, for He speaks peace
unto His people, and unto His saints, and they turn not
back to folly.
9 Only, His salvation [is] near to those fearing Him, that
honor may dwell in our land.
10 Kindness and truth have met, righteousness and
peace have kissed,
11 truth springs up from the earth, and righteousness
looks out from heaven,
12 Jehovah also gives that which is good, and our land
does give its increase.
13 Righteousness goes before Him, and makes His
footsteps for a way!

Psalm 86

1 A Prayer of David. Incline, O Jehovah, Your^{S} ear,
answer me, for I [am] poor and needy.
2 Keep my soul, for I [am] pious, save Your^{S} servant —
who is trusting to You^{S}, O You^{S}, my God.
3 Favor me, O Lord, for I call all the day to You^{S}.
4 Rejoice the soul of Your^{S} servant, for unto You^{S}, O
Lord, I lift up my soul.
5 For You^{S}, Lord, [are] good and forgiving. And
abundant in kindness to all calling You^{S}.
6 Hear, O Jehovah, my prayer, and attend to the voice
of my supplications.
7 I call You^{S} in a day of my distress, for You^{S} do answer
me.
8 There is none like You^{S} among the gods, O Lord, and
there are none like Your^{S} works.
9 All nations that You^{S} have made come and bow
themselves before You^{S}, O Lord, and give honor to Your^{S}
name.
10 For You^{S} [are] great, and doing wonders, You^{S} [are]
God Yourself^{S} alone.
11 Show me, O Jehovah, Your^{S} way, I walk in Your^{S} truth,
my heart does rejoice to fear Your^{S} name.
12 I confess You^{S}, O Lord my God, with all my heart, and
I honor Your^{S} name to the age.
13 For Your^{S} kindness [is] great toward me, and You^{S}
have delivered my soul from the lowest Sheol.
14 O God, the proud have risen up against me, and a
company of the terrible sought my soul, and have not
placed You^{S} before them,
15 And You^{S}, O Lord, [are] God, merciful and gracious,
slow to anger, and abundant in kindness and truth.
16 Look unto me, and favor me, give Your^{S} strength to
Your^{S} servant, and give salvation to a son of Your^{S}
handmaid.
17 Do with me a sign for good, and those hating me see
and are ashamed, For You^{S}, O Jehovah, have helped me,
yes, You^{S} have comforted me!

Psalm 87

1 By sons of Korah. — A Psalm, a song. His foundation
[is] in holy mountains.
2 Jehovah is loving the gates of Zion above all the
tabernacles of Jacob.
3 Honorable things are spoken in you^{S}, O city of God.
Selah.
4 I mention Rahab and Babel to those knowing Me,
behold, Philistia, and Tyre, with Cush! This [one] was
born there.
5 And of Zion it is said: Each one was born in her, and
He, the Most High, does establish her.

6 Jehovah does recount in the describing of the peoples, 'This [one] was born there.' Selah.
7 Singers also as players on instruments, all my fountains [are] in You^{S}!

Psalm 88

1 A Song, a Psalm, by sons of Korah, to the Overseer, 'Concerning the Sickness of Afflictions.' — An instruction, by Heman the Ezrahite. O Jehovah, God of my salvation, I have cried daily, nightly before You^{S},
2 my prayer comes in before You^{S}, incline Your^{S} ear to my loud cry,
3 for my soul has been full of evils, and my life has come to Sheol.
4 I have been reckoned with those going down [to] the pit, I have been as a man without strength.
5 Among the dead — free, as pierced ones lying in the grave, whom You^{S} have not remembered any more, yes, they have been cut off by Your^{S} hand.
6 You^{S} have put me in the lowest pit, in dark places, in depths.
7 Your^{S} fury has lain upon me, and You^{S} have afflicted [with] all Your^{S} breakers. Selah.
8 You^{S} have put my acquaintance far from me, You^{S} have made me an abomination to them, shut up — I go not forth.
9 My eye has grieved because of affliction, I called You^{S}, O Jehovah, all the day, I have spread out my hands unto You^{S}.
10 Do You^{S} do wonders to the dead? Do Rephaim rise? do they thank You^{S}? Selah.
11 Is Your^{S} kindness recounted in the grave? Your^{S} faithfulness in destruction?
12 Are Your^{S} wonders known in the darkness? And Your^{S} righteousness in the land of forgetfulness?
13 And I, unto You^{S}, O Jehovah, I have cried, and my prayer does come before You^{S} in the morning.
14 Why, O Jehovah, cast You^{S} off my soul? You^{S} hide Your^{S} face from me.
15 I [am] afflicted, and expiring from youth, I have borne Your^{S} terrors — I pine away.
16 Your^{S} wrath has passed over me, Your^{S} terrors have cut me off,
17 They have surrounded me as waters all the day, they have gone round against me together,
18 You^{S} have put lover and friend far from me, my acquaintance [is] the place of darkness!

Psalm 89

1 An instruction, by Ethan the Ezrahite. Of the kind acts of Jehovah, to the age I sing, I make known to all generations Your^{S} faithfulness with my mouth,
2 for I said, 'To the age is kindness built, the heavens! You^{S} do establish Your^{S} faithfulness in them.'
3 I have made a covenant for My chosen, I have sworn to David My servant:
4 'Even to the age do I establish your^{S} seed, and have built your^{S} throne to generation and generation. Selah.
5 And the heavens confess Your^{S} wonders, O Jehovah, Your^{S} faithfulness also [is] in an assembly of holy ones.
6 For who in the sky, compares himself to Jehovah? Among sons of the mighty is like to Jehovah?
7 God is very terrible, in the secret counsel of His holy ones, and fearful over all surrounding Him.
8 O Jehovah, God of Hosts, who [is] like You^{S} — a strong Jah? And Your^{S} faithfulness [is] round about You^{S}.
9 You^{S} [are] ruler over the pride of the sea, in the lifting up of its billows You^{S} do restrain them.
10 You^{S} have bruised Rahab, as one wounded. You^{S} have scattered Your^{S} enemies with the arm of Your^{S} strength.
11 Yours^{S} [are] the heavens — the earth also [is] Yours^{S}, the habitable world and its fullness, You^{S} have founded them.
12 North and south You^{S} have appointed them, Tabor and Hermon do sing in Your^{S} name.
13 You^{S} have an arm with might, strong is Your^{S} hand — Your^{S} right hand high.
14 Righteousness and judgment [are] the fixed place of Your^{S} throne, kindness and truth go before Your^{S} face.
15 O the happiness of the people knowing the shout, O Jehovah, they walk habitually in the light of Your^{S} face.
16 They rejoice all the day in Your^{S} name, and they are exalted in Your^{S} righteousness,
17 For You^{S} [are] the beauty of their strength, and our horn is exalted in Your^{S} good will,
18 For of Jehovah [is] our shield, and of the Holy One of Israel our king.
19 Then You^{S} have spoken in vision, to Your^{S} saint, yes, You^{S} say, I have placed help upon a mighty one, exalted a chosen one out of the people,
20 I have found David My servant, I have anointed him with My holy oil.
21 With whom My hand is established, My arm also does strengthen him.
22 An enemy exacts not upon him, and a son of

perverseness afflicts him not.
23 And I have beaten down his adversaries before him, and I plague those hating him,
24 and My faithfulness and kindness [are] with him, and his horn is exalted in My name.
25 And I have set his hand on the sea, and his right hand on the rivers.
26 He proclaims Me: 'You[S] [are] my Father, My God, and the rock of my salvation.'
27 I also do appoint him first-born, Highest of the kings of the earth.
28 To the age I keep My kindness for him, and My covenant [is] steadfast with him.
29 And I have set his seed for ever, and his throne as the days of the heavens.
30 If his sons forsake My law, and do not walk in My judgments;
31 if they pollute My statutes, and do not keep My commands,
32 I have looked after their transgression with a rod, and their iniquity with strokes,
33 and I break not My kindness from him, nor do I deal falsely in My faithfulness.
34 I profane not My covenant, and I change not that which is going forth from My lips.
35 Once I have sworn by My holiness, I lie not to David,
36 His seed is to the age, and his throne [is] as the sun before Me,
37 As the moon it is established — to the age, and the witness in the sky is steadfast. Selah.
38 And You[S], You[S] have cast off, and do reject, You[S] have shown Yourself[S] angry with Your[S] anointed,
39 have rejected the covenant of Your[S] servant, You[S] have polluted his crown to the earth,
40 You[S] have broken down all his hedges, You[S] have made his fenced places a ruin.
41 All passing by the way have spoiled him, he has been a reproach to his neighbors,
42 You[S] have exalted the right hand of his adversaries, You[S] have caused all his enemies to rejoice.
43 Also — You[S] turn back the sharpness of his sword, and have not established him in battle,
44 have caused [him] to cease from his brightness, and have cast down his throne to the earth.
45 You[S] have shortened the days of his youth, have covered him over [with] shame. Selah.
46 Till when, O Jehovah, are You[S] hidden? Does Your[S] fury burn as fire for ever?
47 Remember, I pray You[S], what [is] life-time? For what reason in vain have You[S] created all the sons of men?
48 Who [is] the man that lives, and does not see death? He delivers his soul from the hand of Sheol. Selah.
49 Where [are] Your[S] former kindnesses, O Lord. You[S] have sworn to David in Your[S] faithfulness,
50 Remember, O Lord, the reproach of Your[S] servants, I have borne all the strivings of the peoples in my bosom,
51 with which Your[S] enemies reproached, O Jehovah, with which they have reproached the steps of Your[S] anointed.
52 Blessed [is] Jehovah to the age. Amen, and amen!

Psalm 90

1 A Prayer of Moses, the man of God. Lord, a habitation You[S] — You[S] have been, to us — in generation and generation,
2 Before mountains were brought forth, and You[S] did form the earth and the world, even from age unto age You[S] [are] God.
3 You[S] turn man unto a bruised thing, and says, Turn back, you[P] sons of men.
4 For a thousand years in Your[S] eyes [are] as yesterday, for it passes on, yes, a watch by night.
5 You[S] have inundated them, they are asleep, in the morning he changes as grass.
6 In the morning it flourishes, and has changed, at evening it is cut down, and has withered.
7 For we were consumed in Your[S] anger, and we have been troubled in Your[S] fury.
8 You[S] have set our iniquities before You[S], our hidden things at the light of Your[S] face,
9 For all our days pined away in Your[S] wrath, we consumed our years as a meditation.
10 Days of our years, in them [are] seventy years, and if, by reason of might, eighty years, yet their enlargement [is] labor and vanity, for it has been cut off hastily, and we fly away.
11 Who knows the power of Your[S] anger? And according to Your[S] fear — Your[S] wrath?
12 To number our days aright let [us] know, and we bring the heart to wisdom.
13 Turn back, O Jehovah, till when? And repent concerning Your[S] servants.
14 Satisfy us at morn [with] Your[S] kindness, and we sing and rejoice all our days.
15 Cause us to rejoice according to the days in which You[S] have afflicted us, the years we have seen evil.

16 Let Your[S] work appear unto Your[S] servants, and Your[S] honor on their sons.

17 And let the pleasantness of Jehovah our God be upon us, and the work of our hands establish on us, yes, the work of our hands establish it!

Psalm 91

1 He who is dwelling in the secret place of the Most High, lodges habitually in the shade of the Mighty,

2 He is saying of Jehovah, 'My refuge, and my bulwark, my God, I trust in Him,'

3 For He delivers you[S] from the snare of a fowler, from a calamitous pestilence.

4 With His wing He covers you[S] over, and under His wings you[S] do trust, a shield and buckler [is] His truth.

5 You[S] are not afraid of fear by night, of arrow that flies by day,

6 of pestilence that walks in thick darkness, of destruction that destroys at noon,

7 there fall a thousand at your[S] side, and a myriad at your[S] right hand, it comes not near unto you[S].

8 But with your[S] eyes you[S] look, and you[S] see the reward of the wicked,

9 (For You[S], O Jehovah, [are] my refuge,) you[S] made the Most High your habitation.

10 Evil happens not unto you[S], and a plague comes not near your[S] tent,

11 for He charges His messengers for you[S], to keep you[S] in all your[S] ways,

12 they bear you[S] up on the hands, for fear that you[S] strike your foot against a stone.

13 You[S] tread on lion and asp, you[S] tramp young lion and dragon.

14 Because in Me he has delighted, I also deliver him — I set him on high, because he has known My name.

15 He does call Me, and I answer him, I [am] with him in distress, I deliver him, and honor him.

16 I satisfy him with length of days, and I cause him to look on My salvation!

Psalm 92

1 A Psalm. — A Song for the sabbath-day. Good to give thanks to Jehovah, and to sing praises to Your[S] name, O Most High,

2 to declare Your[S] kindness in the morning, and Your[S] faithfulness in the nights.

3 On ten strings and on psaltery, On higgaion, with harp.

4 For You[S] have caused me to rejoice, O Jehovah, in Your[S] work, I sing concerning the works of Your[S] hands.

5 How great have been Your[S] works, O Jehovah, Your[S] thoughts have been very deep.

6 A brutish man does not know, and a fool understands this not; —

7 when the wicked flourish as a herb, and all workers of iniquity do blossom — for their being destroyed for ever and ever!

8 And You[S] [are] high to the age, O Jehovah.

9 For, behold, Your[S] enemies, O Jehovah, for, behold, Your[S] enemies, do perish, all workers of iniquity do separate themselves.

10 And You[S] exalt my horn as a reem, I have been anointed with fresh oil.

11 And my eye looks on my enemies, of those rising up against me, the evil doers, do my ears hear.

12 The righteous flourishes as a palm-tree, he grows as a cedar in Lebanon.

13 Those planted in the house of Jehovah, in the courts of our God do flourish.

14 Still they bring forth in old age, they are fat and flourishing,

15 To declare that Jehovah my rock [is] upright, And there is no perverseness in Him!

Psalm 93

1 Jehovah has reigned, He has put on excellency, Jehovah put on strength, He girded Himself, also — established is the world, unmoved.

2 Established is Your[S] throne since then, You[S] [are] from the age.

3 Floods have lifted up, O Jehovah, floods have lifted up their voice, Floods lift up their breakers.

4 Than the voices of many mighty waters, breakers of a sea, mighty on high [is] Jehovah,

5 Your[S] testimonies have been very steadfast, to Your[S] house holiness [is] comely, O Jehovah, for length of days!

Psalm 94

1 God of vengeance — Jehovah! God of vengeance, shine forth.

2 Be lifted up, O Judge of the earth, send back a

recompense on the proud.

3 Till when [do] the wicked, O Jehovah? Till when do the wicked exult?

4 They utter — they speak an old saw, all working iniquity do boast themselves.

5 Your[S] people, O Jehovah, they bruise, and they afflict Your[S] inheritance.

6 They slay widow and guest, and they murder fatherless ones.

7 And they say, 'Jehovah does not see, and the God of Jacob does not consider.'

8 Consider, you[P] brutish among the people, and you[P] foolish, when do you[P] act wisely?

9 He who plants the ear does He not hear? He who forms the eye does He not see?

10 He who is instructing nations, does He not reprove? He who is teaching man knowledge [is] Jehovah.

11 He knows the thoughts of man, that they [are] vanity.

12 O the happiness of the man whom You[S] instruct, O Jah, and teaches him out of Your[S] law,

13 To give rest to him from days of evil, while a pit is dug for the wicked.

14 For Jehovah leaves not His people, and forsakes not His inheritance.

15 For judgment turns back to righteousness, and after it all the upright of heart,

16 Who rises up for me with evil doers? Who stations himself for me with workers of iniquity?

17 Unless Jehovah [were] a help to me, my soul had almost inhabited silence.

18 If I have said, 'My foot has slipped,' Your kindness, O Jehovah, supports me.

19 In the abundance of my thoughts within me, Your[S] comforts delight my soul.

20 Is a throne of mischief joined [with] You[S]? A framer of perverseness by statute?

21 They decree against the soul of the righteous, and innocent blood declare wicked.

22 And Jehovah is for a high place to me, and my God [is] for a rock — my refuge,

23 and turns back their iniquity on them, and cuts them off in their wickedness; Jehovah our God does cut them off!

Psalm 95

1 Come, we sing to Jehovah, we shout to the rock of our salvation.

2 We come before His face with thanksgiving, we shout to Him with psalms.

3 For a great God [is] Jehovah, and a great king over all gods.

4 In whose hand [are] the deep places of earth, and the strong places of hills [are] His.

5 Whose is the sea, and He made it, and His hands formed the dry land.

6 Come in, we bow ourselves, and we bend, we kneel before Jehovah our Maker.

7 For He [is] our God, and we the people of His pasture, and the flock of His hand, today, if you[P] listen to His voice,

8 Harden not your[P] heart as [in] Meribah, as [in] the day of Massah in the wilderness,

9 Where your[P] fathers have tried Me, have proved Me, yes, have seen My work.

10 Forty years I am weary of the generation, and I say, 'A people erring in heart — they! And they have not known My ways:'

11 Where I swore in My anger, 'If they come in unto My rest — !'

Psalm 96

1 Sing to Jehovah a new song, sing to Jehovah all the earth.

2 Sing to Jehovah, bless His name, proclaim His salvation from day to day.

3 Declare His honor among nations, His wonders among all the peoples.

4 For great [is] Jehovah, and praised greatly, He [is] fearful over all gods.

5 For all the gods of the peoples [are] nothing, and Jehovah made the heavens.

6 Honor and majesty [are] before Him, strength and beauty in His sanctuary.

7 Ascribe to Jehovah, O families of the peoples, ascribe to Jehovah honor and strength.

8 Ascribe to Jehovah the honor of His name, lift up a present and come in to His courts.

9 Bow yourselves[P] to Jehovah, in the honor of holiness, be afraid of His presence, all the earth.

10 Say among nations, 'Jehovah has reigned, also — established is the world, unmoved, He judges the peoples in uprightness.'

11 The heavens joy, and the earth is joyful, the sea and its fullness roar.

12 The field exults, and all that [is] in it, then all trees of the forest do sing,
13 before Jehovah, for He has come, for He has come to judge the earth. He judges the world in righteousness, and the peoples in His faithfulness!

Psalm 97

1 Jehovah has reigned, the earth is joyful, many isles rejoice.
2 Cloud and darkness [are] round about Him, righteousness and judgment the basis of His throne.
3 Fire goes before Him, and burns round about His adversaries.
4 His lightnings have lightened the world, the earth has seen, and is pained.
5 Hills, like wax, melted before Jehovah, before the Lord of all the earth.
6 The heavens declared His righteousness, and all the peoples have seen His honor.
7 Ashamed are all servants of a graven image, those boasting themselves in idols, bow yourselves[P] to him, all you[P] gods.
8 Zion has heard and rejoices, and daughters of Judah are joyful, because of Your[S] judgments, O Jehovah.
9 For You[S], Jehovah, [are] Most High over all the earth, You[S] have been greatly exalted over all gods.
10 You[P] who love Jehovah, hate evil, He is keeping the souls of His saints, he delivers them from the hand of the wicked.
11 Light [is] sown for the righteous, and for the upright of heart — joy.
12 Rejoice, you[P] righteous, in Jehovah, and give thanks at the remembrance of his holiness!

Psalm 98

1 A Psalm. Sing you[P] a new song to Jehovah, for wonders He has done, His right hand and His holy arm has given salvation to Him.
2 Jehovah has made known His salvation, before the eyes of the nations, He has revealed His righteousness,
3 He has remembered His kindness, and His faithfulness to the house of Israel, all ends of earth have seen the salvation of our God.
4 Shout to Jehovah, all the earth, break forth, and cry aloud, and sing.
5 Sing to Jehovah with harp, with harp, and voice of praise,
6 With trumpets, and voice of a cornet, shout you[P] before the king Jehovah.
7 The sea and its fullness does roar, the world and the inhabitants in it.
8 Floods clap hand, together hills cry aloud,
9 before Jehovah, for He has come to judge the earth, He judges the world in righteousness, and the people in uprightness!

Psalm 99

1 Jehovah has reigned, peoples tremble, the Inhabitant of the cherubs, the earth shakes.
2 Jehovah [is] great in Zion, and He [is] high over all the peoples.
3 They praise Your[S] name, 'Great, and fearful, holy [it] is.'
4 And the strength of the king has loved judgment, You[S] — You[S] have established uprightness; judgment and righteousness in Jacob, You[S] — You[S] have done.
5 Exalt you[P] Jehovah our God, and bow yourselves[P] at His footstool, holy [is] He.
6 Moses and Aaron among His priests, and Samuel among those proclaiming His name. They are calling unto Jehovah, and He does answer them.
7 In a pillar of cloud He speaks unto them, they have kept His testimonies, and the statute He has given to them.
8 O Jehovah, our God, You[S] have afflicted them, You[S] have been to them a God forgiving, and taking vengeance on their actions.
9 Exalt you[P] Jehovah our God, and bow yourselves[P] at His holy hill, for holy [is] Jehovah our God!

Psalm 100

1 A Psalm of Thanksgiving. Shout to Jehovah, all the earth.
2 Serve Jehovah with joy, come before him with singing.
3 Know that Jehovah He [is] God, He made us, and we are His, His people — and the flock of His pasture.
4 Enter you[P] His gates with thanksgiving, His courts with praise, give you[P] thanks to Him, bless you[P] His Name.
5 For good [is] Jehovah, His kindness to the age, and His faithfulness to generation and generation!

Psalm 101

1 A Psalm of David. Kindness and judgment I sing, to
You^{S}, O Jehovah, I sing praise.
2 I act wisely in a perfect way, when do You^{S} come in
unto me? I walk habitually in the integrity of my heart,
in the midst of my house.
3 I set not a worthless thing before my eyes, I have
hated the work of those turning aside, it adheres not to
me.
4 A perverse heart turns aside from me, I know not
wickedness.
5 Whoso slanders his neighbor in secret, him I cut off,
the high of eyes and proud of heart, him I endure not.
6 My eyes are on the faithful of the land, to dwell with
me, whoso is walking in a perfect way, he serves me.
7 He dwells not in my house who is working deceit,
whoso is speaking lies is not established before my eyes.
8 At morning I cut off all the wicked of the land, to cut
off all the workers of iniquity from the city of Jehovah!

Psalm 102

1 A Prayer of the afflicted when he is feeble, and pours
out his lament before Jehovah. O Jehovah, hear my
prayer, yes, my cry comes to You^{S}.
2 Hide not You^{S} Your^{S} face from me, in a day of my
adversity, incline Your^{S} ear unto me, in the day I call,
hurry, answer me.
3 For my days have been consumed in smoke, and my
bones have burned as a fire-brand.
4 Afflicted as the herb, and withered, is my heart, for I
have forgotten to eat my bread.
5 From the voice of my sighing has my bone clung to
my flesh.
6 I have been like to a pelican of the wilderness, I have
been as an owl of the dry places.
7 I have watched, and I am as a bird alone on the roof.
8 All the day my enemies reproached me, those mad at
me have sworn against me.
9 Because I have eaten ashes as bread, and have mingled
my drink with weeping,
10 from Your^{S} indignation and Your^{S} wrath, for You^{S} have
lifted me up, and do cast me down.
11 My days [are] stretched out as a shadow, and I — I
am withered as the herb.
12 And You^{S}, O Jehovah, abide to the age, and Your^{S}
memorial to all generations.
13 You^{S} — You^{S} rise — You^{S} pitied Zion, for the time to
favor her, for the appointed time has come.
14 For Your^{S} servants have been pleased with her stones,
and they favor her dust.
15 And nations fear the name of Jehovah, and all kings
of the earth Your^{S} honor,
16 for Jehovah has built Zion, He has been seen in His
honor,
17 He turned unto the prayer of the destitute, and He
has not despised their prayer.
18 This is written for a later generation, and the people
created do praise Jah.
19 For He has looked from the high place of His
sanctuary. Jehovah looked attentively from heaven unto
earth,
20 to hear the groan of the prisoner, to loose sons of
death,
21 to declare the name of Jehovah in Zion, and His praise
in Jerusalem,
22 in the peoples being gathered together, and the
kingdoms — to serve Jehovah.
23 He has humbled my power in the way, He has
shortened my days.
24 I say, 'My God, take me not up in the midst of my
days,' through all generations [are] Your^{S} years.
25 Beforetime You^{S} did found the earth, and the heavens
[are] the work of Your^{S} hands.
26 They — they perish, and You^{S} remain, and all of them
become old as a garment, You^{S} change them as clothing,
and they are changed.
27 And You^{S} [are] the same, and Your^{S} years are not
finished.
28 The sons of Your^{S} servants do continue, and their
seed is established before You^{S}!

Psalm 103

1 By David. Bless, O my soul, Jehovah, and all my inward
parts — His Holy Name.
2 Bless, O my soul, Jehovah, and forget not all His
benefits,
3 Who is forgiving all your^{S} iniquities, Who is healing
all your^{S} diseases,
4 Who is redeeming your^{S} life from destruction, Who is
crowning you^{S} — kindness and mercies,
5 Who is satisfying your^{S} desire with good, renew itself
as an eagle does your^{S} youth.

6 Jehovah is doing righteousness and judgments for all
the oppressed.
7 He makes known His ways to Moses, His acts to the
sons of Israel.
8 Merciful and gracious [is] Jehovah, slow to anger,
and abundant in mercy.
9 Not for ever does He strive, nor does He watch to the
age.
10 He has not done to us according to our sins, nor has
He conferred benefits upon us according to our
iniquities.
11 For, as the height of the heavens [is] above the earth,
His kindness has been mighty over those fearing Him.
12 As the distance of east from west He has put our
transgressions far from us.
13 As a father has mercy on sons, Jehovah has mercy
on those fearing Him.
14 For He has known our frame, remembering that we
[are] dust.
15 Mortal man! his days [are] as grass, so he flourishes
as a flower of the field;
16 for a wind has passed over it, and it is not, and its
place does not discern it any more.
17 And the kindness of Jehovah [is] from age even unto
age on those fearing Him, and His righteousness to sons'
sons,
18 to those keeping His covenant, and to those
remembering His precepts to do them.
19 Jehovah has established His throne in the heavens,
and has ruled over all His kingdom.
20 Bless Jehovah, you[P] His messengers, mighty in power
— doing His word, to listen to the voice of His Word.
21 Bless Jehovah, all you[P] His hosts, His ministers —
doing His pleasure.
22 Bless Jehovah, all you[P] His works, in all places of
His dominion. Bless, O my soul, Jehovah!

Psalm 104

1 Bless, O my soul, Jehovah! Jehovah, my God, You[S] have
been very great, You[S] have put on honor and majesty.
2 Covering himself [with] light as a garment, stretching
out the heavens as a curtain,
3 Who is laying the beam of His upper chambers in the
waters, Who is making thick clouds His chariot, Who is
walking on wings of wind,
4 making His messengers — the winds, His ministers
— the flaming fire.
5 He has founded earth on its bases, it is not moved to
the age and for ever.
6 The abyss! You[S] have covered it as with clothing,
above hills do waters stand.
7 They flee from Your[S] rebuke, hurry away from the voice
of Your[S] thunder.
8 They go up hills — they go down valleys, unto a
place You[S] have founded for them.
9 You[S] have set a border, they pass not over, they turn
not back to cover the earth.
10 Who is sending forth fountains in valleys, they go
on between hills.
11 They water every beast of the field, wild asses break
their thirst.
12 By them the fowl of the heavens does dwell, from
between the branches they give forth the voice.
13 Watering hills from His upper chambers, from the
fruit of Your[S] works is the earth satisfied.
14 Causing grass to spring up for cattle, and herb for
the service of man, to bring forth bread from the earth,
15 and wine — it rejoices the heart of man, to cause the
face to shine from oil, and bread — it supports the heart
of man.
16 Satisfied [are] the trees of Jehovah, cedars of
Lebanon that He has planted,
17 where birds do make nests, the stork — the firs [are]
her house.
18 The high hills [are] for wild goats, rocks [are] a refuge
for conies,
19 He made the moon for seasons, the sun has known
his place of entrance.
20 You[S] set darkness, and it is night, every beast of the
forest does creep in it.
21 The young lions are roaring for prey, and to seek
their food from God.
22 The sun rises, they are gathered, and they crouch in
their dens.
23 Man goes forth to his work, and to his service — till
evening.
24 How many have been Your[S] works, O Jehovah, You[S]
have made all of them in wisdom, the earth is full of Your[S]
possessions.
25 This, the sea, great and broad of sides, there [are]
moving things — innumerable, living creatures — small
with great.
26 There do ships go: leviathan, that You[S] have formed
to play in it.
27 All of them do look unto You[S], to give their food in
its season.

28 You[S] do give to them — they gather, You[S] do open Your[S] hand — they [are] satisfied [with] good.

29 You[S] hide Your[S] face — they are troubled, You[S] gather their spirit — they expire, and they turn back unto their dust.

30 You[S] send out Your[S] Spirit, they are created, and You[S] renew the face of the ground.

31 The honor of Jehovah is to the age, Jehovah rejoices in His works,

32 who is looking to earth, and it trembles, He comes against hills, and they smoke.

33 I sing to Jehovah during my life, I sing praise to my God while I exist.

34 Sweet is my meditation on Him, I — I do rejoice in Jehovah.

35 Sinners are consumed from the earth, and the wicked are no more. Bless, O my soul, Jehovah. Praise you[P] Jehovah!

Psalm 105

1 Give you[P] thanks to Jehovah — call you[P] in His name, make known His acts among the peoples.

2 Sing you[P] to Him — sing praise to Him, meditate you[P] on all His wonders.

3 Boast yourselves[S] in His Holy Name, the heart of those seeking Jehovah rejoices.

4 Seek you[P] Jehovah and His strength, seek you[S] His face continually.

5 Remember His wonders that He did, His signs and the judgments of His mouth.

6 O seed of Abraham, His servant, O sons of Jacob, His chosen ones.

7 He [is] Jehovah our God, His judgments [are] in all the earth.

8 He has remembered His covenant to the age, the word He commanded to a thousand generations,

9 that He has made with Abraham, and His oath to Isaac,

10 and does establish it for a statute to Jacob, to Israel — a covenant age-during,

11 saying, ' I give the land of Canaan to you[S], the portion of your[S] inheritance,'

12 in their being few in number, but a few, and sojourners in it.

13 And they go up and down, from nation unto nation, from a kingdom unto another people.

14 He has not allowed any to oppress them and He reproves kings for their sakes.

15 'Strike not against My anointed, and do not evil to My prophets.'

16 And He calls a famine on the land, He has broken the whole staff of bread.

17 He has sent a man before them, Joseph has been sold for a servant.

18 They have afflicted his feet with fetters, iron has entered his soul,

19 till the time of the coming of His word the saying of Jehovah has tried him.

20 The king has sent, and loosed him, the ruler of the peoples, and draws him out.

21 He has made him lord of his house, and ruler over all his possessions.

22 To bind his chiefs at his pleasure, and he makes his elders wise.

23 And Israel comes in to Egypt, and Jacob has sojourned in the land of Ham.

24 And He makes His people very fruitful, and makes it mightier than its adversaries.

25 He turned their heart to hate His people, to conspire against His servants.

26 He has sent Moses His servant, Aaron whom He had fixed on.

27 They have set among them the matters of His signs, and wonders in the land of Ham.

28 He has sent darkness, and it is dark, and they have not provoked His word.

29 He has turned their waters to blood, and puts their fish to death.

30 Their land has teemed [with] frogs, in the inner chambers of their kings.

31 He has said, and the beetle comes, lice into all their border.

32 He has made their showers hail, a flaming fire [is] in their land.

33 And He afflicts their vine and their fig, and shatters the trees of their border.

34 He has said, and the locust comes, and the cankerworm — innumerable,

35 and it consumes every herb in their land, and it consumes the fruit of their ground.

36 And He strikes every first-born in their land, the first-fruit of all their strength,

37 and brings them out with silver and gold, and there is not a feeble one in its tribes.

38 Egypt has rejoiced in their going forth, for their fear had fallen upon them.

39 He has spread a cloud for a covering, and fire to

enlighten the night.
40 They have asked, and He brings quails, and satisfies them [with] bread of heaven.
41 He has opened a rock, and waters issue, they have gone on in dry places — a river.
42 For He has remembered His holy word, with Abraham His servant,
43 and He brings forth His people with joy, His chosen ones with singing.
44 And He gives to them the lands of nations, and they possess the labor of peoples,
45 that they may observe His statutes, and may keep His laws. Praise you[P] Jehovah!

Psalm 106

1 Praise you[P] Jah, give thanks to Jehovah, for good, for to the age, [is] His kindness.
2 Who does utter the mighty acts of Jehovah? Sounds all His praise?
3 O the happiness of those keeping judgment, doing righteousness at all times.
4 Remember me, O Jehovah, with the favor of Your[S] people, look after me in Your[S] salvation.
5 To look on the good of Your[S] chosen ones, to rejoice in the joy of Your[S] nation, to boast myself with Your[S] inheritance.
6 We have sinned with our fathers, we have done perversely, we have done wickedly.
7 Our fathers in Egypt, have not wisely considered Your[S] wonders, they have not remembered the abundance of Your[S] kind acts, and provoke by the sea, at the sea of Suph.
8 And He saves them for His name's sake, to make known His might,
9 and rebukes the sea of Suph, and it is dried up, and causes them to go through depths as a wilderness.
10 And He saves them from the hand of him who is hating, and redeems them from the hand of the enemy.
11 And waters cover their adversaries, not one of them has been left.
12 And they believe in His words, they sing His praise,
13 they have hurried — forgotten His works, they have not waited for His counsel.
14 And they lust greatly in a wilderness, and try God in a desert.
15 And He gives their request to them, and sends leanness into their soul.
16 And they are envious of Moses in the camp, of Aaron, Jehovah's holy one.
17 Earth opens, and swallows up Dathan, and covers over the company of Abiram.
18 And fire burns among their company, a flame sets the wicked on fire.
19 They make a calf in Horeb, and bow themselves to a molten image,
20 and change their honor into the form of an ox eating herbs.
21 They have forgotten God their savior, the doer of great things in Egypt,
22 of wonderful things in the land of Ham, of fearful things by the sea of Suph.
23 And He says to destroy them, unless Moses, His chosen one, had stood in the breach before Him, to turn back His wrath from destroying.
24 And they kick against the desirable land, they have not given credence to His word.
25 And they murmur in their tents, they have not listened to the voice of Jehovah.
26 And He lifts up His hand to them, to cause them to fall in a wilderness,
27 and to cause their seed to fall among nations, and to scatter them through lands.
28 And they are coupled to Baal-Peor, and eat the sacrifices of the dead,
29 and they provoke to anger by their actions, and a plague breaks forth upon them,
30 and Phinehas stands, and executes judgment, and the plague is restrained,
31 and it is reckoned to him to righteousness, to all generations — unto the age.
32 And they cause wrath by the waters of Meribah, and it is evil to Moses for their sakes,
33 for they have provoked his spirit, and he speaks wrongfully with his lips.
34 They have not destroyed the peoples, as Jehovah had said to them,
35 and mix themselves among nations, and learn their works,
36 and serve their idols, and they are to them for a snare.
37 And they sacrifice their sons and their daughters to destroyers,
38 and they shed innocent blood — blood of their sons and of their daughters, whom they have sacrificed to idols of Canaan, and the land is profaned with blood.
39 And they are defiled with their works, and commit whoredom in their habitual doings.

40 And the anger of Jehovah is kindled against His
people, and He does abominate His inheritance.
41 And gives them into the hand of nations, and those
hating them rule over them,
42 and their enemies oppress them, and they are
humbled under their hand.
43 He does deliver them many times, and they rebel in
their counsel, and they are brought low in their iniquity.
44 And He looks on their distress when He hears their
cry,
45 and remembers His covenant for them, and is
comforted, according to the abundance of His kindness.
46 And He appoints them for mercies before all their
captors.
47 Save us, O Jehovah our God, and gather us from the
nations, to give thanks to Your[S] holy name, to glory in
Your[S] praise.
48 Blessed [is] Jehovah, God of Israel, from the age even
unto the age. And all the people said, 'Amen, praise Jah!'

Psalm 107

1 'Give you[P] thanks to Jehovah, for good, for to the age
[is] His kindness:'
2 Let the redeemed of Jehovah say, whom He redeemed
from the hand of an adversary.
3 And has gathered them from the lands, from east and
from west, from north, and from the sea.
4 They wandered in a wilderness, in a desert by the
way, they have not found a city of habitation.
5 Hungry — yes — thirsty, their soul becomes feeble in
them,
6 and they cry unto Jehovah in their adversity, He
delivers them from their distress,
7 and causes them to tread in a right way, to go unto a
city of habitation.
8 They confess to Jehovah His kindness, and His
wonders to the sons of men.
9 For He has satisfied a longing soul, and has filled a
hungry soul [with] goodness.
10 Inhabitants of dark places and death-shade, prisoners
of affliction and of iron,
11 because they changed the saying of God, and
despised the counsel of the Most High.
12 And He humbles their heart with labor, they have
been feeble, and there is no helper.
13 And they cry unto Jehovah in their adversity, He
saves them from their distresses.
14 He brings them out from the dark place, and death-
shade, and He draws their bands away.
15 They confess to Jehovah His kindness, and His
wonders to the sons of men.
16 For He has broken doors of brass, and He has cut
bars of iron.
17 Fools, by means of their transgression, and by their
iniquities, afflict themselves.
18 Their soul does abominate all food, and they come
near unto the gates of death,
19 and cry unto Jehovah in their adversity, He saves
them from their distresses,
20 He sends His word and heals them, and delivers from
their destructions.
21 They confess to Jehovah His kindness, and His
wonders to the sons of men,
22 and they sacrifice sacrifices of thanksgiving, and
recount His works with singing.
23 Those going down [to] the sea in ships, doing
business in many waters,
24 they have seen the works of Jehovah, and His
wonders in the deep.
25 And He says, and appoints a tempest, and it lifts up
its billows,
26 They go up [to] the heavens, they go down [to] the
depths, their soul is melted in evil.
27 They reel to and fro, and move as a drunkard, and all
their wisdom is swallowed up.
28 And they cry to Jehovah in their adversity, and He
brings them out from their distresses.
29 He establishes a whirlwind to a calm, and hushed are
their billows.
30 And they rejoice because they are quiet, and He leads
them to the haven of their desire.
31 They confess to Jehovah His kindness, and His
wonders to the sons of men,
32 and they exalt Him in the assembly of the people,
and praise Him in the seat of the elders.
33 He makes rivers become a wilderness, and fountains
of waters become dry land.
34 A fruitful land becomes a barren place, for the
wickedness of its inhabitants.
35 He makes a wilderness become a pool of water, and a
dry land become fountains of waters.
36 And He causes the hungry to dwell there, and they
prepare a city of habitation.
37 And they sow fields, and plant vineyards, and they
make fruits of increase.
38 And He blesses them, and they multiply exceedingly,

and He does not diminish their cattle.
39 And they are diminished, and bow down, by restraint,
evil, and sorrow.
40 He is pouring contempt upon nobles, and causes
them to wander in vacancy — no way.
41 And sets the needy on high from affliction, and places
families as a flock.
42 The upright do see and rejoice, and all perversity
has shut her mouth.
43 Who [is] wise, and observes these? They understand
the kind acts of Jehovah!

Psalm 108

1 A Song, a Psalm of David. Prepared is my heart, O
God, I sing, yes, I sing praise, also my honor.
2 Awake, psaltery and harp, I awake the dawn.
3 I thank You[S] among peoples, O Jehovah, and I praise
You[S] among the nations.
4 For Your[S] kindness [is] great above the heavens, and
Your[S] truth unto the clouds.
5 Be You[S] exalted above the heavens, O God, and Your[S]
honor above all the earth.
6 That Your[S] beloved ones may be delivered, save [with]
Your[S] right hand, and answer us.
7 God has spoken in His holiness: I exult, I apportion
Shechem, and I measure the valley of Succoth,
8 Mine [is] Gilead, mine [is] Manasseh, And Ephraim
[is] the strength of my head, Judah [is] my lawgiver,
9 Moab [is] a pot for my washing, I cast my shoe upon
Edom, I shout habitually over Philistia.
10 Who does bring me in to the fenced city? Who has
led me unto Edom?
11 Have not You[S], O God, cast us off? And You[S] go not
out, O God, with our hosts!
12 Give help to us from adversity, and vain is the
salvation of man.
13 In God we do mightily, and He does tread down our
adversaries!

Psalm 109

1 To the Overseer. — A Psalm of David. O God of my
praise, be not silent,
2 for the mouth of wickedness, and the mouth of deceit,
they have opened against me, they have spoken with
me — a tongue of falsehood, and words of hatred!
3 They have compassed me about, and they fight me
without cause.
4 For my love they oppose me, and I — prayer!
5 And they set evil for good against me, and hatred for
my love.
6 Appoint You[S] the wicked over him, and an adversary
stands at his right hand.
7 In his being judged, he goes forth wicked, and his
prayer is for sin.
8 His days are few, another takes his oversight,
9 His sons are fatherless, and his wife a widow.
10 And his sons do wander continually, yes, they have
begged, and have sought out of their dry places.
11 An exactor lays a snare for all that he has, and
strangers spoil his labor.
12 He has none to extend kindness, nor is there one
showing favor to his orphans.
13 His posterity is for cutting off, their name is blotted
out in another generation.
14 The iniquity of his fathers is remembered unto
Jehovah, and the sin of his mother is not blotted out.
15 They are before Jehovah continually, and He cuts
off their memorial from earth.
16 Because that he has not remembered to do kindness,
and pursues the poor man and needy, and the afflicted
of heart — to slay,
17 and he loves reviling, and it meets him, and he has
not delighted in blessing, and it is far from him.
18 And he puts on reviling as his robe, and it comes in
as water into his midst, and as oil into his bones.
19 It is to him as apparel — he covers himself, and he
girds it on for a continual girdle.
20 This [is] the wage of my accusers from Jehovah, and
of those speaking evil against my soul.
21 And You[S], O Jehovah Lord, deal with me for Your[S]
name's sake, because Your[S] kindness [is] good, deliver
me.
22 For I [am] poor and needy, and my heart has been
pierced in my midst.
23 As a shadow when it is stretched out, I have gone, I
have been driven away as a locust.
24 My knees have been feeble from fasting, and my
flesh has failed of fatness.
25 And I — I have been a reproach to them, they see
me, they shake their head.
26 Help me, O Jehovah my God, save me, according to
Your[S] kindness.
27 And they know that this [is] Your[S] hand, You[S], O
Jehovah, You[S] have done it.

28 They revile, and You[S] do bless, they have risen, and are ashamed, and Your[S] servant does rejoice.

29 My accusers put on blushing, and are covered, their shame [is] as an upper robe.

30 I thank Jehovah greatly with my mouth, and I praise Him in the midst of many,

31 for He stands at the right hand of the needy, to save from those judging his soul.

Psalm 110

1 A Psalm of David. The affirmation of Jehovah to my Lord: 'Sit at My right hand, till I make Your[S] enemies Your[S] footstool.'

2 Jehovah does send the rod of Your[S] strength from Zion, rule in the midst of Your[S] enemies.

3 Your[S] people [are] free-will gifts in the day of Your[S] strength, in the honors of holiness, from the womb, from the morning, You[S] have the dew of Your[S] youth.

4 Jehovah has sworn, and does not repent, 'You[S] [are] a priest to the age, according to the order of Melchizedek.'

5 The Lord on Your[S] right hand struck kings in the day of His anger.

6 He does judge among the nations, He has completed the carcasses, has struck the head over the mighty earth.

7 He drinks from a brook in the way, for that reason He does lift up the head!

Psalm 111

1 Praise you[P] Jah! I thank Jehovah with the whole heart, in the secret meeting of the upright, and of the company.

2 Great [are] the works of Jehovah, sought out by all desiring them.

3 His work is honorable and majestic, and His righteousness is standing for ever.

4 He has made a memorial of His wonders, gracious and merciful [is] Jehovah.

5 He has given prey to those fearing Him, He remembers His covenant to the age.

6 He has declared the power of His works to His people, to give the inheritance of nations to them.

7 The works of His hands [are] true and just, steadfast [are] all His appointments.

8 They are sustained for ever to the age. They are made in truth and uprightness.

9 He has sent redemption to His people, He has appointed His covenant to the age, holy and fearful [is] His name.

10 The beginning of wisdom [is] fear of Jehovah, all doing them have good understanding, His praise [is] standing for ever!

Psalm 112

1 Praise you[P] Jah! O the happiness of one fearing Jehovah, he has delighted greatly in His commands.

2 Mighty is his seed in the earth, the generation of the upright is blessed.

3 Wealth and riches [are] in his house, and his righteousness is standing for ever.

4 Light has risen in darkness to the upright, gracious, and merciful, and righteous.

5 Good [is] the man — gracious and lending, he sustains his matters in judgment.

6 For — to the age he is not moved; for the righteous is a memorial age-during.

7 He is not afraid of an evil report, prepared is his heart, confident in Jehovah.

8 Sustained is his heart — he fears not, till that he look on his adversaries.

9 He has scattered — has given to the needy, his righteousness is standing for ever, his horn is exalted with honor.

10 The wicked sees, and has been angry, he gnashes his teeth, and has melted, the desire of the wicked does perish!

Psalm 113

1 Praise you[P] Jah! Praise, you[P] servants of Jehovah. Praise the name of Jehovah.

2 The name of Jehovah is blessed, from this time forth, and unto the age.

3 From the rising of the sun unto its going in, praised [is] the name of Jehovah.

4 High above all nations [is] Jehovah, His honor [is] above the heavens.

5 Who [is] as Jehovah our God, He is exalting [Himself] to sit?

6 He is humbling [Himself] to look on the heavens and on the earth.

7 He is raising up the poor from the dust, He exalts the needy from a dunghill.

8 To cause to sit with princes, with the princes of His people.
9 Causing the barren one of the house to sit, a joyful mother of sons; praise you^{P} Jah!

Psalm 114

1 In the going out of Israel from Egypt, the house of Jacob from a strange people,
2 Judah became His sanctuary, Israel his dominion.
3 The sea has seen, and flees, the Jordan turns backward.
4 The mountains have skipped as rams, heights as sons of a flock.
5 What — to you^{S}, O sea, that you^{S} flee? O Jordan, you^{S} turn back!
6 O mountains, you^{P} skip as rams! O heights, as sons of a flock!
7 From before the Lord be afraid, O earth, from before the God of Jacob,
8 He is turning the rock to a pool of waters, the flint to a fountain of waters!

Psalm 115

1 Not to us, O Jehovah, not to us, but give honor to Your^{S} name, for Your^{S} kindness, for Your^{S} truth.
2 Why do the nations say, 'Where, pray, [is] their God?'
3 And our God [is] in the heavens, all that He has pleased He has done.
4 Their idols [are] silver and gold, work of man's hands,
5 they have a mouth, and they speak not, they have eyes, and they see not,
6 they have ears, and they hear not, they have a nose, and they smell not,
7 their hands, but they handle not, their feet, and they walk not;
8 nor do they mutter through their throat, their makers are like them, every one who is trusting in them.
9 O Israel, trust in Jehovah, 'Their help and their shield [is] He.'
10 O house of Aaron, trust in Jehovah, 'Their help and their shield [is] He.'
11 You^{P} fearing Jehovah, trust in Jehovah, 'Their help and their shield [is] He.'
12 Jehovah has remembered us, He blesses, He blesses the house of Israel, He blesses the house of Aaron,
13 He blesses those fearing Jehovah, the small with the great.
14 Jehovah adds to you^{P}, to you^{P}, and to your^{P} sons.
15 Blessed [are] you^{P} of Jehovah, maker of heaven and earth,
16 the heavens — the heavens [are] Jehovah's, and He has given the earth to sons of men,
17 The dead praise not Jah, nor any going down to silence.
18 And we, we bless Jah, from this time forth, and unto the age. Praise you^{P} Jah!

Psalm 116

1 I have loved, because Jehovah hears my voice, my supplication,
2 because He has inclined His ear to me, and during my days I call.
3 Cords of death have compassed me, and straits of Sheol have found me, I find distress and sorrow.
4 And I call in the name of Jehovah: I pray You^{S}, O Jehovah, deliver my soul,
5 gracious [is] Jehovah, and righteous, yes, our God [is] merciful,
6 Jehovah [is] a preserver of the simple, I was low, and He gives salvation to me.
7 Turn back, O my soul, to your rest, for Jehovah has conferred benefits on you^{S}.
8 For You^{S} have delivered my soul from death, my eyes from tears, my feet from overthrowing.
9 I walk habitually before Jehovah in the lands of the living.
10 I have believed, for I speak, I — I have been afflicted greatly.
11 I said in my haste, 'Every man [is] a liar.'
12 What do I return to Jehovah? All His benefits [are] upon me.
13 I lift up the cup of salvation, and I call in the name of Jehovah.
14 Let me complete my vows to Jehovah, I pray you^{P}, before all His people.
15 The death for His saints [is] precious in the eyes of Jehovah.
16 Cause [it] to come, O Jehovah, for I [am] Your^{S} servant. I [am] Your^{S} servant, son of Your^{S} handmaid, You^{S} have opened my bonds.
17 I sacrifice a sacrifice of thanks to You^{S}, and I call in the name of Jehovah.

18 Let me complete my vows to Jehovah, I pray you[P],
before all His people,
19 in the courts of the house of Jehovah, in your[S] midst,
O Jerusalem, praise you[P] Jah!

Psalm 117

1 Praise Jehovah, all you[P] nations, glorify Him, all you[P]
peoples.
2 For His kindness has been mighty to us, and the truth
of Jehovah [is] to the age. Praise you[P] Jah!

Psalm 118

1 Give you[P] thanks to Jehovah, for good, for His
kindness [is] to the age.
2 I pray you[P], let Israel say, that, His kindness [is] to the
age.
3 I pray you[P], let the house of Aaron say, that, His
kindness [is] to the age.
4 I pray you[P], let those fearing Jehovah say, that, His
kindness [is] to the age.
5 I called Jah from the distress, Jah answered me in a
broad place.
6 Jehovah [is] for me, I do not fear what man does to
me.
7 Jehovah [is] for me among my helpers, and I — I look
on those hating me.
8 Better to take refuge in Jehovah than to trust in man,
9 better to take refuge in Jehovah, than to trust in
princes.
10 All nations have compassed me about, I surely cut
them off in the name of Jehovah.
11 They have compassed me about, yes, they have
compassed me about, I surely cut them off in the name
of Jehovah.
12 They compassed me about as bees, they have been
extinguished as a fire of thorns, I surely cut them off in
the name of Jehovah.
13 You[S] have sorely thrust me to fall, and Jehovah has
helped me.
14 My strength and song [is] Jah, and He is for salvation
to me.
15 A voice of singing and salvation, [is] in the tents of
the righteous, the right hand of Jehovah is doing
valiantly.
16 The right hand of Jehovah is exalted, the right hand
of Jehovah is doing valiantly.
17 I do not die, but live, and recount the works of Jah,
18 Jah has sorely chastened me, and has not given me
up to death.
19 Open you[P] gates of righteousness to me, I enter into
them — I thank Jah.
20 This [is] the gate to Jehovah, the righteous enter
into it.
21 I thank You[S], for You[S] have answered me, and are to
me for salvation.
22 A stone the builders refused has become head of a
corner.
23 This has been from Jehovah, it [is] wonderful in our
eyes,
24 This [is] the day Jehovah has made, we rejoice and
are glad in it.
25 I beg You[S], O Jehovah, save, I pray You[S], I beg You[S],
O Jehovah, prosper, I pray You[S].
26 Blessed [is] he who is coming in the name of Jehovah,
we blessed you[P] from the house of Jehovah,
27 God [is] Jehovah, and He gives light to us, direct
you[P] the festal-sacrifice with cords, unto the horns of
the altar.
28 You[S] [are] my God, and I confess You[S], My God, I
exalt You[S].
29 Give you[P] thanks to Jehovah, for good, for to the
age, [is] His kindness!

Psalm 119

1 [Aleph.] O the happiness of those perfect in the way,
they are walking in the law of Jehovah,
2 O the happiness of those keeping His testimonies,
they seek Him with the whole heart.
3 Yes, they have not done iniquity, they have walked in
His ways.
4 You[S] have commanded us to keep Your[S] precepts
diligently,
5 O that my ways were prepared to keep Your[S] statutes,
6 Then I am not ashamed in my looking unto all Your[S]
commands.
7 I confess You[S] with uprightness of heart, in my learning
the judgments of Your[S] righteousness.
8 I keep Your[S] statutes, leave me not utterly!
9 [Beth.] With what does a young man purify his path?
To observe — according to Your[S] word.
10 With all my heart I have sought You[S], let me not err
from Your[S] commands.

11 I have hid Your[S] saying in my heart, that I sin not
before You[S].
12 Blessed [are] You[S], O Jehovah, teach me Your[S]
statutes.
13 I have recounted with my lips all the judgments of
Your[S] mouth.
14 I have joyed in the way of Your[S] testimonies, as over
all wealth.
15 I meditate in Your[S] precepts, and I behold Your[S] paths
attentively.
16 I delight myself in Your[S] statutes, I do not forget Your[S]
word.
17 [Gimel.] Confer benefits on Your[S] servant, I live, and
I keep Your[S] word.
18 Uncover my eyes, and I behold wonders out of Your[S]
law.
19 I [am] a sojourner on earth, hide not Your[S] commands
from me.
20 My soul has broken for desire unto Your[S] judgments
at all times.
21 You[S] have rebuked the cursed proud, who are erring
from Your[S] commands.
22 Remove reproach and contempt from me, for I have
kept Your[S] testimonies.
23 Princes also sat — they spoke against me, Your[S]
servant does meditate in Your[S] statutes,
24 Your[S] testimonies also [are] my delight, the men of
my counsel!
25 [Daleth.] My soul has clung to the dust, quicken me
according to Your[S] word.
26 I have recounted my ways, and You[S] answer me, teach
me Your[S] statutes,
27 Cause me to understand the way of Your[S] precepts,
and I meditate in Your[S] wonders.
28 My soul has dropped from affliction, establish me
according to Your[S] word.
29 Turn aside the way of falsehood from me and favor
me with Your[S] law.
30 I have chosen the way of faithfulness, I have
compared Your[S] judgments,
31 I have adhered to Your[S] testimonies, O Jehovah, put
me not to shame.
32 I run the way of Your[S] commands, for You[S] do enlarge
my heart!
33 [He.] Show me, O Jehovah, the way of Your[S] statutes,
and I keep it — [to] the end.
34 Cause me to understand, and I keep Your[S] law, and
observe it with the whole heart.
35 Cause me to tread in the path of Your[S] commands, for
I have delighted in it.
36 Incline my heart unto Your[S] testimonies, and not unto
dishonest gain.
37 Remove my eyes from seeing vanity, quicken You[S]
me in Your[S] way.
38 Establish Your[S] saying to Your[S] servant, that [is]
concerning Your[S] fear.
39 Remove my reproach that I have feared, for Your[S]
judgments [are] good.
40 Behold, I have longed for Your[S] precepts, quicken
You[S] me in Your[S] righteousness,
41 [Waw.] And Your[S] kindness does meet me, O Jehovah,
Your[S] salvation according to Your[S] saying.
42 And I answer him who is reproaching me a word, for
I have trusted in Your[S] word.
43 And You[S] take not utterly away the word of truth
from my mouth, because I have hoped for Your[S]
judgment.
44 And I keep Your[S] law continually, to the age and for
ever.
45 And I walk habitually in a broad place, for I have
sought Your[S] precepts.
46 And I speak of Your[S] testimonies before kings, and I
am not ashamed.
47 And I delight myself in Your[S] commands, that I have
loved,
48 And I lift up my hands unto Your[S] commands, that I
have loved, and I do meditate on Your[S] statutes!
49 [Zain.] Remember the word to Your[S] servant, on which
You[S] have caused me to hope.
50 This [is] my comfort in my affliction, that Your[S] saying
has quickened me.
51 The proud have utterly scorned me, I have not turned
aside from Your[S] law.
52 I remembered Your[S] judgments of old, O Jehovah,
and I comfort myself.
53 Horror has seized me, because of the wicked forsaking
Your[S] law.
54 Your[S] statutes have been songs to me, in the house
of my sojournings.
55 I have remembered Your[S] name in the night, O
Jehovah, and I do keep Your[S] law.
56 This has been to me, that I have kept Your[S] precepts!
57 [Cheth.] My portion [is] Jehovah; I have said — to
keep Your[S] words,
58 I appeased Your[S] face with the whole heart, favor me
according to Your[S] saying.
59 I have reckoned my ways, and turn back my feet unto
Your[S] testimonies.

60 I have made haste, and delayed not, to keep Your^{S}
commands.
61 Cords of the wicked have surrounded me, I have not
forgotten Your^{S} law.
62 At midnight I rise to give thanks to You^{S}, for the
judgments of Your^{S} righteousness.
63 I [am] a companion to all who fear You^{S}, and to those
keeping Your^{S} precepts.
64 Of Your^{S} kindness, O Jehovah, the earth is full, teach
You^{S} me Your^{S} statutes!
65 [Teth.] You^{S} did good with Your^{S} servant, O Jehovah,
according to Your^{S} word.
66 Teach me the goodness of reason and knowledge,
for I have believed in Your^{S} commands.
67 Before I am afflicted, I — I am erring, and now I have
kept Your^{S} saying.
68 You^{S} [are] good, and doing good, teach me Your^{S}
statutes.
69 The proud have forged falsehood against me, I keep
Your^{S} precepts with the whole heart.
70 Their heart has been dead as fat, I — I have delighted
in Your^{S} law.
71 Good for me that I have been afflicted, that I might
learn Your^{S} statutes.
72 The law of Your^{S} mouth [is] better to me than
thousands of gold and silver!
73 [Yod.] Your^{S} hands made me and establish me, cause
me to understand, and I learn Your^{S} commands.
74 Those fearing You^{S} see me and rejoice, because I
have hoped for Your^{S} word.
75 I have known, O Jehovah, that righteous [are] Your^{S}
judgments, and You^{S} have afflicted me [in]
faithfulness.
76 Let, I pray You^{S}, Your^{S} kindness be to comfort me,
according to Your^{S} saying to Your^{S} servant.
77 Your^{S} mercies do meet me, and I live, for Your^{S} law
[is] my delight.
78 Ashamed are the proud, for they dealt perversely
with me [with] falsehood. I meditate in Your^{S}
precepts.
79 Those fearing You^{S} turn back to me, and those
knowing Your^{S} testimonies.
80 My heart is perfect in Your^{S} statutes, so that I am not
ashamed.
81 [Kaph.] My soul has been consumed for Your^{S}
salvation, I have hoped for Your^{S} word.
82 My eyes have been consumed for Your^{S} word, saying,
'When does it comfort me?'
83 For I have been as a bottle in smoke, I have not
forgotten Your^{S} statutes.
84 How many [are] the days of Your^{S} servant? When do
You^{S} execute judgment against my pursuers?
85 The proud have dug pits for me, that [are] not
according to Your^{S} law.
86 All Your^{S} commands [are] faithfulness, they have
pursued me [with] falsehood, help You^{S} me.
87 They have almost consumed me on earth, and I — I
have not forsaken Your^{S} precepts.
88 Quicken You^{S} me according to Your^{S} kindness, and I
keep the testimony of Your^{S} mouth!
89 [Lamed.] To the age, O Jehovah, Your^{S} word is set up
in the heavens.
90 Your^{S} faithfulness to all generations, You^{S} did
establish earth, and it stands.
91 They have stood this day according to Your^{S}
ordinances, for the whole [are] Your^{S} servants.
92 Unless Your^{S} law [were] my delights, then had I
perished in my affliction.
93 To the age I forget not Your^{S} precepts, for You^{S} have
quickened me by them.
94 I [am] Yours^{S}, save You^{S} me, for I have sought Your^{S}
precepts.
95 Your^{S} wicked waited for me to destroy me, I
understand Your^{S} testimonies.
96 I have seen an end of all perfection, broad [is] Your^{S}
command — exceedingly!
97 [Mem.] O how I have loved Your^{S} law! It [is] my
meditation all the day.
98 Your^{S} command makes me wiser than my enemies, for
it [is] before me to the age.
99 I have acted wisely above all my teachers. For Your^{S}
testimonies [are] my meditation.
100 Above elders I understand more, for I have kept
Your^{S} precepts.
101 I restrained my feet from every evil path, so that I
keep Your^{S} word.
102 I turned not aside from Your^{S} judgments, for You^{S}
— You^{S} have directed me.
103 How sweet to my palate has been Your^{S} saying,
above honey to my mouth.
104 From Your^{S} precepts I have understanding, for that
reason I have hated every false path!
105 [Nun.] Your^{S} word [is] a lamp to my foot, and a light
to my path.
106 I have sworn, and I confirm [it], to keep the
judgments of Your^{S} righteousness.
107 I have been afflicted very much, O Jehovah, quicken
me, according to Your^{S} word.

108 Free-will-offerings of my mouth, accept, I pray You[S],
O Jehovah, and teach You[S] me Your[S] judgments.
109 My soul [is] in my hand continually, and I have not
forgotten Your[S] law.
110 The wicked have laid a snare for me, and I wandered
not from Your[S] precepts.
111 I have inherited Your[S] testimonies to the age, for
they [are] the joy of my heart.
112 I have inclined my heart to do Your[S] statutes, to the
age — [to] the end!
113 [Samech.] I have hated doubting ones, and I have
loved Your[S] law.
114 You[S] [are] My hiding place and my shield, for I have
hoped Your[S] word.
115 Turn aside from me, you[P] evil-doers, and I keep the
commands of my God.
116 Sustain me according to Your[S] saying, and I live,
and You[S] put me not to shame because of my hope.
117 Support You[S] me, and I am saved, and I look on
Your[S] statutes continually.
118 You[S] have trodden down all going astray from Your[S]
statutes, for falsehood [is] their deceit.
119 Worthless! You[S] have caused to cease all the wicked
of the earth; for that reason I have loved Your[S]
testimonies.
120 My flesh has trembled from Your[S] fear, and I have
been afraid from Your[S] judgments!
121 [Ain.] I have done judgment and righteousness,
leave me not to my oppressors.
122 Make sure Your[S] servant for good, let not the proud
oppress me.
123 My eyes have been consumed for Your[S] salvation.
And for the saying of Your[S] righteousness.
124 Do with Your[S] servant according to Your[S] kindness.
And teach You[S] me Your[S] statutes.
125 I [am] Your[S] servant — cause me to understand,
and I know Your[S] testimonies.
126 Time for Jehovah to work! they have made void
Your[S] law.
127 For that reason I have loved Your[S] commands above
gold — even fine gold.
128 For that reason I have declared all my appointments
wholly right, I have hated every path of falsehood!
129 [Pe.] Wonderful [are] Your[S] testimonies, for that
reason has my soul kept them.
130 The opening of Your[S] words enlightens, instructing
the simple.
131 I have opened my mouth, yes, I pant, for, for I have
longed Your[S] commands.
132 Look unto me, and favor me, as customary to those
loving Your[S] name.
133 Establish my steps by Your[S] saying, and any iniquity
does not rule over me.
134 Ransom me from the oppression of man, and I
observe Your[S] precepts,
135 Cause Your[S] face to shine on Your[S] servant, and
teach me Your[S] statutes.
136 Rivulets of waters have come down my eyes,
because they have not kept Your[S] law!
137 [Tzade.] Righteous [are] You[S], O Jehovah, and
upright [are] Your[S] judgments.
138 You[S] have appointed Your[S] testimonies, righteous
and exceeding faithful,
139 My zeal has cut me off, for my adversaries forgot
Your[S] words.
140 Tried [is] Your[S] saying exceedingly, and Your[S]
servant has loved it.
141 I [am] small, and despised, I have not forgotten Your[S]
precepts.
142 Your[S] righteousness [is] righteousness to the age,
and Your[S] law [is] truth.
143 Adversity and distress have found me, Your[S]
commands [are] my delights.
144 The righteousness of Your[S] testimonies [is] to cause
me to understand, and I live!
145 [Koph.] I have called with the whole heart, answer
me, O Jehovah, I keep Your[S] statutes,
146 I have called You[S], save You[S] me, and I do keep Your[S]
testimonies.
147 I have gone forward in the dawn, and I cry, I have
hoped for Your[S] word.
148 My eyes have gone before the watches, to meditate
in Your[S] saying.
149 My voice hear, according to Your[S] kindness,
Jehovah, quicken me according to Your[S] judgment.
150 My wicked pursuers have been near, they have been
far off from Your[S] law.
151 Near [are] You[S], O Jehovah, and all Your[S] commands
[are] truth.
152 I have known Your[S] testimonies of old, that You[S]
have founded them to the age!
153 [Resh.] See my affliction, and deliver You[S] me, for I
have not forgotten Your[S] law.
154 Plead my plea, and redeem me, quicken me according
to Your[S] saying.
155 Far from the wicked [is] salvation, for they have not
sought Your[S] statutes.
156 Your[S] mercies [are] many, O Jehovah, quicken me

according to Your^{S} judgments.
157 Many [are] my pursuers, and adversaries, I have not turned aside from Your^{S} testimonies.
158 I have seen treacherous ones, and grieve myself, because they have not kept Your^{S} saying.
159 See, for I have loved Your^{S} precepts, Jehovah, quicken me according to Your^{S} kindness.
160 The sum of Your^{S} word [is] truth, and every judgment of Your^{S} righteousness [is] to the age!
161 [Shin.] Princes have pursued me without cause, and because of Your^{S} words was my heart afraid.
162 I do rejoice concerning Your^{S} saying, as one finding abundant spoil.
163 I have hated falsehood, yes I abominate [it], I have loved Your^{S} law.
164 I have praised You^{S} seven [times] in a day, because of the judgments of Your^{S} righteousness.
165 Those loving Your^{S} law have abundant peace, and they have no stumbling-block.
166 I have waited for Your^{S} salvation, O Jehovah, and I have done Your^{S} commands.
167 My soul has kept Your^{S} testimonies, and I do love them exceedingly.
168 I have kept Your^{S} precepts and Your^{S} testimonies, for all my ways are before You^{S}!
169 [Taw.] My loud cry comes near before You^{S}, O Jehovah; according to Your^{S} word cause me to understand.
170 My supplication comes in before You^{S}, deliver You^{S} me according to Your^{S} saying.
171 My lips do utter praise, for You^{S} do teach me Your^{S} statutes.
172 My tongue does sing of Your^{S} saying, for all Your^{S} commands [are] righteous.
173 Your^{S} hand is for a help to me, for I have chosen Your^{S} commands.
174 I have longed for Your^{S} salvation, O Jehovah, and Your^{S} law [is] my delight.
175 My soul lives, and it does praise You^{S}, and Your^{S} judgments do help me.
176 I wandered as a lost sheep, seek Your^{S} servant, for I have not forgotten Your^{S} precepts!

Psalm 120

1 A Song of the Ascents. I have called unto Jehovah in my distress, and He answers me.
2 O Jehovah, deliver my soul from a lying lip, from a deceitful tongue!
3 What does He give to you^{S}? And what does He add to you^{S}? O deceitful tongue!
4 Sharp arrows of a mighty one, with broom-coals.
5 Woe to me, for I have inhabited Mesech, I have dwelt with tents of Kedar.
6 Too much has my soul dwelt with him who is hating peace.
7 I [am] peace, and when I speak they [are] for war!

Psalm 121

1 A Song of the Ascents. I lift up my eyes unto the hills, from where does my help come?
2 My help [is] from Jehovah, maker of heaven and earth,
3 He allows your^{S} foot not to be moved, your^{S} preserver slumbers not.
4 Behold, He slumbers not, nor sleeps, He who is preserving Israel.
5 Jehovah [is] your^{S} preserver, Jehovah [is] your^{S} shade on your^{S} right hand,
6 By day the sun does not afflict you^{S}, nor the moon by night.
7 Jehovah preserves you^{S} from all evil, He does preserve your^{S} soul.
8 Jehovah preserves your^{S} going out and your^{S} coming in, from this time forth even unto the age!

Psalm 122

1 A Song of the Ascents, by David. I have rejoiced in those saying to me, 'We go to the house of Jehovah.'
2 Our feet have been standing in your^{S} gates, O Jerusalem!
3 Jerusalem — the built one — [is] as a city that is joined together to itself.
4 For there have tribes gone up, tribes of Jah, companies of Israel, to give thanks to the name of Jehovah.
5 For there have sat thrones of judgment, thrones of the house of David.
6 Ask you^{P} the peace of Jerusalem, those loving you^{S} are at rest.
7 Peace is in your bulwark, rest in your^{S} high places,
8 For the sake of my brethren and my companions, let me speak, I pray you^{S}, 'Peace [be] in you.'
9 For the sake of the house of Jehovah our God, I seek good for you^{S}!

Psalm 123

1 A Song of the Ascents. I have lifted up my eyes unto You^{S}, O dweller in the heavens.
2 Behold, as eyes of men-servants [are] unto the hand of their masters, as eyes of a maid-servant [are] unto the hand of her mistress, so [are] our eyes unto Jehovah our God, till that He does favor us.
3 Favor us, O Jehovah, favor us, for greatly have we been filled with contempt,
4 Greatly has our soul been filled with the scorning of the easy ones, with the contempt of the arrogant!

Psalm 124

1 A Song of the Ascents, by David. Save [for] Jehovah — who has been for us, (pray, let Israel say),
2 save [for] Jehovah — who has been for us, in the rising up of man against us,
3 then they had swallowed us up alive, in the burning of their anger against us,
4 then the waters had overflowed us, the stream passed over our soul,
5 then the proud waters had passed over our soul.
6 Blessed [is] Jehovah who has not given us, a prey to their teeth.
7 Our soul has escaped as a bird from a snare of fowlers, the snare was broken, and we have escaped.
8 Our help [is] in the name of Jehovah, maker of the heavens and earth!

Psalm 125

1 A Song of the Ascents. Those trusting in Jehovah [are] as Mount Zion, it is not moved — it abides to the age.
2 Jerusalem! mountains [are] round about her, and Jehovah [is] round about His people, from this time forth even unto the age.
3 For the rod of wickedness rests not on the lot of the righteous, that the righteous put not forth their hands on iniquity.
4 Do good, O Jehovah, to the good, and to the upright in their hearts.
5 As to those turning [to] their crooked ways, Jehovah causes them to go with workers of iniquity. Peace on Israel!

Psalm 126

1 A Song of the Ascents. In Jehovah's turning back [to] the captivity of Zion, we have been as dreamers.
2 Then is our mouth filled [with] laughter, and our tongue [with] singing, then do they say among nations, 'Jehovah did great things with these.'
3 Jehovah did great things with us, we have been joyful.
4 Turn again, O Jehovah, [to] our captivity, as streams in the south.
5 Those sowing in tears, do reap with singing,
6 whoso goes on and weeps, bearing the basket of seed, surely comes in with singing, bearing his sheaves!

Psalm 127

1 A Song of the Ascents, by Solomon. If Jehovah does not build the house, its builders have labored at it in vain, if Jehovah does not watch a city, a watchman has waked in vain.
2 Vain for you^{P} who are rising early, who delay sitting, eating the bread of griefs, so He gives one sleep to His beloved.
3 Behold, sons [are] an inheritance of Jehovah, the fruit of the womb [is[a reward.
4 As arrows in the hand of a mighty one, so [are] the sons of the young men.
5 O the happiness of the man who has filled his quiver with them, they are not ashamed, for they speak with enemies in the gate!

Psalm 128

1 A Song of the Ascents. O the happiness of every one fearing Jehovah, who is walking in His ways.
2 You^{S} surely eat the labor of your^{S} hands, happy [are] you^{S}, and good [is] to you^{S}.
3 Your^{S} wife [is] as a fruitful vine in the sides of your^{S} house, your^{S} sons as olive plants around your^{S} table.
4 Behold, surely thus is the man blessed who is fearing Jehovah.
5 Jehovah does bless you^{S} out of Zion, look, then, on the good of Jerusalem, all the days of your^{S} life,
6 and see the sons of your^{S} sons! Peace on Israel!

Psalm 129

1 A Song of the Ascents. Often they distressed me from
my youth, pray, let Israel say:
2 Often they distressed me from my youth, yet they
have not prevailed over me.
3 Plowers have plowed over my back, they have made
their furrows long.
4 Jehovah [is] righteous, He has cut apart cords of the
wicked.
5 Confounded and do turn backward, all hating Zion.
6 They are as grass of the roofs, that withered before it
was drawn out,
7 that has not filled the hand of a reaper, and the bosom
of a binder of sheaves.
8 And the passers by have not said, 'The blessing of
Jehovah [is] on you^{P}, We blessed you^{P} in the Name of
Jehovah!'

Psalm 130

1 A Song of the Ascents. From depths I have called
You^{S}, Jehovah.
2 Lord, listen to my voice, Your^{S} ears are attentive to the
voice of my supplications.
3 If You^{S} do observe iniquities, O Lord, who does stand?
4 But with You^{S} [is] forgiveness, that You^{S} may be feared.
5 I hoped [for] Jehovah — my soul has hoped, and I
have waited for His word.
6 My soul [is] for the Lord, more than those watching
for morning, watching for morning!
7 Israel does wait on Jehovah, for with Jehovah [is]
kindness, and redemption [is] abundant with Him.
8 And He does redeem Israel from all his iniquities!

Psalm 131

1 A Song of the Ascents, by David. Jehovah, my heart
has not been arrogant, nor have my eyes been high, nor
have I walked in great things, and in things too
wonderful for me.
2 Have I not compared, and kept my soul silent, as a
weaned one by its mother? As a weaned one by me [is]
my soul.
3 Israel does wait on Jehovah, from this time forth, and
unto the age!

Psalm 132

1 A Song of the Ascents. Remember, Jehovah, for David,
all his afflictions.
2 Who has sworn to Jehovah. He has vowed to the
Mighty One of Jacob:
3 'If I enter into the tent of my house, if I go up on the
couch of my bed,
4 If I give sleep to my eyes, to my eyelids — slumber,
5 till I do find a place for Jehovah, Tabernacles for the
Mighty One of Jacob.
6 'Behold, we have heard it in Ephratah, we have found
it in the fields of the forest.
7 We come in to His tabernacles, we bow ourselves at
His footstool.
8 Arise, O Jehovah, to Your^{S} rest, You^{S}, and the ark of
Your^{S} strength,
9 Your^{S} priests do put on righteousness, and Your^{S} pious
ones cry aloud.
10 For the sake of David Your^{S} servant, turn not back
the face of Your^{S} anointed.
11 Jehovah has sworn truth to David, He turns not back
from it: of the fruit of your^{S} body, I set on the throne for
you^{S}.
12 If your^{S} sons keep My covenant, and My testimonies
that I teach them, their sons also for ever and ever, do
sit on the throne for you^{S}.
13 For Jehovah has fixed on Zion, He has desired [it]
for a seat to Himself,
14 This [is] My rest for ever and ever, here do I sit, for I
have desired it.
15 I greatly bless her provision, I satisfy her needy ones
[with] bread,
16 and I clothe her priests [with] salvation, and her pious
ones do sing aloud.
17 There I cause to spring up a horn for David, I have
arranged a lamp for My anointed.
18 His enemies I do clothe [with] shame, and his crown
does flourish upon him!

Psalm 133

1 A Song of the Ascents, by David. Behold, how good
and how pleasant the dwelling of brethren — even
together!
2 As the good oil on the head, coming down on the
beard, the beard of Aaron, that comes down on the skirt

of his robes,
3 as dew of Hermon — that comes down on hills of
Zion, for there Jehovah commanded the blessing — life
unto the age!

Psalm 134

1 A Song of the Ascents. Behold, bless Jehovah, all
servants of Jehovah, who are standing in the house of
Jehovah by night.
2 Lift up your[P] hands [in] the sanctuary, and bless you[P]
Jehovah.
3 Jehovah does bless you[S] out of Zion, the maker of the
heavens and earth!

Psalm 135

1 Praise you[P] Jah! Praise you[P] the name of Jehovah,
praise, you[P] servants of Jehovah,
2 who are standing in the house of Jehovah, in the courts
of the house of our God.
3 Praise you[P] Jah! for Jehovah [is] good, sing praise to
His name, for [it is] pleasant.
4 For Jah has chosen Jacob for Himself, Israel for His
peculiar treasure.
5 For I have known that Jehovah [is] great, yes, our
Lord [is] above all gods.
6 All that Jehovah pleased He has done, in the heavens
and in earth, in the seas and all deep places,
7 Causing vapors to ascend from the end of the earth,
lightnings for the rain He has made, bringing forth wind
from His treasures.
8 Who destroyed the first-born of Egypt, from man unto
beast.
9 He sent tokens and wonders into your[S] midst, O Egypt,
on Pharaoh and on all his servants.
10 Who destroyed many nations, and slew strong kings,
11 Even Sihon king of the Amorite, and Og king of
Bashan, and all kingdoms of Canaan.
12 And He gave their land an inheritance, an inheritance
to Israel His people,
13 O Jehovah, Your[S] name [is] to the age, O Jehovah,
Your[S] memorial to all generations.
14 For Jehovah does judge His people, and comforts
Himself for His servants.
15 The idols of the nations [are] silver and gold, work
of the hands of man.
16 They have a mouth, and they speak not, they have
eyes, and they see not,
17 they have ears, and they give not ear, nose — there
is no breath in their mouth!
18 Their makers are like them, every one who is trusting
in them.
19 O house of Israel, bless you[P] Jehovah, O house of
Aaron, bless you[P] Jehovah,
20 O house of Levi, bless you[P] Jehovah, those fearing
Jehovah, bless you[P] Jehovah.
21 Blessed [is] Jehovah from Zion, inhabiting Jerusalem
— praise you[P] Jah!

Psalm 136

1 Give you[P] thanks to Jehovah, for good, for His
kindness [is] to the age.
2 Give you[P] thanks to the God of gods, For His kindness
[is] to the age.
3 Give you[P] thanks to the Lord of lords, For His kindness
[is] to the age.
4 To Him doing great wonders by Himself alone, for His
kindness [is] to the age.
5 To Him making the heavens by understanding, for
His kindness [is] to the age.
6 To Him spreading the earth over the waters, for His
kindness [is] to the age.
7 To Him making great lights, for His kindness [is] to
the age.
8 The sun to rule by day, for His kindness [is] to the
age.
9 The moon and stars to rule by night, for His kindness
[is] to the age.
10 To Him afflicting Egypt in their first-born, for His
kindness [is] to the age.
11 And bringing forth Israel from their midst, for His
kindness [is] to the age.
12 By a strong hand, and a stretched-out-arm, for His
kindness [is] to the age.
13 To Him cutting the sea of Suph into parts, for His
kindness [is] to the age,
14 and caused Israel to pass through its midst, for His
kindness [is] to the age,
15 and shook out Pharaoh and his force in the sea of
Suph, for His kindness [is] to the age.
16 To Him leading His people in a wilderness, for His
kindness [is] to the age.
17 To Him destroying great kings, for His kindness [is]

to the age.
18 Yes, He does slay honorable kings, for His kindness
[is] to the age.
19 Even Sihon king of the Amorite, for His kindness [is]
to the age.
20 And Og king of Bashan, for His kindness [is] to the
age.
21 And He gave their land for inheritance, for His
kindness [is] to the age.
22 An inheritance to Israel His servant, for His kindness
[is] to the age.
23 Who in our lowliness has remembered us, for His
kindness [is] to the age.
24 And He delivers us from our adversaries, for His
kindness [is] to the age.
25 Giving food to all flesh, for His kindness [is] to the
age.
26 Give you^{P} thanks to the God of the heavens, for His
kindness [is] to the age!

Psalm 137

1 By rivers of Babylon — There we did sit, yes, we wept
when we remembered Zion.
2 We hung our harps on willows in its midst.
3 For there our captors asked us the words of a song,
and our spoilers — joy: 'Sing you^{P} to us of a song of
Zion.'
4 How do we sing the song of Jehovah, on the land of a
stranger?
5 If I forget you^{S}, O Jerusalem, my right hand forgets!
6 My tongue does adhere to my palate, if I do not
remember you^{S}, if I do not exalt Jerusalem above my chief
joy.
7 Remember, Jehovah, for the sons of Edom, the day of
Jerusalem, those saying, 'Raze, raze to its foundation!'
8 O daughter of Babylon, O destroyed one, O the
happiness of him who repays your^{S} deed to you, that
you^{S} have done to us.
9 O the happiness of him who does seize, and has
dashed your^{S} sucklings on the rock!

Psalm 138

1 By David. I confess You^{S}, with all my heart, I do praise
You^{S} before the gods.
2 I bow myself toward Your^{S} holy temple, and I confess
Your^{S} name, for Your^{S} kindness, and for Your^{S} truth, for
You^{S} have made Your^{S} saying great above all Your^{S} name.
3 In the day I called, when You^{S} do answer me, You^{S} do
strengthen me in my soul [with] strength.
4 O Jehovah, all kings of earth confess You^{S}, when they
have heard the sayings of Your^{S} mouth.
5 And they sing in the ways of Jehovah, for great [is]
the honor of Jehovah.
6 For high [is] Jehovah, and He sees the lowly, and He
knows the arrogant from afar.
7 If I walk in the midst of distress You^{S} quicken me, You^{S}
send forth Your^{S} hand against the anger of my enemies,
and Your^{S} right hand does save me.
8 Jehovah does perfect for me, O Jehovah, Your^{S}
kindness [is] to the age, let not fall the works of Your^{S}
hands!

Psalm 139

1 To the Overseer. — A Psalm by David. Jehovah, You^{S}
have searched me, and know.
2 You^{S} — You^{S} have known my sitting down, and my
rising up, You^{S} have attended to my thoughts from afar.
3 You^{S} have fanned my path and my couch, and have
been acquainted [with] all my ways.
4 For there is not a word in my tongue, behold, O
Jehovah, You^{S} have known it all!
5 Behind and before You^{S} have besieged me, and You^{S}
do place Your^{S} hand on me.
6 Knowledge too wonderful for me, it has been set on
high, I am not able for it.
7 Where do I go from Your^{S} Spirit? And where do I flee
from Your^{S} face?
8 If I ascend the heavens — there You^{S} [are], and spread
out a couch in Sheol, behold, You^{S}!
9 I take the wings of morning, I dwell in the uttermost
part of the sea,
10 Your^{S} hand does lead me there also, and Your^{S} right
hand does hold me.
11 And I say, 'Surely darkness bruises me, then night
[is] light to me.
12 Also darkness hides not from You^{S}, and night shines
as day, as [is] darkness so [is] light.
13 For You^{S} — You^{S} have possessed my reins, You^{S} do
cover me in my mother's belly.
14 I confess You^{S}, because that I have been
distinguished [with] wonders. Wonderful [are] Your^{S}
works, and my soul is knowing [it] well.

15 My substance was not hid from You^S, when I was made in secret, curiously worked in the lower part of earth.
16 Your^S eyes saw my unformed substance, and all of them are written on Your^S book, the days they were formed — and not one among them.
17 And how precious Your^S thoughts have been to me, O God, how great has been their sum!
18 I recount them! they are more than the sand, I have waked, and I am still with You^S.
19 Do You^S slay, O God, the wicked? Then, men of blood, turn aside from me!
20 Who exchange You^S for wickedness, lifted up to vanity [are] Your^S enemies.
21 Do not I hate, Jehovah, those hating You^S? And grieve myself with Your^S withstanders?
22 [With] perfect hatred I have hated them, enemies they have become to me.
23 Search me, O God, and know my heart, try me, and know my thoughts,
24 and see if a grievous way be in me, And lead me in a way age-during!

Psalm 140

1 To the Overseer. — A Psalm of David. Deliver me, O Jehovah, from an evil man, keep You^S me from one of violence.
2 Who have devised evils in the heart, all the day they assemble [for] wars.
3 They sharpened their tongue as a serpent, poison of an adder [is] under their lips. Selah.
4 Preserve me, Jehovah, from the hands of the wicked, keep You^S me from one of violence, who have devised to overthrow my steps.
5 The proud hid a snare for me — and cords, they spread a net by the side of the path, they have set snares for me. Selah.
6 I have said to Jehovah, ' You^S [are] my God, hear, Jehovah, the voice of my supplications.'
7 O Jehovah, my Lord, strength of my salvation, You^S have covered my head in the day of armor.
8 Grant not, O Jehovah, the desires of the wicked, bring not forth his wicked device, they are high. Selah.
9 The chief of my surrounders, the perverseness of their lips covers them.
10 They cause burning coals to fall on themselves, He does cast them into fire, into deep pits — they arise not.
11 A talkative man is not established in the earth, one of violence — evil hunts to overflowing.
12 I have known that Jehovah does execute the judgment of the afflicted, the judgment of the needy.
13 Only — the righteous give thanks to Your^S name, the upright do dwell with Your^S presence!

Psalm 141

1 A Psalm, by David. O Jehovah, I have called You^S, hurry to me, give ear [to] my voice when I call to You^S.
2 My prayer is prepared — incense before You^S, the lifting up of my hands — the evening present.
3 Set, O Jehovah, a watch for my mouth, watch You^S over the door of my lips.
4 Incline not my heart to an evil thing, to habitually do actions in wickedness, with men working iniquity, yes, I eat not of their pleasant things.
5 The righteous do beat me [in] kindness. And do reprove me, my head disallows not oil of the head, for still my prayer [is] about their vexations.
6 Their judges have been released by the sides of a rock, and they have heard my sayings, for they have been pleasant.
7 As one tilling and ripping up in the land, have our bones been scattered at the command of Saul.
8 But to You^S, O Jehovah, my Lord, [are] my eyes, I have trusted in You^S, make not my soul bare.
9 Keep me from the gin they laid for me, even snares of workers of iniquity.
10 The wicked fall in their nets together, till I pass over!

Psalm 142

1 An Instruction of David, a prayer when he is in the cave. My voice [is] unto Jehovah, I cry, my voice [is] unto Jehovah, I entreat grace.
2 I pour forth my meditation before Him, I declare my distress before Him.
3 When my spirit has been feeble in me, then You^S have known my path; in the way [in] which I walk, they have hid a snare for me.
4 Looking on the right hand — and seeing, and I have none recognizing; refuge has perished from me, there is none inquiring for my soul.
5 I have cried unto You^S, O Jehovah, I have said, 'You^S [are] my refuge, my portion in the land of the living.'

6 Attend You[S] unto my loud cry, for I have become very low, deliver You[S] me from my pursuers, for they have been stronger than I.
7 Bring forth my soul from prison to confess Your[S] name, the righteous do compass me about, when You[S] confer benefits upon me!

Psalm 143

1 A Psalm of David. O Jehovah, hear my prayer, give ear unto my supplications, answer me in Your[S] faithfulness — in Your[S] righteousness.
2 And enter not into judgment with Your[S] servant, for no one living is justified before You[S].
3 For an enemy has pursued my soul, he has bruised my life to the earth, he has caused me to dwell in dark places, as the dead of old.
4 And my spirit in me is become feeble, within me is my heart become desolate.
5 I have remembered days of old, I have meditated on all Your[S] acts, I contemplate on the work of Your[S] hand.
6 I have spread forth my hands unto You[S], my soul [is] as a weary land for You[S]. Selah.
7 Hurry, answer me, O Jehovah, my spirit has been consumed, hide not You[S] Your[S] face from me, or I have been compared with those going down [to] the pit.
8 Cause me to hear Your[S] kindness in the morning, for I have trusted in You[S], cause me to know the way that I go, for I have lifted up my soul unto You[S].
9 Deliver me from my enemies, O Jehovah, near You[S] I am covered.
10 Teach me to do Your[S] good pleasure, for You[S] [are] my God — Your[S] Spirit [is] good, lead me into a land of uprightness.
11 For Your[S] name's sake O Jehovah, You[S] do quicken me, in Your[S] righteousness, You[S] bring my soul out from distress,
12 and cut off my enemies in Your[S] kindness, and have destroyed all the adversaries of my soul, for I [am] Your[S] servant!

Psalm 144

1 By David. Blessed [is] Jehovah my rock, who is teaching my hands for war, my fingers for battle.
2 My kind one, and my bulwark, my tower, and my deliverer, my shield, and in whom I have trusted, who is subduing my people under me!
3 Jehovah, what [is] man that You[S] know him? Son of man, that You[S] esteem him?
4 Man has been like to vanity, his days [are] as a shadow passing by.
5 Jehovah, incline Your[S] heavens and come down, strike against mountains, and they smoke.
6 Send forth lightning, and scatter them, send forth Your[S] arrows, and trouble them,
7 send forth Your[S] hand from on high, free me, and deliver me from many waters, from the hand of sons of a stranger,
8 because their mouth has spoken vanity, and their right hand [is] a right hand of falsehood.
9 O God, I sing a new song to You[S], I sing praise to You[S] on a psaltery of ten strings.
10 Who is giving deliverance to kings, who is freeing His servant David from the sword of evil.
11 Free me, and deliver me from the hand of sons of a stranger, because their mouth has spoken vanity, and their right hand [is] a right hand of falsehood,
12 because our sons [are] as plants, becoming great in their youth, our daughters as hewn stones, polished — the likeness of a palace,
13 Our storehouses [are] full, bringing out from kind to kind, our flocks are bringing forth thousands, ten thousands in our out-places,
14 our oxen are carrying, there is no breach, and there is no outgoing, and there is no crying in our broad places.
15 O the happiness of the people that is thus, O the happiness of the people whose God [is] Jehovah!

Psalm 145

1 Praise by David. I exalt You[S], my God, O king, and bless Your[S] name to the age and for ever.
2 Every day do I bless You[S], and praise Your[S] name to the age and for ever.
3 Great [is] Jehovah, and praised greatly, and of His greatness there is no searching.
4 Generation to generation praises Your[S] works, and they declare Your[S] mighty acts.
5 The honor — the glory of Your[S] majesty, and I declare the matters of Your[S] wonders.
6 And they tell the strength of Your[S] fearful acts, and I recount Your[S] greatness.
7 They send forth the memorial of the abundance of Your[S] goodness. And they sing Your[S] righteousness.

8 Gracious and merciful [is] Jehovah, slow to anger, and great in kindness.
9 Jehovah [is] good to all, and His mercies [are] over all His works.
10 Confess You[S] O Jehovah, do all Your[S] works, and Your[S] saints do bless You[S].
11 They tell the honor of Your[S] kingdom, and they speak [of] Your[S] might,
12 To make known His mighty acts to sons of men, the honor of the majesty of His kingdom.
13 Your[S] kingdom [is] a kingdom of all ages, and Your[S] dominion [is] in all generations.
14 Jehovah is supporting all who are falling, and raising up all who are bowed down.
15 The eyes of all do look unto You[S], and You[S] are giving to them their food in its season,
16 opening Your[S] hand, and satisfying the desire of every living thing.
17 Righteous [is] Jehovah in all His ways, and kind in all His works.
18 Near [is] Jehovah to all those calling Him, to all who call Him in truth.
19 He does the desire of those fearing Him, and He hears their cry, and saves them.
20 Jehovah preserves all those loving Him, and He destroys all the wicked.
21 My mouth speaks the praise of Jehovah, and all flesh does bless His holy name, to the age and for ever!

Psalm 146

1 Praise you[P] Jah! Praise, O my soul, Jehovah.
2 I praise Jehovah during my life, I sing praise to my God while I exist.
3 Trust not in princes — in a son of man, for he has no deliverance.
4 His spirit goes forth, he returns to his earth, his thoughts have perished in that day.
5 O the happiness of him who has the God of Jacob for his help, his hope [is] on Jehovah his God,
6 making the heavens and earth, the sea and all that [is] in them, who is keeping truth to the age,
7 doing judgment for the oppressed, giving bread to the hungry.
8 Jehovah is loosing the prisoners, Jehovah is opening (the eyes of) the blind, Jehovah is raising the bowed down, Jehovah is loving the righteous,
9 Jehovah is preserving the strangers, He causes the fatherless and widow to stand, and He turns the way of the wicked upside down.
10 Jehovah does reign to the age, your[S] God, O Zion, to generation and generation, praise you[P] Jah!

Psalm 147

1 Praise you[P] Jah! For [it is] good to praise our God, for pleasant — comely [is] praise.
2 Jehovah [is] building Jerusalem, He gathers the driven away of Israel.
3 Who is giving healing to the broken of heart, and is binding up their griefs.
4 Appointing the number of the stars, He gives names to all them.
5 Great [is] our Lord, and abundant in power, there is no narration of His understanding.
6 Jehovah is causing the meek to stand, making the wicked low unto the earth.
7 Answer you[P] to Jehovah with thanksgiving, sing you[P] to our God with a harp.
8 Who is covering the heavens with clouds, who is preparing rain for the earth, who is causing grass to spring up [on] mountains,
9 giving to the beast its food, to the young of the ravens that call.
10 Not in the might of the horse does He delight, not in the legs of a man is He pleased.
11 Jehovah is pleased with those fearing Him, with those waiting for His kindness.
12 Glorify, O Jerusalem, Jehovah, praise your[S] God, O Zion.
13 For He did strengthen the bars of your[S] gates, He has blessed your[S] sons in your midst.
14 Who is making your[S] border peace, He satisfies you[S] [with] the fat of wheat.
15 Who is sending forth His saying [on] earth, His word does run very speedily.
16 Who is giving snow like wool, He scatters hoar-frost as ashes.
17 Casting forth His ice like morsels, who does stand before His cold?
18 He sends forth His word and melts them, He causes His wind to blow — the waters flow.
19 Declaring His words to Jacob, His statutes and His judgments to Israel.
20 He has not done so to any nation, as to judgments, they have not known them. Praise you[P] Jah!

Psalm 148

1 Praise you[P] Jah! Praise you[P] Jehovah from the heavens, praise you[P] Him in high places.
2 Praise you[P] Him, all His messengers, praise you[P] Him, all His hosts.
3 Praise you[P] Him, sun and moon, praise you[P] Him, all stars of light.
4 Praise you[P] Him, heavens of heavens, and you[P] waters that are above the heavens.
5 They do praise the name of Jehovah, for He commanded, and they were created.
6 And He establishes them for ever to the age, He gave a statute, and they pass not over.
7 Praise you[P] Jehovah from the earth, dragons and all deeps,
8 fire and hail, snow and vapor, whirlwind doing His word;
9 the mountains and all heights, fruit tree, and all cedars,
10 the wild beast, and all cattle, creeping thing, and winged bird,
11 kings of earth, and all peoples, chiefs, and all judges of earth,
12 young men, and also maidens, aged men, with youths,
13 they praise the name of Jehovah, for His name alone has been set on high, His honor [is] above earth and heavens.
14 And He exalts the horn of His people, the praise of all His saints, of the sons of Israel, a people near Him. Praise you[P] Jah!

Psalm 149

1 Praise you[P] Jah! Sing you[P] a new song to Jehovah, His praise in an assembly of saints.
2 Israel does rejoice in his Maker, sons of Zion do joy in their king.
3 They praise His name in a dance, sing praise to Him with timbrel and harp.
4 For Jehovah is pleased with His people, He beautifies the humble with salvation.
5 Saints do exult in honor, they sing aloud on their beds.
6 The exaltation of God [is] in their throat, and a two-edged sword in their hand.
7 To do vengeance among nations, punishments among the peoples.
8 To bind their kings with chains, and their honored ones with fetters of iron,
9 To do among them the judgment written, an honor it [is] for all his saints. Praise you[P] Jah!

Psalm 150

1 Praise you[P] Jah! Praise you[P] God in His holy place, praise Him in the expanse of His strength.
2 Praise Him in His mighty acts, praise Him according to the abundance of His greatness.
3 Praise Him with blowing of trumpet, praise Him with psaltery and harp.
4 Praise Him with timbrel and dance, praise Him with stringed instruments and organ.
5 Praise Him with cymbals of sounding, praise Him with cymbals of shouting.
6 All that does breathe does praise Jah! Praise you[P] Jah!

The Book Of
PROVERBS

Chapter 1

1 Proverbs of Solomon, son of David, king of Israel:
2 For knowing wisdom and instruction, for understanding
sayings of intelligence,
3 for receiving the instruction of wisdom, righteousness,
judgment, and uprightness,
4 for giving to simple ones — prudence, to a youth —
knowledge and discretion.
5 (The wise does hear and increases learning, and the
intelligent does obtain counsels.)
6 For understanding a proverb and its sweetness, words
of the wise and their acute sayings.
7 Fear of Jehovah [is] a beginning of knowledge, fools
have despised wisdom and instruction!
8 Hear, my son, the instruction of your^{S} father, and leave
not the law of your^{S} mother,
9 for they [are] a graceful wreath to your^{S} head, and
chains to your^{S} neck.
10 My son, be not willing if sinners entice you^{S}.
11 If they say, 'Come with us, we lay wait for blood, we
watch secretly for the innocent without cause,
12 we swallow them as Sheol — alive, and whole — as
those going down [to] the pit,
13 we find every precious substance, we fill our houses
[with] spoil,
14 you^{S} do cast your lot among us, one purse is — to
all of us.'
15 My son! go not in the way with them, withhold your^{S}
foot from their path,
16 for their feet do run to evil, and they hurry to shed
blood.
17 Surely in vain is the net spread out before the eyes
of any bird.
18 And they lay wait for their own blood, they watch
secretly for their own lives.
19 So [are] the paths of every gainer of dishonest gain,
it takes the life of its owners.
20 Wisdom cries aloud in an out-place, she gives forth
her voice in broad places,
21 At the head of the multitudes she calls, in the
openings of the gates, in the city she says her sayings:
22 'Till when, you^{P} simple, do you^{P} love simplicity? And
have scorners desired their scorning? And do fools hate
knowledge?
23 Turn back at my reproof, behold, I pour forth my
spirit to you^{P}, I make my words known with you^{P}.
24 Because I have called, and you^{P} refuse, I stretched
out my hand, and none is attending,
25 and you^{P} slight all my counsel, and you^{P} have not
desired my reproof.
26 I also do laugh in your^{P} calamity, I deride when your^{P}
fear comes,
27 when your^{P} fear comes as destruction, and your^{P}
calamity does come as a hurricane, when adversity and
distress come on you^{P}.
28 Then they call me, and I do not answer, they seek me
earnestly, and find me not.
29 Because that they have hated knowledge, and have
not chosen the fear of Jehovah.
30 They have not consented to my counsel, they have
despised all my reproof,
31 and they eat of the fruit of their way, and they are
filled from their own counsels.
32 For the turning of the simple slays them, and the
security of the foolish destroys them.
33 And whoso is listening to me dwells confidently, and
[is] quiet from fear of evil!'

Chapter 2

1 My son, if you^{S} do accept my sayings, and do lay up
my commands with you^{S},
2 to cause your^{S} ear to attend to wisdom, you^{S} incline
your heart to understanding,
3 for, if you^{S} call for intelligence, your^{S} voice gives forth
for understanding,
4 if you^{S} do seek her as silver, and search for her as hid
treasures,
5 then you^{S} understand fear of Jehovah, and you^{S} find

knowledge of God.

6 For Jehovah gives wisdom, from His mouth knowledge and understanding.

7 Even to lay up substance for the upright, a shield for those walking uprightly.

8 To keep the paths of judgment, and He preserves the way of His saints.

9 Then you[S] understand righteousness, and judgment, and uprightness — every good path.

10 For wisdom comes into your heart, and knowledge to your soul is pleasant,

11 thoughtfulness does watch over you[S], understanding does keep you[S],

12 to deliver you[S] from an evil way, from any speaking perverse things,

13 who are forsaking paths of uprightness, to walk in ways of darkness,

14 who are rejoicing to do evil, they delight in perverseness of the wicked,

15 whose paths [are] crooked, yes, they are perverted in their ways.

16 To deliver you[S] from the strange woman, from the stranger who has made her sayings smooth,

17 who is forsaking the guide of her youth, and has forgotten the covenant of her God.

18 For her house has inclined unto death, and her paths unto Rephaim.

19 None going in unto her turn back, nor do they reach the paths of life.

20 That you[S] do go in the way of the good, and do keep the paths of the righteous.

21 For the upright do inhabit the earth, and the perfect are left in it,

22 And the wicked are cut off from the earth, and treacherous dealers plucked out of it!

Chapter 3

1 My son! forget not my law, and let your[S] heart keep my commands,

2 for length of days and years, they do add life and peace to you[S].

3 Let not kindness and truth forsake you[S], bind them on your[S] neck, write them on the tablet of your[S] heart,

4 and find grace and good understanding in the eyes of God and man.

5 Trust unto Jehovah with all your[S] heart, and lean not unto your[S] own understanding.

6 Know you[S] Him in all your[S] ways, and He does make your[S] paths straight.

7 Be not wise in your[S] own eyes, fear Jehovah, and turn aside from evil.

8 It is healing to your[S] navel, and moistening to your[S] bones.

9 Honor Jehovah from your[S] substance, and from the beginning of all your[S] increase;

10 and filled are your[S] barns [with] plenty, and your[S] presses break forth [with] new wine.

11 My son, despise not chastisement of Jehovah, and be not vexed with His reproof,

12 for whom Jehovah loves He reproves, even as a father the son He is pleased with.

13 O the happiness of a man [who] has found wisdom, and of a man [who] brings forth understanding.

14 For better [is] her merchandise than the merchandise of silver, and than gold — her increase.

15 She [is] precious above rubies, and all your[S] pleasures are not comparable to her.

16 Length of days [is] in her right hand, in her left [are] wealth and honor.

17 Her ways [are] ways of pleasantness, and all her paths [are] peace.

18 A tree of life she [is] to those laying hold on her, and whoso is retaining her [is] happy.

19 Jehovah did found the earth by wisdom, He prepared the heavens by understanding.

20 By His knowledge depths have been rent, and clouds do drop dew.

21 My son! let them not turn from your[S] eyes, keep you[S] wisdom and thoughtfulness,

22 and they are life to your[S] soul, and grace to your[S] neck.

23 Then you[S] go your[S] way confidently, and your[S] foot does not stumble.

24 If you[S] lie down, you[S] are not afraid, yes, you[S] have lain down, and sweet has been your[S] sleep.

25 Be not afraid of sudden fear, and of the desolation of the wicked when it comes.

26 For Jehovah is at your[S] side, and He has kept your[S] foot from capture.

27 Withhold not good from its owners, when your[S] hand [is] toward God to do [it].

28 Say you[S] not to your[S] friend, 'Go, and return, and tomorrow I give,' And substance with you[S].

29 Devise not evil against your[S] neighbor, and he sitting confidently with you[S].

30 Strive not with a man without cause, if he have not

done you[S] evil.
31 Be not envious of a man of violence, nor fix you[S] on
any of his ways.
32 For the perverted [is] an abomination to Jehovah,
and His secret counsel [is] with the upright.
33 The curse of Jehovah [is] in the house of the wicked.
And He blesses the habitation of the righteous.
34 If He does scorn the scorners, yet He does give grace
to the humble.
35 The wise do inherit honor, and fools are bearing away
shame!

Chapter 4

1 Hear, you[P] sons, the instruction of a father, and give
attention to know understanding.
2 For good learning I have given to you[P], forsake not
my law.
3 For, I have been a son to my father — tender, and an
only one before my mother.
4 And he directs me, and he says to me: 'Let your[S] heart
retain my words, keep my commands, and live.
5 Get wisdom, get understanding, do not forget, nor
turn away from the sayings of my mouth.
6 Forsake her not, and she does preserve you[S], love
her, and she does keep you[S].
7 The first thing [is] wisdom — get wisdom, and with all
your[S] getting get understanding.
8 Exalt her, and she does lift you[S] up, she honors you[S],
when you do embrace her.
9 She gives a wreath of grace to your[S] head, she does
give you[S] a crown of beauty freely.
10 Hear, my son, and receive my sayings, and years of
life [are] multiplied to you[S].
11 I have directed you[S] in a way of wisdom, I have
caused you[S] to tread in paths of uprightness.
12 In your[S] walking your[S] step is not confined, and if
you[S] run, you[S] stumble not.
13 Lay hold on instruction, do not desist, keep her, for
she [is] your[S] life.
14 Enter not into the path of the wicked, and be not
happy in a way of evil doers.
15 Avoid it, pass not over into it, turn aside from it, and
pass on.
16 For they sleep not if they do not evil, and their sleep
has been taken violently away, if they cause not [some]
to stumble.
17 For they have eaten bread of wickedness, and they
drink wine of violence.
18 And the path of the righteous [is] as a shining light,
going and brightening till the day is established,
19 the way of the wicked [is] as darkness, they have
not known at what they stumble.
20 My son, give attention to my words, incline your[S]
ear to my sayings,
21 let them not turn aside from your[S] eyes, preserve
them in the midst of your[S] heart.
22 For they [are] life to those finding them, and healing
to all their flesh.
23 Keep your[S] heart above every charge, for out of it
[are] the outgoings of life.
24 Turn aside a perverse mouth from you[S], and put from
you[S] far from you[S],
25 your[S] eyes do look straightforward, and your[S] eyelids
look straight before you[S].
26 Ponder you[S] the path of your[S] feet, and all your[S] ways
[are] established.
27 Incline not [to] the right or to the left, turn aside your[S]
foot from evil!

Chapter 5

1 My son! give attention to my wisdom, incline your[S]
ear to my understanding,
2 to observe thoughtfulness, and your[S] lips do keep
knowledge.
3 For the lips of a strange woman drop honey, and her
mouth [is] smoother than oil,
4 and her latter end [is] bitter as wormwood, sharp as a
sword [with] mouths.
5 Her feet are going down to death, Sheol take hold of
do her steps.
6 The path of life — for fear that you[S] ponder, moved
have her paths — you[S] know not.
7 And now, you[P] sons, listen to me, and turn not from
sayings of my mouth.
8 Keep your[S] way far from off her, and come not near
unto the opening of her house,
9 for fear that you[S] give your[S] honor to others, and your[S]
years to the fierce,
10 for fear that strangers be filled [with] your[S] power,
and your[S] labors in the house of a stranger,
11 and you[S] have howled in your[S] latter end, in the
consumption of your[S] flesh and your[S] food,
12 and have said, 'How I have hated instruction, and
my heart has despised reproof,

13 and I have not listened to the voice of my directors, and have not inclined my ear to my teachers.
14 As a little thing I have been all evil, in the midst of an assembly and a company.
15 Drink waters out of your[S] own cistern, even flowing ones out of your[S] own well.
16 Let your[S] fountains be scattered abroad, in broad places rivulets of waters.
17 Let them be to you[S] for yourself[S], and not to strangers with you[S].
18 Let your[S] fountain be blessed, and rejoice because of the wife of your[S] youth,
19 a hind of loves, and a roe of grace! Let her loves satisfy you[S] at all times, magnify yourself[S] in her love continually.
20 And why do you[S] magnify yourself[S], my son, with a stranger? And embrace the bosom of a strange woman?
21 For over-against the eyes of Jehovah are the ways of each, and He is pondering all his paths.
22 His own iniquities do capture the wicked, and he is held with the ropes of his sin.
23 He dies without instruction, and magnifies himself in the abundance of his folly!

Chapter 6

1 My son! if you[S] have been surety for your[S] friend, have stricken your[S] hand for a stranger,
2 have been snared with sayings of your[S] mouth, have been captured with sayings of your[S] mouth,
3 do this now, my son, and be delivered, for you[S] have come into the hand of your[S] friend. Go, trample on yourself[S], and strengthen your[S] friend,
4 give not sleep to your[S] eyes, and slumber to your[S] eyelids,
5 be delivered as a roe from the hand, and as a bird from the hand of a fowler.
6 Go unto the ant, O slothful one, see her ways and be wise;
7 which has not captain, overseer, and ruler,
8 she does prepare her bread in summer, she has gathered her food in harvest.
9 Till when, O slothful one, do you[S] lie? When do you[S] arise from your[S] sleep?
10 A little sleep, a little slumber, a little clasping of the hands to rest,
11 and your[S] poverty has come as a traveler, and your[S] want as an armed man.
12 A man of worthlessness, a man of iniquity, walking [with] perverseness of mouth,
13 winking with his eyes, speaking with his feet, directing with his fingers,
14 perverseness [is] in his heart, devising evil at all times, he sends forth contentions.
15 For that reason suddenly comes his calamity, instantly he is broken — and no healing.
16 These six Jehovah has hated, yes, seven [are] abominations to His soul.
17 Eyes high — tongues false — and hands shedding innocent blood —
18 a heart devising thoughts of vanity — feet hurrying to run to evil —
19 a false witness [who] does breathe out lies — and one sending forth contentions between brethren.
20 Keep, my son, the command of your[S] father, and leave not the law of your[S] mother.
21 Bind them on your[S] heart continually, tie them on your[S] neck.
22 In your[S] going up and down, it leads you[S], in your[S] lying down, it watches over you[S], and you[S] have awaked — it talks [with] you[S].
23 For a lamp [is] the command, and the law a light, and a way of life [are] reproofs of instruction,
24 to preserve you[S] from an evil woman, from the flattery of the tongue of a strange woman.
25 Desire not her beauty in your[S] heart, and let her not take you[S] with her eyelids.
26 For a harlot consumes unto a cake of bread, and an adulteress hunts the precious soul.
27 Does a man take fire into his bosom, and are his garments not burnt?
28 Does a man walk on the hot coals, and are his feet not scorched?
29 So [is] he who has gone in unto the wife of his neighbor, none who does touch her is innocent.
30 They do not despise the thief, when he steals to fill his soul when he is hungry,
31 and being found he repays sevenfold, he gives all the substance of his house.
32 He who commits adultery [with] a woman lacks heart, he who does it is destroying his soul.
33 He does find a stroke and shame, and his reproach is not wiped away,
34 for jealousy [is] the fury of a man, and he does not spare in a day of vengeance.
35 He accepts not the appearance of any atonement, yes, he does not consent, though you[S] do multiply bribes!

Chapter 7

1 My son! keep my sayings, and lay up my commands with you[S].
2 Keep my commands, and live, and my law as the pupil of your[S] eye.
3 Bind them on your[S] fingers, write them on the tablet of your[S] heart.
4 Say to wisdom, ' You[S] [are] my sister.' And cry to understanding, 'Kinswoman!'
5 To preserve you[S] from a strange woman, from a stranger who has made her sayings smooth.
6 For, at a window of my house, I have looked out through my casement,
7 and I do see among the simple ones, I discern among the sons, a young man lacking understanding,
8 passing on in the street, near her corner, and he does step the way [to] her house,
9 in the twilight — in the evening of day, in the darkness of night and blackness.
10 And, behold, a woman to meet him — (a harlot's dress, and watchful of heart,
11 she [is] noisy, and stubborn, her feet rest not in her house.
12 Now in an out-place, now in broad places, and near every corner she lies in wait) —
13 And she laid hold on him, and kissed him, she has hardened her face, and says to him,
14 'Sacrifices of peace-offerings [are] by me, today I have completed my vows.
15 For that reason I have come forth to meet you[S], to seek your[S] face earnestly, and I find you[S].
16 I decked my couch [with] ornamental coverings, carved works — cotton of Egypt.
17 I sprinkled my bed — myrrh, aloes, and cinnamon.
18 Come, we are filled [with] loves till the morning, we delight ourselves in loves.
19 For the man is not in his house, he has gone on a long journey.
20 He has taken a bag of money in his hand, at the day of the new moon he comes to his house.'
21 She turns him aside with the abundance of her speech, she forces him with the flattery of her lips.
22 He is going after her straightway, he comes as an ox unto the slaughter, and as a fetter unto the chastisement of a fool,
23 till an arrow does split his liver, as a bird has hurried unto a snare, and has not known that it [is] for its life.
24 And now, you[P] sons, listen to me, and give attention to sayings of my mouth.
25 Let not your[S] heart turn unto her ways, do not wander in her paths,
26 for many [are] the wounded she caused to fall, and mighty [are] all her slain ones.
27 The ways of Sheol — her house, going down unto inner chambers of death!

Chapter 8

1 Does not wisdom call? And understanding give forth her voice?
2 At the head of high places by the way, between the paths she has stood,
3 at the side of the gates, at the mouth of the city, the entrance of the openings, she cries aloud,
4 'Unto you[P], O men, I call, and my voice [is] unto the sons of men.
5 Understand, you[P] simple ones, prudence, and you[P] fools, understand the heart,
6 listen, for I speak noble things, and the opening of my lips [is] uprightness.
7 For my mouth does utter truth, and wickedness [is] an abomination to my lips.
8 In righteousness [are] all the sayings of my mouth, nothing in them is obstinate and perverse.
9 All of them [are] plain to the intelligent, and upright to those finding knowledge.
10 Receive my instruction, and not silver, and knowledge rather than choice gold.
11 For wisdom [is] better than rubies, yes, all delights are not comparable with it.
12 I, wisdom, have dwelt with prudence, and I find out a knowledge of devices.
13 The fear of Jehovah [is] to hate evil; pride, and arrogance, and an evil way, and a obstinate mouth, I have hated.
14 Mine [is] counsel and substance, I [am] understanding, I have might.
15 By me kings reign, and princes decree righteousness,
16 By me do chiefs rule, and nobles, all judges of the earth.
17 I love those loving me, and those seeking me earnestly do find me.
18 Wealth and honor [are] with me, lasting substance and righteousness.
19 My fruit [is] better than gold, even fine gold, and my

increase than choice silver.
20 I cause to walk in a path of righteousness, in midst
of paths of judgment,
21 to cause my lovers to inherit substance, yes, I fill
their treasures.
22 Jehovah possessed me — the beginning of His way,
before His works since then.
23 From the age I was anointed, from the first, from
former states of the earth.
24 In there being no depths, I was brought forth, in there
being no fountains heavy [with] waters,
25 Before mountains were sunk, before heights, I was
brought forth.
26 While He had not made the earth, and out-places,
and the top of the dusts of the world.
27 In His preparing the heavens I [am] there, in His
decreeing a circle on the face of the deep,
28 in His strengthening clouds above, in His making
strong fountains of the deep,
29 in His setting for the sea its limit, and the waters
transgress not His command, in His decreeing the
foundations of earth,
30 then I am near Him, a workman, and I am a delight —
day by day. Rejoicing before Him at all times,
31 rejoicing in the habitable part of His earth, and my
delights [are] with the sons of men.
32 And now, you[P] sons, listen to me, yes, happy are
they who keep my ways.
33 Hear instruction, and be wise, and slight not.
34 O the happiness of the man listening to me, to watch
at my doors day by day, to watch at the door-posts of
my entrance.
35 For whoso is finding me, has found life, and brings
out good-will from Jehovah.
36 And whoso is missing me, is wronging his soul, all
hating me have loved death!

Chapter 9

1 Wisdom has built her house, she has hewn out her
pillars — seven.
2 She has slaughtered her slaughter, she has mingled
her wine, yes, she has arranged her table.
3 She has sent forth her damsels, she cries on the tops
of the high places of the city:
4 'Who [is] simple? let him turn aside here.' Whoso lacks
heart: she has said to him,
5 'Come, eat of my bread, and drink of the wine I have
mingled.
6 Forsake you[P], the simple, and live, and be happy in
the way of understanding.
7 The instructor of a scorner is receiving for it — shame,
and a reprover of the wicked — his blemish.
8 Reprove not a scorner, for fear that he hate you, give
reproof to the wise, and he loves you[S].
9 Give to the wise, and he is wiser still, make known to
the righteous, and he increases learning.
10 The commencement of wisdom [is] the fear of
Jehovah, and a knowledge of the Holy Ones [is]
understanding.
11 For your[S] days do multiply by me, and years of life
are added to you[S].
12 If you[S] have been wise, you[S] have been wise for
yourself[S], and you[S] have scorned — yourself[S] bears [it].
13 A foolish woman [is] noisy, simple, and has not
known what.
14 And she has sat at the opening of her house, on a
throne — the high places of the city,
15 to call to those passing by the way, who are going
straight [on] their paths.
16 'Who [is] simple? let him turn aside here.' And whoso
lacks heart — she said to him,
17 'Stolen waters are sweet, and hidden bread is
pleasant.'
18 And he has not known that Rephaim [are] there, her
invited ones in deep places of Sheol!

Chapter 10

1 Proverbs of Solomon. A wise son causes a father to
rejoice, and a foolish son [is] an affliction to his
mother.
2 Treasures of wickedness profit not, and righteousness
delivers from death.
3 Jehovah causes not the soul of the righteous to
hunger, and He thrusts away the desire of the wicked.
4 Poor [is] he who is working — a slothful hand, and
the hand of the diligent makes rich.
5 Whoso is gathering in summer [is] a wise son, whoso
is sleeping in harvest [is] a son causing shame.
6 Blessings [are] for the head of the righteous, and the
mouth of the wicked does cover violence.
7 The remembrance of the righteous [is] for a blessing,
and the name of the wicked does rot.
8 The wise in heart accepts commands, and a talkative
fool kicks.

9 Whoso is walking in integrity walks confidently, and
whoso is perverting his ways is known.
10 Whoso is winking the eye gives grief, and a talkative
fool kicks.
11 A fountain of life [is] the mouth of the righteous, and
the mouth of the wicked does cover violence.
12 Hatred awakes contentions, and love covers over all
transgressions.
13 Wisdom is found in the lips of the intelligent, and a
rod [is] for the back of him who is lacking
understanding.
14 The wise lay up knowledge, and the mouth of a fool
[is] near ruin.
15 The wealth of the rich [is] his strong city, the ruin of
the poor [is] their poverty.
16 The wage of the righteous [is] for life, the increase of
the wicked for sin.
17 A traveler to life [is] he who is keeping instruction,
and whoso is forsaking rebuke is erring.
18 Whoso is covering hatred with lying lips, and whoso
is bringing out an evil report is a fool.
19 In the abundance of words transgression ceases not,
and whoso is restraining his lips [is] wise.
20 The tongue of the righteous [is] chosen silver, the
heart of the wicked — as a little thing.
21 The lips of the righteous delight many, and fools die
for lack of heart.
22 The blessing of Jehovah — it makes rich, and He
adds no grief with it.
23 To execute inventions [is] as play to a fool, and
wisdom to a man of understanding.
24 The feared thing of the wicked it meets him, and the
desire of the righteous is given.
25 As the passing by of a hurricane, so the wicked is
not, and the righteous is a foundation age-during.
26 As vinegar to the teeth, and as smoke to the eyes, so
[is] the slothful to those sending him.
27 The fear of Jehovah adds days, and the years of the
wicked are shortened.
28 The hope of the righteous [is] joyful, and the
expectation of the wicked perishes.
29 The way of Jehovah [is] strength to the perfect, and
ruin to workers of iniquity.
30 The righteous to the age is not moved, and the wicked
inhabit not the earth.
31 The mouth of the righteous utters wisdom, and the
tongue of perverseness is cut out.
32 The lips of the righteous know a pleasing thing, and
the mouth of the wicked perverseness!

Chapter 11

1 Balances of deceit [are] an abomination to Jehovah,
and a perfect weight [is] His delight.
2 Pride has come, and shame comes, and wisdom [is]
with the lowly.
3 The integrity of the upright leads them, and the
perverseness of the treacherous destroys them.
4 Wealth profits not in a day of wrath, and righteousness
delivers from death.
5 The righteousness of the perfect makes right his way,
and the wicked does fall by his wickedness.
6 The righteousness of the upright delivers them, and
the treacherous are captured in mischief.
7 In the death of a wicked man, hope perishes, and the
expectation of the wicked has been lost.
8 The righteous is drawn out from distress, and the
wicked goes in instead of him.
9 A hypocrite corrupts his friend with the mouth, and
the righteous are drawn out by knowledge.
10 A city exults in the good of the righteous, and [is]
singing in the destruction of the wicked.
11 A city is exalted by the blessing of the upright, and
thrown down by the mouth of the wicked.
12 Whoso is despising his neighbor lacks heart, and a
man of understanding keeps silence.
13 A busybody is revealing secret counsel, and the
faithful of spirit is covering the matter.
14 Without counsels do a people fall, and deliverance
[is] in a multitude of counselors.
15 Evil [one] suffers when he has been surety [for] a
stranger, and whoso is hating suretyship is confident.
16 A gracious woman retains honor, and terrible [men]
retain riches.
17 A kind man is rewarding his own soul, and the fierce
is troubling his own flesh.
18 The wicked is getting a lying wage, and whoso is
sowing righteousness — a true reward.
19 Rightly [is] righteousness for life, and whoso is
pursuing evil — for his own death.
20 The perverse of heart [are] an abomination to
Jehovah, and the perfect of the way [are] His delight.
21 Hand to hand, the wicked is not acquitted, and the
seed of the righteous has escaped.
22 A ring of gold in the nose of a sow — a fair woman
and stubborn of behavior.
23 The desire of the righteous [is] only good, the hope
of the wicked [is] transgression.

24 There is who is scattering, and yet is increased, and
who is keeping back from uprightness, only to want.
25 A liberal soul is made fat, and whoso is watering, he
also is watered.
26 Whoso is withholding corn, the people curse him,
and a blessing [is] for the head of him who is selling.
27 Whoso is earnestly seeking good seeks a pleasing
thing, and whoso is seeking evil — it meets him.
28 Whoso is confident in his wealth he falls, and as a
leaf, the righteous flourish.
29 Whoso is troubling his own house inherits wind,
and the fool [is] a servant to the wise of heart.
30 The fruit of the righteous [is] a tree of life, and whoso
is taking souls [is] wise.
31 Behold, the righteous in the earth is recompensed,
surely also the wicked and the sinner!

Chapter 12

1 Whoso is loving instruction, is loving knowledge, and
whoso is hating reproof [is] brutish.
2 The good brings forth favor from Jehovah, and He
condemns the man of wicked devices.
3 A man is not established by wickedness, and the root
of the righteous is not moved.
4 A virtuous woman [is] a crown to her husband, and as
rottenness in his bones [is] one causing shame.
5 The thoughts of the righteous [are] justice, the
counsels of the wicked — deceit.
6 The words of the wicked [are]: 'Lay wait for blood,'
and the mouth of the upright delivers them.
7 Overthrow the wicked, and they are not, and the house
of the righteous stands.
8 A man is praised according to his wisdom, and the
perverted of heart becomes despised.
9 Better [is] the lightly esteemed who has a servant,
than the self-honored who lacks bread.
10 The righteous knows the life of his beast, and the
mercies of the wicked [are] cruel.
11 Whoso is tilling the ground is satisfied [with] bread,
and whoso is pursuing vanities is lacking heart,
12 the wicked has desired the net of evil doers, and the
root of the righteous gives.
13 In transgression of the lips [is] the snare of the
wicked, and the righteous goes out from distress.
14 From the fruit of the mouth [is] one satisfied [with]
good, and the deed of man's hands returns to him.
15 The way of a fool [is] right in his own eyes, and
whoso is listening to counsel [is] wise.
16 The fool — his anger is known in a day, and the
prudent is covering shame.
17 Whoso utters faithfulness declares righteousness,
and a false witness — deceit.
18 A rash speaker is like piercings of a sword, and the
tongue of the wise is healing.
19 The lip of truth is established for ever, and for a
moment — a tongue of falsehood.
20 Deceit [is] in the heart of those devising evil, and to
those counseling peace [is] joy.
21 No iniquity is desired by the righteous, and the
wicked have been full of evil.
22 Lying lips [are] an abomination to Jehovah, and
steadfast doers [are] his delight.
23 A prudent man is concealing knowledge, and the heart
of fools proclaims folly.
24 The hand of the diligent rules, and slothfulness
becomes tributary.
25 Sorrow in the heart of a man bows down, and a good
word makes him glad.
26 The righteous searches his companion, and the way
of the wicked causes them to err.
27 The slothful roasts not his hunting, and the wealth
of a diligent man is precious.
28 In the path of righteousness [is] life, and in the way
of [that] path [is] no death!

Chapter 13

1 A wise son — the instruction of a father, and a scorner
— he has not heard rebuke.
2 From the fruit of the mouth a man eats good, and the
soul of the treacherous — violence.
3 Whoso is keeping his mouth, is keeping his soul,
whoso is opening wide his lips — ruin to him!
4 The soul of the slothful is desiring, and has not. And
the soul of the diligent is made fat.
5 The righteous hates a false word, and the wicked
causes abhorrence, and is confounded.
6 Righteousness keeps him who is perfect in the way,
and wickedness overthrows a sin offering.
7 There is who is making himself rich, and has nothing,
who is making himself poor, and wealth [is] abundant.
8 The ransom of a man's life [are] his riches, and the
poor has not heard rebuke.
9 The light of the righteous rejoices, and the lamp of
the wicked is extinguished.

10 A vain man causes debate through pride, and wisdom [is] with the counseled.
11 Wealth from vanity becomes little, and whoso is gathering by the hand becomes great.
12 Hope prolonged is making the heart sick, and a tree of life [is] the coming desire.
13 Whoso is despising the Word is destroyed for it, and whoso is fearing the Command is repaid.
14 The law of the wise [is] a fountain of life, to turn aside from snares of death.
15 Good understanding gives grace, and the way of the treacherous [is] hard.
16 Every prudent one deals with knowledge, and a fool spreads out folly.
17 A wicked messenger falls into evil, and a faithful ambassador is healing.
18 Whoso is refusing instruction — poverty and shame, and whoso is observing reproof is honored.
19 A desire accomplished is sweet to the soul, and an abomination to fools [is]: turn from evil.
20 Whoso is walking with wise men is wise, and a companion of fools suffers evil.
21 Evil pursues sinners, and good recompenses the righteous.
22 A good man causes sons' sons to inherit, and laid up for the righteous [is] the sinner's wealth.
23 Abundance of food — the tillage of the poor, and substance is consumed without judgment.
24 Whoso is sparing his rod is hating his son, and whoso is loving him has swiftly chastised him.
25 The righteous is eating to the satiety of his soul, and the belly of the wicked lacks!

Chapter 14

1 Every wise woman has built her house, and the foolish breaks it down with her hands.
2 Whoso is walking in his uprightness is fearing Jehovah, and the perverted [in] his ways is despising Him.
3 In the mouth of a fool [is] a rod of pride, and the lips of the wise preserve them.
4 Without oxen a stall [is] clean, and great [is] the increase by the power of the ox.
5 A faithful witness lies not, and a false witness breathes out lies.
6 A scorner has sought wisdom, and it is not, and knowledge to the intelligent [is] easy.
7 Go from before a foolish man, or you have not known the lips of knowledge.
8 The wisdom of the prudent [is] to understand his way, and the folly of fools [is] deceit.
9 Fools mock at a guilt-offering, and among the upright — a pleasing thing.
10 The heart knows its own bitterness, and a stranger does not intermeddle with its joy.
11 The house of the wicked is destroyed, and the tent of the upright flourishes.
12 There is a way — right before a man, and its latter end [are] ways of death.
13 Even in laughter is the heart pained, and the latter end of joy [is] affliction.
14 From his ways is the backslider filled in heart, and a good man — from his fruits.
15 The simple gives credence to everything, and the prudent attends to his step.
16 The wise is fearing and turning from evil, and a fool is transgressing and is confident.
17 Whoso is short of temper does folly, and a man of wicked devices is hated.
18 The simple have inherited folly, and the prudent are crowned [with] knowledge.
19 The evil have bowed down before the good, and the wicked at the gates of the righteous.
20 The poor is hated even of his neighbor, and those loving the rich [are] many.
21 Whoso is despising his neighbor sins, whoso is favoring the humble, O his happiness.
22 Do not they err who are devising evil? And kindness and truth [are] to those devising good,
23 there is advantage in all labor, and a thing of the lips [is] only to want.
24 The crown of the wise is their wealth, the folly of fools [is] folly.
25 A true witness is delivering souls, and a deceitful one breathes out lies.
26 In the fear of Jehovah [is] strong confidence, and to His sons there is a refuge.
27 The fear of Jehovah [is] a fountain of life, to turn aside from snares of death.
28 In the multitude of a people [is] the honor of a king, and in lack of people the ruin of a prince.
29 Whoso is slow to anger [is] of great understanding, and whoso is short in temper is exalting folly.
30 A healed heart [is] life to the flesh, and rottenness to the bones [is] envy.
31 An oppressor of the poor reproaches his Maker, and

whoso is honoring Him is favoring the needy.
32 The wicked is driven away in his wickedness, and trustful in his death [is] the righteous.
33 Wisdom does rest in the heart of the intelligent. and it is known in the midst of fools.
34 Righteousness exalts a nation, and the goodliness of peoples [is] a sin-offering.
35 The favor of a king [is] to a wise servant, and an object of his wrath is one causing shame!

Chapter 15

1 A soft answer turns back fury, and a grievous word raises up anger.
2 The tongue of the wise makes knowledge good, and the mouth of fools utters folly.
3 In every place are the eyes of Jehovah, watching the evil and the good.
4 A healed tongue [is] a tree of life, and perverseness in it — a breach in the spirit.
5 A fool despises the instruction of his father, and whoso is regarding reproof is prudent.
6 [In] the house of the righteous [is] abundant strength, and in the increase of the wicked — trouble.
7 The lips of the wise scatter knowledge, and the heart of fools [is] not right.
8 The sacrifice of the wicked [is] an abomination to Jehovah, and the prayer of the upright [is] His delight.
9 An abomination to Jehovah [is] the way of the wicked, and He loves whoso is pursuing righteousness.
10 Chastisement [is] grievous to him who is forsaking the path, whoso is hating reproof dies.
11 Sheol and destruction [are] before Jehovah, surely also the hearts of the sons of men.
12 A scorner loves not his reprover, he goes not unto the wise.
13 A joyful heart makes the face glad, and the spirit is afflicted by grief of heart.
14 The heart of the intelligent seeks knowledge, and the mouth of fools enjoys folly.
15 All the days of the afflicted [are] evil, and gladness of heart [is] a perpetual banquet.
16 Better [is] a little with the fear of Jehovah, than much treasure, and tumult with it.
17 Better [is] an allowance of green herbs and love there, than a fatted ox, and hatred with it.
18 A man of fury stirs up contention, and the slow to anger appeases strife.
19 The way of the slothful [is] as a hedge of briers, and the path of the upright is raised up.
20 A wise son rejoices a father. And a foolish man is despising his mother.
21 Folly is joy to one lacking heart, and a man of intelligence directs [his] going.
22 Without counsel [is] the making void of purposes, and it is established in a multitude of counselors.
23 Joy [is] to a man in the answer of his mouth, and a word in its season — how good!
24 A path of life [is] on high for the wise, to turn aside from Sheol beneath.
25 Jehovah pulls down the house of the proud, and He sets up the border of the widow.
26 An abomination to Jehovah [are] thoughts of wickedness, and pure [are] sayings of pleasantness.
27 A dishonest gainer is troubling his house, and whoso is hating gifts lives.
28 The heart of the righteous meditates to answer, and the mouth of the wicked utters evil things.
29 Far [is] Jehovah from the wicked, and He hears the prayer of the righteous.
30 The light of the eyes rejoices the heart, a good report makes fat the bone.
31 An ear that is hearing the reproof of life does lodge among the wise.
32 Whoso is refusing instruction is despising his soul, and whoso is hearing reproof is getting understanding.
33 The fear of Jehovah [is] the instruction of wisdom, and before honor [is] humility!

Chapter 16

1 Of man [are] arrangements of the heart, and from Jehovah an answer of the tongue.
2 All the ways of a man are pure in his own eyes, and Jehovah is pondering the spirits.
3 Roll your[S] works unto Jehovah, and your[S] purposes are established,
4 Jehovah has worked all things for Himself, and also the wicked [works] for a day of evil.
5 An abomination to Jehovah [is] every proud one of heart, hand to hand he is not acquitted.
6 Iniquity is pardoned in kindness and truth, and turn you aside from evil in the fear of Jehovah.
7 When a man's ways please Jehovah, even his enemies, he causes to be at peace with him.
8 Better [is] a little with righteousness, than abundance

of increase without justice.
9 The heart of man devises his way, and Jehovah establishes his step.
10 An oath [is] on the lips of a king, in judgment his mouth trespasses not.
11 A just beam and balances [are] Jehovah's, His work [are] all the stones of the bag.
12 An abomination to kings [is] doing wickedness, for a throne is established by righteousness.
13 The delight of kings [are] righteous lips, and he loves whoso is speaking uprightly,
14 the fury of a king [is] messengers of death, and a wise man pacifies it.
15 In the light of a king's face [is] life, and his good-will [is] as a cloud of the latter rain.
16 To get wisdom — how much better than gold, and to get understanding to be chosen than silver!
17 A highway of the upright [is], 'Turn from evil,' whoso is preserving his soul is watching his way.
18 Before destruction [is] pride, and before stumbling — a haughty spirit.'
19 Better is humility of spirit with the poor, than to apportion spoil with the proud.
20 The wise finds good in any matter, and whoso is trusting in Jehovah, O his happiness.
21 To the wise in heart is called, 'Intelligent,' and sweetness of lips increases learning.
22 A fountain of life [is] understanding to its possessors, the instruction of fools is folly.
23 The heart of the wise causes his mouth to act wisely, and by his lips he increases learning,
24 Sayings of pleasantness [are] a honeycomb, sweet to the soul, and healing to the bone.
25 There is a way right before a man, and its latter end — ways of death.
26 A laboring man has labored for himself, for his mouth has caused [him] to bend over it.
27 A worthless man is preparing evil, and on his lips — as a burning fire.
28 A perverse man sends forth contention, a tale-bearer is separating a familiar friend.
29 A violent man entices his neighbor, and has caused him to go in a way not good.
30 Consulting his eyes to devise perverse things, moving his lips he has accomplished evil.
31 A crown of beauty [are] gray hairs, it is found in the way of righteousness.
32 Better [is] the slow to anger than the mighty, and the ruler over his spirit than he who is taking a city.
33 Into the center is the lot cast, and from Jehovah [is] all its judgment!

Chapter 17

1 Better [is] a dry morsel, and rest with it, than a house full of the sacrifices of strife.
2 A wise servant rules over a son causing shame, and in the midst of brethren he apportions an inheritance.
3 A refining pot [is] for silver, and a furnace for gold, and the trier of hearts [is] Jehovah.
4 An evil doer is attentive to lips of vanity, falsehood is giving ear to a mischievous tongue.
5 Whoso is mocking at the poor has reproached his Maker, whoso is rejoicing at calamity is not acquitted.
6 Sons' sons [are] the crown of old men, and the glory of sons [are] their fathers.
7 A lip of excellency is not comely for a fool, much less a lip of falsehood for a noble.
8 A stone of grace [is] the bribe in the eyes of its possessors, to whatever place it turns, it prospers.
9 Whoso is covering transgression is seeking love, and whoso is repeating a matter is separating a familiar friend.
10 Rebuke comes down on the intelligent more than a hundred stripes on a fool.
11 An evil man seeks only rebellion, and a fierce messenger is sent against him.
12 The meeting of a bereaved bear by a man, and — not a fool in his folly.
13 Whoso is returning evil for good, evil moves not from his house.
14 The beginning of contention [is] a letting out of waters, and leave the strife before it is meddled with.
15 Whoso is justifying the wicked, and condemning the righteous, even both of these [are] an abomination to Jehovah.
16 Why [is] this — a price in the hand of a fool to buy wisdom, and a heart there is none?
17 At all times is the friend loving, and a brother is born for adversity.
18 A man lacking heart is striking hands, he becomes a surety before his friend.
19 Whoso is loving transgression is loving debate, whoso is making his entrance high is seeking destruction.
20 The perverse of heart finds not good, and the turned in his tongue falls into evil.
21 Whoso is fathering a fool has affliction for it, yes,

the father of a fool rejoices not.
22 A rejoicing heart does good to the body, and an
afflicted spirit dries the bone.
23 The wicked takes a bribe from the bosom, to turn
aside the paths of judgment.
24 The face of the intelligent [is] to wisdom, and the
eyes of a fool — at the end of the earth.
25 A foolish son [is] a provocation to his father, and
bitterness to her that bare him.
26 Also, to fine the righteous is not good, to afflict
nobles for uprightness.
27 One acquainted with knowledge is sparing his words,
and the cool of temper [is] a man of understanding.
28 Even a fool keeping silence is reckoned wise, he who
is shutting his lips intelligent!

Chapter 18

1 He who is separated does seek for [an object of] desire,
he interferes with all wisdom.
2 A fool delights not in understanding, but — in
uncovering his heart.
3 With the coming of the wicked come also has
contempt, and with shame — reproach.
4 Deep waters [are] the words of a man's mouth, the
fountain of wisdom [is] a flowing brook.
5 Acceptance of the face of the wicked [is] not good, to
turn aside the righteous in judgment.
6 The lips of a fool enter into strife, and his mouth calls
for stripes.
7 The mouth of a fool [is] ruin to him, and his lips [are]
the snare of his soul.
8 The words of a tale-bearer [are] as self-inflicted
wounds, and they have gone down [to] the inner parts
of the heart.
9 He also that is remiss in his work, he [is] a brother to a
destroyer.
10 A tower of strength [is] the name of Jehovah, into it
the righteous runs, and is set on high.
11 The wealth of the rich [is] the city of his strength,
and as a wall set on high in his own imagination.
12 Before destruction the heart of man is high, and
before honor [is] humility.
13 Whoso is answering a matter before he hears, it is
folly to him and shame.
14 The spirit of a man sustains his sickness, and who
does bear an afflicted spirit?
15 The heart of the intelligent gets knowledge, and the
ear of the wise seeks knowledge.
16 The gift of a man makes room for him, and it leads
him before the great.
17 Righteous [is] the first in his own cause, his neighbor
comes and has searched him.
18 The lot causes contentions to cease, and between
the mighty it separates.
19 A brother transgressed against is as a strong city,
and contentions as the bar of a palace.
20 From the fruit of a man's mouth is his belly satisfied,
he is satisfied [from the] increase of his lips.
21 Death and life [are] in the power of the tongue, and
those loving it eat its fruit.
22 [Whoso] has found a wife has found good, and
brings out good-will from Jehovah.
23 The poor does speak [with] supplications, and the
rich answers fierce things.
24 A man with friends [is] to show himself friendly, and
there is a lover adhering more than a brother!

Chapter 19

1 Better [is] the poor walking in his integrity, than the
perverse [in] his lips, who [is] a fool.
2 Also, without knowledge the soul [is] not good, and
the hasty in feet is sinning.
3 The folly of man perverts his way, and his heart is
angry against Jehovah.
4 Wealth adds many friends, and the poor is separated
from his neighbor.
5 A false witness is not acquitted, whoso breathes out
lies is not delivered.
6 Many entreat the face of the noble, and all have made
friendship to a man of gifts.
7 All the brethren of the poor have hated him, surely
also his friends have been far from him, he is pursuing
words — they are not!
8 Whoso is getting heart is loving his soul, he is keeping
understanding to find good.
9 A false witness is not acquitted, and whoso breathes
out lies perishes.
10 Luxury is not comely for a fool, much less for a servant
to rule among princes.
11 The wisdom of a man has deferred his anger, and his
glory [is] to pass over transgression.
12 The wrath of a king [is] a growl as of a young lion,
and his good-will as dew on the herb.
13 A calamity to his father [is] a foolish son, and the

contentions of a wife [are] a continual dropping.
14 House and wealth [are] the inheritance of fathers,
and from Jehovah [is] an understanding wife.
15 Sloth causes deep sleep to fall, and an lazy soul does
hunger.
16 Whoso is keeping the command is keeping his soul,
whoso is despising His ways dies.
17 Whoso is lending [to] Jehovah is favoring the poor,
and He repays his deed to him.
18 Chastise your son, for there is hope, and lift not up
your soul to put him to death.
19 A man of great wrath is bearing punishment, for, if
you do deliver, yet again you do add.
20 Hear counsel and receive instruction, so that you
are wise in your latter end.
21 Many [are] the purposes in a man's heart, and the
counsel of Jehovah it stands.
22 The desirableness of a man [is] his kindness, and
better [is] the poor than a liar.
23 The fear of Jehovah [is] to life, and satisfied he
remains — he is not charged with evil.
24 The slothful has hidden his hand in a dish, he brings
it not back even unto his mouth.
25 A scorner afflicts, and the simple acts prudently, and
give reproof to the intelligent, he understands
knowledge.
26 Whoso is spoiling a father causes a mother to flee, a
son causing shame, and bringing confusion.
27 Cease, my son, to hear instruction — to err from
sayings of knowledge.
28 A worthless witness scorns judgment, and the mouth
of the wicked swallows iniquity.
29 Judgments have been prepared for scorners, and
stripes for the back of fools!

Chapter 20

1 Wine [is] a scorner — strong drink [is] noisy, and any
going astray in it is not wise.
2 The fear of a king [is] a growl as of a young lion, he
who is causing him to be angry is wronging his soul.
3 Cessation from strife is a honor to a man, and every
fool interferes.
4 Because of winter the slothful plows not, he asks in
harvest, and there is nothing.
5 Counsel in the heart of a man [is] deep water, and a
man of understanding draws it up.
6 A multitude of men proclaim each his kindness, and
who does find a man of steadfastness?
7 The righteous is walking habitually in his integrity, O
the happiness of his sons after him!
8 A king sitting on a throne of judgment, is scattering
all evil with his eyes,
9 Who says, 'I have purified my heart, I have been
cleansed from my sin?'
10 A stone and a stone, an ephah and an ephah, even
both of them [are] an abomination to Jehovah.
11 Even by his actions a youth makes himself known,
whether his work be pure or upright.
12 A hearing ear, and a seeing eye, Jehovah has made
even both of them.
13 Love not sleep, for fear that you become poor, open
your eyes — be satisfied [with] bread.
14 'Bad, bad,' says the buyer, and going his way then
he boasts himself.
15 Substance, gold, and a multitude of rubies, yes, a
precious vessel, [are] lips of knowledge.
16 Take his garment when a stranger has been surety,
and pledge it for strangers.
17 Sweet to a man [is] the bread of falsehood, and
afterwards is his mouth filled [with] gravel.
18 You[S] do establish purposes by counsel, and make
you[S] war with plans.
19 A revealer of secret counsels is the busybody, and
make not yourself[S] surety for a deceiver [with] his lips.
20 Whoso is vilifying his father and his mother,
extinguished is his lamp in blackness of darkness.
21 An inheritance gotten wrongly at first, even its latter
end is not blessed.
22 Do not say, 'I recompense evil,' wait for Jehovah,
and He delivers you[S].
23 An abomination to Jehovah [are] a stone and a stone,
and balances of deceit [are] not good.
24 From Jehovah [are] the steps of a man, and man —
how understands he his way?
25 A snare to a man [is] he has swallowed a holy thing,
and to make inquiry after vows.
26 A wise king is scattering the wicked, and turns back
the wheel on them.
27 The breath of man [is] a lamp of Jehovah, searching
all the inner parts of the heart.
28 Kindness and truth keep a king, and he has supported
his throne by kindness.
29 The beauty of young men is their strength, and the
honor of old men is gray hairs.
30 You[S] remove the bandages of a wound with the evil,
also the plagues of the inner parts of the heart!

Chapter 21

1 Rivulets of waters [is] the heart of a king in the hand of Jehovah, wherever He pleases He inclines it.
2 Every way of a man [is] right in his own eyes, and Jehovah is pondering hearts.
3 To do righteousness and judgment, is chosen of Jehovah rather than sacrifice.
4 Loftiness of eyes, and breadth of heart, tillage of the wicked [is] sin.
5 The purposes of the diligent [are] only to advantage, and of every hasty one, only to want.
6 The making of treasures by a lying tongue, [is] a vanity driven away of those seeking death.
7 The spoil of the wicked catches them, because they have refused to do judgment.
8 Perverse [is] the way of a man who is vile, and the pure — upright [is] his work.
9 Better to sit on a corner of the roof, than [with] a woman of contentions and a house of company.
10 The soul of the wicked has desired evil, not gracious in his eyes is his neighbor.
11 When the scorner is punished, the simple becomes wise, and in giving understanding to the wise he receives knowledge.
12 The Righteous One is acting wisely towards the house of the wicked, He is overthrowing the wicked for wickedness.
13 Whoso is shutting his ear from the cry of the poor, he also does cry, and is not answered.
14 A gift in secret pacifies anger, and a bribe in the bosom strong fury.
15 To do justice [is] joy to the righteous, but ruin to workers of iniquity.
16 A man who is wandering from the way of understanding, rests in an assembly of Rephaim.
17 Whoso [is] loving mirth [is] a poor man, whoso is loving wine and oil makes no wealth.
18 The wicked [is] an atonement for the righteous, and for the upright the treacherous dealer.
19 Better to dwell in a wilderness land, than [with] a woman of contentions and anger.
20 A treasure to be desired, and oil, [is] in the habitation of the wise, and a foolish man swallows it up.
21 Whoso is pursuing righteousness and kindness, finds life, righteousness, and honor.
22 A city of the mighty has the wise gone up, and brings down the strength of its confidence.
23 Whoso is keeping his mouth and his tongue, is keeping his soul from adversities.
24 Proud, haughty, scorner [is] his name, who is working in the wrath of pride.
25 The desire of the slothful slays him, for his hands have refused to work.
26 All the day desiring he has desired, and the righteous gives and withholds not.
27 The sacrifice of the wicked [is] abomination, much more when he brings it in wickedness.
28 A false witness does perish, and an attentive man for ever speaks.
29 A wicked man has hardened by his face, and the upright — he prepares his way.
30 There is no wisdom, nor understanding, nor counsel, over-against Jehovah.
31 A horse is prepared for a day of battle, and the deliverance [is] of Jehovah!

Chapter 22

1 A name is chosen rather than much wealth, than silver and than gold — good grace.
2 Rich and poor have met together, the Maker of them all [is] Jehovah.
3 The prudent has seen the evil, and is hidden, and the simple have passed on, and are punished.
4 The end of humility [is] the fear of Jehovah, riches, and honor, and life.
5 Thorns — snares [are] in the way of the perverse, whoso is keeping his soul is far from them.
6 Give instruction to a youth about his way, even when he is old he turns not from it.
7 The rich rules over the poor, and a servant [is] the borrower to the lender.
8 Whoso is sowing perverseness reaps sorrow, and wears out the rod of his anger.
9 The good of eye — he is blessed, for he has given of his bread to the poor.
10 Cast out a scorner — and contention goes out, and strife and shame cease.
11 Whoso is loving cleanness of heart, grace [are] his lips, a king [is] his friend.
12 The eyes of Jehovah have kept knowledge, and He overthrows the words of the treacherous.
13 The slothful has said, 'A lion [is] without, I am slain in the midst of the broad places.'
14 A deep pit [is] the mouth of strange women, the

abhorred of Jehovah falls there.
15 Folly is bound up in the heart of a youth, the rod of
chastisement puts it far from him.
16 He is oppressing the poor to multiply to him, he is
giving to the rich — only to want.
17 Incline your[S] ear, and hear words of the wise, and set
your[S] heart to my knowledge,
18 For they are pleasant when you[S] do keep them in
your[S] heart, they are prepared together for your[S] lips.
19 That your[S] trust may be in Jehovah, I caused you[S] to
know today, even you[S].
20 Have I not written to you[S] three times with counsels
and knowledge?
21 To cause you[S] to know the certainty of sayings of
truth, to return sayings of truth to those sending you[S].
22 Rob not the poor because he [is] poor, and bruise
not the afflicted in the gate.
23 For Jehovah pleads their cause, and has spoiled the
soul of their spoilers.
24 Show not yourself[S] friendly with an angry man, and
go not in with a man of fury,
25 for fear that you[S] learn his paths, and have received
a snare to your[S] soul.
26 Be not you[S] among those striking hands, among
sureties [for] burdens.
27 If you[S] have nothing to pay, why does he take your[S]
bed from under you[S]?
28 Remove not a border of olden times, that your[S] fathers
have made.
29 Have you[S] seen a man speedy in his business? He
does station himself before kings, he stations not himself
before obscure men!

Chapter 23

1 When you[S] sit to eat with a ruler, you[S] consider
diligently that which [is] before you[S],
2 And you[S] have put a knife to your[S] throat, if you[S]
[are] a man of appetite.
3 Have no desire to his dainties, seeing it [is] lying food.
4 Labor not to make wealth, cease from your[S] own
understanding, do you[S] cause your[S] eyes to fly upon
it? Then it is not.
5 For wealth makes wings to itself, it flies as an eagle to
the heavens.
6 Eat not the bread of an evil eye, and have no desire to
his dainties,
7 For as he has thought in his soul, so [is] he, 'Eat and
drink,' says he to you[S], and his heart [is] not with you[S].
8 You[S] do vomit up your[S] morsel you[S] have eaten, and
have marred your[S] words that [are] sweet.
9 Speak not in the ears of a fool, for he treads on the
wisdom of your[S] words.
10 Remove not a border of olden times, and enter not
into fields of the fatherless,
11 for their Redeemer [is] strong, He does plead their
cause with you[S].
12 Bring in your[S] heart to instruction, and your[S] ear to
sayings of knowledge.
13 Withhold not chastisement from a youth, he dies not
when you[S] strike him with a rod.
14 You[S] strike him with a rod, and you[S] deliver his soul
from Sheol.
15 My son, if your[S] heart has been wise, my heart
rejoices, even mine,
16 and my reins exult when your[S] lips speak uprightly.
17 Let not your[S] heart be envious at sinners, but — in
the fear of Jehovah all the day.
18 For, is there a posterity? Then your[S] hope is not cut
off.
19 Hear you[S], my son, and be wise, and make your[S] heart
happy in the way,
20 Be not you[S] among greedy drinkers of wine, among
gluttonous ones of flesh,
21 for the greedy drinker and glutton become poor, and
drowsiness clothes with rags.
22 Listen to your[S] father, who fathered you[S], and despise
not your[S] mother when she has become old.
23 Buy truth, and sell not, wisdom, and instruction, and
understanding,
24 the father of the righteous rejoices greatly, the father
of the wise rejoices in him.
25 Your father and your mother do rejoice, yes, she that
bare you is joyful.
26 Give, my son, your[S] heart to me, and let your[S] eyes
watch my ways.
27 For a harlot [is] a deep ditch, and a strange woman
[is] a narrow pit.
28 She also, as catching prey, lies in wait, and she
increases the treacherous among men.
29 Who has woe? Who has sorrow? Who has
contentions? Who has complaint? Who has wounds
without cause? Who has redness of eyes?
30 Those tarrying by the wine, those going in to search
out mixed wine.
31 See not wine when it shows itself red, when it gives
its color in the cup, it goes up and down through the

upright.
32 Its latter end — it bites as a serpent, and it stings as
a basilisk.
33 Your[S] eyes see strange women, and your[S] heart
speaks perverse things.
34 And you[S] have been as one lying down in the heart
of the sea, and as one lying down on the top of a mast.
35 'They struck me, I have not been sick, they beat me,
I have not known. When I awake — I seek it yet again!'

Chapter 24

1 Be not envious of evil men, and desire not to be with
them.
2 Their heart does meditate for destruction, and their
lips do speak perverseness.
3 A house is built by wisdom, and it establishes itself
by understanding.
4 And by knowledge the inner parts are filled, [with] all
precious and pleasant wealth.
5 Mighty [is] the wise in strength, and a man of
knowledge is strengthening power,
6 for you[S] make for yourself[S] war by plans, and
deliverance [is] in a multitude of counselors.
7 Wisdom [is] high for a fool, in the gate he opens not
his mouth.
8 Whoso is devising to do evil, they call him a master of
wicked thoughts.
9 The thought of folly [is] sin, and a scorner [is] an
abomination to man.
10 You[S] have showed yourself[S] weak in a day of
adversity, confined is your[S] power,
11 if [from] delivering those taken to death, and those
slipping to the slaughter — you[S] keep back.
12 When you[S] say, 'Behold, we knew not this.' Is not
the Ponderer of hearts He who understands? And the
Keeper of your[S] soul He who knows? And He has
rendered to man according to his work.
13 Eat my son, honey that [is] good, and the honeycomb
— sweet to your[S] palate.
14 So [is] the knowledge of wisdom to your[S] soul, if
you[S] have found that there is a posterity and your[S] hope
is not cut off.
15 Lay not wait, O wicked one, at the habitation of the
righteous. Do not spoil his resting-place.
16 For seven [times] does the righteous fall and rise,
and the wicked stumble in evil.
17 Rejoice not in the falling of your[S] enemy, and let not
your[S] heart be joyful in his stumbling,
18 for fear that Jehovah see, and [it be] evil in His eyes,
and He has turned His anger from off him.
19 Fret not yourself[S] at evil doers, be not envious at the
wicked,
20 for there is not a posterity to the evil, the lamp of the
wicked is extinguished.
21 Fear Jehovah, my son, and the king, mix not up
yourself with changers,
22 for suddenly does their calamity rise, and the ruin of
them both — who knows!
23 These also are for the wise: — to discern faces in
judgment is not good.
24 Whoso is saying to the wicked, 'You[S] [are] righteous,'
peoples execrate him — nations abhor him.
25 And to those reproving it is pleasant, and a good
blessing comes on them.
26 Lips he kisses who is returning straightforward
words.
27 Prepare your[S] work in an out-place, and make it ready
in the field — go afterwards, then you[S] have built your[S]
house.
28 Be not a witness for nothing against your[S] neighbor,
or you[S] have enticed with your[S] lips.
29 Say not, 'As he did to me, so I do to him, I render to
each according to his work.'
30 I passed by near the field of a slothful man, and near
the vineyard of a man lacking heart.
31 And behold, it has gone up — all of it — thorns!
Covered its face have nettles, and its stone wall has been
broken down.
32 And I see — I — I do set my heart, I have seen — I
have received instruction,
33 a little sleep — a little slumber — a little folding of
the hands to lie down.
34 And your[S] poverty has come [as] a traveler, and your[S]
want as an armed man!

Chapter 25

1 Also these are Proverbs of Solomon, that men of
Hezekiah king of Judah transcribed: —
2 The honor of God [is] to hide a thing, and the honor
of kings to search out a matter.
3 The heavens for height, and the earth for depth, and
the heart of kings — [are] unsearchable.
4 Take away dross from silver, and a vessel for the refiner
goes forth,

5 Take away the wicked before a king, and his throne is established in righteousness.
6 Honor not yourself^{S} before a king, and stand not in the place of the great.
7 For better [that] he has said to you^{S}, ‘Come you^{S} up here,’ than [that] he humble you^{S} before a noble, whom your^{S} eyes have seen.
8 Go not forth to strive, hurry, turn, what do you^{S} in its latter end, when your^{S} neighbor causes you^{S} to blush?
9 Plead your^{S} cause with your neighbor, and reveal not the secret counsel of another,
10 for fear that the hearer put you^{S} to shame, and your^{S} evil report turn not back.
11 Apples of gold in imagery of silver, [is] the word spoken at its fit times.
12 A ring of gold, and an ornament of pure gold, [is] the wise reprover to an attentive ear.
13 As a vessel of snow in a day of harvest, [so is] a faithful ambassador to those sending him, and he refreshes the soul of his masters.
14 Clouds and wind, and rain there is none, [is] a man boasting himself in a false gift.
15 By long-suffering is a ruler persuaded, and a soft tongue breaks a bone.
16 Honey you^{S} have found — eat your^{S} sufficiency, for fear that you^{S} be satiated [with] it, and have vomited it.
17 Withdraw your^{S} foot from your^{S} neighbor’s house, for fear that he be satiated [with] you^{S}, and have hated you^{S}.
18 A maul, and a sword, and a sharp arrow, [is] the man testifying a false testimony against his neighbor.
19 A bad tooth, and a tottering foot, [is] the confidence of the treacherous in a day of adversity.
20 Whoso is taking away a garment in a cold day, [is as] vinegar on nitre, and a singer of songs on a sad heart.
21 If he who is hating you^{S} does hunger, cause him to eat bread, and if he thirst, cause him to drink water.
22 For you^{S} are putting coals on his head, and Jehovah gives recompense to you^{S}.
23 A north wind brings forth rain, and a secret tongue — indignant faces.
24 Better to sit on a corner of a roof, than [with] a woman of contentions, and a house of company.
25 [As] cold waters for a weary soul, so [is] a good report from a far country.
26 A spring troubled, and a fountain corrupt, [is] the righteous falling before the wicked.
27 The eating of much honey is not good, nor a searching out of one’s own honor — honor.
28 A city broken down without walls, [is] a man without restraint over his spirit!

Chapter 26

1 As snow in summer, and as rain in harvest, so honor [is] not comely for a fool.
2 As a bird by wandering, as a swallow by flying, so reviling without cause does not come.
3 A whip is for a horse, a bridle for an ass, and a rod for the back of fools.
4 Answer not a fool according to his folly, for fear that you^{S} be like to him — even you^{S}.
5 Answer a fool according to his folly, for fear that he be wise in his own eyes.
6 He is cutting off feet, he is drinking injury, who is sending things by the hand of a fool.
7 Weak have been the two legs of the lame, and a parable in the mouth of fools.
8 As one who is binding a stone in a sling, so [is] he who is giving honor to a fool.
9 A thorn has gone up into the hand of a drunkard, and a parable in the mouth of fools.
10 Great [is] the Former of all, and He is rewarding a fool, and is rewarding transgressors.
11 As a dog has returned to its vomit, a fool is repeating his folly.
12 You^{S} have seen a man wise in his own eyes, more hope of a fool than of him!
13 The slothful has said, ‘A lion [is] in the way, a lion [is] in the broad places.’
14 The door turns round on its hinge, and the slothful on his bed.
15 The slothful has hid his hand in a dish, he is weary of bringing it back to his mouth.
16 Wiser [is] the slothful in his own eyes, than seven [men] returning a reason.
17 Laying hold on the ears of a dog, [is] a passer-by making himself angry for strife not his own.
18 As [one] pretending to be feeble, who is casting sparks, arrows, and death,
19 so has a man deceived his neighbor, and has said, ‘Am not I playing?’
20 Without wood is fire going out, and without a tale-bearer, contention ceases,
21 coal to burning coals, and wood to fire, and a man of contentions to kindle strife.
22 The words of a tale-bearer [are] as self-inflicted

wounds, and they have gone down [to] the inner parts of the heart.
23 Silver of dross spread over potsherd, [are] burning lips and an evil heart.
24 A hater does dissemble by his lips, and he places deceit in his heart,
25 when his voice is gracious trust not in him, for seven abominations [are] in his heart.
26 Hatred is covered by deceit, revealed is its wickedness in an assembly.
27 Whoso is digging a pit falls into it, and the roller of a stone, it turns to him.
28 A lying tongue hates its bruised ones, and a flattering mouth works an overthrow!

Chapter 27

1 Boast not yourself[S] of tomorrow, for you[S] know not what a day brings forth.
2 Let another praise you[S], and not your[S] own mouth, a stranger, and not your[S] own lips.
3 A stone [is] heavy, and the sand [is] heavy, and the anger of a fool is heavier than they both.
4 Fury [is] fierce, and anger [is] overflowing, and who stands before jealousy?
5 Better [is] open reproof than hidden love.
6 Faithful are the wounds of a lover, and abundant the kisses of an enemy.
7 A satiated soul treads down a honeycomb, and [to] a hungry soul every bitter thing [is] sweet.
8 As a bird wandering from her nest, so [is] a man wandering from his place.
9 Ointment and perfume rejoice the heart, and the sweetness of one's friend — from counsel of the soul.
10 Your[S] own friend, and the friend of your[S] father, forsake not, and enter not the house of your[S] brother in a day of your[S] calamity, better [is] a near neighbor than a afar off brother.
11 Be wise, my son, and rejoice my heart. And I return my reproacher a word.
12 The prudent has seen the evil, he is hidden, the simple have passed on, they are punished.
13 Take his garment, when a stranger has been surety, and pledge it for a strange woman.
14 Whoso is saluting his friend with a loud voice, rising early in the morning, a light thing it is reckoned to him.
15 A continual dropping in a day of rain, and a woman of contentions are alike,
16 whoso is hiding her has hidden the wind, and the ointment of his right hand calls out.
17 Iron is sharpened by iron, and a man sharpens the face of his friend.
18 The keeper of a fig-tree eats its fruit, and the preserver of his master is honored.
19 As [in] water the face [is] to face, so the heart of man to man.
20 Sheol and destruction are not satisfied, and the eyes of man are not satisfied.
21 A refining pot [is] for silver, and a furnace for gold, and a man according to his praise.
22 If you[S] do beat the foolish in a mortar, among washed things — with a pestle, his folly turns not aside from off him.
23 Know well the face of your[S] flock, set your[S] heart to the droves,
24 For riches [are] not to the age, nor a crown to generation and generation.
25 Revealed was the hay, and seen the tender grass, and gathered the herbs of mountains.
26 Lambs [are] for your[S] clothing, and the price of the field [are] he-goats,
27 and a sufficiency of goats' milk [is] for your[S] bread, for bread to your[S] house, and life to your[S] damsels!

Chapter 28

1 The wicked have fled and there is no pursuer. And the righteous is confident as a young lion.
2 By the transgression of a land many [are] its heads. And by an intelligent man, who knows right — it is prolonged.
3 A man — poor and oppressing the weak, [is] a sweeping rain, and there is no bread.
4 Those forsaking the law praise the wicked, those keeping the law plead against them.
5 Evil men understand not judgment, and those seeking Jehovah understand all.
6 Better [is] the poor walking in his integrity, than the perverse of ways who is rich.
7 Whoso is keeping the law is an intelligent son, and a friend of gluttons, does cause his father to blush.
8 Whoso is multiplying his wealth by biting and usury, for one favoring the poor does gather it.
9 Whoso is turning his ear from hearing the law, even his prayer [is] an abomination.
10 Whoso is causing the upright to err in an evil way,

he does fall into his own pit, and the perfect do inherit good.
11 A rich man is wise in his own eyes, and the intelligent poor searches him.
12 In the exulting of the righteous the glory [is] abundant, and in the rising of the wicked man is apprehensive.
13 Whoso is covering his transgressions prospers not, and he who is confessing and forsaking has mercy.
14 O the happiness of a man fearing continually, and whoso is hardening his heart falls into evil.
15 A growling lion, and a ranging bear, [is] the wicked ruler over a poor people.
16 A leader lacking understanding multiplies oppressions, whoso is hating dishonest gain prolongs days.
17 A man oppressed with the blood of a soul, flees unto the pit, none takes hold on him.
18 Whoso is walking uprightly is saved, and the perverted of ways falls at once.
19 Whoso is tilling his ground is satisfied [with] bread, and whoso is pursuing vanity, is filled [with] poverty.
20 A steadfast man has multiplied blessings, and whoso is hurrying to be rich is not acquitted.
21 To discern faces is not good, and for a piece of bread does a man transgress.
22 Troubled for wealth [is] the man [with] an evil eye, and he knows not that want does meet him.
23 Whoso is reproving a man afterwards finds grace, more than a flatterer with the tongue.
24 Whoso is robbing his father, or his mother, and is saying, 'It is not transgression,' he is a companion to a destroyer.
25 Whoso is proud in soul stirs up contention, and whoso is trusting on Jehovah is made fat.
26 Whoso is trusting in his heart is a fool, and whoso is walking in wisdom is delivered.
27 Whoso is giving to the poor has no lack, and whoso is hiding his eyes multiplied curses.
28 In the rising of the wicked a man is hidden, and in their destruction the righteous multiply!

Chapter 29

1 A man often reproved, hardening the neck, is suddenly broken, and there is no healing.
2 In the multiplying of the righteous the people rejoice, and in the ruling of the wicked the people sigh.
3 A man loving wisdom rejoices his father, and a friend of harlots destroys wealth.
4 A king establishes a land by judgment, and one receiving gifts throws it down.
5 A man taking a portion above his neighbor, spreads a net for his own steps.
6 In the transgression of the evil [is] a snare, and the righteous does sing and rejoice.
7 The righteous knows the plea of the poor, the wicked understands not knowledge.
8 Men of scorning ensnare a city, and the wise turn back anger.
9 A wise man is judged by the foolish man, and he has been angry, and he has laughed, and there is no rest.
10 Men of blood hate the perfect, and the upright seek his soul.
11 A fool brings out all his mind, and the wise restrains it till afterwards.
12 A ruler who is attending to lying words, all his ministers [are] wicked.
13 The poor and the man of frauds have met together, Jehovah is enlightening the eyes of them both.
14 A king that is judging the poor truly, his throne is established for ever.
15 A rod and reproof give wisdom, and a youth let away is shaming his mother.
16 In the multiplying of the wicked transgression multiplies, and the righteous do look on their fall.
17 Chastise your[S] son, and he gives you[S] comfort, yes, he gives delights to your[S] soul.
18 Without a vision is a people made naked, and whoso is keeping the law, O his happiness!
19 A servant is not instructed by words though he understand, and there is nothing answering.
20 You[S] have seen a man hasty in his words! More hope of a fool than of him.
21 Whoso is bringing up his servant delicately, from youth, [at] his latter end also he is continuator.
22 An angry man stirs up contention, and a furious man is multiplying transgression.
23 The pride of man humbles him, and humility of spirit upholds honor.
24 Whoso is sharing with a thief is hating his own soul, execration he hears, and tells not.
25 Fear of man causes a snare, and the confident in Jehovah is set on high.
26 Many are seeking the face of a ruler, and the judgment of each [is] from Jehovah.
27 The perverse man an abomination to the righteous,

and an abomination to the wicked [is] the upright in the way!

Chapter 30

1 Words of a Gatherer, son of an obedient one, the declaration, an affirmation of the man: — I have wearied myself [for] God, I have wearied myself [for] God, and am consumed.
2 For I am more brutish than any one, and have not the understanding of a man.
3 Nor have I learned wisdom, yet I know the knowledge of Holy Ones.
4 Who went up to heaven, and comes down? Who has gathered the wind in his fists? Who has bound waters in a garment? Who established all ends of the earth? What [is] His name? and what His son's name? Surely you know!
5 Every saying of God [is] tried, He [is] a shield to those trusting in Him.
6 Add not to His words, for fear that He reason with you[S], and you[S] have been found false.
7 I have asked two things from You[S], withhold not from me before I die.
8 Put vanity and a lying word far from me, give not poverty or wealth to me, cause me to eat the bread of my portion,
9 for fear that I become satiated, and have denied, and have said, 'Who [is] Jehovah?' and for fear that I be poor, and have stolen, and have laid hold of the name of my God.
10 Accuse not a servant unto his lord, for fear that he disesteem you[S], and you[S] be found guilty.
11 A generation [is], that lightly esteems their father, and their mother does not bless.
12 A generation — pure in their own eyes, but not washed from their own filth.
13 A generation — how high are their eyes, yes, their eyelids are lifted up.
14 A generation — swords [are] their teeth, and knives — their jaw-teeth, to consume the poor from earth, and the needy from [among] men.
15 To the leech [are] two daughters, 'Give, give, behold, three things are not satisfied, four have not said 'Sufficiency;'
16 Sheol, and a restrained womb, earth — it [is] not satisfied [with] water, and fire — it has not said, 'Sufficiency,'
17 An eye that mocks at a father, and despises to obey a mother, ravens do dig it out of the valley, and young eagles do eat it.
18 Three things have been too wonderful for me, yes, four that I have not known:
19 the way of the eagle in the heavens, the way of a serpent on a rock, the way of a ship in the heart of the sea, and the way of a man in youth.
20 So — the way of an adulterous woman, she has eaten and has wiped her mouth, and has said, 'I have not done iniquity.'
21 Earth has been troubled for three things, and for four — it is not able to bear:
22 for a servant when he reigns, and a fool when he is satisfied with bread,
23 for a hated one when she rules, and a maid-servant when she succeeds her mistress.
24 Four [are] little ones of earth, and they are made wiser than the wise:
25 the ants [are] a people not strong, and they prepare their food in summer,
26 Conies [are] a people not strong, and they place their house in a rock,
27 There is not a king to the locust, and it goes out — each one shouting,
28 Take hold a spider with two hands, and is in the palaces of a king.
29 Three there are going well, yes, four are good in going:
30 an old lion — mighty among beasts, that turns not back from the face of any,
31 a girt one of the loins, or a he-goat, and a king — no rising up with him.
32 If you[S] have been foolish in lifting up yourself[S], and if you[S] have devised evil — hand to mouth!
33 For the churning of milk brings out butter, and the wringing of the nose brings out blood, and the forcing of anger brings out strife!

Chapter 31

1 Words of Lemuel a king, a declaration that his mother taught him:
2 'What, my son? and what, son of my womb? And what, son of my vows?
3 Give not your[S] strength to women, and your[S] ways to wiping away of kings.
4 Not for kings, O Lemuel, not for kings, to drink wine,

and for princes a desire of strong drink.
5 For fear that he drink, and forget the decree, and
change the judgment of any of the sons of affliction.
6 Give strong drink to the perishing, and wine to the
bitter in soul,
7 He drinks, and forgets his poverty, and his misery he
remembers not again.
8 Open your[S] mouth for the dumb, for the right of all
sons of change.
9 Open your[S] mouth, judge righteously, both the cause
of the poor and needy!'
10 Who does find a woman of worth? Yes, her price [is]
far above rubies.
11 The heart of her husband has trusted in her, and he
lacks not spoil.
12 She has done him good, and not evil, all days of her life.
13 She has sought wool and flax, and she works [with]
her hands with delight.
14 She has been as ships of the merchant, she brings in
her bread from afar.
15 Yes, she rises while yet night, and gives food to her
household, and a portion to her damsels.
16 She has considered a field, and takes it, from the fruit
of her hands she has planted a vineyard.
17 She has girded her loins with might, and does
strengthen her arms.
18 She has perceived when her merchandise [is] good,
her lamp is not extinguished in the night.
19 She has sent forth her hands on a spindle, and her
hands have held a distaff.
20 She has spread forth her hand to the poor, yes, she
sent forth her hands to the needy.
21 She is not afraid of her household from snow, for all
her household are clothed [with] scarlet.
22 She has made ornamental coverings for herself, silk
and purple [are] her clothing.
23 Her husband is known in the gates, in his sitting
with elders of the land.
24 She has made linen garments, and sells, and she has
given a girdle to the merchant.
25 Strength and honor [are] her clothing, and she
rejoices at a latter day.
26 She has opened her mouth in wisdom, and the law of
kindness [is] on her tongue.
27 She [is] watching the ways of her household, and
she eats not bread of sloth.
28 Her sons have risen up, and pronounce her happy,
her husband, and he praises her,
29 'Many [are] the daughters who have done worthily,
you[S] have gone up above them all.'
30 The grace [is] false, and the beauty [is] vain, a woman
fearing Jehovah, she may boast herself.
31 Give you[P] to her of the fruit of her hands, and her
works do praise her in the gates!

CPSIA information can be obtained at www.ICGtesting.com
Printed in the USA
LVOW050310281112

308985LV00003BA/98/A